# G·L·O·B·A·L  S·T·U·D·I·E·S

# JAPAN
## AND THE PACIFIC RIM
### FIFTH EDITION

# Japan and the Pacific Rim

## OTHER BOOKS IN THE GLOBAL STUDIES SERIES

- Africa
- China
- India and South Asia
- Latin America
- The Middle East
- Russia, the Eurasian Republics,
  and Central/Eastern Europe
- Western Europe

Cataloging in Publication Data
Main Entry under title: Global Studies: Japan and the Pacific Rim. 5/E
     1. East Asia—History—20th century–. 2. East Asia—Politics and government—20th century–. I. Title: Japan and the Pacific Rim. II. Collinwood, Dean W., *comp*.
ISBN 0–07–024948–2

©1999 by Dushkin/McGraw-Hill Companies, Guilford, Connecticut 06437.

Fifth Edition

Printed in the United States of America     1234567890BAHBAH5432109     Printed on Recycled Paper

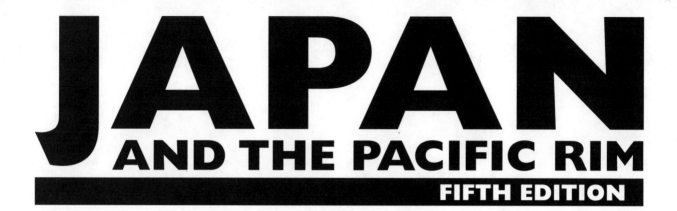

# G·L·O·B·A·L  S·T·U·D·I·E·S

# JAPAN
## AND THE PACIFIC RIM
### FIFTH EDITION

**Dr. Dean W. Collinwood**

**University of Utah**

**Dushkin/McGraw-Hill Company**
**Sluice Dock, Guilford, Connecticut 06437**

**Visit us on the Internet—http://www.dushkin.com**

## STAFF

| | |
|---|---|
| **Ian A. Nielsen** | Publisher |
| **Brenda S. Filley** | Production Manager |
| **Lisa M. Clyde** | Developmental Editor |
| **Roberta Monaco** | Editor |
| **Charles Vitelli** | Designer |
| **Cheryl Greenleaf** | Permissions Coordinator |
| **Lisa Holmes-Doebrick** | Administrative Coordinator |
| **Lara M. Johnson** | Design/Advertising Coordinator |
| **Laura Levine** | Graphics |
| **Michael Campbell** | Graphics |
| **Tom Goddard** | Graphics |
| **Juliana Arbo** | Typesetting Supervisor |

# Japan and the Pacific Rim

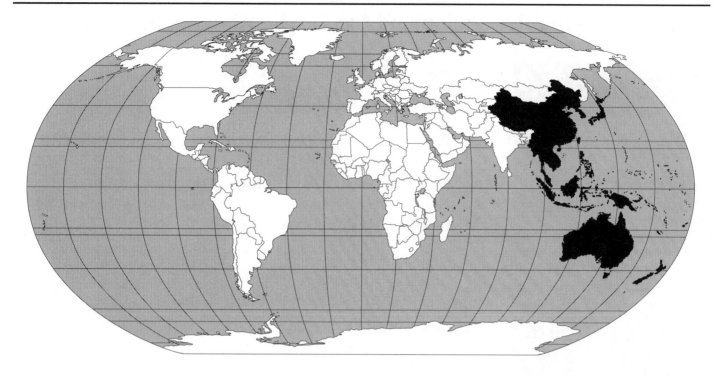

## AUTHOR/EDITOR

### Dr. Dean W. Collinwood

The author/editor of *Global Studies: Japan and the Pacific Rim* received his Ph.D. from the University of Chicago, an M.Sc. in international relations from the University of London, and a B.A. in political science with a minor in Japanese from Brigham Young University. He was a Fulbright scholar at the University of Tokyo and Tsuda College in Japan and has conducted research in Asia and the Pacific. Dr. Collinwood is research professor of management at the University of Utah, where he serves as associate director of global business and director of the U.S.–Japan and U.S.–China Centers. He is also executive director of the Utah Asian Studies Consortium (UCON). He is the immediate past president of the Western Conference of the Association for Asian Studies and is a member of the Pacific Council on International Policy. Dr. Collinwood is the author of books and articles on Japan, Korea, and other countries. Some of his books have been used by the U.S. State Department to train foreign service personnel.

## SERIES CONSULTANT

### H. Thomas Collins
PROJECT LINKS
George Washington University

# Contents

## Global Studies: Japan and the Pacific Rim, Fifth Edition

*Pacific Rim    Page 5*

*Pacific Islands    Page 20*

*Japan    Page 31*

*Hong Kong    Page 56*

*New Zealand    Page 75*

*Thailand    Page 101*

# Using Global Studies: Japan and the Pacific Rim

## THE GLOBAL STUDIES SERIES

The Global Studies series was created to help readers acquire a basic knowledge and understanding of the regions and countries in the world. Each volume provides a foundation of information—geographic, cultural, economic, political, historical, artistic, and religious—that will allow readers to better assess the current and future problems within these countries and regions and to comprehend how events there might affect their own well-being. In short, these volumes present the background information necessary to respond to the realities of our global age.

Each of the volumes in the Global Studies series is crafted under the careful direction of an author/editor—an expert in the area under study. The author/editors teach and conduct research and have traveled extensively through the regions about which they are writing.

In this *Japan and the Pacific Rim* edition, the author/editor has written regional essays on the Pacific Rim and the Pacific Islands and country reports for each of the countries covered, including a special report on Japan.

## MAJOR FEATURES OF THE GLOBAL STUDIES SERIES

The Global Studies volumes are organized to provide concise information on the regions and countries within those areas under study. The major sections and features of the books are described here.

### Regional Essays

For *Global Studies: Japan and the Pacific Rim,* the author/editor has written two narrative essays focusing on the religious, cultural, sociopolitical, and economic differences and similarities of the countries and peoples in the region: "The Pacific Rim: Diversity and Interconnection," and "The Pacific Islands: Opportunities and Limits." Detailed maps accompany each essay.

### Country Reports

Concise reports are written for each of the countries within the region under study. These reports are the heart of each Global Studies volume. *Global Studies: Japan and the Pacific Rim, Fifth Edition,* contains 20 country reports, including a lengthy report on Japan.

The country reports are composed of five standard elements. Each report contains a detailed map visually positioning the country among its neighboring states; a summary of statistical information; a current essay providing important historical, geographical, political, cultural, and economic information; a historical timeline, offering a convenient visual survey of a few key historical events; and four "graphic indicators," with summary statements about the country in terms of development, freedom, health/welfare, and achievements.

### *A Note on the Statistical Reports*

The statistical information provided for each country has been drawn from a wide range of sources. (The most frequently referenced are listed on page 215.) Every effort has been made to provide the most current and accurate information available. However, occasionally the information cited by these sources differs to some extent; and, all too often, the most current information available for some countries is dated. Aside from these difficulties, the statistical summary of each country is generally quite complete and up to date. Care should be taken, however, in using these statistics (or, for that matter, any published statistics) in making hard comparisons among countries. We have also provided comparable statistics for the United States and Canada, which can be found on pages x and xi.

### World Press Articles

Within each Global Studies volume is reprinted a number of articles carefully selected by our editorial staff and the author/editor from a broad range of international periodicals and newspapers. The articles have been chosen for currency, interest, and their differing perspectives on the subject countries. There are 29 articles in *Global Studies: Japan and the Pacific Rim, Fifth Edition.*

The articles section is preceded by an annotated table of contents as well as a topic guide. The annotated table of contents offers a brief summary of each article, while the topic guide indicates the main theme(s) of each article. Thus, readers desiring to focus on articles dealing with a particular theme, say, environment, may refer to the topic guide to find those articles.

### WWW Sites

An extensive annotated list of selected World Wide Web sites can be found on the facing page (ix) in this edition of *Global Studies: Japan.* In addition, the URL addresses for country-specific Web sites are provided on the statistics page of most countries. All of the Web site addresses were correct and operational at press time. Instructors and students alike are urged to refer to those sites often to enhance their understanding of the region and to keep up with current events.

### Glossary, Bibliography, Index

At the back of each Global Studies volume, readers will find a glossary of terms and abbreviations, which provides a quick reference to the specialized vocabulary of the area under study and to the standard abbreviations (NIC, ASEAN, etc.) used throughout the volume.

Following the glossary is a bibliography, which lists general works, national histories, and current-events publications and periodicals that provide regular coverage on Japan and the Pacific Rim.

The index at the end of the volume is an accurate reference to the contents of the volume. Readers seeking specific information and citations should consult this standard index.

### Currency and Usefulness

*Global Studies: Japan and the Pacific Rim,* the like other Global Studies volumes, is intended to provide the most current and useful information available necessary to understand the events that are shaping the cultures of the region today.

This volume is revised on a regular basis. The statistics are updated, regional essays and country reports revised, and world press articles replaced. In order to accomplish this task, we turn to our author/editor, our advisory boards, and—hopefully—to you, the users of this volume. Your comments are more than welcome. If you have an idea that you think will make the next edition more useful, an article or bit of information that will make it more current, or a general comment on its organization, content, or features that you would like to share with us, please send it in for serious consideration.

# Selected World Wide Web Sites for Japan and the Pacific Rim

(Some Web sites continually change their structure and content, so the information listed here may not always be available. Check our Web site at: http://www.dushkin.com/online —Ed.)

## GENERAL SITES

CNN Online Page—**http://www.cnn.com**—U.S. 24-hour video news channel. News is updated every few hours.

C-SPAN ONLINE—**http://www.c-span.org**—See especially C-SPAN International on the Web for International Programming Highlights and archived C-SPAN programs.

International Network Information Center at University of Texas—**http://inic.utexas.edu**—Gateway has pointers to international sites, including Japan, China, and Taiwan.

I-Trade International Trade Resources & Data Exchange—**http://www.i-trade.com**—Monthly exchange-rate data, U.S. Document Export Market Information (GEMS), U.S. Global Trade Outlook, and the CIA Worldfact Book.

Political Science RESOURCES—**http://www.psr.keele. ac.uk/psr.htm**—Dynamic gateway to country sources available via European addresses.

ReliefWeb—**http://wwwnotes.reliefweb.int**—UN's Department of Humanitarian Affairs clearinghouse for international humanitarian emergencies.

Social Science Information Gateway (SOSIG)—**http://sosig. esrc.bris.ac.uk**—Project of the Economic and Social Research Council (ESRC). It catalogs 22 subjects and lists developing-countries' URL addresses.

United Nations System—**http://www.unsystem.org**—The official Web site for the United Nations system of organizations.

U.S. Agency for International Development (USAID)—**http://www.info.usaid.gov**—Graphically presented U.S. trade statistics related to Japan, China, Taiwan, and other Pacific Rim countries are available at this site.

U.S. Central Intelligence Agency Home Page—**http://www.odci.gov/cia/**—This site includes publications of the CIA, current Worldfact Book, and maps.

U.S. Department of State Home Page—**http://www.state. gov/index.html**—Organized alphabetically: Country Reports, Human Rights, International Organizations, etc.

World Bank Group—**http://www.worldbank.org/html/Welcome. html**—News (i.e., press releases, summary of new projects, speeches), publications, topics in development, countries and regions. Links to other financial organizations.

World Health Organization (WHO)—**http://www.who.ch/**—Maintained by WHO's headquarters in Geneva, Switzerland, uses Excite search engine to conduct keyword searches.

World Trade Organization—**http://www.wto.org**—Topics include legal frameworks, trade and environmental policies, recent agreements, etc.

WWW Virtual Library Database—**http://conbio.rice.edu/vl/database/**—Easy search for country-specific sites that provide news, government, and other information.

## ASIA

Aseanweb—**http://www.asean.or.id**—Menu includes "What's New?" and data on economics, politics, security, and print publications on the nations of ASEAN—the Association of Southeast Asian Nations.

Asia Gateway—**http://www.asiagateway.com/index.html**—Country profiles, including lifestyles, business, and other data. Look in "What's New" for news highlights.

Asiatour—**http://asiatour.com/index.htm**—Travel and historical information for many Asian countries.

Asia-Yahoo—**http://www.yahoo.com/Regional/Regions/Asia/**—Specialized Yahoo search site permits keyword search on Asian events, countries, or topics.

NewsDirectory.com—**http://www.newsd.com/web/about/**—This site, a Guide to English-Language Media Online, lists over 7,000 actively updated papers and magazines.

Orientation Asia—**http://as.orientation.com**—Links to specific countries, late-breaking news.

Signposts to Asia and the Pacific—**http://jsa-44.hum.uts.edu. au/signposts/index.html**—Databases, news, key country contacts, articles, and links to other relevant sites.

South-East Asia Information—**http://sunsite.nus.sg/asiasvc. html**—Excellent gateway for country-specific research. Information on Internet Providers and Universities in Southeast Asia, links to Asian online services.

## CHINA

Chinese Security Home Page—**http://members.aol.com/mehampton/chinasec.html**—Information is listed under Chinese Military Links, Data Sources on Chinese Security Issues, Key Newspapers and News Services, and Key Scholarly Journals and Magazines.

Inside China Today—**http://www.insidechina.com**—The European Information Network is organized under Headline News, Government, and Related Sites, Mainland China, Hong Kong, Macau, and Taiwan.

Internet Guide for China Studies—**http://sun.sino.uni-heidelberg.de/igcs/index.html**—Coverage of news media, politics, legal and human-rights information, as well as China's economy, philosophy and religion, society, arts, culture, and history may be found here.

## JAPAN

Japan Ministry of Foreign Affairs—**http://www.mofa.go.jp**—"What's New" lists events, policy statements, press releases. Foreign Policy section has speeches; archive; information under Countries and Region, Friendship.

Japan Policy Research Institute (JPRI)—**http://www.nmjc. org/jpri/**—Headings include "What's New" and Publications before 1996.

The Japan Times Online—**http://www.japantimes.co.jp**—This daily online newspaper is offered in English and contains late-breaking news.

# The United States

## GEOGRAPHY
*Area in Square Miles (Kilometers):*
3,618,770 (9,578,626)
*Capital (Population):* Washington, D.C.
(567,100)
*Environmental Concerns:* air pollution
resulting in acid rain generating from
fossil fuels; water pollution from runoff
of pesticides and fertilizers
*Geographical Features:* vast central plain,
mountains in the west, hills and low
mountains in the east; rugged mountains
and broad river valleys in Alaska;
volcanic topography in Hawaii.
*Climate:* temperate

## PEOPLE

### Population
*Total:* 267,954,800
*Annual Growth Rate:* 0.89%
*Rural/Urban Population Ratio:* 24/76
*Major Languages:* predominantly English;
a sizable Spanish-speaking minority;
many others
*Ethnic Makeup:* 73% white; 12% black;
10% Latino; 5% Asian, Pacific Islander,
American Indian, Eskimo, and Aleut
*Religions:* 55% Protestant; 36% Roman
Catholic; 4% Jewish; 5% Muslim and
others

### Health
*Life Expectancy at Birth:* 73 years (male);
80 years (female)
*Infant Mortality Rate (Ratio):* 6.55/1,000
*Average Caloric Intake:* 138% of FAO
minimum
*Physicians Available (Ratio):* 1/381

### Education
*Adult Literacy Rate:* 97.9% (official)
(estimates vary widely)
*Compulsory (Ages):* 7–16; free

## COMMUNICATION
*Telephones:* 1 per 1.6 people
*Daily Newspaper Circulation:* 228 per
1,000 people; approximately 63,000,000
circulation
*Televisions:* 1 per 1.2 people

## TRANSPORTATION
*Highways in Miles (Kilometers):*
3,906,960 (6,261,154)
*Railroads in Miles (Kilometers):* 149,161
(240,000)
*Usable Airfields:* 13,387
*Motor Vehicles in Use:* 200,500,000

## GOVERNMENT
*Type:* federal republic
*Independence Date:* July 4, 1776
*Head of State:* President William ("Bill")
Jefferson Clinton
*Political Parties:* Democratic Party;
Republican Party; others of minor
political significance
*Suffrage:* universal at 18

## MILITARY
*Military Expenditures (% of GDP):* 3.8%
*Current Disputes:* none

## ECONOMY
*Per Capita Income/GDP:* $28,600/$7.61
trillion
*GDP Growth Rate:* 2.4%
*Inflation Rate:* 3.0%
*Unemployment Rate:* 5.4%
*Labor Force:* 13,943,000
*Natural Resources:* metallic and
nonmetallic minerals; petroleum;
arable land
*Agriculture:* food grains; feed crops;
oil-bearing crops; livestock; dairy
products
*Industry:* diversified in both capital-
and consumer-goods industries
*Exports:* $584.7 billion (primary partners
Canada, Western Europe, Japan, Mexico)
*Imports:* $771.0 billion (primary partners
Canada, Western Europe, Japan, Mexico)

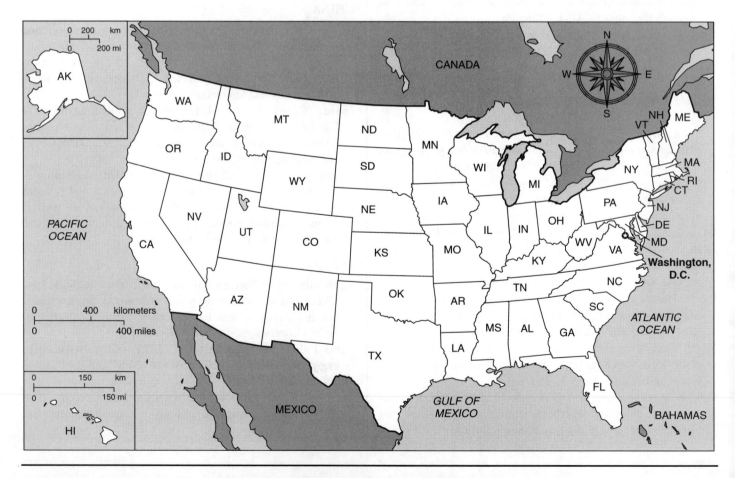

# Canada

## GEOGRAPHY

*Area in Square Miles (Kilometers):* 3,850,790 (9,976,140) (slightly larger than the United States)

*Capital (Population):* Ottawa (1,000,000)

*Environmental Concerns:* air pollution and resulting acid rain severely affecting lakes and damaging forests

*Geographical Features:* permafrost in the north hinders development, mountains in the west, central plains, and a maritime culture in the east

*Climate:* from temperate in south to subarctic and arctic in north

## PEOPLE

### Population

*Total:* 30,337,400

*Annual Growth Rate:* 1.13%

*Rural/Urban Population Ratio:* 23/77

*Major Languages:* both English and French are official

*Ethnic Makeup:* 40% British Isles origin; 27% French origin; 20% other European; 1.5% indigenous Indian and Eskimo; 11.5% mixed

*Religions:* 46% Roman Catholic; 16% United Church; 10% Anglican; 28% others

### Health

*Life Expectancy at Birth:* 76 years (male); 82 years (female)

*Infant Mortality Rate (Ratio):* 5.7/1,000

*Average Caloric Intake:* 127% of FAO minimum

*Physicians Available (Ratio):* 1/464

### Education

*Adult Literacy Rate:* 97%

*Compulsory (Ages):* primary school

## COMMUNICATION

*Telephones:* 1 per 1.7 people

*Daily Newspaper Circulation:* 189 per 1,000 people

*Televisions:* 1 per 1.5 people

## TRANSPORTATION

*Highways in Miles (Kilometers):* 637,104 (1,021,000)

*Railroads in Miles (Kilometers):* 48,764 (78,148)

*Usable Airfields:* 1,139

*Motor Vehicles in Use:* 16,700,000

## GOVERNMENT

*Type:* confederation with parliamentary democracy

*Independence Date:* July 1, 1867

*Head of State/Government:* Queen Elizabeth II; Prime Minister Jean Chrétien

*Political Parties:* Progressive Conservative Party; Liberal Party; New Democratic Party; Reform Party; Bloc Québécois

*Suffrage:* universal at 18

## MILITARY

*Military Expenditures (% of GDP):* 1.53%

*Current Disputes:* none

## ECONOMY

*Currency ($U.S. Equivalent):* 1.53 Canadian dollars = $1

*Per Capita Income/GDP:* $25,000/$721 billion

*Inflation Rate:* 1.4%

*Total Foreign Debt:* $253 billion

*Labor Force:* 15.1 million

*Natural Resources:* petroleum; natural gas; fish; minerals; cement; forestry products; fur

*Agriculture:* grains; livestock; dairy products; potatoes; hogs; poultry and eggs; tobacco

*Industry:* oil production and refining; natural-gas development; fish products; wood and paper products; chemicals; transportation equipment

*Exports:* $195.4 billion (primary partners United States, Japan, United Kingdom, Germany, South Korea, Netherlands, China)

*Imports:* $169.5 billion (primary partners United States, Japan, United Kingdom, Germany, Mexico, Taiwan, South Korea)

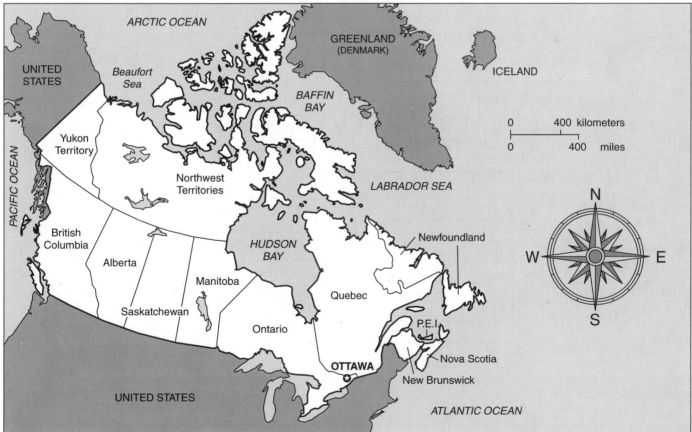

# GLOBAL 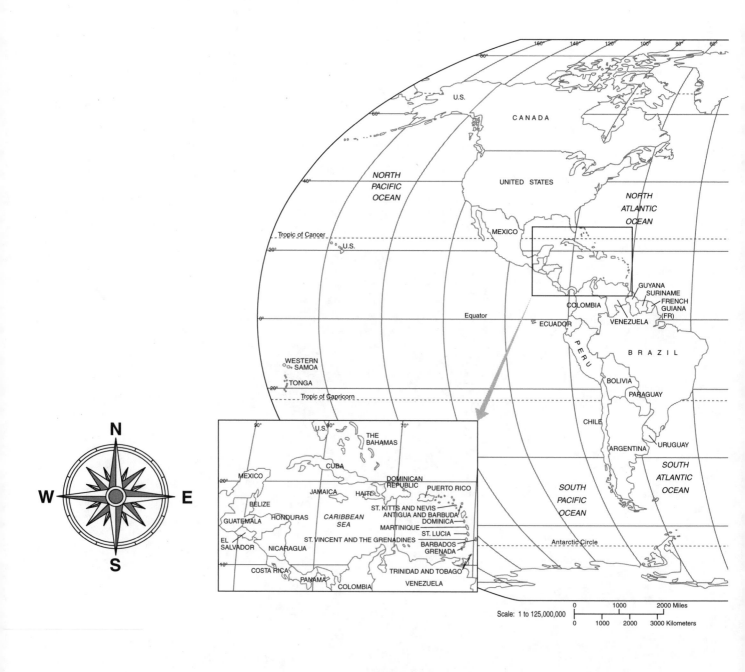 STUDIES

This map is provided to give you a graphic picture of where the countries of the world are located, the relationships they have with their region and neighbors, and their positions relative to the superpowers and power blocs. We have focused on certain areas to illustrate these crowded regions more clearly.

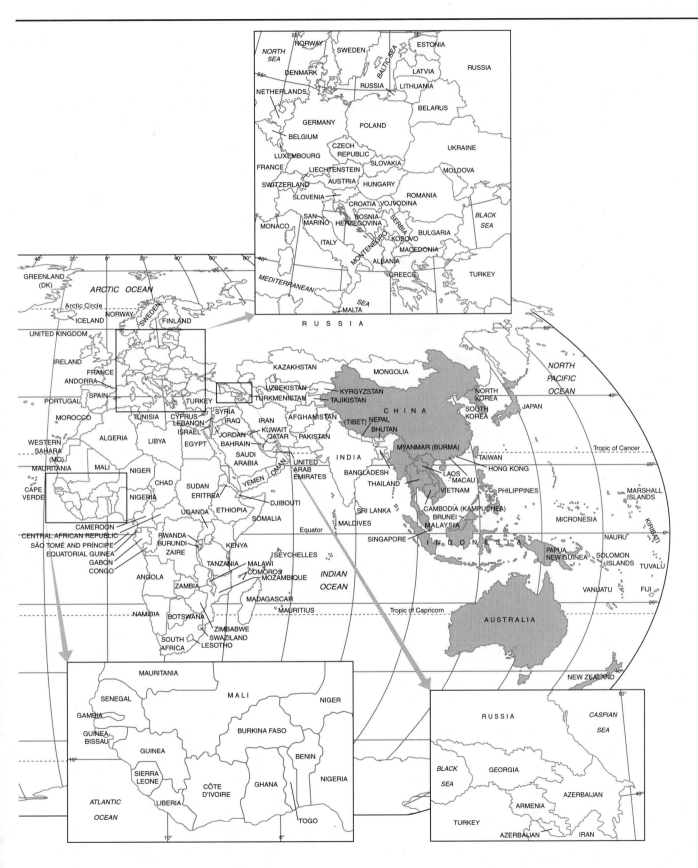

# Pacific Rim Map

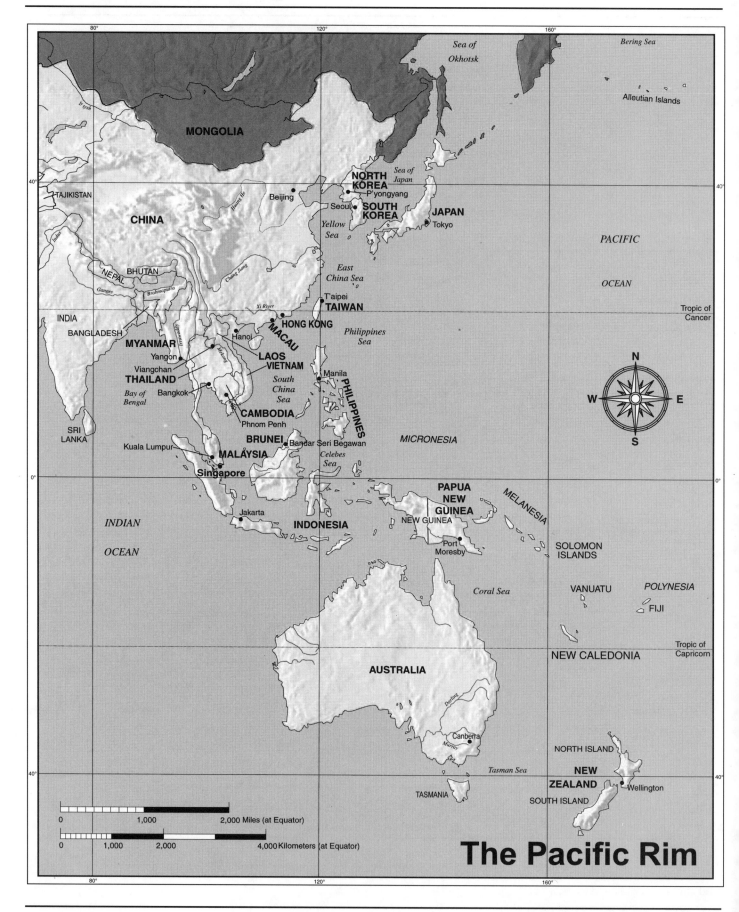

The Pacific Rim

# The Pacific Rim: Diversity and Interconnection

## WHAT IS THE PACIFIC RIM?

The term *Pacific Rim,* as used in this book, refers to 20 countries or administrative units along or near the Asian side of the Pacific Ocean, plus the numerous islands of the Pacific. Together, they are home to approximately 30 percent of the world's population and produce about 20 percent of the world's gross national product (GNP).

It is not a simple matter to decide which countries to include in a definition of the Pacific Rim. For instance, if we were thinking geographically, we might include Mexico, Chile, Canada, the United States, Russia, and numerous other countries that border the Pacific Ocean, while eliminating Myanmar (Burma) and Laos, since they are not technically on the rim of the Pacific. But our definition, and hence our selected inclusions, stem from fairly recent developments in economic and geopolitical power that have affected the countries of Asia and the Pacific in such a way that these formerly disparate regions are now being referred to by international corporate and political leaders as a single bloc.

Most people living in the region that we have thus defined do not think of themselves as "Pacific Rimmers." In addition, many social scientists, particularly cultural anthropologists and comparative sociologists, would prefer not to apply a single term to such a culturally, politically, and sociologically diverse region. It is true that many of the countries in question share certain cultural influences, such as Buddhism and rice cultivation. But these commonalities have not prevented the region from fracturing into dozens of societies, often very antagonistic toward one another.

For more than 2 decades, something has been occurring in the region that seems to be having the effect of uniting the area in a way it has never been united before. If current trends continue, it is likely that the entire Pacific Rim will one day share a single economic system (some version of free market, or at least state capitalism) and some fundamental lifestyle values (materialism and consumerism). There will also be a common awareness of the value of peaceful interdependence of the various nations to guarantee a steady improvement in the various nations to guarantee a steady improvement in the standard of living for all, and the capacity of the region to, for the first time in history, supply the basic survival needs of its inhabitants.

What are the powerful forces that are fueling these trends? There are many, including nationalism and the rapid advances in global communications. But the one that for the past 2 decades has stood out as the defining force in the region is the yen—the Japanese currency—and its accompanying Japanese business strategy. For more than 20 years, Japanese money has been flowing throughout the Pacific Rim in the form of aid and investment, while Japan's high-tech, export-oriented approach to making money has been facilitating development and helping other regional countries to create their own engines of economic growth in a way that none of them had experienced before.

It is true that, during the 1990s, Japan's economy stagnated and the yen weakened in value. It is also true that Japan's banking sector suffered heavy losses during those years, due to sloppy lending and bad loan management. Those events led some observers to speculate that Japan's role as the economic engine of the Pacific Rim is coming to an end; they predicted that other countries, like China, would assume the lead in the future. Those predictions are probably wrong, and certainly premature; for even after a decade of recession, Japan remains the second-largest economy in the world (after the United States), and its economic output continues to dwarf all other Pacific Rim economies *combined.* Moreover, many Japanese corporations still make large profits, even during these hard times, and the government continues to provide economic aid to many Asian countries. Furthermore, the long-term effects of Japan's multi-billion-dollar investments in Asia will remain for years to come.

In the 1960s, when the Japanese economy had completely recovered from the devastation of World War II, the Japanese looked to North America and Europe for markets for their increasingly high-quality products. Japanese business continues to seek out markets and resources globally; but, in the 1980s, in response to the movement toward a truly common European economic community as well as in response to free trade agreements among North American countries, Japan began to invest more heavily in countries nearer its own borders. The Japanese hoped to guarantee themselves market and resource access should they find their products frozen out of the emerging European and North American economic blocs. The unintended, but not unwelcome, consequences of this policy were the revitalization of many Asia–Pacific economies and the solidification of lines of communication between governments and private citizens within the region. Recognizing this interconnection has prompted many people to refer to the countries we treat in this book as a single unit, the Pacific Rim.

## TROUBLES IN THE RIM

In the 1980s, media images of billionaire Japanese businesspeople buying up priceless artworks at auction houses and pampered chauffeur-driven Hong Kong Chinese far overshadowed the harsh realities of life for most people in the Rim. For the most part, Pacific Rim countries have not met the needs of their peoples. Whether it is the desire of affluent Japanese for larger homes and two-car garages, or of rice farmers in Myanmar (formerly called Burma) for the right to sell their grain for personal profit, or of Chinese students to speak their minds without repression—in these and many other ways, the Pacific Rim has failed its peoples. In Vietnam, Myanmar, Laos, and Cambodia, for example, life is so difficult that thousands of families have risked their lives to leave their homelands. Some have swum across the wide Mekong River on moonless nights to avoid detection by guards, while others have sailed into the South China Sea on creaky and overcrowded boats (hence the name commonly given such refugees: "boat people"), hoping that people of goodwill, rather than marauding pirates, will find them and transport them to a land of safety. Despite the cut-off of refugee-support funds from the United Nations (UN), thousands of refugees remain unrepatriated, languishing in camps in Thailand, Malaysia, and other countries. Thousands of villagers driven from their homes by the Myanmar Army await return. Meanwhile, the number of defectors from North Korea has been increasing steadily.

Between 1975 and 1994, almost 14,000 refugees reached Japan by boat, along with 3,500 Chinese nationals who posed as refugees in hopes of being allowed to live outside China. In 1998, the Malaysian government, citing its own economic problems, added to the dislocation of many people when it began large-scale deportations of foreign workers, many from Indonesia. Many of these individuals had lived in Malaysia for years. This "Operation Get Out" was expected to affect at least 850,000 people. These examples, and many others not

(Photo by Lisa Clyde)

The small island of Macau was acknowledged by China as a Portuguese settlement in 1557. The Portuguese influence is obvious in the architecture of the downtown plaza pictured above. Today Macau is a gambling mecca, drawing an enormous number of avid fans from Hong Kong. This last outpost of European colonial power is scheduled to be returned to Chinese control on December 20, 1999.

mentioned here, stand as tragic evidence of the social and political instability of many Pacific Rim nations and of the intense ethnic rivalries that divide the people of the Rim.

**Warfare**

Of all the Rim's troubles, warfare has been the most devastating. In Japan and China alone, an estimated 15.6 million people died as a result of World War II. Not only have there been wars in which foreign powers like Britain, the United States, France, and the former Soviet Union have been involved, but there have been and continue to be numerous battles between local peoples of different tribes, races, and religions.

The potential for serious conflict remains in most regions of the Pacific Rim. Despite international pressure, the military dictators of Myanmar continue to wage war against the Karens and other ethnic groups within its borders; Japan remains locked in a dispute with Russia over ownership of islands to the north of Hokkaido; Taiwan and China still lay claim to each other's territory, as do the two Koreas; and it was not so long ago that Vietnam and China were engaged in battle over their mutual boundary. The list of disputed borders, lands, islands, and waters in the Pacific Rim is very long; indeed, there are some 30 unresolved disputes involving almost every country of Asia and some of the Pacific Islands.

Of growing concern is a 340,000-square-mile area of the South China Sea. When the likelihood of large oil deposits near the rocks and reefs of the Spratly Islands was announced in the 1970s, China, Taiwan, Vietnam, the Philippines, Malaysia, and Brunei instantly laid claim to the area. By 1974, the Chinese Air Force and Navy were bombing a South Vietnamese settlement on the islands; by 1988, Chinese warships were attacking Vietnamese transport ships in the area. Both China and Vietnam have granted nearby oil-drilling concessions to different U.S. oil companies, so the situation remains tense, especially because China claims sovereignty over almost the entire South China Sea and has been flexing its muscles in the area by stopping, boarding, and sometimes confiscating other nations' ships in the area.

In addition to these national disputes, ethnic tensions—most Asian nations are composed of hundreds of different ethnic groups with their own languages and religions—are sometimes severe. In Fiji, it is the locals versus the immigrant Indians; in Southeast Asia, it is the locals versus the Chinese or the Muslims versus the Christians; in China, it is the Tibetans and most other ethnic groups versus the Han Chinese.

With the end of the cold war in the late 1980s and early 1990s, many Asian nations found it necessary to seek new military, political, and economic alliances. For example, South Korea made a trade pact with Russia, a nation that, during the Soviet era, would have dealt only with North Korea; and, forced to withdraw from its large naval base in the Philippines, the United States increased its military presence in Singapore. The United States also began encouraging its ally Japan to assume a larger military role in the region. However, the thought of Japan re-arming itself causes considerable fear among Pacific Rim nations, almost all of which suffered defeat at the hands of the Japanese military only half a century ago. Nevertheless, Japan has acted to increase its military preparedness, within the narrow confines of its constitutional prohibition against re-armament. It now has the second-largest military budget in the world (its actual expenses are huge, but because its economy is so large, Japan spends only about 1 percent of its budget on defense).

In response, China has increased its purchases of military equipment, especially from cash-strapped Russia. As a result, whereas the arms industry is in decline in some other world regions, it is big business in Asia. Four of the nine largest armies in the world are in the Pacific Rim. Thus, the tragedy of warfare, which has characterized the region for so many centuries, could continue unless governments manage conflict very carefully and come to understand the need for mutual cooperation.

In some cases, mutual cooperation is already replacing animosity. Thailand and Vietnam are engaged in sincere efforts to resolve fishing-rights disputes in the Gulf of Thailand and water-rights disputes on the Mekong River; North and South Korea have agreed to allow some cross-border visita-tion; and even Taiwan and China have amicably settled issues relating to fisheries, immigration, and hijackings. Yet greed and ethnic and national pride are far too often just below the surface; left unchecked, they could catalyze a major confrontation in that region.

### Overpopulation

Another serious problem in the Pacific Rim is overpopulation. There are well over 2 billion people living in the region. Of those, approximately 1.2 billion are Chinese. Even though China's government has implemented the strictest family-planning policies in world history, the country's annual growth rate is such that more than 1 million inhabitants are added *every month*. This means that more new Chinese are born each year than make up the entire population of Australia! The World Health Organization (WHO) reports, however, that about 217 million people in East Asia use contraceptives today, as compared to only 18 million in 1965. Couples in some countries, including Japan, Taiwan, and South Korea, have been voluntarily limiting family size. Other states, such as China and Singapore, have promoted family planning

(UN photo by Shaw McCutcheon)

The number of elderly people in China will triple by the year 2025. Even though it limits each family to only one child, China will be faced with the increasing need of caring for retirement-age citizens. This group of elders in a village near Chengdu represents just the tip of an enormous problem for the future.

though government incentives and punishments. The effort is paying off. The United Nations now estimates that the proportion of the global population living in Asia will remain relatively unchanged between now and the year 2025, and China's share will decline. In fact, in some countries, especially Japan, South Korea, and Thailand, single-child families and an aging population are creating problems in their own right as the ratio of productive workers to the overall population declines.

Still, so many children have already been born that Pacific Rim governments simply cannot meet their needs. For these new Asians, schools must be built, health facilities provided, houses constructed, and jobs created. This is not an easy challenge for many Rim countries. Moreover, as the population density increases, the quality of life decreases. In crowded New York City, for example, the population is about 1,100 per square mile, and residents, finding the crowding to be too uncomfortable, frequently seek more relaxed lifestyles in the suburbs. Yet in Tokyo, the density is approximately 2,400 per square mile; and in Manila, it is 51,000! Today, many of the world's largest cities are in the Pacific Rim: Shanghai, China, has about 12 million people; Jakarta, Indonesia, has more than 8.6 million; Manila, the Philippines, is home to over 8.5 million, while Bangkok, Thailand, has about 6.5 million residents. And migration to the cities continues despite miserable living conditions for many (in some Asian cities, 50 percent of the population live in slum housing). One incredibly rapid-growth country is the Philippines; home to only about 7 million in 1898, when it was acquired by the United States, it is projected to have 130 million people in the year 2020.

Absolute numbers alone do not tell the whole story. In many Rim countries, 40 percent or more of the population are under age 15. Governments must provide schooling and medical care as well as plan for future jobs and housing for all these children. Moreover, as these young people age, they will require increased medical and social care. Scholars point out that, between 1985 and 2025, the numbers of old people will double in Japan, triple in China, and quadruple in Korea. In Japan, where replacement-level fertility was achieved in the 1960s, government officials are already concerned about the ability of the nation to care for the growing number of retirement-age people while paying the higher wages that the increasingly scarce younger workers are demanding.

## Political Instability

One consequence of the overwhelming problems of population growth, urbanization, and continual military or ethnic conflict is disillusionment with government. In many countries of the Pacific Rim, people are challenging the very right of their governments to rule or are demanding a complete change in the political philosophy that undergirds governments.

For instance, despite the risk of death, torture, or imprisonment, many college students in Myanmar have demonstrated against the current military dictatorship, and rioting students and workers in Indonesia were successful in bringing down the corrupt government of President Suharto. In some Rim

---

### TYPES OF GOVERNMENT IN SELECTED PACIFIC RIM COUNTRIES

**PARLIAMENTARY DEMOCRACIES**
Australia*
Fiji
New Zealand*
Papua New Guinea

**CONSTITUTIONAL MONARCHIES**
Brunei
Japan
Malaysia
Thailand

**REPUBLICS**
Indonesia
The Philippines
Singapore
South Korea
Taiwan

**SOCIALIST REPUBLICS**
China
Laos
Myanmar (Burma)
North Korea
Vietnam

**OVERSEAS TERRITORIES/COLONIES**
French Polynesia
Macau†
New Caledonia

*Australia and New Zealand have declared their intention of becoming completely independent republics.
†Macau reverts to Chinese control in 1999.

---

countries, opposition groups armed with sophisticated weapons obtained from foreign nations roam the countryside, capturing towns and military installations. In less than a decade, the government of the Philippines endured six coup attempts; elite military dissidents have wanted to impose a patronage-style government like that of former president Ferdinand Marcos, while armed rural insurgents have wanted to install a Communist government. Thousands of students have been injured or killed protesting the governments of South Korea and China. Thailand has been beset by numerous military coups, the former British colony of Fiji recently endured two coups, and half a million residents of Hong Kong took to the streets to oppose Great Britain's decision to turn over the territory to China in 1997. Military takeovers, political assassinations, and repressive policies have been the norm in most of the countries in the region. Millions have spent their entire lives under governments they have never agreed with, and unrest is bound to continue, because people are showing less and less patience with imposed government.

Part of the reason for political unrest is that the region is so culturally fractured, both between countries and, especially, within countries. In some states, dozens of different languages are spoken, people practice very different religions, families trace their roots back to diverse racial and ethnic origins, and wealth is distributed so unfairly that, while some people are well educated and well fed, others nearby remain illiterate and malnourished. Under these conditions, it has been difficult for the peoples of the Rim to agree upon the kinds of government that will best serve them; all are afraid that their particular language, religion, ethnic group, and/or social class will be negatively affected by any leader not of their own background.

## Identity Confusion

A related problem is that of confusion about personal and national identity. Many nation-states in the Pacific Rim were created in response to Western pressure. Before Western influences came to be felt, many Asians, particularly Southeast Asians, did not identify themselves with a nation but, rather, with a tribe or an ethnic group. National unity has been difficult in many cases, because of the archipelagic nature of some countries or because political boundaries have changed over the years, leaving ethnic groups from adjacent countries inside the neighbor's territory. The impact of colonialism has left many people, especially those in places like Singapore, Hong Kong, and the Pacific islands, unsure as to their roots; are they European or Asian/Pacific, or something else entirely?

(UN/DPI Photo by Eskinder Debebe)

In this era of political instability, Pacific Rim countries are increasingly using the forum afforded by regional and international organizations to try to work out their problems. Here, Secretary General Kofi Annan of the United Nations greets President Kim Dae Jung of South Korea at the UN's New York headquarters in June 1998.

Indonesia illustrates this problem. People think of it as an Islamic country, as overall its people are 87 percent Muslim. But in regions like North Sumatra, 30 percent are Protestant; in Bali, 94 percent are Hindu; and in East Timor, 49 percent are Catholic and 51 percent are animist. The Philippines is another example. With 88 different languages spoken, its people spread out over 12 large islands, and a population explosion (the average age is just 16), it is a classic case of psychological (and economic and political) fragmentation. Coups and countercoups rather than peaceful political transitions seem to be the norm, as people have not yet developed a sense of unified nationalism.

## Uneven Economic Development

While millionaires in Singapore, Hong Kong, and Japan wrestle with how best to invest their wealth, far more others worry about how they will obtain their next meal. Such disparity illustrates another major problem afflicting the Pacific Rim: uneven economic development.

Many Asians, especially those in the Northeast Asian countries of Japan, Korea, and China, are finding that rapid economic change seems to render the traditions of the past meaningless. For instance, most people will state that Japan is a Buddhist country, yet few Japanese today claim any actual religious affiliation. Moreover, economic success has produced a growing Japanese interest in maximizing investment returns, with the result that Japan (and, increasingly, South Korea, Taiwan, Singapore, and Hong Kong) is successfully searching out more ways to make money, while resource-poor regions like the Pacific islands lag behind.

The *developed nations* are characterized by political stability and long-term industrial success. Their per capita income is comparable to Canada, Northern Europe, and the United States, and they have achieved a level of economic sustainability. These countries are closely linked to North America economically. Japan, for instance, exports one third of its products to the United States.

The *newly industrializing countries* (NICs) are currently capturing world attention because of their rapid growth. Hong Kong, for example, has exported more manufactured products per year for the past decade than did the former Soviet Union and Central/Eastern Europe combined. Taiwan, famous for cameras and calculators, has had the highest gross national product (GNP) growth in the world for the past 20 years. South Korea is tops in shipbuilding and steel manufacturing and is the tenth-largest trading nation in the world.

The *resource-rich developing nations* have tremendous natural resources but have been held back economically by political and cultural instability and by insufficient capital to develop a sound economy. An example of a country attempting to overcome these drawbacks is Malaysia. Ruled by a coalition government representing nearly a dozen ethnic-based parties, Malaysia is richly endowed with tropical forests and large oil and natural-gas reserves. Developing these resources has taken years (the oil and gas fields began pro-

(UN photo by John Isaac)

Some of the Pacific Rim nations are resource-rich, but development has been curtailed by political instability and a strong traditional culture. This worker is farming as his ancestors did with techniques that have not changed for hundreds of years.

duction as recently as 1978) and has required massive infusions of investment monies from Japan and other countries. By the mid-1990s, more than 3,000 companies were doing business in Malaysia, and the country was moving into the ranks of the world's large exporters.

*Command economies* lag far behind the rest, not only because of the endemic inefficiency of the system but because military dictatorships and continual warfare have sapped the strength of the people. Yet significant changes in some of these countries are now emerging. China and Vietnam, in particular, are eager to modernize their economies and institute market-based reforms. Historically having directed its trade to North America and Europe, Japan is now finding its Asian/Pacific neighbors—especially the socialist-turning-capitalist ones—to be convenient recipients of its powerful economic and cultural influence.

Many of the *less developed countries* (LDCs) are the small micro-states of the Pacific with limited resources and tiny internal markets. Others, like Papua New Guinea, have only recently achieved political independence and are searching for a comfortable role in the world economy.

### Environmental Destruction and Social Ills

Environmental destruction in the Pacific Rim is a problem of mammoth proportions. For more than 20 years, the former Soviet Union dumped nuclear waste into the Sea of Japan; China's use of coal in industrial development has produced acid rain over Korea and Japan; deforestation in Thailand, Myanmar, and other parts of Southeast Asia and China has destroyed many thousands of acres of watershed and wildlife habitat. On the Malaysian island of Sarawak, for example, loggers work through the night, using floodlights, to cut timber to satisfy the demands of international customers, especially Japanese. The forests there are disappearing at a rate of 3 percent a year. Highway and hydroelectric-dam construction in many countries in Asia has seriously altered the natural environment. But environmental damage is perhaps most noticeable in the cities: mercury pollution in Jakarta Bay has led to brain disorders among children in Indonesia's capital city; air pollution in Manila and Beijing ranks among the world's worst, while not far behind are Bangkok and Seoul; water pollution in Hong Kong has forced the closure of many beaches.

An environmentalist's nightmare came true in 1997 and 1998 in Asia, when thousands of acres of timber went up in a cloud of smoke. Fueled by the worst El Niño–produced drought in 30 years and started by farmers seeking an easy way to clear land for farming, wildfires in Malaysia, Indonesia, and Brunei covered much of Southeast Asia in a thick blanket of smoke for months. Singapore reported its worst pollution-index record ever. All countries in the region complained that Indonesia, in particular, was not doing enough to put out the fires. Foreign-embassy personnel, citing serious health risks, left the region until rains—or the lack of anything more to burn—extinguished the flames. Airports had to close, hundreds of people complaining of respiratory problems sought help at hospitals, and many pedestrians and even those inside buildings donned face masks. With valuable timber becoming more scarce all the time, many people around the world reacted with anger at the callous disregard for the Earth's natural resources.

While conservationists are raising the alarm about the region's polluted air and declining green spaces, medical professionals are expressing dismay at the speed with which serious diseases such as AIDS are spreading in Asia. The Thai government now believes that more than 2.4 million Thais are HIV-positive. World Health Organization data suggest that the AIDS epidemic is growing faster in Asia (and Africa) than anywhere else in the world. Added to these problems are drug and alcohol addictions and the attendant impact on family stability.

### GUARDED OPTIMISM

Warfare, overpopulation, political instability, identity confusion, uneven development, and environmental and social ills would seem to be an irresolvable set of problems for the people of the Pacific Rim, but the start of the new millenium also gives reason for guarded optimism. Unification talks continue off

In this United Nations Development Program project, people dig and move earth into flood-damaged areas in North Korea for future crop planting.

and on between North and South Korea, as do talks between Japan and Russia on the Northern Territories dispute. Other important issues are also under discussion all over the region, and the UN peacekeeping effort in Cambodia seems to have paid off—at least there is a legally elected government in place, and most belligerents have put down their arms.

Until the Asian financial and currency crises of 1998–1999, the world media carried glowing reports on the burgeoning economic strength of many Pacific Rim countries. Typical was the *CIA World Factbook 1996–1997,* which reported high growth in gross national product (GNP) per capita for most Rim countries: South Korea, 9.0 percent; Hong Kong, 5.0 percent; Indonesia, 7.5 percent; Japan (due to recession), 0.3 percent; Malaysia, 9.5 percent; Singapore, 8.9 percent; and Thailand, 8.6 percent. By comparison, the U.S. GNP growth rate was 2.1 percent; Great Britain, 2.7 percent; and Canada, 2.1 percent. Other reports on the Rim compared 1990s investment and savings percentages with those of 20 years earlier; in almost every case, there had been a tremendous improvement in the economic capacity of these countries.

Throughout the 1980s and most of the 1990s, the rate of economic growth in the Pacific Rim was indeed astonishing. In 1987, for example, the rate of real gross domestic product (GDP) growth in the United States was 3.5 percent over the previous year. By contrast, in Hong Kong, the rate was 13.5 percent; in Taiwan, 12.4 percent; in Thailand, 10.4 percent;

and in South Korea, 11.1 percent. In 1992, economic growth throughout Asia averaged 7 percent, as compared to only 4.8 percent for the rest of the world. But recession in Japan, near financial collapse in Indonesia, and problems in other Asian countries have slowed the growth rates throughout the region. Still, Singapore, and many other Pacific Rim economies are expected to grow faster than European and North American economies, and even politically chaotic Indonesia believes that its economy will stabilize very soon.

The significance of high growth rates, in addition to improvements in the standard of living, is the shift in the source of development capital, from North America to Asia. Historically, the economies of North America were regarded as the engine behind Pacific Rim growth; and yet today, growth in the United States and Canada trails many of the Rim economies. This anomaly can be explained, in part, by the hard work and savings ethics of Pacific Rim peoples and by their external-market–oriented development strategies. But, without venture capital and foreign aid, hard work and clever strategies would not have produced the rapid economic improvement that Asia has experienced over the past several decades. Japan's contribution to this improvement, through investments, loans, and donations, and often in much larger amounts than other investor nations such as the United States, cannot be overstated. This is why Japan is considered central to our definition of the Pacific Rim as an identifiable unit.

## ECONOMIC DEVELOPMENT IN SELECTED PACIFIC RIM COUNTRIES

*Economists have divided the Rim into five zones, based on the level of development, as follows:*

**DEVELOPED NATIONS**
  Australia
  Japan
  New Zealand

**NEWLY INDUSTRIALIZING COUNTRIES (NICs)**
  Hong Kong
  Singapore
  South Korea
  Taiwan

**RESOURCE-RICH DEVELOPING ECONOMIES**
  Brunei
  Indonesia
  Malaysia
  The Philippines
  Thailand

**COMMAND ECONOMIES***
  Cambodia
  China
  Laos
  Myanmar (Burma)
  North Korea
  Vietnam

**LESS DEVELOPED COUNTRIES (LDCs)**
  Papua New Guinea
  Pacific Islands

*China, Vietnam, and, to a much lesser degree, North Korea are moving toward free-market economies.*

Some subregions are also emerging. There is, of course, the Association of Southeast Asian Nations (ASEAN) regional trading unit; but the one that is gaining world attention is the informal region that people are calling "Greater China," consisting of the emerging capitalist enclaves of the People's Republic of China, Hong Kong, and Taiwan. Copying Japanese strategy and aided by a common written language and culture, this region has the potential of exceeding even the mammoth U.S. economy in the future. For now, however, and despite recent sluggish growth, Japan will remain the major player in the region.

Japan has been investing in the Asia/Pacific region for several decades. However, growing protectionism in its traditional markets as well as changes in the value of the yen and the need to find cheaper sources of labor (labor costs are 75 percent less in Singapore and 95 percent less in Indonesia) have raised Japan's level of involvement so high as to give it the upper hand in determining the course of development and political stability for the entire region. This heightened level of investment started to gain momentum in the mid-1980s.

Between 1984 and 1989, Japan's overseas development assistance to the ASEAN countries amounted to $6.1 billion. In some cases, this assistance translated to more than 4 percent of a nation's annual national budget and nearly 1 percent of GDP. Private Japanese investment in ASEAN countries plus Hong Kong, Taiwan, and South Korea was $8.9 billion between 1987 and 1988. In more recent years, the Japanese government or Japanese business invested $582 million in an auto-assembly plant in Taiwan, $5 billion in an iron and steel complex in China, $2.3 billion in a bullet-train plan for Malaysia, and $530 million in a tunnel under the harbor in Sydney, Australia. Japan is certainly not the only player in Asian development (Japan has "only" about 20 projects under way in Vietnam, for example, as compared to 80 for Hong Kong and 39 for Taiwan), but the volume of Japanese investment is staggering. In Australia alone, nearly 900 Japanese companies are now doing business. Throughout Asia, Japanese is becoming a major language of business.

Although Japan works very hard at globalizing its markets and its resource suppliers, it has also developed closer ties with its nearby Rim neighbors. In a recent year, out of 20 Rim countries, 13 listed Japan as their first- or second-most-important trading partner, and several more put Japan third. Japan receives 42 percent of Indonesia's exports and 26 percent of Australia's; in return, 23 percent of South Korea's imports, 29 percent of Taiwan's, 30 percent of Thailand's, 24 percent of Malaysia's, and 23 percent of Indonesia's come from Japan. Pacific Rim countries are clearly becoming more interdependent—but simultaneously more dependent on Japan—for their economic success.

## JAPANESE INFLUENCE, PAST AND PRESENT

This is certainly not the first time in modern history that Japanese influence has swept over Asia and the Pacific. A major thrust began in 1895, when Japan, like the European powers, started to acquire bits and pieces of the region. By 1942, the Japanese were in control of Taiwan, Korea, Manchuria and most of the populated parts of China, and Hong Kong; what are now Myanmar, Vietnam, Laos, and Cambodia; Thailand; Malaysia; Indonesia; the Philippines; part of New Guinea; and dozens of Pacific islands. In effect, by the 1940s, the Japanese were the dominant force in precisely the area that they have are influencing now and that we are calling the Pacific Rim.

The similarities do not end there, for, while many Asians of the 1940s were apprehensive about or openly resistant to Japanese rule, many others welcomed the Japanese invaders and even helped them to take over their countries. This was because they believed that Western influence was out of place in Asia and that Asia should be for Asians. They hoped that the Japanese military would rid them of Western rule—and it did: After the war, very few Western powers were able to regain control of their Asian and Pacific colonies.

Today, many Asians and Pacific islanders are concerned about Japanese financial and industrial influence in their countries, but they welcome Japanese investment anyway because they believe that it is the best and cheapest way to rid their countries of poverty and underdevelopment. So far, they are right—by copying the Japanese model of economic development, and thanks to Japanese trade, foreign aid, and investment, the entire region—some countries excepted—has increased its wealth and positioned itself to be a major player in the world economy for the foreseeable future.

It is important to note, however, that many Rim countries, such as Taiwan, Hong Kong, and South Korea, are strong challengers to Japan's economic dominance; in addition, Japan has not always felt comfortable about its position as head of the pack, for fear of a backlash. For example, Japan's higher regional profile has prompted complaints against the Japanese military's World War II treatment of civilians in Korea and China and forced Japan to pledge $1 billion to various Asian countries as a symbolic act of apology.

Why have the Japanese re-created a modern version of the old Greater East Asian Co-Prosperity Sphere of the imperialistic 1940s? We cannot find the answer in the propaganda of wartime Japan—fierce devotion to emperor and nation and belief in the superiority of Asians over all other races are no longer the propellants in the Japanese economic engine. Rather, Japan courts Asia and the Pacific today to acquire resources to sustain its civilization. Japan is about the size of California, but it has 5 times as many people and not nearly as much arable land. Much of Japan is mountainous; many other parts are off limits because of active volcanoes (one tenth of all the active volcanoes in the world are in Japan); and, after 2,000-plus years of intensive and uninterrupted habitation, the natural forests are long since consumed, as are most of the other natural resources—most of which were scarce to begin with.

In short, Japan continues to extract resources from the rest of Asia and the Pacific because it is the same Japan as before—environmentally speaking, that is. Take oil. In the early 1940s, Japan needed oil to keep its industries (as well as its military machine) operating, but the United States wanted to punish Japan for its military expansion in Asia, so it shut off all shipments to Japan of any kind, including oil. That may have seemed politically right to the policymakers of the day, but it did not change Japan's resource environment; Japan still did not have its own oil, and it still needed as much oil as before. So Japan decided to capture a nearby nation that did have natural reserves of oil—in 1941, it attacked Indonesia and obtained by force the resource it had been denied through trade.

Japan has no more domestic resources now than it did half a century ago, and yet its demands—for food, minerals, lumber, paper—are greater. Except for fish, you name it—Japan does not have it. A realistic comparison is to imagine trying to feed half the population of the United States solely from the natural output of the state of Montana. As it happens, however, Japan sits next to the continent of Asia, which is rich in almost all the materials it needs. For lumber, there are the forests of Malaysia; for food, there are the farms and ranches

(UN photo by Nichiro Gyogyo)

These men work on a Japanese factory ship, a floating cannery that processes salmon harvested from the Pacific.

of New Zealand and Australia; and for oil, there are Indonesia and Brunei, the latter of which sells 50 percent of its exports to Japan. The quest for resources is why Japan flooded its neighbors with Japanese yen in recent decades and why it will continue to maintain an active engagement with all Pacific Rim countries well into the future.

**Catalyst for Development**

In addition to the need for resources, Japan has turned to the Pacific Rim in an attempt to offset the anti-Japanese import or protectionist policies of its historic trading partners. Because so many import tariffs are imposed on products sold directly from Japan, Japanese companies find that they can avoid or minimize tariffs if they cooperate on joint ventures in Rim countries and have products shipped from there. The result is that both Japan and its host countries are prospering as never before. Sony Corporation, for example, assembles parts made in both Japan and Singapore to construct videocassette recorders at its Malaysian factory, for export to North America, Europe, and other Rim countries. Toyota Corporation intends to build its automobile transmissions in the Philippines and its steering-wheel gears in Malaysia, and to build the final product in whichever country intends to buy its cars.

So helpful has Japanese investment been in spawning indigenous economic powerhouses that many other Rim countries are now reinvesting in the region. In particular, Hong Kong, Singapore, Taiwan, and South Korea are now in a position to seek cheaper labor markets in Indonesia, Malaysia, the Philippines, and Thailand. In recent years, they have invested billions of dollars in the resource- and labor-rich economies of Southeast Asia, increasing living standards and adding to the growing interconnectivity of the region. An example is a Taiwanese company that has built the largest eel-production facility in the world—in Malaysia—and ships its entire product to Korea and Japan.

Eyed as a big consumer as well as a bottomless source of cheap labor is the People's Republic of China. Many Rim countries, such as South Korea, Taiwan, Hong Kong, and Japan, are working hard to increase their trade with China. In 1990, two-way trade between Taiwan and China was already more than $4 billion; between Hong Kong and China, it was $50 billion. Japan was especially eager to resume economic aid to China in 1990 after temporarily withholding aid because of the Tiananmen Square massacre. For its part, China is establishing free-enterprise zones that will enable it to participate more fully in the regional economy. Already the Bank of China is the second-largest bank in Hong Kong.

Japan and a handful of other economic powerhouses of the Rim are not the only big players in Rim economic development. The United States and Canada remain major investors in the Pacific Rim (in computers and automobiles, for example), and Europe maintains its historical linkages with the region (such as oil). But there is no question that Japan has been the main catalyst for development. As a result, Japan itself has become wealthy. The Japanese stock market rivals the New York Stock Exchange, almost all of the top 20 banks in the world are Japanese, and many of the world's wealthiest individuals are Japanese. Loans secured by now-deflated land prices have damaged the Japanese banking industry in recent years, but it is likely that the banks will recover and that Japan will retain its preeminence in the region.

Not everyone is pleased with the way Japan has been giving aid and making loans in the region. Money invested by the Japan International Development Organization (JIDO) has usually been closely connected to the commercial interests of Japanese companies. For instance, commercial-loan agreements have often required that the recipient of low-interest loans purchase Japanese products.

Nevertheless, it is clear that many countries would be a lot worse off without Japanese aid. In a recent year, JIDO aid around the world was $10 billion. Japan is the dominant supplier of foreign aid to the Philippines and a major investor; in Thailand, where U.S. aid recently amounted to $20 million, Japanese aid was close to $100 million. Some of this aid, moreover, gets recycled from one country to another within the Rim—Thailand, for example, receives more aid from Japan than any other country, but in turn, it supplies major amounts of aid to other nearby countries. Thus we can see the growing interconnectivity of the region, a reality now recognized formally by the establishment of the Asia Pacific Economic Cooperation Council (APEC).

During the militaristic 1940s, Japanese dominance in the region produced antagonism and resistance. However, it also gave subjugated countries new highways, railways, and other infrastructural improvements. Today, while host countries continue to benefit from infrastructural advances, they also receive quality manufactured products. Once again, Northeast Asian, Southeast Asian, and South Pacific peoples have begun to talk about Japanese domination. The difference is that this time, few seem upset about it; many countries no longer believe that Japan has military aspirations against them, and they regard Japanese investment as a first step toward becoming economically strong themselves. Many people are eager to learn the Japanese language; in some cities, such as Seoul, Japanese has displaced English as the most valuable business language. Nevertheless, to deter negative criticism arising from its prominent position in the Rim, Japan has increased its gift giving, such that now it has surpassed the United States as the world's most generous donor of foreign aid.

## ASIAN FINANCIAL CRISIS

All over Asia, but especially in Thailand, Indonesia, Malaysia, South Korea, and the Philippines, business leaders and government economists are scrambling to minimize the damage from the worst financial crisis in decades, a crisis that exploded in late 1997. With their economies in deep trouble, the governments are shutting down some of their consular offices in other countries, canceling costly public-works projects, and enduring abuse heaped on them by suddenly unemployed citizens.

For years, Southeast Asian countries copied the Japanese model: They stressed exports, and they allowed their governments to decide which industries to develop. This economic-development approach worked very well for a while, but governments were not eager to let natural markets guide production. So, even when profits from government-supported industries were down, the governments believed that they should continue to maintain these industries through loans from Japan and other sources. But banks can loan only so much, especially if it is "risky" money, and eventually the banks' creditworthiness was called into question. Money became tighter. Currencies were devalued, making it harder still to pay off loans and forcing many companies and banks into bankruptcy. Stock markets nose-dived. Thousands of workers were laid off, and many of the once-booming Asian economies hit hard times.

Japan's own economic sluggishness meant that it was not able to serve as the engine behind Asia's economic growth with the same vigor as it did in the 1980s and early 1990s. One after another, the affected countries requested bailout assistance from the International Monetary Fund (IMF), a pool of money donated by some 183 nations. IMF funding seems to have halted the flow of red ink at least temporarily.

But this is not without a cost: Each recipient is required to restructure its economy, which will mean that many unprofitable companies and banks will go under and many workers will have to tighten their belts until the cycle rights itself.

The crisis has revealed how interconnected are the economies of the region and how much Asia has depended on Japan to stimulate growth. It is no wonder that IMF officials say Japan is the key; it must first fix its own problems before the rest of Asia will rebound.

## POLITICAL AND CULTURAL CHANGES

Although economic issues are important to an understanding of the Pacific Rim, political and cultural changes are also crucial. The new, noncombative relationship between the United States and the former Soviet bloc means that special-interest groups and governments in the Rim will be less able to rely on the strength and power of those nations to help advance or uphold their positions. Communist North Korea, for instance, can no longer rely on the Soviet bloc for trade and ideological support. North Korea may begin to look for new ideological neighbors or, more significantly, to consider major modifications in its own approach to organizing society.

Similarly, ideological changes are afoot in Myanmar, where the populace are tiring of life under a military dictatorship. The military can no longer look for guaranteed support from the crumbling socialist world.

In the case of Hong Kong, the British government shied away from extreme political issues and agreed to the peaceful annexation in 1997 of a capitalist bastion by a Communist nation, China. It is highly unlikely that such a decision would have been made had the issue of Hong Kong's political status arisen during the anti-Communist years of the cold war. One must not get the impression, however, that suddenly peace has arrived in the Pacific Rim. But outside support for extreme ideological positions seems to be giving way to a pragmatic search for peaceful solutions. This should have a salutary effect throughout the region.

The growing pragmatism in the political sphere is yielding changes in the cultural sphere. Whereas the Chinese formerly looked upon Western dress and music as decadent, most Chinese now openly seek out these cultural commodities and are finding ways to merge these things with the Communist polity under which they live. It is also increasingly clear to most leaders in the Pacific Rim that international mercantilism has allowed at least one regional country, Japan, to rise to the highest ranks of world society, first economically and now culturally and educationally. The fact that one Asian nation has accomplished this leap fosters hope that others can do so also.

Rim leaders also see, however, that Japan achieved its position of prominence because it was willing to change traditional mores and customs and accept outside modes of thinking and acting. Religion, family life, gender relations, recreation, and many other facets of Japanese life have altered during Japan's rapid rise to the top. Many other Pacific Rim nations—including Thailand, Singapore, and South Korea—seem determined to follow Japan's lead in this regard. Therefore, we are witnessing in certain high-growth Rim economies significant cultural changes: a reduction in family size, a secularization of religious impulses, a desire for more leisure time and better education, and a move toward acquisition rather than "being" as a determinant of one's worth. That is, more and more people are likely to judge others' value by what they own rather than what they believe or do. Buddhist values of self-denial, Shinto values of respect for nature, and Confucian values of family loyalty are giving way slowly to Western-style individualism and the drive for personal comfort and monetary success. Formerly close-knit communities, such as those in American Samoa, are finding themselves struggling with drug abuse and gang-related violence, just as in the more metropolitan countries. These changes in political and cultural values are at least as important as economic growth in projecting the future of the Pacific Rim.

# The Pacific Islands

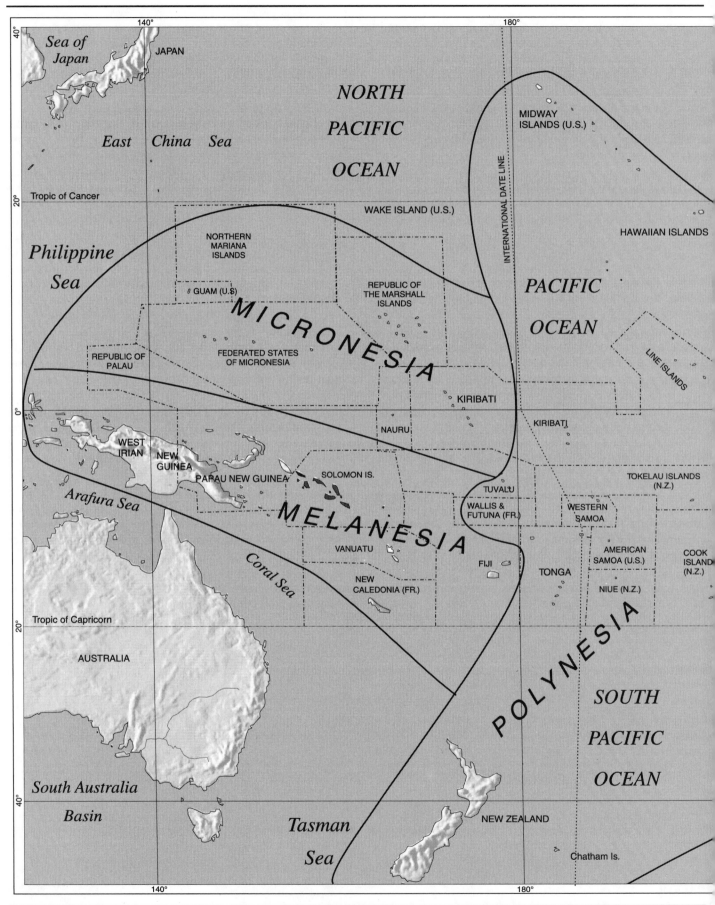

Sea of Japan

JAPAN

NORTH PACIFIC OCEAN

East China Sea

MIDWAY ISLANDS (U.S.)

INTERNATIONAL DATE LINE

Tropic of Cancer

WAKE ISLAND (U.S.)

HAWAIIAN ISLANDS

Philippine Sea

NORTHERN MARIANA ISLANDS

GUAM (U.S)

REPUBLIC OF THE MARSHALL ISLANDS

PACIFIC OCEAN

M I C R O N E S I A

REPUBLIC OF PALAU

FEDERATED STATES OF MICRONESIA

LINE ISLANDS

KIRIBATI

WEST IRIAN

NEW GUINEA

NAURU

KIRIBATI

Arafura Sea

PAPAU NEW GUINEA

SOLOMON IS.

TOKELAU ISLANDS (N.Z.)

M E L A N E S I A

TUVALU

WALLIS & FUTUNA (FR.)

WESTERN SAMOA

Coral Sea

VANUATU

FIJI

AMERICAN SAMOA (U.S.)

COOK ISLAND (N.Z.)

NEW CALEDONIA (FR.)

TONGA

NIUE (N.Z.)

Tropic of Capricorn

AUSTRALIA

P O L Y N E S I A

SOUTH PACIFIC OCEAN

South Australia Basin

Tasman Sea

NEW ZEALAND

Chatham Is.

14

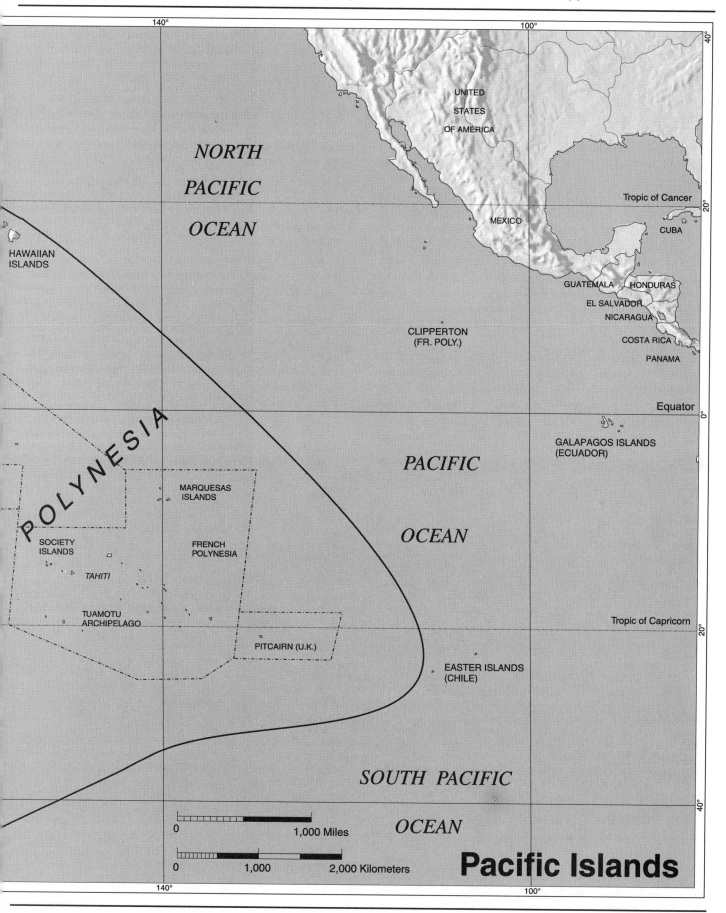

NORTH

PACIFIC

OCEAN

HAWAIIAN
ISLANDS

UNITED
STATES
OF AMERICA

Tropic of Cancer

MEXICO

CUBA

GUATEMALA   HONDURAS

EL SALVADOR

NICARAGUA

COSTA RICA

PANAMA

CLIPPERTON
(FR. POLY.)

P O L Y N E S I A

PACIFIC

OCEAN

Equator

GALAPAGOS ISLANDS
(ECUADOR)

MARQUESAS
ISLANDS

SOCIETY
ISLANDS

FRENCH
POLYNESIA

TAHITI

TUAMOTU
ARCHIPELAGO

Tropic of Capricorn

PITCAIRN (U.K.)

EASTER ISLANDS
(CHILE)

SOUTH  PACIFIC

OCEAN

0                    1,000 Miles

0          1,000          2,000 Kilometers

## Pacific Islands

## PLENTY OF SPACE, BUT NO ROOM

There are about 30,000 islands in the Pacific Ocean. Most of them are found in the South Pacific and have been classified into three mammoth regions: Micronesia, composed of some 2,000 islands with such names as Palau, Nauru, and Guam; Melanesia, where 200 different languages are spoken on such islands as Fiji and the Solomon Islands; and Polynesia, composed of such islands as Hawaii, Samoa, and Tahiti.

Straddling both sides of the equator, these territories are characterized as much by what is *not* there as by what *is*—that is, between every tiny island lie hundreds and often thousands of miles of open ocean. A case in point is the Cook Islands. Associated with New Zealand, this 15-island group contains only 92 square miles of land but is spread over 714,000 square miles of open sea. So expansive is the space between islands that early explorers from Europe and the Spanish lands of South America often unknowingly bypassed dozens of islands that lay just beyond view in the vastness of the 64 million square miles of the Pacific—the world's largest ocean.

However, once the Europeans found and set foot on the islands, they inaugurated a process that irreversibly changed the history of island life. Their goals in exploring the Pacific were to convert islanders to Christianity and to increase the power and prestige of their homelands (and themselves) by obtaining resources and acquiring territory. They thought of themselves and European civilization as superior to others and often treated the "discovered" peoples with contempt. An example is the "discovery" of the Marquesas Islands (from whence came some of the Hawaiian people) by the Peruvian Spaniard Alvaro de Mendana. Mendana landed in the Marquesas in 1595 with some women and children—and, significantly, 378 soldiers. Within weeks, his entourage had planted three Christian crosses, declared the islands to be the possession of the king of Spain, and killed 200 islanders. Historian Ernest S. Dodge describes the inhumanity of the first contacts:

> The Spaniards opened fire on the surrounding canoes for no reason at all. To prove himself a good marksman one soldier killed both a Marquesan and the child in his arms with one shot as the man desperately swam for safety.... The persistent Marquesans again attempted to be friendly by bringing fruit and water, but again they were shot down when they attempted to take four Spanish water jars. Magnanimously the Spaniards allowed the Marquesans to stand around and watch while mass was celebrated. . . . When [the islanders] attempted to take two canoe loads of . . . coconuts to the ships half the unarmed natives were killed and three of the bodies hung in the rigging in grim warning. The Spaniards were not only killing under orders, they were killing for target practice.

*—Islands and Empires; Western Impact on the Pacific and East Asia*

(UN photo by Nagata Jr.)

In the South Pacific area of Micronesia, some 2,000 islands are spread over an ocean area of 3 million square miles. There remain many relics of the diverse cultures found on these islands; these boys are walking among the highly prized stone discs that were used as money on the islands of the Yap District.

All over the Pacific, islanders were "pacified" through violence or deception inflicted on them by the conquering nations of France, England, Spain, and others. Rivalries among the European nations were often acted out in the Pacific. For example, the Cook Islands, inhabited by a mixture of Polynesian and Maori peoples, were partly controlled by the Protestant Mission of the London Missionary Society until the threat of incursions by French Catholics from Tahiti persuaded the British to declare the islands a protectorate of Britain. New Zealand eventually annexed the islands, and it controlled them until 1965.

Business interests frequently took precedence over islanders' sovereignty. In Hawaii, for instance, when Queen Liliuokalani proposed to limit the influence of the business community in island governance, a few dozen American business leaders—without the knowledge of the U.S. president or Congress yet with the unauthorized help of 160 U.S. Marines—overthrew the Hawaiian monarch, installed Sanford Dole (of Dole Pineapple fame) as president, and petitioned Congress for annexation as a U.S. territory.

Whatever the method of acquisition, once the islands were under European or American control, the colonizing nations insisted that the islanders learn Western languages, wear Western clothing, convert to Christianity, and pay homage to faraway rulers whom they had never seen.

This blatant Eurocentrism ignored the obvious—that the islanders already had rich cultural traditions that both predated European culture and constituted substantial accomplishments in technology, the arts, and social structure. Islanders were skilled in the construction of boats suitable for navigation on the high seas and of homes and religious buildings of varied architecture; they had perfected the arts of weaving and cloth-making, tattooing (the word itself is Tahitian), and dancing. Some cultures organized their political affairs much as had early New Englanders, with village meetings to decide issues by consensus, while others had developed strong chieftainships and kingships with an elaborate variety of rituals and taboos (a Tongan word) associated with the ruling elite. Island trade involving vast distances brought otherwise disparate people together; and, although reading and writing was not known on most islands, some evidence of an ancient writing system has been found.

Despite these cultural attributes and a long history of skill in interisland or intertribal warfare, the islanders could not withstand the superior force of European firearms. Within just a few generations, the entire Pacific had been conquered and colonized by Britain, France, Holland, Germany, the United States, and other nations.

## CONTEMPORARY GROUPINGS

The Pacific islands today are classified into three racial/cultural groupings. The first, Micronesia, with a population of approximately 414,000 people, contains seven political entities, four of which are politically independent and three

## TYPES OF ISLAND GOVERNMENTS

The official names of some of the Pacific island nations indicate the diversity of government structures found there:

Republic of Fiji
Federated States of Micronesia
Republic of Palau
Independent State of Papua New Guinea
Kingdom of Tonga
Republic of Vanuatu
Independent State of Western Samoa

of which are affiliated with the United States. Guam is perhaps the best known of these islands. Micronesians share much in common genetically and culturally with Asians. The term *Micronesia* refers to the small size of the islands in this group.

The second grouping, Melanesia, with a population of some 5.5 million (if New Guinea is included), contains six political entities, four of which are independent and two of which are affiliated with colonial powers. The best known of these islands is probably Fiji. The term *Melanesia* refers to the dark skin of the inhabitants, who, despite appearances, apparently have no direct ties with Africa.

Polynesia, the third grouping, with a population of 536,000, contains 12 political entities, three of which are independent, while the remaining are affiliated with colonial powers. *Polynesia* means "many islands," the most prominent of which is probably Hawaii. Most of the cultures in Polynesia have some ancient connections with the Marquesas Islands or Tahiti.

Subtracting the atypically large population of the island of New Guinea leaves about 2.2 million people in the region that we generally think of as the Pacific islands. Although it is possible that some of the islands may have been peopled by or had contact with ancient civilizations of South America, the overwhelming weight of scholarship places the origins of the Pacific islanders in Southeast Asia, Indonesia, and Australia.

Geologically, the islands may be categorized into the tall, volcanic islands, which are well endowed with water, flora, and fauna and are suitable for agriculture; and the dry, flat, coral islands, which have fewer resources (though some are rich in phosphate). It also appears that the farther away an island is from the Asian or Australian continental landmass, the less varied and plentiful the flora and fauna.

## THE PACIFIC COMMUNITY

During the early years of Western contact and colonization, maltreatment of the indigenous peoples and diseases such as measles and influenza greatly reduced their numbers and their cultural strength. Moreover, the carving up of the Pacific by different Western powers superimposed a cultural fragmentation on the region that added to the separateness resulting naturally

## THE CASE OF THE DISAPPEARING ISLAND

It wasn't much to begin with, but the way things are going, it won't be *anything* very soon. Nauru, a tiny, 8½-square-mile dot of phosphate dirt in the Pacific, is being gobbled up by the Nauru Phosphate Corporation. Made of bird droppings (guano) mixed with marine sediment, Nauru's high-quality phosphate has a ready market in Australia, New Zealand, Japan, and other Pacific Rim countries, where it is used in industry, medicine, and agriculture.

Many Pacific islanders with few natural resources to sell to the outside world envy the 4,500 Nauruans. The Nauruans pay no taxes, yet the government, thanks to phosphate sales, is able to provide them with free health and dental care, bus transportation, newspapers, and schooling (including higher education if they are willing to leave home temporarily for Australia, with the trip paid for by the government). Rent for government-built homes, supplied with telephones and electricity, is only about $5 a month. Nor do Nauruans have to work particularly hard for a living. Most laborers in the phosphate pits are imported from other islands; most managers and other professionals come from Australia, New Zealand, and Great Britain.

Phosphate is Nauru's only export, and yet the country makes so much money from it that, technically speaking, Nauru is the richest country per capita in the world. Unable to spend all the export earnings (even though it owns and operates several Boeing 737s, a number of hotels on other islands, and the tallest skyscraper in Melbourne, Australia), the government puts lots of the money away in trust accounts for a rainy day.

It all sounds nice, but the island is literally being mined away. Already there is only just a little fringe of green left along the shore, where everyone lives, and the government is debating what should happen when even the ground under people's homes is mined and shipped away. Some think that topsoil should be brought in to see if the moonlike surface of the excavated areas can be revitalized. Others think that moving away makes sense—with all its money, the government could just buy another island somewhere and move everyone (an idea that Australia suggested years ago, even before Nauru's independence in 1968). Of course, since the government owns the phosphate company, it could just put a halt to any more mining. But if it does, what would Nauru be to anybody? On the other hand, if it doesn't, will Nauru *be* at all?

from distance. Today, however, improved medical care is allowing the populations of the islands to rebound, and the withdrawal or realignment of European and American political power under the post–World War II United Nations policy of decolonization has permitted the growth of regional organizations.

First among the postwar regional groups was the South Pacific Commission. Established in 1947, when Western powers were still largely in control, many of its functions have since been augmented or superseded by indigenously created organizations such as the South Pacific Forum, which was organized in 1971 and has since spawned numerous other associations, including the South Pacific Regional Trade and Economic Agency and the South Pacific Islands Fisheries Development Agency. These associations handle, through an executive body (the South Pacific Bureau for Economic Cooperation), such issues as relief funds, the environment, fisheries, trade, and regional shipping. These organizations have produced a variety of duty-free agreements among countries and yielded joint decisions about regional transportation and cultural exchanges. As a result, regional art festivals and sports competitions are now a regular feature of island life. And a regional university in New Zealand attracts several thousand island students a year, as do schools in Hawaii.

Some regional associations have been able to deal forcefully with much more powerful countries. For instance, when the regional fisheries association set higher licensing fees for foreign fishing fleets (most fleets are foreign, because island fishermen usually cannot provide capital for such large enterprises), the Japanese protested vehemently. Nevertheless, the association held firm, and many islands terminated their contracts with the Japanese rather than lower their fees. In 1994,

the Cook Islands, the Federated States of Micronesia, Fiji, Kiribati, the Marshall Islands, Nauru, Niue, Papua New Guinea, the Solomon Islands, Tonga, Tuvalu, Vanuatu, and Western Samoa signed an agreement with the United States to establish a joint commercial commission to foster private-sector businesses and to open opportunities for trade, investment, and training. Through this agreement, the people of the islands hope to increase the attractiveness of their products to the U.S. market.

Increasingly important issues in the Pacific are the testing of nuclear weapons and the disposal of toxic waste. Island leaders, with the occasional support of Australia and the strong support of New Zealand, have spoken out vehemently against the continuation of nuclear testing in the Pacific by the French government (Great Britain and the United States tested hydrogen bombs on coral atolls for years, but have now stopped) and against the burning of nerve gas stockpiles by the United States on Johnston Atoll. In 1985, the 13 independent or self-governing countries of the South Pacific adopted their first collective agreement on regional security, the South Pacific Nuclear Free Zone Treaty. Encouraged by New Zealand and Australia, the group declared the Pacific a nuclear-free zone and issued a communique deploring the dumping of nuclear waste in the region. Some island leaders, however, see the storage of nuclear waste as a way of earning income to compensate those who were affected by the nuclear testing on Bikini and Enewetak Islands. The Marshall Islands, for example, are interested in storing nuclear waste on already contaminated islands, although the nearby Federated States of Micronesia, which were observers at the Nuclear Free Zone Treaty talks, oppose the idea and have asked the Marshalls not to proceed.

In 1982, world leaders met in Jamaica to sign into international law the Law of the Sea. This law, developed under the auspices of the United Nations, gave added power to the tiny Pacific island nations because it extended the territory under their exclusive economic control to 12 miles beyond their shores or 200 miles of undersea continental shelf. This put many islands in undisputed control of large deposits of nickel, copper, magnesium, and other valuable metals. The seabed areas away from continents and islands were declared the world's common heritage, to be mined by an international company, with profits channeled to developing countries. The United States has negotiated for years to increase the role of industrialized nations in mining the seabed areas; if modifications are made to the treaty, the United States will likely sign the document.

## COMING OF AGE?

If the Pacific islands are finding more reason to cooperate economically and politically, they are still individually limited by the heritage of cultural fragmentation left them by their colonial pasts. Western Samoa, for example, was first annexed by Germany in 1900, only to be given to New Zealand after Germany's defeat in World War I. Today, the tiny nation of mostly Christian Polynesians, independent since 1962, uses both English and Samoan as official languages and embraces a formal governmental structure copied from Western parliamentary practice. Yet the structure of its hundreds of small villages remains decidedly traditional, with clan chiefs ruling over large extended families, who make their not particularly profitable livings by farming breadfruit, taro, yams, bananas, and copra.

Political independence also has not been easy for those islands that have embraced it nor for those colonial powers that continue to deny it. Two military coups toppled the elected government of Fiji (a former British colony) in 1987, and anticolonial unrest continues on many of the other islands (especially the French islands). Concern over economic viability has led most islands to remain in some sort of loose association with their former colonial overseers. After the defeat of Japan in World War II, the Marshall Islands, the Marianas, and the Carolines were assigned by the United Nations to the United States as a trust territory. The French Polynesian islands have remained overseas "departments" of France. In such places as New Caledonia, however, there has been a growing desire for autonomy, which France has attempted to meet in various ways while still retaining sovereignty. The UN decolonization policy has made it possible for most Pacific islands to achieve independence if they wish, but many are so small that true economic independence in the modern world will never be possible.

Indeed, no amount of political realignment can overcome the economic dilemma of most of the islands. Japan, the single largest purchaser of island products, as well as the United States and others, are good markets for the Pacific economies, but exports are primarily of mineral and agricultural products (coffee, tea, cocoa, sugar, tapioca, coconuts, mother-of-pearl) rather than of the more profitable manufactured or "value-added" items produced by industrial nations. In addition, there will always be the cost of moving products from the vastness of the Pacific to the various mainland markets.

## THIS IS LIBERATION?

In 1994, the people of the U.S. Territory of Guam celebrated the 50th anniversary of their liberation by U.S. Marines and Army Infantry from the occupying troops of the Japanese Army. During the three years that they controlled the tiny, 30-mile-long island, the Japanese massacred some of the Guamanians and subjected many others to forced labor and internment in concentration camps.

Their liberation, therefore, was indeed a cause for celebration. But the United States quickly transformed the island into its military headquarters for the continuing battle against the Japanese. The entire northern part of the island was turned into a base for B-29 bombers, and the Pacific submarine fleet took up residence in the harbor. Admiral Nimitz, commander-in-chief of the Pacific, made Guam his headquarters. By 1946, the U.S. military government in Guam had laid claim to nearly 80 percent of the island, displacing entire villages and hundreds of individual property owners.

Since then, some of the land has been returned, and large acreages have been handed over to the local civilian government—which was to have distributed most of it, but has not yet done so. The local government still controls about one third of the land, and the U.S. military controls another third, meaning that only one third of the island is available to the residents for private ownership. Litigation to recover the land has been bitter and costly (more than $40 million in legal expenses since 1975). The controversy has prompted some local residents to demand a different kind of relationship with the United States, one that would allow for more autonomy. It has also spurred the growth of nativist organizations such as the Chamorru Nation, which promotes the Chamorru language (the language of the original Malayo–Polynesian inhabitants; spelled *Chamorro* by the Spanish) and organizes acts of civil disobedience against both civilian and military authorities.

Guam was first overtaken by Spain in 1565. It has been controlled by the United States since 1898, except for the brief Japanese interlude. Whether the local islanders, who now constitute a fascinating mix of Chamorro, Spanish, Japanese, and American cultures, will be able to gain a larger measure of autonomy after 435 years of colonization by outsiders is difficult to predict, but the ever-present island motto, *Tano Y Chamorro* ("Land of the Chamorros"), certainly spells out the objective of many of those who call Guam home.

(UN photo/atb)

Bartering is still a common practice in Papua New Guinea. Here, coastal and inland dwellers are shown exchanging fish for yams, taro, and other agricultural products.

Another problem is that many of the profits from the island's resources do not redound to the benefit of the islanders. Tuna, for example, is an important and profitable fish catch, but most of the profits return to the Taiwanese, Korean, Japanese, and American fleets that ply the Pacific. Similarly, tourism profits largely end up in the hands of the multinational hotel owners. About 80 percent of visitors to the island of Guam since 1982 have been Japanese (more than half a million people annually)—seemingly a gold mine for local Guamanians, since each traveler typically spends more than $2,000. Close inspection of those expenditures, however, reveal that the Japanese tend to purchase their tickets on Japanese airlines and book rooms in Japanese-owned or -managed hotels. Thus, of the $92 million spent in 1992 by Japanese tourists in connection with their Guam vacations, well over 60 percent of it never made it into the hands of the Guamanians.

The poor economies, especially in the outer islands, have prompted many islanders to move to larger cities (about 1 million islanders now live in the Pacific's larger cities) to find work. Indeed, there is currently a tremendous mixing of all of the islands' peoples. Hawaii, for example, is peopled now with Samoans, Filipinos, and many other islanders; pure Hawaiians are a minority, and despite efforts to preserve the Hawaiian language, it is used less and less. Similarly, Fiji is now populated by more immigrants from India than by native Fijians. New Caledonians are outnumbered by Indonesians, Vietnamese, French, and others. And, of course, whites have long outnumbered the Maoris on New Zealand. Guam is peopled with islanders from all of Micronesia as well as from Samoa and other islands. In addition to interisland migration, many islanders emigrate to Australia, New Zealand, the United States, or other countries and then send money back home to sustain their families. Those remittances are important to the economies of the islands, but the absence of parents or adult children for long periods of time does considerable damage to the social fabric. In a few cases, such as in the Cook Islands and American Samoa, there are more islanders living abroad than remain on the islands. Those who leave often find life abroad quite a shock, for the island culture, influenced over the decades by the missionary efforts of Mormons, Methodists, Seventh-day Adventists, and especially the London Missionary Society, is conservative, cautious, and personal. Metropolitan life, by contrast, is considered by some islanders to be wild and impersonal. Some young emigrants respond to the "cold" environment and marginality of big-city life by engaging in deviant behavior themselves, such as selling drugs and joining gangs.

Island society itself, moreover, is not immune from the social problems that plague larger societies. Many islands report an increasing number of crimes and suicides. Young Samoans, for example, are afflicted with many of the same problems—gangs, drugs, and unemployment—as are their U.S. inner-city counterparts. Samoan authorities now report increases in incidences of rape, robbery, and other socially dysfunctional behaviors. In addition, the South Pacific Commission and the World Health Organization are now reporting an alarming increase in AIDS and other sexually transmitted diseases. Out of 22 Pacific island groupings, 13 reported cases of HIV or AIDS as of 1994—a 500 percent increase since 1989.

For decades, and notwithstanding the imposition of foreign ways, islanders have shared a common culture; most people know how to raise bananas, coconuts, and yams, how to roast pigs and fish, and how to make breadfruit, tapioca, and poi. But much of island culture has depended on an identity shaped and preserved by isolation from the rest of the world. Whether the essence of island life—and especially the identity of the people—can be maintained in the face of increasing integration into a much larger world remains to be seen.

# Japan

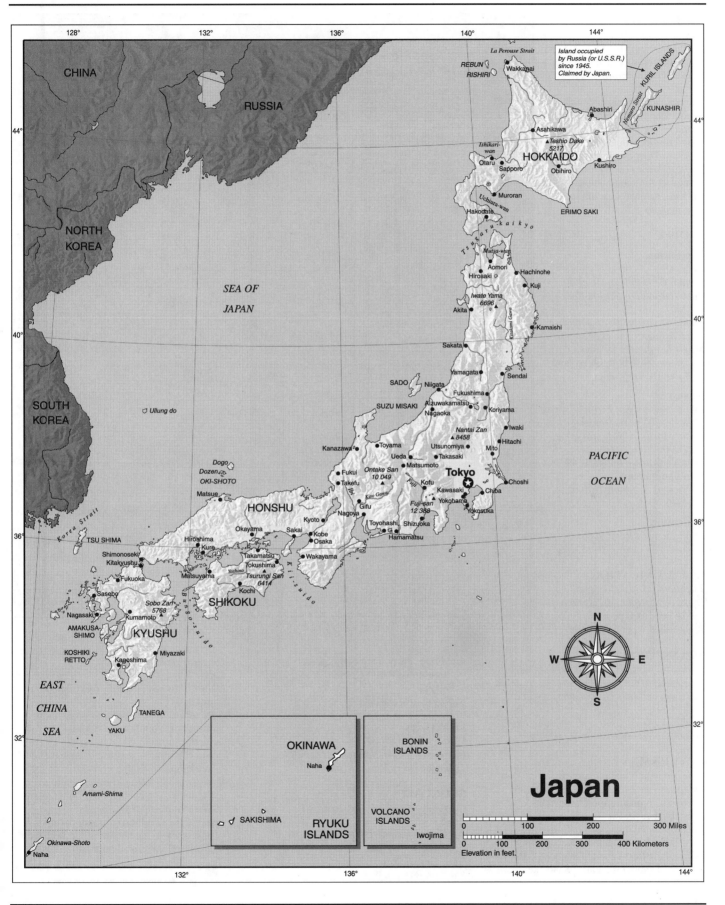

CHINA

RUSSIA

*La Perouse Strait*

*REBUN*
*RISHIRI*

Wakkanai

Island occupied by Russia (or U.S.S.R.) since 1945. Claimed by Japan.

KURIL ISLANDS

Abashiri

*Nemuro Strait*

KUNASHIR

Asahikawa

*Teshio Dake* 5217

*Ishikari-wan*

HOKKAIDO

NORTH KOREA

Otaru  Sapporo

Obihiro

Kushiro

Muroran

*Uchiura-wan*

ERIMO SAKI

Hakodate

*Tsugaru-kaikyo*

*Mutsu-wan*

SEA OF JAPAN

Aomori  Hachinohe

Hirosaki  Kuji

*Iwate Yama* 6696

*Kitakami Gawa*

Akita  Kamaishi

SOUTH KOREA

Sakata

Yamagata  Sendai

*Ullung do*

SADO  Niigata

SUZU MISAKI  Fukushima

Aizuwakamatsu  Koriyama

Nagaoka

*Nantai Zan* 8458  Iwaki

Hitachi

Kanazawa  Toyama

*Dogo*  *Dozen*  OKI-SHOTO

Fukui  Ueda  Utsunomiya  Mito

*Ontake San* 10 049  Matsumoto  Takasaki

Takefu  **Tokyo**

Matsue  Kofu  Choshi

*Fuji* 

HONSHU

Gifu  Kawasaki  Chiba

Kyoto  Nagoya  *Fuji-san* 12 388  Yokohama

*Kiso Gawa*  Yokosuka

Okayama  Sakai  Toyohashi  Shizuoka

TSU SHIMA  Hiroshima  Kobe  Hamamatsu

Shimonoseki  Kure  Osaka

Kitakyushu  Takamatsu  Wakayama

Fukuoka  Matsuyama  Tokushima

*Yoshino*  *Tsurugi San* 6414

Sasebo  Kochi

*Ibu*  *Kii-suido*

*Bungo-suido*

Nagasaki  *Sobo Zan* 5768  SHIKOKU

Kumamoto

AMAKUSA-SHIMO  KYUSHU

KOSHIKI RETTO  Kagoshima  Miyazaki

EAST CHINA SEA

PACIFIC OCEAN

TANEGA

YAKU

*Amami-Shima*

N
W    E
S

*Okinawa-Shoto*
Naha

OKINAWA

Naha

BONIN ISLANDS

SAKISHIMA

RYUKU ISLANDS

VOLCANO ISLANDS

Iwojima

## Japan

0  100  200  300 Miles

0  100  200  300  400 Kilometers

Elevation in feet.

# Japan (Nippon)

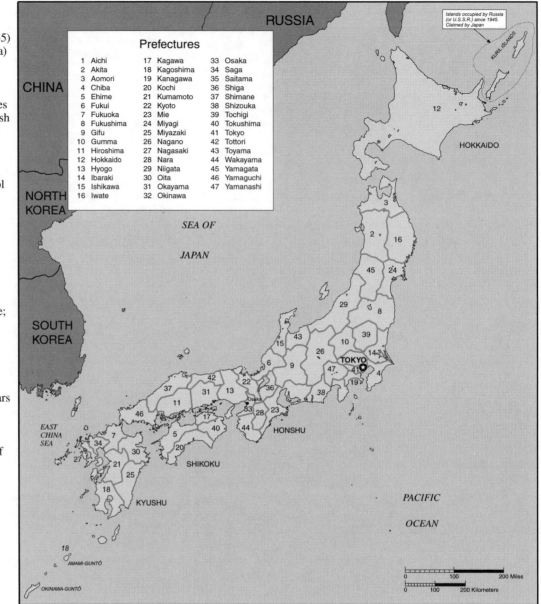

## GEOGRAPHY

*Area in Square Miles (Kilometers):* 145,882 (377,835) (slightly smaller than California)
*Capital (Population):* Tokyo (26,959,000)
*Environmental Concerns:* air pollution; acidification of lakes and reservoirs; depletion of fish and timber around the world due to Japanese demand
*Geographical Features:* mostly rugged and mountainous
*Climate:* tropical in south to cool temperate in north

## PEOPLE

### Population
*Total:* 125,733,000
*Annual Growth Rate:* 0.23%
*Rural/Urban Population Ratio:* 23/77
*Ethnic Makeup:* 99.4% Japanese; 0.6% others (mostly Korean)
*Major Language:* Japanese
*Religions:* 84% both Shinto and Buddhist; 16% others

### Health
*Life Expectancy at Birth:* 77 years (male); 84 years (female)
*Infant Mortality Rate (Ratio):* 4/1,000
*Average Caloric Intake:* 124% of FAO minimum
*Physicians Available (Ratio):* 1/546

### Education
*Adult Literacy Rate:* 99%
*Compulsory (Ages):* 6–15; free

## COMMUNICATION

*Telephones:* 1 per 2 people
*Daily Newspaper Circulation:* 576 per 1,000 people
*Televisions:* 1 per 1.5 people

## TRANSPORTATION

*Highways in Miles (Kilometers):* 686,616 (1,144,360)
*Railroads in Miles (Kilometers):* 14,202 (23,671)
*Usable Airfields:* 164
*Motor Vehicles in Use:* 66,900,000

## GOVERNMENT

*Type:* constitutional monarchy
*Independence Date:* traditional founding 660 B.C. (constitutional monarchy established 1947)
*Head of State/Government:* Emperor Akihito; Prime Minister Keizo Obuchi
*Political Parties:* Liberal Democratic Party; Social Democratic Party; Sakigake; New Frontier Party; Democratic Party; Japan Communist Party; Komeito Party; Sun Party
*Suffrage:* universal at 20

## MILITARY

*Military Expenditures (% of GDP):* 1.0%
*Current Disputes:* various territorial disputes with Russia, others

## ECONOMY

*Currency ($ U.S. Equivalent):* 112.46 yen = $1
*Per Capita Income/GDP:* $22,700/$2.85 trillion
*GDP Growth Rate:* 3.6%
*Inflation Rate:* 0.3%
*Unemployment Rate:* 3.4%
*Labor Force:* 67,230,000
*Natural Resources:* negligible oil and minerals
*Agriculture:* rice; sugar beets; vegetables; fruit; pork; poultry; dairy and eggs; fish
*Industry:* metallurgy; engineering; electrical and electronics; textiles; chemicals; automobiles; fishing
*Exports:* $385 billion (primary partners Southeast Asian countries, United States, Western European countries)
*Imports:* $329 billion (primary partners Southeast Asian countries, United States, Western European countries)

 http://www.odci.gov/cia/publications/factbook/country-frame.html

# Japan: Driving Force in the Pacific Rim

## HISTORICAL BACKGROUND

The Japanese nation is thought to have begun about 250 B.C., when ancestors of today's Japanese people began cultivating rice, casting objects in bronze, and putting together the rudiments of the Shinto religion. However, humans are thought to have inhabited the Japanese islands as early as 20,000 B.C. Some speculate that remnants of these or other early peoples may be the non-Oriental Ainu people (now largely Japanized) who still occupy parts of the northern island of Hokkaido. Asiatic migrants from China and Korea and islanders from the South Pacific occupied the islands between 250 B.C. and A.D. 400, contributing to the population base of modern Japan.

Between A.D. 300 and 710, military aristocrats from some of the powerful clans into which Japanese society was divided established their rule over large parts of the country. Eventually, the Yamato clan leaders, claiming divine approval, became the most powerful. Under Yamato rule, the Japanese began to import ideas and technology from nearby China, including the Buddhist religion and the Chinese method of writing—which the elite somewhat awkwardly adapted to spoken Japanese, an entirely unrelated language. The Chinese bureaucratic style of government and architecture was also introduced; Japan's first permanent capital was constructed at the city of Nara between the years 710 and 794.

As Chinese influence waned in the period 794–1185, the capital was relocated to Kyoto, with the Fujiwara family wielding real power under the largely symbolic figurehead of the emperor. A warrior class controlled by *shoguns,* or generals, held power at Kamakura between 1185 and 1333 and successfully defended the country from invasion by the Mongols. Buddhism became the religion of the masses, although Shintoism was often embraced simultaneously. Between 1333 and 1568, a very rigid class structure developed, along with a feudalistic economy controlled by *daimyos,* feudal lords who reigned over their own mini-kingdoms.

In 1543, Portuguese sailors landed in Japan, followed a few years later by the Jesuit missionary Francis Xavier. An active trade with Portugal began, and many Japanese (perhaps half a million), including some feudal lords, converted to Christianity. The Portuguese introduced firearms to the Japanese and perhaps taught them Western-style techniques of building castles with moats and stone walls. Wealthier feudal lords were able to utilize these innovations to defeat weaker rivals; by 1600, the country was unified under a military bureaucracy, although feudal lords still retained substantial sovereignty over their fiefs. During this time, the general Hideyoshi attempted an unsuccessful invasion of nearby Korea.

### The Tokugawa Era

In the period 1600 to 1868, called the Tokugawa Era, the social, political, and economic foundations of modern Japan were put in place. The capital was moved to Tokyo, cities began to grow in size, and a merchant class arose that was powerful enough to challenge the hegemony of the centuries-old warrior class. Strict rules of dress and behavior for each of the four social classes (samurai, farmer, craftsman, and merchant) were imposed, and the Japanese people learned to discipline themselves to these codes. Western ideas came to be seen as a threat to the established ruling class. The military elite expelled foreigners and put the nation into $2\frac{1}{2}$ centuries of extreme isolation from the rest of the world. Christianity was banned, as was most trade with the West. Even Japanese living abroad were forbidden from returning, for fear that they might have been contaminated with foreign ideas.

During the Tokugawa Era, indigenous culture expanded rapidly. Puppet plays and a new form of drama called *kabuki* became popular, as did *haiku* poetry and Japanese pottery and painting. The samurai code, called *bushido,* along with the concept of *giri,* or obligation to one's superiors, suffused Japanese society. Literacy among males rose to about 40 percent, higher than most European countries of the day. Samurai busied themselves with the education of the young, using teaching methods that included strict discipline, hard work, and self-denial.

During the decades of isolation, Japan grew culturally strong but militarily weak. In 1853, a U.S. naval squadron appeared in Tokyo Bay to insist that Japan open up its ports to foreign vessels needing supplies and desiring to trade. Similar requests had been denied in the past, but the sophistication of the U.S. ships and their advanced weaponry convinced the Japanese military rulers that they no longer could keep Japan isolated from the outside.

### The Era of Modernization: The Meiji Restoration

Treaties with the United States and other Western nations followed, and the dislocations associated with the opening of the country to the world soon brought discredit to the ruling shoguns. Provincial samurai took control of the government. The emperor, long a figurehead in Kyoto, away from the center of power, was moved to Tokyo in 1868, beginning the period known as the Meiji Restoration.

Although the Meiji leaders came to power with the intention of ousting all the foreigners and returning Japan to its former state of domestic tranquillity, they quickly realized that the nations of the West were determined to defend their newly won access to the ports of Japan. To defeat the foreigners, they reasoned, Japan must first acquire their knowledge and technology.

Thus, beginning in 1868, the Japanese leaders launched a major campaign to modernize the nation. Ambassadors and scholars were sent abroad to learn about Western-style government, education, and warfare. Implementing these ideas resulted in the abolition of the feudal system and the division of Japan into 43 prefectures, or states, and other administrative districts under the direct control of the Tokyo government. Legal codes that established the formal separation of society into social classes were abolished; and Western-style dress, music, and education were embraced. The old samurai class turned its attention from warfare to leadership in the government, in schools, and in business. Factories and rail-

(Japan National Tourist Organization)

The Japanese emperor has long been a figurehead in Japan. In 1926, Hirohito, pictured above, became emperor and ushered in the era named *Showa.* He died on January 7, 1989, having seen Japan through World War II and witnessed its rise to the economic world power it is today. He was succeeded by his son, Akihito, who named his reign *Heisei,* meaning "Achieving Peace."

roads were constructed, and public education was expanded. By 1900, Japan's literacy rate was 90 percent, the highest in all of Asia. Parliamentary rule was established along the lines of the government in Prussia, agricultural techniques were imported from the United States, and banking methods were adopted from Great Britain.

Japan's rapid modernization soon convinced its leaders that the nation was strong enough to begin doing what other advanced nations were doing: acquiring empires. Japan went to war with China, acquiring the Chinese island of Taiwan in 1895. In 1904, Japan attacked Russia and successfully acquired Korea and access to Manchuria (both areas having been in the sphere of influence of Russia). Siding against Germany in World War I, Japan was able to acquire Germany's Pacific empire—the Marshall, Caroline, and Mariana Islands. Western nations were surprised at Japan's rapid empire-building but did little to stop it.

The Great Depression of the 1930s caused serious hardships in Japan because, being resource-poor yet heavily populated, the country had come to rely on trade to supply its basic

needs. Many Japanese advocated the forced annexation of Manchuria as a way of providing needed resources. This was accomplished easily, albeit with much brutality, in 1931. With militarism on the rise, the Japanese nation began moving away from democracy and toward a military dictatorship. Political parties were eventually banned, and opposition leaders were jailed and tortured.

## WORLD WAR II AND THE JAPANESE EMPIRE

The battles of World War II in Europe, initially won by Germany, promised to substantially re-align the colonial empires of France and other European powers in Asia. The military elite of Japan declared its intention of creating a Greater East Asia Co-Prosperity Sphere—in effect, a Japanese empire created out of the ashes of the European empires in Asia that were then dissolving. In 1941, under the guidance of General Hideki Tojo and with the tacit approval of the emperor, Japan captured the former French colony of Indochina (Vietnam, Laos, and Cambodia), bombed Pearl Harbor in Hawaii, and captured oil-rich Indonesia. These victories were followed by others: Japan captured all of Southeast Asia, including Burma (now called Myanmar), Thailand, and Malaya, the Philippines, and parts of New Guinea; and expanded its hold in China and in the islands of the South Pacific. Many of these conquered peoples, lured by the Japanese slogan of "Asia for the Asians," were initially supportive of the Japanese, believing that Japan would rid their countries of European colonial rule. It soon became apparent, however, that Japan had no intention of relinquishing control of these territories and would go to brutal lengths to subjugate the local peoples. Japan soon dominated a vast empire, the constituents of which were virtually the same as those making up what we call the Pacific Rim today.

In 1941, the United States launched a counteroffensive against the powerful Japanese military. (American history books refer to this offensive as the Pacific Theater of World War II, but the Japanese call it the *Pacific War.* We use the term *World War II* in this text, for reasons of clarity and consistency.) By 1944, the U.S. troops had ousted the Japanese from most of their conquered lands and were beginning to attack the home islands themselves. Massive firebombing of Tokyo and other cities, combined with the dropping of two atomic bombs on Hiroshima and Nagasaki, convinced the Japanese military rulers that they had no choice but to surrender.

This was the first time in Japanese history that Japan had been conquered, and the Japanese were shocked to hear their emperor, Hirohito—whose voice had never been heard on radio—announce on August 14, 1945, that Japan was defeated. The emperor cited the suffering of the people—almost 2 million Japanese had been killed—devastation of the cities brought about by the use of a "new and most cruel bomb," and the possibility that, without surrender, Japan as a nation might be completely "obliterated." Emperor Hirohito then encouraged his people to look to the future, to keep pace with progress, and to help

(U.S. Navy)

On December 7, 1941, Japan entered World War II as a result of its of bombing of Pearl Harbor in Hawaii. This photograph, taken from an attacking Japanese plane, shows Pearl Harbor and a line of American battleships.

build world peace by accepting the surrender ("enduring the unendurable and suffering what is insufferable").

This attitude smoothed the way for the American Occupation of Japan, led by General Douglas MacArthur. Defeat seemed to inspire the Japanese people to adopt the ways of their more powerful conquerors and to eschew militarism. Under the Occupation forces, the Japanese Constitution was rewritten in a form that mimicked that of the United States. Industry was restructured, labor unions encouraged, land reform accomplished, and the nation as a whole demilitarized. Economic aid from the United States, as well as the prosperity in Japan that was occasioned by the Korean War in 1953, allowed Japanese industry to begin to recover from the devastation of war. The United States returned the governance of Japan back to the Japanese people by treaty in 1951 (although some 60,000 troops still remain in Japan as part of an agreement to defend Japan from foreign attack).

By the late 1960s, the Japanese economy was more than self-sustaining and the United States was Japan's primary trading partner (it remains so today, with about a third of Japanese exports purchased by Americans and similarly a substantial portion of Japanese food imports coming from the United States). Japan's trade with its former Asian empire, however, was minimal, because of lingering resentment against Japan for its wartime brutalities. (In the late 1970s, for

example, anti-Japanese riots and demonstrations occurred upon the visit of the Japanese prime minister to Indonesia.)

Nevertheless, between the 1960s and early 1990s, Japan experienced an era of unprecedented economic prosperity. Annual economic growth was 3 times as much as in other industrialized nations. Japanese couples voluntarily limited their family size so that each child born could enjoy the best of medical care and social and educational opportunities. The fascination with the West continued, but eventually, rather than "modernization" or "Americanization," the Japanese began to speak of "internationalization," reflecting both their capacity for and their actual membership in the world community, politically, culturally, and economically (but not militarily, because Japan's Constitution forbids Japan from engaging in war).

The Japanese government as well as private industry began to accelerate the drive for diversified markets and resources in the mid-1980s. This was partly in response to protectionist trends in countries in North America and Europe with which Japan had accumulated huge trade surpluses, but it was also due to changes in Japan's own internal social and economic conditions. Japan's recent resurgence of interest in its neighboring countries and the origin of the bloc of nations we are calling the Pacific Rim can be explained by both external protectionism and internal changes. This time, however, Japanese influence—no longer linked with militarism—is being welcomed by virtually all nations in the region.

## DOMESTIC CHANGE

What internal conditions are causing Japan's renewed interest in Asia and the Pacific? One change involves wage structure. For several decades, Japanese exports were less expensive than competitors' because Japanese workers were not paid as well as workers in North America and Europe. Today, however, the situation is reversed: Average manufacturing wages in Japan are now higher than those paid to workers in the United States. Schoolteachers, college professors, and many white-collar workers are also better off in Japan. These wage differentials are the result of successful union activity and demographic changes.

Whereas prewar Japanese families—especially those in the rural areas—were large, today's modern household typically consists of a couple and only one or two children. As Japan's low birth rate began to affect the supply of labor, companies were forced to entice workers with higher wages. An example is McDonald's, increasingly popular in Japan as a fast-food outlet. Whereas young people working at McDonald's outlets in the United States are paid at or slightly above the legal minimum wage of $5.15 an hour, McDonald's employees in

Japan are paid more than $7.00 an hour, simply because there are fewer youths available (many schools prohibit students from working during the school year). The cost of land, homes, food—even Japanese-grown rice—is so much higher in Japan than in most of its neighbor countries that employees in Japan expect high wages (household income in Japan is higher even than in the United States).

Given conditions like these, many Japanese companies have found that they cannot be competitive in world markets unless they move their operations to countries like the Philippines or Singapore, where an abundance of laborers keeps wage costs 75 to 95 percent lower than in Japan. Abundant, cheap labor (as well as a desire to avoid import tariffs) is also the reason why so many Japanese companies have been constructed in the economically depressed areas of the U.S. Midwest and South.

Another internal condition that is spurring Japanese interest in the Pacific Rim is a growing public concern for the domestic environment. Beginning in the 1970s, the Japanese courts handed down several landmark decisions in which Japanese companies were held liable for damages to people caused by chemical and other industrial wastes. Japanese industry, realizing that it no longer had a carte blanche to make profits at the expense of the environment, began moving some of its

(United Motor Manufacturing)

As the economy of Japan developed, manufacturing wages rose to a point where Japanese products were less competitive in world markets. In response, Japanese industry began to build manufacturing facilities abroad in partnership with foreign companies. These American workers are busy in a Toyota–General Motors plant in the United States.

smokestack industries to new locations in developing-world countries, just as other industrialized nations had done. This has turned out to be a wise move economically for many companies, as it has put their operations closer to their raw materials. This, in combination with cheaper labor costs, has allowed them to remain globally competitive. It also has been a tremendous benefit to the host countries, although environmental groups in many Rim countries are also now becoming active, and industry in the future may be forced to effect actual improvements in their operations rather than move polluting technologies to "safe" areas.

Attitudes toward work are also changing in Japan. Although the average Japanese worker still works about 6 hours more per week than the typical North American, the new generation of workers—those born and raised since World War II—are not so eager to sacrifice as much for their companies as were their parents. Recent policies have eliminated weekend work in many industries, and sports and other recreational activities are becoming increasingly popular. Given these conditions, Japanese corporate leaders are finding it more cost effective to move operations abroad to countries like South Korea, where labor legislation is weaker and long work hours remain the norm.

## MYTH AND REALITY OF THE ECONOMIC MIRACLE

The Japanese economy, like any other economy, must respond to market as well as social and political changes to stay vibrant. It just so happened that, for several decades, Japan's attempt to keep its economic boom alive created the conditions that, in turn, furthered the economies of all the countries in the Asia /Pacific region. That a regional "Yen Bloc" (so called because of the dominance of the Japanese currency, the yen) had been created was revealed in the late 1990s when sluggishness in the Japanese economy contributed to dramatic downturns in the economies of surrounding countries.

For many years, world business leaders were of the impression that whatever Japan did—whether targeting a certain market or reorienting its economy toward regional trade—turned to gold, as if the Japanese possessed some secret that no one else understood. But when other countries in Asia began to copy the Japanese model, their economies also improved—until, that is, lack of moderation and an inflexible application of the model produced a major correction in 1997 and 1998. Japanese success in business, education, and other fields has been the result of, among other things, hard work, advance planning, persistence, and outside financial help.

However, even with those ingredients in place, Japanese enterprises often fall short. In many industries, for example, Japanese workers are less efficient than are workers in other countries. Japan's national railway system was once found to have 277,000 more employees on its payroll than it needed. At one point, investigators revealed that the system had been so poorly managed for so many years that it had accumulated a public debt of $257 billion. Multimillion-dollar train sta-

tions had been built in out-of-the-way towns, for no other reason than that a member of the *Diet* (the Japanese Parliament) happened to live there and had pork-barreled the project. Both government and industry have been plagued by bribery and corruption, as occurred in the Recruit Scandal of the late 1980s, which caused many implicated government leaders, including the prime minister, to resign.

Nor is the Japanese economy impervious to global market conditions. Values of stocks traded on the Tokyo Stock Exchange took a serious drop in 1992; investors lost millions of dollars, and many had to declare bankruptcy. Moreover, the tenacious recession that hit Japan in the early 1990s and that is likely to continue into the 2000s has forced Japanese companies to reduce overtime work and slow down expansion plans.

## THE COMMANDMENTS OF JAPAN'S ECONOMIC SUCCESS

Still, Japan's rise from the devastation of military defeat to the second-largest economy in the world has been phenomenal, and it would be helpful to review in detail some of the bases of that success. We might call these the 10 commandments of Japan's economic success:

**1.** Some of Japan's entrenched business conglomerates, called *zaibatsu*, were broken up by order of the U.S. Occupation commander after World War II; this allowed competing businesses to get a start. Similarly, the physical infrastructure—roads, factories—was destroyed during the war. This was a blessing in disguise, for it paved the way for newer equipment and technologies to be put in place quickly.

**2.** The United States, seeing the need for an economically strong Japan in order to offset the growing attraction of Communist ideology in Asia, provided substantial reconstruction aid. For instance, Sony Corporation got started with help from the Agency for International Development (AID)—an organization to which the United States is a major contributor. Mazda Motors got its start by making Jeeps for U.S. forces during the Korean War. (Other Rim countries that are now doing well can also thank U.S. generosity: Taiwan received $5.6 billion and South Korea received $13 billion in aid during the period 1945–1978.)

**3.** Japanese industry looked upon government as a facilitator and received useful economic advice as well as political and financial assistance from government planners. (In this regard, it is important to note that many of Japan's civil servants are the best graduates of Japan's colleges and universities.) Also, the advice and help coming from the government were fairly consistent over time, because the same political party, the Liberal Democratic Party, remained in power for almost the entire postwar period.

**4.** Japanese businesses selected an export-oriented strategy that stressed building market share over immediate profit.

**5.** Except in certain professions, such as teaching, labor unions in Japan were not as powerful as in Europe and the United States. This is not to suggest that unions were not effective in gaining benefits for workers, but the structure of the union movement—individual company unions rather than industry-wide unions—moderated the demands for improved wages and benefits.

**6.** Company managers stressed employee teamwork and group spirit and implemented policies such as "lifetime employment" and quality-control circles, which contributed to group morale. In this they were aided by the tendency of Japanese workers to grant to the company some of the same level of loyalty traditionally reserved for families. In certain ways, the gap between workers and management was minimized.

**7.** Companies benefited from the Japanese ethic of working hard and saving much. For most of Japan's postwar history, workers labored 6 days a week, arriving early and leaving late. The paychecks were carefully managed to include a substantial savings component—generally between 15 and 25 percent. This guaranteed that there were always enough cash reserves for banks to offer company expansion loans at low interest.

**8.** The government spent relatively little of its tax revenues on social-welfare programs or military defense, preferring instead to invest public funds in private industry.

**9.** A relatively stable family structure (i.e., few divorces and substantial family support for young people, many of whom remained at home until marriage at about age 27), produced employees who were reliable and psychologically stable.

**10.** The government as well as private individuals invested enormous amounts of money and energy into education, on the assumption that, in a resource-poor country, the mental energies of the people would need to be exploited to their fullest.

Some of these conditions for success are now part of immutable history; but others, such as the emphasis on education, are open to change as the conditions of Japanese life change. A relevant example is the practice of lifetime employment. Useful as a management tool when companies were small and *skilled* laborers were difficult to find, it is now giving way to a freer labor-market system. In some Japanese industries, as many as 30 percent of new hires quit after 2 years on the job. In other words, the aforementioned conditions for success were relevant to one particular era of Japanese and world history and may not be as effective in other countries or other times. Selecting the right strategy for the right era has perhaps been the single most important condition for Japanese economic success.

## CULTURAL CHARACTERISTICS

All these conditions notwithstanding, Japan would never have achieved economic success without its people possessing certain social and psychological characteristics, many of which can be traced to the various religious/ethical philosophies that have suffused Japan's 2,000-year history. Shintoism, Buddhism, Confucianism, Christianity, and other philosophies of living have shaped the modern Japanese mind. This is not to suggest that Japanese are tradition-bound;

nothing could be further from the truth. Even though many Westerners think "tradition" when they think Japan, it is more accurate to think of Japanese people as imitative, preventive, pragmatic, obligative, and inquisitive rather than traditional. These characteristics are discussed in this section.

### Imitative

The capacity to imitate one's superiors is a strength of the Japanese people; rather than representing an inability to think creatively, it constitutes one reason for Japan's legendary success. It makes sense to the Japanese to copy success, whether it is a successful boss, a company in the West, or an educational curriculum in Europe. It is true that imitation can produce conformity; but, in Japan's case, it is often conformity based on respect for the superior qualities of someone or something rather than simple, blind mimicry.

Once Japanese people have mastered the skills of their superiors, they believe that they have the moral right to a style of their own. Misunderstandings on this point arise often when East meets West. One American schoolteacher, for example, was sent to Japan to teach Western art to elementary-school children. Considering her an expert, the children did their best to copy her work to the smallest detail. Misunderstanding that this was at once a compliment and the first step toward creativity, the teacher removed all of her art samples from the classroom in order to force the students to paint something from their own imaginations. Because the

(Sony Corporation of America)

A contributing factor in the modern economic development of Japan was investment from the Agency for International Development. The Sony Corporation is an example of just how successful this assistance could be. These workers are assembling products that will be sold all over the world.

students found this to be a violation of their approach to creativity, they did not perform well, and the teacher left Japan believing that Japanese education teaches conformity and compliance rather than creativity and spontaneity.

This episode is instructive about predicting the future role of Japan vis-à-vis the West. After decades of imitating the West, Japanese people are now beginning to feel that they have the skills and the moral right to create styles of their own. We can expect to see, therefore, an explosion of Japanese creativity in the near future. Some observers have noted, for example, that the fashion industry seems to be gaining more inspiration from designers in Tokyo than from those in Milan, Paris, or New York. And, as of the mid-1980s, the Japanese have annually registered more new patents with the U.S. Patent Office than has any other nation except the United States. The Japanese are also now winning more Nobel prizes than in the past.

### Preventive

Japanese individuals, families, companies, and the government generally prefer long-range over short-range planning, and they greatly prefer foreknowledge over postmortem analysis. Assembly-line workers test and retest every product to prevent customers from receiving defective products. Some store clerks plug in and check electronic devices in front of a customer in order to prevent bad merchandise from sullying the good reputation of the store, and commuter trains in Japan have 3 times as many "Watch your step" or similar notices as do trains in the United States and Europe. Insurance companies do a brisk business in Japan; even though all Japanese citizens are covered by the government's national health plan, many people buy additional coverage—for example, cancer insurance—just to be safe.

This concern with prevention trickles down to the smallest details. At train stations, multiple recorded warnings are given of an approaching train to commuters standing on the platform. Parent–teacher associations send teams of mothers around the neighborhood to determine which streets are the safest for the children. They then post signs designating certain roads as "school passage roads" and instruct children to take those routes even if it takes longer to walk to school. The Japanese think that it is better to avoid an accident than to have an emergency team ready when a child is hurt. Whereas Americans say, "If it ain't broke, don't fix it," the Japanese say, "Why wait 'til it breaks to fix it?"

### Pragmatic

Rather than pursue a plan because it ideologically fits some preordained philosophy, the Japanese try to be pragmatic on most points. Take drugs as an example. Many nations say that drug abuse is an insurmountable problem that will, at best, be contained but probably never eradicated, because to do so would violate civil liberties. But, as a headline in the *Asahi Evening News* proclaimed a few years ago, "Japan Doesn't Have a Drug Problem and Means to Keep It That Way."

Reliable statistics support this claim, but that is not the whole story. In 1954, Japan had a serious drug problem, with 53,000 drug arrests in one year. At the time, the authorities concluded that they had a big problem on their hands and must do whatever was required to solve it. The government passed a series of tough laws restricting the production, use, exchange, and possession of all manner of drugs, and it gave the police the power to arrest all violators. Users were arrested as well as dealers: It was reasoned that if the addicts were not left to buy the drugs, the dealers would be out of business. Their goal at the time was to arrest all addicts, even if it meant that certain liberties were briefly circumscribed. The plan, based on a do-what-it-takes pragmatism, worked; today, Japan is the only industrialized country without a widespread drug problem. In this case, to pragmatism was added the Japanese tendency to work for the common rather than the individual good.

This approach to life is so much a part of the Japanese mind-set that many Japanese cannot understand why the United States and other industrialized nations have so many unresolved social and economic problems. For instance, when it comes to the trade imbalance, it is clear that one of the West's most serious problems is a low savings rate (making money scarce and interest rates high); another is inferior-quality products. Knowing that these are problems, the Japanese wonder why North Americans and Europeans do not just start saving more and working more carefully. They think, "We did it; why can't you?"

### Obligative

The Japanese have a great sense of duty toward those around them. Thousands of Japanese workers work late without pay to improve their job skills so that they will not let their fellow workers down. Good deeds done by one generation are remembered and repaid by the next, and lifelong friendships are maintained by exchanging appropriate gifts and letters. North Americans and Europeans are often considered untrustworthy friends because they do not keep up the level of close, personal communications that the Japanese expect of their own friends; nor do the Westerners have as strong a sense of place, station, or position.

Duty to the group is closely linked to respect for superior authority. Every group—indeed, every relationship—is seen as a mixture of people with inferior and superior resources. These differences must be acknowledged, and no one is disparaged for bringing less to the group than someone else. However, equality is assumed when it comes to basic commitment to or effort expended for a task. Slackers are not welcome. Obligation to the group along with respect for superiors motivated Japanese pilots to fly suicide missions during World War II, and it now causes workers to go the extra mile for the good of the company.

That said, it is also true that changes in the intensity of commitment are becoming increasingly apparent. More Japanese than ever before are beginning to feel that their own personal goals are more important than those of their companies or extended families. This is no doubt a result of the Westernization of the culture since the Meiji Restoration, in the late 1800s, and especially of the experiences of the growing number of Japanese—approximately half a million in a given year—who live abroad and then take their newly acquired values back to Japan. (About half of these "away Japanese" live in North America and Western Europe.)

There is no doubt that the pace of "individualization" of the Japanese psyche is increasing and that, more and more, the Japanese attitude toward work is approaching that of the West. Many Japanese companies are now allowing employees to set their own "flex-time" work schedules, and some companies have even asked employees to stop addressing superiors with their hierarical titles and instead refer to everyone as "*san*," or Mr. or Ms.

## Inquisitive

The image of dozens of Japanese businesspeople struggling to read a book or newspaper while standing inside a packed commuter train is one not easily forgotten, symbolizing as it does the intense desire among the Japanese for knowledge, especially knowledge of foreign cultures. Nearly 6 million Japanese travel abroad each year (many to pursue higher education), and for those who do not, the government and private radio and television stations provide a continuous stream of programming about everything from Caribbean cuisine to French ballet. The Japanese have a yen for foreign styles of dress, foreign cooking, and foreign languages. The Japanese study languages with great intensity. Every student

is required to study English; many also study Chinese, Greek, Latin, Russian, Arabic, and other languages, with French being the most popular after English.

Observers inside and outside of Japan are beginning to comment that the Japanese are recklessly discarding Japanese culture in favor of foreign ideas and habits, even when they make no sense in the Japanese context. A tremendous intellectual debate, called *Nihonjin-ron*, is now taking place in Japan over the meaning of being Japanese and the Japanese role in the world. There is certainly value in these concerns, but, as was noted previously, the secret about Japanese traditions is that they are not traditional. That is, the Japanese seem to know that, in order to succeed, they must learn what they need to know for the era in which they live, even if it means modifying or eliminating the past. This is probably the reason why the Japanese nation has endured for more than 2,000 years while many other empires have fallen. In this sense, the Japanese are very forward-looking people and, in their thirst for new modes of thinking and acting, they are, perhaps, revealing their most basic and useful national personality characteristic: inquisitiveness. Given this attitude toward learning, it should come as no surprise that formal schooling in Japan is a very serious business to the government and to families. It is to that topic that we now turn.

## SCHOOLING

Probably most of the things that the West has heard about Japanese schools are distortions or outright falsehoods. We hear that Japanese children are highly disciplined, for example; yet, in reality, Japanese schools at the elementary and junior high levels are rather noisy, unstructured places, with children racing around the halls during breaks and getting into fights with classmates on the way home. Japan actually has a far lower percentage of its college-age population enrolled in higher education than is the case in the United States—35 percent as compared to 50 percent. Moreover, the Japanese government does not require young people to attend high school (they must attend only until age 15), although 94 percent do anyway. Given these and other realities of school life in Japan, how can we explain the consistently high scores of Japanese on international tests and the general agreement that Japanese high school graduates know almost as much as college graduates in North America?

Structurally, schools in Japan are similar to those in many other countries: There are kindergartens, elementary schools, junior high schools, and high schools. Passage into elementary and junior high is automatic, regardless of student performance level. But admission to high school and college is based on test scores from entrance examinations. Preparing for these examinations occupies the full attention of students in their final year of both junior high and high school, respectively. Both parents and school authorities insist that studying for the tests be the primary focus of a student's life at those times. For instance, members of a junior high soccer team may be allowed to play on the team only for their first 2 years;

(AP Wirephoto by Elaine Kurtenbach)

The Japanese take education very seriously. Half of the children start kindergarten at the age of three, and early on they are instilled with respect for authority.

Doing well in school is seen by Japanese students as fulfilling their obligation to their families. Education is held in high regard and is seen as a critical element in achieving a better life; it is supported very strongly by parents.

during their last year, they are expected to be studying for their high school entrance examinations. School policy reminds students that they are in school to learn and to graduate to the next level, not to play sports. Many students even attend after-hours "cram schools" (*juku*) several nights a week to prepare for the exams.

Time for recreational and other nonschool activities is restricted, because Japanese students attend school 240 days out of the year (as compared to about 180 in U.S. schools), including some Saturday mornings. Summer vacation is only about 6 weeks long, and students often attend school activities during most of that period. Japanese youths are expected to treat schooling as their top priority over part-time jobs (usually prohibited by school policy during the school year, except for the needy), sports, dating, and even family time.

Children who do well in school are generally thought to be fulfilling their obligations to the family. The reason for this focus is that parents realize that only through education can Japanese youths find their place in society. Joining the military is generally not an option, opportunities for farming are limited because of land scarcity, and most major companies will not hire a new employee who has not graduated from college or a respectable high school. Thus, the Japanese find it important to focus on education—to do one thing and do it well.

Teachers are held in high regard in Japan, partly because, when mass education was introduced, many of the high-status samurai took up teaching to replace their martial activities. In addition, in modern times, the Japan Teacher's Union has been active in agitating for higher pay for teachers. As a group, teachers are the highest-paid civil servants in Japan. They take their jobs very seriously. Public-school teachers, for example, visit the home of each student each year to merge the authority of the home with that of the school, and they insist that parents (usually mothers) play active supporting roles in the school.

Some Japanese youths dislike the system, and discussions are currently under way among Japanese educators on how to improve the quality of life for students. Occasionally the pressure of taking examinations (called "exam hell") produces such stress that a desperate student will commit suicide rather than try and fail. Stress also appears to be the cause of *ijime,* or bullying of weaker students by stronger peers. In recent years, the Ministry of Education has worked hard to help students deal with school stress, with the result that Japan's youth suicide rate has dropped dramatically, far lower than the rate in the United States, for example. Despite these and other problems, most Japanese youths enjoy school and value the time they have to be with their friends, whether in class, walking home, or attending cram school. Some of those who fail their college entrance exams continue to study privately, some for many years, and take the exam each year until they pass. Others travel abroad and enroll in foreign universities that do not have such rigid entrance requirements. Still others enroll in vocational training schools. But everyone in Japan realizes that education—not money, name, or luck—is the key to success.

Parents whose children are admitted to the prestigious national universities—such as Tokyo and Kyoto Universities—consider that they have much to brag about. Other parents are willing to pay as much as $35,000 on average for 4 years of college at the private (but usually not as prestigious) universities. Once admitted, students find that life slows down a bit. For one thing, parents typically pay more than 65 percent of the costs, and approximately 3 percent is covered by scholarships. This leaves only about 30 percent to be earned by the students; this usually comes from tutoring high school students who are studying for the entrance exams. Contemporary parents are also willing to pay the cost of a son's or daughter's traveling to and spending a few months in North America or Europe either before college begins or during summer breaks—a practice that is becoming *de rigueur* for Japanese students, much as taking a "grand tour" of Europe was expected of young, upper-class Americans and Canadians at the turn of the century.

College students may take 15 or 16 courses at a time, but classes usually meet only once or twice a week, and sporadic attendance is the norm. Straight lecturing rather than class discussion is the typical learning format, and there is very little homework beyond studying for the final exam. Students generally do not challenge the professors' statements in class, but some students develop rather close, avuncular-type relationships with their professors outside of class. Hobbies, sports, and club activities (things the students did not have time to do while in public school) occupy the center of life for many college students. Equally important is the cementing of friendships that will last a lifetime and be useful in one's career and private life.

## THE JAPANESE BUSINESS WORLD

Successful college graduates begin their work careers in April, when most large companies do their hiring (although this practice is slowly giving way to individual hiring throughout the year). They may have to take an examination to determine how much they know about electronics or stocks and bonds, and they may have to complete a detailed personality profile. Finally, they will have to submit to a very serious interview with company management. During interviews, the managers will watch their every move; the applicants will be careful to avoid saying anything that will give them "minus points."

Once hired, individuals attend training sessions in which they learn the company song and other rituals as well as company policy on numerous matters. They may be housed in company apartments (or may continue to live at home),

permitted to use a company car or van, and advised to shop at company grocery stores. Almost never are employees married at this time, and so they are expected to live a rather spartan life for the first few years.

Employees are expected to show considerable deference to their section bosses, even though, on the surface, bosses do not appear to be very different from other employees. Bosses' desks are out in the open, near the employees; they wear the same uniform; they socialize with the employees after work; even in a factory, they are often on the shop floor rather than sequestered away in private offices. Long-term employees often come to see the section leader as an uncle figure (bosses are usually male) who will give them advice about life, be the best man at their weddings, and provide informal marital and family counseling as needed.

Although there are cases of abuse or unfair treatment of employees, Japanese company life can generally be described as somewhat like a large family rather than a military squad; employees (sometimes called *associates*) often obey their superiors out of genuine respect rather than forced compliance. Moreover, competition between workers is reduced because everyone hired at the same time receives more or less the same pay and most workers receive promotions at about the same time. Only later in one's career are individualistic promotions given.

Employees are expected to work hard, for not only are Japanese companies in competition with foreign businesses, but they also must survive the fiercely competitive business climate at home. Indeed, the Japanese skill in international business was developed at home. There are, for example, hundreds of electronics companies and thousands of textile enterprises competing for customers in Japan. And whereas the United States has only four automobile-manufacturing companies, Japan has nine. All these companies entice customers with deep price cuts or unusual services, hoping to edge out unprepared or weak competitors. Many companies fail. There were once, for instance, almost 40 companies in Japan that manufactured calculators, but today only six remain, the rest victims of tough internal Japanese competition.

At about age 27, after several years of working and saving money for an apartment, a car, and a honeymoon, the typical Japanese male worker marries. The average bride, about age 25, will have taken private lessons in flower arranging, the tea ceremony, sewing, cooking, and perhaps a musical instrument like the *koto,* the Japanese harp. She probably will not have graduated from college, although she may have attended a specialty college for a while. If she is working, she likely is paid much less than her husband, even if she has an identical position (despite equal-pay laws). She may spend her time in the company preparing and serving tea for clients and employees, dusting the office, running errands, and answering telephones. When she has a baby, she will be expected to quit—although more women today are choosing to remain on the job, and some are advancing into management or are leaving to start their own companies.

Because the wife is expected to serve as the primary caregiver for the children, the husband is expected always to make his time available for the company. He may be asked to work weekends, to stay out late most of the week (about four out of seven nights), or even to be transferred to another branch in Japan or abroad without his family. This loyalty is rewarded in numerous ways: Unless the company goes bankrupt or the employee is unusually inept, he may be permitted to work for the company until he retires, usually at about age 55 or 60, even if the company no longer really needs his services; he and his wife will be taken on company sightseeing trips; the company will pay most of his health-insurance costs (the government pays the rest); and he will have the peace of mind that comes from being surrounded by lifelong friends and workmates. His association with company employees will be his main social outlet, even after retirement; upon his death, it will be his former workmates who organize and direct his Buddhist funeral services.

## THE FAMILY

The loyalty once given to the traditional Japanese extended family, called the *ie,* has been transferred to the modern company. This is logical from a historical perspective, since the modern company once began as a family business and was gradually expanded to include more workers, or "siblings." Thus, whereas the family is seen as the backbone of most societies, it might be more accurate to argue that the *kaisha,* or company, is the basis of modern Japanese society. As one Japanese commentator explained, "In the West, the home is the cornerstone of people's lives. In Tokyo, home is just a place to sleep at night. . . . Each family member—husband, wife, and children—has his own community centered outside the home."

Thus, the common image that Westerners hold of the centrality of the family to Japanese culture may be inaccurate. For instance, father absence is epidemic in Japan. It is an unusual father who eats more than one meal a day with his family. He may go shopping or to a park with his family when he has free time from work, but he is more likely to go golfing with a workmate. Schooling occupies the bulk of the children's time, even on weekends. And with fewer children than in earlier generations and with appliance-equipped apartments, many Japanese women rejoin the workforce after their children are self-maintaining.

Japan's divorce rate, while rising, is still considerably lower than in other industrialized nations, a fact that may seem incongruent with the conditions described above. Yet, as

(Reuters/Bettmann)

In the Japanese business world, one's job is taken very seriously and is often seen as a lifelong commitment. These workers have jobs that, in many ways, may be more a part of their lives than are their families.

explained by one Japanese sociologist, Japanese couples "do not expect much emotional closeness; there is less pressure on us to meet each other's emotional needs. If we become close, that is a nice dividend, but if we do not, it is not a problem because we did not expect it in the first place."

Despite these modifications to the common Western image of the Japanese family, Japanese families have significant roles to play in society. Support for education is one of the most important. Families, especially mothers, support the schools by being actively involved in the parent–teacher association, by insisting that children be given plenty of homework, and by saving for college so that the money for tuition is available without the college student having to work.

Another important function of the family is mate selection. Somewhat less than half of current Japanese marriages are arranged by the family or have occurred as a result of far more family involvement than in North America. Families sometimes ask a go-between (an uncle, a boss, or another trusted person) to compile a list of marriageable candidates. Criteria such as social class, blood type, and occupation are considered. Photos of prospective candidates are presented to the unmarried son or daughter, who has the option to veto any of them or to date those he or she finds acceptable. Young people, however, increasingly select their mates with little or no input from parents.

Finally, families in Japan, even those in which the children are married and living away from home, continue to gather for the purpose of honoring the memory of deceased family members or to enjoy one another's company for New Year's Day, Children's Day, and other celebrations.

## WOMEN IN JAPAN

Ancient Confucian values held that women were legally and socially inferior to men. This produced a culture in feudal Japan in which the woman was expected to walk several steps behind her husband when in public, to eat meals only after the husband had eaten, to forgo formal education, and to serve the husband and male members of the family whenever possible. A "good woman" was said to be one who would endure these conditions without complaint. This pronounced gender difference (though minimized substantially over the centuries since Confucius) can still be seen today in myriad ways, including in the preponderance of males in positions of leadership in business and politics, in the smaller percentage of women college graduates, and in the pay differential between women and men.

Given the Confucian values noted above, one would expect that all top leaders would be males. However, women's roles are also subject to the complexity of both ancient and modern cultures. Between A.D. 592 and 770, for instance, of the 12 reigning emperors, half were women. In rural areas today, women take an active decision-making role in farm associations. In the urban workplace, some women occupy typically pink-collar positions (nurses, clerks, and so on), but many women are also doctors and business executives; 28,000 are company presidents.

(UN photo by Jan Corash)

In Japan, not unlike in many other parts of the world, economic well-being often requires two incomes. Still, there is strong social pressure on women to stop working once they have a baby. All generations of family members take part in childrearing.

Thus, it is clear that within the general framework of gender inequality imposed by Confucian values, Japanese culture, especially at certain times, has been rather lenient in its application of those values. There is still considerable social pressure on women to stop working once they marry, and particularly after they have a baby, but it is clear that many women are resisting that pressure: one out of every three employees in Japan is female, and nearly 60 percent of the female workforce are married. An equal-pay law was enacted in 1989 that makes it illegal to pay women less for doing comparable work (although it may take years for companies to comply fully). And the Ministry of Education has mandated that home economics and shop classes now be required for both boys and girls; that is, both girls and boys will learn to cook and sew as well as construct things out of wood and metal.

In certain respects, Japanese women seem more assertive than women in the West. For example, in a recent national election, a wife challenged her husband for his seat in the House of Representatives (something that has not been done in the United States, where male candidates usually expect their wives to stump for them). Significantly, too, the former head of the Japan Socialist Party was an unmarried woman, Takako Doi. Women have been elected to the powerful Tokyo Metropolitan Council and awarded professorships at prestigious universities such as

Tokyo University. And, while women continue to be used as sexual objects in pornography and prostitution, certain kinds of misogynistic behavior, such as rape and serial killing, are less frequent in Japan than in Western societies. Indeed, Western women visiting Japan often report that they felt free to walk outside alone at night for the first time in their lives. However, a spate of bizarre killings by youths in recent years is causing the sense of personal safety in Japan to dissipate. Signs in train stations warn of pickpockets, and signs on infrequently traveled paths warn of molesters.

Recent studies show that many Japanese women believe that their lives are easier than those of most Westerners. With their husbands working long hours and their one or two children in school all day, Japanese women find they have more leisure time than Western women. Gender-based social divisions remain apparent throughout Japanese culture, but modern Japanese women have learned to blend these divisions with the realities and opportunities of the contemporary workplace and home.

## RELIGION/ETHICS

There are many holidays in Japan, most of which have a religious origin. This fact, as well as the existence of numerous shrines and temples, may leave the impression that Japan is a rather religious country. This is not true, however. Most Japanese people do not claim any active religious affiliation, but many will stop by a shrine occasionally to ask for divine help in passing an exam, finding a mate, or recovering from an illness.

Nevertheless, modern Japanese culture sprang from a rich religious heritage. The first influence on Japanese culture came from the animistic Shinto religion, from whence modern Japanese acquired their respect for the beauty of nature. Confucianism brought a respect for hierarchy and education. Taoism stressed introspection, and Buddhism taught the need for good behavior now in order to acquire a better life in the future.

Shinto was selected in the 1930s as the state religion and was used as a divine justification for Japan's military exploits of that era, but most Japanese today will say that Japan is, culturally, a Buddhist nation. Some new Buddhist denominations have attracted thousands of followers. The rudiments of Christianity are also a part of the modern Japanese consciousness, but few Japanese have actually joined Christian churches. Sociologically, Japan, with its social divisions and hierarchy, is probably more of a Confucian society than it is Buddhist or any other philosophy.

(The Bettmann Archive)

Religion in Japan, while not having a large active affiliation, is still an intricate part of the texture and history of the culture. This temple in Kyoto was founded in the twelfth century.

Most Japanese regard morality as springing from within the group rather than pronounced from above. That is, a Japanese person may refrain from stealing so as not to offend the owner of an object or bring shame upon the family, rather than because of a divine prohibition against stealing. Thus we find in Japan a relatively small rate of violent—that is, public—crimes, and a much larger rate of white-collar crimes such as embezzlement, in which offenders believe that they can get away with something without creating a public scandal for their families.

## THE GOVERNMENT

The Constitution of postwar Japan became effective in 1947 and firmly established the Japanese people as the ultimate source of sovereignty, with the emperor as the symbol of the nation. The national Parliament, or *Diet,* is empowered to pass legislation. The Diet is divided into two houses: the House of Representatives, with 511 members elected for 4-year terms; and the House of Councillors, with 252 members elected for 6-year terms from each of the 47 prefectures (states) of Japan as well as nationally. The prime minister, assisted by a cabinet, is also the leader of the party with the most seats in the Diet. Prefectures are governed by an elected governor and an assembly, and cities and towns are governed by elected mayors and town councils. The Supreme Court, consisting of a chief judge and 14 other judges, is independent of the legislative branch of government.

Japan's Constitution forbids Japan from engaging in war or from having military capability that would allow it to attack another country. Japan does maintain a well-equipped self-defense force, but it relies on a security treaty with the United States in case of serious aggression against it. In recent years, the United States has been encouraging Japan to assume more of the burden of the military security of the Asian region, and Japan has increased its expenditures in absolute terms. But until the Constitution is amended, Japan is not likely to initiate any major upgrading of its military capability. This is in line with the general wishes of the Japanese people, who, since the devastation of Hiroshima and Nagasaki, have become firmly committed to a pacifist foreign policy. Moreover, Japanese leaders fear that any significant increase in military capability would re-ignite dormant fears about Japanese intentions within the increasingly vital Pacific Rim area.

This tendency toward not wanting to get involved militarily is reflected in one of Japan's most recent performances on the world stage. The Japanese were slow to play any significant part in supporting military expenditures for the Persian Gulf War, even when the outcome had a direct potential effect on their economy. The Iraqi invasion of Kuwait in August 1990 brought on the wrath—against Japan—of a coalition of countries led by the United States in January 1991, but it generated an initial commitment from Japan of only $2 billion (later increased to $9 billion, still a small fraction of the cost) and no personnel of any kind. This meager support was criticized by some foreign observers, who pointed out that Japan relies heavily on Gulf oil.

In 1992, the Japanese government announced its intention of building its own F-16–type jet-fighter planes; and subsequently, amid protests from the public, the Diet voted to send as many as 1,800 Japanese soldiers—the first to go abroad since World War II—to Cambodia to assist in the UN–supervised peacekeeping effort. Countries that had experienced the full force of Japanese domination in the past, such as China and Korea, expressed dismay at these evidences of Japan's modern military capability, but the United States welcomed the moves as an indication of Japan's willingness to share the costs of providing military security to Asia.

The Japanese have formed numerous political parties to represent their views in government. Among these have been the Japan Communist Party, the Social Democratic Party, and the New Frontier Party. For nearly 40 years, however, the most powerful party was the Liberal Democratic Party (LDP). Formed in 1955, it guided Japan to its current position of economic strength, but a series of sex and bribery scandals caused it to lose control of the government in 1993. A shaky coalition of eight parties took control for about a year but was replaced by an even more unlikely coalition of the LDP and

UN/DPI photo by Greg Kinch

Japan's government has been toppled frequently in recent years by charges of corruption and other scandals. Keizo Obuchi, longtime official of the Liberal Democratic Party, was elected prime minister in July 1998. He is shown here addressing the United Nations General Assembly in September of that year.

| Prepottery, paleolithic culture 20,000–4,500 B.C. | Jomon culture with distinctive pottery 4,500–250 B.C. | Yayoi culture with rice agriculture, Shinto religion, and Japanese language 250 B.C.–A.D. 300 | The Yamato period; warrior clans import Chinese culture A.D. 300–700 | The Nara period; Chinese-style bureaucratic government at the capital at Nara 710–794 | The Heian period; the capital is at Kyoto 794–1185 | The Kamakura period; feudalism and shoguns; Buddhism is popularized 1185–1333 | The Muromachi period; Western missionaries and traders arrive; feudal lords control their own domains 1333–1568 | The Momoyama period; feudal lords become subject to one central leader; attempted invasion of Korea 1568–1600 |
| --- | --- | --- | --- | --- | --- | --- | --- | --- |

the Japan Socialists—historic enemies who were unable to agree on most policies. Eventually, the LDP was able to regain some of its lost political clout; but, with some half a dozen changes in the prime ministership in the 1990s and party realignments in 1994, 1996, and 1998, it would be an understatement to say that Japan's government is in flux.

Part of the reason for this instability can be explained by Japan's party faction system. Party politics in Japan has always been a mixture of Western-style democratic practice and feudalistic personal relationships. Japanese parties are really several parties rolled into one. That is, parties are divided into several factions, each comprised of a group of loyal younger members headed by a powerful member of the Diet. The senior member has a duty to pave the way for the younger members politically, but they, in turn, are obligated to support the senior member in votes and in other ways. The faction leader's role in gathering financial support for faction members is particularly important, because Diet members are expected by the electorate to be patrons of numerous causes, from charity drives to the opening of a constituent's fast-food business. Because parliamentary salaries are inadequate to the task, outside funds, and thus the faction, are crucial. The size and power of the various factions are often the critical elements in deciding who will assume the office of prime minister and who will occupy which cabinet seats. The role of these intraparty factions is so central to Japanese politics that attempts to ban them have never been successful.

The factional nature of Japanese party politics means that cabinet and other political positions are frequently rotated. This would yield considerable instability in governance were it not for the stabilizing influence of the Japanese bureaucracy. Large and powerful, the career bureaucracy is responsible for drafting more than 80 percent of the bills submitted to the Diet. Many of the bureaucrats are graduates from the finest universities in Japan, particularly Tokyo University, which provides some 80 percent of the senior officials in the more than 20 national ministries. Many of them consider their role in long-range forecasting, drafting legislation, and implementing policies to be superior to that of the elected officials under whom they work. They reason that, whereas the politicians are bound to the whims of the people they represent, bureaucrats are committed to the nation of Japan— to, as it were, the *idea* of Japan. Thus, government service is considered a higher calling than are careers in private business, law, or other fields.

In addition to the bureaucracy, Japanese politicians have leaned heavily on big business to support their policies of postwar reconstruction, economic growth, and social reform.

Business has accepted heavy taxation so that social-welfare programs such as the national health plan are feasible, and they have provided political candidates with substantial financial help. In turn, the government has seen its role as that of facilitating the growth of private industry (some critics claim that the relationship between government and business is so close that Japan is best described not as a nation but as "Japan, Inc."). Consider, for example, the powerful Ministry of International Trade and Industry (MITI). Over the years, it has worked closely with business, particularly the Federation of Economic Organizations (Keidanren) to forecast potential market shifts, develop strategies for market control, and generally pave the way for Japanese businesses to succeed in the international marketplace. The close working relationship between big business and the national government is an established fact of life in Japan, and, despite criticism from countries with a more laissez faire approach to business, it will undoubtedly continue into the future, because it has served Japan well.

### THE FUTURE

In the postwar years of political stability, the Japanese have accomplished more than anyone, including themselves, thought possible. Japan's literacy rate is 99 percent, 99 percent of Japanese households have telephones, 99 percent have color televisions, and 75 percent own automobiles. Nationalized health care covers every Japanese citizen, and the Japanese have the longest life expectancy in the world. With only half the population of the United States, a land area about the size of Great Britain, and extremely limited natural resources (it has to import 99.6 percent of its oil, 99.8 percent of its iron, and 86.7 percent of its coal), Japan has nevertheless created the second-largest economy in the world. Where does it go from here?

When the Spanish were establishing hegemony over large parts of the globe, they were driven in part by the desire to bring Christianity to the "heathen." The British, for their part, believed that they were taking "civilization" to the "savages" of the world. China and the former Soviet Union were once strongly committed to the ideals of communism, while the United States has felt that its mission is that of expanding democracy and capitalism.

What about Japan? For what reason do Japanese businesses buy up hotels in New Zealand and skyscrapers in New York? What role does Japan have to play in the world in addition to spawning economic development? What values will guide and perhaps temper Japan's drive for economic dominance?

These are questions that the Japanese people themselves are attempting to answer; but, finding no ready answers, they

The Tokugawa Era; self-imposed isolation from the West
**1600–1868**

The Meiji Restoration; modernization; Taiwan and Korea are under Japanese control
**1868–1912**

The Taisho and Showa periods; militarization leads to war and Japan's defeat
**1912–1945**

Japan surrenders; the U.S. Occupation imposes major changes in the organization of society
**1945**

Sovereignty is returned to the Japanese people by treaty
**1951**

The newly merged Liberal-Democratic Party wins control of the government
**1955**

Japan passes the threshold of economic self-sustainability
**1960s**

Student activism; the Nuclear Security Treaty with the United States is challenged
**late 1960s**

The ruling party is hit by scandals but retains control of the government; Emperor Hirohito dies; Emperor Akihito succeeds
**1980s**

**1990s**

Japan reacts to protectionism in major markets by turning its attention to the Pacific Rim

Japan sends troops to maintain peace in Cambodia; Japan remains the second-largest economy in the world

The Liberal Democratic Party loses control of the government after 38 years in power but recovers power in 1996

A devastating earthquake in Kobe kills more than 5,000 people

After years of a slow economy, Japan officially admits it is in a recession

are beginning to encounter more and more difficulties with the world around them and within their own society. Animosity over the persistent trade imbalance in Japan's favor continues to simmer in Europe and North America as well as in some countries of the Pacific Rim. To deflect these criticisms, Japan has substantially increased its gift-giving to foreign governments, including allocating money for the stabilization or growth of democracy in Central/Eastern Europe and for easing the foreign debt burden of Mexico and other countries.

What Japan has been loathe to do, however, is remove the "structural impediments" that make it difficult for foreign companies to do business in Japan. For example, 50 percent of the automobiles sold in Iceland are Japanese, which means less profit for the American and European manufacturers who used to dominate car sales there. Yet, because of high tariffs and other regulations, very few American and European cars have been sold in Japan. Beginning in the mid-1980s, Japan reluctantly began to dismantle many of these trade barriers, and the process has been so successful that Japan now has a lower overall average tariff on nonagricultural products than the United States—its severest critic in this arena.

But Japanese people worry that further opening of their markets may destroy some fundamentals of Japanese life. Rice, for instance, costs much more in Japan than it should, because the Japanese government protects rice farmers with subsidies and limits most rice imports from abroad. The Japanese would prefer to pay less for rice at the supermarket, but they also argue that foreign competition would prove the undoing of many small rice farmers, whose land would then be sold to housing developers. This, in turn, would destroy more of Japan's scarce arable land and weaken the already shaky traditions of the Japanese countryside—the heart of traditional Japanese culture and values.

Today, thousands of foreign firms do business in Japan; some of them, like Polaroid and Schick, control the Japanese market in their products. Foreign investment in Japan has grown about 16 percent annually since 1980. In the case of the United States, the profit made by American firms doing business in Japan (nearly 800 of them) in a single year is just about equal to the amount of the trade imbalance between Japan and the United States. Japanese supermarkets are filled with foreign foodstuffs, and the radio and television airwaves are filled with the sounds and sights of Western music and dress. Japanese youths are as likely to eat at McDonald's or Kentucky Fried Chicken outlets as at traditional Japanese restaurants, and many Japanese have never worn a kimono nor learned to play a Japanese musical instrument. It is clear to many observers that, culturally, Japan already imports much more from the West than the West does from Japan.

Given this overwhelming Westernization of Japan as well as Japan's current capacity to continue imbibing Western culture, even the change-oriented Japanese are beginning to ask where they, as a nation, are going. Will national wealth, as it slowly trickles down to individuals, produce a generation of hedonistic youths who do not appreciate the sacrifices of those before them? Will wealthy Japanese people be satisfied with the small homes and tiny yards that their forebears had to accept? Will there ever be a time when, strapped for resources, the Japanese will once again seek hegemony over other nations? What future role should Japan assume in the international arena, apart from economic development? If these questions remain to be answered, circumstances of international trade have at least provided an answer to the question of Japan's role in the Pacific Rim countries: It is clear that, for the next several decades, Japan will continue to shape the pace and nature of economic development, and thus the political environment, of the entire Pacific Rim.

## DEVELOPMENT

Japan is now entering a post-smokestack era in which primary industries are being moved abroad, producing a hollowing effect inside Japan and increasing the likelihood of rising unemployment. Nevertheless, prospects for continued growth are excellent, despite the current economic woes.

## FREEDOM

Japanese citizens enjoy full civil liberties, and opposition parties and ideologies are seen as natural and useful components of democracy. Certain people, however, such as those of Korean ancestry, have been subject to both social and official discrimination—an issue that is gaining the attention of the Japanese.

## HEALTH/WELFARE

The Japanese live longer on average than any other people on earth. Every citizen is provided with inexpensive medical care under a national health-care system, but many people still prefer to save substantial portions of their income for health emergencies and old age.

## ACHIEVEMENTS

Japan has achieved virtually complete literacy. Although there are poor areas, there are no slums inhabited by a permanent underclass. The gaps between the social classes appear to be less pronounced than in many other societies. The country seems to be entering an era of remarkable educational and technological achievement.

# Australia (Commonwealth of Australia)

## GEOGRAPHY

*Area in Square Miles (Kilometers):* 2,867,896 (7,686,850) (slightly smaller than the United States)

*Capital (Population):* Canberra (310,000)

*Environmental Concerns:* soil erosion and excessive salinity; desertification; wildlife habitat loss; degradation of Great Barrier Reef; limited freshwater resources

*Geographical Features:* mostly low plateau with deserts; fertile plain in southeast

*Climate:* generally arid to semiarid; temperate to tropical

## PEOPLE

### Population
*Total:* 18,439,000

*Annual Growth Rate:* 0.96%

*Rural/Urban Population (Ratio):* 15/85

*Major Languages:* English; indigenous languages

*Ethnic Makeup:* 95% European ancestry; 4% Asian; 1% Aboriginal and others

*Religions:* 26% Anglican; 26% Roman Catholic; 24% other Christian; 24% other or none

### Health
*Life Expectancy at Birth:* 77 years (male); 83 years (female)

*Infant Mortality Rate (Ratio):* 5.4/1,000

*Average Caloric Intake:* 118% of FAO minimum

*Physicians Available (Ratio):* 1/438

### Education
*Adult Literacy Rate:* 100%

*Compulsory (Ages):* 6–15; free

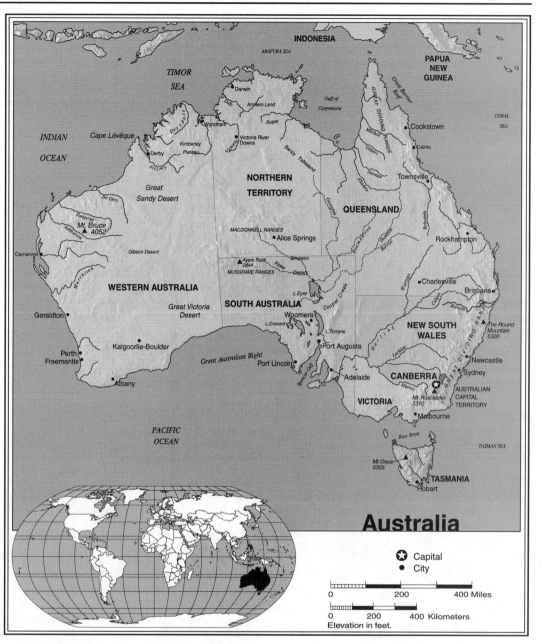

Australia

⭐ Capital
● City

0    200    400 Miles

0    200    400 Kilometers

Elevation in feet.

## COMMUNICATION
*Telephones:* 1 per 2 people

*Daily Newspaper Circulation:* 258 per 1,000 people

*Televisions:* 1 per 2 people

## TRANSPORTATION
*Highways in Miles (Kilometers):* 537,018 (895,030)

*Railroads in Miles (Kilometers):* 25,096 (40,478)

*Usable Airfields:* 439

*Motor Vehicles in Use:* 11,200,000

## GOVERNMENT
*Type:* federal parliamentary state

*Independence Date:* January 1, 1901

*Head of State/Government:* Queen Elizabeth II; Prime Minister John Howard

*Political Parties:* Liberal Party; National Party; Australian Labour Party; Australian Democratic Party; Green Party

*Suffrage:* universal and compulsory at age 18

## MILITARY
*Military Expenditures (% of GDP):* 2.4%

*Current Disputes:* none

## ECONOMY
*Currency ($ U.S. Equivalent):* 1.56 Australian dollars = $1

*Per Capita Income/GDP:* $20,720/$374.6 billion

*GDP Growth Rate:* 3.6%

*Inflation Rate:* 3.1%

*Unemployment Rate:* 8.5%

*Labor Force:* 8,400,000

*Natural Resources:* bauxite; diamonds; coal; copper; iron; oil; gas; other minerals

*Agriculture:* beef; wool; mutton; wheat; barley; sugarcane; fruit

*Industry:* mining; industrial and transportation equipment; food processing; chemicals; steel; motor vehicles

*Exports:* $59.5 billion (primary partners Japan, South Korea, New Zealand, and United States)

*Imports:* $59.7 billion (primary partners United States, Japan, United Kingdom)

## THE LAND NO ONE WANTED

Despite its out-of-the-way location, far south of the main trading routes between Europe and Asia, seafarers from England, Spain, and the Netherlands began exploring parts of the continent of Australia in the seventeenth century. The French later made some forays along the coast, but it was the British who first found something to do with a land that others had disparaged as useless: They decided to send their prisoners there. The British had long believed that the easiest solution to prison overcrowding was expulsion from Britain. Convicts had been sent to the American colonies for many years, but after American independence was declared in 1776, Britain began to send prisoners to Australia.

Australia seemed like the ideal spot for a penal colony: It was isolated from the centers of civilization; it had some good harbors; and, although much of the continent was a flat, dry, riverless desert with only sparse vegetation, the coastal fringes were well suited to human habitation. Indeed, although the British did not know it in the 1700s, they had come across a huge continent endowed with abundant natural resources. Along the northern coast (just south of present-day Indonesia and New Guinea) was a tropical zone with heavy rainfall and tropical forests. The eastern coast was wooded with valuable pine trees, while the western coast was dotted with eucalyptus and acacia trees. Minerals, especially coal, gold, nickel, petroleum, iron, and bauxite, were plentiful, as were the many species of unique animals: kangaroos, platypus, and koalas, to name a few.

Today, grazing and agricultural activities generally take place in the central basin of the country, which consists of thousands of miles of rolling plains. The bulk of the population resides along the coast, where good harbors can be found, although they are relatively few in number. Australia's lakes are often saltwater lakes left over from an inland sea, nor does Australia have many high mountain ranges to supply water; rather, much of the interior is watered by deep artesian wells that are drilled by local ranchers.

The British chose to build their first penal colony alongside a good harbor that they called Sydney. By the 1850s, when the practice of transporting convicts stopped, more than 150,000 prisoners, including hundreds of women, had been sent there and to other colonies. Most of them were illiterate English and Irish from the lower socioeconomic classes. Once they completed their sentences, they were set free to settle on the continent. These individuals, their guards, and gold prospectors constituted the beginning of modern Australian society. Today, despite its 18.4 million inhabitants, Australia remains a sparsely populated continent.

## RACE RELATIONS

Convicts certainly did not constitute the beginning of human habitation on the continent. Tens of thousands of Aborigines (literally, "first inhabitants") inhabited Australia and the nearby island of Tasmania when Europeans first made contact. Living in scattered tribes and speaking hundreds of entirely unrelated languages, the Aborigines, whose origin is unknown (various scholars see connections to Africa, the Indian subcontinent, and the Melanesian Islands), survived by fishing and nomadic hunting. Succumbing to

(Australian Information Service photo)

Most Aborigines eventually adapted to the Europeans' customs, but some continue to live in their traditional ways on tribal reservations.

European diseases, violence, forced removal from their lands, and, finally, neglect, thousands of Aborigines died during the first centuries of contact. Indeed, the entire Tasmanian grouping of people (originally numbering 5,000) is now extinct. Today's Aborigines continue to suffer discrimination. A 1997 bill that would have liberalized land rights for Aborigines failed to gain enough votes to pass in the Australian Parliament.

Most Aborigines eventually adopted European ways, including Christianity. Today, many live in the cities or work for cattle and sheep ranchers. Others reside on reserves (tribal reservations) in the central and northern parts of Australia. Yet modernization has affected even the reservation Aborigines—some have telephones, and some dispersed tribes in the Northern Territories communicate with one another by satellite-linked video conferencing— but in the main, they continue to live as they have always done, organizing their religion around plant or animal sacred symbols, or totems, and initiating youth into adulthood through lengthy and sometimes painful rituals.

Whereas the United States began with 13 founding colonies, Australia started with six, none of which felt a compelling need to unite into a single nation until the 1880s, when other European powers began taking an interest in settling the continent. It was not until 1901 that Australians formally separated from Britain (while remaining within the British Commonwealth with the Queen of England as head of state). Populated almost entirely by whites from Britain or Europe (people of European descent still constitute about 95 percent of Australia's population), Australia has maintained close cultural and diplomatic links with Britain and the West, at the expense of ties with the geographically closer nations of Asia.

Reaction against Polynesians, Chinese, and other Asian immigrants in the late 1800s produced an official "White Australia" policy, which remained intact until the 1960s and effectively excluded nonwhites from settling in Australia. During the 1960s, however, the government made an effort to relax these restrictions and to restore land and some measure of self-determination to Aborigines. In the 1990s, Aborigines successfully persuaded the federal government to block a dam project on Aboriginal land that would have destroyed sacred sites. The federal government sided with the Aborigines against white developers and local government officials. In 1993, despite some public resistance, the government passed laws protecting the land claims of Aborigines

and set up a fund to assist Aborigines with land purchases. Evidence of continued racism can be found, however, in such graffiti painted on walls of high-rise buildings as "Go home Japs!" (in this case, the term *Jap,* or, alternatively, *wog,* refers to any Asian, regardless of nationality). The unemployment rate of Aborigines is four times that of the nation as a whole, and a 1995 survey revealed substantially higher rates of chronic health problems and death by infectious diseases among this population.

## ECONOMIC PRESSURES
Despite lingering discriminatory attitudes against nonwhites, events since World War II have forced Australians to reconsider their position, at least economically, vis-à-vis Asia and Southeast Asia. Australia has never been conquered by a foreign power (not even by Japan during World War II), but the impressive industrial strength of Japan now allows its people to enjoy higher per capita income than that of Australians, and Singapore is not far behind. Moreover, since Australia's economy is based on the export of primary goods (for example, minerals, wheat, beef, and wool) rather than the much more lucrative consumer products manufactured from raw resources, it is likely that Australia will continue to lose ground to the more economically aggressive and heavily populated Asian economies.

This inexorable alteration in socioeconomic status will be a new and difficult experience for Australians, whose standard of living has been the highest in the Pacific Rim for decades. Building on a foundation of sheep (imported in the 1830s and now supplying more than a quarter of the world's supply of wool), mining (gold was discovered in 1851), and agriculture (Australia is nearly self-sufficient in food), the country has developed its manufacturing sector such that Australians are able to enjoy a standard of living equal in most respects to that of North Americans.

But Australians are wary of the growing global tendency to create mammoth regional trading blocs, such as the North American Free Trade Association, consisting of the United States, Canada, Mexico, and others; the European Union (formerly the European Community), eventually including, perhaps, parts of Central/Eastern Europe; the ASEAN nations of Southeast Asia; and an informal "yen bloc" in Asia, headed by Japan. These blocs might exclude Australian products from preferential trade treatment or eliminate them from certain markets altogether. Beginning in 1983, the Labour government of then–prime minister Robert Hawke began to establish collaborative trade agreements

with Asian countries, a plan that seemed to have the support of the electorate, even though it meant reorienting Australia's foreign policy away from its traditional posture Westward.

In the early 1990s, under Labour prime minister Paul Keating, the Asianization plan intensified. The Japanese prime minister and the governor of Hong Kong visited Australia, while Australian leaders made calls on the leaders of South Korea, China, Thailand, Vietnam, Malaysia, and Laos. Trade and security agreements were signed with Singapore and Indonesia, and a national curriculum plan was implemented whereby 60 percent of Australian schoolchildren will be studying Japanese and other Asian languages by the year 2010. The Liberal Party prime minister, John Howard, elected in 1996, has also moderated his views on Asian immigration and now advocates a nondiscriminatory immigration policy rather than the restrictive policy he promoted in the 1980s.

Despite such initiatives (and a few successes: Japan now buys more beef from Australia than from the United States), the economic threat to Australia remains. Even in the islands of the Pacific, an area that Australia and New Zealand generally have considered their own domain for economic investment and foreign aid, investments by Asian countries are beginning to winnow Australia's sphere of influence. U.S. president Bill Clinton, in a 1996 visit to Australia, promised Australian leaders that they would not be left out of the emerging economic structures of the region, but years of recession and an unemployment rate estimated at 8.5 percent in 1996, with nearly 2 million people living in poverty, leave Australians concerned about their economic future.

Labor tension erupted in 1998 when dockworkers found themselves locked out of work by employers who claimed they were inefficient workers. Eventually the courts found in favor of the workers, but not until police and workers clashed and national attention was drawn to the protracted sluggish economy.

## THE AMERICAN CONNECTION
By any standard, Australia is a democracy solidly embedded in the traditions of the West. Political power is shared back and forth between the Labour Party and the Liberal-National Country Party coalition, and the Constitution is based on both British parliamentary tradition and the U.S. model. Thus, it has followed that Australia and the United States have built a warm friendship as both political and military allies. A military mutual-assistance agree-

| European exploration of the Australian coastline begins **1600s** | British explorers first land in Australia **1688** | The first shipment of English convicts arrives **1788** | The gold rush lures thousands of immigrants **1851** | Australia becomes independent within the British Commonwealth **1901** |
| --- | --- | --- | --- | --- |

ment, ANZUS (for Australia, New Zealand, and the United States), was concluded after World War II (New Zealand withdrew in 1986). And just as it had sent troops to fight Germany during World Wars I and II, Australia sent troops to fight in the Korean War in 1950 and the Vietnam War in the 1960s—although anti–Vietnam War sentiment in Australia strained relations with the United States at that time. Australia also joined the United States and other countries in 1954 in establishing the Southeast Asia Treaty Organization, an Asian counterpart to the North Atlantic Treaty Organization designed to contain the spread of communism.

In 1991, when the Philippines refused to renew leases on U.S. military bases there, there was much discussion about transferring U.S. operations to the Cockburn Sound Naval Base in Australia. Singapore was eventually chosen for some of the operations, but the incident reveals the close relationship of the two nations. U.S. military aircraft already land in Australia, and submarines and other naval craft call at Australian ports. The Americans also use Australian territory for surveillance facilities. There is historical precedence for this level of close cooperation: Before the U.S. invasion of the Japanese-controlled Philippines in the 1940s, the United States based its Pacific-theater military headquarters in Australia; moreover, Britain's inability to lead the fight against Japan forced Australia to look to the United States.

A few Australians resent the violation of sovereignty represented by the U.S. bases, but most regard the United States as a solid ally. Indeed, many Australians regard their country as the Southern Hemisphere's version of the United States: Both countries have immense space and vast resources, both were founded as disparate colonies that eventually united and obtained independence from Britain, and both share a common language and a Western cultural heritage.

There is yet another way that Australia is, or might like to be, like the United States: It may want to be a republic. A little less than half the population say that they can see no reason to remain a constitutional monarchy, with the king or queen of England as the head of state. Therefore, in 1993, the prime minister met with Queen Elizabeth II to announce his intention of turning Australia into a republic (within the British Commonwealth) by the year 2001. The queen indicated that she would respect the wishes of the people, but what the people want is still not clear—in 1996, they chose a new antirepublic leader, John Howard of the Liberal Party, who enthusiastically swore alle-

(San Diego Convention and Visitors Bureau)

Australia has a number of animals that are, in their native form, unique in the world. The koala is found only in the eastern coastal region, where it feeds, very selectively, on the leaves of the eucalyptus tree. It is a marsupial and bears its young every other year. Pictured above is a very rare baby albino koala with its mother.

| Australia is threatened by Japan during World War II **1940s** | Australia proposes the South Pacific Commission **1947** | Australia joins New Zealand and the United States in the ANZUS military security agreement **1951** | Australia joins the South East Asian Treaty Organization **1954** | Relations with the United States are strained over the Vietnam War **1960s** | The Australian Labour Party wins for the first time in 23 years; Gough Whitlam is prime minister **1972** | After a constitutional crisis, Whitlam is replaced by opposition leader J. M. Fraser **1975** | Australia begins to strengthen its economic ties with Asian countries | Depletion of the ozone layer is believed to be responsible for a rapidly rising incidence of skin cancer among Australians **1980s** | **1990s** |

After 13 years in power, the Labour Party is defeated by Liberal Party leader John Howard

Australia condemns nuclear testing in the Pacific, recalls French ambassador

Australia prepares to host the Summer Olympics in 2000

giance to the queen upon his inauguration as prime minister.

Unlike New Zealand, which has distanced itself from the United States by refusing to allow nuclear-armed ships to enter its ports and has withdrawn from ANZUS, Australia has joined with the United States in attempting to dissuade South Pacific states from declaring the region a nuclear-free zone. Yet it has also maintained good ties with the small and vulnerable societies of the Pacific through its leadership in such regional associations as the South Pacific Commission, the South Pacific Forum, and the ever-more-influential Asia Pacific Economic Cooperation Group (APEC). It has also condemned nuclear bomb testing programs in French-controlled territories.

## AUSTRALIA AND THE PACIFIC

Australia was not always possessed of good intentions toward the islands around it. For one thing, white Australians thought of themselves as superior to the brown-skinned islanders; and for another, Australia preferred to use the islands' resources for its own economic gain, with little regard for the islanders themselves. At the end of World War I, for example, the phosphate-rich island of Nauru, formerly under German control, was assigned to Australia as a trust territory. Until phosphate mining was turned over to the islanders in 1967, Australian farmers consumed large quantities of the island's phosphates but paid just half the market price. Worse, only a tiny fraction of the proceeds went to the people of Nauru. Similarly, in Papua New Guinea, Australia controlled the island without taking significant steps toward its domestic development until the 1960s, when, under the guidance of the United Nations, it

did an about-face and facilitated changes that advanced the successful achievement of independence in 1975.

In addition to forgoing access to cheap resources, Australia was reluctant to relinquish control of these islands because it saw them as a shield against possible military attack. It learned this lesson well in World War II. In 1941, Japan, taking advantage of the Western powers' preoccupation with Adolf Hitler, moved quickly to expand its imperial designs in Asia and the Pacific. The Japanese first disabled the U.S. Navy by attacking its warships docked in Pearl Harbor, Hawaii. They then moved on to oust the British in Hong Kong and the Gilbert Islands, and the Americans in Guam and Wake Island. Within a few months, the Japanese had taken control of Burma, Malaya, Borneo, the Philippines, Singapore, and hundreds of tiny Pacific islands, which they used to create an immense defensive perimeter around the home islands of Japan. They also had captured part of New Guinea and were keeping a large force there, which greatly concerned the Australians. Yet fighting was kept away from Australia proper when the Japanese were successfully engaged by Australian and American troops in New Guinea. Other Pacific islands were regained from the Japanese at a tremendous cost in lives and military hardware. Japan's defeat came only when islands close enough to Japan to be attacked by U.S. bomber aircraft were finally captured. Japan surrendered in 1945, but the colonial powers had learned that possession of small islands could have strategic importance. This experience is part of the reason for colonial powers' reluctance to grant independence to the vast array of islands over which they have exercised control. Australia is now faced

with the question of whether or not to grant independence to the 4,000 inhabitants of Christmas Island who recently voted to become a self-ruling territory within Australia.

There is no doubt that stressful historical periods and events such as World War II drew the English-speaking countries of the South Pacific closer together and closer to the United States. But recent realignments in the global economic system are creating strains. When the United States insists that Japan take steps to ease the U.S.–Japan trade imbalance, Australia sometimes comes out the loser. For instance, both Australia and the United States are producers of coal, and, given the nearly equal distance between those two countries and Japan, it would be logical to expect that Japan would buy coal at about the same price from both countries. In fact, however, Japan pays $7 a ton more for American coal than for Australian coal, a discrepancy directly attributable to Japan's attempt to reduce the trade imbalance with the United States. Resentment against the United States over such matters is likely to grow, and managing such international tensions will no doubt challenge the skills of the leadership of Australia well into the next century.

## DEVELOPMENT

Mining of nickel, iron ore, and other metals continues to supply a substantial part of Australia's gross domestic product. In recent years, Japan has become Australia's primary trading partner rather than Great Britain. Seven out of 10 of Australia's largest export markets are Asian countries.

## FREEDOM

Australia is a parliamentary democracy adhering to the ideals incorporated in English common law. Constitutional guarantees of human rights apply to all of Australia's 18.4 million citizens. However, social discrimination continues, and, despite improvements since the 1960s, the Aborigines remain a neglected part of Australian society.

## HEALTH/WELFARE

Like New Zealand, Australia has developed a complex and comprehensive system of social welfare. Education is the province of the several states. Public education is compulsory. Australia boasts several world-renowned universities. The world's first voluntary euthanasia law passed in Northern Territory in 1996, but legal challenges prevent its use.

## ACHIEVEMENTS

The vastness and challenge of Australia's interior lands, called the "outback," have inspired a number of Australian writers to create outstanding poetry and fictional novels. In 1973, Patrick White became the first Australian to win a Nobel Prize in Literature. Jill Ker Conway, Thomas Keneally, and Colleen McCullough are other well-known Australian authors.

# Brunei (Negara Brunei Darussalam)

## GEOGRAPHY

*Area in Square Miles (Kilometers):*
2,228 (5,770) (about the size of Delaware)

*Capital (Population):* Bandar Seri Begawan (187,000)

*Environmental Concerns:* water pollution

*Geographical Features:* flat coastal plain rises to mountains in east; hilly lowlands in west

*Climate:* tropical; hot, humid, rainy

## PEOPLE

### Population

*Total:* 307,600

*Annual Growth Rate:* 2.5%

*Rural/Urban Population (Ratio):* 30/70

*Major Languages:* Malay; English; Chinese; Iban; native dialects

*Ethnic Makeup:* 64% Malay; 20% Chinese; 16% others

*Religions:* 63% Muslim; 15% indigenous beliefs; 14% Buddhist; 8% Christian

### Health

*Life Expectancy at Birth:* 70 years (male); 73 years (female)

*Infant Mortality Rate (Ratio):* 23.8/1,000

*Average Caloric Intake:* na

*Physicians Available (Ratio):* 1/1,398

### Education

*Adult Literacy Rate:* 88%

*Compulsory (Ages):* 5–14; free

## COMMUNICATION

*Telephones:* 1 per 4.2 people

*Televisions:* 1 per 4.1 people

## TRANSPORTATION

*Highways in Miles (Kilometers):* 676 (1,120)

*Railroads in Miles (Kilometers):* 8 (13)

*Usable Airfields:* 2

*Motor Vehicles in Use:* 128,000

## GOVERNMENT

*Type:* constitutional sultanate

*Independence Date:* January 1, 1984

*Head of State/Government:* Sultan and Prime Minister His Majesty Paduka Seri Baginda Sultan Haji Hassanal Bolkiah Mu'izzaddin Waddaulah is both head of state and head of government

*Political Parties:* Brunei United National Party (inactive); Brunei National Solidarity Party (the first legal party, now banned); Brunei People's Party (banned); Brunei National Democratic Party (deregistered)

*Suffrage:* none

## MILITARY

*Military Expenditures (% of GDP):* 6.2%

*Current Disputes:* none

## ECONOMY

*Currency ($ U.S. Equivalent):* 1.4 Bruneian dollars = $1

*Per Capita Income/GDP:* $15,800/$4.6 billion

*GDP Growth Rate:* 2%

*Inflation Rate:* 2.5%

*Unemployment Rate:* 4.8%

*Labor Force:* 119,000 (including army)

*Natural Resources:* oil; natural gas; forests

*Agriculture:* rice; vegetables; fruits

*Industry:* oil; rubber; pepper; lumber; gravel; animal hides

*Exports:* $2.7 billion (primary partners Japan, United Kingdom, Thailand)

*Imports:* $2.0 billion (primary partners Singapore, United Kingdom, United States)

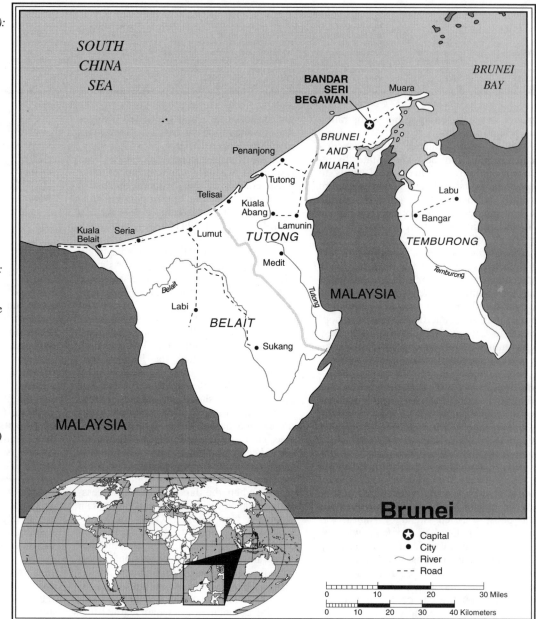

 http://www.odci.gov/cia/publications/factbook/country-frame.html

| Brunei is first visited by Europeans A.D. 1521 | Brunei is known as haven for pirates 1700 | Briton James Brooke is given Sarawak as reward for help in a civil war 1800s | The island of Labuan is ceded to Britain 1847 | Britain attacks and ends pirate activities in Brunei 1849 | The remainder of Brunei becomes a British protectorate 1888 | The first Brunei Constitution is promulgated 1959 | Brunei rejects confederation with Malaysia 1963 | Brunei gains its independence 1984 |
|---|---|---|---|---|---|---|---|---|

1990s

| The sultan of Brunei, Hassanal Bolkiah, is said to be the richest person in the world, with assets of $37 billion | Foreign workers are "imported" to ease the labor shortage; Brunei joins the International Monetary Fund | Scandal erupts when it appears that the sultan's brother has absconded with billions of dollars |
|---|---|---|

## A WEALTHY COUNTRY

Home to only 307,600 people, Brunei rarely captures the headlines. But perhaps it should, for, despite its tiny size, the country boasts one of the highest living standards in the world. Moreover, the sultan of Brunei, with assets of $37 billion, is considered the richest person in the world. The secret? Oil. First exploited in Brunei in the late 1920s, today oil and natural gas almost entirely support the sultanate's economy. The government's annual income is nearly twice its expenditures, despite the provision of free education and medical care, subsidized food and housing, and the absence of income taxes. Currently, Brunei is in the middle of a 5-year plan designed to diversify its economy and lessen its dependence on oil revenues, but 98 percent of the nation's revenues continue to derive from the sale of oil and natural gas. Japan purchases more than 60 percent of Brunei's exports; the other nations of the Asia Pacific buy most of the remainder. Brunei's imports come primarily from Asia, especially Japan, and from the United States.

Muslim sultans ruled over the entire island of Borneo and other nearby islands during the sixteenth century. Advantageously located on the northwest coast of the island of Borneo, along the sea lanes of the South China Sea, Brunei was a popular resting spot for traders; and, during the 1700s, it became known as a haven for pirates. Tropical rain forests and swamps occupy much of the country—conditions that are maintained by heavy monsoon rains for about 5 months each year. Oil and natural-gas deposits are found both on- and offshore.

In the 1800s, the sultan then in power agreed to the kingdom becoming a protectorate of Britain, in order to safeguard his domain from being further whittled away by aggressors bent on empire-building. The Japanese easily overtook Brunei in 1941, when they launched their Southeast Asian offensive in search of oil and gas for their war machine. Today, the Japanese Mitsubishi Corporation has a one-third interest in the Brunei gas company.

In the 1960s, it was expected that Brunei, which is cut in two and surrounded on three sides by Malaysia, would join the newly proposed Federation of Malaysia; but it refused to do so, preferring to remain under British control. The decision to remain a colony was made by Sultan Sir Omar Ali Saifuddin. Educated in British Malaya, the sultan retained a strong affection for British culture and frequently visited the British Isles. (Brunei's 1959 Constitution, promulgated during Sir Omar's reign, reflected this attachment: It declared Brunei a self-governing state, with its foreign affairs and defense remaining the responsibility of Great Britain.)

In 1967, Sir Omar abdicated in favor of his son, who became the 29th ruler in succession. Sultan (and Prime Minister) Sir Hassanal Bolkiah Mu'izzaddin Waddaulah (a shortened version of his name) oversaw Brunei's gaining of independence, in 1984. Not all Bruneians are pleased with the sultan's control over the political process, but opposition voices have been silenced. There are, in effect, no operative political parties in Brunei, and there have been no elections in the country since 1965, despite a constitutional provision for them.

Brunei's largest ethnic group is Malay, accounting for 64 percent of the population. Indians and Chinese constitute sizable minorities, as do indigenous peoples such as Ibans and Dyaks. Despite Brunei's historic ties with Britain, Europeans make up only a tiny fraction of the population.

Brunei is an Islamic nation with Hindu roots. Islam is the official state religion, and in recent years, the sultan has proposed bringing national laws more closely in line with Islamic ideology. Modern Brunei is officially a constitutional monarchy, headed by the sultan, a chief minister, and a Council; in reality, however, the sultan and his family control all aspects of state decision making. The extent of the sultan's control of the government is revealed by his multiple titles: in addition to sultan, he is Brunei's prime minister, minister of defense, and minister of finance. The Constitution provides the sultan with supreme executive authority in the state. In late 1995, Brunei joined with other ASEAN countries in declaring their region a nuclear-free zone.

In recent years, Brunei has been plagued by a chronic labor shortage. The government and Brunei Shell (a consortium owned jointly by the Brunei government and Shell Oil) are the largest employers in the country. They provide generous fringe benefits and high pay. Non-oil private-sector companies with fewer resources find it difficult to recruit in-country and have, therefore, employed many foreign workers. Indeed, one third of all workers today in Brunei are foreigners. This situation is of considerable concern to the government, which is worried that social tensions between foreigners and residents, as is happening in other countries, may flare up at any time.

## DEVELOPMENT

Brunei's economy is a mixture of the modern and the ancient: foreign and domestic entrepreneurship, government regulation and welfare statism, and village tradition. Chronic labor shortages are managed by the importation of thousands of foreign workers.

## FREEDOM

Although Islam is the official state religion, the government practices religious tolerance. The Constitution provides the sultan with supreme executive authority, which he has used to suppress opposition groups and political parties.

## HEALTH/WELFARE

The country's massive oil and natural gas revenues support wide-ranging benefits to the population, such as subsidized food, fuel, and housing, and free medical care and education. This distribution of wealth is reflected in Brunei's generally favorable quality-of-life indicators.

## ACHIEVEMENTS

An important project has been the construction of a modern university accommodating 1,500 to 2,000 students. Since independence, the government has tried to strengthen and improve the economic, social, and cultural life of its people.

# Cambodia (Kingdom of Cambodia)

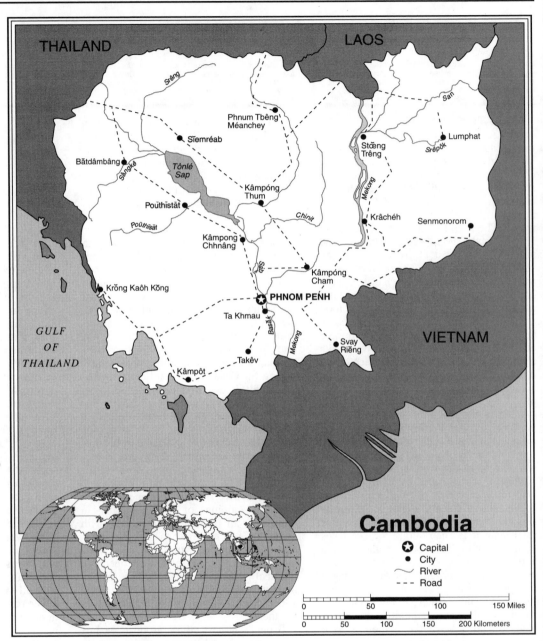

**Cambodia**

- ⭐ Capital
- • City
- ∿ River
- --- Road

## GEOGRAPHY
*Area in Square Miles (Kilometers):* 69,881 (181,040) slightly smaller than Oklahoma)
*Capital (Population):* Phnom Penh (920,000)
*Environmental Concerns:* habitat loss and declining biodiversity; soil erosion; deforestation; lack of access to potable water
*Geographical Features:* mostly low, flat plains; mountains in the southwest and north
*Climate:* tropical

## PEOPLE

### Population
*Total:* 11,164,000
*Annual Growth Rate:* 2.72%
*Rural/Urban Population (Ratio):* 79/21
*Major Languages:* Khmer; French
*Ethnic Makeup:* 90% Khmer (Cambodian); 5% Chinese; 5% others
*Religions:* 95% Theravada Buddhist; 5% others

### Health
*Life Expectancy at Birth:* 49 years (male); 52 years (female)
*Infant Mortality Rate (Ratio):* 106/1,000
*Average Caloric Intake:* 85% of FAO minimum
*Physicians Available (Ratio):* 1/7,900

### Education
*Adult Literacy Rate:* 35%
*Compulsory Ages:* 6–12

## COMMUNICATION
*Telephones:* 1 per 1,890 people
*Televisions:* 1 per 125 people

## TRANSPORTATION
*Highways in Miles (Kilometers):* 21,461 (35,769)
*Railroads in Miles (Kilometers):* 365 (603)
*Usable Airfields:* 14
*Motor Vehicles in Use:* 48,000

## GOVERNMENT
*Type:* liberal democracy under a constitutional monarchy
*Independence Date:* November 9, 1949
*Head of State/Government:* King Norodom Sihanouk; president/prime minister in transition

*Political Parties:* National United Front ... (Funcinpec); Cambodian People's Party; Buddhist Liberal Democratic Party; Democratic Kampuchea (Khmer Rouge); National Liberation Movement; Khmer Nation Party
*Suffrage:* universal at 18

## MILITARY
*Military Expenditures (% of GDP):* na
*Current Disputes:* border disputes with Thailand and Vietnam; civil war

## ECONOMY
*Currency ($ U.S. Equivalent):* 2,723 riels = $1
*Per Capita Income/GDP:* $710/$7.7 billion
*GDP Growth Rate:* 7%

*Inflation Rate:* 5%
*Labor Force:* 2,500,000–3,000,00
*Natural Resources:* timber; gemstones; iron ore; manganese; phosphates; hydropower potential
*Agriculture:* rice; rubber; maize; beans; soybeans
*Industry:* rice processing; fishing; wood and wood products; rubber; cement; gem mining
*Exports:* $464 million (primary partners Vietnam, Japan, India)
*Imports:* $1.4 billion (primary partners China, Singapore, Malaysia, Thailand)

 http://www.cambodia-web.net
http://www.odci.gov/cia/publication/factbook/country-frame.html

## A LAND OF TRAGEDY

In Khmer (Cambodian), the word *Kampuchea*, which for a time during the 1980s was the official name of Cambodia, means "country where gold lies at the foothill." Always an agricultural economy, Cambodia's monsoon rains contribute to the numerous large rivers that sustain farming on the country's large central plain and produce tropical forests consisting of such useful trees as coconuts, palms, bananas, and rubber. But Cambodia is certainly not a land of gold, nor of food, freedom, or stability. Despite a new Constitution, massive United Nations aid, and a formal cease-fire, the horrific effects of Cambodia's bloody Civil War continue.

Cambodia was not always a place to be pitied. In fact, at times it was the dominant power of Southeast Asia. Around the fourth century A.D., India, with its pacifist Hindu ideology, began to influence in earnest the original Chinese base of Cambodian civilization. The Indian script came to be used, the name of its capital city was an Indian word, its kings acquired Indian titles, and many of its Khmer people believed in the Hindu religion. The mile-square Hindu temple Angkor Wat, built in the twelfth century, still stands as a symbolic reminder of Indian influence, Khmer ingenuity, and the Khmer Empire's glory.

But the Khmer Empire, which at its height included parts of present-day Myanmar (Burma), Thailand, Laos, and Vietnam, was gradually reduced both in size and power until, in the 1800s, it was paying tribute to both Thailand and Vietnam. Continuing threats from these two countries as well as wars and domestic unrest at home led the king of Cambodia to appeal to France for help. France, eager to offset British power in the region, was all too willing to help. A protectorate was established in 1863, and French power grew apace until, in 1887, Cambodia became a part of French Indochina, a conglomerate consisting of the countries of Laos, Vietnam, and Cambodia.

The Japanese temporarily evicted the French in 1945 and, while under Japanese control, Cambodia declared its "independence" from France. Heading the country was the young King Norodom Sihanouk. Controlling rival ideological factions, some of which were pro-West while others were pro-Communist, was difficult for Sihanouk, but he built unity around the idea of permanently expelling the French, who finally left in 1955. King Sihanouk then abdicated his throne in favor of his father so that he could, as premier, personally enmesh himself in political governance. He took the title Prince Sihanouk, by which he is known to most people today, although

in 1993 he declared himself, once again, king of Cambodia.

From the beginning, Sihanouk's government was bedeviled by border disputes with Thailand and Vietnam and by the incursion of Communist Vietnamese soldiers into Cambodia. Sihanouk's ideological allegiances were (and remain) confusing at best; but, to his credit, he was able to keep Cambodia officially out of the Vietnam War, which raged for years (1950–1975) on its border. In 1962, Sihanouk announced that his country would remain neutral in the cold war struggle.

Neutrality, however, was not seen as a virtue by the United States, whose people were becoming more and more eager either to win or to quit the war with North Vietnam. A particularly galling point for the U.S. military was the existence of the so-called Ho Chi Minh Trail, a supply route through the tropical mountain forests of Cambodia. For years, North Vietnam had been using the route to supply its military operations in South Vietnam, and Cambodia's neutrality prevented the United States, at least legally, from taking military action against the supply line.

All this changed in 1970, when Sihanouk, out of the country at the time, was evicted from office by his prime minister, General Lon Nol, who was supported by the United States and South Vietnam. Shortly thereafter, the United States, then at its peak of involvement in the Vietnam War, began extensive military action in Cambodia. The years of official neutrality came to a bloody end.

## THE KILLING FIELDS

Most of these international political intrigues were lost on the bulk of the Cambodian population, only half of whom could read and write, and almost all of whom survived, as their forebears had before them, by cultivating rice along the Mekong River Valley. The country had almost always been poor, so villagers had long since learned that, even in the face of war, they could survive by hard work and reliance on extended-family networks. Most farmers probably thought that the war next door would not seriously alter their lives. But they were profoundly wrong, for, just as the United States had an interest in having a pro–U.S. government in Cambodia, the North Vietnamese desperately wanted Cambodia to be pro-Communist.

North Vietnam wanted the Cambodian government to be controlled by the Khmer Rouge, a Communist guerrilla army led by Pol Pot, one of a group of former students influenced by the left-wing ideology taught in Paris universities during the

1950s. Winning control in 1975, the Khmer Rouge launched a hellish 3½-year extermination policy, resulting in the deaths of between 1 million and 3 million fellow Cambodians—that is, between one fifth and one third of the entire Cambodian population. The official goal was to eliminate anyone who had been "polluted" by prerevolutionary thinking, but what actually happened was random violence, torture, and murder.

It is impossible to fully describe the mayhem and despair that engulfed Cambodia during those years. Cities were emptied of people. Teachers and doctors were killed or sent as slaves to work in the rice paddies. Despite the centrality of Buddhism to Cambodian culture (Hinduism having long since been displaced by Buddhist thought), thousands of Buddhist monks were killed or died of starvation as the Khmer Rouge carried out its program of eliminating religion. Some people were killed for no other reason than to terrorize others into submission. Explained Leo Kuper in *International Action Against Genocide*:

> Those who were dissatisfied with the new regime were . . . "eradicated," along with their families, by disembowelment, by beating to death with hoes, by hammering nails into the backs of their heads and by other cruel means of economizing on bullets.
>
> Persons associated with the previous regime were special targets for liquidation. In many cases, the executions included wives and children. There were summary executions too of intellectuals, such as doctors, engineers, professors, teachers and students, leaving the country denuded of professional skills.

The Khmer Rouge wanted to alter the society completely. Children were removed from their families, and private ownership of property was eliminated. Money was outlawed. Even the calendar was started over, at year 0. Vietnamese military leader Bui Tin explained just how totalitarian the rulers were:

> [In 1979] there was no small piece of soap or handkerchief anywhere. Any person who had tried to use a toothbrush was considered bourgeois and punished. Any person wearing glasses was considered an intellectual who must be punished.

It is estimated that, before the Khmer Rouge came to power in 1975, Cambodia had 1,200 engineers, 21,000 teachers, and

| France gains control of Cambodia A.D. **1863** | Japanese invasion; King Norodom Sihanouk is installed **1940s** | Sihanouk wins Cambodia's independence of France **1953** | General Lon Nol takes power in a U.S.–supported coup **1970** | The Khmer Rouge, under Pol Pot, overthrows the government and begins a reign of terror **1975** | Vietnam invades Cambodia and installs a puppet government **1978** | **1990s** |

Vietnam withdraws troops from Cambodia; a Paris cease-fire agreement is violated by the Khmer Rouge

1993 elections result in a new Constitution, reenthronement of Sihanouk as king, and establishment of dual premiership

First Premier Ranariddh is deposed in a bloody coup by Second Premier Hun Sen, followed by the death of Pol Pot

500 doctors. After the purges, the country was left with only 20 engineers, 3,000 teachers, and 54 doctors.

A kind of bitter relief came in late 1978, when Vietnamese troops (traditionally Cambodia's enemy) invaded Cambodia, drove the Khmer Rouge to the borders of Thailand, and installed a puppet government headed by Hun Sen, a former Khmer Rouge soldier who defected and fled to Vietnam in the 1970s. Although almost everyone was relieved to see the Khmer Rouge pushed out of power, the Vietnamese intervention was almost universally condemned by other nations. This was because the Vietnamese were taking advantage of the chaos in Cambodia to further their aim of creating a federated state of Vietnam, Laos, and Cambodia. Its virtual annexation of Cambodia eliminated Cambodia as a buffer state between Vietnam and Thailand, destabilizing the relations of the region even more.

## COALITION GOVERNANCE

The United States and others refused to recognize the Vietnam-installed regime, instead granting recognition to the Coalition Government of Democratic Kampuchea. This entity consisted of three groups: the Communist Khmer Rouge, led by Khieu Samphan and Pol Pot and backed by China; the anti-Communist Khmer People's National Liberation Front, led by former prime minister Son Sann; and the Armee Nationale Sihanoukiste, led by Sihanouk. Although it was doubtful that these former enemies could constitute a workable government for Cambodia, the United Nations granted its Cambodia seat to the coalition and withheld its support from the Hun Sen government.

Vietnam had hoped that its capture of Cambodia would be easy and painless. In-

stead, the Khmer Rouge and others resisted so much that Vietnam had to send in 200,000 troops, of which 25,000 died. Moreover, other countries, including the United States and Japan, strengthened their resolve to isolate Vietnam in terms of international trade and development financing. After 10 years, the costs to Vietnam of remaining in Cambodia were so great that Vietnam announced it would pull out its troops.

A 1992 diplomatic breakthrough allowed the United Nations to establish a peacekeeping force in the country of some 22,000 troops, including Japanese soldiers—the first Japanese military presence outside Japan since World War II. These troops were to keep the tenacious Khmer Rouge faction under control. The agreement, signed in Paris by 17 nations, called for the release of political prisoners; inspections of prisons; and voter registration for national elections, to be held in 1993. Most important, the warring factions, consisting of some 200,000 troops, including 25,000 Khmer Rouge troops, agreed to disarm under UN supervision.

Unfortunately, the Khmer Rouge, although a signatory to the agreement, refused to abide by its provisions. With revenues gained from illegal trading in lumber and gems with Thailand, it launched new attacks on villages, trains, and even the UN peacekeepers themselves, and it refused to participate in the elections of 1993, although it had been offered a role in the new government if it would cooperate.

Despite a violent campaign, 90 percent of those eligible voted in elections that, after some confusion, resulted in a new Constitution; the reenthronement of Sihanouk as king; and the appointment of Sihanouk's son, Prince Norodom Ranariddh of the Royalist Party, as first prime minister and

Hun Sen of the Cambodian People's Party as second prime minister.

The new Parliament outlawed the Khmer Rouge. Both premiers began negotiating with separate factions of the Khmer Rouge to entice them to lay down arms or else join with government forces in return for amnesty. Thousands accepted the offers, weakening the rebel army. Soon, Hun Sen claimed that Ranariddh was attempting to stage a coup by recruiting Khmer Rouge soldiers for a personal army. Hun Sen effected his own coup by deposing Ranariddh, although Ranariddh's father, the king, eventually granted him amnesty, and Ranariddh returned to Cambodia. In the midst of these events, the notorious Khmer Rouge leader, Pol Pot, died, closing the chapter on the saddest of all eras in Cambodian history.

## DEVELOPMENT

In the past, China, the United States, and others built roads and industries in Cambodia, but the country remains an impoverished state whose economy rests on fishing and farming. Continual warfare for 2 decades has prevented industrial development. The economy is sustained primarily by massive foreign aid.

## FREEDOM

Few Cambodians can remember political stability, much less political freedom. Every form of human-rights violation has been practiced in Cambodia since even before the arrival of the barbaric Khmer Rouge. Suppression of dissent continues: Journalists have been killed, and opponents of the government— including the king's brother—have been expelled from the country.

## HEALTH/WELFARE

Almost all of Cambodia's doctors were killed or died during the Khmer Rouge regime, and warfare disrupted normal agriculture. Thus, disease was rampant, as was malnutrition. The few trained international relief workers remaining in Cambodia today are hard-pressed to make a dent in the country's enormous problems.

## ACHIEVEMENTS

Despite violence and intimidation, 90% of the Cambodian people voted in the 1993 elections, restoring an elected government, a limited monarchy, and acceding to a new Constitution. The new government has nearly eliminated the influence of the Khmer Rouge. In 1998 and early 1999, Second Premier Hun Sen negotiated the surrender of key Khmer Rouge leaders.

# China (People's Republic of China)

## GEOGRAPHY

*Area in Square Miles (Kilometers):* 3,723,000 (9,596,960) (slightly smaller than the United States)

*Capital (Population):* Beijing (11,299,000)

*Environmental Concerns:* air and water pollution; water shortages; desertification; trade in endangered species; acid rain; loss of agricultural land to soil erosion and economic development

*Geographical Features:* mostly mountains, high plateaus, deserts in the west; plains, deltas, and hills in the east

*Climate:* extremely diverse; tropical to subarctic

## PEOPLE

### Population

*Total:* 1,223,000,000

*Annual Growth Rate:* 0.93%

*Rural/Urban Population Ratio:* 71/29

*Major Languages:* Standard Chinese (Putonghua) or Mandarin; Yue (Cantonese); Wu (Shanghainese); Minbei (Fuzhou); Minuan (Hokkien-Taiwanese); Xiang; Gan; Hahka

*Ethnic Makeup:* 92% Han Chinese; 8% minority groups (the largest being Chuang, Hui, Uighur, Yi, and Miao)

*Religions:* officially atheist; but Taoism, Buddhism, Islam, Christianity, ancestor worship, and animism do exist

### Health

*Life Expectancy at Birth:* 69 years (male); 71 years (female)

*Infant Mortality Rate (Ratio):* 37.9/1,000

*Average Caloric Intake:* 104% of FAO minimum

*Physicians Available (Ratio):* 1/630

### Education

*Adult Literacy Rate:* 81.5%

*Compulsory (Ages):* 7–16

## COMMUNICATION

*Telephones:* 1 per 30 people

*Daily Newspaper Circulation:* 23 per 1,000 people

*Televisions:* 1 per 5.3 people

## TRANSPORTATION

*Highways in Miles (Kilometers):* 670,200 (1,117,000)

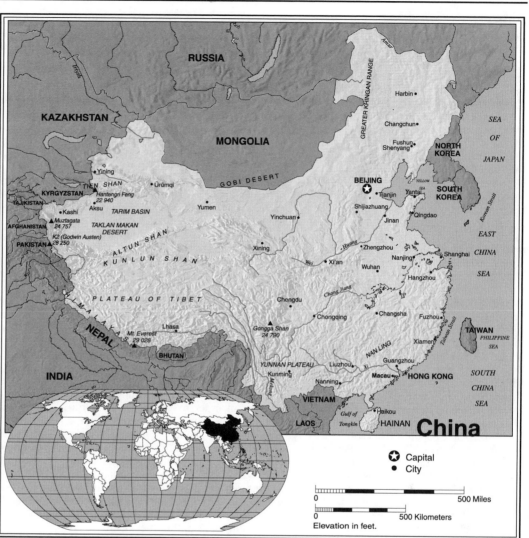

Capital
City

0 — 500 Miles
0 — 500 Kilometers
Elevation in feet.

*Railroads in Miles (Kilometers):* 37,500 (62,500)

*Usable Airfields:* 206

*Motor Vehicles in Use:* 7,900,000

## GOVERNMENT

*Type:* one-party Communist state

*Independence Date:* October 1, 1949

*Head of State/Government:* President Jiang Zemin; Premier Li Peng

*Political Parties:* Chinese Communist Party; eight registered small parties controlled by the CCP

*Suffrage:* universal at 18

## MILITARY

*Military Expenditures (% of GDP):* na

*Current Disputes:* boundary disputes with India, Russia, North Korea, others

## ECONOMY

*Currency ($ U.S. Equivalent):* 8.28 yuan = $1

*Per Capita Income/GDP:* $2,500/$2.97 trillion

*GDP Growth Rate:* 8.8%

*Inflation Rate:* 10%

*Unemployment Rate:* officially 3% in urban areas; probably 8%–10%

*Labor Force:* 614,700,000

*Natural Resources:* coal; petroleum; iron ore; tin; tungsten; antimony; lead; zinc; vanadium; magnetite; uranium

*Agriculture:* food grains; cotton; oil seeds; pork; fish; tea; potatoes; peanuts

*Industry:* iron and steel; coal; machinery; light industry; textiles and apparel; food processing; consumer durables and electronics; telecommunications; armaments

*Exports:* $151 billion (primary partners Hong Kong, Japan, United States)

*Imports:* $138.8 billion (primary partners Japan, United States, Taiwan)

http://www.chinaexpo.com/main.html
http://www.odci.gov/cia/publication/factbook/country-frame.html

## CHINA

The first important characteristic to note about China is its age. Human civilization appeared in China as early as 20,000 years ago, and the first documented Chinese dynasty, the Shang, began about 1523 B.C. Unproven legends suggest the existence of an even earlier Chinese dynasty (about 2000 B.C.), making China one of the oldest societies with a continuing cultural identity. Over the centuries of documented history, the Chinese people have been ruled by a dozen imperial dynasties; have enjoyed hundreds of years of stability and amazing cultural progress; and have endured more hundreds of years of chaos, military mayhem, and hunger. Yet China and the Chinese people remain intact—a strong testament to the tenacity of human culture.

A second major characteristic is that the People's Republic of China (P.R.C.) is very big. It is the fourth-largest country in the world, accounting for 6.5 percent of the world's landmass. Much of China—about 40 percent—is mountainous; but large, fertile plains have been created by China's numerous rivers, most of which flow toward the Pacific Ocean. China is blessed with substantial reserves of oil, minerals, and many other natural resources. Its large size and geopolitical location—it is bordered by Russia, Kazakhstan, Pakistan, India, Nepal, Bhutan, Myanmar, Laos, Vietnam, North Korea, and Mongolia—have caused the Chinese people over the centuries to think of their land as the "Middle Kingdom": that is, the center of world civilization.

However, its unwieldy size has been the undoing of numerous emperors who found it impossible to maintain its borders in the face of outside "barbarians" determined to possess the riches of Chinese civilization. During the Ch'in Dynasty (221–207 B.C.), a 1,500-mile-long, 25-foot-high wall, the so-called Great Wall, was erected along the northern border of China, in the futile hope that invasions from the north could be stopped. Although China's national boundaries are now recognized by international law, recent Chinese governments have found it necessary to "pacify" border areas by settling as many Han Chinese there as possible (for example, in Tibet), to prevent secession by China's numerous ethnic minorities.

Another important characteristic of modern China is its huge population. With 1.2 billion people, China is home to about 20 percent of all human beings alive today. About 92 percent of China's people are Han, or ethnic, Chinese; the remaining 8 percent are divided into more than 50 separate minority groups. Many of these ethnic groups speak mutually unintelligible languages, and although they often appear to be Chinese, they derive from entirely different cultural roots; some are Muslims, some are Buddhists, some are animists. As one moves away from the center of Chinese civilization in the eastern provinces, the influence of the minorities increases. The Chinese government has accepted the reality of ethnic influence and has granted a degree of limited autonomy to some provinces with heavy populations of minorities.

In the 1950s, Chairman Mao Zedong encouraged couples to have many children, but this policy was reversed in the 1970s, when a formal birth-control program was inaugurated. Urban couples today are permitted to have only one child and are penalized if they have more. Penalties include expulsion from the Chinese Communist Party (CCP), dismissal from work, or a 10 percent reduction in pay for up to 14 years after the birth of the second child. The policy is strictly enforced in the cities, but it has had only a marginal impact on overall population growth because three quarters of China's people live in rural areas, where they are allowed more children in order to help with the farmwork. In the city of Shanghai, with a population of about 13 million people, authorities have recently removed second-child privileges for farmers living near the city and for such former exceptional cases as children of revolutionary martyrs and workers in the oil industry. Despite these and other restrictions, it is estimated that 15 million to 17 million new Chinese are being born each year.

Over the centuries, millions of people have found it necessary or prudent to leave China in search of food, political stability, or economic opportunity. Those who emigrated a thousand or more years ago are now fully assimilated into the cultures of Southeast Asia and elsewhere and identify themselves accordingly. More recent émigrés (in the past 200 years or so), however, constitute visible, often wealthy, minorities in their new host countries, where they have become the backbone of the business community. Ethnic Chinese constitute the majority of the population in Singapore and a sizable minority in Malaysia. Important world figures such as Corazon Aquino, the former president of the Philippines, and Goh Chok Tong, the prime minister of Singapore, are part or full Chinese. The Chinese constituted the first big wave of the 6.5 million Asian Americans to call the United States home. Large numbers of Hong Kong Chinese emigrated to Canada in the mid-1990s. Thus the influence of China continues to spread far beyond its borders.

Another crucial characteristic of China is its history of imperial and totalitarian rule. Except for a few years in the early part of this century, China has been controlled by imperial decree, military order, and patriarchal privilege. Confucius taught that a person must be as loyal to the government as a son should be to his father. Following Confucius by a generation or two was Shang Yang, of a school of governmental philosophy called Legalism, which advocated unbending force and punishment against wayward subjects. Compassion and pity were not considered qualities of good government.

Mao Zedong, building on this heritage as well as that of the Soviet Union's Joseph Stalin and Vladimir Lenin, exercised strict control over both the public and private lives of the Chinese people. Dissidents were summarily executed (generally people were considered guilty once they were arrested), the press was strictly controlled, and recalcitrants were forced to undergo "reeducation" to correct their thinking. Religion of any kind was suppressed, and churches were turned into warehouses. It is estimated that, during the first 3 years of CCP rule, more than 1 million opponents of Mao's regime were executed. During the Cultural Revolution (1966–1976), Mao, who apparently thought that a new mini-revolution in China might restore his eroding stature in the Chinese Communist Party, encouraged young people to report to the authorities anyone suspected of owning books from the West or having contact with Westerners. Even party functionaries were purged if it were believed that their thinking had been corrupted by Western influences.

## THE TEACHINGS OF CONFUCIUS

Confucius (550–478 B.C.) was a Chinese intellectual and minor political figure. He was not a religious leader, nor did he ever claim divinity for himself or divine inspiration for his ideas. As the feudalism of his era began to collapse, he proposed that society could best be governed by paternalistic kings who set good examples. Especially important to a stable society, he taught, were respect and reverence for one's elders. Within the five key relationships of society (ruler and subject, husband and wife, father and son, elder brother and younger brother, and friend and friend), people should always behave with integrity, propriety, and goodness.

The writings of Confucius—or, rather, the works written about him by his followers and called the *Analects*—eventually became required knowledge for anyone in China claiming to be an educated person. However, rival ideas such as

Legalism (a philosophy advocating authoritarian government) were at times more popular with the elite; at one point 460 scholars were buried alive for teaching Confucianism. Nevertheless, much of the hierarchical nature of Asian culture today can be traced to Confucian ideas.

## ORIGINS OF THE MODERN STATE

Historically, authoritarian rule in China has been occasioned, in part, by China's mammoth size; by its unwieldy population; and by the ideology of some of its intellectuals. The modern Chinese state has arisen from these same pressures as well as some new ones. It is to these that we now turn.

The Chinese had traded with such non-Asian peoples as the Arabs and Persians for hundreds of years before European contact. But in the 1700s and 1800s, the British and others extracted something new from China in exchange for merchandise from the West: the permission for foreign citizens to live in parts of China without being subject to Chinese authority. Through this process of granting extraterritoriality to foreign powers, China slowly began to lose control of its sovereignty. The age of European expansion was not, of course, the first time in China's long history that its ability to rule itself was challenged; the armies of Kublai Khan successfully captured the Chinese throne in the 1200s, as did the Manchurians in the 1600s. But these outsiders, especially the Manchurians, were willing to rule China on-site and to imbibe as much Chinese culture as they could; eventually they became indistinguishable from the Chinese.

The European powers, on the other hand, preferred to rule China (or, rather, parts of it) from afar as a vassal state, with the proceeds of conquest being drained away from China to enrich the coffers of the European monarchs. Aggression against Chinese sovereignty increased in 1843 when the British forced China to cede Hong Kong Island. Britain, France, and the United States all extracted unequal treaties from the Chinese that gave them privileged access to trade and ports along the eastern coast. By the late 1800s, Russia was in control of much of Manchuria, Germany and France had wrested special economic privileges from the ever-weakening Chinese government, and Portugal had long since controlled Macau. Further affecting the Chinese economy was the loss of many of its former tributary states in Southeast Asia. China lost Vietnam to France, Burma (today called Myanmar) to Britain, and Korea to Japan. During the violent Boxer Rebellion of 1900, the Chi-

nese people showed how frustrated they were with the declining fortunes of their country.

Thus weakened internally and embarrassed internationally, the Manchu rulers of China began to initiate reforms that would strengthen their ability to compete with the Western and Japanese powers. A constitutional monarchy was proposed by the Manchu authorities but was preempted by the republican revolutionary movement of Western-trained Sun Yat-sen. Sun and his armies wanted an end to imperial rule; their dreams were realized in 1912, when Sun's Kuomintang (Nationalist Party, or KMT) took control of the new Republic of China.

Sun's Western approach to government was received with skepticism by many Chinese who distrusted the Western European model and preferred the thinking of Karl Marx and the philosophy of the Soviet Union. In 1921, Mao Zedong and others organized the Soviet-style Chinese Communist Party (CCP), which grew quickly and began to be seen as an alternative to the Kuomintang. After Sun's death, in 1925, Chiang Kai-shek assumed

control of the Kuomintang and waged a campaign to rid the country of Communist influence. Although Mao and Chiang cooperated when necessary—for example, to resist Japanese incursions into Manchuria—they eventually came to be such bitter enemies that they brought a ruinous civil war to all of China.

Mao derived his support from the rural areas of China, while Chiang depended on the cities. In 1949, facing defeat, Chiang Kai-shek's Nationalists retreated to the island of Taiwan, where, under the name Republic of China (R.O.C.), they continued to insist on their right to rule all of China. The Communists, however, controlled the mainland (and have done so for more than 4 decades) and insisted that Taiwan was just a renegade province of the People's Republic of China. These two antagonists are officially (but not in actuality) still at war. Sometimes tensions between Taiwan and China reach dangerous levels. In the 1940s, the United States had to intervene to prevent an attack from the mainland. In 1996, U.S. warships once again patrolled the 150 miles of ocean called the Taiwan Strait to warn China not

(UN photo/John Issac)

In China today, urban couples are permitted to have only one child, and they can be severely penalized if they dare to have a second or if they marry before the legal ages of 22 for men and 20 for women.

to turn its military exercises, including the firing of missiles in the direction of Taiwan, into an actual invasion. China used the blatantly aggressive actions as a warning to the newly elected Taiwanese president not to take any steps toward declaring Taiwan an independent nation.

For many years after World War II, world opinion sided with Taiwan's claim to be the legitimate government of China. Taiwan was granted diplomatic recognition by many nations and given the China seat in the United Nations. In the 1970s, however, many nations, including the United States, came to believe that it was dysfunctional to withhold recognition and standing from such a large and powerful nation as the P.R.C. Because both sides insisted that there could not be two Chinas, nor one China and one Taiwan, the UN proceeded to give the China seat to mainland China, and dozens of countries broke off formal diplomatic relations with Taiwan in order to establish a relationship with China.

## PROBLEMS OF GOVERNANCE

The China that Mao came to control was a nation with serious economic and social problems. Decades of civil war had disrupted families and wreaked havoc on the economy. Mao believed that the solution to China's ills was to wholeheartedly embrace socialism. Businesses were nationalized, and state planning replaced private initiative. Slowly, the economy improved. In 1958, however, Mao decided to enforce the tenets of socialism more vigorously so that China would be able to take an economic "Great Leap Forward." Workers were assigned to huge agricultural communes and were denied the right to grow crops privately. All enterprises came under the strict control of the central government. The result was economic chaos and a dramatic drop in both industrial and agricultural output.

Exacerbating these problems was the growing rift between the P.R.C. and the Soviet Union. China insisted that its brand of communism was truer to the principles of Marx and Lenin and criticized the Soviets for selling out to the West. As relations with (and financial support from) the Soviet Union withered, China found itself increasingly isolated from the world community, a circumstance worsened by serious conflicts with India, Indonesia, and other nations. To gain friends, the P.R.C. provided substantial aid to Communist insurgencies in Vietnam and Laos, thus contributing to the eventual severity of the Vietnam War.

In 1966, Mao found that his power was waning in the face of Communist Party leaders who favored a more moderate approach to internal problems and external relations. To regain lost ground, Mao urged young students called Red Guards to fight against anyone who might have liberal, capitalist, or intellectual leanings. He called it the Great Proletarian Cultural Revolution, but it was an *anti*cultural purge: Books were burned, and educated people were arrested and persecuted. In fact, the entire country remained in a state of domestic chaos for more than a decade.

Soon after Mao died, in 1976, Deng Xiaoping, who had been in and out of Communist Party power several times before, came to occupy the senior position in the CCP. A pragmatist, he was willing to modify or forgo strict socialist ideology if he believed that some other approach would work better. Despite pressure by hard-liners to tighten governmental control, he nevertheless was successful in liberalizing the economy and permitting exchanges of scholars with the West. In 1979, he accepted formalization of relations with the United States—an act seen as a signal of China's opening up to the world.

China's opening has been dramatic, not only in terms of its international relations but also internally. During the 1980s, the P.R.C. joined the World Bank, the International Monetary Fund, the Asian Development Bank, and other multilateral organizations. It also began to welcome foreign investment of almost any kind and permitted foreign companies to sell their products within China itself. Trade between Taiwan and China (still legally permitted only via a third country) was nearly $6 billion by the early 1990s. And while Hong Kong was investing some $25 billion in China, China was investing $11 billion in Hong Kong. More Chinese firms were permitted to export directly and to keep more of the profits. Special Economic Zones—capitalist enclaves adjacent to Hong Kong and along the coast into which were sent the most educated of the Chinese population—were established to catalyze the internal economy. In coastal cities, especially in south China, construction of apartment complexes, new manufacturing plants, and roads and highways began in earnest. Indeed, the south China area, along with Hong Kong and Taiwan, seemed to be emerging as a mammoth trading bloc—"Greater China"—which economists began to predict would exceed the economy of Japan by the year 2000 and eclipse the economy of the United States by 2012. Stock exchanges opened in Shanghai and Shenzhen. Dramatic changes were implemented even in the inner rural areas. The collectivized farm system imposed by Mao was replaced by a household contract system with hereditary contracts (that is, one step away from actual private land ownership), and free markets replaced most of the system of mandatory agricultural sales to the government. New industries were established in

(UN/photo by A. Holcombe)

During Mao Zedong's "Great Leap Forward," huge agricultural communes were established, and farmers were denied the right to grow crops privately. The government's strict control of these communes met with chaotic results; there were dramatic drops in agricultural output.

The Shang Dynasty is the first documented Chinese dynasty **1523–1027 B.C.**

The Chou Dynasty and the era of Confucius, Laotze, and Mencius **1027–256 B.C.**

The Ch'in Dynasty, from which the word *China* is derived **211–207 B.C.**

The Han Dynasty **202 B.C.–A.D. 220**

The Three Kingdoms period; the Tsin and Sui Dynasties **A.D. 220–618**

The T'ang Dynasty, during which Confucianism flourished **618–906**

The Five Dynasties and Sung Dynasty periods **906–1279**

The Yuan Dynasty is founded by Kublai Khan **1260–1368**

The Ming Dynasty **1368–1644**

The Manchu or Ch'ing Dynasty **1644–1912**

rural villages, and incomes improved such that many families were able to add new rooms onto their homes or to purchase two-story and even three-story homes. Predictions of China's economic dominance have had to be revised downward in the face of the Asian financial crisis, but the country's economy remains a force to be reckoned with.

## TIANANMEN SQUARE
Throughout the country in the 1980s, a strong spirit of entrepreneurship took hold; and many people, especially the growing body of educated youth, interpreted economic liberalization as the overture to political democratization. College students, some of whom had studied abroad, pressed the government to crack down on corruption in the Chinese Communist Party and to permit greater freedom of speech and other civil liberties.

In 1989, tens of thousands of college students staged a prodemocracy demonstration in Beijing's Tiananmen Square. The call for democratization received wide international media coverage and soon became an embarrassment to the Chinese leadership, especially when, after several days of continual protest, the students constructed a large statue in the square similar in appearance to the Statue of Liberty in New York Harbor. Some party leaders seemed inclined at least to talk with the students, but hard-liners apparently insisted that the prodemocracy movement be crushed in order that the CCP remain in control of the government. The official policy seemed to be that it would be the Communist Party, and not some prodemocracy movement, that would lead China to capitalism.

The CCP leadership had much to fear; it was, of course, aware of the quickening pace of Communist party power dissolution in the Soviet Union and Central/Eastern Europe, but it was even more concerned about corruption and the breakdown of CCP authority in the rapidly capitalizing rural regions of China, the very areas that had spawned the Communist Party under Mao. Moreover, economic liberalization had spawned inflation, higher prices, and spot shortages, and the general public was disgruntled. Therefore, after several weeks of pained restraint, the authorities moved against the students in what has become

known as the Tiananmen Square massacre. Soldiers injured thousands and killed hundreds of students; hundreds more were systematically hunted down and brought to trial for sedition and for spreading counterrevolutionary propaganda.

In the wake of the brutal crackdown, many nations reassessed their relationships with the People's Republic of China. The United States, Japan, and other nations halted or canceled foreign assistance, exchange programs, and special tariff privileges. The people of Hong Kong, anticipating the return of their British colony to P.R.C. control in 1997, staged massive demonstrations against the Chinese government's brutality. Foreign tourism all but ceased, and foreign investment declined abruptly.

The withdrawal of financial support and investment was particularly troublesome to the Chinese leadership, as it realized that the economy was far behind other nations. Even Taiwan, with a similar heritage and a common history until the 1950s, but having far fewer resources and much less land, had long since eclipsed the mainland in terms of economic prosperity. The Chinese understood that they needed to modernize (although not, they hoped, to Westernize), and they knew that large capital investments from such countries as Japan, Hong Kong, and the United States were crucial to their economic reform program. Moreover, they knew that they could not tolerate a cessation of trade with their new economic partners. By the end of the 1980s, about 13 percent of China's imports came from the United States, 18 percent from Japan, and 25 percent from Hong Kong. Similarly, Japan received 16 percent of China's exports, and Hong Kong received 43 percent.

Fortunately for the Chinese economy, the investment and loan-assistance programs from other countries have been reinstated in most cases as the repercussions of the events of 1989 wane. China was even able to close a $1.2 billion contract with McDonnell Douglas Corporation to build 40 jetliners; and U.S. President Bill Clinton, as a result of a decision to separate China's human-rights issues from trade issues, has repeatedly renewed China's "most favored nation" trade status. Bill Clinton and China's leader, Jiang Zemin, engaged in an unprecedented

public debate on Chinese television in June 1998, and Clinton was allowed to engage students and others in direct dialogue in which he urged religious freedom, free speech, and the protection of other human rights. These events and others suggest that China is trying to address some of the concerns voiced against it by the industrialized world, one of which is copyright violations by Chinese companies. Some have estimated that as much as 88 percent of China's exports of CDs consists of illegal copies. A 1995 copyright agreement is having some effect, but still, much of China's trade deficit with the United States, which is now higher than Japan's, comes from illegal products.

Improved trade notwithstanding, the Tiananmen Square massacre and the continuing brutality against citizens have convinced many people, both inside and outside China, that the Communist Party has lost, not necessarily its legal, but certainly its moral, authority to govern. Amnesty International's 1996 report claimed that human-rights violations in China occur "on a massive scale" and noted that torture is used on political prisoners held in *laogai,* Chinese gulags similar to those in the former Soviet Union. Increasing international attention is turning to Tibet, which China invaded in 1959 and where Chinese officials have been purging monks and others who resist Beijing's authority.

## THE SOCIAL ATMOSPHERE
In 1997, the aged Deng Xiaoping died. He was replaced by a decidedly more forward-looking leader, Jiang Zemin. Under his charge, the country was able to avoid many of the financial problems that affected other Asian nations in the late 1990s (although many Chinese banks are dangerously overextended, and real-estate speculation in Shanghai and other major cities has left many high-rise office buildings severely underoccupied). Despite many problems yet to solve, including serious human-rights abuses, it is clear that the Chinese leadership has actively embraced capitalism and has effected a major change in Chinese society. Historically, the loyalty of the masses of the people was placed in their extended families and in feudal warlords, who, at times of weakened imperial rule, were nearly sovereign

Trading rights and Hong Kong Island are granted to Britain
**1834**

The Sino-Japanese War
**1894–1895**

Sun Yat-sen's republican revolution ends centuries of imperial rule; the Republic of China is established
**1912**

The Chinese Communist Party is organized
**1921**

Chiang Kai-shek begins a long civil war with the Communists
**1926**

Mao Zedong's Communist Army defeats Chiang Kai-shek
**1949**

A disastrous economic reform, the Great Leap Forward, is launched by Mao
**1958**

The Cultural Revolution; Mao dies
**1966–1976**

Economic and political liberalization begins under Deng Xiaoping; the P.R.C. and Britain agree to return Hong Kong to the Chinese
**1980s**

China expands its relationship with Taiwan; the Tiananmen Square massacre provokes international outrage

**1990s**

Crackdowns on dissidents and criminals result in hundreds of arrests and executions; tensions begin to ease

Deng Xiaoping dies; Jiang Zemin becomes president

U.S. president Bill Clinton debates Chinese leader Jiang Zemin on Chinese television

in their own provinces. Communist policy has been to encourage the masses to give their loyalty instead to the centrally controlled Communist Party. The size of families has been reduced to the extent that "family" as such has come to play a less important role in the lives of ordinary Chinese.

Historical China was a place of great social and economic inequality between the classes. The wealthy feudal lords and their families and those connected with the imperial court and bureaucracy had access to the finest in educational and cultural opportunities, while around them lived illiterate peasants who often could not feed themselves, let alone pay the often heavy taxes imposed on them by feudal and imperial elites. The masses often found life to be bitter, but they found solace in the teachings of the three main religions of China (often adhered to simultaneously): Confucianism, Taoism, and Buddhism. Islam, animism, and Christianity have also been significant to many people in China.

The Chinese Communist Party under Mao, by legal decree and by indoctrination, attempted to suppress people's reliance on religious values and to reverse the ranking of the classes; the values of hard, manual work and rural simplicity were elevated, while the refinement and education of the urban elites were denigrated. Homes of formerly wealthy capitalists were taken over by the government and turned into museums, and the opulent life of the capitalists was disparaged. During the Cultural Revolution, high school students who wanted to attend college had first to spend 2 years in manual labor in factories and on farms to help them learn to relate to the peasants and the working class. So much did revolutionary ideology and national fervor take precedence over education that schools and colleges were

shut down for several years during the 1960s and 1970s and the length of compulsory education was reduced.

One would imagine that, after 40 years of communism, the Chinese people would have discarded the values of old China. However, the reverse seems to be true. When the liberalization of the economy began in the late 1970s, many of the former values also came to the fore: the Confucian value of scholarly learning and cultural refinement, the desirability of money, and even Taoist and Buddhist religious values. Religious worship is now permitted, with restrictions, in China.

Thousands of Chinese are studying abroad with the goal of returning to China to establish or manage profitable businesses. Indeed, some Chinese, especially those with legitimate access to power, such as ranking Communist Party members, have become extremely wealthy. Along with the privatization of state enterprises has come the unemployment of hundreds of thousands of "redundant" workers (2 million workers lost their jobs in one province in a single year in the early 1990s). Many others have had to settle for lower pay or unsafe work conditions as businesses strive to enter the world of competitive production. Demonstrations and more than 300 strikes by angry laborers exploded in early 1994. Even those with good jobs were finding it difficult to keep up with inflation, which in recent years has been as high as 22 percent. Nevertheless, those with an entrepreneurial spirit were finding ways to make more money than they had ever dreamed possible in an officially communist country.

Some former values may help revitalize Chinese life, while others, once suppressed by the Communists, may not be so desirable. For instance, Mao (despite being an unabashed womanizer himself)

attempted to eradicate prostitution, eliminate the sale of women as brides, and prevent child marriages. Today some of those customs are returning, and gender-based divisions of labor are making their way into the workplace.

Interest in things foreign however, is having a big impact on daily life in China, in ways both large and small. For example, increasingly entranced by Western culture, the Chinese flocked to movie theaters to see *Titanic*. Breaking box-office records across China, the film's theme song also reached the top of the charts, and scalpers sold tickets for packed screenings. Other movies are also popular; but, when translated into Chinese characters and then re-translated back into English, their titles are often comical: *The Full Monty* is translated to *Six Naked Pigs*; Oliver Stone's *Nixon* becomes *The Big Liar*; *The English Patient* becomes *Do Not Ask Me Who I Am, Ever*; *Fargo* becomes *Mysterious Murder in Snowy Cream*; and *Secrets and Lies* becomes *Dreadful, Difficult People*.

Predicting the future is difficult, but it is very unlikely that the economic reform process will be slowed by political problems. The economy seems to have taken be taking on a life of its own, and, once a solid middle class has developed, it is likely that political changes will follow, for that has been the history of the world. China, despite its size and longevity, cannot realistically expect to bypass the natural history of social change.

## DEVELOPMENT

In the early years of Communist control, authorities stressed the value of establishing heavy industry and collectivizing agriculture. More recently, China has attempted to reduce its isolation by establishing trading relationships with the United States, Japan, and others and by constructing free-enterprise zones. The world's largest dam is currently under construction, despite the objections of environmentalists.

## FREEDOM

Until the late 1970s, the Chinese people were controlled by Chinese Communist Party cadres who monitored both public and private behavior. Some economic and social liberalization occurred in the 1980s. However, the 1989 Tiananmen Square massacre reminded Chinese and the world that despite some reforms, China is still very much a dictatorship.

## HEALTH/WELFARE

The Communist government has overseen dramatic improvements in the provision of social services for the masses. Life expectancy has increased from 45 years in 1949 to 68 years (overall) today. Diverse forms of health care are available at low cost to the patient. The government has attempted to eradicate such diseases as malaria and tuberculosis.

## ACHIEVEMENTS

Chinese culture has, for thousands of years, provided the world with classics in literature, art, pottery, ballet, and other arts. Under communism the arts have been marshaled in the service of ideology and have lost some of their dynamism. Since 1949, literacy has increased dramatically and now stands at 73 percent—the highest in Chinese history.

# Hong Kong (China Special Administrative Region)

## GEOGRAPHY

*Area in Square Miles (Kilometers):* 671 (1,054) (about 6 times the size of Washington, D.C.)

*Capital (Population):* Victoria (na)

*Environmental Concerns:* air and water pollution resulting from the pressures of urbanization

*Geographical Features:* hilly to mountainous, with steep slopes; lowlands in the north

*Climate:* tropical monsoon

## PEOPLE

### Population

*Total:* 6,547,000

*Annual Growth Rate:* 2.59%

*Rural/Urban Population Ratio:* 9/91

*Major Languages:* Chinese (Cantonese); English

*Ethnic Makeup:* 95% Chinese (mostly Cantonese); 5% others

*Religions:* 90% a combination of Buddhism and Taoism; 10% Christian

### Health

*Life Expectancy at Birth:* 76 years (male); 82 years (female)

*Infant Mortality Rate (Ratio):* 5.3/1,000

*Physicians Available (Ratio):* 1/1,000

### Education

*Adult Literacy Rate:* 92%

## TRANSPORTATION

*Highways in Miles (Kilometers):* 1,030 (1,717)

*Railroads in Miles (Kilometers):* 22 (34)

*Usable Airfields:* 2

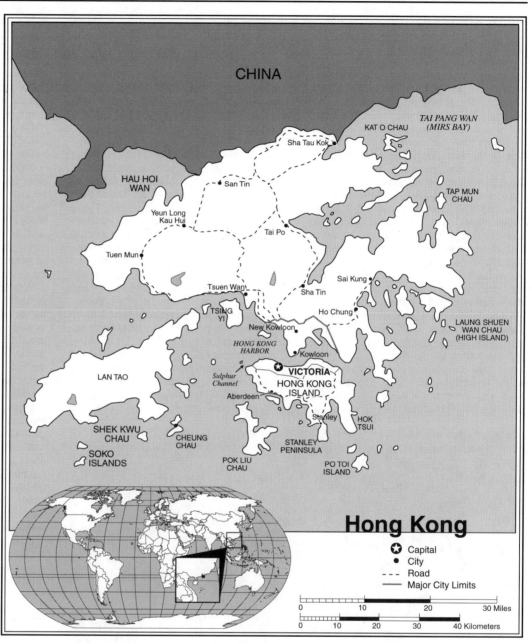

**Hong Kong**

⊛ Capital
• City
- - - Road
— Major City Limits

## GOVERNMENT

*Type:* special administrative region of the People's Republic of China; Chinese sovereignty reestablished on July 1, 1997

*Head of State:* Tung Chee-hwa

*Political Parties:* United Democrats of Hong Kong; Liberal Democratic Federation; Hong Kong Democratic Federation; Association for Democracy and People's Livelihood; Progressive Hong Kong Society

*Suffrage:* residents over age 21 who have lived in Hong Kong for at least 7 years

## MILITARY

*Military Expenditures (% of GDP):* 0.2%

*Current Disputes:* none

## ECONOMY

*Currency ($ U.S. Equivalent):* 7.74 Hong Kong dollars = $1

*Per Capita Income/GDP:* $26,000/$163.6 billion

*GDP Growth Rate:* 4.7%

*Inflation Rate:* 6.5%

*Unemployment Rate:* 3.1%

*Labor Force:* 3,251,000

*Natural Resources:* outstanding deepwater harbor; feldspar

*Agriculture:* vegetables; poultry

*Industry:* textiles; clothing; tourism; electronics; plastics; toys; clocks

*Exports:* $197.2 billion (primary partners China, United States, Japan)

*Imports:* $217.2 billion (primary partners China, Japan, Taiwan)

 http://www.info.gov.hk/sitemap.htm
http://www.odci.gov/cia/publication/factbook/country-frame.html

## HONG KONG'S BEGINNINGS

Opium started it all for Hong Kong. The addictive drug from which such narcotics as morphine, heroin, and codeine are made, opium had become a major source of income for British merchants in the early 1800s. When the Chinese government declared the opium trade illegal and confiscated more than 20,000 large chests of opium that had been on their way for sale to the increasingly addicted residents of Canton, the merchants persuaded the British military to intervene and restore their trading privileges. The British Navy attacked and occupied part of Canton. Three days later, the British forced the Chinese to agree to their trading demands, including a demand that they be ceded the tiny island of Hong Kong (meaning "Fragrant Harbor"), where they could pursue their trading and military business without the scrutiny of the Chinese authorities.

Initially, the British government was not pleased with the acquisition of Hong Kong; the island, which consisted of nothing more than a small fishing village, had been annexed without the foreknowledge of the authorities in London. Shortly, however, the government found the island's harbor a useful place to resupply ships and

to anchor military vessels in the event of further hostilities with the Chinese. The harbor turned out to be one of the finest natural harbors along the coast of China. On August 29, 1842, China reluctantly signed the Treaty of Nanking, which ended the first Opium War and gave Britain ownership of Hong Kong Island "in perpetuity."

Twenty years later, a second Opium War caused China to lose more of its territory; Britain acquired permanent lease rights over Kowloon, a tiny part of the mainland facing Hong Kong Island. By 1898, Britain had realized that its miniscule Hong Kong naval base would be too small to defend itself against sustained attack by French or other European navies seeking privileged access to China's markets. The British were also concerned about the scarcity of agricultural land on Hong Kong Island and nearby Kowloon Peninsula. In 1898, they persuaded the Chinese to lease them more than 350 square miles of land adjacent to Kowloon. Thus, Hong Kong consists today of Hong Kong Island (as well as numerous small, uninhabited islands nearby), the Kowloon Peninsula, and the agricultural lands that came to be called the New Territories.

From its inauspicious beginnings, Hong Kong grew into a dynamic, modern society, wealthier than its promoters would have ever dreamed in their wildest imaginations. Hong Kong is now home to 6.5 million people. Most of the New Territories are mountainous or are needed for agriculture, so the bulk of the population is packed into about one tenth of the land space. This gives Hong Kong the dubious honor of being one of the most densely populated human spaces ever created. Millions of people live stacked on top of one another in 30-story-high public tenement buildings. Even Hong Kong's excellent harbor has not escaped the population crunch: Approximately 10 square miles of former harbor have been filled in and now constitute some of the most expensive real estate on Earth.

Why are there so many people in Hong Kong? One reason is that, after occupation by the British, many Chinese merchants moved their businesses to Hong Kong, under the correct assumption that trade would be given a freer hand there than on the mainland. Eventually, Hong Kong became the home of mammoth trading conglomerates. The laborers in these profitable enterprises came to Hong Kong, for the most part, as political refugees from mainland China in the early 1900s. Another wave of immigrants arrived in the 1930s upon the invasion of Manchuria by the Japanese, and yet another influx came after the Communists took over China in 1949. Thus, like Taiwan, Hong Kong became a place of refuge for those in economic or political trouble on the mainland.

Overcrowding plus a favorable climate for doing business have produced extreme social and economic inequalities. Some of the richest people on Earth live in Hong Kong, alongside some of the most wretchedly poor, notable among whom are recent refugees from China and Southeast Asia (more than 300,000 Vietnamese sought refuge in Hong Kong after the Communists took over South Vietnam), some of whom have joined the traditionally poor boat peoples living in Aberdeen Harbor. Although surrounded by poverty, many of Hong Kong's economic elites have not found it inappropriate to indulge in ostentatious displays of wealth, such as riding in chauffeured, pink Rolls-Royces or wearing full-length mink coats.

Workers are on the job six days a week, morning and night, yet the average pay for a worker in industry is only about $5,000 per year. With husband, wife, and older children all working, families can survive; some even make it into the ranks of the fabulously wealthy. Indeed, the desire to make money was the primary reason why

(Photo by L. Clyde)

Land is so expensive in Hong Kong that most residences and businesses today are located in skyscrapers. While the buildings are thoroughly modern, construction crews typically erect bamboo scaffolding as the floors mount up, protected by netting. The skyscrapers that appear darker in color in the center of this photo are being built with this technique.

(Photo by L. Clyde)

A fishing family lives on this houseboat in Aberdeen Harbor. On the roof, cut-up fish is hung to dry.

Hong Kong was settled in the first place. That fact is not lost on anyone who lives there today. Noise and air pollution, traffic congestion, and dirty and smelly streets do not deter people from abandoning the countryside in favor of the consumptive lifestyle of the city.

Yet materialism has not wholly effaced the cultural arts and social rituals that are essential to a cohesive society. Indeed, with the vast majority of Hong Kong's residents hailing originally from mainland China, the spiritual beliefs and cultural heritage of China's long history abound. Some residents hang small eight-sided mirrors outside windows to frighten away malicious spirits, while others burn paper money in the streets each August to pacify the wandering spirits of deceased ancestors. Business owners carefully choose certain Chinese characters for the names of their companies or products, which they hope will bring them luck. Even skyscrapers are designed following ancient Chinese customs so that their entrances are in balance with the elements of nature.

Buddhist and Taoist beliefs remain central to the lives of many residents. In the back rooms of many shops, for example, are erected small religious shrines; joss sticks burning in front of these shrines are thought to bring good fortune to the pro-

prietors. Elaborate festivals, such as those at New Year's, bring the costumes, art, and dance of thousands of years of Chinese history to the crowded streets of Hong Kong. And the British legacy may be found in the cricket matches, ballet troupes, philharmonic orchestras, English-language radio and television broadcasts, and the legal system under which capitalism flourished.

**THE END OF AN ERA**
Britain was in control of this tiny speck of Asia for nearly 160 years. Except during World War II, when the Japanese occupied Hong Kong for about 4 years, the territory was governed as a Crown colony of Great Britain, with a governor appointed by the British sovereign. In 1997, China recovered control of Hong Kong from the British. In 1984, British prime minister Margaret Thatcher and Chinese leader Deng Xiaoping concluded 2 years of acrimonious negotiations over the fate of Hong Kong upon the expiration of the New Territories' lease in 1997. Great Britain claimed the right to control Hong Kong Island and Kowloon forever—a claim disputed by China, which argued that the treaties granting these lands to Britain had been imposed on them by military force. Hong Kong Island and Kowloon, however, constitute only about 10 percent of the colony; the other 90 percent

was to return automatically to China at the expiration of the lease. The various parts of the colony having become fully integrated, it seemed desirable to all parties to keep the colony together as one administrative unit. Moreover, it was felt that Hong Kong Island and Kowloon could not survive alone.

The British government had hoped that the People's Republic of China would agree to the status quo, or that it would at least permit the British to maintain administrative control over the colony should it be returned to China. Many Hong Kong Chinese felt the same way, since they had, after all, fled to Hong Kong to escape the Communist regime in China. For its part, the P.R.C. insisted that the entire colony be returned to its control by 1997. After difficult negotiations, Britain agreed to return the entire colony to China as long as China would grant important concessions. Foremost among these were that the capitalist economy and lifestyle, including private-property ownership and basic human rights, would not be changed for 50 years. The P.R.C. agreed to govern Hong Kong as a Special Administrative Region (SAR) within China and to permit British and local Chinese to serve in the administrative apparatus of the territory. The first direct elections for the 60-member Legislative

The British begin to occupy and use Hong Kong Island; the first Opium War
A.D. **1839–1842**

The Treaty of Nanking cedes Hong Kong to Britain
**1842**

The Chinese cede Kowloon and Stonecutter Island to Britain
**1856**

England gains a 99-year lease on the New Territories
**1898**

The Boxer Rebellion
**1898–1900**

Sun Yat-sen overthrows the emperor of China to establish the Republic of China
**1911**

The Japanese attack Pearl Harbor and take Hong Kong
**1941**

The Communist victory in China produces massive immigration into Hong Kong
**1949**

Great Britain and China agree to the return of Hong Kong to China
**1980s**

Mass demonstrations in Hong Kong against the Tiananmen Square massacre

**1990s**

China resumes control of Hong Kong on July 1, 1997; Tung Chee-hwa becomes chief executive

Prodemocracy politicians sweep the 1998 elections

The Asian financial crisis begins to make itself felt in Hong Kong

Council were held in September 1991, while the last British governor, Chris Patten, attempted to expand democratic rule in the colony as much as possible before the 1997 Chinese takeover—reforms that the Chinese dismantled to some extent after 1997.

The Joint Declaration of 1984 was drafted by top governmental leaders, with very little input from the people of Hong Kong. This fact plus fears about what P.R.C. control would mean to the free-wheeling lifestyle of Hong Kong's ardent capitalists caused thousands of residents, with billions of dollars in assets in tow, to abandon Hong Kong for Canada, Bermuda, Australia, the United States, and Great Britain. Surveys found that as many as one third of the population of Hong Kong wanted to leave the colony before the Chinese takeover. In the year before the change to Chinese rule, so many residents—16,000 at one point—lined up outside the immigration office to apply for British passports that authorities had to open up a nearby sports stadium to accommodate them. About half of Hong Kong residents already held British citizenship, but many of the rest, particularly recent refugees from China, wanted to secure their futures in case life under Chinese rule became suppressive. Immigration officials received more than 100,000 applications for British passports in a single month in 1996!

Emigration and unease over the future have unsettled, but by no means ruined, Hong Kong's economy. According to the World Bank, Hong Kong is home to the world's eighth-largest stock market, the fifth-largest banking center and foreign-exchange market (and the second largest in Asia after Japan), and its economy is the sixth richest in the world. Close to 9,000 multinational corporations have offices in Hong Kong, while some of the world's wealthiest people call Hong Kong home. Moreover, over the objections of

the Chinese government, the outgoing British authorities embarked on several ambitious infrastructural projects that will allow Hong Kong to continue to grow economically in the future. Chief among these is the airport on Chek Lap Kok Island. At a cost of $21 billion, the badly needed airport was one of the largest construction projects in the Pacific Rim. Opinion surveys showed that, despite fears of angering the incoming Chinese government, most Hong Kong residents appeared to support efforts to improve the economy and to democratize the government by lowering the voting age and allowing direct election rather than appointment by Beijing of more officials. In the 1998 elections, more than 50 percent of registered voters cast ballots—more than voted in Hong Kong's last election under British rule. Results indicated a desire by the people of Hong Kong for more democracy.

These results as well as anti-Beijing demonstrations before and after Hong Kong's return to Chinese control might suggest that the people of Hong Kong preferred to remain a British colony. However, while there were large British and American communities in Hong Kong, and although English has been the medium of business and government for many years (China is now proposing the elimination of English as a language of instruction in most schools), many residents over the years had little or no direct emotional involvement with British culture and no loyalty to the British Crown. They asserted that they were, first and foremost, Chinese. This, of course, does not amount to a popular endorsement of Beijing's rule, but it does imply that some residents of Hong Kong feel that, if they have to be governed by others, they would rather it be by the Chinese. Moreover, some believe that the Chinese government

may actually help rid Hong Kong of financial corruption and allocate more resources to the poor—although with tourism down since the handover to China and the Hong Kong stock market suffering from the general Asian financial problems of 1998 and 1999, there may be fewer resources to distribute in the future.

Hong Kong's natural links with China had been expanding steadily for years before the handover. In addition to a shared language and culture, there are in Hong Kong thousands of recent immigrants with strong family ties to the People's Republic. And there are increasingly important commercial ties. Hong Kong has always served as south China's entrepôt to the rest of the world for both commodity and financial exchanges. For instance, for years Taiwan has circumvented its regulations against direct trade with China by transshipping its exports through Hong Kong. Commercial trucks plying the highways between Hong Kong and the P.R.C. form a bumper-to-bumper wall of commerce between the two regions. Already nearly 50 percent of Hong Kong's imports come from China (about 15 percent from Japan), while 25 percent of its exports go to China (about 25 percent to the United States). The P.R.C. realizes that Hong Kong needs to remain more or less as it is—therefore, the transition to Chinese rule may be less jarring to residents than was expected. Most people think that Hong Kong will remain a major financial and trading center for Asia.

## DEVELOPMENT

Hong Kong is one of the financial and trading dynamos of the world. Hong Kong annually exports billions of dollars worth of products. Hong Kong's political future may be uncertain after 1997, but its fine harbor as well as its new $21 billion airport, currently under construction, are sure to continue to fuel its economy.

## FREEDOM

Hong Kong was an appendage to one of the world's foremost democracies for 160 years. Thus, its residents enjoyed the civil liberties guaranteed by British law. Under the new Basic Law of 1997, the Chinese government has agreed to maintain the capitalist way of life and other freedoms for 50 years.

## HEALTH/WELFARE

Schooling is free and compulsory in Hong Kong through junior high school. The government has devoted large sums for low-cost housing, aid for refugees, and social services such as adoption. Housing, however, is cramped and inadequate for the population.

## ACHIEVEMENTS

Hong Kong has the capacity to hold together a society where the gap between rich and poor is enormous. The so-called boat people have been subjected to discrimination, but most other groups have found social acceptance and opportunities for economic advancement.

# Indonesia (Republic of Indonesia)

## GEOGRAPHY
*Area in Square Miles (Kilometers):*
740,903 (1,919,440) (nearly 3 times the size of Texas)
*Capital (Population):* Jakarta (8,621,000)
*Environmental Concerns:* air and water pollution; sewage; deforestation
*Geographical Features:* coastal lowlands; larger islands have interior mountains
*Climate:* tropical; cooler in highlands

## PEOPLE

### Population
*Total:* 209,774,000
*Annual Growth Rate:* 1.51%
*Rural/Urban Population Ratio:* 64/36
*Major Languages:* Bahasa Indonesian; English; Dutch; Javanese; many others
*Ethnic Makeup:* 45% Javanese; 14% Sundanese; 7.5% Madurese; 7.5% coastal Malay; 26% others
*Religions:* 87% Muslim; 9% Christian; 2% Hindu; 2% Buddhist and others

### Health
*Life Expectancy at Birth:* 60 years (male); 64 years (female)
*Infant Mortality Rate (Ratio):* 61.2/1,000
*Average Caloric Intake:* 105% of FAO minimum
*Physicians Available (Ratio):* 1/7,402

### Education
*Adult Literacy Rate:* 84%
*Compulsory (Ages):* 7–16

## COMMUNICATION
*Telephones:* 1 per 59 people
*Daily Newspaper Circulation:* 20 per 1,000 people
*Televisions:* 1 per 16 people

## TRANSPORTATION
*Highways in Miles (Kilometers):* 226,800 (378,000)
*Railroads in Miles (Kilometers):* 3,875 (6,450)
*Usable Airfields:* 413
*Motor Vehicles in Use:* 3,750,000

## GOVERNMENT
*Type:* republic
*Independence Date:* December 27, 1949 (legally)
*Head of State:* President Bacharuddin Jusuf Habibie
*Political Parties:* Golkar Party (quasi-official); Indonesia Democracy Party; Development Unity Party
*Suffrage:* universal at age 17 and married persons regardless of age

## MILITARY
*Military Expenditures (% of GDP):* 1.3%

*Current Disputes:* territorial disputes with Portugal and Malaysia; internal strife

## ECONOMY
*Currency ($ U.S. Equivalent):* 8,050 Indonesian rupiahs = $1
*Per Capita Income/GDP:* $3,770/$779.7 billion
*GDP Growth Rate:* 0%
*Inflation Rate:* 9.3%
*Unemployment Rate:* 3% (official rate; underemployment 40%)
*Labor Force:* 67,000,000
*Natural Resources:* petroleum; tin; natural gas; nickel; plywood; bauxite; copper; fertile soils; coal; gold; silver
*Agriculture:* rice; cassava; peanuts; rubber; cocoa; coffee; copra; other tropical products; poultry; beef; pork; eggs
*Industry:* petroleum; natural gas; textiles; mining; cement; chemical fertilizer; food; rubber
*Exports:* $49.8 billion (primary partners Japan, United States, Singapore)
*Imports:* $42.9 billion (primary partners Japan, United States, Germany)

http://www.uni-stuttgart.de/indonesia
http://www.hkkk.fi/libwww/asian/indonesia/indonesia.html#general

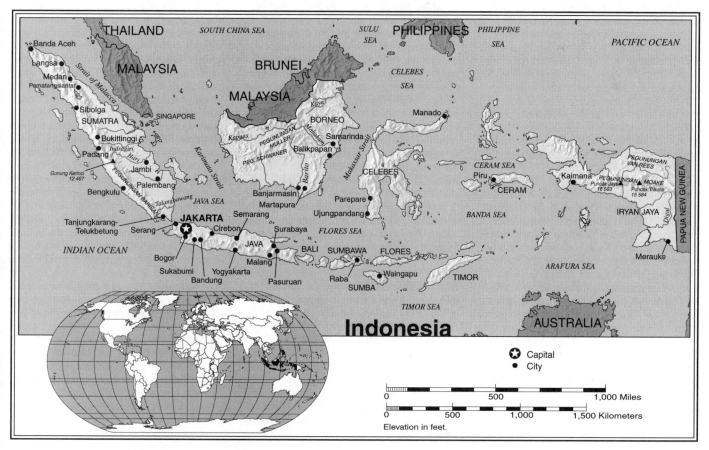

## A KALEIDOSCOPIC CULTURE

Present-day Indonesia is a kaleidoscope of some 300 languages and more than 100 ethnic groups. Beginning about 5000 B.C., people of Mongoloid stock settled the islands that today constitute Indonesia, in successive waves of migration from China, Thailand, and Vietnam. Animism—the nature-worship religion of these peoples—was altered substantially (but never completely lost) about A.D. 200, when Hindus from India began to settle in the area and wield the dominant cultural influence. Several hundred years later, Buddhist missionaries and settlers began converting Indonesians in a proselytizing effort that produced strong political and religious antagonisms. In the thirteenth century, Muslim traders began the Islamization of the Indonesian people; today, 87 percent of the population claim the Muslim faith—meaning that there are more Muslims in Indonesia than in any other country of the world, including the countries of the Middle East. Commingling with all these influences were cultural inputs from the islands of Polynesia.

The real roots of the Indonesian people undoubtedly go back much further than any of these historic cultures. In 1891, the fossilized bones of a hominid who used stone tools, camped around a fire, and probably had a well-developed language were found on the island of Java. Named *Pithecanthropus erectus* ("erect ape-man"), these important early human fossils, popularly called Java Man, have been dated at about 750,000 years of age. Fossils similar to Java Man have been found in Europe, Africa, and Asia.

Modern Indonesia was sculpted by the influence of many outside cultures. Portuguese Catholics, eager for Indonesian spices, made contact with Indonesia in the 1500s and left 20,000 converts to Catholicism, as well as many mixed Portuguese–Indonesian communities and dozens of Portuguese "loan words" in the Indonesian-style Malay language. In the following century, Dutch Protestants established the Dutch East India Company to exploit Indonesia's riches. Eventually the Netherlands was able to gain complete political control; it reluctantly gave it up in the face of insistent Indonesian nationalism only as recently as 1950. Before that, however, the British briefly controlled one of the islands, and the Japanese ruled the country for 3 years during the 1940s.

Indonesians, including then-president Sukarno, initially welcomed the Japanese as helpers in their fight for independence from the Dutch. Everyone believed that the Japanese would leave soon. Instead, the Japanese military forced farmers to give food to the Japanese soldiers, made everyone worship the Japanese emperor, neglected local industrial development in favor of military projects, and took 270,000 young men away from Indonesia to work elsewhere as forced laborers (fewer than 70,000 survived to return home). Military leaders who attempted to revolt against Japanese rule were executed. Finally, in August 1945, the Japanese abandoned their control of Indonesia, according to the terms of surrender with the Allied powers.

Consider what all these influences mean for the culture of modern Indonesia. Some of the most powerful ideologies ever espoused by humankind—supernaturalism, Islam, Hinduism, Buddhism, Christianity, mercantilism, colonialism, and nationalism—have had an impact on Indonesia. Take music, for example. Unlike Western music, which most people just listen to, Indonesian music, played on drums and gongs, is intended as a somewhat sacred ritual in which all members of a community are expected to participate. The instruments themselves are considered sacred. Dances are often the main element in a religious service whose goal might be a good rice harvest, spirit possession, or exorcism. Familiar musical styles can be heard here and there around the country. In the eastern part of Indonesia, the Nga'dha peoples, who were converted to Christianity in the early 1900s, sing Christian hymns to the accompaniment of bronze pot gongs and drums. On the island of Sumatra, Minang Kabau peoples, who were converted to Islam in the 1500s, use local instruments to accompany Islamic poetry singing. Communal feasts in Hindu Bali, circumcision ceremonies in Muslim Java, and Christian baptisms among the Bataks of Sumatra all represent borrowed cultural traditions. Thus, out of many has come one rich culture.

But the faithful of different religions are not always able to work together in harmony. For example, in the 1960s, when average Indonesians were trying to distance themselves from radical Communists, many decided to join Christian faiths. Threatened by this tilt toward the West and by the secular approach of the government, many fundamentalist Muslims resorted to violence. They burned Christian churches, threatened Catholic and Baptist missionaries, and opposed such projects as the construction of a hospital by Baptists. Indonesia is one of the most predominately Muslim countries in the world, and the hundreds of Islamic socioreligious and political organizations intend to keep it that way.

## A LARGE LAND, LARGE DEBTS

Unfortunately, Indonesia's economy is not as rich as its culture. Three quarters of the population live in rural areas; more than half of the people engage in fishing and small-plot rice and vegetable farming. The average income per person is only $3,770 a year, based on gross domestic product, and inflation consumes about 9 percent of that annually. A 1993 law increased the minimum wage in Jakarta to $2.00 *per day*.

Also worrisome is the level of government debt. Indonesia is blessed with large oil reserves (Pertamina is the state-owned oil company) and minerals and timber of every sort (also state-owned), but to extract these natural resources has required massive infusions of capital, most of it borrowed. In fact, Indonesia has borrowed more money than any other country in Asia. Corporate debt alone is a staggering $68 billion. The country must allocate 40 percent of its national budget just to pay the interest on loans. Low oil prices in the 1980s made it difficult for the country to keep up with its debt burden.

To cope with these problems, Indonesia has relaxed government control over foreign investment and banking, and it seems to be on a path toward privatization of other parts of the economy. Still, the gap between the modernized cities and the traditional countryside continues to plague the government.

Indonesia's financial troubles seem puzzling, because in land, natural resources, and population, the country appears quite well-off. Indonesia is the second-largest country in Asia (after China). Were it superimposed on a map of the United States, its 13,677 tropical islands would stretch from California, past New York, and out to Bermuda in the Atlantic Ocean. Oil and hardwoods are plentiful, and the population is large enough to constitute a viable internal consumer market. But transportation and communication are problematic and costly in archipelagic states. Before the financial crisis of 1998–1999 hit, Indonesia's national airline, Garuda Indonesia, had hoped to launch a $3.6 billion development program that would have brought into operation 50 new aircraft stopping at 13 new airports. New seaports are also under construction. But the cost of linking together the 6,000 inhabited islands is a major drain on the economy. Moreover, exploitation of Indonesia's amazing panoply of resources is drawing the ire of more and more people around the world who fear the destruction of the world's ecosystem.

Indonesia's population of 209.7 million is one of the largest in the world, but 16 percent of adults cannot read or write.

| Java Man lived here 750,000 B.C. | Buddhism gains the upper hand A.D. 600 | Muslim traders bring Islam to Indonesia A.D. 1200 | The Portuguese begin to trade and settle in Indonesia 1509 | Dutch traders begin to influence Indonesian life 1596 | The Japanese defeat the Dutch 1942 | Indonesian independence from the Netherlands; President Sukarno retreats from democracy and the West 1949–1950 | General Suharto takes control of the government from Sukarno and establishes his New Order, pro-Western government 1966 | Anti-Japanese riots take place in Jakarta 1974 | Indonesia annexes East Timor 1975 |
|---|---|---|---|---|---|---|---|---|---|

1990s

Economic reforms aim to increase foreign investment and employment opportunities

Oil revenues slump; the rupiah is devalued; earthquakes kill 2,500 in 1992 and injure 1,500 in 1994

Rioting breaks out; Suharto steps down after 32 years in power

Only about 600 people per 100,000 attend college, as compared to 3,580 in nearby Philippines. Moreover, since almost 70 percent of the population reside on or near the island of Java, on which the capital city, Jakarta, is located, educational and development efforts have concentrated there, at the expense of the communities on outlying islands. Many children in the out-islands never complete the required 6 years of elementary school. Some ethnic groups, on the islands of Irian Jaya (New Guinea) and Kalimantan (Borneo), for example, continue to live isolated in small tribes, much as they did thousands of years ago. By contrast, the modern city of Jakarta, with its classical European-style buildings, is home to millions of people. Social problems have been ameliorated somewhat by Indonesia's strong economic growth (an average of 6 percent over the past 20 years), which has reduced the official poverty rate (from 60 percent in 1970 to 15 percent in 1990).

With 2.3 million new Indonesians entering the labor force every year and half the population under age 20, serious efforts must be made to increase employment opportunities. For the 1990s, the government earmarked millions of dollars to promote tourism. Nevertheless, the most pressing problem was to finish the many projects for which World Bank and Asian Development Bank loans had already been received.

## MODERN POLITICS
Establishing the current political and geographic boundaries of the Republic of Indonesia has been a bloody and protracted task. So fractured is the culture that many people doubt whether there really is a single country that one can call Indonesia. During the first 15 years of independence (1950–1965), there were revolts by Muslims and pro-Dutch groups, indecisive elections, several military coups, battles

against U.S.–supported rebels, and serious territorial disputes with Malaysia and the Netherlands. In 1966, nationalistic President Sukarno, who had been a founder of Indonesian independence, lost power to Army General Suharto. (Many Southeast Asians had no family names until influenced by Westerners; Sukarno and Suharto have each used only one name.) Anti-Communist feeling grew during the 1960s, and thousands of suspected members of the Indonesian Communist Party (PKI) and other Communists were killed before the PKI was banned in 1966.

In 1975, ignoring the disapproval of the United Nations, President Suharto invaded and annexed East Timor, a Portuguese colony. Although the military presence in East Timor has since been reduced, separatists were beaten and killed by the Indonesian Army as recently as 1991; and in 1993, a separatist leader was sentenced to 20 years in prison. In late 1995, Amnesty International accused the Indonesian military of raping and executing human-rights activists in East Timor, while the 20th anniversary of the Indonesian take-over was marked by Timorese storming foreign embassies and demanding asylum and redress for the kidnapping and killing of protesters. In 1996, antigovernment rioting in Jakarta resulted in the arrest of more than 200 opposition leaders and the disappearance of many others. The rioters were supporters of the Indonesian Democracy Party and its leader, Megawati Sukarnoputri, daughter of Sukarno.

Suharto's so-called New Order government ruled with an iron hand, suppressing student and Muslim dissent and controlling the press and the economy. With the economy in serious trouble in 1998, and with the Indonesian people tired of government corruption and angry at the control of Suharto and his six children over much of the economy, rioting broke out all over the country. Some 15,000 people

took to the streets, occupied government offices, burned cars, and fought with police. The International Monetary Fund suspended vital aid because it appeared that Suharto would not conform to the belt-tightening required of IMF aid recipients. With unemployed migrant workers streaming back to Indonesia from Malaysia and surrounding countries, with the government unable to control forest fires burning thousands of acres and producing a haze all over Southeast Asia, with even his own lifetime political colleagues calling for him to step down, Suharto at last resigned, ending a 32-year dictatorship. The new leader, President Bacharuddin Jusuf Habibie, has pledged to honor IMF commitments and restore dialogue on the East Timor dispute. Antigovernment demonstrations continued in 1999.

Among other urgent measures, the new government will need to encourage foreign investment, particularly from such important trading partners as Japan. (Indonesia sends 27 percent of its exports to Japan and buys 23 percent of its imports from Japan.) And Japanese investment money, now much scarcer than before, will need to continue to flow to Indonesia, as elsewhere in the Pacific Rim. In the past, companies like Toyota invested millions in Indonesia's ASTRA automobile company, while Japanese banks supported the expansion of Indonesia's tourist industry. If the new government can prove to the world that it will govern wisely, it is possible that foreign investment will help lead Indonesia out of its current quagmire.

## DEVELOPMENT

Indonesia continues to be hamstrung by its heavy reliance on foreign loans, a burden inherited from the Sukarno years. Current Indonesian leaders speak of "stabilization" and "economic dynamism."

## FREEDOM

Demands for Western-style human rights are frequently heard, but only the army has the power to impose order on the numerous and competing political groups, many imbued with religious fervor.

## HEALTH/WELFARE
Indonesia has one of the highest birth rates in the Pacific Rim. Many children will grow up in poverty, never learning even to read or write their national language, Bahasa Indonesian.

## ACHIEVEMENTS

Balinese dancers' glittering gold costumes and unique choreography epitomize the "Asian-ness" of Indonesia.

# Laos (Lao People's Democratic Republic)

## GEOGRAPHY

*Area in Square Miles (Kilometers):* 91,400 (236,800) (about the size of Utah)

*Capital (Population):* Viangchan (Vientiane) (442,000)

*Environmental Concerns:* deforestation; soil erosion; lack of access to potable water

*Geographical Features:* mostly rugged mountains; some plains and plateaus

*Climate:* tropical monsoon

## PEOPLE

### Population

*Total:* 5,117,000

*Annual Growth Rate:* 2.78%

*Rural/Urban Population (Ratio):* 79/21

*Major Languages:* Lao; French; English; various ethnic languages

*Ethnic Makeup:* 50% Lao; 20% tribal Thai; 15% Phoutheung (Kha); 15% Meo, Hmong, Yao, and others

*Religions:* 60% Buddhist; 40% indigenous beliefs and others

### Health

*Life Expectancy at Birth:* 52 years (male); 55 years (female)

*Infant Mortality Rate (Ratio):* 94.3/1,000

*Average Caloric Intake:* 94% of FAO minimum

*Physicians Available (Ratio):* 1/3,555

### Education

*Adult Literacy Rate:* 57%

*Compulsory (Ages):* for 5 years between 6–15

## COMMUNICATION

*Telephones:* 1 per 239 people

*Televisions:* 1 per 119 people

## TRANSPORTATION

*Highways in Miles (Kilometers):* 10,892 (18,153)

*Railroads in Miles (Kilometers):* none

*Usable Airfields:* 39

*Motor Vehicles in Use:* 20,000

## GOVERNMENT

*Type:* Communist state

*Independence Date:* July 19, 1949

*Head of State/Government:* President Nouhak Phoumsavan; Prime Minister (General) Khamtai Siphandon

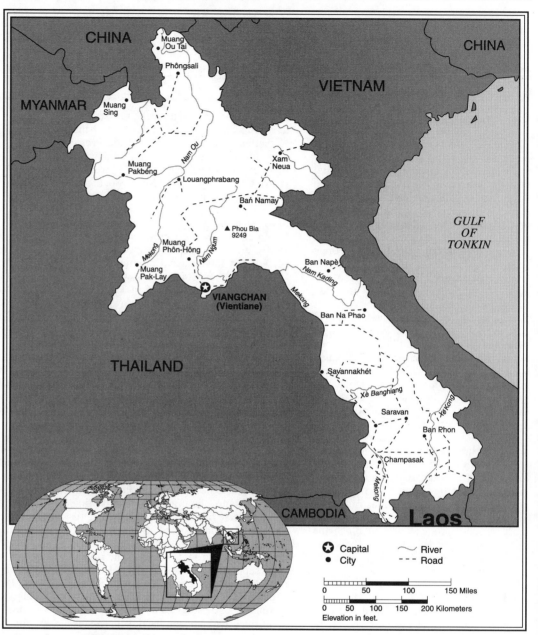

*Political Parties:* Lao People's Revolutionary Party; other parties proscribed

*Suffrage:* universal at 18

## MILITARY

*Military Expenditures (% of GDP):* 8.1%

*Current Disputes:* internal strife

## ECONOMY

*Currency ($ U.S. Equivalent):* 961 new kips = $1

*Per Capita Income/GDP:* $1,150/$5.7 billion

*GDP Growth Rate:* 7.5%

*Inflation Rate:* 15%

*Unemployment Rate:* 5.6% in urban areas

*Labor Force:* 1,000,000–1,500,000

*Natural Resources:* timber; hydropower; gypsum; tin; gold; gemstones

*Agriculture:* rice; potatoes; vegetables; coffee; sugarcane; cotton

*Industry:* tin mining; timber; electric power; agricultural processing

*Exports:* $240 million (primary partners Thailand, Japan, France)

*Imports:* $570 million (primary partners Thailand, China, Japan)

 http://www.tdb.gov.sg/country/laos/bizlaos.html

http://www.stockton.edu/~gilmorew/consorti/1reasia.htm

## A NATION DIVIDED

Laos seems a sleepy place. Almost everyone lives in small villages where the only distraction might be the Buddhist temple gong announcing the day. Water buffalo plow quietly through centuries-old rice paddies, while young Buddhist monks in saffron-colored robes make their silent rounds for rice donations. Villagers build their houses on stilts for safety from annual river flooding and top them with thatch or tin. Barefoot children play under the palm trees or wander to the village Buddhist temple for school in the outdoor courtyard. Mothers stay home to weave brightly colored cloth for the family and to prepare meals—on charcoal or wood stoves—of rice, bamboo shoots, pork, duck, and snakes seasoned with hot peppers and ginger.

Below this serene surface, however, Laos is a nation divided. Although the name Laos is taken from the dominant ethnic group, there are actually about 70 ethnic groups in the country. Over the centuries, they have battled one another for supremacy, for land, and for tribute money. The constant feuding has weakened the nation and served as an invitation for neighboring countries to annex portions of Laos forcibly or to align themselves with one or another of the Laotian royal families or generals for material gain. China, Burma (today called Myanmar), Vietnam, and especially Thailand—with which Laotian people share many cultural and ethnic similarities—have all been involved militarily in Laos.

Historically, a cause of unrest was often palace jealousies that led one member of the royal family to fight against a relative for dominance. More recently, Laos has been seen as a pawn in the battle of the Western powers for access to the rich natural resources of Southeast Asia or as a "domino" that some did and others did not want to fall to communism. Former members of the royal family continue to find themselves on the opposite sides of many issues.

The results of these struggles have been devastating. Laos is now one of the poorest countries in the world. There are few industries in the country, so most people survive by subsistence farming and fishing, raising or catching just what they need to eat rather than growing food to sell. In fact, some "hill peoples" (about two thirds of the Laotian people live in the mountains) in the long mountain range that separates Laos from Vietnam continue to use the most ancient farming technique known, slash-and-burn farming, an unstable method of land use that allows only a few years of good crops before the soil is depleted and the farmers must move to new ground. Today, soil erosion and deforestation pose threats to economic growth.

Even if all Laotian farmers used the most modern techniques and geared their production to cash crops, it would still be difficult to export food (or, for that matter, anything else) because of Laos's woefully inadequate transportation network. There are no railroads, and muddy, unpaved roads make many mountain villages completely inaccessible by car or truck. Only one bridge in Laos, the Thai-Lao Friendship Bridge near the capital city of Vientiane, spans the famous Mekong River. Moreover, Laos is landlocked. In a region of the world where wealth flows toward those countries with the best ports, having no access to the sea is a serious impediment to economic growth. In addition, for years the economy has been strictly controlled. Foreign investment and trade have not been welcomed, and tourists were not allowed until 1989. But the economy began to open up in the late 1980s. The government's "New Economic Mechanism" in 1986 called for foreign investment in all sectors and anticipated GDP growth of 8 percent per year. The year 1999 was declared "Visit Laos Year," and the government set a goal of drawing 1 million tourists. With its technological infrastructure abysmally underdeveloped, tourism seemed like the easiest way for the country to gain some foreign currency and create jobs. Some likely tourist sites, such as Luan Prabang, an ancient royal city with a 112-pound gold statue of Buddha, have changed little in a thousand years, so tourists wishing to see "Old Asia" may indeed find Laos a draw.

Some progress has been made in the past decade. Laos is once again self-sufficient in its staple crop, rice; and surplus electricity generated from dams along the Mekong River is sold to Thailand to earn foreign exchange. Laos imports various commodity items from Thailand, Singapore, Japan, and other countries, and it has received foreign aid from the Asian Development Bank and other organizations. Exports to Thailand, China, and the United States include teakwood, tin, and various minerals.

Despite the 1995 "certification" by the United States that Laos is a cooperating country in the world antidrug effort, Laos is also the source of many controlled substances, such as opium, cannabis, and heroin, much of which finds its way to

(UPI/Bettmann)

Laos is one of the poorest countries in the world. With few industries, most people survive by subsistence farming and fishing. These fishermen spend their days catching tiny fish, measuring 2 to 5 inches, that must suffice to feed their families.

| The first Laotian nation is established A.D. 1300s | Vietnam annexes most of Laos 1833 | Laos comes under French control 1885 | The Japanese conquer Southeast Asia 1940s | France grants independence to Laos 1949 | South Vietnamese troops, with U.S. support, invade Laos 1971 | Pathet Lao Communists gain control of the government 1975 | Laos signs military and economic agreements with Vietnam 1977 | The government begins to liberalize some aspects of the economy 1980s |
|---|---|---|---|---|---|---|---|---|

1990s

The Pathet Lao government maintains firm control over the country

Laos and Thailand move toward improved relations

Efforts to maintain high GDP growth are threatened by deforestation and soil erosion

Europe and the United States. The Laotian government is now trying to prevent hill peoples from cutting down valuable forests for opium-poppy cultivation.

## HISTORY AND POLITICS

The Laotian people, originally migrating from south China through Thailand, settled Laos in the thirteenth century A.D., when the area was controlled by the Khmer (Cambodian) Empire. Early Laotian leaders expanded the borders of Laos through warfare with Cambodia, Thailand, Burma, and Vietnam. Internal warfare, however, led to a loss of autonomy in 1833, when Thailand forcibly annexed the country (against the wishes of Vietnam, which also had designs on Laos). In the 1890s, France, determined to have a part of the lucrative Asian trade and to hold its own against growing British strength in Southeast Asia, forced Thailand to give up its hold on Laos. Laos, Vietnam, and Cambodia were combined into a new political entity, which the French called *Indochina.* Between these French possessions and the British possessions of Burma and Malaysia lay Thailand; thus, France, Britain, and Thailand effectively controlled mainland Southeast Asia for several decades.

There were several small uprisings against French power, but these were easily suppressed until the Japanese conquest of Indochina in the 1940s. The Japanese, with their "Asia for Asians" philosophy, convinced the Laotians that European domination was not a given. In the Geneva Agreement of 1949, Laos was granted independence, although full French withdrawal did not take place until 1954.

Prior to independence, Prince Souphanouvong (who died in 1995 at the age of 82) had organized a Communist guerrilla army, with help from Ho Chi Minh and the Vietnamese Communist Viet Minh.

This army called itself the Pathet Lao (meaning "Lao Country"). In 1954, it challenged the authority of the government in Vientiane. Civil war ensued, and by 1961, when a cease-fire was arranged, the Pathet Lao had captured about half of Laos. The Soviet Union supported the Pathet Lao, whose strength was in the northern half of Laos, while the United States supported a succession of pro-Western but fragile governments in the south. A coalition government consisting of Pathet Lao, pro-Western, and neutralist leaders was installed in 1962, but it collapsed in 1965, when warfare once again broke out.

During the Vietnam War, U.S. and South Vietnamese forces bombed and invaded Laos in an attempt to disrupt the North Vietnamese supply line known as the Ho Chi Minh Trail. Americans flew nearly 600,000 bombing missions over Laos (many of the small cluster bombs released during those missions remain unexploded in fields and villages and present a continuing danger). Communist battlefield victories in Vietnam encouraged and aided the Pathet Lao Army, which became the dominant voice in a new coalition government established in 1974. The Pathet Lao controlled the government exclusively by 1975. In the same year, the government proclaimed a new "Lao People's Democratic Republic." It abolished the 622-year-old monarchy and sent the king and the royal family to a detention center to learn Marxist ideology.

Vietnamese Army support and flight by many of those opposed to the Communist regime have permitted the Pathet Lao to maintain control of the government. The ruling dictatorship is determined to prevent the democratization of Laos: In 1993, several cabinet ministers were jailed for 14 years for trying to establish a multiparty democracy.

The Pathet Lao government was sustained militarily and economically by the Soviet Union and other East bloc nations for more than 15 years. However, with the end of the cold war and the collapse of the Soviet Union, Laos has had to look elsewhere, including non-Communist countries, for support. In 1992, Laos signed a friendship treaty with Thailand to facilitate trade between the two historic enemy countries. In 1994, the Australian government, continuing its plan to integrate itself more fully into the strong Asian economy, promised to provide Laos with more than $33 million in aid. In 1995, Laos joined with ASEAN nations to declare the region a nuclear-free zone.

Trying to teach communism to a devoutly Buddhist country has not been easy. Popular resistance has caused the government to retract many of the regulations it has tried to impose on the Buddhist Church (technically, the Sangara, or order of the monks—the Buddhist equivalent of a clerical hierarchy). As long as the Buddhist hierarchy limits its activities to helping the poor, it seems to be able to avoid running afoul of the Communist leadership.

Intellectuals, especially those known to have been functionaries of the French administration, have fled Laos, leaving a leadership vacuum. As many as 300,000 people are thought to have left Laos for refugee camps in Thailand and elsewhere. Many have taken up permanent residence in foreign countries. The exodus has exacted a significant drain on Laos's intellectual resources.

## DEVELOPMENT

Communist rule after 1975 isolated Laos from world trade and foreign investment. The planned economy has not been able to gain momentum on its own. In 1986, the government loosened restrictions so that government companies could keep a portion of their profits. A goal is to integrate Laos economically with Vietnam and Cambodia.

## FREEDOM

Laos is ruled by the political arm of the Pathet Lao Army. Opposition parties and groups as well as opposition newspapers and other media are outlawed. Lack of civil liberties as well as poverty have caused many thousands of people to flee the country.

## HEALTH/WELFARE

Laos is typical of the least developed countries in the world. The birth rate is high, but so is infant mortality. Most citizens eat less than an adequate diet. Life expectancy is low, and many Laotians die from illnesses for which medicines are available in other countries. Many doctors fled the country when the Communists came to power.

## ACHIEVEMENTS

The original inhabitants of Laos, the Kha, have been looked down upon by the Lao, Thai, and other peoples for centuries. But under the Communist regime, the status of the Kha has been upgraded and discrimination formally proscribed.

# Macau

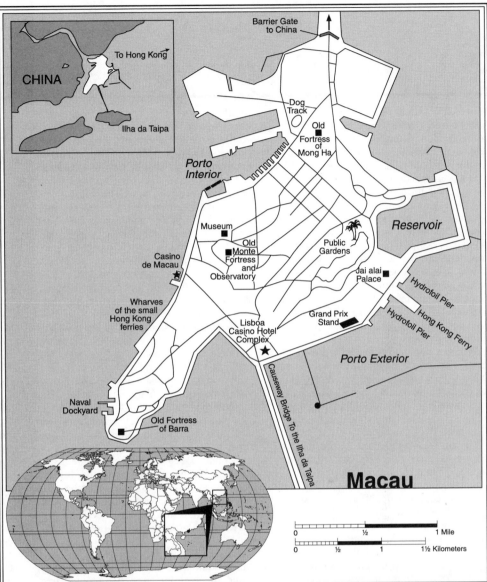

## GEOGRAPHY

*Area in Square Miles (Kilometers):* 6
   (16) (about one tenth the size of
   Washington, D.C.)
*Capital (Population):* Macau (502,325)
*Environmental Concerns:* air and water
   pollution
*Climate:* subtropical; cool winters,
   warm summers

## PEOPLE

### Population
*Total:* 502,325
*Annual Growth Rate:* 1.05%
*Rural/Urban Population Ratio:* 0/100
*Major Languages:* Portuguese;
   Cantonese
*Ethnic Makeup:* 95% Chinese; 3%
   Portuguese; 2% others
*Religions:* 46% unaffiliated; 45%
   Buddhist; 7%; Roman Catholic; 1%
   Protestant; 1% others

### Health
*Life Expectancy at Birth:* 78 years
   (male); 83 years (female)
*Infant Mortality Rate (Ratio):* 5.3/1,000
*Physicians Available (Ratio):* 1/2,470

### Education
*Adult Literacy Rate:* 90%

## TRANSPORTATION
*Highways in Miles (Kilometers):* 67
   (000)
*Railroads in Miles (Kilometers):* none
*Usable Airfields:* 1

## GOVERNMENT
*Type:* Chinese territory under
   Portuguese administration; reverts to
   China on December 20, 1999
*Independence Date:* —
*Head of State/Government:* until
   Macau reverts to China, President
   (of Portugal) Jorge Sampaio;
   Governor General Vasco Joachim Rocha
   Vieira
*Political Parties:* Association to Defend
   the Interests of Macau; Macau
   Democratic Center; Group to Study the
   Development of Macau; Macau
   Independent Group
*Suffrage:* universal at 18

## MILITARY
*Military Expenditures (% of GDP):*
   defense is the responsibility of Portugal
   until the 1999 handover
*Current Disputes:* none

## ECONOMY
*Currency ($ U.S. Equivalent):* 7.73
   patacas = $1 (tied to Hong Kong dollar)
*Per Capita Income/GDP:* $13,600/na
*GDP Growth Rate:* 4%
*Inflation Rate:* 5.5%

*Unemployment Rate:* 2%
*Natural Resources:* fish
*Agriculture:* rice; vegetables
*Industry:* clothing; textiles; toys; plastic
   products; furniture; tourism
*Exports:* $2 billion
*Imports:* $2 billion

   http://www.hkkk/fi/libwww/asian/
   macau.html
   http://www.odci.gov/cia/publication/
   factbook/country-frame.html

A Portuguese trading colony is established at Macau
A.D. 1557

Portugal declares sovereignty over Macau
1849

China signs a treaty recognizing Portuguese sovereignty over Macau
1887

Immigrants from China flood into the colony
1949

Pro-Communist riots in Macau
1967

Portugal begins to loosen direct administrative control over Macau
1970s

Macau becomes a Chinese territory but is still administered by Portugal
1976

China and Portugal sign an agreement scheduling the return of Macau to Chinese control
1987

1990s

50,000 illegal Chinese immigrants seek permanent residency status in Macau

Portugal sends troops to help tamp down gambling-related crime

Macau reverts to Chinese control on December 20, 1999

## MACAU'S HISTORY

Just 17 miles across the Pearl River estuary from Hong Kong is a speck of foreignness on Chinese soil: the Portuguese territory of Macau (sometimes spelled Macao). The oldest permanent outpost of European culture in the Far East, Macau has the highest population density of any political entity in the world: Although it consists of only about 6 square miles of land, it is home to half a million people, crowded onto the peninsula and two small islands. Some 95 percent of these are Chinese. Cantonese is universally spoken, although Portuguese is still the official language. (This official use of Portuguese, however, will end once Macau reverts to China in 1999.)

Macau's population has varied over the years, depending on conditions in China. During the Japanese occupation of China, for instance, Macau's Chinese population is believed to have doubled, and more refugees streamed in when the Communists took over China in 1949.

Macau was frequented by Portuguese traders as early as 1516, but it was not until 1557 that the Chinese agreed to Portuguese settlement of the land; it did not, however, acknowledge Portuguese sovereignty. Indeed, the Chinese government did not recognize the Portuguese right of "perpetual occupation" until 1887.

In 1987, Chinese and Portuguese officials signed an agreement, effective December 20, 1999, to end European control of the first—and last—colonial outpost in China. The agreement ends 450 years of European administration.

The agreement is similar to that signed by Great Britain and China over the fate of Hong Kong. China agreed to allow Macau to maintain its capitalist way of life for 50 years, to permit local elections, and to allow its residents to travel freely without Chinese intervention. Unlike Hong Kong residents, who staged massive demonstrations against future Chinese rule or emigrated from Hong Kong before its return to China, Macau residents—some of whom have been openly pro-Communist—have not seemed bothered by the new arrangements. In fact, a new airport has been opened to bolster the economy, and plans for the reversion to China have gone smoothly. Indeed, businesses in Macau and Hong Kong have contributed to a de facto merging with the mainland by investing more than $20 billion in China since the mid-1990s.

Since it was established in the sixteenth century as a trading colony with interests in oranges, tea, tobacco, and lacquer, Macau has been heavily influenced by Roman Catholic priests of the Dominican and Jesuit orders. Christian churches, interspersed with Buddhist temples, abound. The name of Macau itself reflects its deep and enduring religious roots; the city's official name is "City of the Name of God in China, Macau, There Is None More Loyal." Macau has perhaps the highest density of churches and temples per square mile in the world. Buddhist immigrants from China have reduced the proportion of Christians in the population.

## A HEALTHY ECONOMY

Macau's modern economy is a vigorous blend of light industry, fishing, tourism, and gambling. Revenues from the latter two sources are impressive, accounting for 25 percent of gross domestic product. There are five major casinos and many other gambling opportunities in Macau, which, along with the considerable charms of the city itself, attract more than 5 million foreign visitors a year, more than 80 percent of them Hong Kong Chinese with plenty of money to spend. Macau's gambling industry is run by a syndicate of Chinese businesspeople operating under the name Macau Travel & Amusement Company, which won monopoly rights on all licensed gambling in Macau in 1962. But not everyone is content with that arrangement. Rival gangs, fighting to control parts of the gambling business, produced such a crime spree in 1998 that military troops had to be sent from Portugal to restore order.

Export earnings derived from light-industry products such as textiles, fireworks, plastics, and electronics are also critical to the colony. Macau's leading export markets are the United States, China, Germany, France, and Hong Kong; ironically, Portugal consumes only about 3 percent of Macau's exports.

As might be expected, the success of the economy has a downside. In Macau's case, the hallmarks of modernization—crowded apartment blocks and bustling traffic—are threatening to eclipse the remnants of the old, serene, Portuguese-style seaside town.

## DEVELOPMENT

The development of industries related to gambling and tourism (tourists are primarily from Hong Kong) has been very successful. Most of Macau's foods, energy, and fresh water are imported from China; Japan and Hong Kong are the main suppliers of raw materials.

## FREEDOM

China acquires full sovereignty over Macau in 1999, but local elections will be permitted, as will the capitalist way of life. Under Portuguese rule, the president of Portugal appointed the territory's governor. The 17 members of the Legislative Assembly were elected directly by the people of Macau.

## HEALTH/WELFARE

Macau has very impressive quality-of-life statistics. It has a low infant mortality rate and very high life expectancy for both males and females. Literacy is 90 percent. In recent years, the unemployment rate has been a low 2 percent.

## ACHIEVEMENTS

Considering its unfavorable geographical characteristics, such as negligible natural resources and a port so shallow and heavily silted that oceangoing ships must anchor offshore, Macau has had stunning economic success. Its annual GDP economic growth rate is approximately 4 percent.

# Malaysia

## GEOGRAPHY

*Area in Square Miles (Kilometers):*
121,348 (329,750) (slightly larger than New Mexico)
*Capital (Population):* Kuala Lumpur (1,236,000)
*Environmental Concerns:* air and water pollution; deforestation
*Geographical Features:* coastal plains rising to hills and mountains
*Climate:* tropical; annual monsoons

## PEOPLE

### Population

*Total:* 20,492,000
*Annual Growth Rate:* 2.15%
*Rural/Urban Population Ratio:* 62/38
*Major Languages:* Peninsular Malaysia: Bahasa Malaysia, English, Chinese dialects, Tamil; Sabah: English, Malay, numerous tribal dialects, Mandarin and Hakka dialects; Sarawak: English, Malay, Mandarin, numerous tribal dialects, Arabic, others
*Ethnic Makeup:* 58% Malay and other indigenous; 26% Chinese; 7% Indian; 9% others
*Religions:* Peninsular Malaysia: Malays nearly all Muslim, Chinese predominantly Buddhist, Indians predominantly Hindu; Sabah: 33% Muslim, 17% Christian, 45% others; Sarawak: 35% traditional indigenous, 24% Buddhist and Confucian, 20% Muslim, 16% Christian, 5% others

### Health

*Life Expectancy at Birth:* 67 years (male); 73 years (female)
*Infant Mortality Rate (Ratio):* 23.2/1,000
*Physicians Available (Ratio):* 1/2,638

### Education

*Adult Literacy Rate:* 84% overall
*Compulsory (Ages):* 6–16; free

## COMMUNICATION

*Telephones:* 1 per 6 people
*Daily Newspaper Circulation:* 142 per 1,000 people
*Televisions:* 1 per 6.4 people

## TRANSPORTATION

*Highways in Miles (Kilometers):* 56,385 (33,831)
*Railroads in Miles (Kilometers):* 1,116 (670)
*Usable Airfields:* 106
*Motor Vehicles in Use:* 2,600,000

## GOVERNMENT

*Type:* constitutional monarchy
*Independence Date:* August 31, 1957
*Head of State/Government:* Paramount Ruler Jaafarbin Abdul Rahman; Prime Minister Datuk Mahathir bin Mohamad
*Political Parties:* Peninsular Malaysia: National Front and others; Sabah: National Front and others; Sarawak: National Front and others
*Suffrage:* universal at 21

## MILITARY

*Military Expenditures (% of GDP):* 2.6%
*Current Disputes:* dispute over the Spratly Islands with China, the Philippines, Taiwan, and Vietnam; Sabah is claimed by the Philippines

## ECONOMY

*Currency ($ U.S. Equivalent):* 3.8 ringgits = $1
*Per Capita Income/GDP:* $10,750/$214.7 billion
*GDP Growth Rate:* −1.5%
*Inflation Rate:* 3.5%
*Unemployment Rate:* 2.6%
*Labor Force:* 8,398,000
*Natural Resources:* tin; petroleum; timber; natural gas; bauxite; iron ore; copper; fish
*Agriculture:* rubber; palm oil; rice; coconut oil; pepper; timber
*Industry:* rubber and palm oil manufacturing and processing; light manufacturing; electronics; tin mining and smelting; logging and processing timber; petroleum production and refining; food processing
*Exports:* $84.6 billion (primary partners United States, Singapore, Japan)
*Imports:* $83.2 billion (primary partners Japan, United States, Singapore)

http://st-www.cs.uiuc.edu/users/chai/malaysia.html

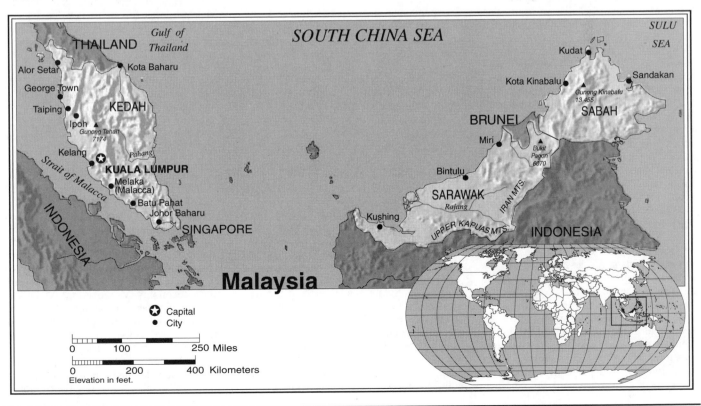

## A FRACTURED NATION

Not much smaller than Japan and famous for its production of natural rubber and tin, Malaysia sounds like a true political, economic, and social entity. But Malaysia, although it has all the trappings of a modern nation-state, is one of the most fragmented nations on Earth.

Consider its land. West Malaysia, wherein reside 86 percent of the population, is located on the Malay Peninsula between Singapore and Thailand; but East Malaysia, with 60 percent of the land, is located on the island of North Borneo, some 400 miles of ocean away.

Similarly, Malaysia's people are divided along racial, religious, and linguistic lines. Fifty-eight percent are Malays and other indigenous peoples, many of whom adhere to the Islamic faith or animist beliefs; 26 percent are Chinese, most of whom are Buddhist, Confucian, or Taoist; 7 percent are Indians and 9 percent are Pakistanis and others, some of whom follow the Hindu faith. Bahasa Malaysia is the official language, but English, Arabic, two forms of Chinese, Tamil, and other languages are also spoken. Thus, although the country is called Malaysia (a name adopted only 30 years ago), many people living in Kuala Lumpur, the capital, or in the many villages in the countryside do not think of themselves first and foremost as Malaysians.

Malaysian culture is further fragmented because each ethnic group tends to replicate the architecture, social rituals, and norms of etiquette peculiar to itself. The Chinese, whose ancestors were imported in the 1800s from south China by the British to work the rubber plantations and tin mines, have become so economically powerful that their cultural influence extends far beyond their actual numbers.

Malaysian history is equally fragmented. Originally controlled by numerous sultans who gave allegiance to no one or only reluctantly to various more powerful states in surrounding regions, Malaysia first came to Western attention in 1511, when the prosperous city of Malacca, founded on the west coast of the Malay Peninsula about A.D. 1400, was conquered by the Portuguese. The Dutch took Malacca away from the Portuguese in 1641. The British seized it from the Dutch in 1824 (the British had already acquired an island off the coast and had established the port of Singapore). By 1888, the British were in control of most of the area that is now Malaysia.

However, British hegemony did not mean total control, for each of the many sultanates—the origin of the 13 states that constitute Malaysia today—continued to act more or less independently of the British, engaging in wars with one another and maintaining an administrative apparatus apart from the British. And some groups, such as the Dayaks, an indigenous people living in the jungles of Borneo, remained more or less aloof from the various intrigues of modern state-making and developed little or no identity of themselves as citizens of any modern nation.

It is hardly surprising, then, that Malaysia has had a difficult time emerging as a modern nation. Indeed, it is not likely that there would have been an independent Malaysia had it not been for the Japanese, who defeated the British in Southeast Asia during World War II and promulgated their alluring doctrine of "Asia for Asians."

After the war, Malaysian demands for independence from European domination grew more persuasive; Great Britain attempted in 1946 to meet these demands by proposing a partly autonomous Malay Union. However, ethnic rivalries and power-sensitive sultans created such enormous tension that the plan was scrapped. In an uncharacteristic display of cooperation, some 41 different Malay groups organized the United Malay National Organization (UMNO) to oppose the British plan. In 1948, a new Federation of Malaya was attempted. It granted considerable freedom within a framework of British supervision, allowed sultans to retain power over their own regions, and placed certain restrictions on the power of the Chinese living in the country.

Opposing any agreement short of full independence, a group of Chinese Communists, with Indonesian support, began a guerrilla war against the government and against capitalist ideology. Known as "The Emergency," the war lasted more than a decade and involved some 250,000 government troops. Eventually, the insurgents withdrew.

The three main ethnic groups—Malayans, represented by UMNO; Chinese, represented by the Malayan Chinese Association, or MCA; and Indians, represented by the Malayan Indian Congress, or MIC—were able to cooperate long enough in 1953 to form a single political party under the leadership of Abdul Rahman. This party demanded and received complete independence for the Federation in 1957, although some areas, such as Brunei, refused to join. Upon independence, the Federation of Malaya (not yet called Malaysia), excluding Singapore and the territories on the island of Borneo, became a member of the British Commonwealth of Nations and was admitted to the United Nations. In 1963, a new Federation was proposed that included Singapore and the lands on Borneo. Again, Brunei refused to join. Singapore joined but withdrew in 1965. Thus, what is known as Malaysia acquired its current form in 1966. It is regarded today as a rapidly developing nation that is attempting to govern itself according to democratic principles.

Political troubles stemming from the deep ethnic divisions in the country, however, remain a constant feature of Malaysian life. With nine of the 13 states controlled by independent sultans, every election is a test of the ability of the National Front, a multiethnic coalition of 11 different parties that has a two-thirds majority in Parliament, to maintain political stability. Particularly troublesome has been the state of Sabah (an area claimed by the Philippines), many of whose residents have wanted independence or, at least, greater autonomy from the federal government. In 1994, however, the National Front was able to gain a slight majority in Sabah elections, indicating the growing confidence that people have in the federal government's economic development policies.

## ECONOMIC DEVELOPMENT

For years, Malaysia's "miracle" economy kept social and political instability in check. Although it had to endure normal fluctuations in market demand for its products, the economy grew at 5 to 8 percent per year from the 1970s to the late 1990s, making it one of the world's top 20 exporters/importers. The manufacturing sector developed to such an extent that it accounted for 70 percent of exports. Then, in 1998, a financial crisis hit. Malaysia was forced to devalue its currency, the ringgit, making it more difficult for consumers to buy foreign products, and dramatically slowing the economy. The government found it necessary to deport thousands of illegal Indonesian and other workers (dozens of whom fled to foreign embassies to avoid deportation) in order to find jobs for Malaysians. In the 1980s and early 1990s, up to 20 percent of the Malaysian workforce had been foreign workers, but the downturn produced "Operation Get Out," in which at least 850,000 "guest workers" were to be deported to their home countries.

Malaysia continues to be rich in raw materials, especially timber (it produces half of the world's timber exports), tin, petroleum, rice, coconut oil, and pepper. Therefore, it is not likely that the crisis of the late 1990s will permanently cripple its economy. Moreover, the Malaysian government has a good record of active planning and support of business ventures—directly modeled after Japan's export-oriented strategy. Malaysia launched a "New Economic" Policy (NEP) in the 1970s that welcomed foreign direct investment and sought to diversify the economic

| The city of Malacca is established; it becomes a center of trade and Islamic conversion A.D. 1403 | The Portuguese capture Malacca 1511 | The Dutch capture Malacca 1641 | The British obtain Malacca from the Dutch 1824 | Japan captures the Malay Peninsula 1941 | The British establish the Federation of Malaya; a Communist guerrilla war begins, lasting for a decade 1948 | The Federation of Malaya achieves independence under Prime Minister Tengku Abdul Rahman 1957 | The Federation of Malaysia, including Singapore but not Brunei, is formed 1963 | Singapore leaves the Federation of Malaysia 1965 | Malaysia attempts to build an industrial base; Datuk Mahathir bin Mohamad becomes prime minister 1980s |

1990s

The NEP is replaced with Vision 2020

Prime Minister Mahathir retains power

Economic crisis; the currency is devalued; "guest workers" are deported

base. Japan, Taiwan, and the United States invested heavily in Malaysia. So successful was this strategy that economic growth targets set for the mid-1990s were actually achieved several years early. In 1991, the government replaced NEP with a new plan, "Vision 2020." Its goal was to bring Malaysia into full "developed nation" status by the year 2020. Sectors targeted for growth included the aerospace industry, biotechnology, microelectronics, and information and energy technology. The government expanded universities and encouraged the creation of some 170 industrial and research parks, including "Free Zones," where export-oriented businesses were allowed duty-free imports of raw materials. Some of Malaysia's most ambitious projects, including a $6 billion hydroelectric dam (strongly opposed by environmentalists), have been shelved, at least until the recent money crisis is resolved. It also appears likely that future years will see much slower growth, but Malaysia's efforts to date have been highly successful and have literally transformed the economy and reduced poverty.

Despite Malaysia's substantial economic successes, serious social problems remain. These problems stem not from insufficient revenues but from inequitable distribution. The Malay portion of the population in particular continues to feel economically deprived as compared to the wealthier Chinese and Indian segments. (At one time, these upper-class households received, on average, 16 times the income of the poorest Malay families.) Furthermore, most Malays are farmers, and rural areas have not benefited from Malaysia's economic boom as much as urban areas have.

In the 1960s and 1970s, riots involving thousands of college students were headlined in the Western press as having their basis in ethnicity. This was true to some degree, but the core issue was economic inequality. Included in the economic master plan of the 1970s were plans (similar to affirmative action in the United States) to change the structural barriers that prevented many Malays from fully enjoying the benefits of the economic boom. Under the leadership of Prime Minister Datuk Mahathir bin Mohamad, plans were developed that would assist Malays until they held a 30 percent interest in Malaysian businesses. In 1990, the government announced that the figure had already reached an impressive 20 percent. Unfortunately, many Malays have insufficient capital to maintain ownership in businesses, so the government has been called upon to acquire many Malay businesses in order to prevent their being purchased by non-Malays. In addition, the system of preferential treatment for Malays has created a Malay elite, detached from the Malay poor, who now compete with the Chinese and Indian elites; interethnic and interracial goodwill is still difficult to achieve. Nonetheless, social goals have been attained to a greater extent than most observers have thought possible. Educational opportunities for the poor have been increased, farmland development has proceeded on schedule, and the poverty rate has dropped to 10 percent.

## THE LEADERSHIP

In a polity so fractured as Malaysia's, one would expect rapid turnover among political elites. But Prime Minister Mahathir, a Malay, had the support of the electorate for more than a decade. His primary challenger has been the Chinese Democratic Action Party (DAP), which has sometimes reduced Mahathir's majority in Parliament but has not been able to top his political strength. The policies that have sustained Mahathir's reputation as a credible leader include the NEP, with its goals of economic diversification, privatization, and wealth equalization, and his nationalist—but moderate—foreign policy. Malaysia has been an active member of ASEAN and has courted Japan and other Pacific Rim nations for foreign investment and export markets (Mahathir's "Look East" policy). Anticipating negative economic consequences from the growing strength of the European Union and the North American Free Trade Agreement, Mahathir promoted a plan to create an Asian free-trade zone that would exclude the United States and other Western nations. Failing in that, he refused to attend the Asia-Pacific Economic Cooperation group meetings held in 1993 in the United States, at which more than a dozen regional leaders discussed economic cooperation. Rocky economic relations between Malaysia and some Western nations were improved somewhat in 1996 by the visit of the Australian prime minister to Prime Minister Mahathir.

Malaysia's success has not been achieved without some questionable practices. The government seems unwilling to regulate economic growth, even though strong voices have been raised against industrialization's deleterious effects on the old-growth teak forests and other parts of the environment. Moreover, the blue-collar workers who are the muscle behind Malaysia's economic success are prohibited from forming labor unions, and outspoken critics have been silenced. Charges of government corruption are becoming more frequent and more strident. The environmentalists' case was substantially strengthened in 1998 when forest and peat-bog fires in Malaysia and Indonesia engulfed Kuala Lumpur in a thick haze for weeks. The government, unable to snuff out the fires, ordered sprinklers installed atop the city's skyscrapers to settle the dust and lower temperatures.

**DEVELOPMENT**

Malaysia continues to struggle to move its economy away from agriculture. Attempts at industrialization have been successful: Malaysia is the third-largest producer of semiconductors in the world, and manufacturing now accounts for about 30% of the gross domestic product.

**FREEDOM**

Malaysia is attempting to govern according to democratic principles. Ethnic rivalries, however, severely hamper the smooth conduct of government and limit such individual liberties as the right to form labor unions.

**HEALTH/WELFARE**

City dwellers have ready access to educational, medical, and social opportunities, but the quality of life declines dramatically in the countryside. Malaysia has one of the highest illiteracy rates in the Pacific Rim. It spends only a small percentage of its GDP on education.

**ACHIEVEMENTS**

Malaysia has made impressive economic advancements. The government's New Economic Policy has achieved a measure of wealth redistribution to the poor. Since the 1970s, the economy has grown at an impressive rate. Malaysia has also made impressive social and political gains.

# Myanmar (Union of Myanmar; commonly known as Burma)

## GEOGRAPHY

*Area in Square Miles (Kilometers):* 261,901 (678,500) (slightly smaller than Texas)

*Capital (Population):* Yangon (Rangoon) (3,873,000)

*Environmental Concerns:* deforestation; air, soil, and water pollution; inadequate sanitation and water treatment

*Geographical Features:* central lowlands ringed by steep, rugged highlands

*Climate:* tropical monsoon

## PEOPLE

### Population

*Total:* 46,822,000

*Annual Growth Rate:* 1.8%

*Rural/Urban Population Ratio:* 74/26

*Major Languages:* Burmese; various minority languages

*Ethnic Makeup:* 68% Burman; 9% Shan; 7% Karen; 4% Rakhine; 3% Chinese; 9% Mon, Indian, and others

*Religions:* 89% Buddhist; 4% Muslim; 4% Christian; 3% animist and others

### Health

*Life Expectancy at Birth:* 55 years (male); 58 years (female)

*Infant Mortality Rate (Ratio):* 78.5/1,000

*Average Caloric Intake:* 106% of FAO minimum

*Physicians Available (Ratio):* 1/3,554

### Education

*Adult Literacy Rate:* 83%

*Compulsory (Ages):* 5–10; free

## COMMUNICATION

*Telephones:* 1 per 317 people

*Daily Newspaper Circulation:* 23 per 1,000 people

*Televisions:* 1 per 200 people

## TRANSPORTATION

*Highways in Miles (Kilometers):* 17,000 (27,600)

*Railroads in Miles (Kilometers):* 2,110 (3,569)

*Usable Airfields:* 73

*Motor Vehicles in Use:* 86,000

## GOVERNMENT

*Type:* military regime

*Independence Date:* January 4, 1948

*Head of State/Government:* Chairman of the State Law and Order Restoration Council (General) Than Shwe; Prime Minister (General) Than Shwe

*Political Parties:* Union Solidarity and Development Association; National League for Democracy; National Unity Party; others

*Suffrage:* universal at 18

## MILITARY

*Current Disputes:* internal strife

## ECONOMY

*Currency ($ U.S. Equivalent):* 6.06 kyats = $1

*Per Capita Income/GDP:* $1,120/$51.5 billion

*GDP Growth Rate:* 7%

*Inflation Rate:* 30%–40%

*Labor Force:* 16,007,000

*Natural Resources:* petroleum; tin; timber; antimony; zinc; copper; tungsten; lead; coal; marble; limestone; precious stones; natural gas

*Agriculture:* teak; rice; corn; oilseed; sugarcane; pulses

*Industry:* agricultural processing; textiles; footwear; wood and wood products; petroleum refining; copper, tin, tungsten, and iron mining; construction materials; pharmaceuticals; fertilizer

*Exports:* $1.1 billion (primary partners Singapore, China, Thailand)

*Imports:* $2 billion (primary partners Singapore, Hong Kong, Japan)

 http://www.myanmar.com

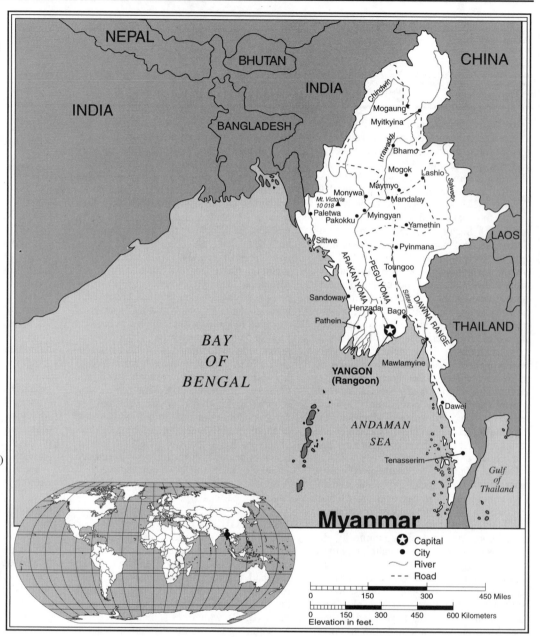

Myanmar

★ Capital
● City
∼ River
--- Road

0    150    300    450 Miles
0   150  300  450  600 Kilometers
Elevation in feet.

## THE CONTROLLED SOCIETY

For more than 3 decades, Myanmar (as Burma was officially renamed in 1989) has been a tightly controlled society. Telephones, radio stations, railroads, and many large companies have been under the direct control of a military junta that has brutalized its opposition and forced many to flee the country. For many years, tourists were allowed to stay only 2 weeks (for a while the limit was 24 hours), could stay only at military-approved hotels, and could visit only certain parts of the country. Citizens too were highly restricted: They could not leave their country by car or train to visit nearby countries because all the roads were sealed off by government decree and rail lines terminated at the border. Even Western-style dancing was declared illegal. Until a minor liberalization of the economy was achieved in 1989, all foreign exports—every grain of rice, every peanut, every piece of lumber—though generally owned privately, had to be sold to the government rather than directly to consumers.

Observers attribute this state of affairs to military commanders who overthrew the legitimate government in 1962, but the roots of Myanmar's political and economic dilemma actually go back to 1885, when the British overthrew the Burmese government and declared Burma a colony of Britain. In the 1930s, European-educated Burmese college students organized strikes and demonstrations against the British. Seeing that the Japanese Army had successfully toppled other European colonial governments in Asia, the students determined to assist the Japanese during their invasion of the country in 1941. Once the British had been expelled, however, the students organized the Anti-Fascist People's Freedom League (AFPFL) to oppose Japanese rule.

When the British tried to resume control of Burma after World War II, they found that the Burmese people had given their allegiance to U Aung San, one of the original student leaders. He and the AFPFL insisted that the British grant full independence to Burma, which they reluctantly did in 1948. So determined were the Burmese to remain free of foreign domination that, unlike most former British colonies, they refused to join the British Commonwealth of Nations, an economic association of former British colonies. This was the first of many decisions that would have the effect of isolating Burma from the global economy.

Unlike Japan, with its nearly homogeneous population and single national language, Myanmar is a multiethnic state; in fact, only about 60 percent of the people speak Burmese. The Burman people are genetically related to the Tibetans and the Chinese; the Chin are related to peoples of nearby India; the Shan are related to Thais; and the Mon migrated to Burma from Cambodia. In general, these ethnic groups live in separate political states within Myanmar—the Kachin State, the Shan State, the Karen State, and so on; and for hundreds of years, they have warred against one another for dominance. Upon the withdrawal of the British in 1948, some ethnic groups, particularly the Kachins, the Karens, and the Shans, embraced the Communist ideology of change through violent revolution. Their rebellion against the government in the capital city of Yangon (the new name of Rangoon) had the effect of removing from government control large portions of the country. Headed by U Nu (U Aung San and several of the original government leaders having been assassinated shortly before independence), the government considered its position precarious and determined that to align itself with the Communist forces then ascendant in the People's Republic of China and other parts of Asia would strengthen the hand of the ethnic separatists, whereas to form alliances with the capitalist world would invite a repetition of decades of Western domination. U Nu thus attempted to steer a decidedly neutral course during the cold war era and to be as tolerant as possible of separatist groups within Burma. Burma refused U.S. economic aid, had very little to do with the warfare afflicting Vietnam and the other Southeast Asian countries, and was not eager to join the Southeast Asian Treaty Organization or the Asian Development Bank.

Some factions of Burmese society were not pleased with U Nu's relatively benign treatment of separatist groups. In 1958, a political impasse allowed Ne Win, a military general, to assume temporary control of the country. National elections were held in 1962, and a democratically elected government was installed in power. Shortly thereafter, however, Ne Win staged a military coup. The military has controlled Burma/Myanmar ever since. Under Ne Win, competing political parties were banned, the economy was nationalized, and the country's international isolation became even more pronounced.

Years of ethnic conflict, inflexible socialism, and self-imposed isolation have severely damaged economic growth in Myanmar. In 1987, despite Burma's abundance of valuable teak and rubber trees in its forests, sizable supplies of minerals in the mountains to the north, onshore oil, rich farmland in the Irrawaddy Delta, and a reasonably well-educated population, the United Nations declared Burma one of the least developed countries in the world (it had once been the richest country in Southeast Asia). Debt incurred in the 1970s exacerbated the country's problems, as did the government's fear of foreign investment. Thus, by 1996, Myanmar's per capita income was less than $1,000 a year.

Myanmar's industrial base is still very small; about two thirds of the population of nearly 47 million make their living by farming (rice is a major export) and by fishing. The tropical climate yields abundant forest cover, where some 250 species of valuable trees abound. Good natural harbors and substantial mineral deposits of coal, natural gas, and others also bless the land. Only about 10 percent of gross domestic product comes from the manufacturing sector (as compared to, for example, approximately 45 percent in wealthy Taiwan). In the absence of a strong economy, black marketeering has increased, as have other forms of illegal economic transactions. It is estimated that 80 percent of the heroin smuggled into New York City comes from the jungles of Myanmar and northern Thailand.

Over the years, the Burmese have been advised by economists to open up their country to foreign investment and to develop the private sector of the economy. They have resisted the former idea because of their deep-seated fear of foreign domination; they have similar suspicions of the private sector because it was previously controlled almost completely by ethnic minorities (the Chinese and Indians). The government has relied on the public sector to counterbalance the power of the ethnic minorities.

Beginning in 1987, however, the government began to admit publicly that the economy was in serious trouble. To counter massive unrest in the country, the military authorities agreed to permit foreign investment from countries such as Malaysia, South Korea, Singapore, and Thailand and to allow trade with China and Thailand. In 1989, the government signed oil-exploration agreements with South Korea, the United States, the Netherlands, Australia, and Japan. Both the United States and the former West Germany withdrew foreign aid in 1988, but Japan did not; in 1991, Japan supplied $61 million—more than any other country—in aid to Myanmar.

## POLITICAL STALEMATE

Despite these reforms, Myanmar has remained in a state of turmoil. In 1988, thousands of students participated in 6 months of demonstrations to protest the lack of democracy in the country and to demand multiparty elections. General Saw Maung brutally suppressed the demonstrators, imprisoning many students—and killing more than 3,000 of them. He then took control of the government and reluctantly agreed to multiparty elections. About 170 political parties registered for the elections, which were held in 1990—the first elections in 30 years. Among these were the National Unity Party (a new name for the Burma Socialist Program Party, the only legal party since 1974) and the National League for Democracy, a new party headed by Aung San Suu Kyi, daughter of slain national hero U Aung San.

The campaign was characterized by the same level of military control that had existed in all other aspects of life since the 1960s. Martial law, imposed in 1988, remained in effect; all schools and universities were closed; opposition-party workers were intimidated; and, most significantly, the three most popular opposition leaders were placed under house arrest and barred from campaigning. The United Nations began an investigation of civil-rights abuses during the election and, once again, students demonstrated against the military government. Several students even hijacked a Burmese airliner to demand the release of Aung San Suu Kyi, who had been placed under house arrest.

As the votes were tallied, it became apparent that the Burmese people were eager to end military rule; the National League for Democracy won 80 percent of the seats in the National Assembly. But the military junta refused to step down and remains in control of the government. Under General Than Shwe, who replaced General Saw Maung in 1992, the military has organized various operations against Karen rebels and has so oppressed Muslims that some 40,000 to 60,000 of them have fled to Bangladesh. Hundreds of students who fled the cities during the 1988 crackdown on student demonstrations have now joined rural guerrilla organizations, such as the Burma Communist Party and the Karen National Union, to continue the fight against the military dictatorship. Among those most vigorously opposed to military rule are Buddhist monks. Five months after the elections, monks in the capital city of Yangon boycotted the government by refusing to conduct religious rituals for soldiers. Tens of thousands of people joined in the boycott. The government responded by threatening to shut down monasteries in the cities of Yangon and Mandalay.

The military government calls itself the State Law and Order Restoration Council (SLORC) and appears determined to stay

(Photo credit AP Laser-Photo)

In 1990, Myanmar's first elections in 30 years were held; a new opposition party, the National League for Democracy, headed by Aung San Suu Kyi, pictured above, won 80 percent of the seats in the National Assembly but she was never permitted to take office. Instead, she was placed under house arrest for several years. In 1991, Aung San Suu Kyi was awarded the Nobel Peace Prize.

in power. SLORC has kept Aung San Suu Kyi under house arrest for years and watches her every move. For several years, even her husband and children were forbidden to visit her. While under arrest, she was awarded the Nobel Peace Prize; in 1993, several other Nobelists gathered in nearby Thailand to call for her release—a plea ignored by SLORC. The United Nations has shown its displeasure with the military junta by substantially cutting development funds, as has the United States, which, on the basis of Myanmar's heavy illegal-drug activities, has disqualified the country from receiving most forms of economic aid.

| Burman people enter the Irrawaddy Valley from China and Tibet **800 B.C.** | The Portuguese are impressed with Burmese wealth **1500s** | The First Anglo-Burmese War **1824–1826** | The Second Anglo-Burmese War **1852** | The Third Anglo-Burmese War results in the loss of Burmese sovereignty **1885** | The Japanese invade Burma **1941** | Burma gains independence of Britain **1948** | General Ne Win takes control of the government in a coup **1962** | Economic crisis; the pro-democracy movement is crushed; General Saw Maung takes control of the government **1980s** | Burma is renamed Myanmar (though most people prefer the name Burma) **1989** |

**1990s**

| The military refuses to give up power; Than Shwe becomes head of state | Aung San Suu Kyi's activities remain restricted; Myanmar is granted observer status in ASEAN | The International Red Cross withdraws from Myanmar in protest because it was not allowed access to political prisoners |

But perhaps the greatest pressure on the dictatorship is from within the country itself. Despite brutal suppression, the military seems to be losing control of the people. Both the Kachin and Karen ethnic groups have organized guerrilla movements against the regime; in some cases, they have coerced foreign lumber companies to pay them protection money, which they, in turn, use to buy arms against the junta. Opponents of SLORC control one third of Myanmar, especially along its eastern borders with Thailand and China and in the north alongside India. With the economy in shambles, the military appears to be involved with the heroin trade as a way of acquiring needed funds; it reportedly engages in bitter battles with drug lords periodically for control of the trade. To ease economic pressure, the military rulers have ended their monopoly of some businesses and have legalized the black market, making products from China, India, and Thailand available on the street.

Still, for ordinary people, especially those in the countryside, life is anything but pleasant. A 1994 human-rights study found that as many as 20,000 women and girls living in Myanmar near the Thai border had been abducted to work as prostitutes in Thailand. For several years, SLORC has carried out an "ethnic-cleansing" policy against villagers who have opposed their rule; thousands of people have been carried off to relocation camps, forced to work as slaves or prostitutes for the soldiers, or simply killed. Some 400,000 members of ethnic groups have fled the country, including 300,000 Arakans who escaped to Bangladesh and 5,000 Karenni, 12,000 Mon, and 50,000 Karens who fled to Thailand. Food shortages plague certain regions of the country, and many young children are forced to serve in the various competing armies rather than acquire an education or otherwise enjoy a normal childhood. Despite the lifting of martial law and some minor liberalization of the economy, it appears that it will be a long time before democracy will take hold in Myanmar.

### THE CULTURE OF BUDDHA

For a brief period in the 1960s, Buddhism was the official state religion of Burma. Although this status was repealed by the government in order to weaken the power of the Buddhist leadership, or *Sangha,* vis-à-vis the polity, Buddhism, representing the belief system of 89 percent of the population, remains the single most important cultural force in the country. Even the Burmese alphabet is based, in part, on Pali, the sacred language of Buddhism. Buddhist monks joined with college students after World War II to pressure the British government to withdraw from Burma, and they have brought continual pressure to bear on the current military junta.

Historically, so powerful has been the Buddhist *Sangha* in Burma that four major dynasties have fallen because of it. This has not been the result of ideological antagonism between church and state (indeed, Burmese rulers have usually been quite supportive of Buddhism) but, rather, because Buddhism soaks up resources that might otherwise go to the government or to economic development. Believers are willing to give money, land, and other resources to the religion, because they believe that such donations will bring them spiritual merit; the more merit one acquires, the better one's next life will be. Thus, all over Myanmar, but especially in older cities such as Pagan, one can find large, elaborate Buddhist temples, monuments, or monasteries, some of them built by kings and other royals on huge, untaxed parcels of land. These monuments drained resources from the government but brought to the donor unusual amounts of spiritual merit. As Burmese scholar Michael Aung-Thwin explained it: "One built the largest temple because one was spiritually superior, and one was spiritually superior because one built the largest temple."

Today, the Buddhist *Sangha* is at the forefront of the opposition to military rule. This is a rather unusual position for Buddhists, who generally prefer a more passive attitude toward "worldly" issues. Monks have joined college students in peaceful-turned-violent demonstrations against the junta. Other monks have staged spiritual boycotts against the soldiers by refusing to accept merit-bringing alms from them or to perform weddings and funerals. The junta has retaliated by banning some Buddhist groups altogether and purging many others of rebellious leaders. The military regime now seems to be relaxing its intimidation of the Buddhists, has reopened universities, and has invited some foreign investment. Although the Japanese have continued to invest in Myanmar throughout the military dictatorship, some potential investors from other countries refuse to invest in a regime that is so obviously brutal and which gives little evidence of any desire to return the country to democracy.

### DEVELOPMENT

Primarily an agricultural nation, Myanmar has a poorly developed industrial sector. Until recently, the government forbade foreign investment and severely restricted tourism. In 1989, recognizing that the economy was on the brink of collapse, the government permitted foreign investment and signed contracts with Japan and others for oil exploration.

### FREEDOM

Myanmar is a military dictatorship. Until 1989, only the Burma Socialist Program Party was permitted. Other parties, while now legal, are intimidated by the military junta. The democratically elected National League for Democracy has not been permitted to assume office. The government has also restricted the activities of Buddhist monks and has carried out "ethnic cleansing" against minorities.

### HEALTH/WELFARE

The Myanmar government provides free health care and pensions to citizens, but the quality and availability of these services are erratic, to say the least. Malnourishment and preventable diseases are common, and infant mortality is high. Overpopulation is not a problem; Myanmar is one of the most sparsely populated nations in Asia.

### ACHIEVEMENTS

Myanmar is known for the beauty of its Buddhist architecture. Pagodas and other Buddhist monuments and temples dot many of the cities, especially Pagan, one of Burma's earliest cities. Politically, it is notable that the country was able to remain free of the warfare that engulfed much of Indochina during the 1960s and 1970s.

# New Zealand (Dominion of New Zealand)

## GEOGRAPHY
*Area in Square Miles (Kilometers):* 98,874 (268,680) (about the size of Colorado)
*Capital (Population):* Wellington (158,300)
*Environmental Concerns:* deforestation; soil erosion; damage to native flora and fauna from outside species
*Geographical Features:* mainly mountainous with some large coastal plains
*Climate:* temperate; sharp regional contrasts

## PEOPLE

### Population
*Total:* 3,587,300
*Annual Growth Rate:* 1.08%
*Rural/Urban Population (Ratio):* 14/86
*Major Languages:* English; Maori
*Ethnic Makeup:* 88% European; 9% Maori; 3% Pacific islander
*Religions:* 81% Christian; 18% unaffiliated; 1% others

### Health
*Life Expectancy at Birth:* 74 years (male); 81 years (female)
*Infant Mortality Rate (Ratio):* 6.5/1,000
*Average Caloric Intake:* 132% of FAO minimum
*Physicians Available (Ratio):* 1/301

### Education
*Adult Literacy Rate:* 99%
*Compulsory (Ages):* 6–16; free

## COMMUNICATION
*Telephones:* 1 per 2.1 people
*Daily Newspaper Circulation:* 297 per 1,000 people
*Televisions:* 1 per 2 people

## TRANSPORTATION
*Highways in Miles (Kilometers):* 55,383 (88,613)
*Railroads in Miles (Kilometers):* 2,383 (3,813)
*Usable Airfields:* 112
*Motor Vehicles in Use:* 2,053,000

## GOVERNMENT
*Type:* parliamentary democracy
*Independence Date:* September 26, 1907
*Head of State/Government:* Queen Elizabeth II, represented by Governor General Sir Michael Hardie-Boys; Prime Minister Jenny Shipley
*Political Parties:* National Party; New Zealand Labour Party; New Zealand First Party; Democratic Party; New Zealand Liberal Party; Green Party; Mana Motuhake; others
*Suffrage:* universal at 18

## MILITARY
*Military Expenditures (% of GDP):* 1.1%
*Current Disputes:* disputed territorial claim in Antarctica

## ECONOMY
*Currency ($ U.S. Equivalent):* 1.87 New Zealand dollars = $1
*Per Capita Income/GDP:* $18,500/$65.6 billion
*GDP Growth Rate:* 2.8%
*Inflation Rate:* 2.8%
*Unemployment Rate:* 5.9%
*Labor Force:* 1,634,500
*Natural Resources:* natural gas; iron ore; sand; coal; timber; hydropower; gold; limestone
*Agriculture:* wool; meat; dairy products; wheat; barley; potatoes; pulses; fruits; vegetables; fishing
*Industry:* food processing; wood and paper products; textiles; machinery; transportation equipment; banking; insurance; tourism; mining
*Exports:* $13.7 billion (primary partners Australia, Japan, United Kingdom)
*Imports:* $14.0 billion (primary partners Australia, United States, Japan)

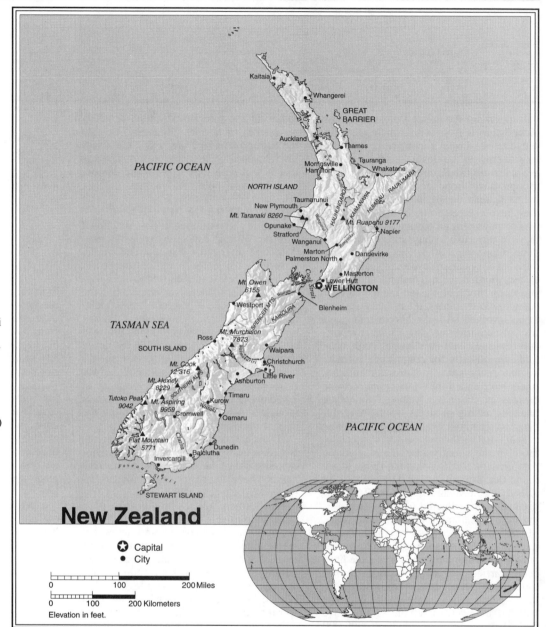

New Zealand

★ Capital
● City

0    100    200 Miles
0    100    200 Kilometers
Elevation in feet.

## ITS PLACE IN THE WORLD

New Zealand, like Australia, is decidedly an anomaly among Pacific Rim countries. Eighty-eight percent of the population are of British descent, English is the official language, and most people, even many of the original Maori inhabitants, are Christians. Britain claimed the beautiful, mountainous islands officially in 1840, after agreeing to respect the property rights of Maoris, most of whom lived on the North Island. Blessed with a temperate climate and excellent soils for crop and dairy farming, New Zealand—divided into two main islands, North Island and South Island—became an important part of the British Empire.

New Zealand, although largely self-governing since 1907 and fully independent as of 1947, has always maintained very close ties with the United Kingdom and is a member of the Commonwealth of Nations. It has, in fact, attempted to re-create British culture—customs, architecture, even vegetation—in the Pacific. So close were the links with Great Britain in the 1940s, for example, that England purchased fully 88 percent of New Zealand's exports (mostly agricultural and dairy products), while 60 percent of New Zealand's imports came from Britain. And believing itself to be very much a part of the British Empire, New Zealand always sided with the Western nations on matters of military defense.

Efforts to maintain a close cultural link with Great Britain do not stem entirely from the common ethnicity of the two nations; they also arise from New Zealand's extreme geographical isolation from the centers of European and North American activity. Even Australia is more than 1,200 miles away. Therefore, New Zealand's policy—until the 1940s—was to encourage the British presence in Asia and the Pacific, by acquiring more lands or building up naval bases, to make it more likely that Britain would be willing and able to defend New Zealand in a time of crisis. New Zealand had involved itself somewhat in the affairs of some nearby islands in the late 1800s and early 1900s, but its purpose was not to provide development assistance or defense. Rather, its aim was to extend the power of the British Empire and put New Zealand in the middle of a mini-empire of its own. To that end, New Zealand annexed the Cook Islands in 1901 and took over German Samoa in 1914. In 1925, it assumed formal control over the atoll group known as the Tokelau Islands.

## REGIONAL RELIANCE

During World War II (or, as the Japanese call it, the Pacific War), Japan's rapid con-

quest of the Malay Archipelago, its seizure of many Pacific islands, and its plans to attack Australia demonstrated to New Zealanders the futility of relying on the British to guarantee their security. After the war, and for the first time in its history, New Zealand began to pay serious attention to the real needs and ambitions of the peoples nearby rather than to focus on

Great Britain. In 1944 and again in 1947, New Zealand joined with Australia and other colonial nations to create regional associations on behalf of the Pacific islands. One of the organizations, the South Pacific Commission, has itself spawned many regional subassociations dealing with trade, education, migration, and cultural and economic development. Al-

(The Peabody Museum of Salem photo)

Maoris occupied New Zealand long before the European settlers moved there. The Maoris quickly realized that the newcomers were intent on depriving them of their land, but it was not until the 1920s that the government finally regulated unscrupulous land-grabbing practices. Today, the Maoris pursue a lifestyle that preserves key parts of their traditional culture while incorporating skills necessary for survival in the modern world.

| Maoris, probably from Tahiti, settle the islands A.D. **1300s** | New Zealand is "discovered" by Dutch navigator A. J. Tasman **1642** | Captain James Cook explores the islands **1769** | Britain declares sovereignty **1840** | A gold rush attracts new immigrants **1865** | New Zealand becomes an almost independent dominion of Great Britain **1907** |
| --- | --- | --- | --- | --- | --- |

though it had neglected the islands that it controlled during its imperial phase, in the early 1900s, New Zealand cooperated fully with the United Nations in the islands' decolonization during the 1960s (although Tokelau, by choice, and the Ross dependency remain under New Zealand's control), while at the same time increasing development assistance. New Zealand's first alliance with Asian nations came in 1954, when it joined the Southeast Asian Treaty Organization.

New Zealand's new international focus certainly did not mean the end of cooperation with its traditional allies, however. In fact, the common threat of the Japanese during World War II strengthened cooperation between Australia and the United States to the extent that, in 1951, New Zealand joined a three-way, regional security agreement known as ANZUS (for Australia, New Zealand, and the United States). Moreover, because the United States was, at war's end, a Pacific/Asian power, any agreement with the United States was likely to bring New Zealand into more, rather than less, contact with Asia and the Pacific. Indeed, New Zealand sent troops to assist in all of the United States' military involvements in Asia: the occupation of Japan in 1945, the Korean War in 1950, and the Vietnam War in the 1960s. And, as a member of the British Commonwealth, it sent troops in the 1950s and 1960s to fight Malaysian Communists and Indonesian insurgents.

## A NEW INTERNATIONALISM
Beginning in the 1970s, especially when the Labour Party of Prime Minister Norman Kirk was in power, New Zealand's orientation shifted even more markedly toward its own region. Under Labour, New Zealand defined its sphere of interest and responsibility as the Pacific, where it hoped to be seen as a protector and benefactor of smaller states. Of immediate concern to many island nations was the issue of nuclear testing in the Pacific. Both the United States and France had undertaken tests by exploding nuclear devices on tiny Pacific atolls. In the 1960s, the United States ceased these tests, but France continued. On behalf of the smaller islands, New Zealand argued before the United Nations against testing, but France still did not stop. Eventually, the desire to end test-

ing congealed into the more comprehensive position that the entire Pacific should be declared a nuclear-free zone. Not only testing but also the transport of nuclear weapons through the area would be prohibited under the plan.

New Zealand's Labour government issued a ban on the docking of ships with nuclear weapons in New Zealand, despite the fact that such ships were a part of the ANZUS agreement. When the National Party regained control of the government in the late 1970s, the nuclear ban was revoked, and the foreign policy of New Zealand tipped again toward its traditional allies. The National government argued that, as a signatory to ANZUS, New Zealand was obligated to open its docks to U.S. nuclear ships. However, under the subsequent Labour government of Prime Minister David Lange, New Zealand once again began to flex its muscles over the nuclear issue. Lange, like his Labour Party predecessors, was determined to create a foreign policy based on moral rather than legal rationales. In 1985, a U.S. destroyer was denied permission to call at a New Zealand port, even though its presence there was due to joint ANZUS military exercises. Because the United States refused to say whether or not its ship carried nuclear weapons, New Zealand insisted that the ship could not dock. Diplomatic efforts to resolve the standoff were unsuccessful; and in 1986, New Zealand, claiming that it was not fearful of foreign attack, formally withdrew from ANZUS.

The issue of use of the Pacific for nuclear weapons testing by superpowers is still of major concern to the New Zealand government. The nuclear test ban treaty signed by the United States in 1963 has limited U.S. involvement in that regard, but France has continued to test atmospheric weapons, and both the United States and Japan have proposed using uninhabited Pacific atolls to dispose of nuclear waste. In 1995, when France ignored the condemnation of world leaders and detonated a nuclear device in French Polynesia, New Zealand recalled its ambassador to France out of protest.

In the early 1990s, a new issue came to the fore: nerve-gas disposal. With the end of the cold war, the U.S. military proposed disposing of most of its European stockpile of nerve gas on an atoll in the Pacific.

The atoll is located within the trust territory granted to the United States at the conclusion of World War II. The plan is to burn the gas away from areas of human habitation, but those islanders living closest (albeit hundreds of miles away) worry that residues from the process could contaminate the air and damage humans, plants, and animals. The religious leaders of Melanesia, Micronesia, and Polynesia have condemned the plan, not only on environmental grounds but also on grounds that outside powers should not be permitted to use the Pacific region without the consent of the inhabitants there—a position with which the Labour government of New Zealand strongly concurs.

## ECONOMIC CHALLENGES
The New Zealand government's new foreign-policy orientation has caught the attention of observers around the world, but more urgent to New Zealanders themselves is the state of their own economy. Until the 1970s, New Zealand had been able to count on a nearly guaranteed export market in Britain for its dairy and agricultural products. Moreover, cheap local energy supplies as well as inexpensive oil from the Middle East had produced several decades of steady improvement in the standard of living. Whenever the economy showed signs of being sluggish, the government would artificially protect certain industries to ensure full employment.

All of this came to a halt in 1973, when Britain joined the European Union (then called the European Economic Community) and when the Organization of Petroleum Exporting Countries sent the world into its first oil shock. New Zealand actually has the potential of near self-sufficiency in oil, but the easy availability of Middle East oil over the years has prevented the full development of local oil and gas reserves. As for exports, New Zealand had to find new outlets for its agricultural products, which it did by contracting with various countries throughout the Pacific Rim. Currently, about one third of New Zealand's trade is within the Pacific Rim. In the transition to these new markets, farmers complained that the manufacturing sector—intentionally protected by the government as a way of diversifying New Zealand's reliance on agriculture—was getting unfair favorable treatment. Sub-

Socialized
medicine is
implemented
**1941**
●

New Zealand
becomes fully
independent
within the
Commonwealth
of Nations
**1947**
●

New Zealand
backs creation of
the South Pacific
Commission
**1947**
●

Restructuring of
export markets
**1950s**
●

The National
Party takes
power; New
Zealand forges
foreign policy
more
independent of
traditional allies
**1970s**
●

The Labour Party
regains power;
New Zealand
withdraws from
ANZUS
**1980s**
●

**1990s**

New Zealanders
consider
withdrawing
from the
Commonwealth

Maoris and white
New Zealanders
face economic
challenges from
other Pacific
Rimmers

Jenny Shipley
becomes New
Zealand's first
woman prime
minister

sequent changes in government policy toward industry resulted in a new phenomenon for New Zealand: unemployment. Moreover, New Zealand had constructed a rather elaborate social-welfare system since World War II, so, regardless of whether economic growth was high or low, social-welfare checks still had to be sent. This untenable position has made for a difficult political situation, for, when the National Party cut some welfare benefits and social services, it lost the support of many voters. The welfare issue, along with a change to a mixed member proportional voting system that enhanced the influence of smaller parties, threatened the National Party's political power. Thus, in order to remain politically dominant, in 1996 the National Party was forced to form a coalition with the United Party—the first such coalition government in more than 60 years.

In the 1970s, for the first time, New Zealanders began to notice a decline in their standard of living. Two decades later, the economy is not greatly improved. New Zealand's economic growth rate is only 2.8 percent per year, as compared to more than 9 percent in Thailand and Singapore (that is, before the financial downturn of 1998–1999); and its per capita income is lower than in Hong Kong, Australia, and Japan. Its inflation rate has dropped, however, to an encouragingly low 2.8 percent.

New Zealanders are well aware of Japan's economic strength and its potential for benefiting their own economy through joint ventures, loans, and trade. Yet they also worry that Japanese wealth may constitute a symbol of New Zealand's declining strength as a culture. For instance, in the 1980s, as Japanese tourists began traveling en masse to New Zealand, complaints were raised about the quality of

New Zealand's hotels. Unable to find the funds for a massive upgrading of the hotel industry, New Zealand agreed to allow Japan to build its own hotels; it reasoned that the local construction industry could use an economic boost and that the better hotels would encourage well-heeled Japanese to spend even more tourist dollars in the country. However, they also worried that, with the Japanese owning the hotels, New Zealanders might be relegated to low-level jobs.

Concern about their status vis-à-vis nonwhites had never been much of an issue to many Anglo-Saxon New Zealanders; they always simply assumed that nonwhites were inferior. Many settlers of the 1800s believed in the Social Darwinistic philosophy that the Maori and other brown- and black-skinned peoples would gradually succumb to their European "betters." It did not take long for the Maoris to realize that, land guarantees notwithstanding, the whites intended to deprive them of their land and culture. Violent resistance to these intentions occurred in the 1800s, but Maori landholdings continued to be gobbled up, usually deceptively, by white farmers and sheep herders. Government control of these unscrupulous practices was lax until the 1920s. Since that time many Maoris (whose population has increased to about 260,000) have intentionally sought to create a lifestyle that preserves key parts of traditional culture while incorporating the skills necessary for survival in a white world.

Now, though, Maoris and whites alike feel the social leveling that is the consequence of years of economic stagnation. Moreover, both worry that the superior financial strength of the Japanese and newly industrializing Asian and Southeast Asian peoples may diminish in some

way the standing of their own cultures. The Maoris, complaining recently about Japanese net fishing and its damage to their own fishing industry, have a history of accommodation and adjustment to those who would rule over them; but for the whites, submissiveness, even if it is imposed from afar and is largely financial in nature, will be a new and challenging experience.

## DEVELOPMENT
Government protection of manufacturing has allowed this sector to grow at the expense of agriculture. Nevertheless, New Zealand continues to export large quantities of dairy products, wool, meat, fruits, and wheat. Full development of the oil and gas deposits could alleviate New Zealand's dependence on foreign oil.

## FREEDOM
New Zealand partakes of the democratic heritage of English common law and subscribes to all the human-rights protections that other Western nations have endorsed. Maoris, originally deprived of much of their land, are now guaranteed the same legal rights as whites. Social discrimination against Maoris is much milder than with many other colonized peoples.

## HEALTH/WELFARE

New Zealand established pensions for the elderly as early as 1898. Child-welfare programs were started in 1907, followed by the Social Security Act of 1938, which augmented the earlier benefits and added a minimum-wage requirement and a 40-hour work week. A national health program was begun in 1941. The government began dispensing free birth-control pills to all women in 1996 in an attempt to reduce the number of abortions.

## ACHIEVEMENTS

New Zealand is notable for its efforts on behalf of the smaller islands of the Pacific. In addition to advocating a nuclear-free Pacific, New Zealand has promoted interisland trade and has established free-trade agreements with Western Samoa, the Cook Islands, and Niue. It provides educational and employment opportunities to Pacific islanders who reside within its borders.

# North Korea (Democratic People's Republic of Korea)*

## GEOGRAPHY

*Area in Square Miles (Kilometers):* 44,358 (120,540) (slightly smaller than Mississippi)

*Capital (Population):* P'yongyang (2,400,000)

*Environmental Concerns:* air and water pollution; insufficient potable water

*Geographical Features:* mostly hills and mountains separated by deep, narrow valleys; coastal plains

*Climate:* temperate

## PEOPLE

### Population

*Total:* 24,317,000

*Annual Growth Rate:* 1.68%

*Rural/Urban Population (Ratio):* 38/62

*Major Language:* Korean

*Ethnic Makeup:* homogeneous Korean

*Religions:* Buddhism and Confucianism (autonomous religious activities now almost nonexistent)

### Health

*Life Expectancy at Birth:* 67 years (male); 74 years (female)

*Infant Mortality Rate (Ratio):* 25/1,000

*Physicians Available (Ratio):* 1/370

### Education

*Adult Literacy Rate:* 99%

*Compulsory (Ages):* 6–17; free

## COMMUNICATION

*Telephones:* 1 per 22 people

*Daily Newspaper Circulation:* 213 per 1,000 people

*Televisions:* 1 per 23 people

## TRANSPORTATION

*Highways in Miles (Kilometers):* 15,000 (24,000)

*Railroads in Miles (Kilometers):* 3,000 (4,800)

*Usable Airfields:* 49

## GOVERNMENT

*Type:* Communist state

*Independence Date:* September 9, 1948

*Head of State/Government:* President Kim Jong Il; Acting Premier Hong Song-nam

*Political Parties:* Korean Workers' Party; Korean Social Democratic Party; Chondoist Chongu Party

*Suffrage:* universal at 17

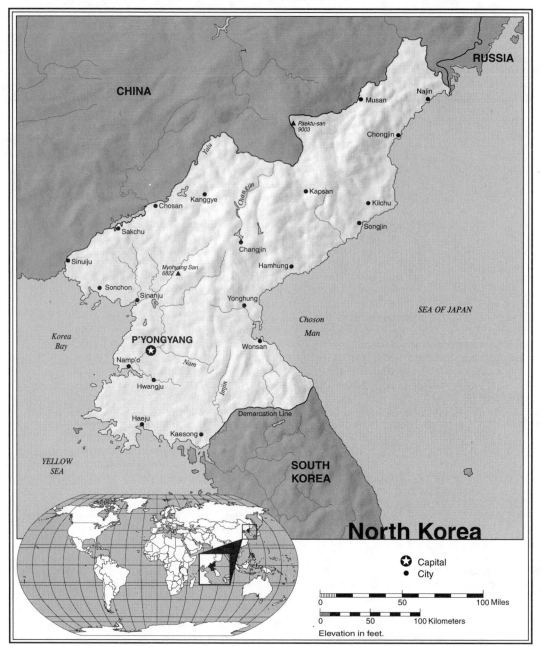

North Korea

Capital
City

Elevation in feet.

## MILITARY

*Military Expenditures (% of GDP):* 25%

*Current Disputes:* Demarcation Line with South Korea; unclear border with China

## ECONOMY

*Currency ($ U.S. Equivalent):* 2.15 wons = $1

*Per Capita Income/GDP:* $900/$20.9 billion

*GDP Growth Rate:* –5%

*Labor Force:* 9,615,000

*Natural Resources:* hydropower; iron ore; copper; lead; salt; zinc; coal; magnesite; gold; tungsten; graphite; pyrites; fluorspar

*Agriculture:* rice; corn; potatoes; soybeans; pulses; livestock and livestock products

*Industry:* machinery; military products; electric power; chemicals; mining; metallurgy; textiles; food processing

*Exports:* $805 million (primary partners China, Japan, South Korea)

*Imports:* $1.24 billion (primary partners China, Japan, Hong Kong)

*Note: Statistics for North Korea are generally estimated due to unreliable information.

 http://www.fe.doe.gov/international/nkorea.html

## A COUNTRY APART

The area that we now call North Korea has, at different times in Korea's long history, been separated from the South. In the fifth century A.D., the Koguryo Kingdom in the North was distinct from the Shilla, Paekche, and Kaya Kingdoms of the South. Later, the Parhae Kingdom in the North remained separate from the expanded Shilla Kingdom in the South. Thus, the division of Korea in 1945 into two unequal parts was not without precedent. Yet this time, the very different paths of development that the North and South chose rendered the division more poignant and, to those separated with little hope of reunion, more emotionally painful.

Beginning in 1945, Kim Il-Song, with the strong backing of the Soviet Union, pursued a hard-line Communist policy for both the political and economic development of North Korea. The Soviet Union's involvement on the Korean Peninsula arose from its opportunistic entry into the war against Japan, just 8 days before Japan's surrender. Thus, when Japan withdrew from its long colonial rule over Korea, the Soviets were in a position to be one of the occupying armies. Reluctantly, the United States allowed the Soviet Union to move troops into position above the 38th Parallel, a temporary dividing line for the respective occupying forces. It was the Soviet Union's intention to establish a Communist buffer state between itself and the capitalist West. Therefore, it moved quickly to establish the area north of the 38th Parallel as a separate political entity. The northern city of P'yongyang was established as the capital.

When United Nations representatives arrived in 1948 to oversee elections and ease the transition from military occupation and years of Japanese rule to an independent Korea, the Soviets would not cooperate. Kim Il-Song took over the reins of power in the North. Separate elections were held in the South, and the beginning of separate political systems got underway. The 38th Parallel came to represent not only the division of the Korean Peninsula but also the boundary between the worlds of capitalism and communism.

## THE KOREAN WAR (1950–1953)

Although not pleased with the idea of division, the South, without a strong army, resigned itself to the reality of the moment. In the North, a well-trained military, with Soviet and Chinese help, began preparations for a full-scale invasion of the South. The North attacked in June 1950, a year after U.S. troops had vacated the South, and quickly overran most of the Korean Peninsula. The South Korean gov-

ernment requested help from the United Nations, which dispatched personnel from 19 nations, under the command of U.S. general Douglas MacArthur. (A U.S. intervention was ordered on June 27 by President Harry Truman.)

MacArthur's troops advanced against the North's armies and by October were in control of most of the peninsula. However, with massive Chinese help, the North once again moved south. In response, UN troops decided to inflict heavy destruction on the North through the use of jet fighter/bomber planes. Whereas South Korea was primarily agricultural, North Korea was the industrialized sector of the peninsula. Bombing of the North's industrial targets severely damaged the economy, forcing several million North Koreans to flee south to escape both the war and the Communist dictatorship under which they found themselves.

Eventually, the UN troops recaptured South Korea's capital, Seoul. Realizing that further fighting would lead to an expanded Asian war, the two sides agreed to cease-fire talks. They signed a truce in 1953 that established a 2.5-mile-wide demilitarized zone (DMZ) for 155 miles across the peninsula and more or less along the former 38th Parallel division. The Korean War took the lives of more than 54,000 American soldiers, 58,000

South Koreans, and 500,000 North Koreans—but when it was over, both sides occupied about the same territory as they had at the beginning. Yet, because neither side has ever declared peace, the two countries remain officially in a state of war.

Peace talks proposed in 1996 gave reason for hope that normalization of relations would follow. Yet the border between North and South remains one of the most volatile in Asia. The North staged military exercises along the border in 1996 and, breaking the cease-fire truce of 1953, fired shots into the DMZ. The South responded by raising its intelligence-monitoring activities to their highest level in years and requesting U.S. AWACS surveillance planes to monitor military movements in the North.

Scholars are still debating whether the Korean War should be called the United States' first losing war and whether or not the bloodshed was really necessary. To understand the Korean War, one must remember that, in the eyes of the world, it was more than a civil war among different kinds of Koreans. The United Nations, and particularly the United States, saw North Korea's aggression against the South as the first step in the eventual communization of the whole of Asia. Just a few months before North Korea attacked, China had fallen to the Communist forces

(UPI/Bettmann photo by Norman Williams)

Pictured above are U.S. Marines with North Koreans captured during the Korean War.

of Mao Zedong, and Communist guerrilla activity was being reported throughout Southeast Asia. The "Red Scare" frightened many Americans, and witchhunting for suspected Communist sympathizers—a college professor who might have taught about Karl Marx in class or a news reporter who might have praised the educational reforms of a Communist country—became the everyday preoccupation of such groups as the John Birch Society and the supporters of U.S. senator Joseph McCarthy.

In this highly charged atmosphere, it was relatively easy for the U.S. military to promote a war whose aim it was to contain communism. Containment rather than defeat of the enemy was the policy of choice, because the West was weary after battling Germany and Japan in World War II. The containment policy also underlay the United States' approach to Vietnam. Practical though it may have been, this policy denied Americans the opportunity of feeling satisfied in victory, since there was to be no victory, just a stalemate. Thus, the roots of the United States' dissatisfaction with the conduct of the Vietnam War actually began in the policies shaping the response to North Korea's offensive in 1950. North Korea was indeed contained, but the communizing impulse of the North remained.

## COLLECTIVE CULTURE

With Soviet backing, North Korean leaders moved quickly to repair war damage and establish a Communist culture. The school curriculum was rewritten to emphasize nationalism and equality of the social classes. Traditional Korean culture, based on Confucianism, had stressed strict class divisions, but the Communist authorities refused to allow any one class to claim privileges over another (although eventually the families of party leaders came to constitute a new elite). Higher education at the more than 600 colleges and training schools was redirected to technical rather than analytical subjects. Industries were nationalized; farms were collectivized into some 3,000 communes; and the communes were invested with much of the judicial and executive powers that other countries grant to cities, counties, and states. To overcome labor shortages, nearly all women were brought into the workforce, and the economy slowly returned to prewar levels.

Today, many young people bypass formal higher education in favor of service in the military. Although North Korea has not published economic statistics for nearly 30 years, it is estimated that military expenses consume about 25 percent of the entire national budget—this despite near-starvation conditions in many parts of the country.

With China and the former Communist-bloc nations constituting natural markets for North Korean products, and with substantial financial aid from both China and the former Soviet Union in the early years, North Korea was able to regain much of its former economic, and especially industrial, strength. Today, North Korea successfully mines iron and other minerals and exports such products as cement and cereals. China has remained North Korea's only reliable ally; trade between the two countries is substantial. In one Chinese province, more than two thirds of the people are ethnic Koreans, most of whom take the side of the North in any dispute with the South.

Tensions with the South have remained high since the war. Sporadic violence along the border has left patrolling soldiers dead, and the assassination of former South Korean president Park Chung Hee and attempts on the lives of other members of the South Korean government have been attributed to North Korea, as was the bombing of a Korean Airlines flight in 1987. Both sides have periodically accused each other of attempted sabotage. In 1996, North Korea tried to send spies to the South via a small submarine; the attempt failed, and most of the spies were killed.

The North, seeing in the growing demand for free speech in the South a chance to further its aim of communizing the peninsula, has been angered by the brutal suppression of dissidents by the South Korean authorities. Although the North's argument is bitterly ironic, given its own brutal suppression of human rights, it is nonetheless accurate in its view that the government in the South has been blatantly dictatorial. To suppress opponents, the South Korean government has, among other things, abducted its own students from Europe, abducted opposition leader Kim Dae Jung from Japan, tortured dissidents, and violently silenced demonstrators. All of this is said to be necessary because of the need for unity in the face of the threat from the North; as pointed out by scholar Gavan McCormack, the South seems to use the North's threat as an excuse for maintaining a rigid dictatorial system.

Under these circumstances, it is not surprising that the formal reunification talks, begun in 1971 with much fanfare, have just recently started to bear fruit. Visits of residents separated by the war were approved in 1985—the first time in 40 years that an opening of the border had even been considered—but real progress came in late 1991, when North Korean premier Yon Hyong Muk and South Korean premier Chung Won Shik signed a nonaggression and reconciliation pact, whose goal was the eventual declaration of a formal peace treaty between the two governments. In 1992, the governments established air, sea, and land links and set up mechanisms for scientific and environmental cooperation. North Korea also signed the nuclear nonproliferation agreement with the International Atomic Energy Agency. This move placated growing concerns about North Korea's rumored development of nuclear weapons and opened the way for investment by such countries as Japan, which had refused to invest until they received assurances on the nuclear question. In 1990, in what many saw as an overture to the United States, North Korea returned the remains of five American soldiers killed during the Korean War.

## THE NUCLEAR ISSUE FLARES UP

The goodwill deteriorated quickly in 1993 and 1994, when North Korea refused to allow inspectors from the International Atomic Energy Agency (IAEA) to inspect its nuclear facilities, raising fears in the United States, Japan, and South Korea that the North was developing a nuclear bomb. When pressured to allow inspections, the North responded by threatening to withdraw from the IAEA and expel the inspectors. Tensions mounted, with all parties engaging in military threats and posturing and the United States, South Korea, and Japan (whose shores could be reached in minutes by the North's new ballistic missiles) threatening economic sanctions. Troops in both Koreas were put on high alert. Former U.S. president Jimmy Carter helped to defuse the issue by making a private goodwill visit to Kim Il-Song in P'yongyang, the unexpected result of which was a promise by the North to hold a first-ever summit meeting with the South. Then, in a near-theatrical turn of events, Kim Il-Song, at 5 decades the longest national office-holder in the world, died, apparently of natural causes. The summit was canceled and international diplomacy was frozen while the North Korean government mourned the loss of its "Great Leader" and informally selected a new one, "Dear Leader" Kim Jong Il, Kim Il-Song's son. Eventually, the North agreed to resume talks, a move interpreted as evidence that, for all its bravado, the North wanted to establish closer ties with the West. In 1994, North Korea agreed to a freeze on nuclear power-plant development as long as the United States would

| Kim Il-Song comes to power **1945** | The People's Democratic Republic of Korea is created **1948** | The Korean War begins **1950** | A truce is arranged between North Korea and UN troops **1953** | A U.S. spy boat, the *Pueblo*, is seized by North Korea **1968** | A U.S. spy plane is shot down over North Korea **1969** | Reunification talks begin **1971** |
|---|---|---|---|---|---|---|

**1990s**

| A nonaggression pact is signed with the South; North and South are granted seats in the UN | Fears of North Korea's nuclear-weapons capacity surge | Kim Il-Song dies and is succeeded by his son, Kim Jong Il; talks with South Korea fail in 1998; food shortages hit the country |
|---|---|---|

supply fuel oil; and in 1996, it agreed to open its airspace to all airlines. Unfortunately, tensions increased when North Korea launched a missile over Japan in 1998 and promised more in 1999.

## THE CHANGING INTERNATIONAL LANDSCAPE

North Korea has good reason to promote better relations with the West, because the world of the 1990s is not the world of the 1950s. In 1989, for instance, several former Soviet-bloc countries cut into the North's economic monopoly by welcoming trade initiatives from South Korea; some even established diplomatic relations. At the same time, the disintegration of the Soviet Union meant that North Korea lost its primary political and military ally. Perhaps most alarming to the North is its declining economy; it has suffered a negative growth for several years. Severe flooding in 1995 destroyed much of the rice harvest and forced the North to do the unthinkable: accept rice donations from the South. More than 100 North Koreans have defected to the South in the past several years, all of them complaining of near-famine conditions. With the South's economy consistently booming and the example of the failed economies of Central/Eastern Europe as a danger signal, the North appears to understand that it must break out of its decades of isolation or lose its ability to govern. Nevertheless, it is not likely that North Koreans will quickly retreat from the Communist model of development that they have espoused for so long.

Kim Il-Song, who controlled North Korea for nearly 50 years, promoted the development of heavy industries, the collectivization of agriculture, and strong linkages with the then–Communist bloc. Governing with an iron hand, Kim denied basic civil rights to his people and forbade any tendency of the people to dress or behave like the "decadent" West. He kept tensions high by asserting his intention of communizing the South. His son, Kim Jong Il, who had headed the North Korean military but was barely known outside his country, was eventually named successor to his father—the first dynastic power transfer in the Communist world. How the younger Kim will influence the direction of North Korea is still unclear, but the somewhat more liberal authorities at his side know that the recent diplomatic initiatives of the South require a response. The North Korean government hopes that recent actions will bring it some badly needed international goodwill. But more than good public relations will be needed if North Korea is to prosper in the new, post–cold war climate in which it can no longer rely on the generosity or moral support of the Soviet bloc. When communism was introduced in North Korea in 1945, the government nationalized major companies and steered economic development toward heavy industry. In contrast, the South concentrated on heavy industry to balance its agricultural sector until the late 1970s but then geared the economy toward meeting consumer demand. Thus, the standard of living in the North for the average resident remains far behind that of the South. Indeed, Red Cross, United Nations, and other observers have documented widespread malnutrition and starvation in North Korea, conditions that are likely to continue well into the twenty-first century unless the North dramatically alters its current economic policies. Conditions are so bad in some areas that there is no electricity nor chlorine to run water-treatment plants, resulting in contaminated water supplies for about 60 percent of the population.

## RECENT TRENDS

There is evidence that some liberalization is taking place within North Korea. In 1988, the government drafted a law that allowed foreign companies to establish joint ventures inside North Korea. Tourism is also being promoted as a way of earning foreign currency, and the government recently permitted two small Christian churches to be established. Nevertheless, years of a totally controlled economy in the North and shifting international alliances indicate many difficult years ahead for North Korea. Moreover, the bad blood between North and South would suggest only the slowest possible reconciliation of the world's most troubled peninsula. Talks that had been stalled for 4 years resumed in 1998, only to end quickly in disagreement and disappointment.

Although political reunification seems to be years away, social changes are becoming evident everywhere as a new generation, unfamiliar with war, comes to adulthood, and as North Koreans are being exposed to outside sources of news and ideas. Many North Koreans now own radios that receive signals from other countries. South Korean stations are now heard in the North, as are news programs from the Voice of America. Modern North Korean history, however, is one of repression and control, first by the Japanese and then by the Kim government, who used the same police surveillance apparatus as did the Japanese during their occupation of the Korean Peninsula. It is not likely, therefore, that a massive push for democracy will be forthcoming soon from a people long accustomed to dictatorship.

## DEVELOPMENT

Already more industrialized than South Korea at the time of the Korean War, North Korea built on this foundation with massive assistance from China and the Soviet Union. Heavy industry was emphasized to the detriment of consumer goods. Economic isolation presages more negative growth ahead.

## FREEDOM

The mainline Communist approach has meant that the human rights commonplace in the West have never been enjoyed by North Koreans. Through suppression of dissidents, a controlled press, and restrictions on travel, the regime has kept North Koreans isolated from the world.

## HEALTH/WELFARE

Under the Kim Il-Song government, illiteracy was greatly reduced. Government housing is available at low cost, but shoppers are often confronted with empty shelves and low-quality goods. Malnutrition is widespread, and mass starvation has been reported in some regions.

## ACHIEVEMENTS

North Korea has developed its resources of aluminum, cement, and iron into solid industries for the production of tools and machinery while developing military superiority over South Korea, despite a population numbering less than half that of South Korea.

# Papua New Guinea (Independent State of Papua New Guinea)

## GEOGRAPHY

*Area in Square Miles (Kilometers):* 178,612 (461,690) (slightly larger than California)

*Capital (Population):* Port Moresby (192,000)

*Environmental Concerns:* deforestation; pollution from mining projects

*Geographical Features:* mostly mountains with coastal lowlands and rolling foothills

*Climate:* tropical; monsoonal

## PEOPLE

### Population

*Total:* 4,496,200

*Annual Growth Rate:* 2.3%

*Rural/Urban Population Ratio:* 85/15

*Major Languages:* English; New Guinea Pidgin; Motu; 715 indigenous languages

*Ethnic Makeup:* predominantly Melanesian and Papuan; some Negrito, Micronesian, and Polynesian

*Religions:* 66% Christian; 34% indigenous beliefs

### Health

*Life Expectancy at Birth:* 57 years (male); 59 years (female)

*Infant Mortality Rate (Ratio):* 58.6/1,000

*Physicians Available (Ratio):* 1/5,584

### Education

*Adult Literacy Rate:* 72%

## COMMUNICATION

*Telephones:* 1 per 99 people

*Daily Newspaper Circulation:* 15 per 1,000 people

*Televisions:* 1 per 345 people

## TRANSPORTATION

*Highways in Miles (Kilometers):* 11,904 (19,200)

*Railroads in Miles (Kilometers):* none

*Usable Airfields:* 451

*Motor Vehicles in Use:* 55,000

## GOVERNMENT

*Type:* parliamentary democracy

*Independence Date:* September 16, 1975

*Head of State/Government:* Queen Elizabeth II; Prime Minister Bill Skate

*Political Parties:* Pangu Party; People's Democratic Movement; People's Action Party; People's Progress Party; United Party; Papua Party; National Party; Melanesian Alliance; others

*Suffrage:* universal at 18

## MILITARY

*Current Disputes:* civil strife

## ECONOMY

*Currency ($ U.S. Equivalent):* 0.745 kina = $1

*Per Capita Income/GDP:* $2,400/$10.7 billion

*GDP Growth Rate:* 2.3%

*Inflation Rate:* 6%

*Labor Force:* 1,941,000

*Natural Resources:* gold; copper; silver; natural gas; timber; oil; fisheries

*Agriculture:* coffee; cocoa; coconuts; palm kernels; tea; rubber; sweet potatoes; fruit; vegetables; poultry; pork

*Industry:* copra crushing; palm oil processing; wood processing and production; mining; construction; tourism

*Exports:* $2.7 billion (primary partners Australia, Japan, United States)

*Imports:* $1.3 billion (primary partners Australia, Japan, United Kingdom)

 http://ww3.datec.com.pg/png/

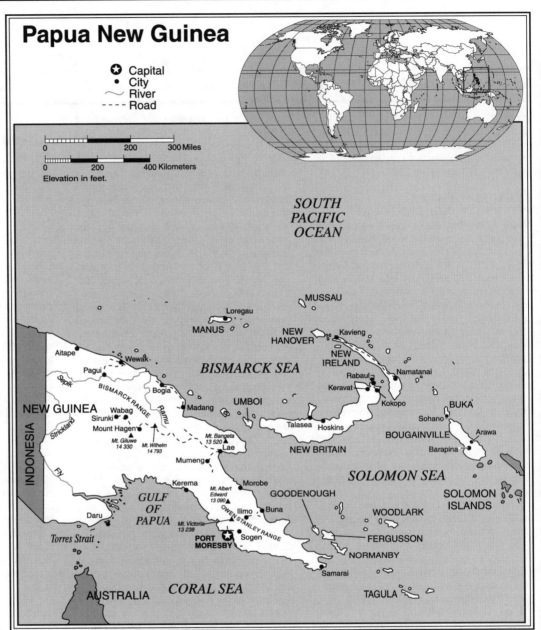

### Papua New Guinea

- ★ Capital
- • City
- ～ River
- --- Road

Elevation in feet.

0 — 200 — 300 Miles
0 — 200 — 400 Kilometers

SOUTH PACIFIC OCEAN

MUSSAU

MANUS
Loregau

NEW HANOVER
Kavieng

NEW IRELAND
Rabaul
Keravat
Namatanai
Kokopo

BUKA
Sohano

BOUGAINVILLE
Arawa
Barapina

INDONESIA

NEW GUINEA

Aitape
Wewak
Pagui
Sepik

BISMARCK RANGE
Bogia
Madang
BISMARCK SEA

UMBOI
Talasea
Hoskins

NEW BRITAIN

SOLOMON SEA

SOLOMON ISLANDS

Wabag
Sirunki
Mount Hagen
Mt. Giluwe 14 330
Mt. Wilhelm 14 793
Ramu
Mt. Bangeta 13 520
Lae

Strickland
Fly

Mumeng
Kerema
Mt. Albert Edward 13 090
Morobe
Buna
Ilimo

GOODENOUGH

WOODLARK

FERGUSSON

GULF OF PAPUA
Daru

OWEN STANLEY RANGE
Mt. Victoria 13 238
PORT MORESBY
Sogen

NORMANBY

Torres Strait

Samarai

TAGULA

AUSTRALIA
CORAL SEA

## TERRA INCOGNITA

Papua New Guinea is an independent nation and a member of the British Commonwealth. Occupying the eastern half of New Guinea (the second-largest island in the world) and many outlying islands, Papua New Guinea is probably the most overlooked of all the nations in the Pacific Rim.

It was not always overlooked, however. Spain claimed the vast land in the mid-sixteenth century, followed by Britain's East India Company in 1793. The Netherlands laid claim to part of the island in the 1800s and eventually came to control the western half (now known as Irian Jaya, a province of the Republic of Indonesia). In the 1880s, German settlers occupied the northeastern part of the island; and in 1884, Britain signed a treaty with Germany, which gave it about half of what is now Papua New Guinea. In 1906, Britain gave its part of the island to Australia. Australia invaded and quickly captured the German area in 1914. Eventually, the League of Nations and, later, the United Nations gave the captured area to Australia to administer as a trust territory.

During World War II, the northern part of New Guinea was the scene of bitter fighting between a large Japanese force and Australian and U.S. troops. The Japanese had apparently intended to use New Guinea as a base for the military conquest of Australia. Australia resumed control of the eastern half of the island after Japan's defeat, and it con-

(Photo credit UN/Witlin)

The interior of Papua New Guinea is geographically very difficult to access. The valuable minerals and exotic timber have caused a push for the development of transportation services. The island has 451 airstrips, some in very isolated areas, along with an increasing development of a road network. The impact on the environment is of great concern.

| The main island is sighted by Portuguese explorers A.D. 1511 | The Dutch annex the west half of the island 1828 | A British protectorate over part of the eastern half of the island; the Germans control the northeast 1884 | Gold is discovered in Papua New Guinea 1890 | Australia assumes control of the British part of the island 1906 | Australia invades and captures the German-held areas 1914 | Australia is given the former German areas as a trust territory 1920 | Japan captures the northern part of the island; Australia resumes control in 1945 1940s | Australia grants independence to Papua New Guinea 1975 | A revolt against the government begins on the island of Bougainville 1988 |
|---|---|---|---|---|---|---|---|---|---|

1990s

An economic blockade of Bougainville is lifted, but violence continues, claiming 3,000 lives

600 army soldiers storm Parliament, demanding higher pay; Prime Minister Julius Chan is forced to step down; he is eventually succeeded by Bill Skate

Thousands are killed, many more made homeless due to massive tidal waves resulting from offshore earthquakes

tinued to administer Papua New Guinea's affairs until 1975, when it granted independence. The capital is Port Moresby, where, in addition to English, the Motu language and a hybrid language known as New Guinea Pidgin are spoken.

## STONE-AGE PEOPLES MEET THE TWENTIETH CENTURY

Early Western explorers found the island's resources difficult to reach. The coastline and some of the interior are swampy and mosquito- and tick-infested, while the high, snow-capped mountainous regions are densely forested and hard to traverse. But perhaps most daunting to early would-be settlers and traders were the local inhabitants. Consisting of hundreds of sometimes warring tribes with totally different languages and customs, the New Guinea populace was determined to prevent outsiders from settling the island. Many adventurers were killed, their heads displayed in villages as victory trophies. The origins of the Papuan people are unknown, but some tribes share common practices with Melanesian islanders. Others appear to be Negritos, and some may be related to the Australian Aborigines. More than 700 languages, often mutually unintelligible, are spoken in Papua New Guinea.

Australians and other Europeans found it beneficial to engage in trade with coastal tribes who supplied them with unique tropical lumbers, such as sandalwood and bamboo, and foodstuffs such as sugarcane, coconut, and nutmeg. Rubber and tobacco were also traded. Tea, which grows well in the highland regions, is an important cash crop.

But the resource that was most important for the economic development of Papua New Guinea was gold. It was discovered there in 1890; two major gold

rushes occurred, in 1896 and 1926. Prospectors came mostly from Australia and were hated by the local tribes; some prospectors were killed and cannibalized. A large number of airstrips in the otherwise undeveloped interior eventually were built by miners who needed a safe and efficient way to receive supplies. Today, copper is more important than gold—copper is, in fact, the largest single earner of export income for Papua New Guinea.

Meanwhile, pollution from mining is increasingly of concern to environmentalists, as is deforestation of Papua New Guinea's spectacular rain forests. A diplomatic flap between Papua New Guinea and Australia occurred in 1992, when Australian environmentalists complained about the environmental damage that a copper and gold mine in Papua New Guinea was causing. They called for its closure. The Papuan government strongly resented the verbal intrusion into its sovereignty and reminded conservationists and the Australian government that it alone would establish environmental standards for companies operating inside its borders. The Papuan government holds a 20 percent interest in the mining company.

The tropical climate that predominates in all areas except the highest mountain peaks produces an impressive variety of plant and animal life. Botanists and other naturalists have been attracted to the island for scientific study for many years. Despite extensive contacts with these and other outsiders over the past century, and despite the establishment of schools and a university by the Australian government, some inland mountain tribes continue to live much as they probably did in the Stone Age. Thus, the country lures not only miners and naturalists but also anthropologists and archaelogists looking for clues to humankind's early lifestyles. One

of the most famous of these was Bronislaw Malinowski, the Polish-born founder of the field of social anthropology. In the early 1900s, he spent several years studying the cultural practices of the tribes of Papua New Guinea, particularly those of the Trobriand Islands.

Most of the 4.5 million Papuans live by subsistence farming. Agriculture for commercial trade is limited by the absence of a good transportation network: Most roads are unpaved, and there is no railway system. Travel on tiny aircraft and helicopters is common, however; New Guinea boasts 451 airstrips, most of them unpaved and dangerously situated in mountain valleys. The harsh conditions of New Guinea life have produced some unique ironies. For instance, Papuans who have never ridden in a car or truck may have flown in a plane dozens of times. In 1998, 23-foot-high tidal waves caused by offshore, undersea earthquakes inundated dozens of villages along the coast and drowned between 3,000 and 6,000 inhabitants.

Given the differences in socialization of the Papuan peoples and the difficult conditions of life on their island, it will likely be many decades before Papua New Guinea, which joined the Asia-Pacific Economic Cooperation group in 1993, is able to participate fully in the Pacific Rim community.

## DEVELOPMENT

Agriculture (especially coffee and copra) is the mainstay of Papua New Guinea's economy. Copper, gold, and silver mining are also important, but large-scale development of other industries is inhibited by rough terrain, illiteracy, and a huge array of spoken languages—more than 700. There are substantial reserves of untapped oil.

## FREEDOM

Papua New Guinea is a member of the British Commonwealth and officially follows the English heritage of law. However, in the country's numerous, isolated small villages, effective control is wielded by village elites with personal charisma; tribal customs take precedence over national law—of which many inhabitants are virtually unaware.

## HEALTH/WELFARE

Even as the new millennium approaches, three quarters of Papua New Guinea's population have no formal education. Daily nutritional intake falls far short of recommended minimums, and tuberculosis and malaria are common diseases.

## ACHIEVEMENTS

Papua New Guinea, lying just below the equator, is world-famous for its varied and beautiful flora and fauna, including orchids, birds of paradise, butterflies, and parrots. Dense forests cover 70 percent of the country. Some regions receive as much as 350 inches of rain a year.

# Philippines (Republic of the Philippines)

## GEOGRAPHY

*Area in Square Miles (Kilometers):* 110,400 (300,000) (slightly larger than Arizona)

*Capital (Population):* Manila (8,594,200)

*Environmental Concerns:* deforestation; air and water pollution; soil erosion; pollution of mangrove swamps

*Geographical Features:* mostly mountainous; coastal lowlands

*Climate:* tropical marine; monsoonal

## PEOPLE

### Population

*Total:* 76,104,000

*Annual Growth Rate:* 2.13%

*Rural/Urban Population Ratio:* 45/55

*Major Languages:* Pilipino (based on Tagalog); English

*Ethnic Makeup:* 95% Malay; 5% Chinese and others

*Religions:* 83% Roman Catholic; 9% Protestant; 5% Muslim; 3% Buddhist and others

### Health

*Life Expectancy at Birth:* 63 years (male); 69 years (female)

*Infant Mortality Rate (Ratio):* 35.2/1,000

*Average Caloric Intake:* 92% of FAO minimum

*Physicians Available (Ratio):* 1/849

### Education

*Adult Literacy Rate:* 95%

*Compusory (Ages):* 7–12; free

## COMMUNICATION

*Telephones:* 1 per 48 people

*Daily Newspaper Circulation:* 65 per 1,000 people

*Televisions:* 1 per 2.1 people

## TRANSPORTATION

*Highways in Miles (Kilometers):* 109,200 (182,000)

*Railroads in Miles (Kilometers):* 499 (800)

*Usable Airfields:* 234

*Motor Vehicles in Use:* 780,000

## GOVERNMENT

*Type:* republic

*Independence Date:* July 4, 1946

*Head of State/Government:* President Joseph Estrada is both head of state and head of government

*Political Parties:* Democratic Filipino Struggle; Nationalista Party; Liberal Party; others

*Suffrage:* universal at 18

## MILITARY

*Military Expenditures (% of GDP):* 0.7%

*Current Disputes:* territorial disputes with China, Malaysia, Taiwan, and Vietnam

## ECONOMY

*Currency ($ U.S. Equivalent):* 38.2 Philippine pesos = $1

*Per Capita Income/GDP:* $2,600/$194.2 billion

*GDP Growth Rate:* 1%

*Inflation Rate:* 8.4%

*Unemployment Rate:* 8.6%

*Labor Force:* 29,130,000

*Natural Resources:* timber; crude oil; nickel; cobalt; silver; gold; salt; copper

*Agriculture:* rice; coconuts; corn; sugarcane; bananas; pineapple; mangoes; animal products; fish

*Industry:* food processing; chemicals; textiles; pharmaceuticals; wood products; electronics assembly; petroleum refining; fishing

*Exports:* $20.5 billion (primary partners United States, Japan, and Singapore, Hong Kong, and United Kingdom)

*Imports:* $33.3 billion (primary partners Japan, United States, Saudi Arabia)

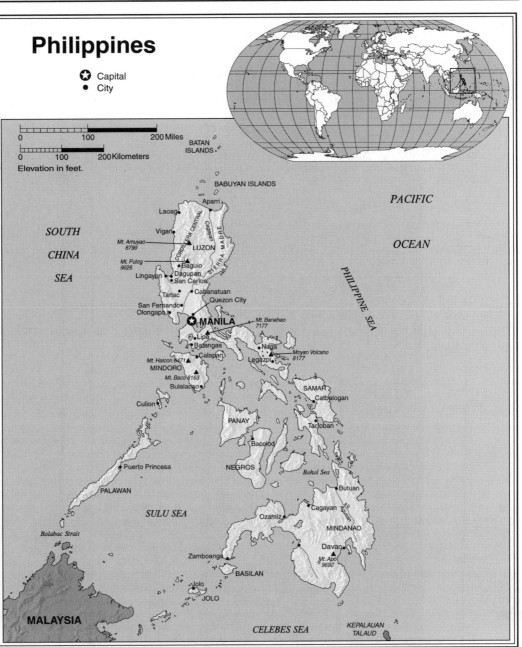

Philippines

- ★ Capital
- ● City

## THIS IS ASIA?

The Philippines is a land with close historic ties to the West. Eighty-three percent of Filipinos, as the people of the Philippines are known, are Roman Catholics, and most speak at least some English. Many use English daily in business and government. In fact, English is the language of instruction at school. Moreover, when they discuss their history as a nation, Filipinos will mention Spain, Mexico, the Spanish-American War, the United States, and cooperative Filipino–American attempts to defeat the Japanese in World War II. The country was even named after a European, King Philip II of Spain. (Currently, 4.4 percent of the United States' foreign-born population, second only to Mexico, are from the Philippines.) If this does not sound like a typical Asian nation, it is because Philippine nationhood essentially began with the arrival of Westerners. That influence continues to dominate the political and cultural life of the country.

Yet the history of the region certainly did not begin with European contact; indeed, there is evidence of human habitation in the area as early as 25,000 B.C. Beginning about 2,000 B.C., Austronesians, Negritos, Malays, and other tribal peoples settled many of the 7,107 islands that constitute the present-day Philippines. Although engaged to varying degrees in trade with China and Southeast Asia, each of these ethnic groups (nearly 60 distinct groups still exist) lived in relative isolation from one another, speaking different languages, adhering to different religions, and, for good or ill, knowing nothing of the concept of national identity.

Although 5 million ethnic peoples remain margined from the mainstream, for most islanders the world changed forever in the mid-1500s, when soldiers and Roman Catholic priests from Spain began conquering and converting the population. Eventually, the disparate ethnic groups came to see themselves as one entity, Filipinos, a people whose lives were controlled indirectly by Spain from Mexico—a fact that, unique among Asian countries, linked the Philippines with the Americas. Thus, the process of national-identity formation for Filipinos actually began in Europe.

Some ethnic groups assimilated rather quickly, marrying Spanish soldiers and administrators and acquiring the language and cultural outlook of the West. The descendants of these mestizos (mixed peoples, including local/Chinese mixes) have become the cultural, economic, and political elite of the country. Others, particularly among the Islamic communities on the Philippine island of Mindanao, resisted assimilation right from the start and continue to challenge the authority of Manila. Indeed, the Communist insurgency, reported so often in the news and the focus of attention of former presidents Ferdinand Marcos and Corazon Aquino, is in part an attempt by marginated ethnics and others to regain the cultural independence that their peoples lost some 400 years ago.

As in other Asian countries, the Chinese community has played an important but controversial role in Philippine life. Dominating trade for centuries, the Philippine Chinese have acquired clout (and enemies) that far exceeds their numbers (fewer than 1 million). Former president Aquino was of part-Chinese ancestry, and some of the resistance to her presidency stemmed from her ethnic lineage. The Chinese-Philippine community, in particular, has been the target of ethnic violence—kidnappings and abductions—because their wealth, relative to other Filipino groups, makes them easy prey.

(United Nations photo by J. M. Micaud)

The Philippines has suffered from the misuse of funds entrusted to the government over the past several decades. The result has been a polarity of wealth, with many citizens living in severe poverty. Slums, such as Tondo in Manila, pictured above, are a common sight in many of the urban areas of the Philippines.

| Negritos and others begin settling the islands **25,000** B.C. | Malays arrive in the islands **2,000** B.C. | Chinese, Arabs, and Indians control parts of the economy and land A.D.**400–1400** | The islands are named for the Spanish king Philip II **1542** | Local resistance to Spanish rule **1890s** |
|---|---|---|---|---|
| ● | ● | ● | ● | ● |

## FOREIGN INTERESTS

Filipinos occupy a resource-rich, beautiful land. Monsoon clouds dump as much as 200 inches of rain on the fertile, volcanic soil. Rice and corn grow well, as do hemp, coconut, sugarcane, and tobacco. Tuna, sponges, shrimp, and hundreds of other kinds of marine life flourish in the ocean. Part of the country is covered with dense tropical forests yielding bamboo and lumber and serving as habitat to thousands of species of plant and animal life. The northern part of Luzon Island is famous for its terraced rice paddies.

Given this abundance, it is not surprising that several foreign powers have taken a serious interest in the archipelago. The Dutch held military bases in the country in the 1600s, the British briefly controlled Manila in the 1800s, and the Japanese overran the entire country in the 1940s. But it was Spain, in control of most of the country for more than 300 years (1565–1898), that established the cultural base for the modern Philippines. Spain's interest in the islands—its only colony in Asia—was primarily material and secondarily spiritual. It wanted to take part in the lucrative spice trade and fill its galleon ships each year with products from Asia for the benefit of the Spanish Crown. It also wanted (or, at least, Rome wanted) to convert the so-called heathens (that is, nonbelievers) to Christianity. The friars were particularly successful in winning converts to Roman Catholicism because, despite some local resistance, there were no competing Christian denominations in the Philippines and because the Church quickly gained control of the resources of the island, which it used to entice converts. Resisting conversion were the Muslims of the island of Mindanao, a group that continues to remain on the fringe of Philippine society but which signed a cease-fire with the government in 1994 after 20 years of guerrilla warfare (although sporadic violence continues, as in 1995, when 200 armed Muslims attacked and burned the town of Ipil on Mindanao). Eventually, a Church-dominated society was established that mirrored in structure—social-class divisions as well as religious and social values—the mother cultures of Spain and Mexico.

Spanish rule in the Philippines came to an inglorious end in 1898, at the end of the Spanish-American War. Spain granted independence to Cuba and ceded the Philippines, Guam, and Puerto Rico to the United States. Filipinos hoping for independence were disappointed to learn that yet another foreign power had assumed control of their lives. Resistance to American rule cost several thousand lives in the early years, but soon Filipinos realized that the U.S. presence was fundamentally different from that of Spain. The United States was interested in trade, and it certainly could see the advantage of having a military presence in Asia, but it viewed its primary role as one of tutelage. American officials believed that the Philippines should be granted independence, but only when the nation was sufficiently schooled in the process of democracy. Unlike Spain, the United States encouraged political parties and attempted to place Filipinos in positions of governmental authority.

Preparations were under way for independence when World War II broke out. The war and the occupation of the country by the Japanese undermined the economy, devastated the capital city of Manila, caused divisions among the political elite, and delayed independence. After Japan's defeat, the country was, at last, granted independence, on July 4, 1946. Manuel Roxas, a well-known politician, was elected president. Despite armed opposition from Communist groups, the country, after several elections, seemed to be maintaining a grasp on democracy.

## MARCOS AND HIS AFTERMATH

Then, in 1965, Ferdinand E. Marcos, a Philippines senator and former guerrilla fighter with the U.S. armed forces, was elected president. He was reelected in 1969. Rather than addressing the serious problems of agrarian reform and trade, Marcos maintained people's loyalty through an elaborate system of patronage, whereby his friends and relatives profited from the misuse of government power and money. Opposition to his rule manifested itself in violent demonstrations and in a growing Communist insurgency. In 1972, Marcos declared martial law, arrested some 30,000 opponents, and shut down newspapers as well as the National Congress. Marcos continued to rule the country by personal proclamation until 1981. He remained in power thereafter, and he

and his wife, Imelda, and their extended family and friends increasingly were criticized for corruption. Finally, in 1986, after nearly a quarter-century of his rule, an uprising of thousands of dissatisfied Filipinos overthrew Marcos, who fled to Hawaii. He died there in 1990.

Taking on the formidable job of president was Corazon Aquino, the widow of murdered opposition leader Benigno Aquino. Aquino's People Power revolution had a heady beginning. Many observers believed that at last Filipinos had found a democratic leader around whom they could unite and who would end corruption and put the persistent Communist insurgency to rest. Aquino, however, was immediately beset by overwhelming economic, social, and political problems.

Opportunists and factions of the Filipino military and political elite still loyal to Marcos attempted numerous coups d'état in the years of Aquino's administration. Much of the unrest came from within the military, which had become accustomed to direct involvement in government during Marcos's martial-law era. Some Communist separatists turned in their arms at Aquino's request, but many continued to plot violence against the government. Thus, the sense of security and stability that Filipinos needed in order to attract more substantial foreign investment and to reestablish the habits of democracy continued to elude them.

Nevertheless, the economy showed signs of improvement. Some countries, particularly Japan and the United States and, more recently, Hong Kong, invested heavily in the Philippines, as did half a dozen international organizations. In fact, some groups complained that further investment was unwarranted, because already-allocated funds had not yet been fully utilized. Moreover, misuse of funds entrusted to the government—a serious problem during the Marcos era—continued, despite Aquino's promise to eradicate corruption.

A 1987 law, enacted after Corazon Aquino assumed the presidency, limited the president to one term in office. Half a dozen contenders vied for the presidency in 1992, including Imelda Marcos and other relatives of former presidents Marcos and Aquino; U.S. West Point graduate General Fidel Ramos, who had thwarted several coup attempts against Aquino and

| A treaty ends the Spanish-American War **1898** | The Japanese attack the Philippines **1941** | General Douglas MacArthur makes a triumphant return' to Manila **1944** | The United States grants complete independence to the Philippines **1946** | Military-base agreements are signed with the United States **1947** | Ferdinand Marcos is elected president **1965** | Marcos declares martial law **1972** | Martial law is lifted; Corazon Aquino and her People Power movement drive Marcos into exile **1980s** |
|---|---|---|---|---|---|---|---|

**1990s**

Marcos dies in exile in Hawaii    The United States closes its military bases    Typhoon Angela destroys 96,000 homes in Luzon; economic crisis

who thus had her endorsement, won the election. It was the first peaceful transfer of power in more than 25 years (although campaign violence claimed the lives of more than 80 people).

In the 1998 presidential campaign, some 83 candidates filed with the election commission, including Imelda Marcos. Despite the deaths of nearly 30 people and some bizarre moments such as when a mayoral candidate launched a mortar attack on his opponents, the election was the most orderly in years. Former movie star Joseph Estrada won by a landslide.

## SOCIAL PROBLEMS
Estrada inherited the leadership of a country awash in problems. Much of the foreign capital coming into the Philippines in the 1990s had been invested in stock and real-estate speculation rather than in agriculture or manufacturing. Thus, with the financial collapse of 1997, there was little of substance to fall back on. Even prior to the financial crisis, inflation had been above 8 percent per year and unemployment was nearing 9 percent. And one problem never seemed to go away: extreme social inequality. As in Malaysia, where ethnic Malays have constituted a seemingly permanent class of poor peasants, Philippine society is fractured by distinct classes. Chinese and mestizos constitute the top of the hierarchy, while Muslims and most country dwellers form the bottom. About half the Filipino population of 76 million make their living in agriculture and fishing; but even in Manila, where the economy is stronger than anywhere else, thousands of residents live in abject poverty as urban squatters. Officially, 55 percent of Filipinos live in poverty. Disparities of wealth are striking. Worker discontent has

been such that the Philippines lost more work days to strikes between 1983 and 1987 than any other Asian country.

Adding to the country's financial woes was the sudden loss of income from the six U.S. military bases that closed in 1991 and 1992. The government had wanted the United States to maintain a presence in the country, but in 1991, the Philippine Legislature, bowing to nationalist sentiment, refused to renew the land-lease agreements that had been in effect since 1947. Occupying many acres of valuable land and bringing as many as 40,000 Americans at one time into the Philippines, the bases had come to be seen as visible symbols of American colonialism or imperialism. But they had also been a boon to the economy. Subic Bay Naval Base alone had provided jobs for 32,000 Filipinos on base and, indirectly, to 200,000 more. Moreover, the United States paid nearly $390 million each year to lease the land and another $128 million for base-related expenses. Base-related monies entering the country amounted to 3 percent of the entire Philippines economy. After the base closures, the U.S. Congress cut other aid to the Philippines, from $200 million in 1992 to $48 million in 1993. To counterbalance the losses, the Philippines accepted a $60 million loan from Taiwan to develop 740 acres of the former Subic Bay Naval Base into an industrial park. The International Monetary Fund also loaned the country $683 million—funds that have been successfully used to transform the former military facilities into commercial zones.

## CULTURE
Philippine culture is a rich amalgam of Asian and European customs. Family life

is valued, and few people have to spend their old age in nursing homes. Divorce is frowned upon. Women have traditionally involved themselves in the worlds of politics and business to a greater degree than have women in other Asian countries. Educational opportunities for women are about the same as those for men; adult literacy in the Philippines is estimated at 95 percent. Unfortunately, many college-educated men and women are unable to find employment befitting their skills. Discontent among these young workers continues to grow, as it does among the many rural and urban poor.

Nevertheless, many Filipinos take a rather relaxed attitude toward work and daily life. They enjoy hours of sports and folk dancing or spend their free time in conversation with neighbors and friends, with whom they construct patron/client relationships. In recent years, the growing nationalism has been expressed in the gradual replacement of the English language with Pilipino, a version of the Malay-based Tagalog language.

## DEVELOPMENT

The Philippines has more than $30 billion in foreign debt. Payback from development projects has been so slow that about half of the earnings from all exports has to be spent just to service the debt. The Philippines sells most of its products to the United States, Japan, Hong Kong, Great Britain, and the Netherlands.

## FREEDOM

Marcos's one-man rule meant that both the substance and structure of democracy were ignored. The Philippine Constitution is similar in many ways to that of the United States. President Aquino attempted to adhere to democratic principles; her successors pledged to do the same. The Communist Party was legalized in 1992.

## HEALTH/WELFARE

Quality of life varies considerably between the city and the countryside. Except for the numerous urban squatters, city residents generally have better access to health care and education. Most people still do not have access to safe drinking water. The gap between the upper-class elite and the poor is pronounced and growing.

## ACHIEVEMENTS
Filipino women often run businesses or hold important positions in government. Folk dancing is very popular, as is the *kundiman*, a unique blend of music and words found only in the Philippines.

# Singapore (Republic of Singapore)

## GEOGRAPHY
*Area in Square Miles (Kilometers):* 252 (633) (about 3½ times the size of Washington, D.C.)
*Capital (Population):* Singapore (2,334,400)
*Environmental Concerns:* pollution; limited fresh water; waste-disposal problems
*Geographical Features:* lowlands; gently undulating central plateau; many small islands
*Climate:* tropical; hot, humid, rainy

## PEOPLE

### Population
*Total:* 3,440,700
*Annual Growth Rate:* 1.67%
*Rural/Urban Population (Ratio):* almost entirely urban
*Major Languages:* Malay; Mandarin Chinese; Tamil; English
*Ethnic Makeup:* 77% Chinese; 15% Malay; 6% Indian; 2% others
*Religions:* 42% Buddhist and Taoist; 18% Christian; 16% Muslim; 5% Hindu; 19% others

### Health
*Life Expectancy at Birth:* 75 years (male); 81 years (female)
*Infant Mortality Rate (Ratio):* 3.9/1,000
*Average Caloric Intake:* 134% of FAO minimum
*Physicians Available (Ratio):* 1/681

### Education
*Adult Literacy Rate:* 91%

## COMMUNICATION
*Telephones:* 1 per 2.1 people
*Daily Newspaper Circulation:* 364 per 1,000 people
*Televisions:* 1 per 2.6 people

## TRANSPORTATION
*Highways in Miles (Kilometers):* 1,873 (2,972)
*Railroads in Miles (Kilometers):* 23 (38)
*Usable Airfields:* 8
*Motor Vehicles in Use:* 461,000

## GOVERNMENT
*Type:* republic within the British Commonwealth
*Independence Date:* August 9, 1965

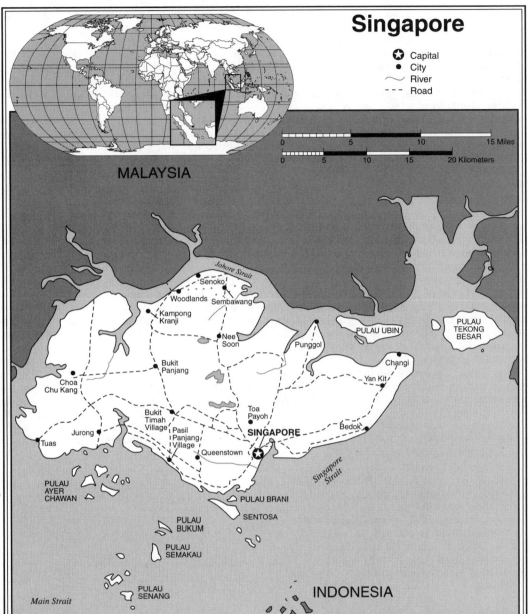

*Head of State/Government:* President Ong Teng Cheong; Prime Minister Goh Chok Tong
*Political Parties:* People's Action Party; Workers' Party; Singapore Democratic Party; National Solidarity Party; Singapore People's Party
*Suffrage:* universal and compulsory at 20

## MILITARY
*Military Expenditures (% of GDP):* 5.2%
*Current Disputes:* territorial dispute with Malaysia

## ECONOMY
*Currency ($ U.S. Equivalent):* 1.67 Singapore dollars = $1

*Per Capita Income/GDP:* $21,200/$72.2 billion
*GDP Growth Rate:* 5%
*Inflation Rate:* 1.3%
*Unemployment Rate:* 2.7%
*Labor Force:* 1,801,000
*Natural Resources:* fish; deepwater ports
*Agriculture:* rubber; copra; fruit; vegetables
*Industry:* petroleum refining; electronics; oil-drilling equipment; rubber processing and rubber products; processed food and beverages; ship repair, financial services; biotechnology
*Exports:* $144.4 billion (primary partners Malaysia, United States, Hong Kong)
*Imports:* $151.1 billion (primary partners Japan, Malaysia, United States)

## SINGAPORE

It is often said that North Americans are well off because they inhabit a huge continent that abounds with natural resources. This explanation for prosperity does not fit even remotely the case of Singapore. The inhabitants of this tiny, flat, humid tropical island, located near the equator off the tip of the Malay Peninsula, must import even their drinking water from another country. With only 252 square miles of land (including 58 mostly uninhabited islets), Singapore is just half the size of Hong Kong; however, it has one of the highest per capita incomes ($21,200) in Asia. With one of the highest population densities in Asia, Singapore might be expected to have the horrific slums that characterize parts of other crowded urban areas. But unemployment in Singapore is less than 3 percent, inflation is only 1.3 percent, and most of its 3.4 million people own their own homes. Eighty percent of the residences are government-built apartments, but they are spacious by Asian standards and are well equipped with labor-saving appliances.

Imperialism, geography, and racism help to explain Singapore's unique characteristics. For most of its recorded history, beginning in the thirteenth century A.D., Singapore was controlled variously by the rulers of Thailand, Java, Indonesia, and even India. In the early 1800s, the British were determined to wrest control of parts of Southeast Asia from the Dutch and expand their growing empire. Facilitating their imperialistic aims was Sir Stamford Raffles, a Malay-speaking British administrator who not only helped defeat the Dutch in Java but also diminished the power of local elites in order to fortify his position as lieutenant governor.

Arriving in Singapore in 1819, Raffles found it to be a small, neglected settlement with an economy based on fishing. Yet he believed that the island's geographic location endowed it with great potential as a transshipment port. He established policies that facilitated its development just in time to benefit from the British exports of tin, rubber, and timber leaving Malaya. Perhaps most important was his declaration of Singapore as a free port. Skilled Chinese merchants and traders, escaping racist discrimination against them by Malays on the Malay Peninsula, flocked to Singapore, where they prospered in the free-trade atmosphere.

In 1924, the British began construction of a naval base on the island, the largest in Southeast Asia, which was nonetheless overcome by the Japanese in 1942. Returning in 1945, the British continued to build Singapore into a major maritime center. Today, oil supertankers from Saudi Arabia must exit the Indian Ocean through the Strait of Malacca and skirt Singapore to enter the South China Sea for deliveries to Japan and other Asian nations. Thus, Singapore has found itself in the enviable position of helping to refine and transship millions of barrels of Middle Eastern oil. Singapore's oil-refining capacities have been ranked the world's third largest since 1973.

Singapore is now the second-busiest port in the world (Rotterdam in the Netherlands is number one). It has become the largest shipbuilding and -repair port in the region and a major shipping-related financial center. Singapore's economy has been growing at rates generally between 6 and 12 percent for the past decade, making it one of the fastest-growing economies in the world, although the Asian financial crisis has cut growth in Singapore to 5 percent or less. In recent years, the government has aggressively sought out investment from non-shipping–related industries in order to diversify the economy. In 1992, Singapore hosted a summit of the Association of Southeast Asian Nations in which a decision was made to create a regional common market by the year 2008. In order to compete with the emerging European and North American regional trading blocs, it was decided that tariffs on products traded within the ASEAN region would be cut to 5 percent or less.

## A UNIQUE CULTURE

Britain maintained an active interest in Singapore throughout its empire period. At its peak, there were some 100,000 British military men and their dependents stationed on the island. The British military remained until 1971. (The U.S. Navy's Seventh Fleet's logistics operations have recently been transferred from the Philippines to Singapore, thereby increasing the number of U.S. military personnel in Singapore to about 300 persons.) Thus, British culture, from the architecture of the buildings, to the leisure of a cricket match, to the prevalence of the English language, is everywhere present in Singapore. Yet, because of the heterogeneity of the population (77 percent Chinese, 15 percent Malay, and 6 percent Indian), Singapore accommodates many philosophies and belief systems, including Confucianism, Buddhism, Islam, Hinduism, and Christianity. In recent years, the government has attempted to promote the Confucian ethic of hard work and respect for law, as well as the Mandarin Chinese language, in order to develop a greater Asian consciousness among the people. But most Singaporeans seem content to avoid extreme ideology in favor of pragmatism; they prefer to be-

(UPI/Corbis-Bettmann photo by Paul Wedel)

Singapore, one of the most affluent nations in Asia, features a wealthy financial district that overlooks a harbor in the island state.

| Singapore is controlled by several different nearby nations, including Thailand, Java, India, and Indonesia A.D. 1200–1400 | British take control of the island 1800s | The Japanese capture Singapore 1942 | The British return to Singapore 1945 | Full elections and self-government; Lee Kuan Yew comes to power 1959 | Singapore, now unofficially independent of Britain, briefly joins the Malaysia Federation 1963 | Singapore becomes an independent republic 1965 | Singapore becomes the second-busiest port in the world and achieves one of the highest per capita incomes in the Pacific Rim 1980s |
| --- | --- | --- | --- | --- | --- | --- | --- |

1990s

Prime Minister Lee steps down; Goh Chok Tong is appointed

The U.S. Navy moves some of its operations from the Philippines to Singapore

A slump in global demand for electronics slows Singapore's economic growth

lieve in whatever approach works—that is, whatever allows them to make money and have a higher standard of living. Fortunately, the financial crisis that has devastated adjacent Malaysia and the rest of Southeast Asia has slowed, but not seriously hurt, Singapore's economy.

Their great material success has come with a price. The government keeps a firm hand on the people. For example, citizens can be fined as much as $250 for dropping a candy wrapper on the street or for driving without a seat belt. Worse offenses, such as importing chewing gum or selling it, carry fines of $6,000 and $1,200 respectively. Death by hanging is the punishment for murder, drug trafficking, and kidnapping, while lashing is inflicted on attempted murderers, robbers, rapists, and vandals. Being struck with a cane is the punishment for crimes such as malicious damage, as an American teenager, in a case that became a brief international *cause célèbre* in 1994, found out when he allegedly sprayed graffitti on cars in Singapore. Later that year, a Dutch businessperson was executed for alleged possession of heroin. The death penalty is required when one is convicted of using a gun in Singapore. The United Nations regularly cites Singapore for a variety of human-rights violations, and the world press frequently makes fun of the Singapore government for such practices as giving prizes for the cleanest public toilet.

Political dissidents may be arrested, and the press cannot publish whatever it wishes without often generating the government's ire. In fact, in 1998, Parliament banned all political advertising on television. Government leaders argue that order and hard work are necessities since, being a tiny island, Singapore could easily be overtaken by the envious and more politi-

cally unstable countries nearby; with few natural resources, Singapore must instead develop its people into disciplined, educated workers. Few deny that Singapore is an amazingly clean and efficient city-state; yet in recent years, younger residents have begun to wish for a greater voice in government.

The law-and-order tone exists largely because, after its separation from Malaysia in 1965, Singapore was controlled by one man and his personal hard-work ethic, Prime Minister Lee Kuan Yew, along with his Political Action Party (PAP). On November 26, 1990, Lee resigned his office (though he remains a powerful figure). Two days later, he was replaced by his chosen successor, Goh Chok Tong. Goh had been the deputy prime minister and was the designated successor-in-waiting since 1984. The transition has been smooth, and the PAP's hold on the government remains intact.

The PAP originally came into prominence in 1959, when the issue of the day was whether Singapore should join the proposed Federation of Malaysia. Singapore joined Malaysia in 1963, but serious differences persuaded Singaporeans to declare independence 2 years later. Lee Kuan Yew, a Cambridge-educated, ardent anti-Communist with old roots in Singapore, gained such strong support as prime minister that not a single opposition-party member was elected for more than 20 years. Only one opposition seat exists today.

The two main goals of the administration have been to utilize fully Singapore's primary resource—its deepwater port—and to develop a strong Singaporean identity. The first goal has been achieved in a way that few would have thought possible; the question of national identity, however, continues to be problematic. Creating a

Singaporean identity has been difficult because of the heterogeneity of the population, a situation that is likely to increase as foreign workers are imported to fill gaps in the labor supply resulting from a very successful birth control campaign started in the 1960s. Identity formation has also been difficult because of Singapore's recent seesaw history. First Singapore was a colony of Britain, then it became an outpost of the Japanese empire, followed by a return to Britain. Next Malaysia drew Singapore into its fold, and finally, in 1965, Singapore became independent. All these changes transpired within the lifetime of many contemporary Singaporeans, so their confusion regarding identity is understandable. Many still have a sense that their existence as a nation is tenuous, and they look for direction. In 1996, Singapore reaffirmed its support for a five-nation defense agreement among itself, Australia, Malaysia, New Zealand, and Great Britain, and it strengthened its economic agreements with Australia.

## DEVELOPMENT

Development of the deepwater Port of Singapore has been so successful that, at any single time, 400 ships are in port. Singapore has also become a base for fleets engaged in offshore oil exploration and a major financial center, the "Switzerland of Southeast Asia." Singapore has key attributes of a developed country.

## FREEDOM

Under Prime Minister Lee Kuan Yew, Singaporeans had to adjust to a strict regimen of behavior involving both political and personal freedoms. Citizens want more freedoms but realize that law and order have helped produce their high quality of life. Political opposition voices have largely been silenced since 1968, when the People's Action Party captured all the seats in the government.

## HEALTH/WELFARE

Eighty percent of Singaporeans live in government-built dwellings. A government-created pension fund, the Central Provident Fund, takes up to one quarter of workers' paychecks; some of this goes into a compulsory savings account that can be used to finance the purchase of a residence. Other forms of social welfare are not condoned. Care of the elderly is the duty of the family, not the government.

## ACHIEVEMENTS

Housing remains a serious problem for many Asian countries, but virtually every Singaporean has access to adequate housing. Replacing swamplands with industrial parks has helped to lessen Singapore's reliance on its deepwater port. Singapore successfully overcame a Communist challenge in the 1950s to become a solid home for free enterprise in the region.

# South Korea (Republic of Korea)

## GEOGRAPHY

*Area in Square Miles (Kilometers):* 38,013 (98,480) (about the size of Indiana)

*Capital (Population):* Seoul (11,609,000)

*Environmental Concerns:* air and water pollution; overfishing

*Geographical Features:* mostly hills and mountains; wide coastal plains in west and south

*Climate:* temperate, with rainfall heaviest in summer

## PEOPLE

### Population

*Total:* 45,949,000

*Annual Growth Rate:* 1.02%

*Rural/Urban Population (Ratio):* 17/83

*Major Language:* Korean

*Ethnic Makeup:* homogeneous Korean

*Religions:* 49% Christianity; 47% Buddhism; 3% Confucianism; 1% Shamanism and Chondokyo

### Health

*Life Expectancy at Birth:* 70 years (male); 78 years (female)

*Infant Mortality Rate (Ratio):* 8/1,000

*Average Caloric Intake:* 119% of FAO minimum

*Physicians Available (Ratio):* 1/817

### Education

*Adult Literacy Rate:* 98%

*Compulsory (Ages):* 6–12; free

## COMMUNICATION

*Telephones:* 1 per 2.4 people

*Daily Newspaper Circulation:* 404 per 1,000 people

*Televisions:* 1 per 3.1 people

## TRANSPORTATION

*Highways in Miles (Kilometers):* 44,937 (74,235)

*Railroads in Miles (Kilometers):* 1,848 (3,081)

*Usable Airfields:* 103

*Motor Vehicles in Use:* 8,500,000

## GOVERNMENT

*Type:* republic

*Independence Date:* August 15, 1948

*Head of State/Government:* President Kim Dae Jung; Prime Minister Ko Kon

*Political Parties:* New Korea Party; United Liberal Democratic Party; National Congress for New Politics

*Suffrage:* universal at 20

## MILITARY

*Military Expenditures (% of GDP):* 3.3%

*Current Disputes:* Demarcation Line disputed with North Korea; Liancourt Rocks, claimed by Japan

## ECONOMY

*Currency ($ U.S. Equivalent):* 1173.5 won = $1

*Per Capita Income/GDP:* $14,200/$647.2 billion

*GDP Growth Rate:* –7%

*Inflation Rate:* 5%

*Unemployment Rate:* 7% (est.)

*Labor Force:* 20,000,000

*Natural Resources:* coal; tungsten; graphite; molybdenum; lead; hydropower

*Agriculture:* rice; root crops; barley; vegetables; fruit; livestock and livestock products; fish

*Industry:* textiles; clothing; footwear; food processing; chemicals; steel; electronics; automobile production; shipbuilding

*Exports:* $130.9 billion (primary partners United States, European Union countries, Japan)

*Imports:* $150.2 billion (primary partners United States, Japan, European Union countries)

 http://www.www-kr.org/Korea/overview.html

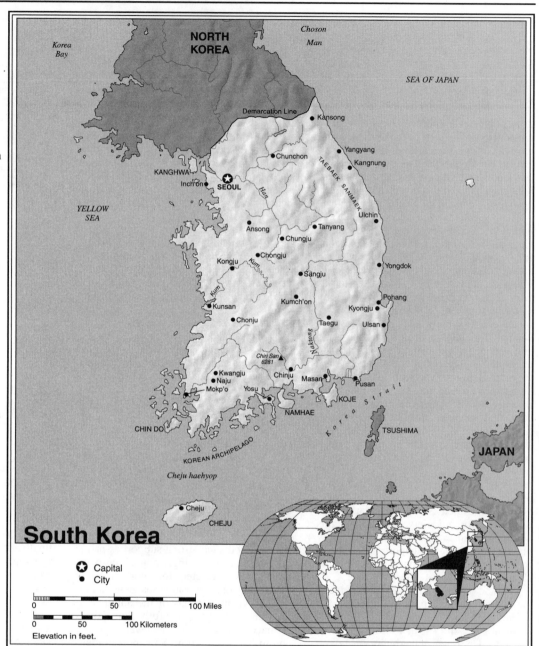

South Korea

⊛ Capital
• City

0    50    100 Miles
0    50    100 Kilometers
Elevation in feet.

## EARLY HISTORY

Korea was inhabited for thousands of years by an early people who may or may not have been related to the Ainus of northern Japan, the inhabitants of Sakhalin Island, and the Siberian Eskimos. Distinct from this early civilization are today's Koreans whose ancestors migrated to the Korean Peninsula from Central Asia and, benefiting from close contact with the culture of China, established prosperous kingdoms as early as 1000 B.C. (legends put the date as early as 2333 B.C.).

The era of King Sejong, who ruled Korea from 1418 to 1450, is notable for its many scientific and humanistic accomplishments. Ruling his subjects according to neo-Confucian thought, Sejong taught improved agricultural methods; published books on astronomy, history, religion, and medicine (the Koreans invented movable metal type); and was instrumental in the invention of sundials, rain gauges, and various musical instruments. Of singular importance was his invention of *han-qul,* a simplified writing system that even uneducated peasants could easily learn. Before *han-qul,* Koreans used the more complicated Chinese characters to represent sounds in the Korean language.

## REGIONAL RELATIONS

For most of its history, Korea has remained at least nominally independent of foreign powers. China, however, always wielded tremendous cultural influence and at times politically dominated the Korean Peninsula. Similarly, Japan often cast longing eyes toward Korea but was never able to control affairs successfully there until the beginning of the twentieth century.

Korean influence on Japanese culture was pronounced in the 1400s and 1500s, when, through peaceful trade as well as forced labor, Korean artisans and technicians taught advanced skills in ceramics, textiles, painting, and other arts to the Japanese. (Historically, the Japanese received most of their cultural influence from China via Korea.)

In this century, the direction of influence reversed—to the current Japan-to-Korea flow—with the result that the two cultures share numerous qualities. Ironically, cultural closeness has not eradicated emotional distance: Modern Japanese continue to discriminate against Koreans who live in Japan, and Japanese brutality during Japan's of occupation of Korea (1905–1945) remains a frequent topic of conversation among Koreans.

Japan achieved its desire to rule Korea in 1905, when Russia's military, along with its imperialistic designs on Korea, was soundly defeated by the Japanese in the Russo–Japanese War; Korea was granted to Japan as part of the peace settlement. Unlike other expansionist nations, Japan was not content to rule Korea as a colony but, rather, attempted the complete cultural and political annexation of the Korean Peninsula. Koreans had to adopt Japanese names, serve in the Japanese Army, and pay homage to the Japanese emperor. Some 1.3 million Koreans were forcibly sent to Japan to work in coal mines or to serve in the military. The Korean language ceased to be taught in school, and more than 200,000 books on Korean history and culture were burned.

Many Koreans joined clandestine resistance organizations. In 1919, a Declaration of Korean Independence was announced in Seoul by resistance leaders, but the brutally efficient Japanese police and military crushed the movement. They killed thousands of demonstrators, tortured and executed the leaders, and set fire to the homes of those suspected of cooperating with the movement. Despite suppression of this kind throughout the 40 years of Japanese colonial rule, a provisional government was established by the resistance in 1919, with branches in Korea, China, and Russia. However, a very large police force—one Japanese for every 40 Koreans—kept resistance in check.

One resistance leader, Syngman Rhee, vigorously promoted the cause of Korean independence to government leaders in the United States and Europe. Rhee, supported by the United States, became the president of South Korea after the defeat of the Japanese in 1945.

Upon the surrender of Japan, the victorious Allied nations decided to divide Korea into two zones of temporary occupation, for the purposes of overseeing the orderly dismantling of Japanese rule and establishing a new Korean government. The United States was to occupy all of Korea south of the 38th Parallel of latitude (a demarcation running east and west across the peninsula, north of the capital city of Seoul), while the Soviet Union was to occupy Korea north of that line. The United States was uneasy about permitting the Soviets to move troops into Korea, as the Soviet Union had entered the war against Japan just 8 days before Japan surrendered, and its commitment to the democratic intentions of the Allies was questionable. Nevertheless, it was granted occupation rights.

(Reuters/Bettmann photo by Tony Chung)

South Korea became an economic powerhouse, following the Japanese model of development. Workers in the Hyundai shipyards are pictured above.

Later, the United Nations attempted to enter the zone occupied by the Soviet Union in order to oversee democratic elections for all of Korea. Denied entry, UN advisers proceeded with elections in the South, which brought Syngman Rhee to the presidency. The North created its own government, with Kim Il-Song at the head. Tensions between the two governments resulted in the elimination of trade and other contacts across the new border. This was difficult for each side, because the Japanese had developed industries in the North while the South had remained primarily agricultural. Each side needed the other's resources; in their absence, considerable civil unrest occurred. Rhee's government responded by suppressing dissent, rigging elections, and using strong-arm tactics on critics. Autocratic rule, not unlike that of the colonial Japanese, has been the norm in South Korea almost ever since, and citizens, particularly university students, have been quick to take to the streets in protest of human-rights violations by the various South Korean governments. Equally stern measures were instituted by the Communist government in the North, so that, despite a half century of Korean rule, the repressive legacy of the Japanese police state remained.

## AN ECONOMIC POWERHOUSE

Upon the establishment of two separate political entities in Korea, the North pursued a Communist model of economic restructuring. South Korea, bolstered by massive infusions of economic and military aid from the United States, pursued a decidedly capitalist strategy. The results of this choice have been dramatic. For many years, South Korea's economic growth has been one of the fastest in the world; before the financial crisis of the late 1990s, it had been predicted that South Korea's per capita income would rival that in European countries by the year 2010. Predictions have since been revised downward, but South Korea's success in improving the living standards of its people has been phenomenal. About 75 percent of South Korean people live in urban centers, where they have access to good education and jobs. Manufacturing accounts for 30 percent of the gross domestic product. Economic success and recent improvements in the political climate seem to be slowing the rate of outward migration. In recent years, some Koreans have even returned home after years abroad.

North Koreans, on the other hand, are finding life unbearable. Hundreds have defected, some via a "safe house" system through China (similar to the famous Underground Railroad of U.S. slavery days). Some military pilots have flown their jets across the border to South Korea. Food shortages are increasingly evident, and some people expect the total collapse of the North Korean economy.

Following the Japanese model, South Korean businesspeople work hard to capture market share rather than to gain immediate profit—that is, they are willing to sell their products at or below cost for several years in order to gain the confidence of consumers, even if they make no profit. Once a sizable proportion of consumers buy their product and trust its reliability, the price is raised to a profitable level.

During the 1980s and much of the 1990s, South Korean businesses began investing in other countries, and South Korea became a creditor rather than a debtor member of the Asian Development Bank, putting it in a position to loan money to other countries. There was even talk that Japan (which is separated from Korea by only 150 miles of ocean) was worried that the two Koreas would soon unify and thus present an even more formidable challenge to its own economy—a situation not unlike some Europeans' concern about the economic strength of a reunified Germany.

The magic ended, however, in late 1997, when the world financial community would no longer provide money to Korean banks. This happened because Korean banks had been making questionable loans to Korean *chaebol,* or business conglomerates, for so long, that the banks' creditworthiness came into question. With companies unable to get loans, with stocks at an 11-year low, and with workers eager to take to the streets in mass demonstrations against industry cutbacks, many businesses went under. One of the more well-known firms that went into receivership in 1998 was Kia Motors Corporation. By 1999, the unemployment rate had reached 7 percent, and South Korea had applied for a financial bailout—with all of its restrictions and forced closures of unprofitable businesses—from the International Monetary Fund. Workers deeply resented the belt-tightening required by the IMF (shouting "No to layoffs!" thousands of them threw rocks at police who responded with tear gas and arrests), but IMF funding probably prevented the entire economy from collapsing.

## SOCIAL PROBLEMS

Economically, South Korea was once, and likely will be again, an impressive showcase for the fruits of capitalism. Politically, however, the country has been wracked with problems. Under Presidents Syngman Rhee (1948–1960), Park Chung Hee (1964–1979), and Chun Doo Hwan (1981–1987), South Korean government was so centralized as to constitute a virtual dictatorship. Human-rights violations, suppression of workers, and other acts incompatible with the tenets of democracies were frequent occurrences. Student uprisings, military revolutions, and political assassinations became more influential than the ballot box in forcing a change of government. President Roh Tae-woo came to power in 1987, in the wake of a mass protest against civil-rights abuses and other excesses of the previous government. Students began mass protests against various candidates long before the 1992 elections that brought to office the first civilian president in more than 30 years, Kim Young-sam. Kim was once a dissident himself and was victimized by government policies against free speech; once elected, he promised to make major democratic reforms. The reforms, however, were not good enough for thousands of striking subway workers, farmers, or students whose demonstrations against low pay, foreign rice imports, or the placement of Patriot missiles in South Korea sometimes had to be broken up by riot police.

Replacing Kim Young-sam as president in 1998 was opposition leader Kim Dae Jung. Kim's election was a profound statement that the Korean people were tired of human-rights abuses, because Kim himself had once been a political prisoner. Convicted of sedition by a corrupt government and sentenced to die, Kim had spent 13 years in prison or house arrest, and then, like Nelson Mandela of South Africa, rose to defeat the system that had abused him. That the Korean people were ready for real democratic reform was also revealed in the 1996 trial of former president Chun Doo Hwan, who was sentenced to death (later commuted) for his role in a 1979 coup.

A primary focus of the South Korean government's attention at the moment is the several U.S. military bases in South Korea, currently home to approximately 43,500 U.S. troops. The government (and apparently most of the 46 million South Korean people), although not always happy with the military presence, believes that the U.S. troops are useful in deterring possible aggression from North Korea, which, despite an enfeebled economy, still invests massive amounts of its budget in its military. Many university students, however, are offended by the presence of these troops. They claim that the Americans have suppressed the growth of democracy by propping up authoritarian regimes—a claim readily admitted by the United States, which believed during the cold war era that the containment of communism was a higher priority. Strong feelings against U.S. involvement in South Korean affairs have precipitated hundreds of violent demonstrations, sometimes in-

| The Yi dynasty begins a 518-year reign over Korea A.D. 935 | Korea pays tribute to Mongol rulers in China 1637 | Korea opens its ports to outside trade 1876 | Japan formally annexes Korea at the end of the Russo-Japanese War 1910 | Korea is divided into North and South 1945 | North Korea invades South Korea: the Korean War begins 1950 | Cease-fire agreement; the DMZ is established 1953 | President Park Chung Hee is assassinated 1979 | Democratization movement; the 1988 Summer Olympic Games are held in Seoul 1980s |

1990s

| Reunification talks; a nonaggression pact is signed with North Korea; cross-border exhanges begin | President Kim Young-sam is replaced by former political prisoner Kim Dae Jung | The economy suffers a major setback; the IMF bails out the economy |

volving as many as 100,000 protesters. The United States' refusal to withdraw its forces from South Korea left an impression with many Koreans that Americans were hard-line, cold war ideologues who were unwilling to bend in the face of changing international alignments.

In 1990, U.S. officials announced that, in an effort to reduce U.S. military costs in the post–cold war era, the United States would pull out several thousand of its troops from South Korea and close three of its five air bases. The United States also declared that it expected South Korea to pay more of the cost of the U.S. military presence, in part as a way to reduce the unfavorable trade balance between the two countries. The South Korean government agreed to build a new U.S. military base about 50 miles south of the capital city of Seoul, where current operations would be relocated. South Korea would pay all construction costs—estimated at about $1 billion—and the United States would be able to reduce its presence within the Seoul metropolitan area, where many of the anti-U.S. demonstrations take place. Although the bases have been a focus of protest by students, surveys now show that about 90 percent of South Koreans want the U.S. military to remain in the country.

A second issue that has occupied the government for years is the question of reunification with North Korea. The division of the country has left many families unable to communicate with or visit relatives in the North, and the threat of a military incursion from the North has forced South Korea to spend large sums of its national budget on defense. Frequent charges of spying, counterspying, and other forms of subversive activities—not to mention the fact that the two nations have not signed a peace treaty since the Korean War, and that the North declared in 1996 that it would no longer recognize

the 1953 armistice—have kept tensions high. High-profile meetings to discuss re-unification have been held for several years, but with little concrete progress, despite a nonaggression and reconciliation pact and agreements on cross-border exchanges and other forms of cooperation. The impetus behind improvements in relations appears to be North Korea's loss of solid diplomatic and economic partners and thus its increasing isolation in the world economy, due to the collapse of the Soviet Union. Some South Koreans have estimated that it will cost $980 billion to reunify with the North.

South Korean government leaders have to face a very active, vocal, and even violent populace when they initiate controversial policies. Among the more vocal groups for democracy and human rights are the various Christian congregations and their Western-ized clergy. Other vocal groups include the college students who hold rallies annually to elect student protest leaders and to plan an-tigovernment demonstrations. In addition to the military-bases question, student protesters are angry at the South Korean government's willingness to open more Korean markets to U.S. products. The students want the United States to apologize for its alleged assistance to the South Korean government in violently suppressing an antigovernment demonstration in 1981 in Kwangju, a southern city that is a frequent locus of antigovernment as well as labor-related demonstrations and strikes. Protesters were particularly angered by then–president Roh Tae-woo's silencing of part of the opposition by convincing two opposition parties to merge with his own to form a large Democratic Liberal Party, not unlike that of the Liberal Democratic Party that governed Japan almost continuously for more than 40 years.

Ironically, demands for changes have increased at precisely the moment that the government has been instituting changes de-

signed to strengthen both the economy and civil rights. Under Roh's administration, for example, trade and diplomatic initiatives were launched with Eastern/Central European nations and with China and the former Soviet Union. Under Kim Young-sam's administration, 41,000 prisoners, including some political prisoners, were granted amnesty, and the powerful chaebol business conglomerates were brought under a tighter rein. Similarly, relaxation of the tight controls on labor-union activity gave workers more leverage in negotiating with management. Unfortunately, union activity, exploding after decades of suppression, has produced crippling industrial strikes—as many as 2,400 a year, and the police have been called out to restore order. In fact, since 1980, riot police have fired an average of more than 500 tear-gas shells a day, at a cost to the South Korean government of tens of millions of dollars.

The sense of unease in the country was tempered, until the late 1990s, by dynamism of the economy. What will happen with the economy in difficult straits is not easy to predict, but economic recovery and democratization will likely continue to be high on the government's agenda. South Korea recently established unofficial diplomatic ties with Taiwan in order to facilitate freer trade. It then signed an industrial pact with China to merge South Korea's technological know-how with China's inexpensive labor force. Relations with Japan have also improved since Japan's apology for atrocities during World War II.

## DEVELOPMENT

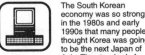

The South Korean economy was so strong in the 1980s and early 1990s that many people thought Korea was going to be the next Japan of Asia. The standard of living was increasing for everyone until a major slowdown in 1997–1998. The resulting difficulties forced companies to abandon plans for wage increases or to decrease work hours.

## FREEDOM

Suppression of political dissent, manipulation of the electoral process, and restrictions on labor union activity have been features of almost every South Korean government since 1948. Martial law has been frequently invoked, and governments have been overthrown by mass uprisings of the people. Reforms have been enacted under Presidents Roh Tae-woo, Kim Young-sam, and Kim Dae Jung.

## HEALTH/WELFARE

Korean men usually marry at about age 27, women at about 24. In 1960, Korean women, on average, gave birth to 6 children; in 1990, the expected births per woman were 1.6. The average South Korean baby born today can expect to live well into its 70s.

## ACHIEVEMENTS

In 1992, Korean students placed first in international math and science tests. South Korea achieved self-sufficiency in agricultural fertilizers in the 1970s and continues to show growth in the production of grains and vegetables. The formerly weak industrial sector is now a strong component of the economy.

# Taiwan (Republic of China)

## GEOGRAPHY

*Area in Square Miles (Kilometers):* 22,320 (36,002) (slightly smaller than Maryland and Delaware combined)

*Capital (Population):* T'aipei (2,626,000)

*Environmental Concerns:* water and air pollution; poaching; contamination of drinking water; radioactive-waste disposal

*Geographical Features:* mostly rugged mountains in east; flat to gently rolling plains in west

*Climate:* tropical; marine

## PEOPLE

### Population

*Total:* 21,701,000

*Annual Growth Rate:* 0.95%

*Rural/Urban Population Ratio:* 25/75

*Major Languages:* Mandarin Chinese; Taiwanese and Hakka dialects also used

*Ethnic Makeup:* 84% Taiwanese; 14% Mainlander Chinese; 2% aborigine

*Religions:* 93% mixture of Buddhism, Confucianism, and Taoism; 4.5% Christian; 2.5% others

### Health

*Life Expectancy at Birth:* 72 years (male); 79 years (female)

*Infant Mortality Rate (Ratio):* 7/1,000

*Physicians Available (Ratio):* 1/804

### Education

*Adult Literacy Rate:* 86%

*Compulsory (Ages):* 6–15; free

## COMMUNICATION

*Telephones:* 1 per 2.3 people

*Televisions:* 1 per 3 people

## TRANSPORTATION

*Highways in Miles (Kilometers):* 11,750 (19,584)

*Railroads in Miles (Kilometers):* 2,760 (4,600)

*Usable Airfields:* 38

*Motor Vehicles in Use:* 4,950,000

## GOVERNMENT

*Type:* multiparty democratic regime

*Head of State/Government:* President Lee Teng-hui; Premier Lien Chan

*Political Parties:* Nationalist Party (Kuomintang); Democratic Progressive Party; Chinese New Democratic Party; Labour Party; New KMT Party

*Suffrage:* universal at 20

## MILITARY

*Military Expenditures (% of GDP):* 3.6%

*Current Disputes:* officially (but not actually) in a state of war with the People's Republic of China; territorial disputes

## ECONOMY

*Currency ($ U.S. Equivalent):* 32.14 New Taiwan dollars = $1

*Per Capita Income/GDP:* $14,700/$315 billion

*GDP Growth Rate:* 5.7%

*Inflation Rate:* 3.1%

*Unemployment Rate:* 2.6%

*Labor Force:* 9,310,000

*Natural Resources:* coal; natural gas; limestone; marble; asbestos

*Agriculture:* rice; tea; bananas; pineapples; sugarcane; sweet potatoes; wheat; soybeans; peanuts

*Industry:* steel; pig iron; aluminum; shipbuilding; cement; fertilizer; paper; cotton; fabrics

*Exports:* $116 billion (primary partners United States, Hong Kong, European Union countries)

*Imports:* $102.4 billion (primary partners Japan, United States, European Union countries)

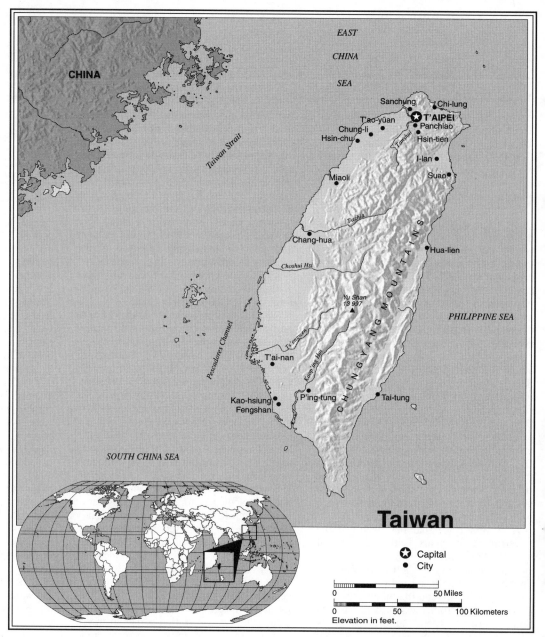

Taiwan

⊗ Capital
• City

0     50 Miles
0   50    100 Kilometers
Elevation in feet.

## A LAND OF REFUGE

It has been called "beautiful island," "treasure island," and "terraced bay island," but to the people who have settled there, Taiwan (formerly known as Formosa) has come to mean "refuge island."

Typical of the earliest refugees of the island were the Hakka peoples of China, who, tired of persecution on the mainland, fled to Taiwan (and to Borneo) before A.D. 1000. In the seventeenth century, tens of thousands of Ming Chinese soldiers, defeated at the hands of the expanding Manchu Army, sought sanctuary in Taiwan. In 1949, a third major wave of immigration to Taiwan brought thousands of Chinese Nationalists, retreating in the face of the victorious Red Chinese armies. Hosting all these newcomers were the original inhabitants of the islands, various Malay–Polynesian-speaking tribes. Their descendants live today in mountain villages throughout the island.

Since 1544, other outsiders have shown interest in Taiwan, too: Portugal, Spain, the Netherlands, Britain, and France have all either settled colonies or engaged in trade along the coasts. But the non-Chinese power that has had the most influence is Japan. Japan treated parts of Taiwan as its own for 400 years before it officially acquired the entire island in 1895, at the end of the Sino–Japanese War. From then until 1945, the Japanese ruled Taiwan with the intent of fully integrating it into Japanese culture. The Japanese language was taught in schools, college students were sent to Japan for their education, and the Japanese style of government was implemented. Many Taiwanese resented the harsh discipline imposed, but they also recognized that the Japanese were building a modern, productive society. Indeed, the basic infrastructure of contemporary Taiwan—roads, railways, schools, and so on—was constructed during the Japanese colonial era (1895–1945). Japan still lays claim to the Senkaku Islands, a chain of uninhabited islands, which the Taiwanese say belong to Taiwan.

After Japan's defeat in World War II, Taiwan became the island of refuge of the anti-Communist leader Chiang Kai-shek and his 3 million Kuomintang (KMT, or Nationalist Party) followers, many of whom had been prosperous and well-educated businesspeople and intellectuals in China. These Mandarin-speaking mainland Chinese, called Mainlanders, now constitute about 14 percent of Taiwan's people.

During the 1950s, Mao Zedong, the leader of the People's Republic of China, planned an invasion of Taiwan. However, Taiwan's leaders succeeded in obtaining military support from the United States to prevent the attack. They also convinced the United States to provide substantial amounts of foreign aid to Taiwan (the U.S. government saw the funds as a way to contain communism) as well as to grant it diplomatic recognition as the only legitimate government for all of China.

China was denied membership in the United Nations for more than 20 years because Taiwan held the "China seat." World opinion on the "two Chinas" issue began to change in the early 1970s. Many countries believed that a nation as large and powerful as the People's Republic of China should not be kept out of the United Nations nor out of the mainstream of world trade in favor of the much smaller Taiwan. In 1971, the United Nations withdrew its China seat from Taiwan and gave it to the P.R.C. Taiwan has consistently reapplied for membership, arguing that there is nothing wrong with there being either two China seats or one China seat and one Taiwan seat; its requests have been denied. The United States and many other countries wished to establish diplomatic relations with China but could not get China to cooperate as long as they recognized the sovereignty of Taiwan. In 1979, desiring access to China's huge market, the United States, preceded by many other nations, switched its diplomatic recognition from Taiwan to China. Foreign-trade offices in Taiwan remained unchanged but embassies were renamed; the U.S. Embassy was called the American Institute in Taiwan. As far as official diplomacy with the United States was concerned, Taiwan became a non-nation, but that did not stop the two countries from engaging in very profitable trade, including a controversial U.S. agreement in 1992 to sell $4 billion to $6 billion worth of F-16 fighter jets to Taiwan. Similarly, Taiwan has refused to establish diplomatic ties, yet continues to trade, with nations that recognize the mainland Chinese authorities as a legitimate government. In 1992, for instance, when South Korea established ties with mainland China, Taiwan immediately broke off formal relations with South Korea and suspended direct airline flights. However, Taiwan continued to permit trade in many commodities. Recognizing a potentially strong market in Vietnam, Taiwan also established air links with Vietnam in 1992, links that had been broken since the end of the Vietnam War. In 1993, a Taiwanese company collaborated with the Vietnamese government to construct a $242 million highway in Ho Chi Minh City (formerly Saigon). Just over 30 states formally recognize Taiwan today, but Taiwan nevertheless maintains close economic ties with more than 140 countries.

## AN ECONOMIC POWERHOUSE

Diplomatic maneuvering has not affected Taiwan's stunning postwar economic growth. Like Japan, Taiwan has been described as an economic miracle. In the past 2 decades, Taiwan has enjoyed more years of double-digit economic growth

(UN photo by Chen Jr.)

Taiwan has one of the highest population densities in the world (about 1,550 people per square mile), but it has been able to expand its agricultural output rapidly and efficiently through utilization of a number of practices. By terracing, using high-yield seeds, and supplying adequate irrigation, Taiwanese can grow a succession of crops on the same piece of land throughout the year.

(UN photo by Chen Jr.)

Taiwan is described as an economic miracle. After World War II, it emerged as a tremendous source for labor-intensive industries, such as electronics and clothing. Many Western manufacturers moved their facilities to Taiwan to take advantage of the savings in labor costs.

than any other nation. With electronics leading the pack of exports, a substantial portion of Taiwan's gross domestic product comes from manufacturing. Taiwan has been open to foreign investment and, of course, to foreign trade. However, for many years, Taiwan insisted on a policy of no contact and no communication with mainland China. Private enterprises eventually were allowed to trade with China— as long as the products were transshipped through a third country, usually Hong Kong. In 1993, government-owned enterprises such as steel and fertilizer plants were allowed to trade with China, on the same condition. By the early 1990s, Taiwanese trade with China had exceeded $13 billion a year and China had become Taiwan's seventh-largest trading partner. The liberalization of trade between China (especially its southern and coastal provinces), Taiwan, and Hong Kong has made the region, now known as Greater China, an economic dynamo. Economists predict that Greater China will someday bypass Japan's economy.

As one of the newly industrializing countries of Asia, Taiwan certainly no longer fits the label "underdeveloped." Taiwan holds large stocks of foreign reserves and carries a trade surplus with the United States (in Taiwan's favor) far greater than Japan's, when counted on a per capita basis. The Taipei stock market

has been so successful—sometimes outperforming both Japan and the United States—that a number of workers reportedly have quit their jobs to play the market, thereby exacerbating Taiwan's already serious labor shortage. (This shortage has led to an influx of foreign workers, both legal and illegal.)

Successful Taiwanese companies have begun to invest heavily in other countries where land and labor are plentiful and less expensive. In 1993, the Philippines accepted a $60 million loan from Taiwan to build an industrial park and commercial port at Subic Bay, the former U.S. naval base; and Thailand, Australia, and the United States have also seen inflows of Taiwanese investment monies. By the early 1990s, some 200 Taiwanese companies had invested $1.3 billion in Malaysia alone (Taiwan supplanted Japan as the largest outside investor in Malaysia). Taiwanese investment in mainland China has also increased.

Taiwan's economic success is attributable in part to its educated population, many of whom constituted the cultural and economic elite of China before the Communist revolution. Despite resentment of the mainland immigrants by native-born Taiwanese, everyone, including the lower classes of Taiwan, has benefited from this infusion of talent and capital. Yet the Taiwanese people are beginning to pay

a price for their sudden affluence. It is said that Taipei, the capital city of Taiwan (and the sixth most expensive city in the world for foreigners), is awash in money, but it is also awash in air pollution and traffic congestion. Traffic congestion in Taipei is rated near the worst in the world. Concrete high-rises have displaced the lush greenery of the mountains. Many residents spend their earnings on luxury foreign cars and on cigarettes and alcohol, the consumption rate of which has been increasing by about 10 percent a year. Many Chinese traditions—for instance, the roadside restaurant serving noodle soup—are giving way to 7-Elevens selling Coca-Cola and ice cream.

Some Taiwanese despair of ever turning back from the growing materialism; they wish for the revival of traditional Chinese (that is, mostly Confucian) ethics, but they doubt that it will happen. Still, the government, which has been dominated since 1949 by the conservative Mandarin migrants from the mainland, sees to it that Confucian ethics are vigorously taught in school. And there remains in Taiwan more of traditional China than in China itself, because, unlike the Chinese Communists, the Taiwanese authorities have had no reason to attempt an eradication of the values of Buddhism, Taoism, or Confucianism. Nor has grinding poverty—often the most serious threat to the cultural arts—nega-

Portuguese sailors are the first Europeans to visit Taiwan
A.D. **1544**

Taiwan becomes part of the Chinese Empire
**1700s**

The Sino-Japanese War ends; China cedes Taiwan to Japan
**1895**

Taiwan achieves independence from Japan
**1945**

Nationalists, under Chiang Kai-shek, retreat to Taiwan
**1947-49**

A de facto separation of Taiwan from China; Chinese aggression is deterred with U.S. assistance
**1950s**

China replaces Taiwan in the United Nations
**1971**

Chiang Kai-shek dies and is succeeded by his son, Chiang Ching-Kuo
**1975**

The first two-party elections in Taiwan's history are held; 38 years of martial law end
**1980s**

Chiang Ching-Kuo dies; Lee Teng-hui is the first native-born Taiwanese to be elected president

**1990s**

Relations with China improve; the United States sells F-16 jets to Taiwan

China conducts military exercises to intimidate Taiwanese voters

Bilateral talks with China resume

tively affected literature and the fine arts, as it has in China. Parents, with incense sticks burning before small religious altars, still emphasize respect for authority, the benefits of harmonious cooperative effort, and the inestimable value of education. Traditional festivals dot each year's calendar, among the most spectacular of which is Taiwan's National Day parade. Marching bands, traditional dancers, and a huge dragon carried by more than 50 young men please the crowds lining the streets of Taipei. Temples are filled with worshipers praying for health and good luck.

But the Taiwanese will need more than luck if they are to escape the consequences of their intensely rapid drive for material comfort. Some people contend that the island of refuge is being destroyed by success. Violent crime, for instance, once hardly known in Taiwan, is now commonplace. Six thousand violent crimes, including rapes, robberies, kidnappings, and murder, were reported in 1989—a 22 percent increase over the previous year, and the upward trend has continued since then. Extortion against wealthy companies and abductions of the children of successful families are causing a wave of fear among the rich.

There are also signs that the economy is heading for a slowdown. Labor shortages have forced some companies to operate at only 60 percent of capacity, and low-interest loans are hard to get because the government fears that too many people will simply invest in get-rich stocks instead of in new businesses.

## POLITICAL LIBERALIZATION
These disturbing trends notwithstanding, in recent years, the Taiwanese people have had much to be grateful for in the political sphere. Until 1986, the government, domi-

nated by the influence of the Chiangs, had permitted only one political party, the Nationalists, and had kept Taiwan under martial law for nearly 4 decades. A marked political liberalization began near the time of Chiang Ching-Kuo's death, in 1987. The first opposition party, the Democratic Progressive Party, was formed; martial law (officially, the "Emergency Decree") was lifted; and the first two-party elections were held, in 1986. In 1988, for the first time a native-born Taiwanese, Lee Teng-hui, was elected to the presidency. He was reelected in 1996 in the first truly democratic, direct presidential election ever held in Taiwan. Although Lee has never promoted the independence of Taiwan, his high-visibility campaign raised the ire of China, which attempted to intimidate the Taiwanese electorate into voting for a more pro-China candidate by conducting military exercises and firing missiles just 20 miles off the coast of Taiwan. As expected, the intimidation backfired, and Lee soundly defeated his opponents.

It is still against the law for any group or person to advocate publicly the independence of Taiwan—that is, to advocate international acceptance of Taiwan as a sovereign state, separate and apart from China. When the opposition Democratic Progressive Party (DPP) resolved in 1990 that Taiwan should become an independent country, the ruling Nationalist government immediately outlawed the DPP platform. Although the Taiwan government still bans direct official contact with Beijing, it nevertheless established the private Straits Exchange Foundation in 1991 to further contact with the mainland, and it resumed bilateral talks in 1998. Some believe that such talks will eventually result in Taiwan being annexed by China, just as in the cases of Hong Kong and Macau (although from a strictly legal-

istic viewpoint, Taiwan has just as much right to annex China). Others believe that dialogue will eventually diminish animosity, allowing Taiwan to move toward independence without China's opposition.

Opinion on this issue is clearly divided. Even some members of the anti-independence Nationalist Party have bolted and formed a new party (the New KMT alliance, or the New Party) to promote closer ties with China. As opposition parties proliferate, the independence issue could become a more urgent topic of political debate. In the meantime, contacts with the P.R.C. increase daily; Taiwanese students are now being admitted to China's universities, and Taiwanese residents by the thousands are now visiting relatives on the mainland. Despite complaints from China, Taiwanese government leaders have been courting their counterparts in the Philippines, Thailand, Indonesia, and South Korea. Moreover, President Lee has publicly promoted better relations with the People's Republic (the first president to do so), but China has vowed to invade Taiwan if it should ever declare independence. Under these circumstances, many—probably most—Taiwanese will likely remain content to let the rhetoric of reunification continue while enjoying the reality of de facto independence.

## DEVELOPMENT

Taiwan has vigorously promoted export-oriented production, particularly of electronic equipment. In the 1980s, manufacturing became a leading sector of the economy, employing more than one third of the workforce. Virtually all Taiwanese households own color televisions, and other signs of affluence are abundant.

## FREEDOM

For nearly 4 decades, Taiwan was under martial law. Opposition parties were not tolerated, and individual liberties were limited. A liberalization of this pattern began in 1986. Taiwan now seems to be on a path toward greater democratization. In 1991, 5,574 prisoners, including many political prisoners, were released in a general amnesty.

## HEALTH/WELFARE
Taiwan has one of the highest population densities in the world. Education is compulsory to age 15, and the country boasts more than 100 institutions of higher learning. Social programs, however, are less developed than those in Singapore, Japan, and some other Pacific Rim countries.

## ACHIEVEMENTS

From a largely agrarian economic base, Taiwan has been able to transform its economy into an export-based dynamo with international influence. Today, only 10 percent of the population work in agriculture, and Taiwan ranks among the top 20 exporters in the world.

# Thailand (Kingdom of Thailand)

## GEOGRAPHY
*Area in Square Miles (Kilometers):* 198,404 (514,000) (slightly more than twice the size of Wyoming)
*Capital (Population):* Bangkok (6,547,000)
*Environmental Concerns:* air and water pollution; deforestation; soil erosion; poaching
*Geographical Features:* central plain; Khorat Plateau in the east; mountains elsewhere
*Climate:* tropical monsoon

## PEOPLE

### Population
*Total:* 59,451,000
*Annual Growth Rate:* 1%
*Rural/Urban Population Ratio:* 80/20
*Major Languages:* Thai; English; dialects; others
*Ethnic Makeup:* 75% Thai; 14% Chinese; 11% Malay and others
*Religions:* 95% Buddhist; 4% Muslim; 1% others

### Health
*Life Expectancy at Birth:* 65 years (male); 73 years (female)
*Infant Mortality Rate (Ratio):* 32.1/1,000
*Average Caloric Intake:* 105% of FAO minimum
*Physicians Available (Ratio):* 1/4,245

### Education
*Adult Literacy Rate:* 94%
*Compulsory (Ages):* 6–15

## COMMUNICATION
*Telephones:* 1 per 17 people
*Daily Newspaper Circulation:* 48 per 1,000 people
*Televisions:* 1 per 85 people

## TRANSPORTATION
*Highways in Miles (Kilometers):* 34,141 (56,903)
*Railroads in Miles (Kilometers):* 2,813 (4,623)
*Usable Airfields:* 100
*Motor Vehicles in Use:* 5,000,000

## GOVERNMENT
*Type:* constitutional monarchy
*Independence Date:* founding date 1238
*Head of State/Government:* King Bhumibol Adulyadej; Prime Minister Chuan Leekpai

*Political Parties:* Thai Nation Party; Democratic Party; National Development Party; others
*Suffrage:* universal at 18

## MILITARY
*Military Expenditures (% of GDP):* 2.5%
*Current Disputes:* boundary disputes with Laos, others

## ECONOMY
*Currency ($ U.S. Equivalent):* 36.45 baht = $1
*Per Capita Income/GDP:* $7,700/$455.7 billion
*GDP Growth Rate:* 6.7%
*Inflation Rate:* 5.9%
*Unemployment Rate:* 2.6%

*Labor Force:* 34,030,000
*Natural Resources:* tin; rubber; natural gas; tungsten; tantalum; timber; lead; fish; gypsum; lignite; fluorite
*Agriculture:* rice; cassava; rubber; corn; sugarcane; coconuts; soybeans
*Industry:* tourism; textiles and garments; agricultural processing; beverages; tobacco; cement; electric appliances and components; electronics; furniture; plastics
*Exports:* $57.3 billion (primary partners Hong Kong, Japan, Singapore)
*Imports:* $72.4 billion (primary partners Japan, United States, Singapore)

 http://www.asiapac.org/research/thailand.htm

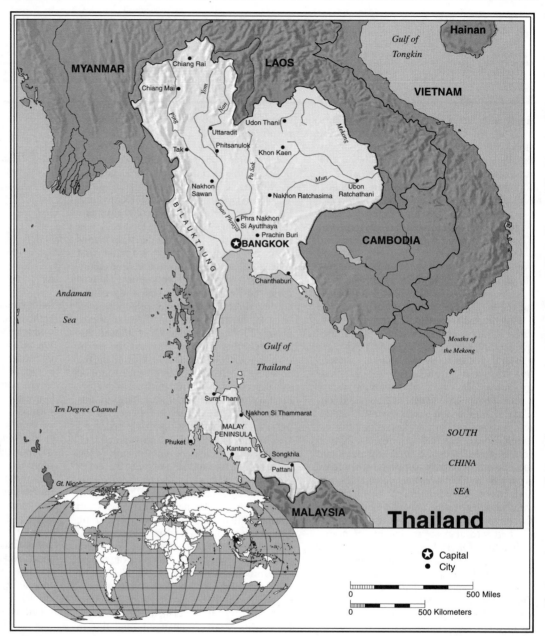

## THAILAND'S ANCIENT HERITAGE

The roots of Thai culture extend into the distant past. People were living in Thailand at least as early as the Bronze Age; by the time Thai people from China (some scholars think from as far away as Mongolia) had established the first Thai dynasty in the Chao Phya Valley, in A.D. 1238, some communities, invariably with a Buddhist temple or monastery at their centers, had been thriving in the area for 600 years. Early Thai culture was greatly influenced by Buddhist monks and traders from India and Sri Lanka (Ceylon).

By the seventeenth century, Thailand's ancient capital, Ayutthaya, boasted a larger population than that of London. Ayutthaya was known around the world for its wealth and for the beauty of its architecture, particularly its religious edifices. Attempts by European nations to obtain a share of the wealth were so inordinate that, in 1688, the king expelled all foreigners from the country. Later, warfare with Cambodia, Laos, and Malaya yielded tremendous gains in power and territory for Thailand, but it was periodically afflicted by Burma (present-day Myanmar), which briefly conquered Thailand in the 1760s (as it had done in the 1560s). The Burmese were finally defeated in 1780, but the destruction of the capital required the construction of a new city, near what, today, is Bangkok.

Generally speaking, the Thai people have been blessed over the centuries with benevolent kings, many of whom have been open to new ideas from Europe and North America. Gathering around them advisers from many nations, they improved transportation systems, education, and farming while maintaining the central place of Buddhism in Thai society. Occasionally royal support for religion overtook other societal needs, at the expense of the power of the government.

The gravest threat to Thailand came during the era of European colonial expansion. However, although both France and Britain forced Thailand to yield some of its holdings in Southeast Asia, Thailand—whose name means "Free Land"—was never completely conquered by European powers. Today, the country occupies a land area about the size of France.

## MODERN POLITICS

Since 1932, when a constitutional monarchy replaced the absolute monarchy, Thailand (formerly known as Siam) has weathered 17 attempted or successful military or political coups d'état (most recently in 1991). The Constitution has been revoked and replaced numerous times; governments have fallen under votes of no-confidence; students have mounted

(Photo credit United Nations/Prince)

Buddhism is an integral part of the Thai culture. Six hundred years ago, Buddhist monks traveled from India and Ceylon (present-day Sri Lanka) and built their temples and monasteries throughout Thailand. These newly ordained monks are meditating in the courtyard of a temple in Bangkok.

violent demonstrations against the government; and the military has, at various times, imposed martial law or otherwise curtailed civil liberties.

Clearly, Thai politics are far from stable. Nevertheless, there is a sense of stability in Thailand. Miraculously, its people were spared the direct ravages of the Vietnam War, which raged nearby for 20 years. Despite all the political upheavals, the same royal family has been in control of the Thai throne for nine generations, although its power has been severely delimited for some 60 years. Furthermore, before the first Constitution was enacted in 1932, the country had been ruled continuously, for more than 700 years, by often brilliant and progressive kings. At the height of Western imperialism, when France, Britain, the Netherlands, and Portugal were in control of every country on or near Thailand's borders, Thailand remained free of Western domination, al-

though it was forced—sometimes at gunpoint—to relinquish sizable chunks of its holdings in Cambodia and Laos to France, and holdings in Malaya to Britain. The reasons for this singular state of independence were the diplomatic skill of Thai leaders, Thai willingness to Westernize the government, and the desire of Britain and France to let Thailand remain interposed as a neutral buffer zone between their respective armies in Burma and Indochina.

The current king, Bhumibol Adulyadej, born in the United States and educated in Switzerland, is highly respected as head of state. The king is also the nominal head of the armed forces, and his support is critical to any Thai government. Despite Thailand's structures of democratic government, any administration that has not also received the approval of the military elites, many of whom hold seats in the Senate, has not prevailed for long. The military has been a rightist force in Thai

(Photo by Lisa Clyde)

Bangkok is one of the largest cities in the world. The city is interlaced with canals, and the population crowds along the banks. With the enormous influx of people who are lured by industrialization and economic opportunity, the environment has been strained to the limit.

politics, resisting reforms from the left that might have produced a stronger labor union movement, more freedom of expression (many television and radio stations in Thailand are controlled directly by the military), and less economic distance between the social classes. Military involvement in government increased substantially during the 1960s and 1970s, when a Communist insurgency threatened the government from within and the Vietnam War destabilized the external environment.

Until the February 1991 coup, there had been signs that the military was slowly withdrawing from direct meddling in the government. This may have been because the necessity for a strong military appeared to have lessened with the end of the cold war. In late 1989, for example, the Thai government signed a peace agreement with the Communist Party of Malaya, which had been harassing villagers along the Thai border for more than 40 years. Despite these political/military improvements, Commander Suchinda Kraprayoon led an army coup against the legally elected government in 1991 and, notwithstanding promises to the contrary, promptly had himself named prime minister. Immediately, Thai citizens, tired of the constant instability in government occasioned by military meddling, began staging mass demonstrations against Suchinda. The protesters were largely middle-class office workers who used their cellular telephones to communicate from one protest site to

another. The demonstrations were the largest in 20 years, and the military responded with violence; nearly 50 people were killed and more than 600 were injured. The public outcry was such that Suchinda was forced to appear on television being lectured by the king; he subsequently resigned. An interim premier dismissed several top military commanders and removed military personnel from the many government departments over which they had come to preside. Elections followed in 1992, and Thailand returned to civilian rule, with the military's influence greatly diminished.

The events of this latest coup show that the increasingly educated and affluent citizens of Thailand wish their country to be a true democracy. Still, unlike some democratic governments that have one dominant political party and one or two smaller opposition parties, party politics in Thailand is characterized by diversity. Indeed, so many parties compete for power that no single party is able to govern without forming coalitions with others. Parties are often founded on the strength of a single charismatic leader rather than on a distinct political philosophy, a circumstance that makes the entire political setting rather volatile. The Communist Party remains banned. Campaigns to elect the 360-seat Parliament often turn violent; in a recent election, 10 candidates were killed when their homes were bombed or sprayed with rifle fire, and nearly 50 gun-

men-for-hire were arrested or killed by police, who were attempting to protect the candidates of the 11 political parties vying for office. Former prime minister Banharn Silpaarcha was under constant attack due to a series of corruption scandals and alleged incompetence. He was eventually replaced.

## FOREIGN RELATIONS

Thailand is a member of the United Nations, the Association of Southeast Asian Nations, and many other regional and international organizations. Throughout most of its modern history, Thailand has maintained a pro-Western political position. During World War I, Thailand joined with the Allies; and during the Vietnam War, it allowed the United States to stage air attacks on North Vietnam from within its borders, and it served as a major rest and relaxation center for American soldiers. During World War II, Thailand briefly allied itself with Japan but made decided efforts after the war to reestablish its former Western ties.

Thailand's international positions have seemingly been motivated more by practical need than by ideology. During the colonial era, Thailand linked itself with Britain because it needed to offset the influence of France; during World War II, it joined with Japan in an apparent effort to prevent its country from being devastated by Japanese troops; during the Vietnam War, it supported the United States because the United States seemed to offer Thailand its only hope of not being directly engaged in military conflict in the region.

Thailand now seems to be tilting away from its close ties with the United States and toward a closer relationship with Japan. In the late 1980s, disputes with the United States over import tariffs and international copyright matters cooled the prior warm relationship (the United States accused Thailand of allowing the manufacture of counterfeit brand-name watches, clothes, computer software, and many other items, including medicines). Moreover, Thailand found in Japan a more ready, willing, and cooperative economic partner than the United States.

During the cold war and especially during the Vietnam War era, the Thai military strenuously resisted the growth of Communist ideology inside Thailand, and the Thai government refused to engage in normal diplomatic relations with the Communist regimes on its borders. Because of military pressure, elected officials refrained from advocating improved relations with the Communist governments. However, in 1988, Prime Minister Prem Tinslanond, a former general in the army who had been in control of the government for 8 years, stepped down from office, and opposition to normalization of relations seemed to mellow. The subsequent prime minister, Chatichai Choonhavan, who was ousted in the 1991 military coup, invited Cambodian leader Hun Sen to visit Thailand; he also made overtures to Vietnam and Laos. Chatichai's goal was to open the way for trade in the region by helping to settle the agonizing Cambodian conflict. He also hoped to bring stability to the region so that the huge refugee camps in Thailand, the largest in the world, could be dismantled and the refugees repatriated. Managing regional relations will continue to be difficult: Thailand fought a brief border war with Communist Laos in 1988. The influx of refugees from the civil wars in adjacent Cambodia and Myanmar continues to strain relations. Currently some 100,000 Karen refugees live precariously in 20 camps in Thailand along the Myanmar border. The Karens, many of whom practice Christianity and are the second-largest

ethnic group in Myanmar, have fought the various governments in their home country for years in an attempt to create an independent Karen state. Despite the patrol efforts of Thai soldiers, Myanmar soldiers frequently cross into Thailand at night to raid, rape, and kill the Karens.

## THE ECONOMY
Part of the thrust behind Thailand's diplomatic initiatives is the changing needs of its economy. For decades, Thailand saw itself as an agricultural country; indeed, more than half of the workforce remain in agriculture today, with rice as the primary commodity. Rice is Thailand's single most important export and a major source of government revenue. Every morning, Thai families sit down on the floor of their homes around bowls of hot and spicy *tom yam goong* soup and a large bowl of rice; holidays and festivals are scheduled to coincide with the various stages of planting and harvesting rice; and, in rural areas, students are dismissed at harvest time so that all members of a family can help in

the fields. So central is rice to the diet and the economy of the country that the Thai verb equivalent of "to eat," translated literally, means "to eat rice." Thailand is the fifth-largest exporter of rice in the world.

Unfortunately, Thailand's dependence on rice subjects its economy to the cyclical fluctuations of weather (sometimes the monsoons bring too little moisture) and market demand. Thus, in recent years, the government has invested millions of dollars in economic diversification. Not only have farmers been encouraged to grow a wider variety of crops, but tin, lumber, and offshore oil and gas production have also been promoted. Foreign investment in export-oriented manufacturing has been warmly welcomed. Japan in particular benefits from trading with Thailand in food and other commodities, and it sees Thailand as one of the more promising places to relocate smokestack industries. For its part, Thailand seems to prefer Japanese investment over that from the United States, because the Japanese seem more willing to engage in joint ventures and to

(UN/photo by Saw Lwin)

Rice is Thailand's most important export. Its production utilizes a majority of the agricultural workforce. Today, the government is attempting to diversify this reliance on rice, encouraging farmers to grow a wider variety of crops that are not so dependent on world markets and the weather.

| The formal beginning of Thailand as a nation A.D. 1200s | King Sukhothai creates the Thai alphabet 1279–1299 | King Rama I ascends the throne, beginning a nine-generation dynasty 1782 | Coup; constitutional monarchy 1932 | The country's name is changed from Siam to Thailand 1939 | Thailand joins Japan and declares war on the United States and Britain 1942 | Thailand resumes its historical pro-Western stance 1946 | Communist insurgency threatens Thailand's stability 1960s–1970s | Student protests usher in democratic reforms 1973 |
|---|---|---|---|---|---|---|---|---|

1990s

Chatichai Choonhavan replaces a former army general as prime minister

Chatichai is deposed in a military coup; mass demonstrations force a return to civilian rule

Currency decisions in Thailand precipitate the Southeast Asian financial crisis

show patience while enterprises become profitable. Indeed, economic ties with Japan are very strong. For instance, in recent years Japan has been the largest single investor in Thailand and has accounted for more than 40 percent of foreign direct investment (Taiwan, Hong Kong, and the United States each have accounted for about 10 percent). About 30 percent of Thai imports come from Japan, and approximately 17 percent of its exports go to Japan.

Thailand's shift to an export-oriented economy paid off until 1997, when pressures on its currency, the baht, required the government to allow it to float instead of having it pegged to the U.S. dollar. That action triggered the Southeast Asian financial crisis. Until that time, Thailand's gross domestic product growth rate had averaged about 10 percent a year—one of the highest in the world, and as high, or higher than, all the newly industrializing countries of Asia (Hong Kong, South Korea, Singapore, Taiwan, and China). Furthermore, unlike the Philippines and Indonesia, Thailand was able to achieve this incredible growth without very high inflation.

## SOCIAL PROBLEMS

Industrialization in Thailand, as everywhere, draws people to the cities. Bangkok is one of the largest cities in the world. Numerous problems, particularly traffic congestion and overcrowding, already complicate life for Bangkok residents. An international airport that opened near Bangkok in 1987 was so overcrowded just 4 years later that a new one had to be planned, and new harbors had to be constructed south of the city to alleviate congestion in the main port. Demographic projections indicate that there will

be a decline in population growth in the future as the birth rate drops and the average Thai household shrinks from the six people it was in 1970 to only three people by 2015. This will alter the social structure of urban families, especially as increased life expectancy adds older people to the population and forces the country to provide more services for the elderly. Today, however, many Thai people still make their living on farms, where they grow rice, rubber, and corn, or tend chickens and cattle, including the ever-present water buffalo. Thus, it is in the countryside (or "upcountry," as everywhere but Bangkok is called in Thailand) that the traditional culture of Thailand may be found. There, one still finds villages of typically fewer than 1,000 inhabitants, with houses built on wooden stilts alongside a canal or around a Buddhist monastery. One also finds, however, unsanitary conditions, higher rates of illiteracy, and lack of access to potable water. Of increasing concern is deforestation, as Thailand's growing population continues to use wood as its primary fuel for cooking and heat. The provision of social services does not meet demand even in the cities, but rural residents are particularly deprived.

Culturally, Thai people are known for their willingness to tolerate (although not necessarily to assimilate) diverse lifestyles and opinions. Buddhist monks, who shave their heads and vow celibacy, do not find it incongruous to beg for rice in districts of Bangkok known for prostitution and wild nightlife. And worshippers seldom object when a noisy, congested highway is built alongside the serenity of an ancient Buddhist temple. (However, the mammoth scale of the proposed $3.2 billion, four-level road and railway system in the city and its likely effect on cultural and relig-

ious sites prompted the Thai cabinet to order the construction underground; but the cabinet had to recant, when the Hong Kong firm designing the project announced that it was technically impossible to build it underground.)

Relative tolerance has mitigated ethnic conflict among Thailand's numerous minority groups. The Chinese, for instance, who are often disliked in other Asian countries because of their dominance of the business sectors, are able to live with little or no discrimination in Thailand; indeed, they constitute the backbone of Thailand's new industrial thrust.

## DEVELOPMENT

Many Thais are small-plot or tenant farmers, but the government has energetically promoted economic diversification. Despite high taxes, Thailand has a reputation as a good place for foreign investment. Electronics and other high-tech industries from Japan, the United States, and other countries have been very successful in Thailand.

## FREEDOM

Since 1932, when the absolute monarchy was abolished, Thailand has endured numerous military coups and countercoups, most recently in February 1991. Combined with the threat of Communist insurgencies, these have resulted in numerous declarations of martial law, press censorship, and suspensions of civil liberties.

## HEALTH/WELFARE

About 2,000 Thais out of every 100,000 inhabitants attend college (as compared to only 200 per 100,000 Vietnamese). Thailand has devoted substantial sums to the care of refugees from Cambodia and Vietnam. The rate of nonimmigrant population growth has dropped substantially since World War II. AIDS has emerged as a significant problem in Thailand.

## ACHIEVEMENTS

Thailand is the only Southeast Asian nation never to have been colonized by a Western power. It was also able to remain detached from direct involvement in the Vietnam War. Unique among Asian cultures, Thailand has a large number of women in business and other professions. Thai dancing is world-famous for its intricacy. In 1996, boxer Somluck Khamsing became the first Thai to win an Olympic gold medal.

# Vietnam (Socialist Republic of Vietnam)

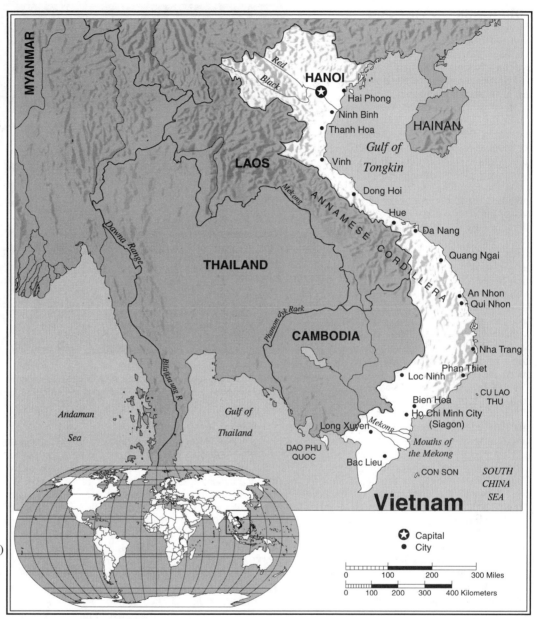

## GEOGRAPHY

*Area in Square Miles (Kilometers):* 121,278 (329,560) (slightly larger than New Mexico)

*Capital (Population):* Hanoi (1,236,000)

*Environmental Concerns:* deforestation; soil degradation; overfishing; water and air pollution; groundwater contamination

*Geographical Features:* low, flat delta in south and north; central highlands; hilly and mountainous in far north and northwest

*Climate:* tropical in south; monsoonal in north

## PEOPLE

### Population

*Total:* 75,124,000

*Annual Growth Rate:* 1.51%

*Rural/Urban Population Ratio:* 81/19

*Major Languages:* Vietnamese; French; Chinese; English; Khmer; tribal languages

*Ethnic Makeup:* 85%–90% Vietnamese; 3% Chinese; 7% Muong, Thai, Meo, and other mountain tribes

*Religions:* Buddhists, Confucians, and Taoists most numerous; Roman Catholics; Cao Dai; animists; Muslims; Protestants

### Health

*Life Expectancy at Birth:* 64 years (male); 68 years (female)

*Infant Mortality Rate (Ratio):* 37.2/1,000

*Average Caloric Intake:* 91% of FAO minimum

*Physicians Available (Ratio):* 1/3,096

### Education

*Adult Literacy Rate:* 94%

*Compulsory (Ages):* 6–11

## COMMUNICATION

*Telephones:* 1 per 95 people

*Daily Newspaper Circulation:* 8 per 1,000 people

*Televisions:* 1 per 23 people

## TRANSPORTATION

*Highways in Miles (Kilometers):* 63,629 (106,048)

*Railroads in Miles (Kilometers):* 1,701 (2,835)

*Usable Airfields:* 48

*Motor Vehicles in Use:* 200,000

## GOVERNMENT

*Type:* Communist state

*Independence Date:* September 2, 1945

*Head of State/Government:* Chairman Nong Duc Manh; Premier Phan Van Khai

*Political Party:* Communist Party of Vietnam

*Suffrage:* universal at 18

## MILITARY

*Military Expenditures (% of GDP):* 2.7%

*Current Disputes:* boundary disputes with Cambodia; border clashes with China; other boundary disputes

## ECONOMY

*Currency ($ U.S. Equivalent):* 11,100 new dong = $1

*Per Capita Income/GDP:* $1,470/$108.7 billion

*GDP Growth Rate:* 3.5%

*Inflation Rate:* 4.5%

*Unemployment Rate:* 25%

*Labor Force:* 32,700,000

*Natural Resources:* phosphates; coal; manganese; bauxite; chromate; oil and gas deposits; forests

*Agriculture:* rice; corn; potatoes; rubber; soybeans; coffee; tea; animal products; fish

*Industry:* food processing; textiles; machine building; mining; cement; chemical fertilizer; glass; tires; oil; fishing

*Exports:* $7.1 billion (primary partners Japan; Singapore, Taiwan)

*Imports:* $11.1 billion (primary partners Singapore, South Korea, Japan)

## FOREIGNERS IN VIETNAM

Foreign powers have tried to control Vietnam for 2,000 years. Most of that time it has been the Chinese who have had their eye on control—specifically of the food and timber resources of the Red River Valley in northern Vietnam.

Most of the northern Vietnamese are ethnically Chinese themselves; but over the years, they forged a separate identity for themselves and came to resent Chinese rule. Vietnam was conquered by China as early as 214 B.C. and again in 111 B.C., when the Han Chinese emperor Wu Ti established firm control. For about 1,000 years (until A.D. 939, and sporadically thereafter by the Mongols and other Chinese), the Chinese so thoroughly dominated the region that the Vietnamese people spoke and wrote in Chinese, built their homes like those of the Chinese, and organized their society according to Confucian values. In fact, Vietnam (*viet* means "people" and *nam* is Chinese for "south") is distinct among Southeast Asian nations because it is the only one whose early culture—in the north, at least—was influenced more by China than by India.

The Chinese did not, however, directly control all of what constitutes modern Vietnam. Until the late 1400s, the southern half of the country was a separate kingdom known as Champa. It was inhabited by people called Chams, who originally came from Indonesia. For a time, Champa was annexed by the north. However, between the northern region called Tonkin and the southern Chams-dominated region was a narrow strip of land occupied by Annamese peoples (a mixture of Chinese, Indonesian, and Indian ethnic groups), who eventually overthrew the Cham rulers and came to dominate the entire southern half of the country. In the 1500s, the northern Tonkin region and the southern Annamese region were ruled separately by two Vietnamese family dynasties. In the 1700s, military generals took power, unifying the two regions and attempting to annex or control parts of Cambodia and Laos as well.

In 1787, Nguyen-Anh, a general with imperial ambitions, signed a military-aid treaty with France. The French had already established Roman Catholic missions in the south, were providing mercenary soldiers for the Vietnamese generals, and were interested in opening up trade along the Red River. The Vietnamese eventually came to resent the increasingly active French involvement in their internal affairs and took steps to curtail French influence. The French, however, impressed by the resources of the Red River Valley in the north and the

(UN/DPI photo by Evan Scheider)

Addressing the UN General Assembly, Pham Gia Khiem, Deputy Prime Minister of Vietnam, expresses Vietnam's concern regarding the escalating worldwide drug problem.

Mekong River Delta in the south, were in no mood to pull out. Vietnam's geography contains rich tropical rain forests in the south, valuable mineral deposits in the north, and oil deposits offshore.

War broke out in 1858, and by 1863, the French had won control of many parts of the country, particularly in the south around the city of Saigon. Between 1884 and 1893, France solidified its gains in Southeast Asia by taking the northern city of Hanoi and the surrounding Tonkin region and by putting Cambodia, Laos, and Vietnam under one administrative unit, which it named *Indochina*.

Ruling Indochina was not easy for the French. For one thing, the region comprised hundreds of different ethnic groups, many of whom had been traditional enemies long before the French arrived. Within the borders of Vietnam proper lived Thais, Laotians, Khmers, northern and southern Vietnamese, and mountain peoples whom the French called Montagnards. Most of the people could not read or write—and those who could wrote in Chinese, because the Vietnamese language did not have a writing system until the French created it. Most people were Buddhists and Taoists, but many also followed animist beliefs.

In addition to the social complexity, the French had to contend with a rugged and

inhospitable land filled with high mountains and plateaus as well as lowland swamps kept damp by yearly monsoon rains. The French were eager to obtain the abundant rice, rubber, tea, coffee, and minerals of Vietnam but found that transporting these commodities to the coast for shipping was extremely difficult.

## VIETNAMESE RESISTANCE

France's biggest problem, however, was local resistance. Anti-French sentiment began to solidify in the 1920s; by the 1930s, Vietnamese youths were beginning to engage in open resistance. Prominent among these was Nguyen ai Quoc, who founded the Indochinese Communist Party in 1930 as a way of encouraging the Vietnamese people to overthrow the French. He is better known to the world today as Ho Chi Minh, meaning "He Who Shines."

Probably none of the resisters would have succeeded in evicting the French had it not been for Adolf Hitler's overrunning of France in 1940 and Japan's subsequent military occupation of Vietnam. These events convinced many Vietnamese that French power was no longer a threat to independence; the French remained nominally in control of Vietnam, but everyone knew that the Japanese had the real power. In 1941, Ho Chi Minh, having been trained in China by Maoist leaders, organized the League for the Independence of Vietnam, or Viet Minh. Upon the defeat of Japan in 1945, the Viet Minh assumed that they would take control of the government. France, however, insisted on reestablishing a French government. Within a year, the French and the Viet Minh were engaged in intense warfare, which lasted for 8 years.

The Viet Minh initially fought the French with weapons supplied by the United States when that country was helping local peoples to resist the Japanese. Communist China later became the main supplier of assistance to the Viet Minh. This development convinced U.S. leaders that Vietnam under the Viet Minh would very likely become another Communist state. To prevent this occurrence, U.S. president Harry S. Truman decided to back France's efforts to recontrol Indochina (although the United States had originally opposed France's desire to regain its colonial holdings). In 1950, the United States gave $10 million in military aid to the French—an act that began a long, costly, and painful U.S. involvement in Vietnam.

In 1954, the French lost a major battle in the north of Vietnam, at Dien Bien Phu, after which they agreed to a settlement with the Viet Minh. The country was to be temporarily divided at the 17th Parallel (a latitude above which the Communist Viet Minh held sway and below which non-Communist Vietnamese had the upper hand), and countrywide elections were to be held in 1956. The elections were never held, however; and under Ho Chi Minh, Hanoi became the capital of North Vietnam, while Ngo Dinh Diem became president of South Vietnam, with its capital in Saigon.

## THE UNITED STATES ENTERS THE WAR

Ho Chi Minh viewed the United States as yet another foreign power trying to control the Vietnamese people through its backing of the government in the South. The United States, concerned about the continuing attacks on the south by northern Communists and by southern Communist sympathizers known as Viet Cong, increased funding and sent military advisers to help prop up the increasingly fragile southern government. By 1963, President John F. Kennedy had sent 12,000 military "advisers" to Vietnam. In 1964, an American destroyer ship was attacked in the Gulf of Tonkin by North Vietnam. The U.S. Congress responded by giving then-president Lyndon Johnson a free hand in ordering U.S. military action against the north; before this time, U.S. troops had not been involved in direct combat.

(United Nations/J. K. Isaac)

Many thousands of Vietnamese have fled the country in recent decades to face new lives of uncertainty in other countries. These Vietnamese are newly arrived in prosperous Hong Kong.

By 1969, some 542,000 American soldiers and nearly 66,000 soldiers from 40 other countries were in battle against North Vietnamese and Viet Cong troops. Despite unprecedented levels of bombing and use of sophisticated electronic weaponry, U.S. and South Vietnamese forces continued to lose ground to the Communists, who used guerrilla tactics and built their successes on latent antiforeign sentiment among the masses as well as extensive Soviet military aid. At the height of the war, as many as 300 U.S. soldiers were being killed every week.

| China begins 1,000 years of control or influence over the northern part of Vietnam 214 B.C. | Northern and southern Vietnam are ruled separately by two Vietnamese families A.D. 1500s | Military generals overthrow the ruling families and unite the country 1700s | General Nguyen-Anh signs a military-aid treaty with France 1787 | After 5 years of war, France acquires its first holdings in Vietnam 1863 | France establishes the colony of Indochina 1893 | Ho Chi Minh founds the Indochinese Communist Party 1930 | The Japanese control Vietnam 1940s | France attempts to regain control Post-1945 |

Watching the war on the evening television news, many Americans began to withdraw support. Anti-Vietnam rallies became a daily occurrence on American university campuses, and many people began finding ways to protest U.S. involvement: dodging the draft by fleeing to Canada, burning down ROTC buildings, and publicly challenging the U.S. government to withdraw. President Richard Nixon had once declared that he was not going to be the first president to lose a war, but, after his expansion of the bombing into Cambodia to destroy Communist supply lines and after significant battlefield losses, domestic resistance became so great that an American withdrawal seemed inevitable. The U.S. attempt to "Vietnamize" the war by training South Vietnamese troops and supplying them with advanced weapons did little to change South Vietnam's sense of having been sold out by the Americans.

Secretary of State Henry Kissinger negotiated a cease-fire settlement with the North in 1973, but most people believed that, as soon as the Americans left, the North would resume fighting and would probably take control of the entire country. This indeed happened, and in April 1975, under imminent attack by victorious North Vietnamese soldiers, the last Americans lifted off in helicopters from the grounds of the U.S. Embassy in Saigon, the South Vietnamese government surrendered, and South Vietnam ceased to exist.

The war wreaked devastation on Vietnam. It has been estimated that nearly 2 million people were killed during just the American phase of the war; another 2.5 million were killed during the French era. In addition, 4.5 million people were wounded, and nearly 9 million lost their homes. U.S. casualties included more than 58,000 soldiers killed and 300,000 wounded.

## A CULTURE, NOT JUST A BATTLEFIELD

Because of the Vietnam War, many people think of Vietnam as if it were just a battlefield. But Vietnam is much more than that. It is a rich culture made up of peoples representing diverse aspects of Asian life. In good times, Vietnam's dinner tables are supplied with dozens of varieties of fish and the ever-present bowl of rice. Sugarcane and bananas are also favorites. Be-

cause about 80 percent of the people live in the countryside, the population as a whole possesses a living library of practical know-how about farming, livestock raising, fishing, and home manufacture. Today, only about 200 out of every 100,000 Vietnamese people attend college, but most children attend elementary school and 94 percent of the adult population can read and write.

Literacy was not always so high; much of the credit is due the Communist government, which, for political-education reasons, has promoted schooling throughout the country. Another thing that the government has done, of course, is to unify the northern and southern halves of the country. This has not been an easy task, for, upon the division of the country in 1954, the North followed a socialist route of economic development, while in the South, capitalism became the norm.

Religious belief in Vietnam is an eclectic affair and reflects the history of the nation; on top of a Confucian and Taoist foundation, created during the centuries of Chinese rule, rests Buddhism (a modern version of which is called Hoa Hao and claims 1 million believers); French Catholicism, which claims about 15 percent of the population; and a syncretist faith called Cao Dai, which claims about 2 million followers. Cao Dai models itself after Catholicism in terms of hierarchy and religious architecture, but it differs in that it accepts many Gods—Jesus, Buddha, Mohammed, Lao-Tse, and others—as part of its pantheon. Many Vietnamese pray to their ancestors and ask for blessings at small shrines located inside their homes. Animism, the worship of spirits believed to live in nature, is also practiced by many of the Montagnards. (About 400 Christianized Montagnards, incidentally, fought the Communists continually since 1975 and have only recently taken refuge outside of Vietnam.)

Freedom of religious worship has been permitted, and church organizational hierarchies have not been declared illegal. In fact, the government, sensing the need to solicit the support of believers (especially the Catholics), has been careful in its treatment of religions and has even avoided collectivizing farms in areas known to have large numbers of the faithful.

## THE ECONOMY

When the Communists won the war in 1975 and brought the capitalist South under its jurisdiction, the United States imposed an economic embargo on Vietnam, which most other nations honored and which remained in effect for 19 years, until President Bill Clinton ended it in 1994. As a consequence of war damage as well as the embargo and the continuing military involvement of Vietnam in the Cambodian War and against the Chinese along their mutual borders, the first decade after the end of the Vietnam War saw the entire nation fall into a severe economic slump. Whereas Vietnam had once been an exporter of rice, it now had to import rice from abroad. Inflation raged at 250 percent a year, and the government was hardpressed to cover its debts. Many South Vietnamese were, of course, opposed to Communist rule and attempted to flee on boats—but, contrary to popular opinion, most refugees left Vietnam because they could not get enough to eat, not because they were being persecuted.

Beginning in the mid-1980s, the Vietnamese government began to liberalize the economy. Under a restructuring plan called *doi moi* (similar in meaning to Soviet *perestroika*), the government began to introduce elements of free enterprise into the economy. Moreover, despite the Communist victory, the South remained largely capitalist; today, with wages lower than almost every other country in Asia, an infrastructure built by France and the United States, and laborers who can speak at least some English or French, foreign nations are finding Vietnam a good place to invest funds. In 1991 alone, Australian, Japanese, French, and other companies spent $3 billion in Vietnam. After the embargo ended, firms poured into Vietnam to do business. By the end of 1994, more than 540 firms, especially from Singapore, Hong Kong, Japan, and France, were doing business in Vietnam, and some 70 other countries had expressed interest. The government's move toward privatization and capitalism, begun in 1986, was so successful that by the early 1990s, nearly 90 percent of the workforce were in the private sector, and loans from the World Bank, the Asian Development Bank, and the International Monetary Fund were flowing in to jumpstart national development.

| The United States begins to aid France to contain the spread of communism **1950s** | Geneva agreements end 8 years of warfare with the French; Vietnam is divided into North and South **1954** | South Vietnam's regime is overthrown by a military coup **1961** | The United States begins bombing North Vietnam **1965** | Half a million U.S. troops are fighting in Vietnam **1969** | The United States withdraws its troops and signs a cease-fire **1973** | North Vietnamese troops capture Saigon and reunite the country; U.S. embargo begins **1975** | Vietnamese troops capture Cambodia; China invades Vietnam **1979** | Communist Vietnam begins liberalization of the economy **1980s** |

**1990s**

Unfortunately, the financial crises in nearby Malaysia, Indonesia, and other countries caused Vietnam to devalue its currency in 1998. Combined with El Niño–caused drought and forest fires (some 900 fires in 1998), the currency devaluation slowed economic growth and gave government leaders an excuse to trumpet the failures of capitalism. Leaders declared that, despite some liberalization, the government is committed to communism.

Much to the worry of government traditionalists, the Vietnamese people seem fascinated with foreign products. They want to move ahead and put the decades of warfare behind them. Western travelers in Vietnam are treated warmly, and the Vietnamese government has cooperated with the U.S. government's demands for more information about missing U.S. soldiers. In 1994, after a 40-year absence, the United States opened up a diplomatic mission in Hanoi as a first step toward full diplomatic recognition. So eager are the Vietnamese to reestablish economic ties with the West that the Communist authorities have even offered to allow the U.S. Navy to lease its former port at Cam Ranh Bay (the offer has not yet been accepted). Diplomatic bridge-building between the United States and Vietnam increased in the 1990s, when a desire to end the agony of the Cambodian conflict created opportunities for the two sides to talk together. Telecommunications were established in 1992, and in the same year, the United States gave $1 million in aid to assist handicapped Vietnamese war veterans. Finally, in 1995, some 20 years after the end of the Vietnam War, the United States established full diplomatic relations with Vietnam.

Despite this gradual warming of relations, however, anti-Western sentiment remains strong in some parts of the population, particularly the military. As recently as 1996, police were still tearing down or covering up signs advertising Western products and anti-open-door policy editorials were still appearing in official newspapers.

**HEARTS AND MINDS**

As one might expect, resistance to the current Vietnamese government comes largely from the South Vietnamese, who, under both French and American tutelage, adopted Western values of capitalism and consumerism. Many South Vietnamese had feared that after the North's victory, South Vietnamese soldiers would be mercilessly killed by the victors; some were in fact killed, but many former government leaders and military officers were instead sent to "reeducation camps," where, combined with hard labor, they were taught the values of socialist thinking. Several hundred such internees remain incarcerated 2 decades after the end of the war. Many of the well-known leaders of the South fled the country when the Communists arrived and now are making new lives for themselves in the United States, Canada, Australia, and other Western countries. Those who have remained—for example, Vietnamese members of the Roman Catholic Church—have occasionally resisted the Communists openly, but their protests have been silenced. Hanoi continues to insist on policies that remove the rights to which the South Vietnamese had

U.S. and Vietnamese officials begin meetings to resolve the Cambodian war

The U.S. economic embargo of Vietnam is lifted; the United States establishes full diplomatic relations

Thousands of refugees are forcibly repatriated from around Southeast Asia; Vietnam devalues its currency

become accustomed. For instance, the regime has halted publication and dissemination of books that it judges to have "harmful contents." There is not much that average Vietnamese can do to change these policies except passive obstruction, which many are doing even though it damages the efficiency of the economy.

**DEVELOPMENT**

Vietnam is again a major exporter of rice. It also produces cement, fertilizer, steel, and coal. Aid and loans from other Asian nations are helping with the construction of roads and other infrastructure, but the per capita income based on gross domestic product is still only $1,140 a year.

**FREEDOM**

Vietnam is nominally governed by an elected National Assembly. Real power, however, resides in the Communist Party and with those military leaders who helped defeat the U.S. and South Vietnamese armies. Civil rights, such as the right of free speech, are curtailed. Private-property rights are limited. In 1995, Vietnam adopts its first civil code providing property and inheritance rights for citizens.

**HEALTH/WELFARE**

Health care has been nationalized and the government operates a social-security system, but the chronically stagnant economy has meant that few Vietnamese receive sufficient health care or have an adequate nutritional intake. The World Health Organization has been involved in disease-abatement programs since reunification of the country in 1975.

**ACHIEVEMENTS**

Vietnam provides free and compulsory schooling for all children. The curricular content has been changed in an attempt to eliminate Western influences. New Economic Zones have been created in rural areas to try to lure people away from the major cities of Hanoi, Hue, and Ho Chi Minh City (formerly Saigon).

# Articles from the World Press

provided lumber and important environmental protection of land and water. Recently, however, cheap imported lumber has caused a drop in the number of people involved in forestry, thus endangering maintenance work.

# Topic Guide to Articles

| TOPIC AREA | TREATED IN | TOPIC AREA | TREATED IN |
|---|---|---|---|
| **Agriculture** | 14. State of the Staple<br>28. Little House on the Paddy | **Economic Investment** | 3. How Asia Went from Boom to Gloom<br>5. End of a "Miracle"<br>10. Sputter, Cough, Choke<br>11. Why Japan Won't Budge<br>12. Arthritic Nation<br>26. Enter at Own Risk |
| **Children** | 13. Once Prized, Japan's Elderly Feel Abandoned and Fearful | | |
| **China** | 18. Agent of Change<br>19. New Order<br>20. China's New Family Values | **Economy** | 2. Controlling Economic Competition in the Pacific Rim<br>3. How Asia Went from Boom to Gloom<br>7. Out of the Ashes?<br>9. In Defense of Japanese Bureaucracy<br>10. Sputter, Cough, Choke<br>11. Why Japan Won't Budge<br>12. Arthritic Nation<br>23. Korean Struggle |
| **Communist Party** | 18. Agent of Change<br>29. Vietnam's Communists Eye New Vices as Market Worries Rise | | |
| **Consumerism** | 29. Vietnam's Communists Eye New Vices as Market Worries Rise | | |
| **Cultural Development** | 1. Asia, a Civilization in the Making<br>4. Asian Values and the Asian Crisis<br>8. Japanese Roots<br>9. In Defense of Japanese Bureaucracy<br>22. Not Fair: Indonesia Feels More Unequal than It Is | **Environment** | 14. State of the Staple<br>15. Far from the Concrete Jungle<br>21. Indonesia's Discontent |
| | | **Family** | 13. Once Prized, Japan's Elderly Feel Abandoned and Fearful<br>17. Cambodian Calamity<br>20. China's New Family Values<br>28. Little House on the Paddy |
| **Cultural Roots** | 1. Asia, a Civilization in the Making<br>4. Asian Values and the Asian Crisis<br>8. Japanese Roots<br>9. In Defense of Japanese Bureaucracy<br>11. Why Japan Won't Budge<br>13. Once Prized, Japan's Elderly Feel Abandoned and Fearful<br>16. Continental Divide<br>25. Between God and Mammon | **Foreign Investments** | 4. Asian Values and the Asian Crisis<br>19. New Order<br>23. Korean Struggle<br>26. Enter at Own Risk |
| | | **Foreign Relations** | 2. Controlling Economic Competition in the Pacific Rim<br>4. Asian Values and the Asian Crisis |
| **Current Leaders** | 6. Out with the Old, In with Something Much Less Familiar<br>7. Out of the Ashes?<br>18. Agent of Change<br>24. Unlocking the Citadel<br>27. Narcopolitics in Burma | **Foreign Trade** | 4. Asian Values and the Asian Crisis<br>5. End of a "Miracle"<br>15. Far from the Concrete Jungle<br>24. Unlocking the Citadel<br>26. Enter at Own Risk |
| **Economic Development** | 2. Controlling Economic Competition in the Pacific Rim<br>3. How Asia Went from Boom to Gloom<br>4. Asian Values and the Asian Crisis<br>5. End of a "Miracle"<br>7. Out of the Ashes?<br>10. Sputter, Cough, Choke<br>17. Cambodian Calamity<br>19. New Order<br>23. Korean Struggle<br>24. Unlocking the Citadel | **Health and Welfare** | 12. Arthritic Nation<br>13. Once Prized, Japan's Elderly Feel Abandoned and Fearful<br>14. State of the Staple<br>16. Continental Divide<br>20. China's New Family Values<br>21. Indonesia's Discontent<br>22. Not Fair: Indonesia Feels More Unequal than It Is<br>28. Little House on the Paddy |

| TOPIC AREA | TREATED IN | TOPIC AREA | TREATED IN |
|---|---|---|---|
| **History** | 1. Asia, a Civilization in the Making<br>4. Asian Values and the Asian Crisis<br>8. Japanese Roots<br>13. Once Prized, Japan's Elderly Feel Abandoned and Fearful<br>16. Continental Divide<br>25. Between God and Mammon | **Political Unrest** | 6. Out with the Old, In with Something Much Less Familiar<br>7. Out of the Ashes?<br>16. Continental Divide<br>21. Indonesia's Discontent<br>27. Narcopolitics in Burma |
| **Hong Kong** | 19. New Order | **Politics** | 6. Out with the Old, In with Something Much Less Familiar<br>9. In Defense of Japanese Bureaucracy<br>10. Sputter, Cough, Choke<br>11. Why Japan Won't Budge<br>18. Agent of Change<br>19. New Order<br>29. Vietnam's Communists Eye New Vices as Market Worries Rise |
| **Human Rights** | 12. Arthritic Nation<br>13. Once Prized, Japan's Elderly Feel Abandoned and Fearful<br>17. Cambodian Calamity<br>19. New Order<br>22. Not Fair: Indonesia Feels More Unequal than It Is<br>26. Enter at Own Risk<br>27. Narcopolitics in Burma | | |
| | | **Religion** | 1. Asia, a Civilization in the Making<br>25. Between God and Mammon |
| **Industrial Development** | 11. Why Japan Won't Budge<br>26. Enter at Own Risk | **Social Reform** | 12. Arthritic Nation<br>13. Once Prized, Japan's Elderly Feel Abandoned and Fearful<br>19. New Order<br>20. China's New Family Values |
| **Khmer Rouge** | 17. Cambodian Calamity | | |
| **Minorities** | 16. Continental Divide<br>17. Cambodian Calamity<br>21. Indonesia's Discontent | **Social Unrest** | 6. Out with the Old, In with Something Much Less Familiar<br>16. Continental Divide<br>21. Indonesia's Discontent<br>22. Not Fair: Indonesia Feels More Unequal than It Is<br>27. Narcopolitics in Burma |
| **Natives** | 8. Japanese Roots<br>16. Continental Divide<br>17. Cambodian Calamity<br>28. Little House on the Paddy | | |
| **Natural Resources** | 14. State of the Staple<br>15. Far from the Concrete Jungle<br>21. Indonesia's Discontent | **Standard of Living** | 3. How Asia Went from Boom to Gloom<br>4. Asian Values and the Asian Crisis<br>13. Once Prized, Japan's Elderly Feel Abandoned and Fearful<br>23. Korean Struggle<br>28. Little House on the Paddy<br>29. Vietnam's Communists Eye New Vices as Market Worries Rise |
| **Political Development** | 1. Asia, a Civilization in the Making<br>9. In Defense of Japanese Bureaucracy<br>18. Agent of Change | | |
| **Political Reform** | 6. Out with the Old, In with Something Much less Familiar<br>7. Out of the Ashes? | | |

*Article 1*

*Foreign Affairs*, July/August, 1996

# Asia, a Civilization in the Making

*Masakazu Yamazaki*

## EAST ASIA, THE PACIFIC, AND THE MODERN AGE

AS THE specter of communism fades, some warn of a new East-West confrontation. The remarkable rise of East Asia in recent decades, they say, has been fostered by a civilization very different from the West's, and this poses dangers for international relations. Such thinking, however, is based on Kiplingesque assumptions about an Asian civilization whose existence it fails to demonstrate. At no time in history has an Asian or Eastern civilization arisen over and above the many national and ethnic civilizations and cultures found in that vast region.

Much writing from the West on the purported divide is economically or militarily alarmist, focusing on huge trade deficits with East Asian countries, China's flexing of military muscle, and a few cases in which Chinese or North Korean arms were reportedly sold to Iraq or Iran. Some go so far as to predict that what they see as East Asian civilization may cozy up to Islamic civilization and make common cause against Western power and values. East Asian writers, on the other hand, tend to be extremely sanguine about their region's recent development and its future, contrasting these with Europe's economic plight and the West's social problems. All participants in the debate, however, emphatically affirm the existence of a distinctive East Asian frame of mind, even if they describe it only by saying that it, unlike its Western counterpart, subscribes to no shared value system like democracy or capitalism.

This very diversity and flexibility, some in East Asia argue, will smooth the way for the integration of their region; even North Korea and Myanmar may be brought in. But such integration requires a binding force capable of overriding the logically incompatible value systems the people of the region espouse. That force could only be a tacitly shared psychology or style of life. Some of the thinkers lined up along the arti-

ficial East-West divide have noted common features among cities all around the Pacific Basin and even speculated about a melding there of Western and what they call Eastern civilization. What few have seen clearly, however, is that the force behind the convergence observable in the region today is modernity, which was born in the West but has radically transformed both East and West in this century.

## AMBIGUOUS ASIA

IN TREATING the question of civilization in Asia, one must first deal with the ambiguity of Asia as a concept. This ambiguity is an irritant to Asians and non-Asians alike and the source of a more than semantic problem in international diplomacy. From around 130 B.C. "Asia" was the name of a province of the Roman Empire on the eastern shore of the Aegean. Today it refers to a sweeping stretch of land and sea from the Middle East to the South Pacific islands—an area too broad to make any sense as a geographical unit. The 1994 Asian Sports Festival in Hiroshima saw Kyrgyz and Tajik athletes from the former Soviet Union in action, but no Hawaiians, Siberians, Australians, or New Zealanders were invited because of the host organization's uncertainty about what constituted Asia. At times, admittedly, countries exploit the confusion over the region's boundaries for political purposes. Many nations along the Pacific Rim—including the United States, Canada, and Chile—participate in the Asia-Pacific Economic Cooperation forum, organized on Australia's initiative, but the white-dominated nations are denied membership in the East Asian Economic Caucus envisaged by Malaysian Prime Minister Mahathir bin Mohamad. And if delineating Asia is a problem, East Asia poses even greater difficulties. This region's energy is palpable but its identity is elusive. Is it a geographical area, an agglomeration of ethic populations, or a civilization in the making?

One thing is certain: the region the West disdained for its "Asiatic stagnation" and whose people suffered because of its lack of economic growth is no more. Flush with Western and

---

MASAKAZU YAMAZAKI is a playwright and Professor of comparative Studies on Cultures at East Asia University. Mask and Sword collects two of his plays in English translations.

Japanese capital and technology, Asian nations are growing vigorously, supplying the rest of the world with products and workers and opening their own markets. Riding the global tide of modernization and industrialization, the region at long last has been integrated into the world economic system. This, however, does not mean that the development that has occurred has been "Asiatic," or that an Asia once seen as dormant is now wide awake.

## CIVILIZATION AS UMBRELLA

TO REPEAT: there has never been an Asian, let alone East Asian, sphere of civilization. Western civilization is dominant in Europe and North America, but Asia has known only the individual national and ethnic cultures and civilizations that have arisen in areas of the region.

Western civilization, whose beginnings I place toward the end of the eighth century A.D., created a world that contained different nationalities while transcending national identity. Earlier civilizations, by contrast, whether Greek, Judaic, or Chinese, were essentially ethnic or national and maintained their identity through unity. Customs and forms adopted from the outside were fused with traditional patterns, never acknowledged as a foreign presence. Everyone and everything outside the group was relegated to the realm of the "barbarous," beyond the civilized pale.

# Asia has known diverse civilizations, never an Asian civilization.

From Constantine until the latter part of the eighth century, the dominant force in the West was Christianity, which fused the Judaic and Hellenic traditions and, thanks to extensive trade and the use of Latin as the official language, constituted a unified sphere of civilization. But toward the end of the eighth century, as Charlemagne consolidated his empire, Islamic control of Mediterranean trade routes forced fundamental changes in the West. Denied any chance at prosperity through commerce, the West became an agricultural society based on large landholdings. This system of land ownership gave rise to decentralization, leading to dual rule by powerful princes and the Catholic Church. Latin's status gradually eroded, allowing local vernaculars to assert themselves as national languages.

The rise of duality in both rule and language marked the beginning of the Western world civilization. Under the civilizational umbrella dating back to the Roman Empire, and within the unifying framework of Christian civilization, the West set out on its journey toward a world civilization that would encompass national and ethnic civilizations and cultures alien to one another. The crucial factor in the process was that no single nation claimed the supranational umbrella as its own. The Greeks had been debilitated, while the Romans had turned Italian and Latin remained the common language only for writing. The Jews preserved their identity but were driven to the bottom of the social scale, with Hebrew consigned to libraries and Yiddish and Ladino taking its place. Westerners, whether English, German, or French, could and still can talk about Judeo-Hellenistic civilization on an equal footing.

Asia has never had a comparable superstructure of civilization. Asians lack an experience of political unification like the West's under the Roman Empire, nor do they possess a common tradition in language, currency, laws, roads, or architecture. In the absence of an overall, if loose, religious framework such as Christianity provided for the West, Confucianism, Buddhism, Taoism, Islam, Christianity, and a variety of indigenous religions have coexisted in Asia. There was no writing system like the alphabet that could spell words from different national languages. There was no universal system of musical notation, nor contemporaneous development of artistic styles as in the West's Romanesque, Gothic, and Renaissance periods. Far larger than Europe, Asia stretches from the Arctic to the tropics, and one cannot find in that swath any fundamental similarity in mores, manners, or customs.

## CHINESE AND BARBARIANS

SOME WOULD contend that Chinese civilization is the basis of an Asian civilization, and China's influence has indeed been extensive. But the Chinese Empire differed greatly from the Roman. It was the homogeneous empire of the Han, conquering the Manchurians, to be sure, but failing to bring the Mongolians, Vietnamese, Koreans, or Japanese under its control. China exported its laws, religions, art forms, and ideographic writing, but their impact was on the same order as, say, French civilization's on the Germans, in no way tantamount to the framework a world civilization provides. Although the use of Chinese ideograms is widespread in neighboring nations, it failed to progress beyond mimicry into the universalization of the civilization; even today, Japanese politicians are reportedly embarrassed when they sign Sino-Japanese diplomatic agreements with brush and ink, as their ancestors learned to do from the Chinese.

The Chinese, for their part, were generally allergic to outside cultural influences and were particularly reluctant to credit alien contributions to the development of their culture. For them, the Japanese and the Vietnamese were always the "eastern barbarians" and the "southern savages." The Italian descendants of the Romans recognize that they can learn something from the English about Latin language and literature, whereas the Chinese have never turned an attentive ear to Japanese interpretations of Confucius. German directors have impressed and moved Englishmen with their productions of Shakespeare, but the Japanese calligrapher Sugawara Michizane's distinguished work has never had the slightest impact on Chinese practitioners of the art.

The primary reason for Chinese civilization's unusual exclusivity is that the Han have endured, for good or for ill, for 4,000 years. Through the Mongol invasion and Manchu domination, the Han preserved their ethnic civilization as a badge of their identity; "Down with the Manchu, long live the Han!" was their motto as late as the end of the last century. And in the eyes of surrounding peoples, Chinese civilization was simply the source of their borrowings; the civilization never suggested that they had claims on it.

That the Chinese strand has dominated so large an area for so long has inhibited the development of an Asian civilization. The dynamism of a civilization derives from mutual influence, intermixture, and the friendly rivalry of different peoples, but no such chemistry has been at work in Asia. National or ethnic civilizations can undergo such changes only under the umbrella of a world civilization, and Asia has never known such a dual structure.

Buddhist civilization could have become Asia's world civilization. Born in India but disowned there, Buddhism spread to China, northeastern Asia, and Southeast Asia, establishing itself as a religion shared by many ethnic groups. But it has left no indelible mark in the Malay Peninsula or Indonesia, and has been emaciated in China and Korea under the Confucian onslaught that began in the fifteenth century. Buddhism has managed to retain some hold on Japan and part of Southeast Asia, but the two centers have little contact, and the faith survives in Asia at large only as a localized religion. The history of Buddhism, in fact, illustrates how difficult it is for any civilization without an ethnic proprietor to attain dominance and for any dual structure of civilization to take root in Asian soil.

Strangely enough, a prototype of a dual structure was once firmly in place in the early monoethnic Japanese civilization. From time immemorial into the modern era, the Japanese regarded Chinese civilization not as another national civilization but as a world civilization and were painfully conscious that their own civilization occupied a subsidiary position. Few, however, had set foot in China, and their knowledge of the civilization was limited to Chinese characters and other imported traits and institutions. They failed to appreciate that Chinese civilization was a living national civilization, mistaking it for a supranational world civilization. Thus they yielded tamely to Chinese influences, and saw themselves as an alien presence tolerated within the supposedly universal civilization. This mindset may well have facilitated Japanese acceptance of Western civilization in the nineteenth century. If exposure to a strange civilization does not set off alarms warning of imminent clashes but is instead taken as an invitation to share in common property, the recipient nation will naturally be more open and tolerant than it would otherwise be.

The dual structure of rule and language in the West significantly aided the acceptance of Arab civilization that started the West on the path of modernization as far back as the twelfth century. When Spaniards and Italians first encountered Arab civilization, they would have subconsciously placed it on the same level as Western world civilization—which would make it common property that they were encouraged to share in. Since the Arabs in real life were regarded as a great peril, how else could the West have accepted their insights on such fundamental subjects as mathematics, science and technology, and even—if Arab mysticism indeed influenced the twelfth-century troubadors, as some scholars believe—love?

Asia, unfortunately, possessed no such dual structure of civilization or the dynamism it generates. In Japan and a few other nations on the periphery, there was some notion of an Eastern world civilization encompassing all of Asia, but in actuality no such thing existed. This absence ensured that the seeds of modernization in Asia would fail to sprout but would lie dormant until the encounter with the West.

## MORNING IN ASIA

MODERN WESTERN civilization has brought the world umbrella to Asia for the first time, and a dual structure of civilization is now taking shape in the region. The Asian world and Asian civilization cited so often of late have their origins not deep in the past but in modernization this century in an Asia in contact with the West.

# The entire fabric of society is being geared toward modernization.

In the past 100 years or so, East Asian nations as a group have set out to modernize, and they have been fairly successful in the endeavor. Progress has extended beyond economic development; the entire fabric of society is being geared to modernization, more rapidly in some fields than in others. The formation of a nation-state under the rule of law and legitimate institutions, the secularization of ethics and mores, the rise of industry, and the growth of market economies integrated into the global economy all have been or soon will be attained in virtually all countries of the region except North Korea.

The world over, as education is extended, mass media grow, and leisure activities and consumer goods gain popularity, a middle class arises that favors democratic development. Although each country in East Asia defines and protects human rights and democratic principles differently, no national leader except perhaps North Korea's Kim Jung Il would deny their legitimacy. Members of the Association of Southeast Asian Nations have nearly reached consensus on such fundamentals as the separation of politics from religion, one man—one vote representation, and public trial. When it comes to social welfare, women's liberation, freedom of conscience, access to modern health care, and other social policies, almost all the countries of the region now speak the same language as the West.

In city after large city in East Asia, one finds glass-and-steel towers soaring, the metric system in use, and intellectuals employing American English as the lingua franca. People drive cars, wear Western-style clothes to work, have electric appliances at home, and enjoy jazz, motion pictures, and soap operas. Often television programs are broadcast across the Pacific Basin. It is getting so that one feels at home on both sides of the Pacific.

# The secular tolerance of Asian religions has been very good for business.

These changes began in the early 1900s in Japan and in mid-century elsewhere in the region, with all countries going through the same process, experiencing its drawbacks as well as rewards, in the space of a single century. Nothing comparable has ever occurred in Africa, the Middle East, or Russia. It is this contemporaneous experience that is the driving force behind East Asia's integration as a region.

### THE BUSINESS OF RELIGION

LOOKING AT the region for common factors that might have made such a transformation possible, the secular tolerance of Asian religions, or the weakness of what is fashionably called fundamentalism, stands out. Asia has had its share of ascetics and spiritual disciplinarians, but they have never joined the establishment. Religions that developed elsewhere tend to slacken in their precepts when they arrive in East Asia. Hinduism as practiced in Bali has reduced the caste system to a mere skeleton, and farmers are permitted to raise hogs for food. Islamic strictures against images and public entertainment, which have led to the closing of movie theaters in Saudi Arabia, are breezily dispensed with in Indonesia, and shadow puppet shows and traditional *gamelan* orchestra music are all the rage.

During the Middle Ages Europeans and Asians alike looked down on commercial profits, and ascetic renunciation of the world was the ideal. But an emphasis on diligence, if not financial gain, is detectable in East Asian religions. By the sixteenth century commerce and its profits were seen as legitimate in Japan and China, and a "secular asceticism" entailing hard work and thrift became established. In his *Religious Ethics*

*and the Merchant Spirit in Early-Modern China,* Ying-shi Yu, a professor of Chinese history at Princeton University, calls this ethos precisely analogous with the Protestant ethic that Max Weber saw as leading to the rise of capitalism and industrialization in Europe.

According to Ying-shi Yu, the notion of secular asceticism originated in China as early as the ninth century in the reforms of Zen Buddhism, then a new sect. The farm and domestic work required of Zen novices came to be equated with prescribed ascetic practices, and the Zen precept, "No eating without producing," was quoted and put into practice in society at large as well as the monasteries. Confucian scholars of the Sung Dynasty (960–1279) came to interpret the ancient ethic of character-building—"Work hard, be frugal, save time"—in terms of whatever daily work one did in the secular world.

In the sixteenth century, with the policies of the latter Ming Dynasty threatening to impoverish them, intellectuals moved away from the classic interpretation of Confucianism and embraced commerce. Business activity took off nationwide, with merchant cliques in Guangxi and Zhejiang provinces in the vanguard. Merchants' social status improved, and they became conscious of their own power. The insight of the neo-Confucian scholar Wang Yangming—"Though their walks of life are different, all four classes of people are on the same road"—became firmly established. His followers acknowledged that hard work and frugality were virtues on the same order as study. After the merchants agreed to high tax rates, the emperor opened the prestigious profession of government service to them. Scholars made themselves available to pen the epitaphs of magnates.

Merchants, for their part, committed themselves to diligence and thrift and sought to earn "profits controlled by justice." The moral code of merchants of the late Ming Dynasty and Ching Dynasty (1644–1912) boiled down to honest dealings, as the merchants took to heart the tenth-century saying, "In sincerity lies the passage to Heaven." Ying-shi Yu equates this animating principle with the old Protestant belief that worldly work crowned by material success is a sign of redemption: for the Chinese merchant, the secular moral value of open and fair dealings with customers and suppliers became a transcendental passage to heaven. The modern character of Japanese merchants of the period was even more pronounced that that of their Chinese counterparts. They strove to gain a reputation for honesty and trustworthiness, lived frugally, regarded their calling as given by Providence, and took pride in their business because it benefited the nation.

Why East Asians nurtured religious tolerance of the secular and a view of secular activity as akin to religious is not easy to explain. One possibility is that East Asia, along with the Protestant West, which underwent an almost identical ideological evolution, is located far from the centers where the ancient religions were born, and that the religions grew less dogmatic as they spread. In any case, when modern Western civilization encountered East Asia, it found civilizations with which it had a strong affinity. Little wonder, then, that it could serve as the framework for the integration of those civilizations.

## CULTURE AND CIVILIZATION

INTEGRATION UNDER Western auspices, however, does not imply the wholesale Westernization of East Asian national civilizations, let alone an East-West fusion of cultures. Culture is a way of life, a conventional order, physically acquired and rooted in subliminal consciousness. Civilization, in contrast, is a consciously recognized ideational order. There is a gray area between the two, but they are distinct. Handiness with machines, for example, is part of culture, while mechanized industry is an aspect of civilization. The performing styles of individual musicians and idiosyncrasies of composers belong to the former, while the diatonic scale and rhythmic system of Western music belong to the latter. Cultures die hard, but their spheres of dominance are limited. Civilizations can become widespread, but they may be deliberately abandoned.

Failure to distinguish clearly between culture and civilization marks the thought of the prophets of the clash of civilizations. The thesis is predicated on the mistaken notions that a civilization can be as predetermined a property of an ethnic group as its culture and that a culture can be as universal and expansive as a civilization. Working from these misconceptions, it follows that a stubborn and irrational culture posing as a civilization could assert itself politically, stirring up conflict.

The rule of culture extends at most from the family, village, or circle of social acquaintances to the tribe or nation. Civilization, in contrast, encompasses different tribes and nations and creates a world. Ancient civilizations, however, had a limited sphere of dominance; in Greece, China, Judea, and elsewhere in the ancient world, the ethnic-national culture covered the same area as the civilization. After Western world civilization arose in the eighth century, the correspondence between cultures and nations still obtained, but civilization assumed a two-level structure: Western world civilization arching over distinct national civilizations. In twentieth-century Britain, a member of Parliament's oratorical style is part of culture, constitutional monarchy is part of national civilization, and democracy is part of Western civilization.

The peoples of East Asia today can be said to partake of modern Western civilization at the topmost stratum of their world, to retain their national civilizations and nation-states in the middle stratum, and to preserve their traditional cultures in their day-to-day lives. In political affairs, human rights and democratic principles belong to the first stratum, distinct bodies of law and political institutions to the second, and political wheeling and dealing to the third. In theater, the dramaturgy common to modern drama is at the topmost stratum, the national languages in which characters' lines are spoken are in the middle, and at ground level are distinctive ethnic styles and figures of speech.

Under the umbrella of modernization, traditional ethnic cultures are being revived with new elements of universality. The Korean agrarian folk music known as *samulnori* attracts percussion aficionados worldwide in the jazz-influenced version popularized by the musician Kim Deoksoo. The Japanese dance troupe Sankaijuku, currently popular in Europe, incorporates steps from Balinese *kechak* dancing, which in turn draws on steps learned from Germans in Bali at the beginning of the century. East Asia has also become a center for cinema, nurturing some promising young filmmakers who bring to their twentieth-century medium exquisite touches of ethnic aesthetics. These developments suggest the imminent birth in the region of what may be called the Pacific-International style.

## Traditionalists fail to understand that a world civilization belongs not to one group but to all.

Charging the West with cultural imperialism or deploring the loss of traditional Asian cultures is the height of foolishness. Under the influence of the reigning world civilization, cultures inevitably change and may lose this or that, since they are living organisms. But some portion of their identity is always kept intact. Traditionalists of a nationalistic bent decry the changes, depicting them as impositions from abroad or trappings of a borrowed civilization. They fail to understand that a world civilization belongs not to any one group but to all.

## THE MODERN MODE

MODERN CIVILIZATION originated in the West, but it is not an evolutionary phase of Western civilization. To the contrary, modernization began in the twelfth century with the rejection of the Western civilization born four centuries before and can be thought of as an 800-year-long progressive denial of Western civilization.

During the Renaissance the West was deeply influenced by Arab civilization and shaken by underground and local folk cultures that it had deemed heretical and had repressed. The investigations of alchemists led to scientific experimentation, and the grotesque pushed the limits of artistic taste. The seventeenth century witnessed the revival of animistic sensitivity as the West rediscovered and sometimes well-nigh worshiped Nature. Romanticism in the late eighteenth and nineteenth centuries fired the imaginations of the era's artist-exiles, and the West felt the impact first of eastern Europe and Russia and then of the East, as evidenced by the flood of chinoiserie and japonisme.

In this century modernization has driven Western cultures to transform themselves as rapidly as Asian ones. American puritanism has declined to the point that homosexuality is widely tolerated, French cuisine is cutting down on fat and alcohol, German has lost its fraktur script, and the British have abandoned their shillings and tuppence for the more rational decimal system. If the social scientist David Riesman, author of *The Lonely Crowd,* is right, self-centrism, once said to be the core of Western culture, is giving way among the masses to a group-oriented culture. And the revolution in information and communications is changing the West and East Asia at the same time and at about the same speed.

As its Latin etymology suggests, modernity (from *modo,* now) is the spirit of living in constant contrast to the past. Despite the conventional wisdom, it does not necessarily have anything to do with progressivism, which sets goals in pursuit of a future utopia. The essence of modernity is not programmed; there is only a patchwork of trial and error and changes in the status quo. Modernity casts a glance back and extrapolates in different directions. In its willingness to reject all previous values and systems, including itself, modernity verges on nihilism but differs from it in its deep faith in *élan vital.*

If a new sphere of East Asia civilization is in the making today, modernity is the topmost stratum of its "world." The most positive outcome for the region would be not merely diversity but an orderly, widely agreed-on framework encompassing a well-regulated market, human rights, and democratic principles. While narrower political considerations will inevitably affect the civilizational process, an East Asian sphere that defied these fundamental values is inconceivable.

But then, Asian peoples no longer need think in terms of an East Asian framework. In view of the prevailing economic, defense, and political relations in the region, it would seem reasonable to take the entire Pacific Basin as the sphere of the emerging civilization. In East Asia as in North America, Mexico, Australia, and New Zealand, the experience of the twentieth century is of crucial significance, which is why one can feel at home traveling between their cities.

The Pacific sphere should not and will not remain closed to the rest of the world for long. As a civilization-in-progress incorporating continually advancing industrial and communications technologies and unfolding mass societies, it will have to collaborate with the Atlantic sphere of civilization that is sharing the experience. As the 21st century begins, humankind must overcome fanatic nationalism and fundamentalism in all their forms. If it is to have historical relevance, the Pacific sphere of civilization must serve as a transitional stronghold in that struggle.

---

*Article 2*                                                 *USA Today Magazine,* May 1998

## USA LOOKS AT THE WORLD

# Controlling Economic Competition in the
# PACIFIC RIM

*The Big Three economic powers in Asia—China, Japan, and the U.S.— must learn to cooperate economically, politically, and militarily if prosperity is to succeed in this burgeoning marketplace.*

by Charles W. Kegley, Jr.

AS ASTONISHED lenders and investors surveyed the wreckage from the chain-reaction near-collapse of Asia's currencies and markets, their former smug self-confidence began to fade. The spread of Asia's economic flu throughout the globalized marketplace has provoked widespread anxiety about the prospects for a 21st century of peace bolstered by prosperity through free trade in a borderless, integrated international economy. The financial typhoon amidst contagious currency devaluations, budget deficits, and bankruptcies has exposed the logical flaws underlying the megalomania during the 1990s' string of boom years. Now, in the face of crisis, the basic fault lines and vulnerabilities in the unmanaged trade and monetary system have been exposed. Policymakers worldwide have ample reasons to fear the future. The economic foundations of peace in the Pacific Rim are precarious and, without Asian regional stability, there exists little chance for the interdependent international political economy to remain stable.

The challenge of building a more stable institutional architecture for order must be faced if the future is to be prosperous and peaceful. The obstacles to cooperation must be confronted collectively to overcome nations' natural temptation to bolster exports at one another's expense. To avert the disaster of another competitive round of "beggar they neighbor" policies that was the tinderbox for the 1930s Great Depression which ignited World War II, the leading powers must overcome their divisions and work together or their national economies will implode. In a globalized economy where states only can help themselves if they help their rivals as well, *all* have a clear stake in the collective management of collective problems. Still, history does not inspire much confidence that parochial impulses can be resisted. How, then, should the pitfalls and prospects for a prosperous and peaceful future be envisioned?

Any understanding of the prospects for the Pacific Rim, and the globe in general, must begin with a sense of history. As British statesman Winston Churchill once observed, in looking to the future, the further back one looks, the further ahead one can see. To find an informed basis for grasping the major challenges that should be faced by the Big Three economic powers in Asia (China, Japan, and the U.S.), one should follow his advice by looking at long-term historical trends and learning from their lessons.

A second analytical axiom for viewing the future is that there exists a tight interface between the political and military preconditions for continued economic growth in the Pacific Rim. A synergistic, interactive interrelationship has developed among economics, politics, and military security, which can not be meaningfully separated. Peace is a precondition for prosperity, and inspired diplomacy to manage economic competitors' trade relations in the global market is, in turn, a precondition for lasting peace.

What are the long-term problems of the past and the core contemporary circumstances that most will affect the future? First, the U.S. still is a military superpower and an economic giant. It once was said that when the American economy sneezed, the rest of the world caught a cold. That assertion no longer is quite true, but the globalization of trade means that the impact of changes in the American economy continue to reverberate throughout the world.

A second feature of today's global realities lies in how the law of gravity applies in international relations. In the historical evolution of the global political economy, as in nature, what goes up must come down. That natural phenomenon pertains to the U.S. It now is recognized widely that, although the recent Japanese economic upheaval has interrupted that nation's ascendancy, Japan and China's economic growth will resume over the long term. China and Japan enjoy massive trade surpluses and hold vast reserves of foreign currency. Their own currencies are not challenged immediately, and, banking crises in Japan notwithstanding, both nations continue to cut into the U.S. share of world output. The American share peaked after World War II at almost 50%, but steadily has slid since.

Simply put, the U.S. is in decline relative to its two Pacific Rim economic rivals. Without a doubt, the next superpower contest will be between the U.S. and China. The question is not if, but when, China will surpass the U.S. as the leading economic power in the world. More problematic is if and how long it might take a recovering, restructuring Japan to challenge U.S. economic supremacy as well. Whatever the timetable, current economic trajectories

suggest that a major power transition likely will occur in the early 21st century, with three great powers wealthy enough to project military might throughout the region.

This leads to a third unfolding trend. In the likely new 21st century global distribution of power, military and economic might increasingly will be diffused. In contrast to bipolarity, where two superpowers held a preponderance of strength compared to all other countries, the multipolar state system of the future appears destined to contain three roughly equal great powers: China, the U.S., and Japan. The changes from this power transition promise to be profound, creating a new hierarchy with the Big Three at the top of a tripolar regional pyramid.

Such a reordering of the global economic pecking order raises important questions about future military and political order in the Pacific Rim and the world at large. Which powers might align with one another? Will these alignments be seen as a threat by others and stimulate the formation of counteralliances? Can a security regime be built to prevent the rise of such rival trade blocs and military coalitions primed for war on the economic and, perhaps, even military battlefield? To frame an answer, let us return to Churchill's advice that prophets need good memories and look at some additional facts surrounding the advent of a new multipolar Pacific Rim.

The diffusion of strength among the world's three economic powers demands attention because, in history, some forms of multipolarity have been more peaceful than others. For instance, the multipolar system of antagonistic blocs that developed on the eve of World War I proved particularly explosive. When many great powers split into rival camps, there is little chance that competitors in one policy arena (for example, trade) will emerge as partners somewhere else (say, defense), so as to mitigate the competition. Rather, the gains made by one side will be seen as losses by the other, ultimately causing minor disagreements to grow into larger face-offs from which neither coalition is willing to retreat. Since the international system of the early 21st century probably will be dominated by the Big Three extremely powerful states whose commercial and security interests are global, it is important that they do not become segregated into rival blocs.

Aside from the danger of trade wars and armed conflict, the security threats of the Pacific Rim future will include such challenges as interdependent monetary affairs, environmental degradation, resource depletion, internal rebellion by minority ethnic populations, the rising tide of refugees, and the cross-border spread of contagious diseases through increased contact, ranging from AIDS to multi-drug-resistant strains of tuberculosis. None of these regional problems can be met without substantial Big Three cooperation; they are transnational issues that necessitate not national, but global solutions. The threats on the horizon require a collective approach, at the very time when the accelerating erosion of national sovereignty is reducing states' control over their national fates and forcing them to confront common problems through multilateral diplomacy.

> "Conflict over political and territorial issues remains much in evidence. While there have been mutual gains made through foreign trade, geostrategic military differences in the interests of the Big Three have not disappeared."

However, whereas the impact of these traditional non-military threats to regional welfare and stability promises to be potent, they do not necessarily mean geo-economics or ecopolitics will replace geopolitics. Conflict over political and territorial issues remains much in evidence. While there have been mutual gains made through foreign trade, geostrategic military differences in the interests of the Big Three have not disappeared. As former U.S. Secretary of State Lawrence S. Eagleburger has pointed out, the world is "returning to a more traditional and complicated time of multipolarity, with a growing number of countries increasingly able to affect the course of events." The primary issues are how well the U.S. can adjust to its decline from overwhelming preponderance, and how well China and Japan will adapt to their new-found importance. "The change will not be easy for any of the players, as such shifts in power relationships have never been easy," Eagleburger cautions. The challenge to be confronted is ensuring that Big Three cooperation, not competition, becomes institutionalized. At issue is whether the traditional politico-military and non-traditional economic security threats that collectively face the greater Asian Pacific will be managed through concerted Big Three action, to preserve the order that has made the extraordinary progress of the past three decades possible.

## Multipolar future options

As power in the Asian Pacific becomes more dispersed, what can be done to prevent the re-emergence of an unstable form of multipolarity? How can the Big Three avoid becoming polarized into antagonist trade and military blocs and avert the use of currency devaluations and protective tariffs as competitive weapons? Three general courses of action exist: they can act unilaterally; they can develop specialized bilateral alliances with another state; or they can engage in some form of collective collaboration with each other.

Of course, each option has many possible variations, and the foreign policies of most great powers contain a mix of acting single-handedly, joining with a partner, and cooperating globally. History shows that what has mattered most for the stability of past multipolar systems has been the relative emphasis placed on "going it alone" vs. "going it with others," and whether joint action was defined in inclusive or exclusive terms.

Unilateral policies, though attractive because they symbolize the nostalgic pursuit of national autonomy, are unlikely to be viable in a multipolar future. The end of the Cold War has reduced public anxieties about foreign dangers. In the U.S., the collapse of the communist threat has led to calls for a reduction in the scale of foreign commitments. In Japan, the Asian financial crisis has prompted the declaration at the December, 1997, Asian Summit that its neighbors could not count on Japan to cushion the cascading economic collapse by opening its market for their exports. In China, echoes of enthusiasm for the Middle Kingdom assertively to chart an independent path can be heard growing more vocal. However, an isolationistic retreat from world affairs by any or all would imperil efforts to deal with the many transnational threats to regional security that require global activity and engagement, and this decreases the incentives for a neo-isolationist withdrawal from existing involvements abroad.

On the other hand, a surge of unilateral activism by any of the Big Three powers would be equally harmful. None of them holds unquestioned hegemonic status with enough power to override all others. Although the U.S. is unrivaled in military might, its offensive capability and unsurpassed military technology is not paralleled by unrivaled financial clout. The U.S. economy faces problems that constrain and inhibit the projection of American power on a global scale. (The U.S. remains the biggest debtor country in history and suffers from extremely low savings rates. Moreover, the American investment in infrastructure is the lowest among all the G-7 industrialized economies.) Given the prohibitive costs of shouldering the financial burden of acting alone, and given the probability that other great powers would be unlikely to accept subordinate positions, unilateralism will be problematic in a multipolar future. The Big Three countries will have to accommodate themselves to the need for internationalist roles so they can coexist and interact with each other.

An alternative to acting unilaterally is joining with selected states in a series of special relationships. On the surface, this option appears attractive. Yet, in a world lacking the stark simplicities of obvious allies and adversaries, differentiating friend from foe is exceedingly difficult, particularly when allies in the realm of military security are the most likely to be trade competitors in a cutthroat global marketplace. Instead of adding restrictive predictability to international affairs, a network of special bilateral relationships and internally active restrictive trade blocs would foster a fear of encirclement among those who perceive themselves as the targets of these combinations.

Whether they entail informal understandings or formal treaties of alliance, all bilateral partnerships have a common drawback: they promote a politics of exclusion that can lead to dangerously polarized forms of multipolarity, in which the competitors align by forming countercoalitions. For example, the formation of new Russo-Sino, Japanese-American, and Sino-American mutual defense agreements have elevated others' security fears. In much the same way, construction of a U.S.-Russian-European Union axis stretching from the Atlantic to the Urals, if institutionalized, greatly would alarm both China and Japan. The trouble with bilateral alliances and multiparty defense and trade coalitions is that they inevitably shun those standing outside the charmed circle. Resentment, revenge, and revisionist efforts to overturn the *status quo* are the predictable consequence. The freewheeling dance of balance-of-power politics typically produces much switching of partners, with some cast aside and thus willing to break-up the whole dance. Arms races fed by beggar-thy-neighbor trade and monetary competition almost always result.

Beyond forming special bilateral alliances, the Big Three have the option of cementing their mutual financial fate in the strengthening of the broad, multilateral associations and cooperative institutions they have created. Two common variants of this option are concerts and collective security organizations. The former involves regularized consultation among those at the top of the global hierarchy; the latter, full par-

ticipation by all states in the region. A concert offers the benefit of helping control the great-power rivalries that often spawn polarized blocs, though at the cost of ignoring the interests of those not belonging to the group.

---

"Creating a new Pacific Rim security structure that enlarges the circle of participation to include all the Big Three in collective decision-making will not be easy, especially in a climate of financial crisis and fear."

---

Alternatively, the all-inclusive nature of collective security allows every voice to be heard, but makes more problematic providing a timely response to threatening situations. Consensus-building is both difficult and delayed, especially in identifying a party to the regime aiming at overturning its rules or preparing for either parochial economic protectionism or, even worse, armed conquest. Collective security mechanisms are deficient in choosing an appropriate response to a challenger to order and in implementing the selected course of deterrent action as well. Since a decision-making body can become unwieldy as its size expands, what is needed to make multilateralism a viable option for the Pacific Rim multipolar future looming on the political horizon is a hybrid that combines elements of a Big Three concert with elements of collective security.

## Assuring collective security

Throughout history, different types of multipolar systems have existed. Some of these systems of diffused power were unstable because they contained antagonistic blocs poised on the brink of trade or military warfare. History shows that the key to the stability of any future multipolar system in Asia lies in the inclusiveness of multilateralism. While not a panacea for all of the region's security problems, it offers the best chance to avoid the kinds of polarized alignment patterns that have proven so destructive in the past.

Creating a new Pacific Rim security structure that enlarges the circle of participation to include all the Big Three in collective decision-making will not be easy, especially in a climate of financial crisis and fear. When seen from today's perspective, however, there is no alternative but to try. The other options—unilateralism or bilateralism—have severe costs, because any of the Big Three is certain to look disfavorably on any great power's hegemonic effort to bully the others, or on an alliance between the other pair that defines its purpose as the third's containment. Restricting security protection and free-trade zones in a way that ostracizes and encircles one of the Big Three is a path to division and destruction of the very pillars of prosperity provided through open regional trade and agreements to facilitate exports.

The Big Three must not ever return to the days of a world divided in separate blocs, each seeking to contain the expansion of the other. Such a *realpolitik* response is likely to produce the very kind of polarization into competing coalitions that would benefit no one and corrode the cooperative trade links that provide the basis for lasting friendship. As countries connected by a web of economic linkages, there are material incentives for the Big Three to avoid policies that will rupture profitable business transactions, such as those that stigmatize any core player in the game as an enemy.

This is not to ignore the stubborn fact that trading relationships involve both costs and benefits. The rewarding aspects of commerce likely will be offset by fierce competition, breeding irritation, disputes, and hostility between winners and losers. In view of the differential growth rates among the Big Three and their anxiety about trade competitiveness in an interdependent global marketplace, their major battles of the future indeed are likely to be clashes on the economic front. Still, the Big Three have it within their power to avoid armed combat among soldiers if they keep their aim set on the business of managing business instead of warfare.

A full-fledged, comprehensive Pacific Rim collective security system, dedicated to containing aggression anywhere at any time, may be too ambitious and doomed to failure. A restricted, concert-based collective security mechanism, though, could bring a modicum of order in a fragile

and disorderly new Pacific Rim multipolar system, and provide the umbrella needed to allow the regional marketplace to contribute to continuing prosperity.

Whether the actions taken by a Pacific Rim concert-based collective security organization can succeed will hinge on how such a body is perceived and the ways members in it are treated. A Big Three consensus on the rules of trade and security regimes is imperative. It also is vital that each of the Big Three be accorded the equal status it deserves in such multilateral institutions, and none be deprived of membership or equal power over decision-making in such organizations.

In this light, China needs to be included in the World Trade Organization and Group of Seven (and agree to abide by its rules for membership as Russia has done in its participation as the G-7's eighth member). Japan has to be seated on the United Nations' Security Council, and the enlarged NATO and European Union must define their agendas with greater sensitivity to the fears enlargement provoked in the minds of leaders in Tokyo, Beijing, and Moscow. Unity for a globalized, increasingly borderless world is the *sine qua non* to future prosperity and peace. The Big Three have special responsibilities to lead in fostering a unified collective spirit, not only in the Pacific Rim, but in the 21st-century global system.

---

*Article 3*                                          *THE WORLD & I,* May 1998

# How Asia Went From Boom to Gloom

*by Andrew Z. Szamosszegi*

In December 1994, East Asian political and economic leaders looked aghast at the meltdown of Mexico's economy and prayed fervently that East would remain East and West would remain West and never the twain would meet.

But three years later, alas, a string of booming East Asian economies nosedived—for reasons similar to the Mexico cataclysm—sending a chill around the world.

The Mexican economy's sudden collapse roiled markets throughout the Western Hemisphere. A U.S.-led bailout eventually calmed regional markets, but the damage to Mexico's economy was substantial and took years to repair. The country's real gross domestic product (GDP) tumbled 6 percent in 1995 and did not reach its precrisis levels until 1997.

Half a world away, in East Asia, nations such as Indonesia, Malaysia, the Philippines, and Thailand, which had attained levels of economic development similar to Mexico's, had similar fundamental economic problems. For example, they ran substantial *current account deficits*—meaning that export earnings did not cover imports and investment income sent abroad.

Although most East Asian countries ran well-publicized trade *surpluses* with the United States, their huge trade *deficits* with Japan guaranteed that, overall, they ran current account deficits.

South Korea, though its companies competed head-on with Japanese and U.S. multinationals, also had a growing current account deficit. To finance these shortfalls, each country borrowed heavily on international markets.

Despite this glaring weakness, the consensus was that Asian economies were safe. Asian countries saved more, consumed less, and invested more than Mexico. These investments, the logic went, would produce enough exports in the future to pay off all the foreigners who were pouring money into the region.

Of course, now we know better. Last year, Indonesia, the Philippines, Thailand, and South Korea were hit by devastating crises that pummeled their currencies and pushed many of their banks and companies into insolvency.

One by one, governments in the region came to the International Monetary Fund (IMF) to forestall default. In exchange for more than $100 billion in foreign currency loans from the IMF and other countries, the once proud

# Roots of the Asia Crisis

➡ South Korea, Indonesia, the Philippines, Thailand, and Malaysia all adopted Japan's industrial policy economic model.

---

➡ Instead of letting market forces guide their economies' development, the governments picked which industries to build up.

---

➡ The regimes ignored realities of world demand and business risk.

---

➡ The bank systems, controlled by the governments, were milked for loans that built up huge debt-to-equity ratios for the favored industries.

---

➡ Stock markets, noting a slowdown in the region's exports began to shed investments, sending the affected countries over a financial precipice.

---

➡ The rottenness at East Asia's economic core was masked by the region's stunning savings and investment rates, which for years fooled even the most astute analysts.

economies are now being asked to reform the economic systems that lifted them from poverty to near prosperity. These systems, once the envy of the world, are now viewed as the root cause of East Asia's troubles.

## IT BEGAN WITH JAPAN

This sudden fall from grace has refocused attention on Japan, Asia's preeminent economy. Such attention, however, could not come at a worse time. Japan is now in its sixth year of stagnation—with barely 1 percent annual growth—and its banking system has accumulated more than $500 billion in poor loans.

Though reeling now, Japan was once Asia's model economy. In a span of 40 years, its economic miracle vaulted it from wartime ruin to one of the world's richest countries.

Japan scholar Chalmers Johnson has observed that the country achieved spectacular growth while ignoring many of the tenets of Western economic thought, much to the West's chagrin. For instance, rather than allow market forces alone to shape its economy, Japan embraced *industrial policy,* defined by Johnson as government guidance and development of industry.

Tokyo bureaucrats created a producer-oriented, government-interventionist, bank-financed economy. Tokyo officials, business leaders, and bank big-

wigs developed a chummy old boys' network that steered huge bank loans to favored manufacturers regardless of the industries' long-term risk and financial prospects. This was in contrast to the free-market, consumer-oriented approach championed by the United States, where financing is accomplished not so much by bank loans as by floating corporate bonds and issuing stock.

The Japanese economy also came to display very healthy signs: high saving and investment rates and large export surpluses. But with the heavy doses of government intervention came an unmistakable bias against foreign products and firms.

Japan's model was attractive to many governments in Asia that were throwing off the colonial yoke. To these nondemocratic or partially democratic regimes, an activist government role aligning the interests of business and state was preferable to the U.S. approach.

Among Asian countries, South Korea tried most to emulate Japan. Indonesia and Thailand, though less like Japan, also chose more government-centered models of development.

For years, many analysts emphasized the differences among these economies, either ignoring or dismissing parallels with Japan. But the current crisis has made the debate moot.

In a recent speech, Deputy Treasury Secretary Lawrence Summers summa-

rized "Asian" economics as "an approach that favored centralized coordination of activities over decentralized market incentives. Governments targeted particular industries, promoted selected exports, and protected domestic industry.

"There was reliance on debt rather than equity," he said, "relation-driven finance not capital markets, and informal rather than formal enforcement mechanisms." It is an approach "that closely tracks the postwar economic success of Japan."

The rush to blame regional industrial policies ignores the banking and currency crises in countries without industrial policies. The United States, for example, had its savings and loan crisis in the 1980s. During the 1990s, a few European countries were also forced to suddenly devalue their currencies. And, of course, there was Mexico.

## INDUSTRIAL POLICY AT FAULT?

A consensus is emerging, however, that industrial policies were a significant cause of East Asia's financial turmoil. They may not have tipped Asia into the financial abyss, but they certainly left it poised at cliff's edge.

One of the fascinating aspects of this collapse is how perceived strengths became glaring weaknesses. Take Asia's legendary investment rates. Economists encourage investment, but Asian economies went overboard.

During the 1990s, South Korea, Indonesia, and Thailand invested nearly 40 percent of their GDP, compared to about 20 percent for the European Union and even less for the United States.

But too much investment can be counterproductive. According to a recent IMF study, investment in Thailand from 1983 to 1989 amounted to 28 percent of GDP and produced an annual growth rate of 8 percent. From 1990 to 1996, investment rates of 40 percent led to growth of only 8.5 percent a year.

In South Korea, overinvestment in steel manufacturing pushed three of the country's conglomerates into bankruptcy in 1997.

The Asian devotion to exporting was also extreme. Government industrial policies—ignoring the dictates of free-market forces—encouraged many manufacturers to build factories with excess capacity, under the assumption that what could not be sold at home would be exported.

This strategy worked for Japan when it was the only game in town, but with East Asian countries today competing for market share in similar products, replicating Japan's success has been difficult. Instead, many Asian companies have flooded global markets with too much product, which lowers export prices and holds down profits.

Economists often remind us that countries export in order to buy imports that are made more efficiently elsewhere. But export-oriented industrial policies turned this logic upside down: In order to export, they imported. That is to say, developing Asian countries had to import large quantities of machinery, key components, technology, and management know-how so they could export. These imports virtually ensured current account deficits for most Asian countries, despite their prodigious exporting.

## BANKS AND THE DEBT BEHEMOTH

To maintain export competitiveness, many Asian countries pegged their currencies to the dollar. That is, they set a fixed, official rate at which businesses and countries around the world could exchange Asian currencies for U.S. dollars. Pegging gave the currencies stability and international confidence.

The link worked well from the mid-1980s to early 1995, a period during which the weaker dollar gave members of the Association of Southeast Asian Nations (ASEAN) a price advantage over Japanese and European-based production and made the region attractive to foreign investors.

This could happen because a weaker dollar—and, consequently, weaker ASEAN currencies—meant that ASEAN-produced goods became relatively cheap compared to those produced in Europe and Japan. In addition, Japanese yen and, say, German deutsche marks became comparatively more valuable and so could purchase more than the usual quantity of ASEAN assets. Not only did ASEAN

equities become comparatively cheap, good buys, but it became comparatively cheaper for Japanese and Europeans to manufacture goods in ASEAN countries than in Japan or Europe.

Moreover, the peg encouraged short- and long-term lending by foreign banks, which received higher interest rates in Asia than from lending at home. (Banks are more cautious when exchange rates float, because sudden fluctuations can lead to huge losses.)

A stable currency and cheap capital are normally economic pluses, but this flood of investment came too fast. As Federal Reserve Board Chairman Alan Greenspan testified before the House of Representatives, "Those economies could not provide adequate profitable opportunities at reasonable risk to absorb such a surge in funds."

Sound financial systems—banks in particular—could have helped check such excesses by refusing to finance projects that had little chance of earning reasonable rates of return. But Asia's financial systems were underdeveloped.

South Korean banks, for example, were government-owned until the late 1970s. Even after the state divested, Seoul still appointed bank presidents and encouraged banks to direct capital to favored business sectors and companies.

The combination of cash-insatiable corporations and rubber-stamp banks produced a national debt-to-equity ratio of about 5–1 in South Korea. For perspective, the ratio for U.S. firms is less than 1–1.

Commercial banks are a relatively new phenomenon in Indonesia, and for years regulatory powers were woefully inadequate. Even after regulations were tightened, implementation remained poor, in large part because many private banks are owned by family members and allies of President Suharto. Thai banks were also poorly supervised and managed.

Instead of being the last line of defense against the excesses of industrial policy, banks borrowed money cheaply from abroad and continued funding dubious domestic investment schemes.

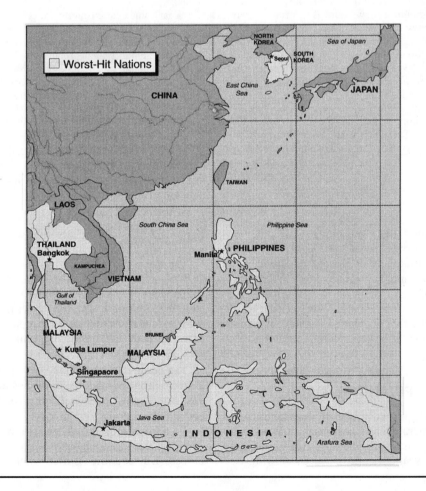

# Japan's Dubious Success

From the devastation, privation, and humiliation of the immediate postwar years, Japan has roared back to become a proud, nearly $3 trillion-a-year economy, the second largest in the world.

But while the Japanese have enthusiastically embraced American baseball, hamburgers, music, clothing, and even democratic politics, they have pointedly turned up their noses at the American free-market economic model.

Instead of adopting a decentralized U.S.-style approach of independent individual corporations in sharp competition with one another, they've built their economy by embracing a system that might be termed *bureaucronomics*—an economics of central planning revolving around decisions made by government bureaucrats on which industries to invest in.

Japan's stunning success with this form of economics—in which the country built an array of glittering high-tech brands from computers to cars to copiers—eventually led to much anguished introspection in U.S. and European circles over whether the North Atlantic community of nations should follow suit. But many observers now say that the verdict is in on what may be the ultimate bankruptcy of Japan's economic model.

Not only have Japan's imitators in much of the rest of East Asia been wrecked economically, almost like houses built on sand, but Japan itself appears to be starting to splinter.

The country has been in the grip of an enervating economic stagnation for the past seven years, with near-zero annual growth. Its banking system, which analysts agree often makes loan decisions on the basis of cronyism, is groaning under the weight of $500–600 billion of bad loans.

And figures released in March show that the economy contracted by 0.7 percent for the last three months of 1997. Indeed, Japan may end the fiscal year with negative growth for the first time since oil prices quadrupled in 1973–74.

"What we're dealing with is a truly sick economy. If anything, we're headed for the worst recession in Japan's postwar history," said Andrew Shipley of Shroders Japan Ltd., a Tokyo-based brokerage.

"You can compare what's happening now in Japan with what happened in Russia in the late 1980s, when the economic system broke down," he said.

Allen Sinai, president of Primark Decision Economics in New York, agreed, saying bluntly, "Japan is back in recession now." The reason, he said, is because half-hearted attempts by Japanese leaders to stimulate the economy in the last year have failed.

What somewhat cushions the economic blow in Japan is that it produces and consumes six times more than International Monetary Fund bailout recipients South Korea, Thailand, and Indonesia combined. And, unlike its cash-strapped neighbors, Japan is second in the world in foreign-reserve holdings ($230 billion) and has a gargantuan $12 trillion in private savings.

Still, unemployment remains near record highs and pessimism is spreading among Japanese. There is a severe credit crunch, a surge in high-profile financial failures, and embarrassing revelations of cozy ties between the Finance Ministry and banks. The public pessimism is causing a sharp slowdown in consumer and business spending, smothering growth.

Prime Minister Ryutaro Hashimoto came into office two years ago as a bold reformer who promised to end collusion among politicians, powerful *keiretsu* business conglomerates, and banks. But he has mainly unfulfilled pledges and unenacted proposals to show so far.

If anything, the country seems to be planning to try to export its way out of its troubles. Japan reported that its trade surplus in autos and other goods skyrocketed by 66 percent in February. The flood of imports into the United States from Japan reflects the yen's 30 percent depreciation against the dollar in the last year—a drop nearly as large as that of other Asian currencies but not as well publicized.

"The only thing [the Japanese] know how to do to grow is export," said Clyde Prestowitz, head of the Economic Strategy Institute. "Japan is an export machine."

The best tonic for Japan's economy, he said, would be a Theodore Roosevelt-style shattering of the keiretsu that control such key industries as trucking, telecommunications, construction, and ports. These monopolies have driven up prices for Japanese consumers by 2 to 10 times those in the rest of the world, sharply inhibiting spending.

*—The Editor*

Rather than enforcing discipline on Asian businesses, the banks added fuel to an already dangerous tinderbox.

In sum, industrial policies in East Asia produced a situation in which the region was investing poorly yet sucking in an avalanche of foreign capital, exporting prodigiously yet importing even more.

## ROLE OF THE FINANCIAL MARKETS

Though industrial policies had left Asia vulnerable to a financial detonation, they did not light the fuse. In the end, the spark was provided by slowing exports and the self-preservationist psychology of global financial markets.

The rapid movement of capital from one country to another is a hallmark of the modern era. It combines the best of twentieth-century technology with postwar economic integration to generate faster growth for borrowing countries and better returns for investors.

The era of global capital markets has delivered for both parties, but it has also left borrowers dependent on investor sentiment.

Countries with bright growth prospects thrive as money flows in from abroad. But countries suffer when foreign investors conclude that growth is no longer a sure bet and head for the exits, leaving behind weaker currencies and stock markets. Because falling exchange rates increase the cost of repaying foreign loans, domestic borrowers also cash out, further intensifying the downward pressure on the economy.

The rout occurs because market forces, like the flames in a burning theater, reward those who get out early and punish those who stay too long. And, once a verdict is rendered in one country, investors look for other countries with similar weaknesses and leave those markets as well.

## DIARY OF A CRISIS

These dynamics played out in Asia during 1996 and '97.

ASEAN countries and South Korea had benefited greatly when the Japanese yen appreciated against the dollar in 1994 and '95, but this trend reversed itself the following year. The yen, which touched 80 per dollar in April 1995, weakened to 115 in January 1997 and to almost 130 by December.

Japanese multinationals that had invested heavily in production from ASEAN manufacturing facilities found it was more profitable to export from Japan again. The ASEAN currencies' dollar peg, an advantage while the yen was strong, had become a liability.

South Korea's currency, the won, though not pegged to the dollar, was similarly affected. Its cost advantage over Japan, which had been expected to result in mounting Korean exports of ships, cars, and semiconductors, suddenly evaporated. Exporters found themselves begging the Blue House (Korea's White House) for a weaker won.

At the same time, market conditions for some of East Asia's key products worsened. Huge investments in memory chip production led to a worldwide glut that sent prices spiraling downward and clobbered some of South Korea's top companies. Global demand for electronics took a breather as well, hurting firms in ASEAN and South Korea.

Thus, exports from developing East Asia slowed markedly. Thai exports, which had grown 20 percent annually from 1992 to 1995, fell by 1 percent in 1996 and continued to flounder in 1997. South Korean export growth dipped from nearly 18 percent growth to 3.7 percent in 1996 and was up 5.3 percent in 1997.

Faltering exports and excessive debt leverage pushed several South Korean conglomerates into bankruptcy. Investors concluded that the region was on an unsustainable path. Banks began calling in some of their loans.

Speculators began testing the resolve of Thailand, the region's weakest economy, to maintain the value of its currency, the baht. The rout had begun.

In early July, Thai authorities decided they were fighting a battle they could not win. After decades of being pegged at about 25 to the dollar, the baht was allowed to float, enabling buyers and sellers to determine its value.

Within months, other ASEAN members had followed suit, further dampening confidence and eroding the exchange rates of countries throughout Asia, Latin America, and eastern Europe.

Asian currencies and stock markets continued to plummet during the fall, but in December came the biggest blow of all as South Korea, the world's 11th-largest economy, found itself without enough foreign currency to meet obligations to foreign banks.

## THE AFTERMATH

The impact has been devastating. By February 1998, the currencies of South Korea, the Philippines, and Thailand had lost about half their value. Indonesia's rupiah declined much further. Malaysia's ringgit has been badly battered.

The region's once-vibrant economies are expected to grow slowly this year, if at all. Higher unemployment and prices are already spawning social unrest.

Asian industrial policies, which once seemed omnipotent, had one glaring weakness: They promoted excess and recklessness in a world that punishes both. Asian countries, perhaps intoxicated by their success, had relied too heavily on investment and exports for their growth and ignored—perhaps even encouraged—weak financial systems that made corporations fat, regardless of their sectors' risk, on easy credit.

The IMF's bailout packages take aim at industrial policies in several ways. They mandate the opening of import markets, discourage government-directed lending, and promote stronger financial systems that would reduce the problem of overinvestment.

Yet the region's embrace of Western-style economic policy is by no means assured. The area's predilection for industrial policies will not disappear overnight. Asia's economic problems, like Mexico's, will fade with time. Yet only time will tell if the industrial policies that produced the boom and the gloom in the region will share the same fate.

---

*Andrew Z. Szamosszegi is senior research associate of the Economic Strategy Institute.*

*Article 4*

*Commentary,* February 1998

# Asian Values and the Asian Crisis

*Francis Fukuyama*

A MERE decade ago, Americans at every level of business and government were being chided for their failure to emulate the example of Asia. The key to that region's economic success was said to be its cultural values—a combination of the work ethic, respect for community and authority, and a tradition of paternalistic government—all of which were contrasted invidiously to the rampant dysfunctionality then plaguing the American economy and American society alike.

Today, as the International Monetary Fund (IMF) imposes Western, market-oriented rules on one desperate Asian country after another, the mood has shifted to the other extreme. Asian values, we are now told, are what led to nepotistic credit allocation, an overly meddlesome state, and a disastrous lack of transparency in financial transactions. From being the cause of Asia's success, Asian values are now seen as the root of last summer's currency crisis and of the ensuing economic meltdown across nearly the whole region.

Neither reading is correct.

## II

THE SUBJECT of Asian values emerged in the early 1990's thanks largely to two politicians: Lee Kuan Yew, then Prime Minister of Singapore, and Prime Minister Mahathir Mohamad of Malaysia. Each was in pursuit of a relatively narrow agenda. Lee, seeking to improve his ties with China, hoped to gain favor in Beijing by promoting a mildly anti-Western sense of Chinese cultural identity. Mahathir, for his part, wanted to fend off the Bush administration's push to create a forum known as Asia-Pacific Economic Cooperation, in favor of a new Asian political bloc that would exclude "white" powers like Australia and the United States.

But the idea of a distinct Asian cultural and political identity had a larger resonance as well. In part, it reflected the genuine pride felt by many people in the region at the stunning success of their economies over the previous two generations. It also, however, served the interests of states eager to shield themselves both from Western criticisms of their human-rights practices and from pressure to open their protected domestic markets to imports and foreign investment. To the "soft"

*FRANCIS FUKUYAMA is Hirst professor of public policy at George Mason University and director of its International Transactions program.*

authoritarian governments ruling Singapore, Malaysia, Indonesia, and increasingly the People's Republic of China, "Asian values" offered an apparently principled defense of their reluctance to broaden political participation.

The idea of Asian values was, however, problematic from the start. As anyone knows who has spent time in that part of the world, there are huge cultural differences not only among the various countries but also among the ethnic groups that make up multicultural societies like Singapore and Malaysia. In southern China, families are both large and cohesive; in Japan, much less large and socially less significant. Whereas in Japan, South Korea, and Taiwan the state has traditionally commanded substantial respect, in many parts of Southeast Asia it has been historically weak or nonexistent. Confucian societies tend to invest more resources in education than do Islamic, Malay, or Catholic ones—indeed, Lee Kuan Yew was forced to pull back from his embrace of Confucianism for the simple reason that it did not reflect the cultural heritage of the 15 percent of Singapore's population that is of Malay descent.

As for the relationship between Asian values and economic success, that is dubious at best. Not only have attitudes toward work and money varied tremendously from one part of Asia to another, but Asia as a whole was rightly regarded as an economic basket-case for much of the first half of the 20th century. As Max Weber pointed out in 1905, no Asian society had ever produced indigenous capitalist institutions; economic growth became possible only after contact with the West and with Western ideas of property rights, the rule of law, scientific rationalism, modern state institutions, and the like. To put it another way, economic growth was contingent on the *rejection* by Asians of important elements of their own cultural heritage, including the Mandarin disdain for commerce and physical labor.

This is not to say that Asian values did not also turn out to be economically valuable: the Confucian emphasis on education and meritocratic advancement, for example, happened to dovetail very nicely with the requirements of a modernizing society. But as in the case of the impoverished Asian immigrants who came to Canada and the United States and made a success there, those values could come into play only when combined with other values and institutions imported from the West.

ASIDE FROM inculcating good work habits, Asian values have also been said to have a political dimension. Thus, Lee and Mahathir have argued that their brand of authoritarian government is well-suited to Confucian traditions of hierarchy and enables the state to focus its resources on economic development while avoiding the high degree of social disorder characteristic of Western democracies.

Unfortunately, the alleged cultural fit between Asian values and authoritarian government is a matter more of convenience than of principle. In any old and complex cultural system—whether Confucianism or Christianity—it is possible to find sources legitimating totally contradictory practices. Historically, Christians reading the same Bible have both promoted and condemned slavery. Similarly, if Lee Kuan Yew can cite Confucian sources to support rule by benevolent authoritarianism, Taiwan's Lee Teng-hui has cited other sources to prove the compatibility of Confucian tradition with the kind of democratic institutions he has sought to build in his island nation. All cultural systems evolve. Given the examples of Japan, South Korea, and Taiwan, who is to say that "Asian values" constitute an insuperable obstacle to the establishment of Western-style democracy?

Nor is the economic efficacy of authoritarian government clear-cut, as the careful studies of Robert Barro and others have shown. When such governments function well, as in the case of Singapore and of South Korea under military rule, they can indeed be very effective at promoting rapid growth; but when they function badly, like Brazil or Peru during the 1970's, their economies tend to perform much more poorly than democracies.

It is true that Asian authoritarians have, on the whole, been more competent and honest than Latin American ones, but, as the current crisis already suggests, there can be no assurance this will continue to be the case over the long run. In the absence of adequate feedback mechanisms and institutional controls on state power, it ends up being a matter of luck whether authoritarian institutions are turned toward the single-minded pursuit of investment and growth or become vehicles for padding the bank accounts of the politicians in charge.

## III

IF ASIAN values are not the cause of either rapid growth or of a superior form of governance, are they, instead, a catalyst of excessive state intervention and "crony capitalism"? And if so, can they be blamed for the economic debacle that occurred in the wake of the collapse of the Thai baht and other regional currencies in the summer of 1997? Alas, in sickness as in health, Asia is a very diverse place, and the causes of crisis vary from country to country.

The trouble in Thailand began when the government's efforts to defend the baht's link to the dollar came under attack in international currency markets. But it was the very stability of that link that had encouraged *private* firms, in Thailand and abroad, to borrow and lend short-term funds to finance specu-

lation in real estate and other questionable ventures. If there was failure at the government level, it lay not in excessive interventionism but in an insufficiency of regulatory power: the Thai state was unable to impose proper reporting, disclosure, and reserve requirements on its banking system. And if there has been longer-term failure at the government level, it is again one of omission rather than commission—a failure, that is, to invest adequately in public education and physical infrastructure.

The problem facing Thailand—overzealous speculative investment fueled by cheap credit—has been a feature of capitalist markets for as long as they have existed. Nor is Thailand alone in the region in this respect. Most Southeast Asian governments have opened their economies to foreign investment and trade, and some, like Singapore and Hong Kong, have been models of state minimalism in the economic realm—not that this has saved them from being buffeted in the global financial markets.

Of course, the crisis today is centered not in any of these places but in Japan and especially South Korea. In both countries, state agencies for the past 45 years have indeed played a hyperactive role in guiding economic life, primarily through the allocation of credit.

Intervening on both a macro- and microeconomic level, the Korean government protected domestic producers from foreign competition and created a government-industry machine that resembled a time bomb waiting to go off. The large Korean conglomerates known as *chaebol* became addicted to cheap, often subsidized credit for ambitious expansion projects. While these paid off during the country's high-growth period from 1961 to 1987, the absence of constraints, either in the form of hard budgets or in the form of shareholder demands for a return on equity, led to spectacular mistakes, as in the 1996 decision by the Samsung conglomerate to become the sixth major Korean automobile manufacturer. The tremendous power vested in government also led to cases of massive corruption; former President Roh Tae Woo stole some $600 million, and politics played a role in the recent collapse of Hanbo Steel.

Japan's sins are by now familiar: lack of openness, regulation, and transparency in the financial sector, coupled with a penchant for keeping faltering firms alive at all costs rather than letting managers and shareholders absorb the consequences of failure. All this has led to a rolling seven-year crisis in the banking system that has seriously weakened the country's still-competitive manufacturing firms. As in the case of Korea, government intervention in markets has persisted long past the point where it makes economic sense.

But the fact that government intervention is no longer functional in places like Japan and South Korea does not mean that it served no purpose in the past. Although many American economists assert dogmatically that state intervention *always* produces inefficiencies, the fact is that these same meddlesome Asian governments presided over periods of growth that were historically unprecedented anywhere in the world. Perhaps one might argue that, in the absence of state intervention, Asian growth from 1950 to the 1990's could have been even higher than it was; but to imagine that one period of unprecedentedly high growth should have yielded to another and even higher one is to indulge in fantasy.

WHICH BRINGS us to the other frequently-named culprit for Asia's present troubles, "crony capitalism." If Northeast and Southeast Asia share a common failing, it is that business decisions are frequently made by other than market criteria. The entire region is permeated with personalistic ties of all sorts, ranging from the mutual obligations that Japanese managers feel toward their workers or their business-network *(keiretsu)* partners to the forthrightly corrupt dealings of Indonesia's Suharto family. In Southeast Asia, family connections link the far-flung overseas Chinese communities; in Northeast Asia, there are long-term corporate alliances or informal connections between government overseers and the firms they ostensibly regulate.

Greater formality, based on the strict rule of law, is a pressing need everywhere in Asia. Nevertheless, "crony capitalism" is a misnomer. The term was initially coined to describe the Philippines under the late Ferdinand Marcos, a place where huge amounts of money were being siphoned off by the dictator's close associates. Historically, despite exceptions like the Philippines, China, and Indonesia, East Asia boasted astonishingly *low* levels of corruption. In light of the huge regulatory powers vested in Japanese, Korean, and Taiwanese bureaucrats over the past two generations, one might reasonably have expected to see nepotism, influence-peddling, and stagnation in these countries on the level of, say, Mobutu's Zaire. Instead, while major scandals have emerged over time, all three countries have demonstrated an ability to build strong, competent, and reasonably honest government institutions that can stimulate a high level of savings and direct them to productive investment.

No society can expect to keep this going forever, which is why formal institutions are critical in the long run. But few countries outside Asia have shown an ability to make "personalism" pay off so spectacularly even in the short run.

In any case, is it so obvious that "personalism" is always a bad thing? Ironically, business-school professors and information-technology gurus have been urging *American* firms to move in precisely that direction. In a sophisticated economy, we are told, work is done by highly educated professionals who must be allowed to organize themselves. To that end, American companies are being advised to replace their large, bureaucratic, hierarchical structures with smaller, flatter ones linked by informal networks. Many high-tech firms have also adopted a policy of "relational contracting," basing their business decisions not on price and performance criteria but on relationships of trust with suppliers or with clients that resemble nothing so much as the Japanese *keiretsu.*

## IV

IF ASIAN values are not central to the saga of Asia's economic rise and recent decline, and will not, in and of themselves, determine the kind of political system that ultimately prevails in that part of the world, what, then, *is* their significance? The answer lies in the sphere of social relations.

Among all the criticisms of the West lodged by proponents of Asian values in the early 1980's, the most cogent focused on the effects of excessive individualism in Western societies, and particularly in the United States. The concept of the autonomous individual as the ground of all rights and duties is indeed unique to the liberal West; it has no counterpart in Asia, where people are born into the world encumbered with a whole series of obligations to others, from the family to the state. This encumbrance can inhibit their ability to take advantage of the good things that we associate with individualism, like innovation and entrepreneurship; but it can also reduce their susceptibility to the bad things, like crime and illegitimacy.

How does this play out in practice? Many modern Asian societies have followed a completely different evolutionary path from Europe and North America. Beginning approximately in the mid-1960's, virtually every country in the industrialized West experienced a rapid increase in crime rates and a breakdown in the nuclear family. The only two countries in the Organization for Economic Cooperation and Development *not* experiencing this disruption were the Asian ones, Japan and Korea.

Since the end of World War II, Japan has shown but a slightly rising divorce rate, while its rate of illegitimacy has been both low and flat, and its crime rate, already one of the lowest in the world, has trended slightly *downward* for the past three decades. Korea underwent a slight rise in crime in the 1970's and has experienced periodic outbreaks of political violence, but there, too, very little social dysfunction has attended industrialization.

Similarly with the countries of Southeast Asia. As their percapita income has risen, they have experienced *declining* rates of both divorce and illegitimacy. To be sure, traditional family structure has changed dramatically, as joint and multigenerational families have turned into nuclear ones; but the breakdown of the nuclear family that is so notable in the West has been all but absent.

Any number of factors may be adduced to explain why these social trends in Asia differ from those in the United States and other Western countries. But, from the perspective of "Asian values," the most important difference—and the one that has yet to be confronted squarely—has to do with the role of women. Here, indeed, is an example of a social value with large effects both in economic life and in politics.

To a much greater extent than in the West, women in Japan and Korea, not to mention in other, less-developed Asian societies, continue to be treated differently from men both in social custom and in law. While female labor-force participation can be high, girls generally work only until they are married, and then drop out to raise families. Women across Asia are also less able to control their own reproductive cycles. Even in Japan, the pill was only recently made legally available.

Until recently, too, Japanese labor laws prohibited women from working double shifts in factories; they were thus effectively barred form the fabled lifetime-employment system of large Japanese corporations. And what has been true of Japan tends to be even truer in the more socially conservative parts of Asia: in one way or another, women are prevented from earning enough to support themselves and their children without a husband.

When Asian spokesmen (at least the male ones) say they do not like Western values, what they often mean is that they do not like Western sexual roles; the individualism that is problematic for them includes not only freewheeling political protest but freewheeling protest within the family. And no wonder: family structure has implications for education, for economic performance, for public safety, and for government investment in such things as crime prevention and health care. Through the selective application of "Asian values," Asian societies have so far preserved the coherence of the nuclear family and have spared themselves the social disruption that has attended economic change in the West.

## V

BUT WHAT of the future? In the long run, there is no reason to think that the nations of Asia cannot resume, if at a slower pace, the trajectory they were on prior to last summer's crisis. It is much less certain, however, that their economic and political institutions will be able to withstand the powerful forces of globalization. If they are to remain competitive, for example, the Japanese *keiretsu* and the Korean *chaebol* will have to undergo massive changes in the next decade. In Northeast Asia, the regulatory hand of the state will have to be relaxed; in Southeast Asia, in order to guarantee the soundness of the financial sector, it will have to be strengthened. All Asian countries will need to rethink the wisdom of pegging their currencies tightly to the U.S. dollar.

A likely result of these and other changes will be an erosion of Asia's social distinctiveness, which is already under siege by a variety of factors. Fertility rates in Japan and Korea are far below replacement levels, and Japan in particular faces not only an older but a dramatically shrinking population. If the country wants to see some semblance of economic growth, it will have to expand its labor force, either through immigration or through allowing more women to work. Caught between these two choices, many Japanese would, I suspect, opt for the latter. But this means that, over time, Japan too will begin to experience Western-style family disruption, and the social problems that grow out of it.

In short, what the current crisis will end up doing is to puncture the idea of Asian exceptionalism. The laws of economics have not been suspended in Asia; as the economies of the region catch up to the West, growth rates will slow and social problems will accumulate. And neither have the laws of politics: the well-documented correlation between stable democracy and a high level of development surely applies to a region where rising educational achievements and the complex nature of industrial or post-industrial societies will increasingly favor the rule of law and greater popular participation.

In order to get to the long run, however, we must first survive the short run. In the near term, most countries in Asia will face a severe challenge restructuring their economies without generating a political backlash, and all sorts of uncertainties may complicate the process of recovery. The likely future behavior of the PRC and North Korea is one such unknown. Another is the reaction in the United States. As Asia's fallen tigers try to export their way back to health on the basis of depreciated currencies, America's trade deficit will swell, increasing the pressure for protectionism already evident in the defeat of the Clinton administration's effort to secure "fast-track" trade legislation. On top of all that, there has already been an upsurge of resentment against the IMF and the United States in Korea, Thailand, and other economically prostrate countries.

The remaining years of the 20th century thus promise to be difficult and eventful ones for people on both sides of the Pacific. It would be nice if, for the duration, we could be spared further lectures either about the special advantages or about the special deficiencies of Asian values.

*Article 5*    MULTINATIONAL MONITOR, January/February 1998

# The End of a "Miracle"

*Speculation, Foreign Capital Dependence and the Collapse of the Southeast Asian Economies*

## by Walden Bello

BANGKOK—Environmentalists received an early Christmas gift when the Malaysian government announced in early December that it was suspending plans to build the controversial Bakun Dam in Sarawak. Constructing the dam would have resulted in the clearcutting of 70,000 hectares of forestland in an area that is already experiencing one of the world's highest rates of deforestation and in the displacement of approximately 9,500 indigenous people.

What years of international and local pressure on and lobbying of the Malaysian government could not do was achieved by the one message that the country's strong-willed leader Mohammed Mahathir could understand: no more dollars. Expected to cost $5 billion, the Bakun Dam—like Mahathir's other vision of building a two kilometer-long "Linear City" that would have been the world's longest building—fell victim to the financial crisis that is presently wracking Southeast Asia.

In the several months, the Philippines and Southeast Asia have been gripped by an economic downturn that has yet to hit bottom. The Philippine peso, the Thai baht, the Malaysian ringgit and the Indonesian rupiah have collapsed, falling in value by as much as 80 percent in the case of the rupiah. Stock markets from Jakarta to Manila have hit record lows, dragging down via a curious "contagion effect" Hong Kong and even Wall Street, at least momentarily.

Governments throughout the region were paralyzed by the crisis. In Thailand, the ruling coalition has lost its last ounce of credibility as people look toward the curious combination of the King and the International Monetary Fund (IMF) for salvation in these frightening times. In the Philippines, the administration of President Fidel Ramos is reduced to telling people to count their blessings because the crisis is worse in Thailand, Malaysia and Indonesia. In Kuala Lumpur, Mahathir rails angrily against what he sees as a conspiracy to debauch

*Walden Bello is professor of sociology and public administration at the University of the Philippines and co-director of Focus on the Global South, a research program at Chulalongkorn University in Bangkok, Thailand. He is author of* A Siamese Tragedy: Development and Disintegration in Modern Thailand. *(Food First Book, 1998).*

© SEAN SPRAGUE/IMPACT VISUALS

Bangkok

Southeast Asia's currencies led by speculator George Soros, also hinting darkly at a Jewish plot against Islamic Malaysia.

Once proud of their freedom from IMF stabilization and structural adjustment programs, the Thai and Indonesian governments have run to the Fund, which has assembled multi-billion dollar bailout funds in return for draconian programs that pull the plug from banks and finance companies, mandate deep spending cuts and accelerate liberalization and deregulation in economies marked by significant state intervention. The Philippines never left IMF management, and it is now likely to postpone its "exit." True to form, Malaysia's Mahathir refused to go to an institution that he sees as part of the problem rather than the solution.

## CRISIS OF A MODEL

Many informed analysts, while dismissing Mahathir's conspiracy theories, have pinned part of the blame for the crisis on the uncontrolled flow of trillions of dollars across borders owing to the globalization of financial markets over the last few years. Increasingly, some assert, capital movements have become irrational and motivated by no more than a herdlike mentality, where one follows the movement of "lead" fund managers like Soros, without really knowing about the "economic fundamentals" of regions they are coming to or withdrawing from.

Surprisingly, Stanley Fischer, the deputy managing director of the IMF, lent support to this interpretation about irrational markets, telling the recent World Bank annual meeting in Hong Kong that "markets are not always right. Sometimes inflows are excessive, and sometimes they may be sustained too long. Markets tend to react late, but then they tend to react fast, sometimes excessively."

The merits of this analysis notwithstanding, it fails to grapple with a more fundamental issue: the pattern of development that has rendered the region so vulnerable to such variations in foreign capital inflows and outflows. To a considerable extent, the current downspin of the region's economies should be seen as the inevitable result of the region's closer integration into the global economy and heavy reliance on foreign capital.

More than in the case of the original newly industrializing countries (NICs) of Northeast Asia, the Southeast Asian NICs have been dependent for their economic growth on foreign capital inflows. The first phase of this process of foreign capital-dependent growth occurred between the mid-eighties and the early 1990s, when a massive inflow of capital from Japan occurred, lifting the region out of recession and triggering a decade of high 7 to 10 percent growth rates that were the envy of the rest of the world.

Central to this development was the Plaza Accord of 1985, which drastically revalued the yen relative to the dollar, leading Japanese corporations to seek out low-cost production sites outside of Japan so they could remain globally competitive. Some $15 billion in Japanese direct investment flowed into the region between 1986 and 1990. This infusion brought with it not only billions more in Japanese aid and bank capital but also an ancillary flow of capital from the first generation NICs of Taiwan, Korea and Hong Kong.

By providing an alternative access to tremendous sums of capital, Japanese investment had another important result: it enabled Southeast Asian countries to slow down the efforts of the IMF and World Bank to carry out the wide-ranging "structural adjustment" of their economies in the direction of greater trade liberalization, deregulation and privatization—something the Fund and Bank were successfully imposing on Latin America and Africa at the time.

By the early 1990s, however, Japanese direct investment inflows were leveling off or, as in the case of Thailand, falling. By that time, the Southeast Asian countries had become addicted to foreign capital. The challenge confronting the political and economic elite of Southeast Asia was how to bridge the massive gap between the limited saving and investments of the Southeast Asian countries and the massive investments they needed for their strategy of "fast track capitalism."

But happily for them, a second source of foreign capital opened up in the early 1990s: the vast amounts of personal savings, pension funds, corporate savings and other funds—largely from the United States—that were deposited in mutual funds and other investment institutions that sought the highest returns available anywhere in the world.

These funds were not, however, going to come in automatically, without a congenial investment climate. To attract the funds, government financial officials throughout Southeast Asia devised come-hither strategies that had three central elements:

- Financial liberalization or the elimination of foreign exchange and other restrictions on the inflow and outflow of capital, fully opening up stock exchanges to the participation of foreign portfolio investors, allowing foreign banks to participate more fully in domestic banking operations and opening up other financial sectors, like the insurance industry, to foreign players.
- Maintaining high domestic interest rates relative to interest rates in the United States and other world financial centers in order to suck in speculative capital that would seek to capture the enormous difference from the spread between, say, interest rates of 5 to 6 percent in New York and 12 or 15 percent in Manila or Bangkok.
- Fixing the exchange rate between the local currency and the dollar to eliminate or reduce risks for foreign investors stemming from fluctuations in the value of the region's currencies. This guarantee was needed if investors were going to come in, change their dollars into pesos, baht or rupiah, play the stock market or buy high-yielding government or corporate bonds, and then transform their capital and their profits back into dollars and move on to other markets where more attractive opportunities awaited them.

This formula had the blessing of the IMF and the World Bank, where one of the key elements of reigning economic doctrine was capital account liberalization.

The policy was wildly successful in achieving its objective of attracting foreign portfolio investment and bank capital. U.S. mutual funds led the way, supplying new capital to the region on the order of $4 billion to $5 billion a year for the past few years.

## THAILAND'S RECORD RISE AND FALL

A close look at two countries—Thailand and the Philippines—reveals the dynamic of the rise and unravelling of foreign capital-driven "fast track capitalism."

In the case of Thailand, net portfolio investment or speculative capital inflow came to around $24 billion in the last three to four years, while another $50 billion came in the form of loans via the innovative Bangkok International Banking Facility (BIBF), which allowed foreign and local banks to make dollar loans to local enterprises at much lower rates of interest than those in baht terms. With the wide spread—6 or 7 per-

# THE KOREAN COLLAPSE

PERHAPS AN EVEN BIGGER surprise than the collapse of the economies of Southeast Asia has been the implosion of the Korean economy. The coming of the IMF has only triggered an even greater loss of confidence, with the nation's currency, the won, dropping even more relative to the dollar and the Seoul stockmarket plunging to near its low for the year after the inking of a rescue agreement with the Fund in the first week of December.

Even as the economies of Southeast Asia were collapsing in dramatic fashion over the summer, things were building up to a climax in Korea, where over the last year, seven of the country's mighty chaebol or conglomerates had come crashing down. The dynamics of the fall in Korea were, however, distinct from that in Southeast Asia.

## The Korean Path

Unlike the Southeast Asian economies, Korea, the classical "NIC" or newly industrializing country, had blazed a path to industrial strength that was based principally on domestic savings, carried out partly through equity-enhancing reforms such as land reform in the early 1950s. Foreign capital had played an important part, no doubt, but local financial resources extracted through a rigorous system of taxation plus profits derived from the sale of goods to a protected domestic market and to foreign markets opened up by an aggressive mercantilist strategy constituted the main source of capital accumulation.

The institutional framework for high-speed industrialization was a close working relationship between the private sector and the state, with the state in a commanding role. By picking winners, providing them subsidized credit through a government-directed banking system and protecting them from competition from multi-nationals in the domestic market, the state nurtured industrial conglomerates that it later pushed out into the international market. In the early 1980s, the state-chaebol combine appeared to be unstoppable in international markets, as the deep pockets of commercial banks that were extremely responsive to government wishes provided the wherewithal for Hyundai, Samsung, LG and other conglomerates to carve out market shares in Europe, Asia and North America. The good years were from 1985 to 1990, when profitability was roughly indicated by the surpluses that the country racked up in its international trade account.

## The squeeze

In the early nineties, however, the tide turned against the Koreans. Two factors, in particular, appear to be central. The first was the failure to invest significantly in research and development. The second was the massive trade blitz visited on Korea by the United States.

On the one hand, failure to invest significantly in research and development (R&D) during the 1980s translated into continuing heavy dependence on Japan for basic machinery, manufacturing inputs and technology, resulting in a worsening trade deficit with that country. Government spending on R&D in the late 1980s came to only 0.4 per cent of gross national product, and reforms needed so the country's educational structure could mass produce a more technically proficient work force were never implemented. By the end of the decade, there were only 32 engineers per 10,000 workers in Korea, compared to 240 in Japan and 160 in the United States.

Management took the easy way out, with many firms choosing to continue to compete on the basis of low-cost unskilled or semi-skilled labor by moving many of their operations to Southeast Asia. Instead of pouring money into R&D to turn out high-value-added commodities and develop more sophisticated production technologies, Korea's conglomerates went for the quick and easy route to profits, buying up real estate or pouring money into stock market speculation. In the 1980s, over $16.5 billion in chaebol funds went into buying land for speculation and setting up luxury hotels. In fact, as of the early

cent—between U.S. interest rates and interest rates on baht loans, local commercial banks could borrow abroad and still make a mean profit relending the dollars to local customers at lower rates than those charged for baht loans.

Thai banks and finance companies had no trouble borrowing abroad. With the ultimate collateral being an economy that was growing at an average rate of 10 percent a year—the fastest in the world in the decade from 1985 to 1995—Bangkok became a debtors' market.

Contrary to the current IMF and World Bank attempts to rewrite history, the massive inflow of foreign capital did not alarm the Fund or the Bank, even as short-term debt came to $41 billion of Thailand's $83 billion foreign debt by 1995. In fact, the Bank and the IMF were not greatly bothered by a conjunction of a skyrocketing foreign debt and a burgeoning current account deficit (a deficit in the country's trade in goods and services) which came to 6 to 8 percent of gross domestic product in the mid 1990s. At the height of the borrowing spree in 1994, the official line of the World Bank on Thailand was: "Thailand provides an excellent example of the dividends to be obtained through outward orientation, receptivity to foreign investment and a market-friendly philosophy backed by conservative macro-economic management and cautious external borrowing policies."

Indeed, as late as 1996, while expressing some concern with the huge capital flows, the IMF was still praising Thai authorities for their "consistent record of sound macroeconomic management policies." While the Fund recommended "a greater degree of exchange rate flexibility," there was certainly no advice to let the baht float freely.

The complacency of the IMF and World Bank when it came to Thailand—and their failure to fully appreciate the danger signals—is traced by some analysts to the fact that the debt was not incurred and financed by the government but by the private actors. Indeed, the high current account deficits of the early 1990s coincided with government budget surpluses. In the Fund/Bank view, since the financial flows were conducted by private sectors, there was no need to worry, as they would be subject to the self-correcting mechanisms of the market. That, at least, was the theory.

1990s, a single U.S. corporation, IBM, was investing much more on R&D than all Korean corporations combined!

Not surprisingly, most of the machines in industrial plants continue to be imported from Japan, and Korean-assembled products from color televisions to laptop computers continue to be made up mainly of Japanese components. For all intents and purposes, Korea has not been able to graduate from its status as a labor-intensive assembly point for Japanese inputs using Japanese technology. Predictably, the result has been a massive trade deficit with Japan, which came to over $15 billion in 1996.

As Korea's balance of trade with Japan was worsening, so was its trade account with the United States. Fearing the emergence of another Japan with whom it would constantly be in deficit, Washington subjected Seoul to a broad-front trade offensive that was much tougher than the one directed at Japan, probably owing to Korea's lack of retaliatory capacity. Among other things, the United States:

• Hit Korean television manufacturers with anti-dumping suits;
• Forced Korea to adopt "voluntary export restraints" on a number of products, including textile, garments and steel;
• Forced the appreciation of the won, the Korean currency, relative to the dollar by 40 per cent between 1986 and 1989 to make Korean goods more expensive to U.S. consumers, thus dampening demand for them;

• Knocked Korea off the list of countries eligible for inclusion in the General System of Preferences (GSP), which grants preferential tariffs to products from Third World countries in order to assist their development;
• Threatened Korea with sanctions for a whole host of alleged offenses, ranging from violation of intellectual property rights to discriminatory tax treatment against large-engine U.S. car imports;
• Forced Korea to open up its markets to U.S. tobacco products and to increase imports of beef and rice;
• Forced Seoul to open an estimated 98 percent of industrial areas and 32 percent of service areas to foreign equity investments and stepped up the pressure for liberalization in telecommunications, maritime services, banking, government procurement and many other areas.

Hemmed in on all fronts, Korea saw its 1987 trade surplus of $9.6 billion with the United States turn into a deficit of $159 million in 1992. By 1996, the deficit with the United States had grown to over $10 billion, and Korea's overall trade deficit hit $21 billion.

**Desperation move**

In a desperate attempt to regain profitability, management tried to ram through parliament in December 1996 a series of laws that would have given it significantly expanded rights to fire labor and reduce the work force, along the lines of a U.S.-style

reform of sloughing off "excess labor" and making the surviving work force more productive [see "Democracy on Trial: South Korean Workers Resist Labor Law Deform," *Multinational Monitor,* March 1997]. When fierce street opposition from workers defeated this effort, many chaebol had no choice but to fall back on their longstanding symbiotic relationship with the government and the banks, this time to draw ever greater amounts of funds to keep money-losing operations alive. The lifeline could not, however, be maintained without the banks themselves being run to the ground.

By October, it was estimated that non-performing loans by Korean enterprises had escalated to over $50 billion. As this surfaced, foreign banks, which already had about $200 billion worth of investments and loans in Korea, became reluctant to release new funds to Seoul. By late November, on the eve of the APEC summit in Vancouver, Seoul, saddled with having to repay some $72 billion out of a total foreign debt of $110 billion within one year, joined Thailand and Indonesia on the IMF queue. The Korean government was able to get a commitment of $57 billion to bail out the economy, but only on condition that it would not only undertake a harsh stabilization program but also do away with the key institutions and practices that had propelled the country into "tigerhood."

The miracle was over          —*W.B.*

## SIAM'S TWIN

Turning to the Philippines, Manila's technocrats were in the early 1990s very hungry for foreign capital since the country had been, for reasons of political instability, skirted by the massive inflow of Japanese investment into the Southeast Asian region in the late 1980s. Eager to join the front ranks of the Asian tigers, the Philippine technocrats saw Thailand as a worthy example to follow and in the next few years, in matters of macroeconomic strategy, the Philippines became Siam's twin.

Cloned by Manila, the formula of financial liberalization, high interest rates and a virtually fixed exchange rate attracted some $19.4 billion of net portfolio investment to the Philippines between 1993 and 1997. And dollar loans via the Foreign Currency Deposit Units—Manila's equivalent of the Bangkok International Banking Facility—rose from $2 billion at the end of 1993 to $11.6 billion in March 1997. As one investment house put it, with the peso "padlocked" at 26.2 to 26.3 to the dollar since September 1995, "they [Filipino banks] are not fools in Manila. They were offered U.S. dollars at 600 basis

points cheaper than the peso rates along with currency protection from the BSP [the central bank]. They took it."

## REAL EVENTS VERSUS THE REAL ECONOMY

Had these foreign capital inflows gone into the truly productive sectors of the economy, like manufacturing and agriculture, the story might have been different. But they went instead principally to fuel asset-inflation in the stock market and real estate, which were seen as the most attractive in terms of providing high yield with a quick turnaround time. Indeed, the promise of easy profits via speculation subverted the real economy as manufacturers in Thailand and the Philippines, instead of plowing their profits into upgrading their technology or skills of their workforce, gambled much of them in real estate and the stock market.

The inflow of foreign portfolio investment and foreign loans into real estate led to a construction frenzy that has resulted in a situation of massive oversupply of residential and commercial properties from Bangkok to Jakarta. By the end of 1996, an estimated $20 billion worth of the residential and commercial property in Bangkok remained unsold. Monuments of the property folly were everywhere evident, such as Bangkok Land Company's massive but virtually deserted residential complex near the Don Muang International Airport and the sleek but near empty 30-story towers in the Bangna-Trat area. Yet developers were still rushing new highrises to completion as late as mid-1997.

In Manila, the question by the beginning of 1997 was no longer if there would be a glut in real estate. The question was how big it would ultimately be, with one investment analyst projecting that by the year 2000, the supply of highrise residential units would exceed demand by 211 percent while the supply of commercial units would outpace demand by 142 percent. In their efforts to cut their losses in the developing glut, real estate developers refrained from major new investments in office space and condos, pouring billions of pesos instead into tourist resorts and golf courses.

Oversupply also overtook property development in Kuala Lumpur and Jakarta.

This all spelled bad news for commercial banks and finance companies in all four countries, since their real estate loan exposure was heavy. As a percentage of commercial banks' total exposure, real estate or real estate-related loans came to 15 to 25 percent in the case of the Philippines and 20 to 25 percent in the case of Malaysia and Indonesia. In Thailand, where the exposure in real estate was grossly underestimated by official figures and calculated by some to come to as high as 40 percent of total bank loans, half of the loans made to property developers were said to be "non-performing" by early 1997.

Unchecked by any significant controls by governments that had internalized the IMF and World Bank theory about the self-correcting mechanisms of the financial market, the frenzied flow of capital had led to the creation of a giant speculative bubble over the real economy that would explode in a highly destabilizing fashion.

## STAMPEDE AND SPECULATION

It was the massive oversupply in the real estate sector that underlined to foreign investors and creditors that, despite creative accounting techniques, many of the country's finance companies that had borrowed heavily, floated bonds or sold equities to them were saddled with billions of dollars worth of bad loans. This led them to reassess their position in Thailand in the beginning of 1997. They began to panic when they saw the real estate glut in the context of the country's deteriorating macroeconomic indicators, like a large current account deficit, an export growth rate of near zero in 1996 and a burgeoning foreign debt of $89 billion, half of which was due in a few months time.

Of these figures, the current account deficit loomed largest in foreign investors' consciousness, because it was thought to indicate that Thailand would not be able to earn enough for-

eign exchange in order to service its foreign debt. Nevertheless, during the boom years, investment analysts shrugged off deficits that came to 8 to 11 percent of gross domestic product (GDP) and continued to give Thailand A to AA+ credit ratings on the strength of its high growth rate. However, the combination of the massive buildup of private debt and the real estate glut put the country's "macroeconomic fundamentals," to borrow investors' jargon, in a new, and to many, scary light in 1997. Thailand's deficit in 1996 came to 8.2 percent of GDP, and this was now emphasized as roughly the same figure as that of Mexico when that economy suffered its financial meltdown in December 1994.

It was time to get out, first, and with over $20 billion jostling around in Bangkok, parked in speculative investment in Thai companies or nestled in nonresident bank accounts, the stampede was potentially catastrophic. It meant the unloading of hundreds of billions of baht for dollars. The result was tremendous downward pressure on the value of the baht, making it difficult to maintain the now-sacrosanct one-dollar-to-25-baht rate.

The scent of panic attracted speculators who sought to make profits from the well-timed purchases and unloading of baht and dollars by gambling on the baht's eventual devaluation. The Bank of Thailand, the country's central monetary authority, tried to defend the baht at around 25 baht to one dollar by dumping its dollar reserves on the market. But the foreign investors' stampede that speculators rode on was simply too strong, with the result that the central bank lost $9 billion of its $39 billion reserves before it threw in the towel and let the baht float "to seek its own value" in July.

Speculators spotted the same skittish foreign investor behavior in Manila, Kuala Lumpur and Jakarta, where the same conjunction of overexposure in the property sector, weak export growth and widening current account deficits was stoking fears of a devaluation of the currency. Speculators rode on the exit of foreign investors, which accelerated tremendously after the effective devaluation of the baht on July 2. Central bank authorities attempted the same strategy of dumping their dollar reserves to defend the value of their currencies, with the only result being the massive rundown of their reserves. By the end of August, the "fixing" of the dollar value of the Malaysian ringgit, Indonesian rupiah and the Philippine peso that had been one of the ingredients of the Southeast Asian "miracle" had been abandoned by all the region's central banks, as the currencies were let go to seek their own value in the brave new world of the free float.

## THE FUTURE

Seldom in economic history has a region fallen so fast from economic grace. From being one of the world's hottest economic zones, Southeast Asia now faces a bleak future marked by the following likely developments:

First, despite statements made by some Southeast Asian governments (as well as by professional Asian miracle boosters like Harvard's Jeffrey Sachs) that the crisis is a short-term one—a phase in the normal ebb and flow of capital—there is a strategic withdrawal of finance capital from the Southeast Asian region. Capital movements may indeed be dedicated by a mixture of rationality and irrationality. But one thing is certain: foreign capital is not so irrational as to return to Southeast Asia anytime soon. For in most investors' minds, the most likely scenario is one of prolonged crisis. The current instability will last from seven to 12 months, if the earlier experiences of Mexico, Finland and Sweden were any indication, says the chair of Salomon Brothers Asia Pacific, during which there will be weak domestic demand and "severe contraction in GDP in some of them."

A second likely development is that foreign investors will follow the lead of the banks and portfolio investors and significantly decrease their commitments to the region.

General Motors is now said to be regretting its 1996 decision to set up a major assembly plant in Thailand to churn out cars for what was then seen as the infinitely growing Southeast Asian market.

How Japanese direct investors who dominate the region will react is, however, the decisive question. Some analysts say that new investment flows from Japan are not likely to be reduced much since the Japanese are continuing to pursue a strategic plan of making Southeast Asia an integrated production base. More than 1,100 Japanese companies are ensconced in Thailand alone, they point out.

However, there are now wrinkles that make the situation different than the early 1990s. Japanese investment strategies in the last few years have targeted Southeast Asia not just as an export platform but increasingly as prosperous middle-class markets to be exploited themselves—and these markets are expected to contract severely. Diverting production from Southeast Asian markets to Japan will be difficult since Japan's recession, instead of giving way to recovery, is becoming even deeper. And redirecting production to the United States is going to be very difficult, unless the Japanese want to provoke the wrath of Washington.

The upshot of all this is that Japan is likely to be burdened with significant overcapacity in its Southeast Asian manufacturing network, and this will trigger a significant plunge in the level of fresh commitments of capital to the region. Already, nearly all of the Japanese vehicle manufacturers—Toyota, Mitsubishi and Isuzu—have either shut down or reduced operations in Thailand.

A third likely development that will lengthen the shadow of gloom in the region is that the United States and the IMF are likely to take advantage of the crisis to press for further liberalization of the ASEAN economies. While many Asian economic managers are now coming around to the position that the weak controls on the flow of international capital ha[ve] been a major cause of the currency crisis, U.S. officials and economists are taking exactly the opposite position: that it was incomplete liberalization that was one of the key causes

of the crisis. The fixing of the exchange rate has been identified as the major culprit by Northern analysts, conveniently forgetting that it was the Northern fund managers who had emphasized the stability that fixed rates brought to the local investment scene and not even the IMF had advocated a truly free float for Third World currencies owing to its fears of the inflationary pressures and other forms of economic instability this might generate.

But the agenda of U.S. economic authorities goes beyond the currency question to include the accelerated deregulation, privatization and liberalization of trade in goods and services.

Formerly, the economic clout of the Southeast Asian countries enabled them to successfully resist Washington's demands for faster trade liberalization. Indeed, they were able to derail Washington's rush to transform the Asia-Pacific Economic Cooperation (APEC) into a free trade area. But with the changed situation, the capacity to resist has been drastically reduced and there is virtually no way to prevent Washington and the IMF from completing the liberalization or structural adjustment of the economies where the process was aborted (with the significant exception of financial liberalization) in the late eighties owing to the cornucopia of Japanese investment.

Indeed, as part of the package of reforms agreed with the IMF, Thai authorities have removed all limitations on foreign ownership of Thai financial firms and are pushing ahead with even more liberal foreign investment legislation to allow foreigners to own land. Even before it sought the help of the IMF, Jakarta abolished a 49 percent limit for foreign investors to buy the initial public offering (IPO) shares in publicly listed companies.

Because of depressive effects of severe spending cuts, currency depreciation and the channeling of national financial resources to service the foreign debt, structural adjustment programs in Latin America and Africa brought a decade of zero or minimal growth in the 1980s. It is likely that with the resumption of structural adjustment that was aborted in the mid-eighties by the cornucopia of Japanese investment, Southeast Asia's economies will see the recession induced by the current crisis turn into a longer period of economic stagnation, possibly leading to political instability.

## FLOTSAM AND JETSAM

All this has translated into a pervasive feeling throughout the region that an era has passed, that the so-called "Southeast Asian miracle" has come to an end. Increasingly, some say that the miracle was a mirage, that high growth rates for a long time put a lid on what was actually a stripmine type of growth that saw the development of the financial and services sector at the expense of agriculture and industry, intensified inequalities and disrupted the environment, probably irretrievably.

In Thailand, where the crisis in the real economy is spreading most quickly, with unemployment rates fast approaching double digits, the balance of costs and benefits of the last decade of fast-track growth is painfully evident. The legacy of this process is an industry whose technology is antiquated, a countryside marked by continuing deep poverty and a distribution of income worse than it was more than two decades ago. Indeed, inequality has reached Latin American (or U.S.) levels, with the income going to the top 20 percent of households rising from 50 percent in 1975 to 53 percent in 1994, while the income of the bottom 40 percent declined from 15 to 14 percent.

As the World Bank admitted in a recent study, this pattern of growing inequality has marked most of the other "tiger" economies.

But it is probably the rapid rundown of natural capital and the massive environmental destabilization that will serve as an enduring legacy of the miracle that has vanished.

In Indonesia, deforestation has accelerated to 2.4 million hectares a year, one of the highest levels in the world. Industrial pollution is pervasive in urban centers like Jakarta and Surabaya, with about 73 percent of water samples taken in Jakarta discovered to be highly contaminated by chemical pollutants. In the East Malaysian state of Sarawak, 30 percent of the forest disappeared in 23 years, while in peninsular Malaysia, only 27 percent of 116 rivers surveyed by authorities were said to be pollution free, the rest being ranked either "biologically dead" or "dying."

In this dimension, too, Thailand is the paradigm. According to government statistics, only 17 percent of the country's land area remains covered by forest, and this is probably an overestimate. The great Chao Phraya River that runs through Bangkok is biologically dead to its lower reaches. Only 50,000 of the 3.5 million metric tons of hazardous waste produced in the country each year are treated, the rest being disposed of in ways that gravely threaten public health, like being dumped in shallow underground pits where seepage can contaminate aquifers. So unhealthy is Bangkok's air that, a few years ago, a University of Hawaii team measuring air pollution reportedly refused to return to the city.

"I ask myself constantly what we have been left with that is positive," Professor Nikhom Chandravithun, one of the country's most respected civic leaders, recently told a public meeting. "And, honestly, I can't think of anything."

---

*Article 6*

*The Economist,* October 10th, 1998

# Out with the old, in with something much less familiar

After the economic devastation, a political upheaval in South-East Asia was inevitable. It has only just begun

BANGKOK

ANWAR IBRAHIM is not short of friends in high places. The second arraignment of Malaysia's former deputy prime minister in Kuala Lumpur this week smoked them out. The charges, five counts of sodomy and five of arranging cover-ups, did not seem to justify the press campaign against him. Mr Anwar's appearance—bruised, black-eyed and then wearing a surgical collar—was shocking.

Expressions of confidence came from the bosses of the World Bank, the IMF and the American Treasury. For them Mr Anwar, who was also finance minister, was a "respected member of the international financial community". But, unusually in a region where diplomatic etiquette bars any meddling in your neighbours' affairs, South-East Asian leaders have also piped up. President Joseph Estrada of the Philippines has said he is loth to visit Malaysia while "my friend Anwar" is behind bars. President B.J. Habibie of Indonesia has told Thai journalists that he is "very concerned over how my friend Anwar has been treated." On October 6th, a planned visit by Mr Habibie to Kuala Lumpur was called off because, it was said, the president was too busy at home. It was to have been his first overseas foray since taking office in May.

These breaches of South-East Asia's hallowed principle of "non-interference" are a tribute to Mr Anwar's great personal charm and years of making friends. But for many intellectuals, politicians and officials in the region, Mr Anwar is more than just a nice man they happen to know. He represents the ideal of a new generation of leaders: clean, cultivated and liberal; patriotic but outward-looking; at home making fiery speeches in Malay *kampongs* and then chairing high-powered international committees in Washington.

If Mr Anwar is guilty of even a fraction of the crimes he has been accused of (which go far beyond those with which he has been formally charged), his fans will consider themselves to have been sadly misled. But for them, his tussle with his former boss, Mahathir Mohamad, the prime minister, is emblematic of a broader struggle across the region. The old order, established in the 1960s, is fading, and the forces of "reform" are battling those of reaction. *Reformasi,* the catch-all slogan of the movement that helped unseat President Suharto of Indonesia in May, has now been taken up by Mr Anwar's supporters. It encompasses a drive against corruption and a change to a more responsive, pluralist political system. In foreign policy, it implies a more assertive style of diplomacy (see box "Time to pass a few judgments?").

Economic turmoil has already wrought one fundamental change in the politics of South-East Asia: the fall of the 32-year-old Suharto regime. Whatever successor government eventually emerges in Indonesia, it will take years to assume the regional dominance enjoyed by Mr Suharto. He was the last of those who presided over the founding in 1967 of the regional club, the Association of South-East Asian Nations (ASEAN), to give up office; and, whatever the methods by which he did it, he had provided stability of a sort. The tumult has also resulted in political change elsewhere. In Thailand, it brought in a new government last year. In the Philippines it helped persuade Fidel Ramos not to try for another spell in the presidency when his constitutional term reached its limit after the elections held in May.

Political ferment still bubbles. In the next year, more elections are likely to be held in both Malaysia and Thailand, though in neither country are they inevitable until 2000. In Cambodia, which is still trying to form a government after its parliamentary election in July, there is the risk of political violence between the forces of the state, run by the winner, Hun Sen, and its opponents. Something similar hangs over Myanmar, where the election held in 1990, which was won by Aung San Suu Kyi's opposition party, has never been honoured. Even Vietnam's ruling Communists will face mounting pressure for reform as the economy slows.

## Everywhere except Malaysia

Indonesia is to hold an election next May; an electoral assembly dominated

# Time to pass a few judgments?

BANGKOK

IT'S a generational thing." That is how one of President B.J. Habibie's advisers explains the staunch resistance to change displayed by Indonesia's long-serving foreign minister, Ali Alatas, at a meeting in Manila in July. It was the annual bash of the Association of South-East Asian Nations (ASEAN). Thailand's foreign minister, Surin Pitsuwan, had suggested ASEAN might ditch, or at least tinker with, its doctrine of noninterference, and contemplate "flexible engagement" instead. The time had come, he argued, for less regional reticence, and more straight talk. After all, the internal policies of one country could affect all.

Yes, indeed. For example, European sanctions imposed on Myanmar because of its repressive regime have disrupted ASEAN-EU relations. But, of Mr Surin's eight ASEAN colleagues, only one, from the Philippines, backed him up. It was hard to persuade the others to accept even a compromise formulation—"enhanced interaction" —which had been watered down to the point of meaninglessness.

The debate is not new. But it heated up last year, with the accession to ASEAN of Myanmar, and the nearly simultaneous coup in Cambodia, which had been due to join at the same time. ASEAN decided to wait to let Cambodia in until its leader, Hun Sen, could make some claim to legitimacy. It is still waiting. At the time, Anwar Ibrahim was acting as Malaysia's prime minister. He wrote an article urging ASEAN to start considering "constructive interventions" in its members' affairs, because "all of us in the region are our brothers' keepers", bound by "core humanitarian values".

It is this vision, shared by Mr Habibie's adviser, that is contested both by ASEAN's old guard (Mahathir Mohamad, for example, and in his day ex-President Suharto) and its newer members: Myanmar, Laos and Vietnam. For them political "stability" is paramount, and it is nobody else's business how it is achieved. With the end of the Suharto era, this view might soon lose the support of Indonesia, much the biggest and still the most influential ASEAN member. And if, as used to be taken for granted, Mr Anwar were to succeed Dr Mahathir, ASEAN as a whole would take on a very different look. No longer would it appear a group of more or less authoritarian countries with a couple of outlandish, unruly democracies (Thailand and the Philippines). Rather it might become an organisation committed to some minimum standards of decent behaviour from its members' governments. As it is, Thai diplomats worry that, at ASEAN's summit in Hanoi in December, even the modest changes approved in Manila may be rolled back, and ASEAN will reassert its non-interfering fundamentals.

That worries not just those who are embarrassed that ASEAN affords a degree of diplomatic cover to vile regimes, but also those who would like to see it play a stronger economic role. During the region's travails, ASEAN has proved itself largely irrelevant to efforts to stop the rot. It is joked that the Asia-Pacific Economic Co-operation trade forum, whose summit in Kuala Lumpur next month will be awkward, comprises four adjectives in search of a noun. ASEAN is looking for a verb.

by the winners is then to pick a new president the following December. But dark hints have been dropped that this timetable may slip if there is too much unrest on the streets. Pessimists remember that both in Mr Suharto's early years in power and in those of Indonesia's first president, Sukarno, there were interludes, like the present one, when freedom flickered, only to be snuffed out as the army took fright.

This time, however, Indonesia has a deeper stratum of educated, younger reformists, who have chafed at the restrictions and injustices of one-man rule. Under Mr Suharto, they went into business, academia, the bureaucracy or a plethora of non-governmental organisations, and pondered, interminably, the looming succession crisis. "If only we had an Anwar!" is how one, now in government, recalls their conclusions. Mr Anwar seemed trusted by his mentor, Dr Mahathir, who had chosen him as his eventual successor, and yet he was different enough in background and outlook to promise change without dislocation. In comparison, Indonesia had a void, which, even now, few of Mr Suharto's critics trust his protégé, Mr Habibie, to fill.

Mr Anwar had also, through his Institute for Policy Research, close intellectual links with the Indonesian elite, including some of Mr Habibie's closest advisers, who had their own think-tank, the Centre for Information and Development Studies. Adi Sasono, once the think-tank's chairman, now sits in Mr Habibie's cabinet, but he is also close to Amien Rais, a leading opposition figure in Indonesia who has been voicing support for Mr Anwar.

In fact, the "friends of Anwar" seem to be thriving everywhere except in Malaysia. Mr Anwar's institute also cultivated contacts in the Philippines, and was involved two years ago in activities to mark the centenary of the execution of the Filipino nationalist hero, Jose Rizal. Some of those friends now form part of President Estrada's large phalanx of advisers. In Thailand, too, some of his intellectual pals are now in office. Sukhumbhand Paribatra, for example, now a deputy foreign minister, telephoned Mr Anwar's wife after her husband's arrest to offer moral support.

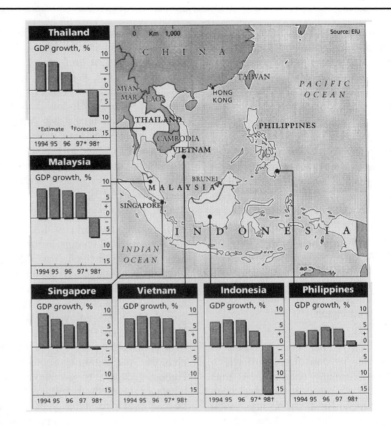

## The whiff of Islamism

In this context, Mr Anwar seems part of a broader generational shift across South-East Asia, a representative of an up-and-coming elite whose attitudes are very different from those of their predecessors. Their rise is welcomed by some westerners, who see them as open-minded liberals, free of the post-colonial chips borne by their elders, and committed to greater pluralism, open markets and clean government.

But in Malaysia and Indonesia Mr Anwar and his friends are not universally viewed as beacons of hope. They prompt alarm in some quarters because of their Islamist backgrounds. Mr Anwar first came to prominence in the 1970s as the leader of an Islamic youth movement. His critics accuse him of having tried, at the time, to import Iranian-style Islamic revolution, and of having switched, 20 years later, to the kind of campaign against corruption and nepotism that swept Mr Suharto out of office in Indonesia. Although it is hard to see Mr Anwar as a closet fundamentalist, some worry that he might not stand up to more extreme Muslims, because they form part of his power base (though not, presumably, for much longer, if convincing evidence of his alleged sexual offences is brought before the courts next month).

## The last of the anti-colonialists

Dr Mahathir, like Mr Suharto before his downfall, draws support from those who fear a drift away from secular politics. In Indonesia, the terrible looting, arson and rape suffered by some members of the country's Chinese minority earlier this year have given a grim warning of what might happen should religion and race become the currency of politics. Neither Dr Mahathir nor the government of the neighbouring state, Singapore, needs reminders of the race riots that pitted Malays against Chinese in their countries some 30 years ago.

The shape of the region's current politics was set in the 1960s, amid post-colonial anxieties and the cold war (at that time being fought, very hotly, in Vietnam). ASEAN's first task was to defuse the legacy of Mr Sukarno's "confrontation" with Malaysia, with which the Philippines also had territorial disputes.

South-East Asia later divided into communist Vietnam, Laos and Cambodia, on the one hand, and staunchly pro-western right-wing regimes elsewhere (with Myanmar, then known as Burma, which opted out of the world in 1962, pursuing non-alignment to the isolationist extreme). After the collapse of communism in Europe in the late 1980s, this arrangement became anachronistic. In Thailand and the Philippines, dictatorship was already giving way to varieties of democracy. ASEAN, which was originally an anti-communist grouping that developed its cohesion by opposing the Vietnamese occupation of Cambodia in the 1980s, admitted Vietnam in 1995.

If Mr Suharto was the last of the region's right-wing dictators, all of whom owed at least some of their power to their credentials as anti-communists, Dr Mahathir is one of the last whose instincts seem animated by an anti-colonial grudge. He still seems ready to believe that all his country's problems are the result of a conspiracy by foreigners to keep his people down. One of the insinuations against Mr Anwar is that he has been the tool of these conspirators.

Politically, Dr Mahathir holds all the cards at the moment. He should be able to ensure himself a convincing victory in a general election this year or next, and so retain his leadership of his party and his prime ministership. But is it possible that Dr Mahathir will find himself, nonetheless, on the wrong side of progress? The outrage his treatment of Mr Anwar has caused at home is in part the result of the success—at least until last year—of his own economic policies. A new Malaysian middle class is no longer willing to believe all the government tells it. And a basic sense of justice has been offended.

If history had indeed ended, Dr Mahathir would be a throwback, whose days were numbered. What has happened to Mr Anwar would be only a setback on the road to liberal democracy. But history is still with us, and it is being especially unkind to South-East Asia at the moment.

It is a handicap for Mr Anwar and his friends around the region that many of them are identified with the IMF's prescriptions for economic health. Indeed, Mr Anwar's policy—of introducing a "virtual" IMF programme in Malaysia without the actual funds—was one source of tension with Dr Mahathir. The Thai government, and Mr Habibie's in Indonesia, have similarly gained some international kudos by being "serious" about introducing painful economic reforms. The trouble with painful economic reforms is that they hurt: Indonesia's economy is likely to shrink 15% this year, Thailand's at least 8% and Malaysia's more than 5% (see charts).

Because Malaysia is not in hock to the IMF, Dr Mahathir has been able to go it alone, imposing stiff exchange controls and isolating the economy from external speculative pressures while he reflates it dangerously at home. This is not likely to work. But nor, by any normal standards, has the IMF's intervention in Thailand and Indonesia. The IMF argues, and has done in these pages, that this is not its fault, and that, given its time again, it would have advocated the same policies in the afflicted countries. This is no comfort to those losing their jobs, their shirts and, in Indonesia at least, their daily supply of enough to eat. Rather, it is a recognition that the world's financial regulators did not know how to fix the trouble in the first place, and still have not found out.

Even two years ago, before South-East Asia received the first of its many subsequent buffetings, many in the region were all too aware of the flaws in their economic and political systems. Living with cronyism, corruption and collusion, they understood the costs, and accepted that sorting them out would involve pain for all. Then they saw the panic spreading to other emerging markets. And now they see Wall Street's admired hedge funds collapse in circumstances very familiar at home (banks lending unwisely to institutions in which their directors have invested). Moreover, they see praise lavished on countries, like China and India, which have failed to open up and liberalise as they have. And they see the world's leading industrial countries take up the call for a reform of the "architecture" of global finance—a call which, a year ago, brought down upon Dr Mahathir the scorn of international financiers and economists alike.

## And now the reaction

In this sense, Dr Mahathir is less throwback than backlash—the first, angry slap in the face of a region that had committed itself to globalisation, only to discover that slump may turn out to be global too. The economic consequences of this are being suffered by millions of Asians. The political consequences may yet be benign: the end of corrupt, nationalistic, repressive, "pragmatic" regimes, in favour of more honest, outward-looking, more liberal, "pragmatic" regimes. Or they may be pernicious, fostering political appeals to racism, xenophobia, and greed. As and when they come to power across the region, Mr Anwar's friends will have their work cut out.

*Article 7*                                        *The Brookings Review,* Summer 1998

# Out of the Ashes?

### Southeast Asia's Struggle through Crisis

## BY STEPHEN PARKER

*Stephen Parker is chief economist for the Asia Foundation,
San Francisco, California.*

The Southeast Asian countries of Thailand, Indonesia, Malaysia, the Philippines, and Singapore have been at the epicenter of the Asian economic crisis. On July 2 last year Thailand floated its baht after months of trying to defend it against market pressures. The baht sank immediately by about a third, followed with surprising speed by similar devaluations by the Philippines, Malaysia, and Indonesia. Even the Singapore dollar soon fell, though considerably less than the other currencies, and pressure on currency values spread to Northeast Asia, eventually to wreak havoc in South Korea by December.

What started as a seemingly innocuous balance-of-payments problem degenerated into a full-scale economic, political, and social crisis that continues today. The breadth and depth of impact has surprised analysts through each stage of the crisis.

In its wake has come political change, economic recession, unprecedented unemployment, surging inflation, and collapsing imports throughout Southeast Asia. To regain stability and confidence, Thailand's democracy changed government leadership in November and shortly after rewrote the constitution to increase government accountability and transparency. Although the Thai baht has strengthened in recent months, the realization of the extent of the economic downturn becomes more sobering with each government report, the latest predicting a recession with output falling about 6 percent for 1998.

As of this writing, Indonesia stands on the brink of systematic collapse, with the resignation of President Suharto after 32 years of leadership of the New Order Regime and the prospect of declines in output of 20–30 percent. The nation is caught in a vicious cycle—with political transition requiring time but with economic collapse adding instability.

The economic fallout on Malaysia, the Philippines, and Singapore has been less severe, largely because of their more limited foreign debt exposure. For these countries, economic growth is expected to decline by at least half, to 0–4 percent.

Nevertheless, Malaysian Prime Minister Mahathir has agreed to dismantle the long-time core of his political strategy, the New Economic Policy, that provided preferences for Malay nationals relative to ethnic-Chinese nationals. The Philippines, in many ways the least affected country in Southeast Asia, faces concerns about populist President-elect Estrada's commitment to continue the successful economic reforms of the Ramos administration. Even Singapore, the most economically developed Southeast Asian country, with respected market and commercial law institutions, is struggling with lower growth and heavy financial exposure to the Indonesian debacle.

Out of this turmoil, however, one catches glimpses of a rejuvenated Southeast Asia with strengthened political and economic institutions. Although the current unraveling in Indonesia (and a weak Japanese economy) casts a pall of concern over the region, many economic forecasts expect the Southeast Asian economies to bottom out over the next six to nine months and to resume moderate economic growth in 1999. After a damaging period of reticence by governments early in the currency crisis, Thailand, Indonesia, Malaysia, and the Philippines are all now implementing a wide range of economic, regulatory, and legal policy reforms. Rather than reversing course and turning inward by increasing protection and fomenting nationalism, all have reconfirmed their commitment to outward-looking development strategies.

The complex, systematic nature of the crisis has revealed strengths and weaknesses—both economic and political—in Southeast Asia's development process. Each country, of course, is different in many ways, but each faces the challenge of adapting its distinctive domestic political and economic systems to the homogenizing forces of globalization. The rapid spread of the crisis from its core in Southeast Asia to the rest of East Asia and then to world markets emphasizes the worldwide integration of financial markets. It also reflects the inability of international and regional mechanisms to monitor and contain the contagion effects of mistakes by governments and the private sector.

What were the main causes of this crisis? What lessons does it offer? What are the implications for U.S. interests? A closer look at the evolution of the crisis yields some interesting insights.

# ANATOMY OF THE CRISIS IN SOUTHEAST ASIA

Almost universally, Southeast Asians and the international community trumpeted the region's strong economic fundamentals and stable political systems leading up to, and even into, the initial stages of the crisis. After all, the Southeast Asian economies had grown in mass by close to 8 percent for decades, lifting tens of millions out of poverty and creating vibrant middle and upper classes. Southeast Asian governments and businesses had gained confidence and influence in regional and international affairs. In fact, however, the economic fundamentals were not as strong as projected in mid-1997, and they are not as weak now as they are presumed.

The region as a whole had been fighting a tendency to overheat since 1993–95. Characteristics of bubble economies were becoming increasingly apparent—prices on assets such as real estate and stock had skyrocketed; imports were growing rapidly while export growth lagged, resulting in substantial current account deficits. These deficits were financed by large inflows of foreign capital, which in turn exerted pressure to keep currency values high. Nominal currency values in the region had remained relatively stable for years, while real rates had appreciated significantly against the U.S. dollar (and even more so against the Japanese yen), lending a sense of security to investors that led many to resist spending the additional amounts needed to hedge their investments as a precaution against currency devaluation. Rapid growth and wealth generation created political environments where vested interests became increasingly virile, while East Asia's vaunted capacity to grow and to improve income distribution came into increasing question. Inflation, on the other hand, had generally declined in 1995 and 1996, reflecting conservative monetary and fiscal policies and the strong currency values.

## SIGNS OF TROUBLE

Four understated weaknesses in the Southeast Asian economies stand out. First, although poorly researched even now, these economies (as did East Asia as a whole) appear to have been losing global competitiveness for at least the past several years. Their dramatic decades-long growth had depended on export growth typically in the 20–40 percent range. Most telling was the collapse in export growth between the summer of 1995 and the summer of 1996 in China, Korea, and Japan, as well as Thailand, Singapore, and the rest of Southeast Asia. Although exports rebounded a bit in 1997, they had not regained their earlier strength.

In addition, much of the region's rapid export growth in the 1990s was due to declining trade and investment barriers that encouraged greater trade in intermediate inputs among multinational production networks that now flourish in Asian economies. Although this encouraged efficiencies in production, it probably overstated growth in regional export value added. Southeast Asian firms had saturated many of their tra-

ditional export sectors such as clothing, footwear, and household electronics. They were facing increasing competition from other low-wage producers, while finding it hard to expand into new, more sophisticated export sectors. At the same time, trade liberalization, strong currencies, and rising domestic demand spurred growth in imports, which combined with weaker export growth to generate the high current account deficits.

The second weakness involved another of what many considered to be a Southeast Asian strength—the rapid inflow of foreign funds. A common view was that since the private sector was more than willing to invest (loan) funds to cover the current account deficits, then these economies must be well-managed, leveraged economies. But two trends were underappreciated. First, the composition of longer-term foreign direct investment was increasingly shifting away from export sectors and more toward nontradable sectors that generally earned revenue in local currencies and that depended on domestic market conditions for success. Second, the composition of financial inflows was shifting away from more stable foreign direct investment toward portfolio investment, and an increasingly large share of the financial inflows was in the form of private debt. For example, in June 1997 foreign debt totaled $69 billion in Thailand and $59 billion in Indonesia. It was also on the rise, though at lower levels, in Malaysia and the Philippines, where it reached $29 billion and $14 billion, respectively.

With interest rates on local debt about twice those on foreign debt, local banks borrowed overseas to cover lending to local business, and corporations borrowed directly from overseas sources. And, as has always been the case in Asia, most of this private debt was relatively short-term, predominantly less than 18 months, though it was often used to finance long-term projects that would require several rollovers to complete the financing cycle. Short-term private debt thus mounted without government authorities or private markets knowing its full extent. The region, especially Indonesia and Thailand, grew increasingly vulnerable to a shock to exchange rates since more and more overseas debt was used to earn revenue in local currency, but had to be paid back in foreign currency.

Third, the efficient use of private debt depends greatly on the effectiveness of an economy's financial intermediation system, which in Southeast Asia is concentrated in bank operations. Bubble economies place considerable stress on banking systems even in developed economies, as the costly U.S. savings and loan crisis did in the 1980s and as the ongoing and even more costly Japanese banking debacle is doing today. The situation is often even worse in developing economies, where regulatory environments are less strictly enforced, vested interests sometimes use preferential access to fund risky investments, and banks are not as skilled at differentiating the risk of investments. Worse still, some Asian banks tend to lend funds based on the asset values of their customers rather than on careful analysis of the cash flow returns of a particular investment. Thus the Asian banks increased their investment while asset values were high, and then, when asset values collapsed, drew back their loans more than necessary. The general lack of transparency of business operations in Asia, relatively unnoticed during the good times (in the case of Southeast Asia, for decades), exacerbated the downturn. Southeast Asia's banking system was not well prepared to absorb the shocks of an economic downturn or a plunge in currency value.

Fourth, governments proved less able than they had been in the past to manage the relatively moderate economic shocks at the beginning of the crisis. Many see Thailand's weak response to numerous economic warnings as early as 1995 and 1996 as the incubator of the crisis. Moody's rating agency had in fact downgraded Thai bonds as early as the summer of 1996.

In this sense, the longstanding cronyism, and often corruption, that accompanied decades of rapid growth in the region were particularly decisive. The bubble-enhanced financial interests tied up government responsiveness as they had not earlier. In 1985, for example, Indonesia had informally restructured its foreign official debt portfolio almost seamlessly following the collapse in oil prices. Technocratic reformers in Thailand and Indonesia, who had traditionally been called in to resolve economic difficulties, actually favored bringing in the IMF to counterbalance the domestic political interests of the status quo who were blocking reform.

One reason for the limited success of the first IMF agreements in Indonesia and Thailand was the IMF's presumption that the technocrats would be given political authority, as they had been in the past, to implement the relatively mild policy changes initially required and to manage the financial restructuring to deal with the still underestimated private debt exposure. When political forces did not pass the torch to the technocrats and instead blocked meaningful change, governments and the IMF lost critical credibility in both domestic and international markets. As a result, they also lost the opportunity to buy time for serious financial restructuring and for distributing the costs of successfully rescheduling the predominantly short-term private foreign debt.

## GLOBALISM VERSUS POLITICAL TRADITION

At the heart of the crisis is a fundamental tension over how governments harness the commercial windfall of globalism while managing the domestic economic, political, and social stresses caused by increased influences from abroad. As Southeast Asia moved toward modern, liberalized financial systems and open international capital markets, its domestic political and economic environment remained characterized by government preferences and by weak government regulation of banks and private foreign borrowing. The combination made the region far more vulnerable to exchange rate risk and balance-of-payments pressures.

The crisis sneaked up on the region in the guise of seemingly benign increases in private capital flows, further disguised by poorly reported statistics. In the end, however, it exposed the weaknesses, in a globalizing market environment, of domestic political systems that depend on traditional, personalized control and manipulation of powerful elite groups rather than on strong, independent institutions and legal systems.

## LESSONS AND IMPLICATIONS OF THE CRISIS

The crisis in Southeast Asia proved much more serious than anyone would have imagined, both because of its systematic economic and political nature and because of the unforgiving makeup and magnitude of short-term, private foreign debt. Lessons abound.

Governments and the private sector in Southeast Asia must develop economic and political environments to regain capital, both domestic and foreign. The situation, however, is much different than it was during the capital booms of the 1980s and early 1990s, when intra-Asian capital flows were dominant. With the economic downturns in Japan, Korea, Hong Kong and Singapore, Asian sources of capital are limited. U.S. funds are thus likely to become more prominent in the region, even though they tend to have more strings attached, especially regarding demands for greater corporate and government transparency and more reliable legal systems. Market forces in this environment, therefore, are likely to reinforce IMF requirements to pressure for further reform.

As foreign firms move to merge and acquire Southeast Asian businesses, we already see clashes of corporate culture over managerial control and the difficulty of completing due diligence to determine the true financial circumstances of many Asian companies. These pressures, traumatic in nature for Asian economies, are likely to modernize economic and corporate governance and market institutions in Southeast Asia in ways that will strengthen their capacities in the future.

A key lesson of the crisis is that open private capital markets do indeed place considerable stress on domestic economic management and on political arrangements. Balancing monetary and exchange rate policy in small, open economies—no simple task at any time—is made particularly precarious if governments desire exchange rate stability and some independence in monetary policy. Similarly, private investors do indeed make mistakes, and governments do need to monitor and manage carefully private capital inflows. And lenders of last resort, such as the IMF, provide limited protection from government or private mistakes.

The crisis clearly calls into question what some Asians have called the "Asian Way," where economic development comes before political development, where business interactions tend to be personalized rather than supported by strong commercial law institutions, where business and the state operate in close quarters with limited independent regulatory oversight. Thailand's maturing democracy raises hopes that stronger political and economic institutions will emerge. Less politically open Singapore, in contrast, remains the bastion of solid market institutions and credibility. Indonesia's patriarchal autocracy proved incapable of balancing the need for distributing losses among domestic vested interests. The development of effective regulatory and commercial law systems is fundamentally a political decision, since independent institutions limit executive and preferential control over allocation of funds and power. There are real costs to maintaining domestic political conditions that limit the development of effective market institutions, especially for countries that rely importantly on foreign capital inflows and that are committed to global integration.

Implications for the United States are less direct. The crisis in Southeast Asia is having a relatively limited impact on U.S. commercial interests. U.S. banks were not heavily exposed to the Asian crisis economies, and U.S. trade interests with Southeast Asia are significant but not substantial. Once it became clear, with the successful negotiation in New York for the roll-over of Korean debt in January, that the Asia crisis would not spill over into Japan and China, and thus would not likely pose a threat to the global economy, the U.S. stock market regained its upward momentum. In fact, the crisis-related reforms enacted by the Southeast Asian governments should open access to U.S. investment and trade, especially in financial services, once regional economies stabilize and begin to grow again.

The decision by most of Southeast Asia's governments to continue on the track of outward-looking growth deflected what could have been the most serious ramification for U.S. policy—a withdrawal by the region into inward, nationalist governments playing off an anti-American backlash. The only remaining question mark is Indonesia, where political and social instability remain a major concern for U.S. strategic and political interests.

---

*Article 8*

*Discover,* June 1998

# Japanese Roots

Just who are the Japanese? Where did they come from and when? The answers are difficult to come by, though not impossible—the real problem is that the Japanese themselves may not want to know.

## BY JARED DIAMOND

*JARED DIAMOND is a longtime contributing editor of DISCOVER, a professor of physiology at UCLA Medical School, and a member of the National Academy of Sciences. Expanded versions of many of his DISCOVER articles appear in his book* The Third Chimpanzee *and in his most recent book,* Guns, Germs, and Steel: The Fates of Human Societies. *For that book, in April, Diamond was awarded this year's Pulitzer Prize for general nonfiction.*

Unearthing the origins of the Japanese is a much harder task than you might guess, among world powers today, the Japanese are the most distinctive in their culture and environment. The origins of their language are one of the most disputed questions of linguistics. These questions are central to the self-image of the Japanese and to how they are viewed by other peoples. Japan's rising dominance and touchy relations with its neighbors make it more important than ever to strip away myths and find answers.

The search for answers is difficult because the evidence is so conflicting. On the one hand, the Japanese people are biologically undistinctive, being very similar in appearance and genes to other East Asians, especially to Koreans. As the Japanese like to stress, they are culturally and biologically rather homogeneous, with the exception of a distinctive people called the Ainu on Japan's northernmost island of Hokkaido. Taken together, these facts seem to suggest that the Japanese reached Japan only recently from the Asian mainland, too recently to have evolved differences from their mainland cousins, and displaced the Ainu, who represent the original inhabitants. But if that were true, you might expect the Japanese language to show close affinities to some mainland language, just as English is obviously closely related to other Germanic languages (because Anglo-Saxons from the continent conquered England as recently as the sixth century A.D.). How can we resolve this contradiction between Japan's presumably ancient language and the evidence for recent origins?

Archeologists have proposed four conflicting theories. Most popular in Japan is the view that the Japanese gradually evolved from ancient Ice Age people who occupied Japan long before 20,000 B.C. Also widespread in Japan is a theory that the Japanese descended from horse-riding Asian nomads who passed through Korea to conquer Japan in the fourth century, but who were themselves—emphatically—not Koreans. A theory favored by many Western archeologists and Koreans, and unpopular in some circles in Japan, is that the Japanese are descendants of immigrants from Korea who arrived with rice-paddy agriculture around 400 B.C. Finally, the fourth theory holds that the peoples named in the other three theories could have mixed to form the modern Japanese.

When similar questions of origins arise about other peoples, they can be discussed dispassionately. That is not so for the Japanese. Until 1946, Japanese schools taught a myth of history based on the earliest recorded Japanese chronicles, which were written in the eighth century. They describe how the sun goddess Amaterasu, born from the left eye of the creator god Izanagi, sent her grandson Ninigi to Earth on the Japanese island of Kyushu to wed an earthly deity. Ninigi's great-grandson Jimmu, aided by a dazzling sacred bird that rendered his enemies helpless, became the first emperor of Japan in 660 B.C. To fill the gap between 660 B.C. and the earliest historically documented Japanese monarchs, the chronicles invented 13 other equally fictitious emperors. Before the end of World War II, when Emperor Hirohito finally announced that he was not of divine descent, Japanese archeologists and historians had to make their interpretations conform to this chronicle account. Unlike American archeologists, who acknowledge that ancient sites in the United States were left by peoples (Native Americans) unrelated to most modern Americans, Japanese archeologists believe all archeological deposits in Japan, no matter how old, were left by ancestors of the modern Japanese. Hence archeology in Japan is supported by astronomical budgets, employs up to 50,000 field-workers each year, and draws public attention to a degree inconceivable anywhere else in the world.

Why do they care so much? Unlike most other non-European countries, Japan preserved its independence and culture while emerging from isolation to create an industrialized society in the late nineteenth century. It was a remarkable achievement. Now the Japanese people are understandably concerned about maintaining their traditions in the face of massive Western cultural influences. They want to believe that their distinctive language and culture required uniquely complex developmental processes. To acknowledge a relationship of the Japanese language to any other language seems to constitute a surrender of cultural identity.

What makes it especially difficult to discuss Japanese archeology dispassionately is that Japanese interpretations of the past affect present behavior. Who among East Asian peoples brought culture to whom? Who has historical claims to whose

MAP BY NENAD JAKESEVIC
During the ice ages, land bridges (striped areas) connected Japan's main islands to one another and to the mainland, allowing mammals—including humans—to arrive on foot.

land? These are not just academic questions. For instance, there is much archeological evidence that people and material objects passed between Japan and Korea in the period A.D. 300 to 700. Japanese interpret this to mean that Japan conquered Korea and brought Korean slaves and artisans to Japan; Koreans believe instead that Korea conquered Japan and that the founders of the Japanese imperial family were Korean.

Thus, when Japan sent troops to Korea and annexed it in 1910, Japanese military leaders celebrated the annexation as "the restoration of the legitimate arrangement of antiquity." For the next 35 years, Japanese occupation forces tried to eradicate Korean culture and to replace the Korean language with Japanese in schools. The effort was a consequence of a centuries-old attitude of disdain. "Nose tombs" in Japan still contain 20,000 noses severed from Koreans and brought home as trophies of a sixteenth-century Japanese invasion. Not surprisingly, many Koreans loathe the Japanese, and their loathing is returned with contempt.

What really was "the legitimate arrangement of antiquity"? Today, Japan and Korea are both economic powerhouses, facing each other across the Korea Strait and viewing each other through colored lenses of false myths and past atrocities. It bodes ill for the future of East Asia if these two great peoples cannot find common ground. To do so, they will need a correct understanding of who the Japanese people really are.

Japan's unique culture began with its unique geography and environment. It is, for comparison, far more isolated than Britain, which lies only 22 miles from the French coast. Japan lies 110 miles from the closest point of the Asian mainland (South Korea), 190 miles from mainland Russia, and 480 miles from mainland China. Climate, too, sets Japan apart. Its rainfall, up to 120 inches a year, makes it the wettest temperate country in the world. Unlike the winter rains prevailing over much of Europe, Japan's rains are concentrated in the summer growing season, giving it the highest plant productivity of any nation in the temperate zones. While 80 percent of Japan's land consists of mountains unsuitable for agriculture and only 14 percent is farmland, an average square mile of that farmland is so fertile that it supports eight times as many people as does an average square mile of British farmland. Japan's high rainfall also ensures a quickly regenerated forest after logging. Despite thousands of years of dense human occupation, Japan still offers visitors a first impression of greenness because 70 percent of its land is still covered by forest.

Japanese forest composition varies with latitude and altitude: evergreen leafy forest in the south at low altitude, deciduous leafy forest in central Japan, and coniferous forest in the north and high up. For prehistoric humans, the deciduous leafy forest was the most productive, providing abundant edible nuts such as walnuts, chestnuts, horse chestnuts, acorns, and beechnuts. Japanese waters are also outstandingly productive. The lakes, rivers, and surrounding seas teem with salmon, trout, tuna, sardines, mackerel, herring, and cod. Today, Japan is the largest consumer of fish in the world. Japanese waters are also rich in clams, oysters, and other shellfish, crab, shrimp, crayfish, and edible seaweeds. That high productivity was a key to Japan's prehistory.

From southwest to northeast, the four main Japanese islands are Kyushu, Shikoku, Honshu, and Hokkaido. Until the late nineteenth century, Hokkaido and northern Honshu were inhabited mainly by the Ainu, who lived as hunter-gatherers with limited agriculture, while the people we know today as Japanese occupied the rest of the main islands.

In appearance, of course, the Japanese are very similar to other East Asians. As for the Ainu, however, their distinctive appearance has prompted more to be written about their origins and relationships than about any other single people on Earth. Partly because Ainu men have luxuriant beards and the most profuse body hair of any people, they are often classified as Caucasoids (so-called white people) who somehow migrated east through Eurasia to Japan. In their overall genetic makeup, though, the Ainu are related to other East Asians, including the Japanese and Koreans. The distinctive appearance and hunter-gatherer lifestyle of the Ainu, and the undistinctive appearance and the intensive agricultural lifestyle of the Japanese, are frequently taken to suggest the straightforward interpretation that the Ainu are descended from Japan's original hunter-gatherer inhabitants and the Japanese are more recent invaders from the Asian mainland.

But this view is difficult to reconcile with the distinctiveness of the Japanese language. Everyone agrees that Japanese does not bear a close relation to any other language in the world. Most scholars consider it to be an isolated member of Asia's Altaic language family, which consists of Turkic, Mongolian, and Tungusic languages. Korean is also often considered to be an isolated member of this family, and within the family Japanese and Korean may be more closely related to each other than to other Altaic languages. However, the similarities between Japanese and Korean are confined to general grammatical features and about 15 percent of their basic vocabularies, rather than the detailed shared features of grammar and vocabulary that link, say, French to Spanish; they are more different from each other than Russian is from English.

Since languages change over time, the more similar two languages are, the more recently they must have diverged. By counting common words and features, linguists can estimate how long ago languages diverged, and such estimates suggest that Japanese and Korean parted company at least 4,000 years ago. As for the Ainu language, its origins are thoroughly in doubt; it may not have any special relationship to Japanese.

After genes and language, a third type of evidence about Japanese origins comes from ancient portraits. The earliest preserved likeness of Japan's inhabitants are statues called haniwa, erected outside tombs around 1,500 years ago. Those statues unmistakably depict East Asians. They do not resemble the heavily bearded Ainu. If the Japanese did replace the Ainu in Japan south of Hokkaido, the replacement must have occurred before A.D. 500.

Our earliest written information about Japan comes from Chinese chronicles, because China developed literacy long before Korea or Japan. In early Chinese accounts of various peoples referred to as "Eastern Barbarians," Japan is described under the name Wa, whose inhabitants were said to be divided into more than a hundred quarreling states. Only a few Korean or Japanese inscriptions before A.D. 700 have been preserved, but extensive chronicles were written in 712 and 720 in Japan and later in Korea. Those reveal massive transmission of culture to Japan from Korea itself, and from China via Korea. The chronicles are also full of accounts of Koreans in Japan and of Japanese in Korea—interpreted by Japanese or Korean historians, respectively, as evidence of Japanese conquest of Korea or the reverse.

The ancestors of the Japanese, then, seem to have reached Japan before they had writing. Their biology suggests a recent arrival, but their language suggests arrival long ago. To resolve this paradox, we must now turn to archeology.

The seas that surround much of Japan and coastal East Asia are shallow enough to have been dry land during the ice ages, when much of the ocean water was locked up in glaciers and sea level lay at about 500 feet below its present measurement. Land bridges connected Japan's main islands to one another, to the Russian mainland, and to South Korea. The mammals walking out to Japan included not only the ancestors of modern

Japan's bears and monkeys but also ancient humans, long before boats had been invented. Stone tools indicate human arrival as early as half a million years ago.

Around 13,000 years ago, as glaciers melted rapidly all over the world, conditions in Japan changed spectacularly for the better, as far as humans were concerned. Temperature, rainfall, and humidity all increased, raising plant productivity to present high levels. Deciduous leafy forests full of nut trees, which had been confined to southern Japan during the ice ages, expanded northward at the expense of coniferous forest, thereby replacing a forest type that had been rather sterile for humans with a much more productive one. The rise in sea level severed the land bridges, converted Japan from a piece of the Asian continent to a big archipelago, turned what had been a plain into rich shallow seas, and created thousands of miles of productive new coastline with innumerable islands, bays, tidal flats, and estuaries, all teeming with seafood.

That end of the Ice Age was accompanied by the first of the two most decisive changes in Japanese history: the invention of pottery. In the usual experience of archeologists, inventions flow from mainlands to islands, and small peripheral societies aren't supposed to contribute revolutionary advances to the rest of the world. It therefore astonished archeologists to discover that the world's oldest known pottery was made in Japan 12,700 years ago. For the first time in human experience, people had watertight containers readily available in any desired shape. With their new ability to boil or steam food, they gained access to abundant resources that had previously been difficult to use: leafy vegetables, which would burn or dry out if cooked on an open fire; shellfish, which could now be opened easily; and toxic foods like acorns, which could now have their toxins boiled out. Soft-boiled foods could be fed to small children, permitting earlier weaning and more closely spaced babies. Toothless old people, the repositories of information in a preliterate society, could now be fed and live longer. All those momentous consequences of pottery triggered a population explosion, causing Japan's population to climb from an estimated few thousand to a quarter of a million.

The prejudice that islanders are supposed to learn from superior continentals wasn't the sole reason that record-breaking Japanese pottery caused such a shock. In addition, those first Japanese potters were clearly hunter-gatherers, which also violated established views. Usually only sedentary societies own pottery: what nomad wants to carry heavy, fragile pots, as well as weapons and the baby, whenever time comes to shift camp? Most sedentary societies elsewhere in the world arose only with the adoption of agriculture. But the Japanese environment is so productive that people could settle down and make pottery while still living by hunting and gathering. Pottery helped those Japanese hunter-gatherers exploit their environment's rich food resources more than 10,000 years before intensive agriculture reached Japan.

Much ancient Japanese pottery was decorated by rolling or pressing a cord on soft clay. Because the Japanese word for cord marking is *jomon*, the term Jomon is applied to the pottery itself, to the ancient Japanese people who made it, and to that whole period in Japanese prehistory beginning with the invention of pottery and ending only 10,000 years later. The earliest Jomon pottery, of 12,700 years ago, comes from Kyushu, the southernmost Japanese island. Thereafter, pottery spread north, reaching the vicinity of modern Tokyo around 9,500 years ago and the northernmost island of Hokkaido by 7,000 years ago. Pottery's northward spread followed that of deciduous forest rich in nuts, suggesting that the climate-related food explosion was what permitted sedentary living.

How did Jomon people make their living? We have abundant evidence from the garbage they left behind at hundreds of thousands of excavated archeological sites all over Japan. They apparently enjoyed a well-balanced diet, one that modern nutritionists would applaud.

One major food category was nuts, especially chestnuts and walnuts, plus horse chestnuts and acorns leached or boiled free of their bitter poisons. Nuts could be harvested in autumn in prodigious quantities, then stored for the winter in underground pits up to six feet deep and six feet wide. Other plant foods included berries, fruits, seeds, leaves, shoots, bulbs, and roots. In all, archeologists sifting through Jomon garbage have identified 64 species of edible plants.

Then as now, Japan's inhabitants were among the world's leading consumers of seafood. They harpooned tuna in the open ocean, killed seals on the beaches, and exploited seasonal runs of salmon in the rivers. They drove dolphins into shallow water and clubbed or speared them, just as Japanese hunters do today. They netted diverse fish, captured them in weirs, and caught them on fishhooks carved from deer antlers. They gathered shellfish, crabs, and seaweed in the intertidal zone or dove for them. (Jomon skeletons show a high incidence of abnormal bone growth in the ears, often observed in divers today.) Among land animals hunted, wild boar and deer were the most common prey. They were caught in pit traps, shot with bows and arrows, and run down with dogs.

The most debated question about Jomon subsistence concerns the possible contribution of agriculture. Many Jomon sites contain remains of edible plants that are native to Japan as wild species but also grown as crops today, including the adzuki bean and green gram bean. The remains from Jomon times do not clearly show features distinguishing the crops from their wild ancestors, so we do not know whether these plants were gathered in the wild or grown intentionally. Sites also have debris of edible or useful plant species not native to Japan, such as hemp, which must have been introduced from the Asian mainland. Around 1000 B.C., toward the end of the Jomon period, a few grains of rice, barley, and millet, the staple cereals of East Asia, began to appear. All these tantalizing clues make it likely that Jomon people were starting to practice some slash-and-burn agriculture, but evidently in a casual way that made only a minor contribution to their diet.

Archeologists studying Jomon hunter-gatherers have found not only hard-to-carry pottery (including pieces up to three feet tall) but also heavy stone tools, remains of substantial houses that show signs of repair, big village sites of 50 or more dwellings, and cemeteries—all further evidence that the Jomon people were sedentary rather than nomadic. Their stay-at-home lifestyle was made possible by the diversity of resource-rich habitats available within a short distance of one central site: inland forests, rivers, seashores, bays, and open oceans. Jomon people lived at some of the highest population densities ever estimated for hunter-gatherers, especially in central and northern Japan, with their nut-rich forests, salmon runs, and productive seas. The estimate of the total population of Jomon Japan at its peak is 250,000—trivial, of course, compared with today, but impressive for hunter-gatherers.

# All through human history, centralized states with metal weapons and armies supported by dense agricultural populations have swept away sparser populations of hunter-gatherers. How did Stone Age Japan survive so long?

With all this stress on what Jomon people did have, we need to be clear as well about what they didn't have. Their lives were very different from those of contemporary societies only a few hundred miles away in mainland China and Korea. Jomon people had no intensive agriculture. Apart from dogs (and perhaps pigs), they had no domestic animals. They had no metal tools, no writing, no weaving, and little social stratification into chiefs and commoners. Regional variation in pottery styles suggests little progress toward political centralization and unification.

Despite its distinctiveness even in East Asia at that time, Jomon Japan was not completely isolated. Pottery, obsidian, and fishhooks testify to some Jomon trade with Korea, Russia, and Okinawa—as does the arrival of Asian mainland crops. Compared with later eras, though, that limited trade with the

outside world had little influence on Jomon society. Jomon Japan was a miniature conservative universe that changed surprisingly little over 10,000 years.

To place Jomon Japan in a contemporary perspective, let us remind ourselves of what human societies were like on the Asian mainland in 400 B.C., just as the Jomon lifestyle was about to come to an end. China consisted of kingdoms with rich elites and poor commoners; the people lived in walled towns, and the country was on the verge of political unification and would soon become the world's largest empire. Beginning around 6500 B.C., China had developed intensive agriculture based on millet in the north and rice in the south; it had domestic pigs, chickens, and water buffalo. The Chinese had had writing for at least 900 years, metal tools for at least 1,500 years, and had just invented the world's first cast iron. Those developments were also spreading to Korea, which itself had had agriculture for several thousand years (including rice since at least 2100 B.C.) and metal since 1000 B.C.

With all these developments going on for thousands of years just across the Korea Strait from Japan, it might seem astonishing that in 400 B.C. Japan was still occupied by people who had some trade with Korea but remained preliterate stone-tool-using hunter-gatherers. Throughout human history, centralized states with metal weapons and armies supported by dense agricultural populations have consistently swept away sparser populations of hunter-gatherers. How did Jomon Japan survive so long?

To understand the answer to this paradox, we have to remember that until 400 B.C., the Korea Strait separated not rich farmers from poor hunter-gatherers, but poor farmers from rich hunter-gatherers. China itself and Jomon Japan were probably not in direct contact. Instead Japan's trade contacts, such as they were, involved Korea. But rice had been domesticated in warm southern China and spread only slowly northward to much cooler Korea, because it took a long time to develop cold-resistant strains of rice. Early rice agriculture in Korea used dry-field methods rather than irrigated paddies and was not particularly productive. Hence early Korean agriculture could not compete with Jomon hunting and gathering. Jomon people themselves would have seen no advantage in adopting Korean agriculture, insofar as they were aware of its existence, and poor Korean farmers had no advantages that would let them force their way into Japan. As we shall see, the advantages finally reversed suddenly and dramatically.

More than 10,000 years after the invention of pottery and the subsequent Jomon population explosion, a second decisive event in Japanese history triggered a second population explosion. Around 400 B.C., a new lifestyle arrived from South Korea. This second transition poses in acute form our question about who the Japanese are. Does the transition mark the replacement of Jomon people with immigrants from Korea, ancestral to the modern Japanese? Or did Japan's original Jomon inhabitants continue to occupy Japan while learning valuable new tricks?

The new mode of living appeared first on the north coast of Japan's southwesternmost island, Kyushu, just across the Korea Strait from South Korea. There we find Japan's first metal tools, of iron, and Japan's first undisputed full-scale agriculture. That agriculture came in the form of irrigated rice fields, complete with canals, dams, banks, paddies, and rice residues revealed by archeological excavations. Archeologists term the new way of living Yayoi, after a district of Tokyo where in 1884 its characteristic pottery was first recognized. Unlike Jomon pottery, Yayoi pottery was very similar to contemporary South Korean pottery in shape. Many other elements of the new Yayoi culture were unmistakably Korean and previously foreign to Japan, including bronze objects, weaving, glass beads, and styles of tools and houses.

While rice was the most important crop, Yayoi farmers introduced 27 new to Japan, as well as unquestionably domesticated pigs. They may have practiced double cropping, with paddies irrigated for rice production in the summer, then drained for dry-land cultivation of millet, barley, and wheat in the winter. Inevitably, this highly productive system of intensive agriculture triggered an immediate population explosion in Kyushu, where archeologists have identified far more Yayoi sites than Jomon sites, even though the Jomon period lasted 14 times longer.

In virtually no time, Yayoi farming jumped from Kyushu to the adjacent main islands of Shikoku and Honshu, reaching the Tokyo area within 200 years, and the cold northern tip of Honshu (1,000 miles from the first Yayoi settlements on Kyushu) in another century. After briefly occupying northern Honshu, Yayoi farmers abandoned that area, presumably because rice farming could not compete with the Jomon hunter-gatherer life. For the next 2,000 years, northern Honshu remained a frontier zone, beyond which the northernmost Japanese island of Hokkaido and its Ainu hunter-gatherers were not even considered part of the Japanese state until their annexation in the nineteenth century.

It took several centuries for Yayoi Japan to show the first signs of social stratification, as reflected especially in cemeteries. After about 100 B.C., separate parts of cemeteries were set aside for the graves of what was evidently an emerging elite class, marked by luxury goods imported from China, such as beautiful jade objects and bronze mirrors. As the Yayoi population explosion continued, and as all the best swamps or irrigable plains suitable for wet rice agriculture began to fill up, the archeological evidence suggests that war became more and more frequent: that evidence includes mass production of arrowheads, defensive moats surrounding villages, and buried skeletons pierced by projectile points. These hallmarks of war in Yayoi Japan corroborate the earliest accounts of Japan in Chinese chronicles, which describe the land of Wa and its hundred little political units fighting one another.

In the period from A.D. 300 to 700, both archeological excavations and frustratingly ambiguous accounts in later chronicles let us glimpse dimly the emergence of a politically unified Japan. Before A.D. 300, elite tombs were small and exhibited a regional diversity of styles. Beginning around A.D. 300, increasingly enormous earth-mound tombs called *kofun,* in the shape of keyholes, were constructed throughout the former Yayoi area from Kyushu to North Honshu. *Kofun* are up to 1,500 feet long and more than 100 feet high, making them possibly the largest earth-mound tombs in the world. The prodigious amount of labor required to build them and the uniformity of their style across Japan imply powerful rulers who commanded a huge, politically unified labor force. Those *kofun* that have been excavated contain lavish burial goods, but excavation of the largest ones is still forbidden because they are believed to contain the ancestors of the Japanese imperial line. The visible evidence of political centralization that the *kofun* provide reinforces the accounts of *kofun*-era Japanese emperors written down much later in Japanese and Korean chronicles. Massive Korean influences on Japan during the *kofun* era— whether through the Korean conquest of Japan (the Korean view) or the Japanese conquest of Korea (the Japanese view)— were responsible for transmitting Buddhism, writing, horseback riding, and new ceramic and metallurgical techniques to Japan from the Asian mainland.

Finally, with the completion of Japan's first chronicle in A.D. 712, Japan emerged into the full light of history. As of 712, the people inhabiting Japan were at last unquestionably Japanese, and their language (termed Old Japanese) was unquestionably ancestral to modern Japanese. Emperor Akihito, who reigns today, is the eighty-second direct descendant of the emperor under whom that first chronicle of A.D. 712 was written. He is traditionally considered the 125th direct descendant of the legendary first emperor, Jimmu, the great-great-great-grandson of the sun goddess Amaterasu.

Japanese culture underwent far more radical change in the 700 years of the Yayoi era than in the ten millennia of Jomon times. The contrast between Jomon stability (or conservatism) and radical Yayoi change is the most striking feature of Japanese history. Obviously, something momentous happened at 400 B.C. What was it? Were the ancestors of the modern Japanese the Jomon people, the Yayoi people, or a combination? Japan's population increased by an astonishing factor of 70 during Yayoi times: What caused that change? A passionate debate has raged around three alternative hypotheses.

One theory is that Jomon hunter-gatherers themselves gradually evolved into the modern Japanese. Because they had already been living a settled existence in villages for thousands of years, they may have been preadapted to accepting agriculture. At the Yayoi transition, perhaps nothing more happened than that Jomon society received cold-resistant rice seeds and information about paddy irrigation from Korea, enabling it to produce more food and increase its numbers. This theory appeals to many modern Japanese because it minimizes the unwelcome contribution of Korean genes to the Japanese gene pool while portraying the Japanese people as uniquely Japanese for at least the past 12,000 years.

A second theory, unappealing to those Japanese who prefer the first theory, argues instead that the Yayoi transition represents a massive influx of immigrants from Korea, carrying Korean farming practices, culture, and genes. Kyushu would have seemed a paradise to Korean rice farmers, because it is warmer and swampier than Korea and hence a better place to grow rice. According to one estimate, Yayoi Japan received several million immigrants from Korea, utterly overwhelming the genetic contribution of Jomon people (thought to have numbered around 75,000 just before the Yayoi transition). If so, modern Japanese are descendants of Korean immigrants who developed a modified culture of their own over the last 2,000 years.

The last theory accepts the evidence for immigration from Korea but denies that it was massive. Instead, highly productive agriculture may have enabled a modest number of immigrant rice farmers to reproduce much faster than Jomon hunter-gatherers and eventually to outnumber them. Like the second theory, this theory considers modern Japanese to be slightly modified Koreans but dispenses with the need for large-scale immigration.

By comparison with similar transitions elsewhere in the world, the second or third theory seems to me more plausible than the first theory. Over the last 12,000 years, agriculture arose at not more than nine places on Earth, including China and the Fertile Crescent. Twelve thousand years ago, everybody alive was a hunter-gatherer; now almost all of us are farmers or fed by farmers. Farming spread from those few sites of origin mainly because farmers outbred hunters, developed more potent technology, and then killed the hunters or drove them off lands suitable for agriculture. In the modern times European farmers thereby replaced native Californian hunters, aboriginal Australians, and the San people of South Africa. Farmers who used stone tools similarly replaced hunters prehistorically throughout Europe, Southeast Asia, and Indonesia. Korean farmers of 400 B.C. would have enjoyed a much larger advantage over Jomon hunters because the Koreans already possessed iron tools and a highly developed form of intensive agriculture.

Which of the three theories is correct for Japan? The only direct way to answer this question is to compare Jomon and Yayoi skeletons and genes with those of modern Japanese and Ainu. Measurements have now been made of many skeletons. In addition, within the last three years molecular geneticists have begun to extract DNA from ancient human skeletons and compare the genes of Japan's ancient and modern populations. Jomon and Yayoi skeletons, researchers find, are on the average readily distinguishable. Jomon people tended to be shorter, with relatively longer forearms and lower legs, more wide-set eyes, shorter and wider faces, and much more pronounced facial topography, with strikingly raised browridges, noses, and nose bridges. Yayoi people averaged an inch or two taller, with

close-set eyes, high and narrow faces, and flat browridges and noses. Some skeletons of the Yayoi period were still Jomon-like in appearance, but that is to be expected by almost any theory of the Jomon-Yayoi transition. By the time of the *kofun* period, all Japanese skeletons except those of the Ainu form a homogeneous group, resembling modern Japanese and Koreans.

In all these respects, Jomon skulls differ from those of modern Japanese and are most similar to those of modern Ainu, while Yayoi skulls most resemble those of modern Japanese. Similarly, geneticists attempting to calculate the relative contributions of Korean-like Yayoi genes and Ainu-like Jomon genes to the modern Japanese gene pool have concluded that the Yayoi contribution was generally dominant. Thus, immigrants from Korea really did make a big contribution to the modern Japanese, though we cannot yet say whether that was because of massive immigration or else modest immigration amplified by a high rate of population increase. Genetic studies of the past three years have also at last resolved the controversy about the origins of the Ainu: they are the descendants of Japan's ancient Jomon inhabitants, mixed with Korean genes of Yayoi colonists and of the modern Japanese.

Given the overwhelming advantage that rice agriculture gave Korean farmers, one has to wonder why the farmers achieved victory over Jomon hunters so suddenly, after making little headway in Japan for thousands of years. What finally tipped the balance and triggered the Yayoi transition was probably a combination of four developments: the farmers began raising rice in irrigated fields instead of in less productive dry fields; they developed rice strains that would grow well in a cool climate; their population expanded in Korea, putting pressure on Koreans to emigrate; and they invented iron tools that allowed them to mass-produce the wooden shovels, hoes, and other tools needed for rice-paddy agriculture. That iron and intensive farming reached Japan simultaneously is unlikely to have been a coincidence.

We have seen that the combined evidence of archeology, physical anthropology, and genetics supports the transparent interpretation for how the distinctive-looking Ainu and the undistinctive-looking Japanese came to share Japan: the Ainu are descended from Japan's original inhabitants and the Japanese are descended from more recent arrivals. But that view leaves the problem of language unexplained. If the Japanese really are recent arrivals from Korea, you might expect the Japanese and Korean languages to be very similar. More generally, if the Japanese people arose recently from some mixture, on the island of Kyushu, of original Ainu-like Jomon inhabitants with Yayoi invaders from Korea, the Japanese language might show close affinities to both the Korean and Ainu languages. Instead, Japanese and Ainu have no demonstrable relationship, and the relationship between Japanese and Korean is distant. How could this be so if the mixing occurred a mere 2,400 years ago? I suggest the following resolution of this paradox: the languages of Kyushu's

Jomon residents and Yayoi invaders were quite different from the modern Ainu and Korean languages, respectively.

The Ainu language was spoken in recent times by the Ainu on the northern island of Hokkaido, so Hokkaido's Jomon inhabitants probably also spoke an Ainu-like language. The Jomon inhabitants of Kyushu, however, surely did not. From the southern tip of Kyushu to the northern tip of Hokkaido, the Japanese archipelago is nearly 1,500 miles long. In Jomon times it supported great regional diversity of subsistence techniques and of pottery styles and was never unified politically. During the 10,000 years of Jomon occupation, Jomon people would have evolved correspondingly great linguistic diversity. In fact, many Japanese place-names on Hokkaido and northern Honshu include the Ainu words for river, nai or betsu, and for cape, shiri, but such Ainu-like names do not occur farther south in Japan. This suggests not only that Yayoi and Japanese pioneers adopted many Jomon place-names, just as white Americans did Native American names (think of Massachusetts and Mississippi), but also that Ainu was the Jomon language only of northernmost Japan.

That is, the modern Ainu language of Hokkaido is not a model for the ancient Jomon language of Kyushu. By the same token, modern Korean may be a poor model for the ancient Yayoi language of Korean immigrants in 400 B.C. In the centuries before Korea became unified politically in A.D. 676, it consisted of three kingdoms. Modern Korean is derived from the language of the kingdom of Silla, the kingdom that emerged triumphant and unified Korea, but Silla was not the kingdom that had close contact with Japan in the preceding centuries. Early Korean chronicles tell us that the different kingdoms had different languages. While the languages of the kingdoms defeated by Silla are poorly known, the few preserved words of one of those kingdoms, Koguryo, are much more similar to the corresponding Old Japanese words than are the corresponding modern Korean words. Korean languages may have been even more diverse in 400 B.C., before political unification had reached the stage of three kingdoms. The Korean language that reached Japan in 400 B.C., and that evolved into modern Japanese, I suspect, was quite different from the Silla language that evolved into modern Korean. Hence we should not be surprised that modern Japanese and Korean people resemble each other far more in their appearance and genes than in their languages.

History gives the Japanese and the Koreans ample grounds for mutual distrust and contempt, so any conclusion confirming their close relationship is likely to be unpopular among both peoples. Like Arabs and Jews, Koreans and Japanese are joined by blood yet locked in traditional enmity. But enmity is mutually destructive, in East Asia as in the Middle East. As reluctant as Japanese and Koreans are to admit it, they are like twin brothers who shared their formative years. The political future of East Asia depends in large part on their success in rediscovering those ancient bonds between them.

---

*Article 9*

*Foreign Affairs,* September/October 1998

# In Defense of Japanese Bureaucracy

*Peter F. Drucker*

## A HERETIC'S VIEW

AMERICAN POLICY on Japan, especially during Asia's economic crisis, is based on five assumptions that have become articles of faith for most American policymakers, Japan scholars, and even a good many business executives. But all of them are either plain wrong or, at best, highly dubious:

1. The government bureaucracy's dominance is assumed to be unique to Japan, like its near-monopoly on policymaking and its control of business and the economy through "administrative guidance."

2. Reducing the bureaucracy's role to what it should be—"the experts on tap but not on top"—would not be that difficult. All that is needed is political will.

3. A ruling elite like the Japanese bureaucracy is both unnecessary in a modern developed society and undesirable in a democracy.

4. The Japanese bureaucracy's resistance to "deregulation," especially now in the financial sector, is nothing but a selfish clinging to power that will do severe damage. By delaying the inevitable, it can only make things worse.

5. Finally, the Japanese—they are intelligent people, after all—put the economy first, as we do.

The right assumptions about Japan, however, are:

1. Bureaucracies dominate almost all developed countries. The United States and a few less populous English-speaking countries such as Australia, New Zealand, and Canada are the exceptions rather than the rule. Indeed, the Japanese bureaucracy is a good deal less overbearing than that of some other developed countries, particularly France.

2. Bureaucratic elites have far greater staying power than we are willing to concede. They manage to keep power for decades despite scandals and proven incompetence.

3. This is because developed countries—with the sole exception of the United States—are convinced that they need a ruling elite, without which they fear social disintegration. As such, they cling to the old elite unless there is a universally accepted replacement, and no such replacement is in sight in Japan.

4. Their experience has proven to the Japanese that procrastination works. Twice during the last 40 years, Japan has overcome major and apparently insoluble social problems not by "solving" them but by delaying until, in the end, the problems evaporated. The procrastination strategy will probably fail this time, considering the shaky structure and solvency of Japan's financial system. Given Japan's earlier experiences, however, procrastination is not an irrational strategy.

5. In fact, it is the logical strategy since for the Japanese policymaker—whether politician, civil servant, or leading business executive—society comes first, not the economy.

## DESCENDING FROM HEAVEN

"DESCENT FROM heaven"—the Japanese term for the practice whereby senior civil servants, having reached their terminal government position around age 45 to 55, become "counselors" to big companies—is seen in the United States as uniquely Japanese. The shift is considered the most visible manifestation of the dominance, power, and privilege of the Japanese bureaucracy. But it is actually a universal custom in all developed countries, including the United States.

To use a personal example, my father was the civil service head of the Austrian Ministry of Commerce just after World War I. When he retired in 1923, not yet 50, he was promptly appointed chairman and CEO of a big bank, as were his predecessor and his successor. So were their counterparts in the Ministry of Finance. Senior Austrian civil servants in key ministries "descend from heaven" to this day.

Japanese counselors who descend from heaven are well paid, but the job is a sinecure. They are usually not even expected to show up at the company's office except to collect their paychecks once a month. By contrast, in most European countries these "retiring" civil servants move into real jobs, as did the Austrian civil servants who became bank CEOs.

Whether this is wise or foolish is beside the point. Such practices are universal. In Germany the second-tier civil servant who will not make it into a top position in a ministry becomes secretary-general of an industry association, a job that not only pays well but has real power. Membership in such associations is compulsory in Germany, and all but the very largest companies must conduct their relations with both government and labor unions through them. If the civil servant is a Social Democrat he gets a similar job—equally well paid and powerful—as chief economist or secretary-general of a labor union. In France, the civil servant who has reached the exalted position of *inspecteur de finance,* usually around age 40 or 45, moves into a top position in industry or finance. Almost every power position in the French economy and society is filled by a former *inspecteur de finance.* Even in the United Kingdom, it remains customary for the top civil servant in a major ministry to chair a big bank or insurance company after his retirement.

In the United States, too, "descending from heaven" is anything but unknown. Scores of generals and admirals have, upon retirement, taken senior executive positions in defense and aerospace companies. An even larger number of congressional staffers and political appointees in the upper and middle levels of executive agencies—together, Washington's ruling elite—routinely come from on high to become well-paid lobbyists or partners in Washington law firms.

Even at the peak of its power circa 1970, the Japanese bureaucracy still had less control of business and the economy than its European counterparts. In both France and Germany, the government directly owns large chunks of the economy. A fifth of Europe's largest automobile producer, Volkswagen, is owned by the state of Saxony, giving it absolute veto power. Until quite recently, the French government owned most of the country's major banks and insurance companies. The same is true in Italy, the third-largest economy on the continent. Japan, by contrast, owns almost nothing of the economy besides the Postal Savings Bank. Where the Japanese make do with "administrative guidance," or control through persuasion, the Europeans rely on *dirigisme,* direct decision-making power as owners and managers, for good or ill.

## ELITES RULE

HOW DIFFICULT could it be to curtail the Japanese bureaucrats' power? After all, the bureaucracy's record is dismal. It reeled from one failure after another for the past 25 years. It failed miserably to pick the winners in the late 1960s and early 1970s, choosing instead such losers as the mainframe supercomputer. As a result, Japan today lags far behind in the information industry and in high-tech altogether.

The bureaucracy failed again in the 1980s. Panicked by a mild recession, it plunged Japan into the wild excess of the speculative fiscal bubble and with it into the present financial crisis. "Administrative guidance" pushed banks, insurance companies, and businesses into stock and real estate investments at insanely inflated prices and into the worst kind of problem loans. When the bubble burst in the early 1990s, the bureaucracy could not get Japan's economy going again. It poured unprecedented amounts of money—far beyond anything the U.S. government tried during the New Deal—into attempts to raise stock prices, real estate prices, consumption, and capital investment, all without any effect. In 1997, the bureaucracy followed that up by totally failing to anticipate the financial crisis in mainland Asia. It still urged Japanese banks and industry to invest more money in Asia even after mainland economies began to totter.

Since then, the bureaucracy has been revealed to be riddled with corruption, even prestigious agencies such as the Bank of Japan or the Ministry of Finance. This cost the bureaucrats their claim to moral leadership. Even the bureaucracy's staunchest supporters, the big companies, have turned against it. Big business' organization, the Keidanren, is now calling for deregulation and clipping the bureaucracy's wings.

Yet nothing happens. Worse, even the tiny, timid, token gestures by politicians to assert control over the bureaucracy, like kicking a powerful bureaucrat upstairs, are quietly reversed a few weeks later. There is, Americans argue, something unusual going on, something "exceptionally Japanese."

But ruling elites—especially those which, like Japan's, are based not on birth or wealth but on function—have remarkable staying power. They remain in power long after they have lost credibility and public respect. Consider the French military. This ruling elite's pretensions were shattered when the Dreyfus scandal of the 1890s showed it to be corrupt, dishonorable, dishonest, and bereft of the "military virtues" that underlie an army's claim to social leadership. Yet it held onto power, even after its abysmal incompetence in World War I proved it capable only of senseless mass slaughter. Totally discredited, especially in the years of widespread West European pacifism after the Great War, it had enough strength in 1936 to defeat an attempt by Léon Blum's government to shift power to a civil service elite. Teaming up with the French communists, the military forced Blum from power. And in 1940, even after it had again proven its utter incompetence by inflicting on France the most humiliating defeat the country had ever suffered, the French military still had enough power to make the Vichy collaborators choose the least discredited of France's military leaders, the nearly senile Marshal Pétain, to win legitimacy and widespread popular support for their puppet regime.

The extraordinary ability of a ruling elite to stalemate any attempt to unhorse it is by no means a Japanese phenomenon. Developed countries, especially developed democracies, are convinced that they need a ruling elite. Without it, society and politics disintegrate—as, in turn, does democracy. Only the United States and the few smaller English-speaking countries are immune to this certainty. American society has not had a ruling elite since the early years of the nineteenth century. Indeed, as almost every foreign observer of America since Toc-

queville has remarked, the truly unique feature of U.S. society is that every group feels itself unappreciated, disrespected, if not discriminated against—a feature many consider the country's greatest strength. But America is the exception. Japan is the rule. In all major developed countries other than the United States, it is considered self-evident that without a ruling elite there can be neither political stability nor social order.

Consider Charles de Gaulle and Konrad Adenauer. Both had been outsiders rejected by the ruling elites of their societies— the French military and German governmental service, respectively. Despite their talents, they were denied preferment and power. De Gaulle did not make general until World War II broke out and even then got only the command of a small brigade. Adenauer was generally recognized as the country's most adroit politician and as an exceptionally able administrator, but he was never offered a cabinet appointment, let alone the chancellorship, for which he was clearly vastly more qualified than Weimar's mediocrities. Both men were bitter about their rejection by the elite, of which both were openly contemptuous. Yet both, upon winning power after the war, immediately set about creating a new ruling elite.

One of de Gaulle's first acts upon becoming president in 1945 was to make a new French civil service the elite it is today by melding a fractured mess of competing bureaucracies into one centrally controlled body, giving the civil servants control of all major positions in government and the economy, making the *inspecteurs de finance* all-powerful, and, finally, creating a new credential, graduation from a new elite school, the école Nationale d'Administration. Out of it, for the last 40 years, has come almost every social, political, or business leader in France, including, of course, practically all *inspecteurs de finance*.

When Adenauer became Germany's chancellor in 1949, he inherited a discredited, demoralized civil service deeply tainted by its subservience to the Nazis. Adenauer immediately set out to restore its elite status. He had himself been twice imprisoned by the Nazis, but despite heavy pressure, especially from the British and Americans, he shielded the civil service from de-Nazification. He restored its job security and the privileges the Nazis had abolished and gave it unprecedented freedom from interference by local politicians. Adenauer thereby gave the German civil service elite greater status than it ever had before, and this time it was not outranked by the military, as it had been under the kaiser and even in the Weimar Republic.

Both de Gaulle and Adenauer were denounced as undemocratic, and both responded by asserting that a modern society—and especially a modern democracy—disintegrates without a ruling elite. They had a point. In Weimar Germany, for one, the military was discredited by the defeat in World War I, although it did retain a veto. The civil service, which before 1918 had run a weak second to the army, was bitterly divided over whether to accept the republic. The new groups on the public stage, such as business leaders and professionals, were still seen as upstarts. The resulting absence of an accepted ruling group proved critical to the disintegration of Weimar. To take another example, the absence of a ruling elite surely has had something to do with Italy's political paralysis and social anomie.

# Developed countries need ruling elites to survive, and Japan's elite is its bureaucracy.

The ruling elites that developed countries need to survive do, of course, cling to power. All rulers do. But elites can maintain themselves in power only because no replacement is in sight. Until such an alternative is provided—and it apparently takes a de Gaulle or an Adenauer to do so—the ruling elite will stay on, even if it is totally discredited and dysfunctional.

No replacement is in sight in Japan. The military, historically the ruling elite (indeed, the militarist regime of the 1930s was largely a replay of the shogunates, the military dictatorships that ruled Japan for most of its history), enjoys no public support whatsoever. Big business now commands unprecedented public respect, but it would not be accepted as society's ruling elite. Nor would the professoriate or professionals. So far the bureaucracy, no matter how discredited, is the only group that fits the bill. Whether America's policymakers like or dislike these facts is irrelevant. They are facts. American policy toward Japan must be based on the assumption that the bureaucracy will remain for the foreseeable future Japan's ruling elite, or at least its most powerful one—"deregulation" or not.

## A POLICY ABOUT NOTHING

JAPAN'S RULING elite does not behave like its rough equivalents in America. American elite groups are political: executive branch appointees and congressional staffers (both, incidentally, uniquely American phenomena alien to the rest of the developed world). But the ruling group in Japan is a bureaucracy, and it acts like one.

Max Weber, the great German sociologist who identified bureaucracy as a universal phenomenon, defined its function as codifying its experiences and converting them into rules of behavior. Three formative experiences in the collective memory of today's Japanese bureaucracy, two successes and one failure, provide the basis for its actions, especially in a major crisis.

The first success was not intervening in the most serious social malady of post-1945 Japan: the problem of an unemployed and unemployable rural majority. Today working farmers in both the United States and Japan make up no more than 2 or 3 percent of the work force. In 1950, more than 20 percent

of U.S. workers were farmers, but in Japan some 60 percent of the population was still living on the land, earning at best a bare subsistence. Most Japanese farmers in the early 1950s were utterly unproductive. Yet the bureaucracy successfully resisted all pressures to have government do anything about the farm problem. "Yes," it in effect admitted, "this enormous and totally unproductive overpopulation on the farms is a tremendous obstacle to economic development. Yes," it conceded, "subsidizing these farmers for producing nothing heavily penalizes the Japanese consumer at a time when most Japanese city dwellers are barely earning enough to pay for necessities." But doing anything to encourage farmers to move off the land or become more productive (which, in many cases, would have meant growing new crops like sorghum or soybeans, or moving out of growing rice and into breeding chicken and livestock) might cause serious social disruption. The only sensible thing to do, the bureaucracy argued, is absolutely nothing—and that is what it did.

Economically, Japan's farm policy has been a disaster. Agriculturally, Japan is worse off than any other developed country. It pays its remaining farmers as much in subsidies as do other developed countries, including the United States, but unlike the others, Japan now needs to import more of its food than ever before—more than any other major developed country. But socially, doing nothing has been a huge success. Japan has proportionately absorbed more former farmers into the urban population than any other developed country without the slightest social disruption.

The second great success of the Japanese bureaucracy was also a case of studied inaction: not tackling the problem of retail distribution. In the late 1950s and early 1960s, Japan had the most antiquated, expensive, and inefficient distribution system in the developed world—more eighteenth-century than nineteenth-century. It consisted of thousands of "mom-and-pop" shops—tiny holes in the wall with such enormous costs and outrageously high margins that each sold barely enough to let the owners scrape by. Economists and business leaders warned that Japan could not have a healthy modern economy until it had an efficient distribution system. The bureaucracy, however, refused to help. On the contrary, it passed regulation after regulation to slow the growth of modern retailers like supermarkets and discounters. "Economically," the bureaucrats agreed, "the existing retail system is an enormous drag. But it is Japan's social safety net. A person who loses his job or is retired at age 55 with just a few months' severance pay can always get a job at subsistence pay in his cousin's mom-and-pop shop." After all, Japan at that time still had no unemployment insurance or pensions.

Forty years later, the problem of retail distribution has disappeared, both socially and economically. The mom-and-pop shops are still there, but most, especially in the larger cities, have become franchisees of big new retail chains. The dank old stores are gone. Today's small shops are clean, well-lit, centrally managed, and computerized. Japan may well now have the world's most efficient and cheapest distribution system, and mom and pop now earn good money.

# The great formative experiences of Japan's bureaucrats taught them inaction's value.

The third formative experience of the Japanese bureaucracy—unlike the first two, a gross failure—also taught it not to act. Indeed, this failure resulted from violating the above lessons and disregarding the wisdom of procrastination and delay. In the early 1980s, Japan had what in most parts of the world would not even be considered a recession but a mild slowdown in economic and employment growth. But this slowdown coincided with the uncoupling of the fixed dollar-yen exchange rate and a rapid fall in the exchange value of the U.S. dollar that panicked export-dependent Japan. The bureaucrats caved in under the resulting public pressure and became Western-style activists. They poured huge sums into attempts to stimulate the economy. Disaster ensued. The government began to run up larger budget deficits than most developed countries; the stock market boomed crazily, driving prices up to price-to-earning ratios of 50 to 1 or higher; there was an even wilder boom in urban real estate prices; and banks, swamped by money for which there were no solid borrowers, lent frenetically to speculators. The bubble burst, of course—the present financial crisis is its legacy—with banks, insurance companies, and thrifts drowning in stock market and real estate losses and uncollectable problem loans.

Subsequent events only confirmed the bureaucracy's conviction that procrastination is wiser than action. For again, in the last two years, due in some measure to pressure from Washington, Japanese politicians and public opinion have pushed the government to pour larger amounts of money into the economy than any other Western country, to absolutely no avail.

## THE SOCIAL CONTRACT

THE WAY the Japanese bureaucracy is now tackling—or, rather not tackling—the Japanese banking system's crisis is commonly seen by Westerners as mere political cowardice, especially by official Washington: the U.S. Treasury, the World Bank, and the International Monetary Fund. But to Tokyo's ruling coterie, procrastination and delay appear the only rational policies.

No one knows yet how much Japanese financial institutions have suffered from the bursting of the bubble. On top of their domestic losses now loom huge additional losses inflicted by the economic crisis in other Asian countries—South Korea,

Thailand, Indonesia, and Malaysia—where Japan's banks were by far the heaviest lenders, as they have also been to China.

Japan faces the largest financial crisis of any developed country since World War II. According to an estimate last May in *Business Week,* the Japanese banking system will eventually have to write off domestic losses of about $1 trillion, not including losses on loans and investment elsewhere in Asia. This sum handily tops even the highest estimate of the losses incurred in the U.S. savings and loan debacle 15 years ago, and this in an economy barely half the size of America's. It amounts to a stunning 12 percent or so of the funds of all Japanese financial institutions.

Even more serious—and much harder to handle—are the banking crisis' social threats. The entire Japanese financial system is already being radically downsized. Japan is grossly overbanked, not so much in the number of institutions as in the number of bank branches, which are both ubiquitous and heavily overstaffed. Japanese and American financial experts estimate that Japan's commercial banks employ three to five times as many people per thousand transactions as do American or European banks. This has made the banking system one of Japan's largest employers, as well as its highest-paying. Most of the redundant though well-paid employees are middle-aged people with limited skills who would find it hard to get other jobs if laid off. Unemployment in Japan has already risen to the highest levels in 40 years—above 4 percent by the official count, and if Japan used American or European definitions of unemployment, it would be 7 or 8 percent. Only 2 years ago the official unemployment rate was still below 3 percent.

Even graver than the threat of unemployment is the threat to the country's social contract, especially the job security of lifetime employment. If the banks laid off large numbers of people, the social contract would shatter. The seriousness with which the Japanese view the social aspects of the crisis is shown by the lengths to which they will go to preserve a few jobs. They took the virtually unthinkable step of allowing (indeed, probably inviting) an American financial firm, Merrill Lynch to take over the main branches of Yamaichi, Japan's fourth-largest brokerage house, when it failed in 1997 simply because Merrill Lynch promised to keep on about a sixth of Yamaichi's employees—a few thousand people. Only six weeks earlier senior officials in the Ministry of Finance, which oversees brokerage firms, had still loudly insisted that they would never let a foreigner do domestic Japanese securities business.

The bank crisis undermines the structure of Japanese business and society. It may dissolve Japan's most distinctive economic organization: the *keiretsu,* the cluster of businesses around a major bank. Contrary to common belief in the West, the *keiretsu* does not primarily serve business purposes. Its first function is to act as the real board of directors for the member companies, since the official board of each individual company is just an internal management committee. The *keiretsu* quietly removes incompetent top management and checks out proposed promotions into the top echelons of member companies. But, above all, the *keiretsu* is a mutual support association. The members of a component company collectively hold enough of each other's shares to give the *keiretsu* effective ownership control. It thus protects each member against outsiders and hostile takeover bids. Moreover, it is the ultimate guarantor of lifetime employment. If a *keiretsu* member gets into such serious trouble that it has to lay off people, the other *keiretsu* companies will provide jobs for them. This lets the fellow *keiretsu* member cut costs and still fulfill its commitment to permanent job security.

Can the *keiretsu* survive the financial crisis? The banks at the core of the typical *keiretsu* have begun to sell off their holdings in the group in order to offset their losses. More *keiretsu* members are, in turn, selling off their shares in other *keiretsu* members to get cash to shore up their balance sheets. But, quite apart from the threat to lifetime employment and job security, what will replace the *keiretsu* as the organizing principle of the Japanese economy?

# Unlike America, Japan places society ahead of the economy.

The great formative experiences of Japan's bureaucrats taught them inaction's value.

There are no answers to these questions. Thus, the only rational course for the Japanese bureaucracy may indeed be to have no policy. That delay will whittle the banking problem down to a manageable size is probably wishful thinking. But surely the West, especially the United States, can only hope that the procrastination strategy will work again. Social unrest in Japan would be a far more serious threat to U.S. political, strategic, and economic interests than anything that U.S. businesses or the U.S. economy could possibly gain through the actions, such as rapid deregulation of the financial sector, which Washington is now pressing on Tokyo.

## IT'S NOT THE ECONOMY, STUPID

IN THE end, the most important key to understanding how the Japanese bureaucracy thinks, works, and behaves is under-

standing Japan's priorities. Americans assume that the economy takes primacy in political decisions, unless national security is seriously threatened. The Japanese—and by no means the bureaucracy alone—accord primacy to society.

Again the United States is the exception and Japan more nearly the rule. In most developed countries other than the United States, the economy is considered a restraint on policies rather than their major, let alone sole, determinant. Ideology and, above all, the impact on society come first.

Even in the United States, the primacy of economics in public life and policy is fairly recent, dating no further back than World War II. Until then, the United States, too, tended to consider society first. Despite the Great Depression, the New Deal put social reform well ahead of economic recovery. America's voters overwhelmingly approved.

But while hardly uniquely Japanese, giving pride of place to society is more important to the Japanese than to most other developed countries, save perhaps France. To the outsider, Japan appears to have extraordinary social strength and cohesion. No other society in history has successfully met such extreme challenges and dislocations: say, the 180-degree turn forced on Japan by Commodore Perry's black ships in the 1860s, as a result of which the world's most isolated country, hermetically sealed for more than two centuries, opened itself to modernity overnight and became Westernized, or, equally traumatic, the radical social turnaround after its defeat in 1945 and the long years of foreign occupation thereafter. The Japanese, however, see their society as fragile. They know how close to collapse and civil war their country came both times; hence the extreme importance, for instance, of lifetime employment as Japan's social glue.

Whether Japanese society is hardy or delicate is beside the point. What matters is that the Japanese take its primacy for granted. If Americans understood this, especially in dealing with a Japan in trouble, they might cling less to myths about the uselessness of the Japanese bureaucracy. Defending the bureaucrats is still heresy, of course, but heresy is often closer to the truth than conventional wisdom.

PETER F. DRUCKER is Clarke Professor of Social Science at Claremont Graduate University.

*Article 10*                                             *The Brookings Review,* Summer 1998

# Sputter, Cough, Choke

## Japan Misfires as the Engine of Asia

By Robert Alan Feldman

**Hopes in Asia Pacific that Japan will help solve the region's financial crisis are all but certain to be dashed. Japan does not have the fiscal power and maneuverability to act as the engine of Asia. More important, it may not have the political will.**

Since the equity and real estate bubble burst in 1990, Japan has abdicated the intellectual leadership of the region. By tinkering with and expanding—rather than junking—the state-capitalist economic model of the postwar period, Japan is offering a "wagons in a circle" example to Asian countries. Even if that strategy were right for Japan (which is doubtful), it is almost certainly not economically optimal for other Asian nations.

But economic optimality may not be driving either Japanese or Asian policy. If "Asian values," rather than the conservatism of wealth, have been the determining factors behind Japan's torpid reform efforts of the 1990s, then the policy choices made by the Asian countries may not accord with Western logic. To the extent that Asian countries imitate the Japanese reform model, economic prospects for the region—and for the firms that operate there—could improve more slowly than now expected.

## JAPAN'S ECONOMY: DOWN AGAIN IN 1998

The Japanese economy is now facing gale-force headwinds from private domestic demand. Fight as it may, the government's demand-support policies are unlikely to generate positive growth in 1998.

*Business investment* has already entered a downturn. Typically, such downturns last two to three years, and so far no sign of revival is visible. In addition to negative profit momentum, tighter credit standards imposed by banks are causing a credit crunch among small and medium-sized businesses. *Housing investment* is in just as serious shape. The effects of low interest rates and government housing programs have worn off, and the outlook for income growth is poor. Moreover, lat-

*Robert Alan Feldman is chief economist for Japan at Morgan Stanley Dean Witter. The views expressed in this article are the author's and not necessarily those of Morgan Stanley Dean Witter.*

est indications suggest that residential land prices are headed for another dive—hardly the time that households will rush to buy. *Inventories* relative to sales are at the highest level since 1975. The March decline of nearly 14 percent in overtime hours in manufacturing is a harbinger of a continued decline of production, income, and demand. Finally, the *export* outlook is cloudy. The drop of shipments to Asian economies, which make up about 40 percent of Japan's exports, will likely cut about 1 percent from Japanese GDP growth. Even the weakening of the yen against the dollar and European currencies and continued upswings in the United States and Europe will barely offset the losses to Asian destinations. (The net export contribution to growth may be positive—but only because Japanese imports are collapsing.)

Both fiscal and monetary policy are fighting against the downturn. Although the initial 1998 budget was contractionary, the stimulus package announced at end-April should generate a modest gain of public works spending during fiscal 1998. Moreover, the package's restoration of the 2 trillion yen of income tax cuts, which had been withdrawn in February 1997, should replace much of income lost to lower overtime and the squeeze on wages. In addition, the Bank of Japan is maintaining its low interest rate policy, and is providing huge quantities of credit through nonstandard routes as a means to offset the credit crunch.

These measures put a floor under the economy for 1998, but are not likely to spark sustainable growth.

## PRICE AND NONPRICE COMPETITION

The yen, already weak against the dollar, is unlikely to strengthen and may weaken further, putting more downward pressure on the currencies of Asia against the dollar. That would exacerbate foreign debt problems in Asia, destabilize financial systems and corporate balance sheets further, and worsen and lengthen the Asian crisis. Certainly in the recent past, weakness in the yen against the dollar has been followed by Asian currency weakness. The yen's fall—to 132 yen to the dollar—in early 1998 coincided with the weakest point for many Asian currencies, and its subsequent rebound coincided with rebounds of some of the Asian currencies as well. At current exchange rates, many Japanese industries remain highly competitive.

Japan also remains strong relative to Asian countries in non-price competitiveness. Product quality and innovation are high. Labor is expensive but high in quality and reliability. Distribution channels are well developed. Technology levels are high. And infrastructure in most areas is far above the levels of Asian competitors—although not necessarily competitors from industrial countries.

In short, in both price (exchange rate) and nonprice factors, Japan remains highly competitive against Asian competitors.

## INTELLECTUAL LEADERSHIP: JAPAN HAS ABDICATED

The most important way for Japan to influence the course of the Asian crisis is by example. Just as Japan's postwar success with an export-based, state-capitalist economy prompted developing Asian countries to follow that same model, Japan's reaction to the equity and land price collapses and banking problems of the 1990s promises to shape Asia's reaction to similar problems. Asian leaders feel more comfortable with Japanese than with Western social philosophy. Japanese economic policies are presumed more consistent with "Asian values" and thus more likely to work than Western solutions.

## DEMAND MANAGEMENT POLICIES

Japan reacted to the problems of the 1990s in several stages. First, it tried aggressive demand-support policies by raising public spending and cutting taxes and interest rates. General government fiscal balance shifted from a surplus of 3 percent of GDP in 1991 to a deficit of more than 4 percent in 1996. The lesson was "when faced with a market crash and a banking crisis, the first thing to do is loosen fiscal and monetary policies."

Japan could try that approach because its initial fiscal position was strong and real interest rates were high. It also had a huge excess of private savings over domestic investment and virtually no net debt denominated in foreign currencies. But conditions in other Asian countries (possibly excepting Taiwan) at the onset of the Asian financial crisis were totally different.

Now that Japan has run out of room for maneuver with both fiscal and monetary policy, what it does next will be the example it provides to Asia. If it tries to inflate its way out of a structurally weak economy, that would suggest to Asia that it try to do the same. In this sense, the fiscal package recently adopted in Japan would be a double-edged sword for Asia. It could support Japanese growth in the short run and hence the market for Asian exports, but it would be a disastrous example to countries already heavily indebted (in foreign currency debt to boot). The short-term gains to Asia from a year

or two of Japanese growth could even be offset by long-term losses if Asia receives the wrong policy message.

## PUBLIC-SECTOR REFORM

Japan also responded to the crises of the 1990s through public-sector reform to try to counter the tendency toward growth in government, in public-sector financial intermediation, and in special corporations. While helpful in earlier phases of growth, these institutions have led to inefficiencies that have been an important drag on growth in both Japan and Asia.

There have been two attempts at public-sector reform—under Prime Minister Murayama in 1994–95 and under Prime Minister Hashimoto in 1997—but both fell far short of hopes. Major privatizations and increases of accountability are yet to be implemented. A Hashimoto-led commission also proposed "administrative reform" to cut the number of ministries from 22 to 12 and shift jurisdictions among ministries. But the wings of that reform were clipped by vested interests in industry, bureaucracy, and politics well before the proposals were drafted into legislation.

Despite private-sector complaints that the public financial system interferes with the private economy, steals business, and operates with unfair advantages, the public system continues to grow. The ratio of total assets of the Trust Fund Bureau (a Ministry of Finance bureau that invests funds of the Postal Savings Bank and Postal Life Insurance, public pension funds, and some other funds) to nominal GDP rose from 57 percent in 1990 to 81 percent in 1997. And recent proposals from the ruling LDP herald even larger lending by public institutions.

In short, Japan has not succeeded in reform of the public sector, despite a broad understanding of the problem, increasingly glaring inefficiencies, and a long series of scandals in a broad range of public-sector functions—hardly a good example for the rest of Asia.

## FINANCIAL-SECTOR REFORM

The financial sector has also been a key focus of reform since 1991, when investors were shocked by even the first estimates of the extent of bad loans—20 trillion yen (about 4 percent of nominal GDP). Japan first tried a strategy of forbearance (not strictly forcing recognition and writeoff of bad loans) combined with demand stimulus in the hope that financial institutions would earn their way out of trouble. But the strategy failed, both because early estimates of bad assets were wildly low (recent estimates are many-fold greater than the initial estimates) and because growth was too weak to generate profits to write off the ballooning bad debts.

The focus of financial-sector support then shifted to tax relief. At a high cost in lost tax revenue, financial institutions were allowed to write off bad loans. Indeed, financial institutions were responsible for much of the plunge of corporate tax revenue from 19 trillion yen in fiscal 1989 to about 13 trillion yen in 1994–96. As estimates of bad debts continued to mount, depositors began shifting deposits out of the private system into the postal savings system.

Reform during 1994–96 also involved a quiet but clear improvement in the rules of financial oversight coupled with creation of a better safety net for depositors. The definition of nonperforming assets was tightened, and requirements for their disclosure were strengthened. The Deposit Insurance Corporation was mobilized to liquidate financial institutions; its resources were augmented by increased premiums on banks, and its scope for borrowing was enhanced. In addition, work was begun on better capital requirements for banks, and life insurance companies were subjected to "solvency ratios," the equivalent of capital standards. But here too there has been backsliding, such as easing the accounting treatment of market assets to allow institutions to avoid declaring trading losses on bonds at book closing. Moreover, by mid-1996, it was clear that a true solution to the financial-sector problem was not in sight.

The third stage of financial-sector reform, announced with great fanfare in autumn 1996, was the Big Bang, a set of legal reforms encompassing a new central bank law, a new foreign exchange law, a new financial oversight agency law, a new holding company law, tightened accounting standards, increased cross-entry of financial firms into each others' traditional business areas, and many other reforms. But the commitment to Big Bang reforms was sorely tested in 1997, when several major financial institutions underwent stress, including bankruptcies.

In the wake of these disruptions, the authorities have embarked on actions that have shaken investor confidence in their willingness to enforce efficiency in the financial sector. For example, they have declared their intent not to allow the exit of any more large banks. And the weak conditionality on the injection of public capital into institutions raised questions about how sharp the authorities' teeth really are. Moreover these injections of public capital are more likely to prolong excess capacity, continue pressure on margins, and extend the caution of banks toward borrowers than to solve any of these problems.

In short, Japan's signals to Asia regarding financial reform have been mixed. While pursuing a clear agenda of improving rules on competition, oversight, and accounting, policymakers seem to be trying to maintain the status quo within the new set of rules. Because the authorities are not willing to take the consequences of recognizing losses, potentially productive resources are being withheld from the economy. The eruption of new scandals, including multiple murders and suicides, has resulted in all-time low confidence in the financial system.

## POLITICAL REFORM

The recession of 1991–93 knocked the LDP out of power for the first time since it was formed in 1957. In the year following the June 1993 general election, a motley coalition of old-line opposition parties and reformist LDP splinter groups managed to pass important political reforms. They eliminated multi-member election districts (2 to 6 members per district) in the Lower House of the Diet and replaced them with the combination of single-member districts and super-regional districts (with many seats allocated on the basis of party votes in the region). They reapportioned all districts to correct inequalities in the weight of votes between different parts of the country. And they strengthened campaign financing laws.

But the reforms have had little effect on economic policy. The LDP regained power in 1994 by forming a coalition with its former arch-rival, the Socialist Party, and in the run-up to the October 1996 general election, the LDP-led government favored such old economic chestnuts as public works spending and bigger subsidies for farmers. The usual coalitions of vested interests have also returned to blocking important deregulation items.

Voters, on balance, have validated the status quo. The fall in voter turnout in recent elections indicates a generalized antipathy toward the state of politics, but it does not alter the incentives felt by national political parties. For example, the 1996 general election virtually wiped out the Socialists and gave the LDP a near majority in the Lower House. And renegades from opposition parties have since joined the LDP, returning it to its past status.

Japanese voters seem to prefer familiar stagnation to the uncertainties of economic reform. Optimistic Western observers hope that the voters' preference grows out of the relative wealth of the Japanese people and that it will not flourish in the poorer Asia-Pacific soil. But the Japanese election results may also stem from the part of Asian social philosophy that values social stability over growth. The Upper House election in July will be the next test of Japanese voter attitudes. Should voters again signal their preference for stability over growth, the lesson is not likely to be lost on leaders of Asia-Pacific nations. If Asian leaders act on that lesson, rather than in line with more aggressive reform models, hopes for rapid economic reform in the region would be clouded by the prospect of a more prolonged period of economic adjustment.

FORTUNE, September 7, 1998

# Why Japan WON'T BUDGE

*Everyone wants Japan to save Asia by gunning its economy. But the country's problems are mind-boggling. Besides, the Japanese still don't want to change.*

BY JUSTIN FOX

IF ONLY JAPAN WOULD TAKE decisive action to get its economic act together, it has been said again and again, the Asian crisis could become the Asian comeback. Demand from Japanese consumers would revitalize industries from Korea to Indonesia; money from Japanese banks would ease the region's credit crunch. If only. But it isn't going to happen. Not now, not anytime soon.

That much can be easily gleaned from a few days spent wandering the dingy halls of the Japanese Ministry of Finance and the fancier digs of Tokyo bankers and economists. The harder question is what exactly *is* going to happen in Japan. Has the "Japanese way" dead-ended, necessitating a U-turn to U.S.-style capitalism? Or are those smug Westerners proclaiming the demise of Japan Inc. going to look really stupid in a few years?

But first, the easy question: Why won't Japan bail out Asia?

For all the talk of unique cultural traits and "human capitalism," the essence of Japan's postwar political, economic, and financial system was this: It squeezed savings out of the country's citizens and, with the Ministry of Finance providing direction, funneled cheap money to strategic industries. The goal: to catch up with the West. By the 1980s the country had more than caught up, and investment capital was no longer in short supply. But changing course is not something the Japanese system does easily, so it kept squeezing out savings and investing them in Japanese industry and, when industry couldn't absorb it all, in real estate and the stock market. Then, after the speculative bubble brought on by all that excess credit began to deflate in Japan, Japanese banks helped create similar bubbles elsewhere in Asia.

Now, nine years of post-bubble economic stagnation and uncertainty about the future have left the Japanese more stuck on saving than ever. As a result, tax cuts end up mostly in savings accounts (or, as confidence in banks wanes, in piggy banks). The nation's shopkeepers are getting sick of this—one

recently interviewed on the evening news said any tax cut should be paid in vouchers so people *have* to spend it.

In the U.S., more savings is a good thing. But in Japan there's not much left to invest all those savings in—manufacturers already have too much production capacity and the government has already built more dams and bridges than the country needs. So nobody in Japan, from the bureaucrats at the MOF to the economists at the foreign investment banks to the man in the street, expects much of the $110 billion stimulus package announced by the new Prime Minister, Keizo Obuchi. Nobody's expecting much from Obuchi, period. He's a member of the same old Liberal Democratic Party machine that has dominated Japanese politics since 1955, and he isn't likely to do more than tinker at the edges of Japan's problems. Besides, as a politician he has limited clout anyway in bureaucrat-ruled Japan.

"We've now moved into a period where the natural direction is down," says Peter Tasker, a strategist with investment bank Dresdner Kleinwort Benson in Tokyo. For years, Japanese banks loaned money assuming that economic growth and asset-price inflation would continue. Now, says Tasker, "that debt has to be liquidated because the expectations behind that debt are gone."

If that debt could be liquidated quickly, by forcing banks to sell off their nonperforming loans, the groundwork would be laid for an economic turnaround. But such tough medicine would surely wipe out some major banks. Both regulators and brokerage-house analysts in Tokyo talk admiringly of the way the U.S. handled the 1980s savings and loan crisis, seemingly unaware that it took years for Congress to act on a problem that was far smaller and more manageable than the Japanese bank mess. Now the Japanese government has put together a package of legislation modeled on the S&L cleanup. But given how spooked Japanese regulators and politicians are by the prospect of bank failures—and how unpopular taxpayer-funded bank bailouts are with Japanese voters—the mess isn't going to be cleaned up quickly.

REPORTER ASSOCIATE *Cindy Kano*

That's why Japan can't help Asia. Which brings us back to the harder question: Can Japan help itself? That one can even ask such a thing is an amazing development. A decade ago Japan seemed on the verge of ruling the world. Five years ago it was still formidable and frightening. Now, of course, *everybody* knows that Japan is a basket case, and a relatively insignificant one at that. China is the country that matters in Asia now. The Japanese way of doing business, emulated by so many East Asian countries, is widely blamed for the financial disaster that hit the region last year. Japan Inc. is bankrupt, both financially and ideologically.

Is it, though? Japan is still running huge trade surpluses. It dominates many of the world's key manufacturing industries. Tokyo remains the most bustling city on earth, its shopping districts packed with people and its skyline dotted with construction cranes. There are a few visible signs of distress: homeless people sleeping at railroad stations, boarded-up Yamaichi Securities branches, shoppers who seem to be browsing more than buying. But it's nothing compared with the sort of havoc that would be wreaked in New York or London by an 80% decline in real estate values, a 60% stock market drop, and a shrinking economy.

Japan has been able to fend off many of the usual symptoms of a recession for two reasons. One is that big Japanese corporations generally react to bad times by cutting pay, not laying off workers—although unemployment is now finally becoming a visible problem. The other is that Japan is a net creditor, not a borrower, and can deal with bad debt and other problems at its own pace. (It could be argued that other East Asian countries are in such dire straits because they *failed* to follow the Japanese model and became indebted to foreigners.) "We have enough money to do whatever we need to do," says Eisuke Sakakibara, the vice minister of finance for international affairs. Referring to the need for a bank rescue, he adds, "If policies changed, we could easily get out of this recession."

The standard U.S. prescription for policy change in Japan is this: Be more like us, let capital markets and consumers run the economy, and don't be afraid of trade deficits. Recent developments seem to indicate that Japan is headed down that road. In the troubled financial sector, foreigners are making remarkable inroads—from Merrill Lynch buying most of the Yamaichi Securities branch network to Citibank becoming the bank of choice for trendy young urban Japanese to GE Capital going on an acquisition flurry all over Japan to young Tokyo University graduates taking jobs with *foreign* investment banks. "Basically, the unthinkable is happening every day," says Jun Makihara, a Goldman Sachs managing director.

Some Japanese are even beginning to talk worriedly of a "Wimbledonization" in which foreign financial institutions come to dominate Tokyo's markets just as foreign players dominate the famous English tennis tournament. If that were to happen, the ramifications for the Japanese economy could be huge: Japanese companies would have to start paying attention to return on equity and shareholder rights, and the country's cozily intertwined corporate system would inevitably start to unravel.

But American business journalists have been erroneously predicting such an unraveling for decades. It wasn't until the late 1980s that Western opinion makers began discussing the possibility that Japan was not a capitalist democracy subject to the same political and market forces as the U.S. but instead was a land where unelected bureaucrats both made policy and allocated capital. "In Western countries the sign of health of an economy is the ability of enterprises to turn a profit," says Dutch journalist Karel van Wolferen, author of the groundbreaking 1989 book *The Enigma of Japanese Power.* "In Japan the sign of a healthy economy is confidence in the ability of administrators to keep things moving."

That confidence has clearly been tested lately. But there's no clamor among the Japanese for an end to lifetime employment or government guidance of the economy. The Wimbledonization alarm is probably a sign that foreign inroads into Japanese financial markets will be allowed to go only so far. That resistance may not be sustainable; Japan may eventually be forced to play by the Anglo-American rules of global capitalism. But if nine years of economic doldrums can't force Japan to give in, what can?

*Article 12*                    *FAR EASTERN ECONOMIC REVIEW,* July 16, 1998

J A P A N

# Arthritic Nation

The greying of Japan isn't a worry for the next millennium: It's already a problem.

Conservative habits of an ageing population have a lot to do with

why Japan can't seem to restructure its economy.

**By Peter Landers in Kiryu, Japan**

No doubt about it, says Shigeo Shimizu, this recession is bad. The neighbourhood near the Kiryu River where he makes black sashes for funeral kimonos used to be lined with textile factories; now they're mostly gone, and people who are still hanging on say orders are sharply down since last year.

Yet when parliamentary elections roll around on July 12, the 66-year-old Shimizu will be voting, as always, for a candidate from the ruling Liberal Democratic Party. He doesn't suppose the LDP will do much to make the bad times better, but the opposition candidates make him uneasy. "I can't vote for someone I don't know. At least I know these guys," he says.

As Japan ages, older voters like Shimizu—wary of risk, averse to changing old habits—have come to make all the difference. In the voting for half of parliament's upper house, the LDP is certain to win more seats than any other single party. It may even capture a majority of the 126 at stake. If past trends hold up, fewer than one in four Japanese in their 20s will vote. But more than two-thirds of those over 65 will—and overwhelmingly they'll vote for the conservative ruling party. In the 1995 upper-house election, those aged 55 and over accounted for an estimated 48% of all voters.

Elections show how the ageing of Japan, once seen as a trend whose impact

was still a few decades away, is already making itself felt. With a solid base of conservative supporters, politicians have no impetus to force through the painful restructuring that's needed to revive Japan's economy—seen as vital to the recovery of Asia. And the frugal spending habits of an ageing population do little to stimulate demand.

Japan isn't an old country, yet. Only 16% of its people are over age 65, a proportion comparable to most European nations. But that's changing. The average Japanese woman lives 83.6 years, and the average man 77. Meanwhile, women are having fewer babies than ever. So by 2035 or so, the government estimates that more than 30% of Japanese will be 65 years or older.

But forecasts like those have prompted even middle-aged Japanese to turn conservative politically, and to try to hang on to their financial assets. Concerned that state-supported pensions will dry up, consumers are clinging to their savings like never before and as a result deepening Japan's recession. And young people feel increasingly left out of a society that doesn't seem to involve them.

Places like Kiryu, a textile manufacturing town of 120,000 people 100 kilometres north of Tokyo, give a sense of things to come. About one in five people in town is over 65, partly because competition from South Korea and China has hurt the textile industry and sent

young people seeking jobs elsewhere. The town's commercial district is filled with clinics, dentists' offices, and companies offering services for the homebound elderly. Night-time is quiet, with only a handful of teenagers hanging out in the main shopping area.

In elections, it's elderly activists who ensure victory. At the Kiryu office of LDP candidate Hirofumi Nakasone—a son of former Prime Minister Yasuhiro Naka-

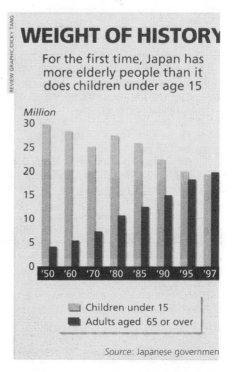

REVIEW GRAPHIC/DICKY TANG

**WEIGHT OF HISTORY**

For the first time, Japan has more elderly people than it does children under age 15

*Million*

- Children under 15
- Adults aged 65 or over

*Source:* Japanese governmen

sone—35 activists gather one night, all but one or two over 60. They're organized block by block, and a sign exhorts them to "steamroller" their neighbourhoods and trade guilds with get-out-the-vote efforts.

That kind of organization virtually assures Nakasone and the other LDP candidate of capturing the two seats open in Gumma Prefecture, which includes Kiryu. The economy is barely discussed; instead, the activists in Kiryu respond to ties of obligation. Many of the prefecture's legislators are on Nakasone's side, says Katsumi Okabe, who owns a dyeing factory. As a result, he tells the group, "We should try to preserve their face by making absolutely sure to get more votes than the other camp."

The scene in Kiryu is repeated in LDP candidates' campaigns nationwide—and that's significant long after the election.

Take Hiroshi Kobayashi, 65, who runs a tiny sash factory with his wife in Kiryu. "We've never had a recession as bad as this," says Kobayashi. Yet he smiles through the bad times, saying he never expected to be rich, anyway. "As long as we have enough to eat, why be gloomy when you can be cheerful?" he asks.

Radical steps such as deregulation or encouraging corporate restructuring don't appeal to elderly voters since the benefits,

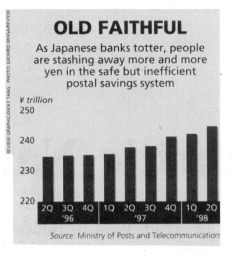

## OLD FAITHFUL

As Japanese banks totter, people are stashing away more and more yen in the safe but inefficient postal savings system

¥ trillion

Source: Ministry of Posts and Telecommunications

as with U.S. deregulation in the late 1970s and 1980s, may take a decade or more to appear. "Older people don't think about what youth needs when voting," says Yumiko Ehara, an associate professor of sociology at Tokyo Metropolitan University. "They vote to protect their own interests and try to keep the status quo."

As Japan's deepening recession over the last year shows, this defensive mentality has spread to millions of middle-aged consumers—who already ranked among the world's biggest savers and have begun preparing for the future by

saving more than ever. Household spending, which accounts for 60% of Japan's gross domestic product, was down in May compared with a year earlier and for the seventh month in a row.

On April 1, 1997, the government increased the national sales tax to 5% from 3%. And on September 1 it doubled the percentage of medical costs that salaried workers must pay out of their own pockets to 20%.

Even before 1997, some experts had warned that Japan would someday need a sales tax of 15%–20% to support its elderly population, and a government panel had warned in November 1996 that Japan's system of universal health care might collapse in the future. The modest steps of 1997 had the effect of persuading Japanese that these dire predictions were likely to come true.

Isamu Ueda, 39, a member of parliament's lower house from the opposition New Peace Party, says the biggest worry of his constituents in a Tokyo suburb isn't the current economic mess: "The largest concern is for the future . . . A lot of people are pessimistic that they won't get their full pension."

It's not an unfounded fear. Under current projections, 30%–35% of national income would have to go toward pensions, medical care and other welfare costs by 2025, up from around 19%. Low

# Going Postal

For an example of the clout older voters wield, look no further than Japan's postal savings and life-insurance system. A year ago, privatization was a hot topic; now, it's off the agenda, even though Tokyo is moving ahead with financial liberalization under its Big Bang programme.

The postal savings system remains unpopular among bankers, who complain that they shouldn't have to compete for deposits against a state institution, which many people perceive as offering unbeatable security at competitive rates of return. And the system, which was founded in 1875 as a vehicle to encourage personal savings, has long outlived its purpose as a source of cash for government "investments." Much of the money is lent to boondoggle projects that can't pay off their loans, leaving taxpayers holding the bag.

Yet the post office not only survives, it thrives. As of June 30, it had far more deposits than any commercial bank in the world—¥244.8 trillion ($1.74 trillion), a 6.5% increase from a year earlier. It also boasts outstanding insurance policies worth ¥208 trillion.

One reason politicians have backed away from reform is the powerful postmasters' lobby, which rounds up votes for ruling-party candidates nationwide at election time. But the post office is enormously popular among older people who make up much of its customer base.

"They're friendly to the elderly," says a 73-year-old former geisha in Kiryu. She can't figure out how to use the automatic cash dispensers, but that's no problem: Tellers are happy to help her withdraw

money the old way. And they don't ask nosy questions, she says.

A Ministry of Posts and Telecommunication survey released in June underlines the age gap in popularity. On an image ranking from 0 (bad) to 100 (good), Japanese over the age of 70 years gave the post office an average rating of 64, compared with 54 for people in their 20s.

Prime Minister Ryutaro Hashimoto has said he plans to make the post office a public corporation separate from the Posts Ministry by 2003, but that's as far as he's gone. Younger Japanese are barely aware of the issue, and older Japanese don't mind the go-slow approach. Banks, meanwhile, aren't in a position to proclaim free-market rhetoric since many need government help themselves to survive. ■ **Peter Landers** interest rates in recent years have worsened the financial position of the state pension system, which provides basic benefits for all. Many private companies, which supplement government payouts, also suffer from vastly underfunded pension plans. Electronics maker Hitachi said in April it will inject ¥180 billion ($1.3 billion) into its pension plan over the next five years to cover shortfalls, and it is also reducing benefits.

Cash-rich companies such as Hitachi can withstand such a blow, but workers at weaker companies fear they won't get the pension money that they're owed. That gives Japanese all the more reason to save as much as possible now just in case.

For their part, young people tend to tune out of the ageing debate altogether. That's not all bad: Spending by teenagers and people in their 20s represents one of the few supports for the economy. But their ambivalence slows political change.

Shio Yamazaki, the main opposition candidate in the district that includes Kiryu, says young people won't listen to politicians' speeches. "For older people, it's part of their life to vote. They don't ask questions. For the younger generation, voting isn't part of their lifestyle," says Yamazaki after a midday campaign speech outside a supermarket, during which not a single person stops to listen.

But Japan need not be doomed to a permanent recession. Consumer sentiment is notoriously fickle; a series of lucky breaks such as a recent heat wave, which has sent sales of air conditioners surging, might be enough to put Japanese in a buying mood. More deregulatory steps, such as allowing larger housing, could create new demand for durable goods.

Nevertheless, over the longer term, Japan needs leaders who can lay out a persuasive vision of the future, say commentators. With government encouragement, companies could raise their retirement ages and institute more flexible wage scales to make use of older workers' experience without hurting the bottom line. Also, raising consumption taxes and reducing the top income-tax rate from the current 65% would ease the relative burden of salaried workers and perhaps even increase total tax revenue by encouraging people to work more. Pensions could be scaled back for wealthier people without erasing the basic guarantees for a secure old age.

At the moment, however, far-sighted leadership is in short supply. LDP leaders tend instead to pander to older people on fixed incomes by calling for higher interest rates, a move economists say would be disastrous. "The public is ready to take in the real story and choose between the true alternatives," says Ueda, the opposition MP. "But politicians aren't bold enough to take the chance."

---

*Article 13*

*The New York Times,* August 4, 1997

# Once Prized, Japan's Elderly Feel Abandoned and Fearful

By NICHOLAS D. KRISTOF

OMIYA, Japan—As Kuni Kanbe fusses over the frail figure of her 84-year-old husband, gaunt and bedridden with cancer, she thinks of her four children, all sympathetic and loving—and a long way away.

When she married 56 years ago, Mrs. Kanbe recalled softly, she lived with her husband's parents and cared for them as they aged and sickened and died. But now, as she and her husband struggle with age and sickness in this little town in central Japan, her house is full of emptiness and resounds with the deafening absence of her grandchildren.

"I took care of my parents-in-law, but nobody will take care of me," she said resignedly.

"I suppose," she mused, and for the first time a hint of bitterness crept into her tone, "it's better for young people this way."

The sense of unfairness endured so stoically by Mrs. Kanbe is common among the elderly in Japan even though, by everyone's standards but their own, the Japanese are models of filial piety. Some 55 percent of Japanese over the age of 65 live with their children, compared with fewer than 20 percent in the United States and virtually every other industrial country.

Indeed, as the baby-boom generation approaches retirement, threatening the bankruptcy of social security systems across the globe, Japan in one sense seems to be the best-positioned of all major countries. It has a flexible and caring system that might be able to cope with retirement of the baby boomers: the family. If retirees can depend on their children for care, the nation is likely to survive the demographic up-heaval relatively smoothly.

Yet in the winding alleys of little towns like Omiya, a farming community in the mist-shrouded hills of the Kii Peninsula nearly 200 miles southeast of Tokyo, the mood is one of disquiet.

A revolutionary shift in attitudes toward the elderly appears to be under way in Japan, and to some extent in Korea and China as well. One result is that now for the first time a considerable share of the elderly in East Asia are growing old apart from their children, and the resulting loneliness and guilt and resentments cast a long shadow on family life across the region.

Even if a bit more than half of people over 65 live with their children in Japan, the proportion has plummeted from 80 percent as recently as 1970. Surveys suggest that Japanese attitudes are changing very rapidly and that many young Japanese feel even less of a debt to their parents than do young Americans.

"Young people are scary," Mrs. Kanbe reflected soberly, as she kneeled on the tatami-mat floor a few feet from her sick husband. "The reason young people can kill humans as if they were insects, or fail to understand the feelings of their own parents, is mostly because they haven't had proper moral education.

"I'm scared of young people now."

Such comments are particularly surprising because Mrs. Kanbe is, by Western standards, well cared for by her children. They visit regularly, and her sons have asked her to come and live with them after her husband dies.

Yet she and many elderly women like her are reluctant to move in with their children because they know they would not occupy the traditional throne of the mother-in-law, that of matriarch of the household. Instead they would be guests, staying by the grace of their daughters-in-law.

Japanese families are sometimes built more on proximity than closeness, and tensions revolve in particular around the traditional axis of home life in East Asia: relations between mother-in-law and daughter-in-law. Deng Xiaoping, during his leadership of China, once gave a major national speech on mother-in-law/daughter-in-law relations; in East Asia, this tie is a central one in society.

Mainly this is because men are out working most of the time and pay little attention to child rearing, so it is the two women who spend the days together and who do battle over the children's future.

In a growing number of cases, this divide between mother-in-law and daughter-in-law has led elderly people to move in, not with their eldest son—the age-old custom—but instead with a daughter.

"Life is upside down now," complained Akemi Hayashi, an 83-year-old widow who lives alone and who has not even received an invitation to live with any of her three children. "The daughter-in-law is on top, and Granny is a nuisance."

Mrs. Hayashi, who was tending her vegetable garden beside a highway, sat down on the grass and grumbled delightedly about the times. The term for widow in Japanese, mibojin, means "a person who has not yet died," and Mrs. Hayashi's plight, as such a person awaiting death and living alone, sends a shudder down the spine of any traditional Japanese. Yet it is becoming steadily more common. The proportion of elderly living alone has almost doubled since the early 1970's, to 13 percent.

"There are tough-talking daughters-in-law around here," Mrs. Hayashi said, "so the grannies just sit around in the shadows and complain."

What if she becomes ill and cannot care for herself?

"I just hope that I die a quick death," she answered promptly.

## The Tradition
## Loyalty to Parents:
## The Core of Society

The elderly grumble in part because they grew up steeped in concepts of filial piety that once pervaded not only Japan but also China and Korea and other countries influenced by Confucianism. In Japan, in fact, filial devotion traditionally ran a close second to loyalty to one's feudal lord, but in the mid-19th century a new Government tried to subvert feudalistic loyalties by re-emphasizing the primacy of filial piety.

Schools taught famous stories about filial piety, like the tale of the couple who decided, after running out of food, to kill their child so they would have more to feed their parents. They were

rewarded for this when they dug the child's grave and found a treasure.

Those were legends, but in the 19th century in the town of Matsue in Japan a real 15-year-old girl named Omasu won acclaim for her piety. She was summoned by a judge to give testimony against her father in a theft case, and she grew fearful of saying something that might get him in trouble. So she paused, and suddenly blood came gushing from her mouth.

Omasu had bitten off her tongue. She survived, unable ever to speak again, and her father was acquitted. A wealthy merchant so admired her devotion that he married her and looked after her father in his old age.

By that exalted standard, it is easier to see that weekend visits from a son fall a bit short.

After World War II, Japan reorganized itself socially and cast off many traditions, like the classes in shushin, or moral education, which had drummed the idea of filial piety into schoolchildren. The notion of special reverence for parents faded, and two years ago Japan even abandoned its traditional law decreeing a harsher punishment for the slaying of a parent or parent-in-law than for other murders.

"In the old days we had shushin to teach us filial piety," said Masae Minami, 86, the matriarch of a family that runs a clothing store in Omiya. "But now that's all gone. I think the old system was better, because society has become very chaotic. Now it's as if you can do anything you like to parents."

That seemed a trifle like hyperbole, because as Mrs. Minami grumbled, she was surrounded by relatives from four generations of her family, all deferring with great respect to her and her 91-year-old husband, Suezo.

So what is there to complain about?

Three patterns of unfilial behavior came to light in her household: the teenagers show no interest in watching the samurai television dramas that their great-grandparents adore; the younger generations like to eat meat instead of the austere rice dishes favored by the elders, and no one observes the old custom of letting Grandpa take a bath first.

"In the old days," Mrs. Minami lamented, "the master of the house would bathe first, and no one could eat until he came home and was ready to eat. That's all gone now."

## The New Generation Caring for Elderly: Shame Is a Motive

Evidence of a far-reaching change of attitudes toward the elderly emerges from opinion polls in which younger Japanese now come across as less devoted to parents than Americans are.

When a broad range of people in both countries were asked what a child's responsibility is to parents who have become disabled, Americans were twice as likely as Japanese to choose the most devoted answer: "Children should look after their parents, even if they have to make sacrifices."

Conversely, Japanese were twice as likely to choose the answer at the other end of the spectrum: "Because children have their own responsibilities, there is no need for them to look after their parents."

Why do Japanese invite their parents to live with them so regularly, even if they do not feel any strong moral debt to them? Why do they act more devoted than they feel?

One explanation may be strong social pressure and a culture of shame, as fundamental a force in Japan as gravity. Even if middle-aged Japanese feel no moral obligation to look after their parents, they would be humiliated by the gossip if they packed them off to a nursing home.

This pressure may explain why only 2 percent of the country's elderly live in nursing homes or similar institutions, compared with 5 percent in America.

"Only recently are people letting their parents enter these facilities," said Dr. Yoshihisa Yamazaki, director of the Firefly Nursing Home, nestled on the edge of a valley against a forested hillside. "Most Japanese basically feel that they should take care of their parents by themselves."

One indication that a good chunk of Japan's filial piety may be a result of community pressure is that once children overcome their reluctance and put their parents in a nursing home, they do not often visit.

"For some families," Dr. Yamazaki said, "visits become very rare, so that the only contact we have with them is a discussion every three months about whether to renew the contract." He added that some people arranged "temporary" stays for bedridden parents, and then hoped the parents would not recover enough to go home.

"We try to help those bedridden old people so that they can walk again," Dr. Yamazaki said. "But family members tell us they don't want their parents walking again."

## The Social Setting A Role for Grandma: Helping at Home

Ironically, the decline in multigenerational living is coming just as it is beginning to offer more practical advantages than before. As in most of the industrialized world, the proportion of mothers in the work force has risen steadily, and it is far easier for a mother to get a job if grandparents are around to help look after the children.

Partly for this reason, the latest boom in Japanese home styles is in the "multigeneration" house. It typically includes a separate wing for the grandparents, with their own entrance, bathroom and kitchen. The idea is to share a home while avoiding a situation in which the elderly wake everyone up when they rise at dawn each day.

A few years ago Kazufumi and Taka Sakai tried a similar compromise, living next to their children instead of with them. Mr. and Mrs. Sakai moved out of their son's home but built a new house right next door.

"My main thought when building this was that by living separately we could avoid troubles," said Mr. Sakai, 66, and he says it is a near-perfect arrangement. There are no longer strains about what to make for dinner, and the grandchildren still drop in all the time to propose a game of catch.

"Grandpa's O.K. at softball," allowed Mr. Sakai's 8-year-old grandson, Fumiya, during one pop-in visit. "But he's not quite good enough to make the third-grade team."

Article 14

*LOOK JAPAN*, June 1997

COVER STORY

# STATE OF THE STAPLE

## CHANGING CONDITIONS IN JAPAN'S RICE MARKETS

**JAPANESE RICE CULTIVATION:**

**A KEY TO UNDERSTANDING ASIA'S FUTURE**

### BY SHŌGENJI SHIN'ICHI

THERE are three points that must be made when considering the future of Japanese agriculture in general and rice production in particular.

The first is Japan's marked lack of self-sufficiency when it comes to food. The country is able to meet only 42% of its requirements (calorie-supply self-sufficiency rate; Ministry of Agriculture, Forestry and Fisheries, 1995).

When the Agricultural Basic Law was passed in 1961, Japan was producing 80% of its food (calorific) requirements. In the intervening years that rate has dropped by half. This is in sharp contrast to other advanced industrial countries, where the self-sufficiency rate has, in the main, been rising. The Ministry of Agriculture, Forestry and Fisheries has calculated the maximum number of calories Japan's agricultural resources could produce assuming minimum nutrition. It says at most 2,100 KCal per person per day (Japanese calorific intake today is an average 2,630 KCal per day). Food is the most necessary of necessities, literally a matter of life and death, and Japan is reaching a precipitous point. For Japan, food is a serious security issue, one that could impinge on its continued existence.

The second point to be considered is the renewed importance of rural, agricultural villages to Japanese society.

After World War II, Japan marshaled all of its resources towards catching up with the more advanced countries of Europe and North America. This was as true of agriculture as any other field, and it remained so from the establishment of the Agricultural Basic Law until very recently. Today, however, Japan has no more examples to mimic. We must create our country and our society from our own concepts. The current debate on agriculture and rural villages must, I think, be seen within this larger context. The "lifestyles" of rural villages must not be preserved merely as relics of the past, but in a living form as a valid choice for members of the society of the future. It is from that perspective that I believe rural villages and agriculture have extremely important roles to play.

The final point is that agriculture in the West is completely different in type and style from that in Japan.

Agriculture in Western Europe basically involves fields, with livestock as an appendage. This entails several problems. Unless a certain amount of what is harvested is returned to the earth in the form of fertilizer, European agriculture becomes an exploitative process that robs the land of its nutrients and causes the topsoil itself to run off. The center of Japanese agriculture, however, is the paddy not the field. This is in some senses a recycling-oriented method, a peculiar use of resources that has enabled the same paddies to be used literally for 2,000 years in a row, something inconceivable in the world of fields.

Until South Korea recently joined their ranks, Japan was the only one of the industrialized countries to have a background in rice cultivation. Other rice producers will eventually join them—Thailand, the Philippines, Vietnam—and as that happens Japan will not be so much a peculiarity as merely a holder of a certain share of production on a redefined world stage. Understanding Japan is the key to foreseeing the future of Asia.

Since the 1980s there has been a growing recognition in Europe and North America that, far from being friendly to the environment, agricultural production is actually a burden on the environment. Certainly Japan shares many of these problems. Fertilizers and agrochemicals are made heavy use of in field crops, while paddies give off methane, but Japanese nonetheless see agriculture in general as contributing to the protection of our environment, including our water and soil resources.

On April 18, the Commission on Basic Problems in Food, Agriculture, and Rural Villages began an intensive and wide-ranging debate on the principles that should underlie agricul-

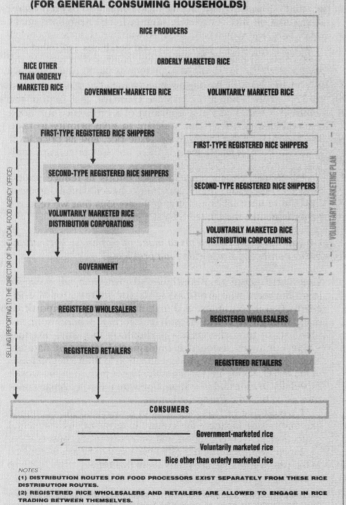

## INTERNATIONAL COMPARISON OF MAJOR AGRICULTURAL INDICATORS

| | JAPAN | GERMANY | FRANCE | U.K. | U.S.A. | SOUTH KOREA (ROK) | |
|---|---|---|---|---|---|---|---|
| DAILY PER CAPITA CALORIES (KCAL) | 2,899 | 3,319 | 3,522 | 3,174 | 3,648 | 3,224 | 1994 |
| TOTAL LAND AREA (MILLION HA) | 37.65 | 34.93 | 55.01 | 24.16 | 915.9 | 9.87 | 1994 |
| AGRICULTURAL LAND AREA (MILLION HA) | 5.1 | 17.29 | 30.12 | 17.09 | 426.9 | 2.15 | 1994 |
| FOREST AND WOODLAND AREA (MILLION HA) | 25.1 | 10.7 | 15.0 | 2.5 | 296.0 | 6.46 | 1994 |
| NUMBER OF FARMS OR FARM HOUSEHOLDS (THOUSAND)* | 3,438 | 601 | 501 | 244 | 2,088 | 1,499 | 1995 (JAPAN, ROK) 1993 (GERMANY, FRANCE, U.K.) 1992 (U.S.A.) |
| AVERAGE SIZE OF AGRICULTURAL LAND PER FARM OR FARM HOUSEHOLD (HA)* | 1.5 | 28.1 | 35.1 | 67.3 | 198.7 | 1.3 | 1992 (U.S.A.) |

*SOURCES:* FOOD AND AGRICULTURE ORGANIZATION
　MINISTRY OF AGRICULTURE, FORESTRY AND FISHERIES (MAFF),
　EUROSTAT,STATISTICS IN FOCUS,
　USDA,
　KOREAN MINISTRY OF AGRICULTURE*

*Background picture: Rice planting in Shirone City, Niigata Prefecture, early May*

## RICE DISTRIBUTION ROUTES UNDER THE NEW SYSTEM (FOR GENERAL CONSUMING HOUSEHOLDS)

NOTES
(1) DISTRIBUTION ROUTES FOR FOOD PROCESSORS EXIST SEPARATELY FROM THESE RICE DISTRIBUTION ROUTES.
(2) REGISTERED RICE WHOLESALERS AND RETAILERS ARE ALLOWED TO ENGAGE IN RICE TRADING BETWEEN THEMSELVES.
*SOURCE:* THE FOOD AGENCY

tural policy in today's internationalized world. Certainly it is time for a general reevaluation of the agricultural framework that has been in place since the war. In sum, we must rethink and rework our divisions between those areas best left up to market mechanisms and those that will require a planned, government-led (local governments and even informal organizations at the village level are included in this) approach.

The new Staple Food Law (Law for Stabilization of Supply-Demand and Price of Staple Food), for example, can be seen as a laudable step in this direction—though it does contain provisions both for free production and sales on the one hand, and for supply and demand regulation and price stabilization on the other, systems which seem to be fundamentally in opposition to each other. Rice distribution has been liberalized to the point that rice can be sold when and where one wills, and the barriers to entry, particularly in downstream sectors, are extremely low. This represents a considerable expansion in the scope given to market mechanisms. Over the long term, I think that upstream areas ought to be liberalized in such a way that production too can run without the need for regulation. Our stock piles as well ought to be maintained in a systematic manner so that we are prepared for unseen occurrences, an idea that was never part of the former Food Control Law.

It is my hope and expectation that over the next year or two we will be able to have a frank, open, public debate on food issues.

It is senseless that 800 million people in the world should be starving while the most advanced countries try to hold back their food production. This is one of the things that makes one despair of market economies. They are equally inept at income distribution. As is commonly noted, when total world production is divided by population, there is no food shortage. The problem lies in unequal distribution of purchasing power. Correcting this is the basic solution to food issues. Starvation is therefore not a problem of food so much as income, and the question eventually boils down to how to increase the food production capacities and incomes of developing countries.

What Japanese need to think about are ways to prevent developing countries from becoming any more dependent on food aid (though emergency assistance is obviously excepted from this). Symbolic of this is the idea of "food for work" found in the World Food Program—assistance that improves supply capacity. This is something I think deserves more thought.

The author is a professor at the Graduate School of Agriculture and Life Sciences at the University of Tokyo, his alma mater (Faculty of Agriculture). His publications (joint ed.) include *Nochi no keizai bunseki, Nogyo keizaigaku* (Economic analysis of agricultural land, agricultural economics) and *Kokoro yutaka-nare: Nihon nogyo shinron* (Be rich at heart: A new theory of Japanese agriculture).

Article 15

LOOK JAPAN, June 1997

CULTURAL CREATORS

# FAR FROM THE CONCRETE JUNGLE

*LOOK JAPAN* takes to the trail with volunteer members of the

Tokyo-based Mountain and Greenery Cooperation Corps

WEARING yellow safety helmets, 38 workers move through dense vegetation on a steep mountain slope in the Kururi National Forest on Chiba Prefecture's Boso Peninsula. They clear away underbrush and cut down young broadleaf trees with sickles and handsaws to provide the cedar and cypress trees with room to grow. But these men and women, both young and old, are not accustomed to handling these tools—or even climbing in the mountains for that matter. This group of businessmen, office ladies, elderly retired people, students, and housewives are participating in a forest volunteer program. With sickles and saws provided by the Chiba Forestry Office and under the direction of Forestry Office staff, the volunteers spent two days clearing and thinning trees, turning part of this mountain—admittedly only a small part—into a suitable plantation for cedar and cypress trees.

On the spring-like days of February 22 and 23, this group toiled in the forest as members of the Mountain and Greenery Cooperation Corps, a volunteer program organized by the Green Earth Center, a NGO (nongovernmental organization) based in Tokyo.

## ROOM TO GROW

Mountains range up the center of the bow-shaped Japanese archipelago like a backbone and they are covered with lush, beautiful forests. The forests not only provide lumber, but also fulfill functions important to land preservation and environmental protection by preventing landslides, storing water resources, and cleaning and filtering water. These days, however, the profitability of national forests has been severely undercut by cheap lumber imports. The number of people involved in forestry and the volume of timber cut for lumber has dropped. Consequently, the administration of the national forests is in difficult straits from both a financial and management standpoint.

Nitta Hitoshi, head of the Global Green Earth Center, says, "Many people are greatly concerned about nature and they want to interact with mountains and nature; they want to take part in preservation activities. Our job is to act as coordinators between the mountains and these people."

Although the center's domestic projects are staged in Japan's national forests, the government doesn't necessarily approve of citizens entering these forests. From the government's perspective, they have to make a special exception for the center's activities and they have to think about their responsibility if a problem should occur.

Over the past several years, Nitta has been gingerly but actively negotiating with the Forestry Agency for permission to enter national forest lands in order to undertake the forest volunteer program. Last year, that permission was finally granted and urban citizens obtained sites to carry out their volunteer activities.

The first program took place in Nagano Prefecture, followed by work in Fujinomiya and Hakone in Kanagawa Prefecture. In the first year, volunteers took to the mountains 13 times.

"Let's work together to preserve all the mountains of Japan," says Nitta. "These programs came together because of the big dream, the romanticism and the significance for the public behind the idea that even though [our work] is only small-scale, we are protecting the whole Earth."

## A SENSE OF RESPONSIBILITY

One of the volunteers in the Kururi forests was Yasuda Shigeru, who works in the clothing and accessories industry. His interest in nature began with the desire to learn the names of the trees he saw during his commute to work. Once he started walking around with a tree identification book, he says, his interest in forests and mountains just grew and grew.

Kawasaki Mayumi, a pharmacist for a pharmaceuticals company, came all the way from Hyogo Prefecture. She had long been interested in greenification activities and wanted to participate herself. After finding out about the Green Earth Center's activities, she volunteered for an afforestation project in Inner Mongolia during the summer of 1995.

"I didn't want to become one of those burned out by overwork," she explains. "Now I live for these volunteer activities; I look forward to them."

Company employee Nomura Hiroyuki of Chiba Prefecture says, "Ultimately, this is a hobby." Nomura loves nature and has participated in this program many times, but he says that if you approach it too seriously like work you won't last long." First and foremost, he says, it has to be fun.

Nakagawa Sayaka, an organization staff member from Tokyo, says, "I like nature. There is nothing attractive about life in the concrete jungle. My motivation is that I want to build and live in a wooden house instead of one made of concrete."

Oishi Isao came from Shizuoka Prefecture. He participated in activities held by the center last September in Fujinomiya, Shizuoka Prefecture. He always wanted to go to the forests and says, "I retired after working for 40 years and [this volunteer work] is my way of expressing my gratitude to society for being able to work for all those years."

Kamimura Hiroshi is one of the few volunteers whose job is related to the work in the mountains. He works for a landscaping company and wants to become a tree doctor.

Kamimura is a serious student of nature. "I highly recommend this," he says, pulling out a pocket tree identification guide.

Although he loves what he is doing, he feels that the relationship between himself and society is very important. The idea of contributing to the community is a strong part of his outlook.

Indeed, when a society has achieved a certain level of economic growth, it is time for the people who have enjoyed that prosperity to rethink in a variety of ways the relationship between themselves and their society.

Japan's economic development pulled people out of the rural villages and reconcentrated them in large urban centers. The result has been the depopulation of rural communities. Without manpower for upkeep, the forests around mountain villages have fallen into disarray. Year by year, deterioration of the forests accelerates. In one way of thinking, the flow of people out of the rural areas and into the cities means that the mass of city dwellers are foisting a disproportionate responsibility onto a relatively few rural citizens. From now on, says Nitta, "Urban citizens have to reduce this burden through their activities."

"Time is experienced differently by humans and nature and in cities and in mountain villages," he says. "Our standard should be the village version of time, not the urban version."

## ACORNS

The Green Earth Center works jointly with the Nagano Forestry Office and the Tokyo Forestry Office, which is in charge of the whole Kanto Region. The center's forest volunteer work is catching on in the Kanto Region, but the real issue is the development of an all-Japan network of volunteer activities. The problem is money. Public financial assistance is vital. While subsidies from the Foreign Ministry and elsewhere, as well as Postal Savings for International Voluntary Aid from the Ministry of Posts and Telecommunications, are extremely effective, when it comes right down to it, funds for activities are short. Because there is a limit on the amount of funding assistance that the government can give, as an NGO, the center needs its independence and also needs political clout.

In order to increase the scope of its activities, the center is appealing for understanding and participation from not only the government, but from corporations and other groups as well. On June 7 and 8, the center—along with the Global Environment Project Group (Environment Network), Shizuoka Prefecture, and the Forestry Office—is holding a work project just below the Fifth Station on Mount Fuji on the Fujinomiya side of the mountain. Volunteers will clear away trees blown down in last year's typhoon and replant broadleaf and deciduous trees. The center expects 700 to 800 people to participate.

This fall, volunteers will return to the same forest again to gather acorns. They will bring the acorns home and plant them in pots. When spring comes, they will return to the mountain with their seedlings and plant them back in the forest. The Green Earth Center plans to continue this program for many years to come.

The center is looking to long-term development. "Mount Fuji is the symbol of Japan and there is talk of developing strategies to clean up what has become a fairly polluted environment," explains Nitta. "We want to develop a movement to enlarge the mixed forests and a movement to protect Mount Fuji."

The center will continue to look for activity sites and sponsor forest volunteer programs. In a way, these forest volunteer programs are planting the seeds for a connection between urban dwellers and mountain villages. The words of the chief of the Chiba Forestry Office come to mind: "It is at least a 40- to 60-year cycle between planting trees and harvesting timber." Perhaps the center would say that the seeds they sow are on the same cycle.

BY **CHIBA HITOSHI**

*Article 16*                                                    THE CHRISTIAN SCIENCE MONITOR, December 8, 1997

# A Continental Divide: Who Owns Aboriginal Lands?

## ■ Australian leader wants to weaken claims of Aborigines—or call a racially tinged election.

**By Lindsey Arkley**

Special to The Christian Science Monitor

MELBOURNE, AUSTRALIA
WHAT if the US Supreme Court ruled that native Americans could lay claim to much of the United States?

In Australia, such a real-life drama involving Aborigines and descendants of white settlers has created a national political crisis.

Two high-court rulings since 1992 involving Aboriginal land have led to Prime Minister John Howard threatening to call national elections if the Senate fails to fix the Native Title Act and protect farmers, ranchers, and mining firms from the claims of Aborigines.

Prime Minister Howard says he is only trying to find a middle ground between Aborigines and present landholders. But opponents worry that he is speeding the nation toward an election that will be emotionally charged with racial issues.

With almost two-thirds of Australia's export earnings coming from farming and mining, the issue of who owns rural land—or at least has the right to use it—is important.

The debate has also set many rural Australians, worried about losing their land and livelihoods, against urban dwellers, many of whom would like to see the acrimonious debate over Aboriginal rights end amicably.

The Senate, where Howard's government lacks a majority, refused to pass the amendments last week. And in a rare session over the weekend, the House of Representatives formally rejected proposals by the Senate to change the amendments in favor of Aborigines.

Howard says he would prefer not to see an election fought over racial issues. But he will resubmit his amendments to the Senate in three months. If the Senate again refuses to pass them, the Constitution allows him to call an early election, possibly in mid-1998, instead of when it is required in 1999. Opposition leaders have urged Howard not to do so, saying the campaign would inevitably center on racial issues and prove divisive.

Howard's conservative coalition won a landslide victory at the polls in March 1996 after 13 years of Labor Party rule. But recent polls show the government trailing the Labor Party opposition right now.

### Ruling enhances claims

The Native Title Act of 1993 was passed by the previous Labor Party government in response to a historic court ruling that, despite more than 200 years of settlement by Europeans, Aborigines still could claim land rights. The act set out a process for Aborigines to claim ownership if they could prove they had a continuous ancestral link to the land.

Mr. Howard's proposed changes follow another 1996 court ruling in what has become known as the Wik case, brought by Aboriginal people in the northeastern state of Queensland.

In that case, Australia's highest court found that Aborigines could claim title to vast areas of land held by farmers, ranchers, and mining companies under long-term "pastoral leases" granted by state governments. About 42 percent of Australia's land falls under these pastoral leases.

Although the court ruled that in the event of irreconcilable differences, the current leaseholders would have primacy, the powerful "pastoral" and mining industries were in an uproar.

The Howard government responded by drawing up the amendments. In the words of Howard's deputy, Tim Fischer, the proposed amendments provide for "bucket-loads of extinguishment" to native title rights.

### Charges fly

In the ensuing bitter debate, one Aboriginal leader has accused some government leaders of being "racist scum," while a government politician from a rural area urged churchgoers to boycott churches with leaders who sided with Aborigines in opposing the amendments.

Government ministers also raised the possibility that native title claims also could be made on land held under "freehold title," the usual form of land ownership in urban Australia, where two-thirds of the population lives.

This possibility was quickly denied by most legal experts and was not emphasized by the government, but it undoubtedly helped inflame passions.

# Oil Firm Works With Aborigines

MELBOURNE, AUSTRALIA

At the same time voices rise over the difficult issue of Aboriginal land rights, Chevron Corp. has signed an historic agreement with Aboriginal landowners for a 1,600-mile natural gas pipeline to cross their traditional lands.

The $1.5 billion project would involve building a pipeline from the Kutubu oil field in the neighboring island country of Papua New Guinea under the Torres Strait to Australia's Cape York Peninsula. From there it could be sold to clients all over eastern Australia, where two-thirds of the population lives.

"This agreement, which has involved numerous traditional owner groups from the tip of Cape York right down through northern and central Queensland [state], shows that Aboriginal people are not opposed to development," says Aboriginal leader Norman Johnson.

"If companies show respect like Chevron has, then native title will work," adds Mr. Johnson, who was appointed to negotiate the deal by the Cape York Land Council, which represents about 12,000 Aborigines.

"We've bridged a gap between matters commercial and matters spiritual," adds John Powell, the project director for Chevron. "We've bridged a gap between black fella and white fella, and how have we done that? We've done it in an environment of respect with honesty and firm negotiation."

The agreement provides for Aboriginal landowners to have first rights to buy equity in the pipeline project. It would be the first such equity arrangement in Australia, according to Gerhardt Pearson, another Aboriginal leader involved in the negotiations with Chevron.

"It's clear that this is the way of the future, that this is what Aboriginal people are expecting," Mr. Pearson says. "They don't just want short-term compensation. Equity ensures long-term and real benefits coming back to their communities."

The amount that Aboriginal groups could invest in the pipeline company would be "much higher" than the undisclosed amount of compensation to be paid to Aboriginal landowners under the agreement with Chevron, he said.

Chevron already has committed about $17 million for feasibility and environmental-impact studies for the project.

The agreement also provides for "cultural heritage" surveys of the land the pipeline would pass through.

These would identify areas of cultural or spiritual significance to Aborigines in need of protection, such as a burial ground, rock art site, or other sacred site.

—**Lindsey Arkley**

Aboriginal leaders remain unanimously and vehemently opposed to amending the legislation, saying the existing act provides the means for Aborigines and others to work together to make use of the land.

According to a recent newspaper poll, 52 percent of Australians fear the issue of Aboriginal land claims could divide the nation over race. The current row has occurred just as the prominence of controversial politician Pauline Hanson had begun to fade.

The prime minister was widely criticized for failing to denounce remarks by Ms. Hanson that were seen by many as racist and counter the damage her comments caused Australia's image overseas. Hanson shot to prominence last year when she said Australia was in danger of being swamped by Asians and criticized welfare programs for Aborigines.

## Aborigines lag behind

By any number of measures, Aborigines are not faring well relative to other Australians. According to official statistics, the average life-span is 15 to 20 years below the national average of 79 years. Only about one-third of Aborigines complete high school, compared with 77 percent overall. And unemployment among Aborigines is four times higher than the national rate of about 9 percent.

"The indigenous unemployment rate could reach 47 percent by 2006 unless there is an unprecedented expansion in job creation," says John Taylor at the Center for Aboriginal Economic Policy Research at the Australian National University in the national capital, Canberra.

The opposition Labor Party agrees with the need for some changes to its Native Title Act to create more certainty over land ownership. Labor Party leader Kim Beazley says changes proposed by his party would make the legislation more practical—and in keeping with the Constitution.

"What we in the opposition have been trying to do in the Parliament is to get right all these things that are wrong with the bill—simply to make sure that it's workable and certain in its operation, and strikes a fair balance," Mr. Beazley says.

"If we want reconciliation between black and white Australians, then the best possible thing we can do is get this bill right, so we don't have this divisive bill over and over again."

Article 17

*The New York Review of Books,* August 13, 1998

# The Cambodian Calamity

## Henry Kamm

Only by comparison with the worst that Cambodia has suffered since it was plunged into the Indochina war in 1970 can the notion of progress be applied at all to this tormented country. The four calamitous years of Pol Pot's rule by maniacal murderers, who extinguished or damaged forever the lives of untold numbers of their own people, blighted Cambodian society and culture and shattered the bases of its economic survival. They established a nadir so low that any change meant an improvement. But some two decades have passed since those brief days of hope when Cambodia emerged from the Khmer Rouge nightmare, thanks to the Vietnamese invasion in 1978 and conquest in early 1979. And today, what is the condition of the country, now numbering more than ten million people?

Today's Cambodia is a basket case. It is a country that hardly nourishes and barely teaches its ever-increasing population, nor does it bind its multiple wounds or cure its many ills. In large measure its workers are exploited, its women ill-used, its children unprotected, its soil studded with treacherous land mines primed to kill. No equitable rule of law or impartial justice shelters Cambodians against a mean-spirited establishment of political and economic power, a cabal, dominated by Prime Minister Hun Sen, that is blind and deaf to the crying needs of an abused people. Their leaders' passions are private: to expand their might and riches. Unlike most politicians elsewhere, they do not even profess high ideals that they then betray. The betterment of the lot of the people whom they govern is rarely even the object of the customary lip service paid by holders of power all over the world. Cambodia's politicians scarcely pretend to serve the Cambodian people.

While those who rule over Cambodians still professed communism, their dogma obliged them to mouth the eternal verities of that religion. Since their respective Chinese and Russian patrons deserted them, they have foresworn the Communist creed in favor of greed, of open, unvarnished avidity. But they have retained the crude methods by which they ruled in the Communist years—terror, torture, and the gun. The democratic innovations that the United Nations installed or encouraged when it organized elections in the early 1990s have worn so thin that they no longer serve even as a threadbare cover for the rulers' disdain for the people or their ruthless resort to brute force against one another. The political settlement to which Sihanouk, Hun Sen, and other leaders committed themselves before the world in 1991 is dead.

The well-being of Cambodians, their constant struggle for food and shelter, health and education, is left in their own hands. Their government ignores their plight without apology. What little help and protection reaches Cambodians comes mainly from outside sources—aid of all kinds from foreign governments, international organizations, and private volunteer groups. Few countries are host to so many of the world's organizations of benevolence as Cambodia is, and they attend helpfully to a wide range of needs. That this only scratches the surface is not their fault.

For there is one fundamental need to which outsiders cannot minister—Cambodia's need of leaders, a class of politicians whose concern it is to guide their nation out of the depths of misery into which it was cast in 1970. Cambodia needs not one man on horseback who will be the savior but an elite of aware men and women of good will and creative energy to whom the fate of fellow Cambodians matters.

The members of the UN General Assembly had an opportunity to help bring this about when they unanimously assigned, with Cambodian consent, the ultimate responsibility for temporarily governing Cambodia and setting it on a path toward a better future to an impartial international authority, the UN Transitional Authority in Cambodia (UNTAC). But the UN force missed its chance to dismantle an illicit regime of brute force and to disarm the Khmers Rouges, an even less legitimate and more brutal rival. It yielded its mandate to the implied threat of force and took satisfaction instead in an exercise, moving and impressive, in letting the people speak their minds in conditions of severely limited freedom.

The people's message was clear; it would have been clearer yet had the fear of the ruling powers been neutralized. Cambodians wanted leaders who did not rule by fear, a government that held out a hope of freedom from all that had oppressed them for so long, materially and spiritually. They were given instead the shadow of democracy, devoid of substance. The leaders who between them gathered almost all their votes in the May 1993 elections cheated them the moment the polls had closed, and the world chose to applaud the shadow and shut its eyes to the absence of substance.

Will there be another chance? I doubt it. Cambodia is no longer a stumbling block to smoother relations between confrontational major powers. Since Cambodia's problems no longer complicate important international relationships, nations that matter globally have no urgent interest in resolving them. Cambodia today is nothing but a pathetically weak, ill-governed, and unproductive country that has vanished from the radar screen that emits signals warning of impending international crises. Cambodia's enduring crisis is strictly its own, that of its survival. Nations do not become extinct; there will always be Cambodians. But their lives can become so impoverished of everything that makes a human being, their leaders so arbitrary, corrupt, and indifferent to everything but their egoism, that a people founders and loses the struggle for national survival.

Not its struggle for survival against a demonic neighbor bent on exterminating the "Khmer race," as is paranoiacally bemoaned by the pernicious advocates of Cambodian chauvinism, from Lon Nol to Pol Pot. Unfortunately it is also bemoaned by men and women of moderation, who are instantly possessed by a raging furor when Vietnam is mentioned. The threat to Cambodia's survival lies in the fatal incompetence of its political class, in the indifference of its leaders to the parlous descent of their people over nearly three decades into ever deeper illness, ignorance, and demoralization.

Meanwhile, Cambodia's western and eastern neighbors, Thailand and Vietnam, vigorous nations of expanding population and an energetic will to rise rapidly to greater heights of prosperity and well-being, may suffer temporary setbacks but can be relied on to grow steadily in strength. Therein, in the yawning disproportion between buoyancy and lassitude, resides the threat to Cambodia's survival as a sovereign nation.

It is not that Thailand and Vietnam are girding to renew the rivalry of earlier centuries of the Kingdoms of Siam and Hue for possession of Khmer soil. Times have changed, and as Vietnam has found, conquest by arms of a neighbor bears the price of international revulsion, even if it overthrows one of the worst rulers in history. But states have not been converted to a religion of international beneficence. Would Cambodia's neighbors resist the temptation to penetrate into a disintegrating country whose regions look ready to fall into a waiting lap?

Cambodia, I fear, is past helping itself. Its future, if it is to have one, cannot be entrusted to the hands of its present leaders, most of their opposition, and the class that they represent. The country has lost its international importance and possesses only its own worth, the life of a nation of ten million. During the past century, its life has been grossly tampered with by many outsiders. By France, for the sake of colonial possession. By Japan, as a piece in its "Greater Asian Co-Prosperity Sphere." By the United States, to facilitate its withdrawal from a war it was losing in Vietnam. By China, because having a friend in Cambodia gave it a foothold in Southeast Asia and a thorn in the side

of Vietnam, a client of the Soviet Union. By Vietnam, to establish its preeminence over an Indochinese bloc of its own design. By the Soviet Union, because those who opposed Vietnam in Cambodia were China's clients.

Will the world for once act in Cambodia for the sake of Cambodians? Can it set aside, for the sake of the survival of a people that has gone in one generation through too many variations on the theme of Hell, its slavish adulation of the principle of national sovereignty as an unquestionable good? It drew close to doing so in the Paris Agreement of 1991 but fell short in its application. Cambodia looks mortally ill, and experience has shown that its own doctors are not up to the task of curing it. When a powerful Cambodian falls ill he goes abroad to be treated. I fear "abroad" would have to come to Cambodia to try to pull the stricken nation through. I see no other way but to place Cambodia's people into caring and disinterested hands for one generation, administer it for its own sake, and gradually hand it back to a new generation of Cambodians, who will have matured with respect for their own people and will be ready to take responsibility for them.

Unrealistic? Of course. Unrealizable? No.

---

*Article 18*  *FAR EASTERN ECONOMIC REVIEW,* July 23, 1998

CHINA

# Agent of Change

Initially dismissed as a transitional figure, Jiang Zemin is now presiding over what may prove to be the most profound changes in China since Deng Xiaoping opened up the economy two decades ago

**By Susan V. Lawrence in Beijing**

On a rainy Saturday in the Chinese capital, the Tree Song Bookstore near Peking University is packed. Customers are leafing through books on subjects that just a year ago were considered taboo. *Farewell to Utopia* documents the failure of socialism worldwide, while in *Ideas and Problems of China,* political scientists Liu Junning argues that "without rights and freedoms for citizens and without limited government, the market economy can only be pie in the sky."

Those books and many like them in the Tree Song Bookstore are testimony to a profound change in the political atmosphere in Beijing over the last nine months. The change has taken place since Chinese leader Jiang Zemin consolidated his power at a party congress and began to put his stamp on China post-Deng Xiaoping. Apparently looking for any help he can get to steer China through the dangerous next stage of economic reform, and to safeguard the gains made in the past 20 years, Jiang has sanctioned an unprecedented public debate about what in which China must change.

Jiang is "looking to see where consensus coalesces," says a seasoned Western observer. Already, the debate has helped create a consensus about the need for rule of law and limits on government power if the market economy is to succeed. Through his advisers, Jiang is hinting at going further, ordering up research projects on how other political systems work.

That's not all. Jiang has made tough decisions about China's economic-reform agenda, giving the go-ahead for a long-postponed overhaul of state enterprises and the financial system. He has shored up China's rocky relationship with the United States. He is promoting transparency and exposing judicial abuses, and he is backing the notion of local accountability through village elections.

Nine years ago, when Jiang first came to Beijing as general secretary of the Chinese Community Party, outside observers did not expect him to last more than a year or two. He was a hastily recruited fill-in for the previous party boss, who was purged in 1989 for siding with the demonstrators in Tiananmen Square. Jiang held office at the whim of his famously mercurial mentor, Deng Xiaoping, who had cashiered two previous choices of successor. And, in meetings with foreign dignitaries and the media, Jiang showed little sign of the steely determination or political skills needed to win the power struggle expected over Deng's death.

Deng held on for nearly eight years after 1989—and Jiang held on, too. But he operated in Deng's shadow, even when the patriarch grew too ill to weigh in on policy. Then, in February last year, Deng finally died, and Jiang began ruling on his own terms. His performance since has proven him to be the canny political operator that his longevity at Deng's side suggested he had to be. Many analysts see in Jiang's recent moves first, an agenda for change, and second, a willingness to break the rules by which China is governed in order to achieve it. He has not yet created a legacy that would put him on a par with Deng, but it now seems at least possible that he might.

Jiang's first priority after Deng's death was strengthening his position in the party leadership. Hong Kong's successful return to Chinese rule a year ago helped. Skilful politicking in the run-up to last September's 15th party congress helped more. At the congress, Jiang dispatched one rival, former National People's Congress Chairman Qiao Shi, and got another, former Premier Li Peng, moved out of involvement in the core portfolios of the economy and foreign affairs and into Qiao's old job. Jiang then embarked on what the Chinese media presented as a hugely successful visit to the U.S., full of photo opportunities portraying him as a statesman who had earned the world's respect.

President Bill Clinton's June 25–July 3 return visit to China strengthened Jiang's position further. Local media made much of the fact that Clinton spent a full eight days in China, and that he brought "half the White House" with him. It was testament, the media said, to American recognition of China's importance, and, by extension, Jiang's.

Jiang is using his newly consolidated power to push forward an agenda set by economic imperatives. At the top of that agenda is the attempt to turn debt-ridden, state-owned dinosaurs into independent, market-driven enterprises. Reforming state-owned industry has long been considered China's most crucial task in its quest to modernize its economy. Leaders had been unwilling to take on the task partly for ideological reasons—public ownership is a cornerstone of socialism—and partly because they knew it would involve massive lay-offs.

But Jiang and his new partner at the top, Premier Zhu Rongji, decided to bite the bullet. Jiang is credited with making the decision at the September party congress to move ahead with state-enterprise reform. Former Shanghai party chief Wu Bangguo has been put in day-to-day charge of the effort.

Such reform requires an overhaul of China's financial system in which banks bail out state firms on orders from the party. Now the market, free from political pressure, must start allocating capital. Another vice-premier, Wen Jiabao, has been named to head a new Central Work Commission on Finance.

Both state-sector and financial reform require changes in the size and function of the party and government bureaucracy. If the economy is run on market principles, it does not need bureaucrats to micro-manage it. Premier Zhu, with Jiang's approval, announced in March a restructuring of government at all levels. By the end of three years, some 4 million officials are slated to lose their jobs in the central government alone.

'The leadership now sees the serious consequences of maintaining the old political system while doing economic liberalization'

—A Beijing intellectual

Eventually, Chinese analysts say, Jiang and Zhu would have come around to the idea that for China's economy to function efficiently and rationally, changes are required in noneconomic fields, too—from law to politics. But the Asian financial crisis has lent an urgency to that logic; it points up the perils of economic development without parallel political and legal reform. And it has led Jiang to start flirting with ideas which, if followed through—that's a big if—could change China as profoundly as did Deng's economic changes in the 1980s.

"The disturbances in Indonesia have had a big impact on the leadership," says a former academic who convenes a bi-weekly discussion group on political change and regularly swaps ideas with policymakers. "The leadership now sees the serious consequences of maintaining the old political system while doing economic liberalization."

He says Chinese leaders saw in Indonesia President Suharto's relatives and cronies using their connections to amass assets, then blocking policies that threatened their interests, but that were needed to make the Indonesian economy healthier. What has particularly shocked the Chinese leadership, he says, is how the crisis has wiped out the fruits of 35 years of Indonesian economic development.

It is far from clear that Jiang Zemin wants to bring fundamental political reform to China. In recent months, however, he has shown at least an interest in alternative models of governance. His point man on such matters is Wang Huning, a professor of politics at Shanghai's Fudan University whom Jiang has recruited to be deputy director of the Policy Research Office under the party secretariat. That office now acts largely as Jiang's private think-tank.

Researchers at the mammoth national think-tank, the Chinese Academy of Social Sciences, confirm that Bai Gang, deputy director of the academy's Institute of Politics, has been assigned to prepare a report on presidential systems around the world. They say that it is widely understood within the academy that the assignment came from Wang Huning.

An academy researcher familiar with the study emphasizes that, so far, it represents just an "exploratory, theoretical forward position" aimed "at the long term." He underlines that "it is not on the agenda of the party or the government."

News of the presidential-systems study is nonetheless being avidly shared among the intelligentsia. Part of the reason for the excitement is that the topic plays into the debate in China about the relationships between party and state. The party and the state operate parallel hierarchies from the highest level of power (the Central Committee and the State Council) to the lowest (the party branch and the village committee). Theoretically, the party sets macro-policy and makes personnel decisions, and the state implements policy. In practice, the party implements policy, too. With

their functions overlapping, the two hierarchies have had a history of friction.

As China's leaders have strengthened their support for rule of law—needed to safeguard economic reform—legal issues in the party vs. state debate have taken on a new prominence. It bothers many legalists that Jiang attends international forums in his capacity as state president when, according to Chinese law, the presidency is a ceremonial post with no real powers. By rights, they say, Premier Zhu should represent the state. Jiang's positions of power are as general secretary of the Communist Party and chairman of the Central Military Commission.

Jiang could create a position of power for himself on the state side—say, an executive presidency on the American or French model. That, Chinese analysts say, could open the way for the party to step back from day-to-day governing. It could confine itself to setting direction for the country and nominating candidates for top posts. The change could stop there. Or, eager liberals say, it could continue. A presidential system would need a legislature with real powers and an independent judiciary. Much later, it might even lead to the sanctioning of opposition parties.

Jiang has given no indication that this is his game plan. Moreover, while establishing a powerful state presidency would require amending the constitution, constitutional scholars say they have heard of no one receiving orders to study such a change. But then, the Western observer notes, "the fact that Jiang Zemin has not made speeches about political change doesn't say anything one way or the other about his views. In that position, you can't and don't want to commit yourself." Jiang, he says, "has people continually testing the waters."

Chinese Academy of Social Sciences researchers say Jiang has also commissioned a study of how different democracies around the world work, and the lessons of their experiences. No one knows what Jiang wants to do with that study, either.

Some analysts see evidence of Jiang's interest in political change in his sanctioning of the public debate about ways forward for China. The debate has produced an intellectual ferment: Liberals, Marxists and nationalists, usually outside the party

and government, are now vying in the pages of books, journals and select newspapers to put forward their varying visions of China's future.

He Qinglian's *The Pitfalls of China's Modernization* is one of the hottest new contributions to the debate. It's part of a high-profile series of books edited by an informal adviser to Jiang, Chinese Academy of Social Sciences Vice-President Liu Ji. In her book, He argues that much of the wealth amassed in China since 1992 went to those who exploited official connections and special privileges to gain access to cut-price assets like real estate and stocks. Only with improved moral education and a legal system which guarantees equal access to economic opportunities can China soothe public resentment, she argues.

Staying enigmatic, Jiang has not commented on the public debate, nor allowed those under him to do so. "If you are an official in the government or the party now, you have to be neutral," explains a researcher at the academy. "You are just supposed to support Jiang Zemin and Zhu Rongji. You are not supposed to support the radical Left or the radical Right." The implicit understanding Jiang and Zhu have with those jousting in public, the researcher says, is: "We will say nothing. You can talk. You can debate. You can go to court. Maybe we'll adopt some of your ideas. We won't interfere."

That makes the debate markedly different from those of a decade ago. In the 1980s, policy discussions took place inside the party, in think-tanks linked to top party officials who used ideas as weapons in internal struggles.

No one is expecting Jiang to put political change firmly on his agenda before the year 2000, at the earliest. The rationale for the current debate—whether it's better protection of individual rights, limits on official power, or the exploration of different models of governance—is that new political solutions are needed to safeguard economic development.

For Jiang, simply steering China through intensifying economic and social dislocation will be a tall enough order. State-enterprise reform could throw as many as 40 million out of work, and Asia's financial crisis is slowing China's growth, hampering efforts to get them re-employed. The potential for unrest is real, and growing.

Jiang is trying to stave off strife by allowing more open debate. If he is the undogmatic reformer liberals hope he is, he may also be looking to the debate to produce a consensus for the political and legal reforms that economic stability demands.

Mao Zedong, says an academic, united China. Deng Xiaoping took China from a period of struggle to one of reform. Jiang, he says, "would just like to have the whole situation stable and growing smoothly." Even if that were all there is to Jiang's legacy, he might yet be ranked in history with China's political titans.

# Authoritarian Streak

## Jiang displays his conservative instincts in handling media

*Among the books travelling with President Bill Clinton on Air Force One during his recent trip to China was* Tiger on the Brink: Jiang Zemin and China's New Elite, *a biography of the Chinese president by* REVIEW *correspondent* **Bruce Gilley.** *Clinton portrayed Jiang as "a man of extraordinary intellect" and "vision" who was taking risks to pull his country into the 21st century. Not mentioned, but amply illustrated in the biography, is Jiang's authoritarian streak—an aspect of his little-known personality that he has displayed most often when handling the Chinese media.*

*From 1985, Jiang was mayor and then party secretary of Shanghai until his appointment as Communist Party general secretary following the 1989 Tiananmen Massacre. During that time, he showed an exceptional sensitivity to what was in the press. From 1986, he held regular meetings with the senior editors of Shanghai's main media organizations to ensure they toed the party line, a task normally delegated to propaganda officials. No issue seemed too small for Jiang's attention. When a fire broke out at a government building in October 1986, for example, Jiang criticized local TV reporters for "alarming people" with their on-the-spot coverage of the disaster.*

*In the following excerpt from* Tiger on the Brink, *Jiang again exhibits his authoritarian instincts in a run-in with the local media. These instincts continue to characterize his handling of several policy areas in addition to the media—areas such as the arts, public security, even political reform. It's a reminder that Jiang, for all his apparent openness, has distinctly conservative impulses.*

On May 4, 1987, following a meeting with local People's Congress delegates, Jiang was accosted by one harried delegate who told him a sorry tale. A water pipe near the new train station had been spewing into the street for close to a year after being severed by careless workers. Several letters from the delegate to the Zhabei district authorities had received only polite replies. "The matter is being handled by relevant departments," they read. The broken pipe was, of course, affecting the image of one of Jiang's own showcase projects in the city. Back in his office, he patched through to the local water-supplies department. "Get someone to fix that pipe now!" he hollered. It was done the same day.

The incident might have passed unremarked. But a few weeks later Xu Jingen, a star reporter for the *Liberation Daily* newspaper, asked the delegate about his campaign to fix the pipe and was told the story of Jiang's personal intervention in the matter. An average reporter for the mainland press might have written a story praising Jiang's respect for the "suggestion" of the People's Congress delegate. But other ideas crossed Xu's mind. The issue was important enough, he thought, to be written up in the "Weekly Forum" column on the front page of the *People's Daily*. Editors there, familiar with Xu's work, agreed immediately.

The column appeared on July 6, 1987. Entitled "The Other Side of Doing Things Yourself," the column was a stinging indictment of Jiang's high-handed meddling in what should have been an administrative affair. "It is totally abnormal for leading cadres to get involved in sorting out every little problem," the column read. "All it will do is

encourage a mentality of dependence and procrastination among those at the lower levels."

Jiang was furious. Though it did not mention him by name, the article left little doubt that he was the "principal city leader" of Shanghai under discussion. The last sentence made the connection even stronger by making a reference to one of Jiang's earlier attempts to hold down taxi fares in Shanghai. "Some newspapers around the country constantly run articles praising the mayors of certain cities for resolving the high costs of taxis," it read. "But what's the point of having a director of the price bureau or a general manager of the taxi company if this kind of thing goes on?"

Jiang was being held up to public ridicule on the front page of the party's flagship national newspaper. Xu's biting sarcasm made a point that the *People's Daily* felt was fair. But Jiang was offended. His assiduous efforts to run this creaky, sprawling city were being dismissed as petty meddling by an insolent young reporter. It wouldn't do.

On July 10, Jiang convened a special meeting of all party and government officials in Shanghai involved in propaganda. "Xu Jingen has not the slightest idea of what it's like to run this city," Jiang charged, pounding his fist on the table. "This supposedly skilful writer really thinks he's impressive," he continued. "Well, I think he should get out of his office more often and have a look around!" Editors from the *Liberation Daily* sat at the meeting hanging their heads in shame. The meeting had turned into a forum for a torrent of abuse against Xu and his superiors.

Jiang by this time was sufficiently aware of the power of the media—even in its heavily controlled form in China—to influence public opinion in favour of or against the government. Not only his effectiveness as mayor but also his image in Beijing depended on keeping close tabs on the press. After lambasting Xu, he proceeded to enumerate the various reasons why he had intervened over the broken pipe. No one spoke a word.

When the meeting adjourned, the editors returned to the newspaper office and informed Xu of his transgression. There was no point debating. Only by showing contrition could Xu hope to save his job. A letter of apology was the first step. On his editors' advice, Xu worked through the night fashioning an apology to Jiang and delivered it by hand the next morning.

It seems that Jiang was not after Xu's head. Indeed, he appears to have been caught off guard by the repentant appeal. "After you've been around me a little longer, you'll realize that I always encourage comrades to appraise each other in an open-hearted way," Jiang responded in a letter to Xu. "But I have this one fault: Sometimes my attitude is a little too harsh. Please excuse me."

It seemed magnanimous. Jiang was admitting that he had gone overboard in calling the special struggle session. But he had made his point. Jiang was like the chief clerk of the city's general-affairs office, as (former Shanghai mayor) Wang Daohan had predicted, and he was determined not to be held to blame for the bureaucratic sclerosis that forced him to intervene in such cases. The chastened Shanghai media never again dared to comment on his style of governance.

*Tiger on the Brink: Jiang Zemin and China's New Elite* **is published by the University of California Press (1998).**

---

*Article 19*                                   *The NEW REPUBLIC*, April 20, 1998

# THE NEW ORDER

*By Edward A. Gargan*

Just weeks after China raised its flag over this former British colony last July, Hong Kong's business district began to echo with the whine of cement drills and the tatoo of jackhammers. Beijing's hand-picked administrator for Hong Kong, a shipping tycoon named Tung Chee-hwa, had decided to erect wrought-iron fences around the low-slung government office buildings scattered across downtown. During 156 years of colonial rule, Hong Kong's British governors had never seen the need to cloister behind fencing. However, Tung clearly felt the gold-tipped, thick-stemmed bars were a top priority. So far, the newly installed gates remain open. But the fences have become a symbol of the new order—a new government that is more secretive, less democratic and, if the polls are right, a good deal less popular than that of the British.

Tung and his fellow Beijing loyalists, of course, maintain that nothing has changed in Hong Kong since the last British governor, Chris Patten, stepped aboard the royal yacht *Britannia* shortly after midnight on July 1 and sailed off into history. "It's business as usual," Tung chirps when people ask how things are going.

In fact, much has changed here, and much continues to change. Until Chinese suzerainty, there was no mistaking Hong Kong for China. Most Hong Kongers were richer and freer than those on the mainland. They were educated differently.

They loudly expressed their views on call-in radio programs. Now, some of those distinctions are being chiseled away. Next year, the number of high schools that teach in English will be cut by 50 percent, and, notwithstanding the uproar from Hong Kong parents, eventually all high schools will be required to teach in Cantonese. More generally, the freedoms Hong Kongers used to take for granted appear increasingly endangered. On his very first day in office, Tung abolished every one of Hong Kong's democratic institutions, right down to the local councils. The most prominent body dismissed was the Hong Kong legislature, which Patten had sought to make somewhat more representative of popular will during his five-year term.

Patten's steps toward democracy had admittedly been rather timid. At his tenure's end, only a third of the 60 legislative seats were directly elected. Meanwhile, one-half of the seats remained "functional constituencies"—meaning they were chosen by corporations or professional, entertainment, and religious groups. The remaining ten seats were appointed by an electoral commission.

Nonetheless, Patten's modest democratization effort was denounced by Beijing as a violation of secret agreements reached with Patten's London masters. The real reason for China's rage was not difficult to fathom: In the first—and last—election under the Patten system (held in 1995), Hong Kong's voters decisively turned out for the Democratic Party, whose platform calls for the introduction of a fully elected legislature and an elected chief executive. Beijing's preferred candidates, by contrast, suffered a crushing defeat. Not surprisingly, after dismissing the 1995 legislature, Beijing appointed a provisional one that included many of the defeated Beijing loyalists.

This May, Hong Kong's citizens will be allowed to elect a new legislature to replace the provisional one. Still, Tung shows little interest in implementing the "Basic Law" that Beijing agreed to for Hong Kong and which calls for gradual movement toward direct elections. Instead, he has scrapped the system of direct contests that was used to fill a third of the seats during the Patton era and replaced it with a new procedure based on proportional representation. This will enable the less popular pro-Beijing parties to at least slightly increase their representation in the legislature because, even though they will not win outright in any constituency, they will get some votes, and their presence in the legislature will be based roughly on the proportion of votes they garner. Furthermore, not only has Tung kept the old "functional constituency" seats in place, he has limited the number of people allowed to choose them from two million to fewer than 200,000.

Tung's changes practically guarantee that the new legislature will be subservient to Beijing. And that's clearly his goal. His electoral scheme, he explains, is designed to move Hong Kong toward democracy "neither too fast nor too slow." Indeed, he has indicated that the transition might take twelve to 15 years. Many Hong Kong residents find it difficult to understand how a society with one of the highest per capita incomes in the world can move too quickly toward democracy. But Tung and his colleagues see no contradiction in letting Hong Kongers decide where to work, how to invest their savings, and where to go on vacation, while denying them the right to choose their government.

The Tung administration also appears unenthusiastic about the vigor with which Hong Kongers are criticizing his government and Beijing. At the annual gathering of China's parliament in Beijing a few weeks ago, a prominent Hong Kong businessman and longtime Beijing supporter denounced Hong Kong's government-funded radio and television network for questioning government policies. The stations, created under the British administration along the lines of the BBC, are supported by tax revenues but have traditionally been independent of government editorial control. Yet Tung, who was also at the meeting, failed to defend the stations in the face of this attack. Instead, he opined that "while freedom of speech is important, it is also important for government policies to be positively presented."

Tung clearly plans to translate this philosophy into action. When Hong Kong's new legislature is seated in May, one of

Tung's first items of business will be to introduce a law on subversion, treason, sedition, and secession. Hong Kong's democrats are understandably concerned about the threat the law might pose to free expression, whether in the press, in public protest, or through political organizations. But Tung, a corporate chief executive accustomed to giving orders, has already displayed his impatience with those who would question his judgment. His taciturn encounters with Hong Kong's raucous and relentless press are a sharp departure from those of his predecessor Patten, who reveled in the contest of wits with reporters. Tung, in short, presents himself as a traditional Chinese patriarch, the authoritarian family figure who, while genuinely absorbed in the welfare of his family, has no truck with rebellious children.

Nevertheless, Tung's administration takes great pains to assure the international business community that, whatever the new limits on democracy in Hong Kong, the rule of law remains sacrosanct. But does it? Last year, a leading democracy activist, Emily Lau, decided to test the extent to which Hong Kong's existing laws applied to Beijing institutions based in Hong Kong. Lau filed a formal request with Xinhua—nominally the New China News Agency but in reality the Chinese Communist Party's office here—for all its files on her and her political activities, many of which involved protests against Beijing policies. Under Hong Kong law, individuals who believe that information is being collected on them by any organization, public or private, may demand copies of their dossier; the organization is required to cough up its files within 40 days. But Xinhua waited ten months and then blandly claimed it had no files on Lau.

Lau then called on Hong Kong's chief legal officer, Elsie Leung, to file charges against Xinhua. Leung refused. And Leung has also declined to charge a prominent pro-Beijing newspaper owner who is accused of conspiring to defraud advertisers, despite mentioning her in the charges filed against her executives. Thus, it seems that institutions and individuals from the mainland are already getting special treatment under Hong Kong law. What consequences this will have as more and more mainland entities set up shop here remains to be seen.

Ironically, Hong Kong's new leaders are rushing to embrace a version of China that many mainlanders wish to escape. While Beijing loyalists in Hong Kong push for greater media controls, government secrecy, patriotic displays, and repression of the democratic activists, places like Shanghai are witnessing a rising tide of unease over communist social and political controls. Thus, China and Hong Kong are beginning to resemble two trains, barreling past each other in opposite directions.

EDWARD A. GARGAN has just completed a tour as the Hong Kong bureau chief for The New York Times. He is the author of China's Fate (Doubleday).

*Article 20*                                      *NEWSWEEK,* August 24, 1998

A S I A

# China's New Family Values

## Unhappy with high divorce rates and too much adultery,

## Beijing gets ready to launch a sexual counterrevolution

BY LESLIE PAPPAS

DR. WANG, BUSY WITH FAMILY AND work, waited more than half a lifetime to tango. And when the 56-year-old physician finally stepped out for dance lessons two years ago, he left his wife of 30 years at home. That, Mrs. Wang suspects, is how he met his lover, a 44-year-old teacher with a husband and college-age son. The doctor hid the affair for six months, acknowledged it when his wife confronted him but still devotes his free time—and most of his salary—to his mistress. The Wangs continue to share a bed, but since he took up ballroom dancing, "we don't have husband-and-wife relations," Mrs. Wang laments. "We live apart but in the same room."

Still, Mrs. Wang wants to save her marriage. So, it seems, does the Chinese government. Alarmed by urban divorce rates approaching 25 percent, what they see as rampant infidelity and a younger generation that gleans its values from Hollywood and MTV, Chinese lawmakers are set to approve a new morality code. If passed, the new law will strictly regulate divorce, mandate waiting periods before marriage and make adultery illegal. Now being written by a select group of law experts, the new legislation will probably take effect after the National People's Congress rubber-stamps it next March. Mrs. Wang can hardly wait. "The law should be strict," says the 53-year-old retiree, who asked that her full name not be published. "It should encourage proper behavior."

Beijing has tried to play Big Brother in the bedroom before. After the 1949 revolution, Chairman Mao Zedong imposed strict moral codes that required the masses to dress in unisex fashion, jailed adulterers and gave commune leaders the power to deny marriages. Under Mao's successor, economic reformer Deng Xiaoping, morality codes— and attitudes—relaxed. People trapped in unhappy unions divorced or took lovers. Sex toys appeared in special "health care"

centers. Brothels disguised as karaoke bars, massage parlors or beauty salons cropped up across the country. One recent survey showed that 68 percent of university students think premarital sex is "morally okay." On campuses, cohabitation today is common. "The disaster caused by sexual freedom is everywhere," bemoaned the Beijing Youth Daily last month.

In an attempt at damage control, legislators plan to discourage hasty weddings and impose stringent guidelines on divorces. One proposal calls for public announcements of engagements followed by a waiting period of weeks—or months—to give anyone opposed to the union a chance to speak up (or forever hold his peace). New divorce laws would strictly define what constitutes sufficient grounds for ending a marriage. Included: a three-year separation, "incurable physical defects," mental illness and adultery. "Everybody has the right to divorce, but there must be standards," says Chen Mingxia, a law professor at the Chinese Academy of Social Sciences, who is helping write the new laws. "We want to make people think."

Other proposals would forbid single motherhood, deny marriage licenses to people with "AIDS or sexual diseases" and require "loyalty" in marriage—essentially making cheating illegal. The law is also likely to define the marriage bond as existing between "men and women," a standard that blocks same-sex unions.

The government has tried to keep the revisions quiet. One of the authors of the proposed legislation told NEWSWEEK that the pending laws are "not for open publication," a status Beijing normally affords state secrets. Nonetheless, details have leaked in the press—and sparked a firestorm. "If adultery becomes a crime," warned a newspaper editorial last month, "judicial authorities will invade the most private domain of people's lives." Women's groups are especially irate. While they have convinced the authors of

---

## New Rules?

If conservative legislators carry the day, China will impose a stringent moral code that reminds some of the Mao regime.

- **Marriage** Waiting periods required. No licenses for those with AIDS or sexual diseases.
- **Divorce** No-fault would be a thing of the past. Only desertion, adultery and the like would qualify.
- **Adultery** Cheating would be illegal—possibly punishable by forced labor. Births out of wedlock would be outlawed.

the proposed legislation to include "domestic violence" as a legitimate reason for divorce, they have failed on other counts. "They don't even admit that there can be rape within marriage," says

Wang Xingjuan, who runs a women's hotline in Beijing.

Will the public outcry be enough to kill off the new regulations? Maybe: the opposition, swelling faster than the conservatives had expected, may force lawmakers to tone down moral guidelines. Until they do, it's a family-values campaign that Chairman Mao himself would have loved.

*Article 21*

*World • Watch,* May/June 1998

# INDONESIA'S DISCONTENT

*For more than 30 years, the rulers of the world's fourth most populous country have pursued an aggressive and seemingly successful development policy. But the economic crisis wracking the country today is one signal that much of that success has been achieved through a relentless exploitation of the country's rich environmental assets—and its still poor people. Many Indonesians now sense that their course has been an unsustainable one. And in many ways, Indonesia's troubles are a reflection of the world's.*

## By Curtis Runyan

When Indonesia began its economic free fall last year, the *New York Times* declared that the collapse "surprised almost everyone." Against all expectation, the Asian economic "miracle" simply stalled out, leaving Indonesia and several of its neighbors looking to the International Monetary Fund for multi-billion-dollar bailouts. Private investment in the country had increased by an average of 11 percent annually in the past decade. But Indonesia—the fourth most populous country in the world, and one of the richest in natural resources—was now staggering and threatening to drag down global markets with it.

Together with reports of President Soeharto's failing health, the economic crisis sent investors running. By January 1998 the value of the rupiah had plunged over 70 percent. Food riots, ethnic violence, and protests against the government mounted.

International attention to the country's crisis has focused on the web of bad lending practices by banks, overborrowing by

companies, and an economic boom driven largely by overpriced real estate, artificially maintained exchange rates, and speculation. But the underlying truth is that Indonesia has been in trouble for decades, and those troubles extend far beyond bad investments and financial management. Since Soeharto came to power at the height of the Cold War, the country has been kept in a state of increasingly precarious imbalance—between the power of its ruling elite and the marginalization of its swelling majority, and between the country's vast natural and cultural assets and the unapologetic ambitions of its government to exploit those assets in ways that promise to rapidly deplete them.

While the country was dazzling investors with 8- to 10-percent annual growth rates, Soeharto's "New Order," as his 32-year reign is called, had been raiding the country's treasurehouse of natural wealth and cheap human labor, maintaining a veneer of impressive exports and returns on investment, but meanwhile liquidating the country's natural capital—and suppressing its dissent—in order to keep appearances up. Despite reports of bloody massacres in East Timor, Aceh, and West Papua, endemic financial and political cronyism in the capital city of Jakarta, and environmental devastation in the outlying provinces, foreign investment in Indonesian stock had reached $59 billion by January 1997. Over the following year, however, the façade began to crumble. By the end of 1997, the stock market had fallen by more than 40 percent, and social unrest was rising rapidly.

By some measures, Indonesia's progress under Soeharto has been impressive. Average incomes have increased from U.S. $50 in 1967 to U.S. $650 in 1994 (though the averages hide huge regional and ethnic inequities), and adult literacy has risen from 36 percent to 77 percent since 1960. The country was the world's largest rice importer in 1974, but is now self-sufficient in production of the grain. And Indonesia's national statistics bureau has released figures claiming that only 15 percent of the population lives in poverty, down from 60 percent of the population 30 years ago. But these figures, often cited by the World Bank, are considered by many to be misleading. "Jakarta's definition of poverty is questioned by economists," writes the *Far Eastern Economic Review.* "For city dwellers, the poverty line is fixed at a mere 930 rupiah [roughly 40 cents] per capita per day; in the countryside, it's 608 rupiah [25 cents]." Indeed, Indonesian economist Faisal Basri calculates that 82 percent of Indonesians live on $30 per month or less.[1]

Having risen to power 32 years ago in a country faced with grinding poverty, Soeharto considers himself Indonesia's "Father of Development," and has aggressively and often ruthlessly promoted economic growth. He has been a key proponent of the "Asian Values" vein of thought, which holds communal harmony in higher esteem than individual rights. He has repeatedly implied that paying heed to human rights and democratization at any expense to economic growth is a luxury that developing countries like Indonesia cannot afford. "In Indonesia, we respect and carry out the principles of human rights in accordance with our system and our own understanding," Soeharto told reporters in response to U.S. criticism of his track record in East Timor last year.

One result of Soeharto's development strategy is that an entire generation has been left to languish with little hope for participation or incentive for advancement. Under the glitzy surface of high returns on international investments, plentiful labor, and abundant resources, there has been a dangerous hollow space—an absence of the kind of opportunity for en-

trepreneurial inventiveness and ambition that can make an open market and a free society thrive. As the Indonesian novelist Mochtar Lubis asks, "How can you expect people to create, to think, if there is no climate of freedom? Without fostering our intellectual strengths, which means letting people say what they think without fear, Indonesians will remain coolies in their own country."

By concentrating all the real opportunity in the hands of just a few people, says Jafar Siddiq Hamzah of the Indonesian Legal Aid Foundation, Soeharto has undermined the country's stability. For three decades, the façade was propped up by the power of the military government to maintain a rigid political conformity and civil order. But the cost of such order has been heavy, says Hamzah: "A strong political elite has meant a weak civil society." To outsiders, civil order was too easily mistaken for fundamental stability, and even experts like World Bank President James Wolfensohn misread the signs. "There is no doubt we got it wrong," said Wolfensohn in the wake of the collapse. "I was not alone in thinking 12 months ago that Indonesia was on a very good path. One thing we should have done was to try to suppress the monopolies and unfair practices [of the Soeharto clan]."[2] It should now be clear to Wolfensohn and other outsiders that Indonesia's crisis will require far more than an economic patch.

## A Javanese Empire?

With more than 17,000 islands, Indonesia is the world's largest archipelago. The country stretches across 5,000 kilometers from east to west—the distance from Baghdad to London. Its total land mass of nearly 2 million square kilometers is larger than that of Belgium, Germany, Italy, Spain, Portugal, and the United Kingdom combined. Include The Netherlands, the colonial power that used to control most of Indonesia (see sidebar, "Another Time, Another World"), and Indonesia is still larger. It is endowed with a wealth of resources, including extensive oil and natural-gas reserves, rich mineral deposits, and dense forests that cover three-quarters of its land. It is home to 10 percent of the world's tropical rainforest—second only to Brazil's in area—and it may be unequaled by any other country in the diversity of its flora and fauna.

With 209 million people, Indonesia ranks only behind China, India, and the United States in total population. More than 120 million Indonesians live on the central island of Java, making this relatively small island the most densely populated island in the world.[3] The "outer" island provinces of Sumatra to the west, and Kalimantan, Sulawesi, and West Papua (which the government calls Irian Jaya) to the east, have served as

1. Eyal Press, "The Soeharto Lobby," *The Progressive,* May 1997.
2. According to analysis by Jeffrey Winters, an Indonesia expert at Northwestern University, at least one-third of all World Bank loans to Indonesia "leak into the government bureaucracy and disappear."
3. Java alone is half the size of United Kingdom but has more than twice the population.

resource banks for the country's development. These outer islands are also home to most of the country's 300 ethnic minority groups.

Indonesia's sprawling geography and demography have significantly shaped the history of the country. One of Soeharto's key accomplishments has been patching together such an intensely diverse nation. But in many cases, where the military has violently imposed unification (see "Unrest in Indonesia"), it has only added to the simmering tensions now threatening to tear Indonesia apart.

Java, with 60 percent of the population and the majority of political and military power, dominates Indonesia. In this century, says one Indonesian critic of Soeharto's regime, the country merely exchanged the long-distance colonial rule of the Dutch for the internal colonialism of the Soeharto regime. Just as the Dutch once made fortunes shipping teak wood and Mollucan spices from Java to Holland, Java now helps itself to great quantities of oil, timber, coal, and gold from the outer islands.

Provincial leaders from the outer islands have complained that their natural resources are being exploited to benefit the Javenese. For example, in the provinces of Aceh (northern Sumatra) and West Papua, the wealth produced per inhabitant is among the highest in Indonesia, but the income per inhabitant is much lower. Irian Java has the sixth highest per capita GDP among Indonesia's 27 provinces, but also has the highest incidence of rural poverty. Much of its GDP is being channeled to Jakarta, and thence to Tokyo, New York, and Melbourne.

The Jakarta regime has been pursuing its own brand of manifest destiny since the inception of Soeharto's New Order. In 1966, when Soeharto, then an obscure General in the army, seized control from Sukarno, the country's charismatic independence leader and first president, he immediately made economic development his highest priority.

Twenty years after declaring independence from the Dutch in 1945, Sukarno's Communist-leaning, economically unstable leadership had left the country deeply impoverished and politically volatile. Sukarno had been unable to fashion a workable constitution around a parliamentary structure; he had tried—and ultimately failed—to balance political power between various factions, the main antagonists being the military and the Communists.

Amid rising tensions, in October 1965 a handful of leftist military officers kidnapped and murdered six top-ranking military officials whom they suspected of disloyalty to Sukarno.

Using the pretext that the Communist party was behind the insurrection, Soeharto quickly stepped in to put down the abortive coup, unleashing social tensions that exploded into nationwide violence.[4] The clashes quickly turned into one of the worst massacres of this century—a pogrom aimed at eliminating all Communists and their sympathizers. The army, and the civilian vigilante groups it encouraged, rounded up and systematically executed 500,000 real and suspected communists (some estimates range to more than 1 million). The U.S. Central Intelligence Agency compared the purge to the Maoist massacres of the 1930s and the Nazi mass murders committed during the Second World War.[5]

Soeharto worked quickly to create a sharp contrast between the extreme poverty and chaos of Sukarno's rule and his own intentions for the country, elevating the goal of economic development to "near-sacred" status.[6] "Development has become one of the ... most important key words" in the Indonesian language, according to Indonesian intellectual Heryanto. "This key word has become a focus of authority and legitimacy, and a departure point from which to reinterpret old facts and direct the future course of history."

Through a series of political maneuvers—expanding military control over the government, placing economic policy in the hands of western-trained "technocrats," and starting a system of political patronage designed to buoy supporters and undermine opponents—Soeharto maintained enough control to set the country on a path of rapid development. Adam Schwarz, author of *A Nation in Waiting: Indonesia in the 1990s,* observes that as Soeharto's efforts to export the country's rich supplies of oil and other natural resources began to pay off, "political 'order' and economic 'development' came to be seen as two sides of the same coin."

"Pervasive Indonesian media campaigns and community education programs equate economic development with moral righteousness as well as economic prosperity," says cultural anthropologist Lorraine Aragon. Government officials brand opponents of development projects as impediments to political order. "Workers who exercise their right to strike; activists who call for democratization; students and human rights lawyers who criticize the government development policy; and urban squatters and traders who create 'disorder' by their mere existence, are all vulnerable to accusations of being 'subversives,' 'communists,' 'terrorists,' or 'traitors,'" reports Amnesty International. "This puts them at risk of arbitrary detention, torture,

---

4. The facts surrounding the aborted coup remain a matter of some debate. While the government's official version pins the coup entirely on the Communists, historical evidence discounts their role.

5. U.S. Central Intelligence Agency, "Intelligence Report: Indonesia—1965, the coup that backfired," 1968.

6. Charles Barber, "Environmental Scarcities, State Capacity, and Civil Violence: The Case of Indonesia," University of Toronto and the American Academy of Arts and Sciences, 1997.

imprisonment, or death, a powerful deterrent to all but the most courageous."

Those who challenge activities that cause ecological devastation, such as deforestation, industrial pollution, mining, or damming of rivers, also run the risk of being branded enemies of the state. For example, four people were killed in September 1993 when police and military forces opened fire on 500 peaceful demonstrators protesting the proposed Nipah dam on the island of Madura. As planned, the dam would have submerged four villages and flooded surrounding farmlands.

The government has pegged the environmental group WALHI (The Indonesian Forum for the Environment)—a coalition of 335 organizations from around the country—as one of 32 "problematic" activist organizations deemed to be "carrying out activities that exceed their charter," writes John McBeth in the *Far Eastern Economic Review*. The military alleges that in 1996, WALHI helped spark riots at the gigantic Freeport gold and copper mine in West Papua, which has close ties to Soeharto. The accusers have offered no evidence to support this claim, and apparently feel no compelling pressure to do so. In Indonesia, where insulting the president can be a capital offense, critics of the country's style of development are forced to tread lightly.

While Soeharto's system of political patronage originally consisted of granting oil, mineral, or timber concessions to military leaders and close business associates, it now stretches into all corners of the economy, from flour milling to petrochemical refining.[7] Even the biggest international players have little chance of getting into the Indonesian game unless they partner up with Soeharto's children, in-laws, or business partners and their giant monopolies. "In recent years," writes Schwarz, "hardly a single major infrastructure contract has been awarded without one Soeharto relative or other having a piece of it." For example, in 1988, when Indonesia's Technology Minister Habibie announced plans to add 350,000 new telephone lines to Jakarta's overloaded system, U.S.-based AT&T teamed up with Soeharto's eldest daughter Siti Hardijanti Rukmana ("Tutut"), who has significant interests in toll roads and agriculture, to bid for the $300 million contract, while Japan's NEC and Simitomo entered a joint bid with Soeharto's younger son, Hutomo Mandala Putra ("Tommy"). After two years of heavy lobbying by the rivals, Habibie doubled the size of the contract and awarded half each to AT&T and NEC/Simitomo, despite the fact that their two bids were the highest of the five bids submitted.[8]

Timber concessions, which require low capital investments and almost guarantee high returns, have been a favorite tool of patronage. Politically connected players like Soeharto's golf partner Bob Hasan "have heavily influenced the allocation of nearly one-third of the nation's territory to private companies for timber utilization," estimates Mark Poffenberger in the May 1997 *Asian Survey*. Moreover, the shearing of Indonesia's forests is only part of a larger pattern of systematic stripping of the country's resources—and undermining of its people's traditional assets. Charles Barber, in his recent study of the country's environmental security, concludes that Indonesia's New Order has become "dependent on cheap raw materials, accustomed to high levels of profit, and able to pass the environmental costs of unsustainable . . . practices on to local communities, the state, and society at large."

## The World's Richest Mine

On April 29, 1996, representatives of about 3,000 members of the Amungme tribe from West Papua filed a lawsuit in a United States district court against a subsidiary of the international mining giant Freeport McMoRan.[9] The $6 billion suit charged that Freeport, during the company's 25 years of mining copper and gold at the Grasberg and Erstberg mines, carved up and poisoned ancestral lands integral to the tribe's survival, and committed human rights abuses such as detention, abduction, torture, and execution to intimidate and eliminate local opposition to the company's actions.

Freeport's operation has closely mirrored Soeharto's fortunes, and is one of the most extreme cases of the systemic troubles underlying Indonesia's shallow style of development. Soeharto, a long-time friend of Freeport CEO Jim Bob Moffet, in 1967 agreed to give the company sole mineral exploration rights to West Papua, along with generous tax and royalty exemptions. The mine was one of Soeharto's first major development projects and remains the country's single largest source of tax revenue. It is the richest mine in the world, with assets exceeding $60 billion, and the Indonesian government received $480 million in 1996 from the 10 percent stake it owns in the operation.

But development of this remote site, which physically occupies more than 10,000 hectares, has taken a heavy toll on the local people and their environment. Each day the operation extracts more than 165,000 tons of ore from the mountain—98 percent of which is subsequently dumped into the Ajkwa river for disposal. The sediment load in the Ajkwa river is now five times its natural concentration, and the mining wastes have contaminated thousands of hectares of forest downstream. Environmental groups claim that the tailings from the mine,

---

7. Several of Soeharto's business cronies—such as Liem Sioe Liong and Bob Hasan, now two of the richest people in Indonesia—worked with him when he was a young colonel in the military.

8. Adam Schwarz, *A Nation in Waiting,* Boulder, CO: Westview Press, 1994.

9. With no legal recourse in Indonesia, the Amugme had no option but to file in the United States, where Freeport is based.

which contain dissolved arsenic, lead, mercury, and other potentially dangerous metals, have killed fish, poisoned sago forests (a traditional food source), and made the water dangerous to drink. The local environmental bureau, after conducting tests in April 1997, declared the water unfit to consume.

Freeport spokesperson Edward Pressman insists that the water in the Ajkwa river poses "no health threat to the local population whatsoever." The *Australian Financial Review* quoted Moffet as saying the environmental impact of the mine was "equivalent to me pissing in the Arafura Sea." However, while the company claims that it monitors the river's water quality, it has refused to allow any independent monitoring. In fact, Danny Kennedy of the mining watchdog group Project Underground was deported in February 1997 for attempting to ship samples of the river's water to the United States for analysis.

Citing environmental concerns at the mine, in 1995 the U.S. Overseas Private Investment Corporation decided to cancel all of its $100 million political-risk insurance policy for Freeport's operation:

"Especially its tailings management and disposal practices have severely degraded the rainforests surrounding the Ajkwa . . .[and] continue to pose unreasonable or major environmental, health, or safety hazards with respect to the rivers that are being impacted by the tailings, the surrounding terrestrial ecosystems, and the local inhabitants."

The operation has already decapitated the Grasberg peak— once one of the highest between the Himalayas and the Andes—reducing its height by 300 meters. And the company has plans to nearly double the output of the mine to 300,000 metric tons of ore per day—enough to fill a line of dump trucks 100 miles long each day.

Meanwhile, the Amungme, Komoro, and other local tribal communities have received little compensation for their lands. The company has provided a clinic, some housing, a school, and a few community programs, but this has been small compensation in light of the $1.9 billion in revenues and $175 million in profits Freeport made from the mine in 1996. The rationale for this deprivation is that Indonesian law requires indigenous peoples "to relinquish their customary rights over land and resources to so-called national development projects, which include mines," writes Carolyn Marr of the environmental group Down to Earth. While the mine has provided the area with about 18,000 jobs, only 1,500 of those are filled by West Papuans—and only 400 of them are filled by local people.10 In addition, West Papuans are paid only one-seventh as much as other employees, according to a report by Radio National in Australia.

Since mining first began, local communities have resisted the presence of Freeport, and the driving force has been a widespread resentment over what is perceived as a neo-colonial interference by outside interests. "The vast majority of West Papuan people resent the Indonesians being there because they've gained very little from it and they have lost control over their own lives," says Jim Elmsley, an expert on West Papuan nationalism. "At the moment . . .they do not have an avenue in which to express dissatisfaction short of basically going to armed conflict. . . . The onus is on the mine to include these people."

In 1977, the state accused the secessionist group the Free Papua Movement (OPM) of using stolen Freeport explosives to blow up a copper slurry pipe. The action spurred military retributions—Indonesian Air Force OV-10 Broncos bombed and strafed local villages—reportedly resulting in the deaths of at least 900 people. In recent years, the military has continued to use repressive measures to silence protests and maintain an atmosphere of intimidation. In 1994, the Australian council for Overseas Aid and the Roman Catholic Church of Jayapura issued reports documenting continued human rights abuses, including the deaths or disappearances of 37 local people.

But it wasn't until anti-Freeport rioters rampaged through the mining town of Timika in March 1996 that Freeport offered any substantial compensation to local people. A number of community leaders rejected the deal, which gave 1 percent of the operation's revenues ($10 to $15 million annually) to a development plan controlled by the military, because local people were not given a say in how the money was to be spent. After a year the plan collapsed, reports journalist John McBeth, largely because of corruption and mismanagement among those who administered it.

Freeport vehemently defends its operation, insisting that company employees have committed no crimes and that its actions have not been illegal. But the company's rejoinder that it operates on the legal side of Indonesian law, whether or not it is true, is a shallow one. Critics say the company has done little within its power to help curb the government's violent repression of local people. Freeport vice president Paul Murphy, in a comment that echoes the statements issued by Shell Oil around the time of the Nigerian government's execution of environmental activist Ken Saro-Wiwa, says that the company has no role in any abuses that government forces may have committed: "Our contract of work . . . requires us to provide logistical support for all government officials who are resident in, or visiting our area, including the army. We provide shelter, food, and logistics."11

10. Richard Vietor, "Freeport Indonesia," Harvard Business School Case Study, March 5, 1997.
11. See "Dying for Oil," *World Watch,* March/April 1996.

Emmy Hafild, head of the environmental group WALHI, remains critical of Freeport's role in human rights abuses: "There is no clear line between the military operations and Freeport's protections," she says. "The line is blurred. For instance, Freeport security guards, many of them, are also military personnel." Freeport has spent $35 million to house and supply the estimated 800 military troops that guard the mine.[12]

Freeport, of course, is not the only company benefiting from Indonesia's economic development-at-any-cost policies—just as the Amungme are not the only people coping with government-sanctioned environmental destruction and human rights abuses. On the island of Kalimantan, where the government is heavily promoting coal mining, more than half of the land has been opened up to mining concessions. With Indonesia's oil supplies expected to run dry in the next 20 years, the country is diligently working to access its 27.7 billion tons of estimated coal reserves. Like many of the country's gold and mineral reserves, these coal deposits lie under some of the world's last remaining frontier forests. Jakarta plans to dramatically increase production from 22.5 million tons in 1992 to 80 million tons by the year 2000. That would be enough coal to fill a line of dump trucks 66 miles long each day.

## Liquidating the Forest

Deforestation of the country's vast rainforests spurs more conflict and controversy than any other development practice of the Soeharto regime. Some 60 million people depend on Indonesia's forests for their survival. According to the Indonesian forest ministry, around 22 million of those people are small-scale slash-and-burn cultivators engaged in long-term rotational farming, a practice that has been sustainable for thousands of years. Yet since 1967 the base of their livelihood has declined at a precipitous rate. In 1950 the country had an estimated 152 million hectares of forest; by 1993 that number had dropped to approximately 92 million hectares. Deforestation rates have reached up to 1.3 million hectares annually. The World Bank estimates current rates of "harvest" to be between 50 and 100 percent higher than can be sustained. And WALHI reports that those rates have continued to increase.

Indonesian timber companies are notoriously inefficient and wasteful, says the World Resources Institute's Charles Barber. Damage to saplings is rampant, and selective cutting guidelines are ignored. Large government subsidies in some cases allow timber companies to convert their degraded concessions to tree plantations, negating any incentive for long-term forest management. In other cases, logging roads lay ecosystems open to migrant farmers, who move in behind the loggers and halt forest regeneration.

Because so much of Indonesia is cloaked in forest, nearly 74 percent of its land is under the jurisdiction of the Ministry of Forestry. The ministry has bestowed logging contracts on just a few politically connected players. In 1995 there were 584 logging contracts in the country covering about 65 million hectares, but that number is misleading. About 50 corporate groups control these concessions and dominate the sector. And these conglomerates are in the hands of just 35 players, according to Mark Poffenberger. "What began as political patronage," says American University Professor Robin Broad, "has metamorphosed into a dense web of connections . . . among an undemocratic government, the military, and business leaders who scratch each other's back for their mutual benefit at the expense of the forest and the public."

The Ministry of Forestry is unable to adequately monitor concessions and enforce those regulations that do exist, often allowing companies to avoid royalty payments to the state outright. Across Indonesia there is only one forest ministry employee for every 127,100 hectares of forest. And companies rarely limit logging to within the boundaries of their concessions.

APKINDO, Indonesia's powerful plywood cartel, for years has been able to stave off attempts by the forest ministry to raise royalties. The cartel, which controls three-quarters of the world's plywood exports, has used its political pull to avoid paying an estimated $500 million per year in royalties that could have gone into the public treasury. APKINDO is headed by Bob Hasan, who controls 2 million hectares of forest concessions.

Even the royalties that are collected have been frequently misused. When last year's fires in Kalimantan and Sumatra spread out of control, environmentalists accused Indonesia of doing too little to combat the problem. The fires spread to more than 2 million hectares, causing an estimated $1.4 billion in damages.[13] When IMF director Michel Camdessus looked into the country's finances earlier this year, he found that the country's multi-billion dollar reforestation fund, collected from taxes on timber, had not been spent to fight the fires or to set up better anti-fire defenses. "When we asked why the money had not been spent," he said, "we were told it was because it had been set aside for the project to create a national car."

Forest destruction is tied up so completely in this system of patronage that local communities and even government officials are often powerless to stop it. For example, Prajogo Pangestu, who has ties to Soeharto's second son, Bambang Trihatmodjo, by the early 1990s had accumulated 5.5 million

---

12. In late 1996, the sub-district of Timika, where the mine is located, was the most heavily militarized area in all of Indonesia.

13. Owing to a nationwide drought and a premature end of the monsoon season, forest fires in Indonesia have flared up again and "are threatening a bigger crisis than last year," according to the *Sydney Morning Herald*. Conditions are similar to those in 1982–83, when the largest fire in the world's recorded history burned more than 3 million hectares in Kalimantan.

# Unrest in Indonesia

At the heart of much of the turmoil in the country today, especially in these "hotspots," stand decades-old tensions over sovereignty, human rights, and the environment.

◆ **Aceh:** In the strongly Muslim province of Aceh, which is rich in oil and natural gas, more than 2,000 Acehnese have been killed by the military since 1989. Many similarities can be drawn between Aceh and Nigeria's Ogoniland, where human rights activist Ken Saro-Wiwa was executed for leading resistance to environmental destruction of his homeland, says exiled Indonesia scholar George Aditjondro. "Popular support for independence has been fuelled in recent years by resentment over the unequal benefits of industrial development in the area, and a perceived lack of respect for local custom and religion by central government and military authorities, and economic migrants," reports Amnesty International.

hectares in forest concessions—an area of land larger than Denmark and valued at more than $5 billion. In 1991, the forest ministry fined Prajogo's Barito Pacific Group $5 million for extensive timber operation violations. But when Barito refused to pay, the case was dropped. It may not be coincidence that Prajogo had just paid $220 million to bail out one of Soeharto's troubled banks.

"How long Indonesia's political hierarchy will allow the interest of 35 'timber kings' to take precedence over the livelihood requirements of one-third of the nation's population remains to be seen," writes Poffenberger.

## Developing a History

To give Soeharto his due, when he first came to power the situation in Indonesia was dire, and the need for some measure

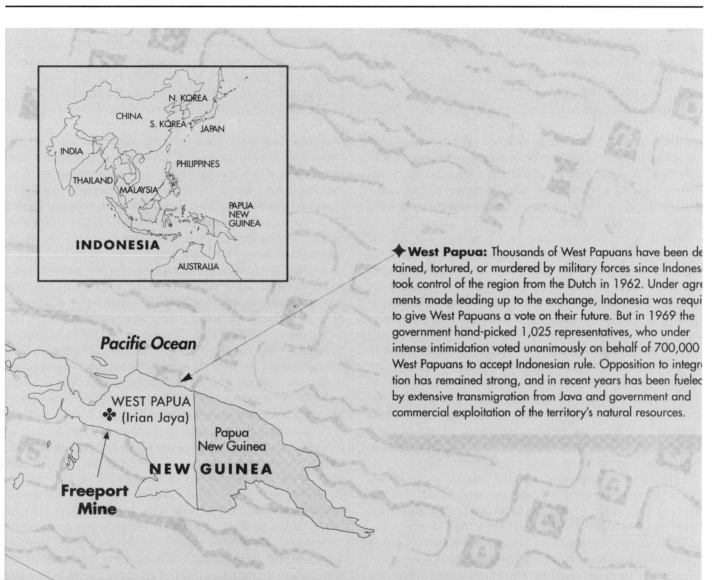

INDONESIA

N. KOREA
CHINA
S. KOREA
JAPAN
INDIA
PHILIPPINES
THAILAND
MALAYSIA
PAPUA
NEW
GUINEA
AUSTRALIA

Pacific Ocean

WEST PAPUA
(Irian Jaya)

Papua
New Guinea

NEW GUINEA

Freeport
Mine

**◆ West Papua:** Thousands of West Papuans have been de tained, tortured, or murdered by military forces since Indonesi took control of the region from the Dutch in 1962. Under agre ments made leading up to the exchange, Indonesia was requi to give West Papuans a vote on their future. But in 1969 the government hand-picked 1,025 representatives, who under intense intimidation voted unanimously on behalf of 700,000 West Papuans to accept Indonesian rule. Opposition to integr tion has remained strong, and in recent years has been fuelec by extensive transmigration from Java and government and commercial exploitation of the territory's natural resources.

**◆ East Timor:** A month after declaring independence from Portugal in November 1975, East Timor was invaded by Indonesia. Fierce resistance stifled Indonesia's hope of a quick takeover. Years of brutal occupation ensued and the costs were high: by 1980 an estimated 200,000 Timorese—nearly a third of the country's popu- lation—had died. While the UN does not recognize Indonesia's claim to East Timor, the military maintains heavy-handed control: in 1991, Indonesian troops opened fire on several thousand peaceful demonstrators in the capital city of Dili, killing at least 50. In December 1996, exiled resistance leader José Ramos Horta and Catholic Bishop Carlos Felipe Belo were awarded the Nobel Peace Prize. "Accounts of Indonesia's behavior in East Timor suggest that the plight of these people may well constitute, relatively speaking, the most serious case of contravention of human rights facing the world at this time," writes journalist Adam Schwarz.

of development was unarguable. Life expectancy in 1960 was just 41 years; infant mortality was 225 per 1,000 live births (compared with 125 for East Asia as a whole); and 64 percent of adults couldn't read. Soeharto's early development strategy called for intensive extraction and export of natural re- sources—not inconsistent with the strategies being promoted by the World Bank throughout the developing world. Under

Sukarno, the export of raw materials had been nearly non-ex- istent. But by 1970, about 60 percent of the country's GDP came from extracting and exporting natural resources.

Primary commodity extraction provided an economic boost for the country, and the government invested revenues from vast oil and timber supplies into the expansion of agriculture and infrastructure, such as schools and clinics. Manufacturing and other sectors have made large inroads, but resource extraction's share of the GDP remains around 40 percent—still a significant share. In addition, the absolute value of resources extracted annually in the 1990s has more than doubled the value extracted in 1970.

Government statistics indicate that under the New Order, the average Indonesian's standard of living has improved substantially: along with the aforementioned improvements in income and literacy, family planning programs have helped to curb runaway population growth, and the economy has grown at three times the world average. Life expectancy had increased to 61 years by 1990, and infant mortality had dropped from 225 to 64 per 1,000 deaths.

But as noted, some of these indicators may not tell the whole story. To begin with, several experts have cautioned that the figures compiled by the Soeharto government are self-serving. The number of Indonesians still living in "absolute" poverty, says the Indonesian Legal Aid Foundation's Hamzah, is considerably higher than the World Bank's estimate of 15 percent. "The World Bank's original figure was more than two times higher," according to Northwestern University's Jeffrey Winters. In reality, suggests one expert, 50 to 70 percent—the majority of the people—are still very poor. Moreover, conditions were so poor in 1960 that any improvement looks dramatic even when conditions are still substandard by world standards. Problems can only be expected to worsen as Indonesia's population is projected to increase to 250 million in the next two decades.

Even taken at face value, national data mask serious regional injustices between Java and the outer islands. Income levels in Jakarta are triple the national levels.[14] Cultural anthropologist Lorraine Aragon observes: "The Indonesian national development program is founded on, and literally fueled by, regional inequities that often entail the rapid debasement of ancestral lands occupied by ethnic minorities who reside on the less populated 'outer islands' of the archipelago."

For example, Indonesian military police arrested more than 60 small-scale farmers last year for setting fires that contributed to the blazes the ultimately ravaged 2 million hectares in Kalimantan, Sumatra, and Sulawesi, and threatened the health of tens of thousands of people. Satellite images revealed, however, that 80 percent of the fires began on timber and palm-oil plantations controlled by a few politically connected growers and timber barons. The growers, taking advantage of dry conditions in the normally saturated rainforests, were trying to clear as much land as possible for future plantations.

While Soeharto was compelled to apologize for the choking smoke that engulfed the region for several months, owners of large plantations escaped sanctions. Rural communities, however, were left to face both the political and environmental fallout of the fires—in October Indonesia's information ministry forbade the country's newspapers to point to connections between the plantations and the fires. In effect, small-scale farmers and shifting cultivators became the scapegoats.

The marginalization of communities on the outer islands has become commonplace: logging companies, mining operations, and large-scale palm and rice plantations are routinely allowed to develop the land of local people, displacing native inhabitants. While Indonesian law claims to respect *adat,* or traditional land tenure, indigenous communities have little guarantee that their lands will not be developed out from under them. Across Kalimantan more than 2.5 million indigenous peoples were displaced or resettled during the 1970s due to logging and other activities. And logging has likely tripled since then. "Indonesia is no exception to the general rule," writes Aragon, "that a state's economic development most adversely affects the environment and human rights of its marginal populations, particularly its ethnic minority groups."

By the mid-1980s, with the help of a $500 million loan from the World Bank, the government had moved more than 3.6 million people from the densely populated island of Java to the outer islands. Half of the area settled was virgin forest, and most of that was land occupied by indigenous peoples.[15] Moreover, for every official migrant, there were two unofficial ones, according to the World Bank's own assessment.

This "transmigration" program, officially established to alleviate population pressures, has primarily served as another form of internal colonialism—a means of separating the indigenous cultures from their lands and resources, and an attempt to bring together the country's disparate native cultures into a "developed" society. "Using Javanese culture as a tool for political and cultural engineering, the New Order government seeks to assimilate and unify the varying cultures of Indonesia into a single way of life," according to the Indonesian forest conservation network SKEPHI.

These transmigrant projects have increased poverty for both host communities and migrants, and worsened ecological destruction. In his explication of World Bank-funded projects, Bruce Rich, an attorney and development expert at the Environmental Defense Fund, estimates that as much as 4 percent of the country's forests—3.7 million hectares—have been felled to make way for transmigrants and their farming attempts. The forest soils of the outer islands are nutrient-poor, and the monsoon climate renders them highly vulnerable to erosion and depletion from runoff if they are opened up to large plantations; they hold up much more sustainably under traditional methods of rotational, small-scale farming, the variety that is being pushed out.

14. Michael Shari and Mark Clifford, "Suharto Capitalism," *Business Week,* 16 June 1997.

15. Indonesia's Department of Transmigration and Resettlement of Forest Dwellers plans to relocate a total of 65 million people, although the program's past efforts have done little to alleviate population pressures on Java.

These poorly planned resettlement sites, more often than not, have turned out to be the sites of "environmental calamities of biblical proportions," writes Rich. Using traditional agricultural methods on "some of the poorest soils on earth," transmigrants have been beset by paltry crop yields, flooding, and plagues of insects, rats, and wild boars. According to Rich, "in wetland and swamp areas, 40 to 50 percent of the settlers simply abandoned the sites." Moreover, the transmigration

scheme has done little to alleviate population pressures in Java, and has managed to simply redistribute poverty.

## Growing Pressure for Change

A reporter for the Jakarta newspaper *Sinar Pagi* was found stabbed to death in the back seat of his car in West Kalimantan in July 1997. Police called the incident a traffic accident. They

# Another Time, Another World

This map of the islands that now form Indonesia was published in 1940, one year before the Japanese attack on Pearl Harbor, as part of a "War Supplement" to *Compton's Pictured Encyclopedia*. The map's purpose was to show the loci of likely warfare in the Pacific during the early years of World War II, and the "radii of effective action" of Great Britain, the United States, and Japan.

Today, the names on this map serve as a reminder of how recently the age of imperialism came to a close. Australia, Papua New Guinea, Burma, Malaysia, and Singapore are all shown as occupied by the British Empire; today's Vietnam, Laos, and Cambodia are occupied by France; the Philippines is occupied by the United States; and Indonesia is occupied by The Netherlands.

One of the millions of Asians living under European rule during this time was the young Soeharto, who spent his first years of adulthood observing first-hand how colonialism works: how people and resources can be exploited to generate political control, and how political power can be backed by military force. More than half a century later, his own regime's control of the "outer islands" of Indonesia appears in many ways to be a direct heritage of the combination of benign dictatorship and resource-exploitation that marked Dutch rule in his formative years.

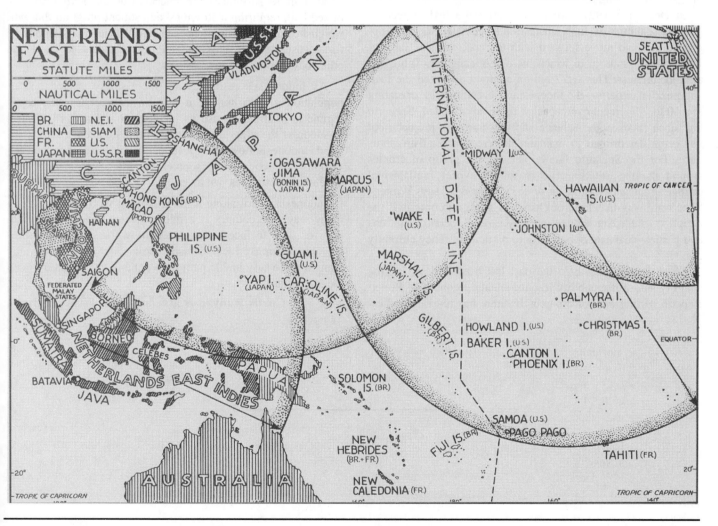

made no link between his death and a story he had written a short time earlier that exposed a timber-smuggling racket in the province. While this may be an extreme case, heavy-handed control of the media is not uncommon in Indonesia.

The government first cracked down on the press following critical reports of riots in 1974. Security forces shut down twelve publications and arrested several journalists. Many more papers have been shut down since then, and the common theme in each case, writes Schwarz, "was that the offending publications were considered destabilizing and harmful to development." While today the government makes no clear statements about what can or can't be discussed, the possibility of harsh reprisals is often enough to make publications censor themselves.

Under Soeharto's rigid style of development, the government accepts little criticism and is increasingly unable to cope with new challenges. The limitations placed on Indonesia's civil society—a heavily censored press, little regard for indigenous rights, a corrupt legal system, a ban on labor unions and strikes, restrictions on the ability to assemble, and an increasingly degraded environment—have given many citizens the sense that they have little control and are somehow spectators in their own country.

In December 1997, two months after the IMF agreed to give the country its first financial-aid package, Soeharto approved plans to move forward with the controversial Tanjung Jati C power station, in which his oldest daughter, Tutut, has a major interest. The $1.77 billion contract alienated the IMF and puzzled experts—the Indonesian electricity grid, operating at a 60 to 70 percent overcapacity, is already flooded. Soeharto has since revoked the scheme and other similar projects, but he seems determined to maintain the crony-capitalism status quo. "For the Soeharto family, and for the group of cronies around them . . . there is no reason to expect fundamental change in the way business is done in Indonesia," says Winters. "The only way that kind of change is going to come is if the people of Indonesia—represented by various social institutions and parties—have an opportunity to participate. They currently don't."

Much of the growth in the past has been hollow, lacking stability and sustainability. Environmental economist Robert Repetto of the World Resources Institute has re-examined estimates of the country's past 8- to 10-percent growth rates. Taking into account the degradation of the country's natural resources—forests, oil, and soil—actual growth rates have been nearer to 4 percent a year, he concluded. Similarly, if the New Order's corrupt political and economic system and its practice of stifling its citizens' freedoms and are considered, the country's past years of intense growth seem at the very least misguided.

Indonesia is at a crossroads. The economic collapse has given critics, activists, and ordinary citizens a renewed voice, a more attentive international audience, and a platform for unprecedented attacks on Soeharto's legitimacy. In growing numbers, students, activists, and Muslim and democratic leaders, among others, have begun to call for serious reform. Indonesians are planting the seeds of change. While Soeharto and the IMF spar over reforms to revamp the country's economy, the Indonesian people are in the thro[e]s of a battle to determine whether they will have a more equitable and sustainable future. The IMF-led economic bailout is one piece of a puzzle. Loan provisions that require economic transparency—aimed at breaking up huge monopolies and cartels, and curtailing corruption and nepotism—are among the first steps needed to build a more sustainable Indonesia. But the IMF deal is a mixed bag, requiring a structural adjustment program that will weigh heavily on those who can least afford it by imposing fiscal austerity measures and cutting subsidies on food and other basic commodities.

As Indonesia's resources are increasingly eroded and as population growth surges, it will be difficult for Soeharto's regime to continue to use its ideological and military control to suppress the pressures building throughout the country. Instead, Indonesia now faces a fundamental choice between developing the country's resources *in spite of* its people, and developing resources *for* its people.

Indonesia is not alone in its reckoning with this choice. In many ways the country is a microcosm of the problems facing—or soon to face—the rest of the world. Many countries are approaching critical decision points; whether to develop along a more sustainable path or to gamble on continuing with the status quo.

**Curtis Runyan** is assistant editor of *World Watch*.

*Article 22*                    *THE ECONOMIST,* July 26th, 1997

# Not fair

## Indonesia feels more unequal than it is

THE tarmac road peters out more than a mile before you reach the village of Rowok, on the southern coast of the island of Lombok, just east of Bali. A bumpy dirt track leads through a lush valley to the foot of the hills and the village itself—or what is left of it. About 40 people are squatting there. Their houses are small and makeshift, built on the packed-earth foundations of what used to be more permanent dwellings. In one house a desperately thin man, nursing a baby with a nasty rash on her face, describes the raid in March last year when several hundred policemen and soldiers descended on Rowok at first light. They burned the houses or pulled them down, shot the chickens, looted the rice, and badly beat some of the villagers. About 400 had to leave, destitute. They could blame their fate on the nearby beach—a spectacular stretch of virgin sand and shingle with towering breakers and a backdrop of magically beautiful islands. It will make a lovely spot for a hotel.

Among those who have noticed this is a consortium of developers including a company owned by a relative of President Suharto and the son of the local provincial governor. The villagers were in the way, and they had no legal title to their land, which belongs to the government. They complain they were encouraged to settle there 12 years ago, after being displaced elsewhere; they want compensation.

Under Indonesia's arcane system of land tenure, disputes between local residents, and between locals and developers, are commonplace. What sets the Rowok villagers apart is their association with a local lawyer, Gusti Putu Ekadana. For months he offered shelter to some of the evacuees, fed them, paid the medical expenses of the injured, and took up their case. About four months ago, he told some of them to go home, to show they had not abandoned their claim. So there they are, waiting for the next raid, eking a living from fishing, planting a few vegetables, and selling long grass for thatch.

Ekadana is not exactly a liberal bleeding heart. He is the head of the local branch of Pemuda Pancasila, a youth organisation named after Indonesia's national ideology, which in other places has a reputation for semi-licensed thuggery. Indeed, Ekadana's secretary likes to boast that his boss used to be a gangster. The man himself demurs, describing himself more as a local Robin Hood figure, who has risen out of poverty.

One young Rowok man greets visitors with a clenched fist and a cry of "*Pancasila!*". In last month's elections he and his friends all voted for Golkar, the government party. But he says he is ready to fight, even to die, to defend his home, his rights and the freedom and justice *pancasila* is supposed to represent. He speaks not in Indonesian, in which he is not fluent, but in the language of the majority ethnic group in Lombok, Sasak.

As elsewhere, social tension is compounded at times by racial animosity, felt by some Muslim Sasaks towards the small Chinese minority, and the Hindu Balinese population. Even if the anger of the Rowok villagers is expressed as support for the government's own ideology, its intensity is worrying for authorities. These people, and millions of disgruntled outsiders like them, pose as much of a threat to stability as organised political opposition.

### Crumbs from rich men's tables

Lombok has fine beaches, beautiful coral, the highest mountain in the region, a benign climate and ambitions to become rich through tourism like its neighbour Bali. Seven areas of the island have been parcelled off as tourism-development zones. One company with big planned investments in the island is Rajawali, part of Bambang Suharto's Bimantara group. Already, parts of the island have a large tourist industry, and villagers have left their homes to make way for new hotels and a planned new airport. But Lombok remains one of the poorest areas of Indonesia, and locals worry that development will not benefit them. They complain that the smart new hotels import their smiling staff from Bali, rather than recruit on the spot.

Local people are well aware of the involvement of well-connected businessmen in the new hotels. When analysts in Jakarta worry about the social consequences of Indonesia's "wealth gap", it is those sorts of people they have in mind. In fact, according to studies undertaken by the World Bank, economic growth, far from widening inequality, has reduced the gap between rich and poor within and between provinces, as well as lifting millions above the poverty line. By conventional measures—comparing the incomes of the richest and the poorest fifth of the population—Indonesia is less unequal than Malaysia, Thailand and the Philippines. And, with the exception of Jakarta and the oil-and-gold-producing provinces, GDP per head is fairly similar across the archipelago.

But that is not the way it feels in Rowok or, indeed, in most places in Indonesia. Even in Jakarta, slums nestle just behind the towering skyscrapers and designer boutiques of the central business district. Many people believe that the new wealth is benefiting only small groups of people—especially those with good government connections, and the Chinese. Far more than racism or Islamic fervour, that explains the riots and their targets.

It is not a "wealth gap" so much as a "justice gap" that people object to. As in other rapidly industrialising countries, economic change is undermining traditional society. The village community used to afford a degree of protection. Now people have to rely more on formal legal and political systems, which are seen as hopelessly biased in favour of the rich and powerful. And the education system, which should offer a channel for social advancement, is seen as failing in that job.

### Beyond literacy

One of the New Order's greatest achievements has been to spread basic education. In 1973, just 60% of Indonesia's children attended primary school. Now enrolment is nearly universal. The illiteracy rate has dropped from 43% of the adult

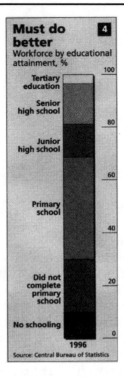

**Must do better** 4

Workforce by educational attainment, %

- Tertiary education
- Senior high school
- Junior high school
- Primary school
- Did not complete primary school
- No schooling

1996
Source: Central Bureau of Statistics

population in the 1970s to 15% now. But the quality of much education is felt to be poor. Comparative studies suggest that reading ability among schoolchildren is much lower than in, for example, Thailand. And nearly a third of all primary schoolchildren fail to graduate. As a result, the educational standard of the Indonesian workforce remains low (see chart). This is one of the biggest obstacles to attracting foreign investment and moving into more sophisticated products.

At the top end of the educational scale, the shortcomings are evident in the large numbers of foreign managers—often from the Philippines or India—working in Indonesian conglomerates. There are 52 state-run universities and 1,284 private ones, some of which are better at making money than at educating their students. Teachers are badly paid and lack motivation. Even people of moderate means scrimp to send their children overseas to be educated. Australia alone has about 15,000 Indonesian students. Thoby Mutis, of Trisakti, the largest private university and one of the most highly-regarded, blames the curriculum, which no longer suits the country's needs. Much of what is taught is still determined by the government, which he claims instils a "narrow nationalism". Another consequence has been monolingualism—which has boosted Malaysia, Singapore and the Philippines, where English is more widely spoken.

---

*Article 23*                                   *Z MAGAZINE,* July/August 1998

# The Korean Struggle

## Aftermath of the IMF takeover

### By James Crotty & Gary Dymski

Just a few months after getting a clean bill of economic health from the OECD in mid 1997, South Korea's economy plunged into a foreign exchange crisis. By December the Korean government had signed a loan agreement with the IMF. The severity of its terms were unprecedented. Koreans quickly spread the bitter joke that the IMF means "I Am Fired." Given the long tradition of labor and student militancy in Korea, and the election to the presidency just days later of populist Kim Dae Jung (who had called the IMF deal a "na-

tional humiliation"), it seemed likely that the virtual takeover of the Korean economy by the IMF would generate resentment and spark resistance in the new year.

But no such resistance appeared. A consensus quickly formed among the U.S., IMF, and Korean political and economic leadership that Korea must dismantle its long-admired model of state-led development, throwing open its borders to overseas goods and money and its asset and banking markets to overseas owners. An embittered, fatalistic acceptance of the inevitability of the Neoliberalization of the Korean economy seemed to infuse the national psyche. U.S. and IMF complicity in this externally imposed revolution was no surprise, but Kim Dae Jung's quick switch from an anti- to a pro-IMF position, which infuriated his labor supporters, certainly did. After all, the IMF program would mean economic collapse, mass layoffs, and a loss of economic sovereignty. Yet mass protests by workers and students did not take place, and by February Korea's crisis was pushed off the front pages of Western newspapers.

These events generated a number of questions in the minds of interested outside observers. Why did Kim Dae Jung suddenly change his view? Did most Koreans share his newfound enthusiasm for neoliberalism? Why were Korea's political leaders willing to walk away from their amazingly successful and longstanding development model and accept its replacement with a Neoliberal model that has brought disaster to labor and the majority of citizens wherever it has been implemented? Where was the expected mass resistance to the IMF takeover of Korea?

We spent the last two weeks of March in Korea at the invitation of Professor Kim Soo Haeng of Seoul National University, Korea's most respected progressive political economist. We had the opportunity to discuss these and other questions with an unusually broad array of Koreans from diverse social positions—top managers and officials in banking and industry, important government officials, leaders of the more militant of the two Korean labor federations, students, and academics. Days of discussion yielded some tentative answers to our questions.

An understanding of the Korean crisis requires historical perspective. For the past three and one-half decades the Korean economy has been organized according to the general principles of the so-called "East Asian economic model," an approach often referred to as state-led growth or the state-governed market economy. The Korean government provided temporary import protection for domestic markets introducing new products or technologies, focused the development of high tech production capabilities on a small number of diversified companies termed chaebol, coordinated chaebol investment decisions, allocated credit toward priority industries and technologies, and tightly regulated the cross border movement of money. At the same time, the government selectively opened markets to import competition and imposed export performance criteria in return for government aid to insure that key industries achieved world-class efficiency.

The Korean economic model has been astoundingly successful. Over the past 35 years it achieved an average annual rate of growth of both real per-person national income and real wages of about 7 percent while maintaining full employment and a relatively equal income distribution. Korea's success was so indisputable that it demonstrated to those not ideologically committed to Neoliberalism that there were practical, superior alternatives to the free market development model. Of course, much of Korea's growth took place under an authoritarian political system, but in 1987 long-term, heroic struggles by the militant Korean labor and student movements finally toppled the military regime that had ruled Korea off and on until that time.

The East Asia alternative development model has become increasingly important in the last 20 years as more and more countries adopted Neoliberal economic policies, sometimes willingly, more often under external pressure. Under the Neoliberal approach, resource allocation is left to the vagaries of market forces, domestic and international financial flows are unregulated, and foreign ownership of domestic assets is encouraged. These economic policies have created a world of globally mobile capital and disenfranchised governments. Most economies in Latin America, Africa, Eastern Europe, and the former Soviet Union have adopted "market-friendly" policies of this sort, and their people have suffered enormously as a result.

East Asia was the last important area of the globe to successfully resist the encroachment of the Neoliberal regime. Should the current crisis signal the end of this resistance, the effects on the people of Asia and, indeed, the rest of the world may be profound. In the stagnant world economy of the 1990s, East and South East Asia, constituting 25 percent of global GDP, have accounted for half of the growth of world GDP. Were Asia to now shift to the slow growth, high unemployment path of the rest of the Neoliberal world, no country could long escape the consequences.

What caused Korea to experience this system-shaking crisis? We posed this question to everyone we interviewed. The most common answer stressed internal problems—not pressure from the U.S. or IMF, pointing an accusing finger first at the chaebol, then the government. In the late 1980s and 1990s the chaebol began to make their presence felt in such up-scale global industries as semi-conductors and automobiles; Samsung, for example, became the world's largest chip-maker. By the early 1990s they believed they were positioned for a serious run at the U.S. and European consumer markets. The ambition of Korea's chaebol to become serious rivals to the most powerful Western and Japanese multinational corporations is thought by most Koreans to have begun the chain of events that terminated in the crisis of 1997.

To achieve their objectives the chaebol had to undertake major new investments in Korea and elsewhere that were so large they could not be financed through profits or equity issues. To help raise the needed funds, the chaebol successfully pressed the government to deregulate domestic financial markets, then proceeded to increase domestic borrowing dramatically. Of particular importance, the government licensed 24 new merchant banks between 1994 and 1996—some with substantial chaebol ownership interests, and in a shocking reversal of tradition, left these banks virtually unregulated. The chaebol also needed assured access to foreign markets, which led to a Korean bid to enter the OECD. The price of entry included a promise to accelerate the deregulation of cross border capital flows as well as domestic financial markets. This suited chaebol interests because their credit needs exceeded the capacity of domestic markets and Korea's interest rates were much higher than global rates. Once capital inflows were deregulated, short-term foreign money—especially bank loans—poured into the country. The new merchant banks proceeded to borrow heavily from foreign banks, relending most of the money to the chaebol. Total foreign bank loans doubled from 1994 to 1997 to about $120 billion, an astounding 60 percent of which had to be repaid within one year.

The stage was now set for the outbreak of a financial crisis. The chaebol had financed a risky long-term capital boom primarily with short-term loans, a large part of which were in foreign currency. Any set of events which led to chaebol profit problems and\or disappointing export earnings—an overvalued won, sluggish export markets, rising foreign interest rats, or a domestic recession—would lead to delayed interest payments and eventually to defaults on foreign loans, triggering a run on the won, a collapse of the Korean stock market, and a mass refusal by foreign banks to roll their loans over.

The government helped them do it. In contrast to the near universal opinion expressed in the Western press, most Koreans correctly understand that their crisis was not caused by too much government regulation, but by too little. It was excessive liberalization, not the traditional East Asia model that failed.

As the Korean financial situation deteriorated, Koreans prepared to vote for a new president. Kim Dae Jung's fortunes rose as he attacked the IMF in public forums. But just days before the election the U.S. and IMF threatened to create economic chaos in Korea unless all three presidential candidates vowed their commitment to an IMF agreement over which two of them had no control and whose provisions they did not even understand. They all capitulated to this extortion. Following his election and thereafter, Kim consistently argued that IMF-mandated neoliberal restructuring would be the salvation of the Korean economy. This position reflected a theme Kim has stressed for 30 years—to break the power of the families who own the chaebol and end their repressive alliance with authoritarian Korean governments, it is necessary to liberalize Korean markets. Kim believed that chaebol domination of the economy, government, and even civil society was the deep seated cause of Korea's current crisis. Most academics, students, government officials, and bankers we talked with echoed this theme—everyone in Korea, we discovered, hates the chaebol.

We were stunned to learn that even many progressive Koreans welcomed IMF intervention, believing it would provide them with weapons they could use to bring about the downfall of the chaebol and the disciplining of the government. They hoped that increased foreign ownership of Korean firms and banks and the breakup of the chaebol empires would drastically reduce the concentration of economic and political power in Korea. As economic power became more dispersed, they argued, labor would become stronger and the government more amenable to democratic control. Meanwhile, the entry of foreign banks and Western banking standards would end the wholesale abuse of the banking system that characterized the mid 1990s.

Conversations with representatives of the chaebol revealed a different perspective on the origins of the crisis. They trace Korea's current problems back to the political struggles that

culminated with the end of the military dictatorship in 1987. In the chaebol's view, labor used the increased power gained through these struggles to obtain real wage gains that exceeded productivity growth, causing a secular crisis of profitability and international competitiveness for the chaebol and thus for the Korean economy. And the government's power to regulate chaebol activity hindered their attempts to respond to this profit crisis. The chaebol were thus forced to undertake their overly ambitious capital accumulation program of the mid 1990s and attack government regulation of financial markets. They sought lower costs by shifting operations overseas and adopting advanced, often labor-saving, technology at home. As the chaebol see it, then, the long-standing conflict between Korean capital and labor was the most deep-seated cause of the current crisis.

These same conversations unearthed an incredible irony: like the progressive academics we spoke with, the chaebol believe they can use the provisions of the IMF agreement to defeat their internal enemies—labor and the government.

The IMF agreement has a number of key demands with profound consequences for the Korean economy: austerity macro policy, very high interest rates plus restrictive fiscal policy, which will cause recession, raise unemployment, and force a tidal wave of bankruptcies, especially among small and medium businesses; the imposition of stringent banking regulations in a financial crisis, when most banks cannot possibly meet them, forcing both bank failures and a drying up of credit for Korea's beleaguered businesses; labor law "reform" which, for the first time, will allow firms to fire workers at will; the removal of all restrictions on foreign ownership of Korean firms and banks; the elimination of restrictions on imports (including Japanese cars, a provision the chaebol fear); and the elimination of all forms of government influence over both domestic and international capital flows, including even the short-term capital inflows that led to the current crisis.

Credit starvation and high interest rates have already launched a self-feeding cycle of bankruptcies, bank failures, declining production, and rising unemployment, which is expected to reach at least 10 percent and perhaps 15 percent or more—in an economy with the flimsiest of social safety nets. The chaebol (as well as foreign investors) expect labor law "reform" and massive unemployment to smash the union movement, while other structural changes will eliminate the government's ability to regulate the private sector. Accelerated liberalization will assure free access to global capital and credit markets. In addition, chaebol family personal wealth will now be free to roam the world in search of high returns. It is thus easy to see why the chaebol see the IMF as their ally. And chaebol support for much of the IMF program in turn helps explain why the Korean government offered so little resistance to its harsh terms.

But though they will terrorize labor, defang the government, and demoralize the people, the IMF agreement will not assure victory to the chaebol. The chaebol are weak and over indebted, even their trading capacity is severely compromised by a lack of credit. They are in desperate need of financial assistance from foreign companies and foreign banks, forced to offer their assets at fire sale prices to others much bigger and more powerful. It is unlikely they will be able to gain the financial support they desperately need without losing control of their empires to their foreign rivals.

But the likelihood that the people can use the IMF to obtain their objectives is smaller yet. The IMF agreement is designed to permanently destroy the institutional foundations of the Korean developmental model—that "East Asian" mix of government strategic planning, industrial ingenuity, high productivity growth, and worker security that spread prosperity so widely across Korea. Regulation through market whimsy, footloose relations between industry and workers, high unemployment, rising inequality, and labor insecurity will become the new norms in Korea, as they are in the rest of the neoliberal world. Many Koreans with whom we spoke held out hope that after the IMF program had reduced the power of the chaebol and the government, they could proceed to reconstruct an even better "East Asian" economy reflecting deep-seated Korean values such as community and labor solidarity. When pressed, however, no one could explain to us how this could be done when foreigners controlled their firms and banks, their economy was fully open to global forces, and the government had been stripped of all power to regulate the economy.

The only people we spoke to who fully appreciated the severity of the threat to the Korean economy posed by the IMF agreement were labor union representatives. They understood that the preservation of Korea's development path would require a fierce and prolonged fight to resist full and permanent implementation of the IMF program. They were preparing for a sustained period of massive and disciplined social protest against the IMF and all the external and internal forces supporting it. At the time of our visit, however, no significant public opposition to the agreement had yet taken place. Confusion, fatalism, passivity and the false hope that the IMF could be used to win domestic battles ruled the day. But as the damage caused by the agreement increases, with unemployment and bankruptcies setting new records with each passing month, the preconditions required for the organization of a mass protest movement are in the process of creation.

There are indications that serious resistance has started. Lee Kap Yong, the newly elected head of the militant Korean Confederation of Trade Unions (KCTU), threatened massive strikes in late May or June to prevent the chaebol's planned massive layoffs (estimated to be at least 500,000 or one-third of their work force). Since his election was understood to be a repudiation by the rank and file of their former leaders for accepting February's labor law "reform," Lee immediately demanded that Kim Dae Jung negotiate a new, more worker-friendly, labor law. This demand, which has the support of the larger, less militant union federation, infuriated Kim, the chaebol, foreign investors, and the IMF. Hyundai Motors union leaders threatened to strike if the company attempted to carry out its layoff plans. Large numbers of unemployed demonstrated in Seoul and Pusan in April; and while the government declared unions of unemployed workers illegal in March, People's Victory 21, a political organization affiliated with the KCTU, organized a national alliance of the unemployed. And 22,000 demonstrators organized by the KCTU gathered in Seoul on May Day to protest the IMF program and the government's role in its implementation. The government reacted to this renewed popular resistance with repressive tactics familiar from the days before Korea's democracy was secured, threatening resistors with imprisonment.

The problem facing the militant labor union movement, the only force presently capable of organizing an effective protest movement, is if they fail to effectively resist the mass layoffs which the chaebol say will begin shortly, they will be severely weakened, perhaps destroyed. But successful resistance to such powerful adversaries in these dangerous conditions will require the creation of a united coalition linking the majority of workers and students, one that has the sympathy of the broad middle class. Unfortunately, the creation of such a coalition may take more time to secure than the unions have available to them. We can only hope that, as on so many occasions in their history, the Korean people will find the courage and strength needed to sustain themselves in this struggle, a struggle of monumental importance to the eventual outcome of the undeclared, ongoing global war between national autonomy, community, and worker security, on one hand, and the privileges and power of Neoliberal capital and global elites on the other.

*Article 24*                    *FAR EASTERN ECONOMIC REVIEW*, March 26, 1998

SOUTH KOREA

# Unlocking The Citadel

President Kim Dae Jung is convinced that opening to the world is the only way to save his country's economy. Now he has to convince the South Korean people.

**By Shim Jae Hoon and Charles S. Lee in Seoul**

In the hip Myong-dong area of downtown Seoul, the narrow streets are packed with Western stores and the signboards climb three or four storeys high. But if you want to grab a bite at American-style eatery T.G.I. Friday's, a curious notice greets you at the entrance. "T.G.I.F. is 100% domestic capital," it says. "We get 90% of our ingredients locally." T.G.I.F. isn't the only one trumpeting its Made-in-Korea credentials. At quintessentially American KFC, a sign next to founder Colonel Sanders' statue announces that the finger-licken' chicken served is 100% homegrown.

Asked why foreign labels have gone from chic to shunned in Myong-dong, President Kim Dae Jung seems surprised. He turns to his aides and asks: "Is this true?" He then replies that such attitudes are out of date and starting to change. After all, he says, "capital doesn't have nationality. A foreign company investing money in Korea becomes a Korean company."

Words like those have won the newly minted South Korean leader many new admirers among foreign investors, who once doubted the longtime opposition chief's free-market credentials. Kim realizes that in order to survive, his troubled nation needs to complete its integration into the world economy by welcoming even more foreign businesses at home. At stake is nothing less than the future of the country, which is facing the worst economic crisis of its postwar history.

A cartoon in the *Munhwa Ilbo* underscores Korean fears that the country will be crushed by hostile mergers and acquisitions.

If Kim succeeds, it will be a watershed for South Korea: Freed of isolationism, the country will resume its transformation into a powerhouse of the East. But if nationalism prevails, it could become an also-ran economy. Several years from now, it might badly trail the likes of China, Taiwan and perhaps even Malaysia.

The fear is not unfounded: A yawning gap exists between President Kim's cosmopolitan views and those of many South Koreans, who see globalization as a one-way street favouring South Korean exports and brand names abroad. They also equate foreign ownership of

local businesses and land with colonial control. When the International Monetary Fund first introduced its shock therapy in early December, most South Koreans wanted to shoot the messenger. The initials IMF immediately became a byword for economic disaster. People talked of "the IMF crisis" and "overcoming the IMF," as if the multilateral agency was responsible for the country's troubles. In a display of black humour, IMF even became an acronym for "I'M Fired."

Fortunately for foreign investors, xenophobic nationalism at least does not seem to be rampant. Even the early wave of finger-pointing never degenerated into outright violence against foreigners, thanks in part to Kim's forthright admission of South Korea's own mistakes.

Indeed, thinking South Koreans see the logic in—and necessity for—opening up to foreign business, management and dollars. Most incidents of hostility towards the outside world tend to spring from emotion, rather than logic. A surly Seoul taxi driver, for example, told his passenger, a European diplomat talking to Korean companions, to "shut up." The driver said hearing foreign languages gave him a headache.

The more common anti-foreign reaction, however, has been directed at imported goods, under the guise of saving precious dollars. Students have staged public burnings of foreign goods and have vowed to boycott other imports. Vandalism of foreign cars has suddenly increased, and some owners complain that some petrol stations have refused service.

Patriotism in an age of globalization is particularly confusing for young Koreans. Han Dare, a 17-year-old pupil at Doksong Junior High School in Seoul, for example, sports a Reebok backpack and attends extracurricular classes in English to prepare herself, as she puts it, "for the global age." But she is determined not to eat at KFC. "We'd be wasting our dollars on foreign food. It can wait until our country is out of the IMF crisis," she says. At least 30% of youngsters surveyed by KFC said they avoided the fast-food chain for the same reason.

For the Korean economy to truly globalize, Kim must overturn the notion—deeply ingrained among not only ordinary Koreans but also bureaucrats and business groups—that keeping foreigners out as much as possible is good for Korea Inc. Already, Kim has instructed his administration officials to refrain from using "Buy Korean" rhetoric and has lectured the nation on television on how Toyota USA is more American than IBM Japan. But as the signs on stores and eateries such as T.G.I.F. show, changing this insular mindset promises to be much more difficult than cracking open the country's exclusive business system—itself no easy task.

The huge chaebols, or conglomerates, are debt-sodden, and the banks empty-pocketed, so there is a fighting chance for greater openness on that front. Indeed, bleeding domestic companies are redoubling their efforts to sell goods overseas and are shedding subsidiaries and real estate in the open market. But there are few domestic buyers rich enough to absorb them. The upshot: only foreign direct investors can fill the void.

Such realities, though, are slow to seep through into popular consciousness. One reason is Korea's long history of foreign invasions and of suffering inflicted by outsiders. Korean social commentators say this has bred a deep-seated, us-versus-them mentality. This way of looking at the world is captured in the Korean word *uri*, roughly translated as "we," "us" or "our."

The key to understanding the notion of uri is a shared experience of hardship and tribulations that is credited with

helping to preserve the Korean identity. In modern-day South Korea, uri has come to mean "our country first" and "foreigners have no business meddling in our business," says Lee Young Gil, a food-industry executive and part-time columnist. The same concept has been pushed to its logical extreme in North Korea in its state ideology of *juche,* or self-reliance.

For many Koreans, the wounds from the country's first attempt to open itself up to the world are painfully fresh. The

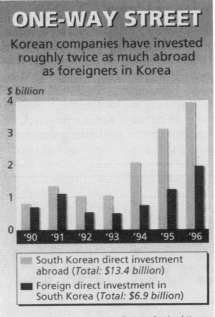

**ONE-WAY STREET**

Korean companies have invested roughly twice as much abroad as foreigners in Korea

- South Korean direct investment abroad (*Total: $13.4 billion*)
- Foreign direct investment in South Korea (*Total: $6.9 billion*)

*Source:* Bank of Korea

signing of the first international treaty in 1876 set in motion a chain of events that led to its outright annexation by Japan in 1910. Soon after, the Japanese colonialists began forcing Korean peasants to sell their land. By 1918, the Japanese owned 40% of Korea's entire land mass. An independent South Korea in 1948 enacted legislation banning ethnic-Chinese Koreans from owning farmland or properties. That law, though repeatedly revised since, still limits foreign ownership of land strictly to business purposes and requires elaborate approval procedures. As a result, a tiny 0.039% of national land belongs to foreigners.

Many intellectuals put the blame for the current crisis on the government's premature financial liberalization, which allowed the growth-fixated chaebols to borrow massively abroad. And many

Korean workers display contempt for Western managers; this extends even to Koreans working in foreign firms—some of the most uncompromising unions are found there. A typical attitude is that voiced by a Yonhap News Agency reporter: "Our media industry, for one, could be wiped out if we permit foreign investors into this area. I would never go to work for a foreign news agency. In fact, I regard those who do so as agents of foreign information imperialism."

Of course, this kind of nationalism isn't exclusive to Koreans. The Japanese suffer from it, even though they haven't had to endure decades of colonization as have Koreans. The Chinese have a bad case, as do people of many other countries. Indeed, the disease is widespread and usually becomes particularly virulent when economic conditions turn sour. In the case of South Korea, it has emerged due to a combination of the economic downturn, ethnic homogeneity and years of playing catch-up to the West and Japan.

For Kim and his internationalist-minded aides, the trick will be to keep up the momentum of reform. Now that the initial shock of crisis has started to wear off, opposition to his policies is likely to grow. "We have to keep the sense of urgency," says You Jong Keun, a trusted economic adviser to the president. "Only then will we maintain a unified purpose, which will act as a restraint against various interests."

Meanwhile, many foreign investors complain they are still getting tripped up by miles of bureaucratic red tape and an official attitude that seems indifferent to their investment concerns. In February, frustrated by Seoul's constantly shifting policies during two years of negotiations, Dow Corning of the U.S. opted to take a $2.8 billion silicone complex—what would have been the largest foreign project in South Korea—to Malaysia instead.

Notwithstanding Dow Corning's decision to take its money elsewhere, foreign companies continue to invest in South Korea. The rub is that they're not doing it as much as some South Koreans would like—especially in such desperate times. The reasons range from stricter due-diligence to debt levels of local firms. Anti-foreign sentiment is also partly responsible for potential investors deciding to take a wait-and-see stance, analysts says.

It's clear South Korea can't climb out of the deep hole it has dug itself into without looking outward. The IMF's bailout programme is already extending more than $57 billion towards helping ease a $187 billion overseas debt. Heeding the IMF's advice, Seoul has duly flung open the tightly shut doors of the domestic stock and bond markets. This is giving an impetus to foreign portfolio investment, and may also perk up foreign direct investment, which in recent years has amounted only to about half of what South Koreans invested abroad.

Both foreign investors and Kim Dae Jung want to speed up reform. This prompted the president to instruct his economic advisers on March 11 to scrap regulations on foreign land purchases and hostile foreign mergers and acquisitions. Attracting more foreign direct investment is a question of "national survival," he said.

A decision on land "is going to be fairly important," says John Seel, associate director at Bear Stearns Asia.

That's not because foreign business people are aching to become Korean landowners, but because permission to own property would "make people more willing to invest in other kinds of assets" that are sometimes backed by real-estate holdings. Seel believes foreign businesses are interested in the long-term prospects of investing in South Korea, and owning land there would provide "a form of security."

Whether South Koreans will take to heart the repeated exhortations from their leader to open up remains a question that defies simple answers. As South Korea stands at another crossroads in its history, profoundly conflicting impulses pull it simultaneously towards the past and the future. Even as conservative government mandarins call for a new exit tax for foreigners using the country's airports, Korea's powerful, nationalistic press is devoting more and more pages to the importance of becoming international. "In this age of globalization, insisting on only using our products can damage our national interest," wrote *Chosun Ilbo,* the largest national daily, in a February editorial. "No country will trade with us or lend us money if we only export our goods and refuse to use imported products."

Perhaps Kim's leadership will help Korea and Koreans to unlock the doors that confine them. His determination to build a national consensus for change and to push the country towards more openness seems sincere. And if the country's meteoric economic rise over the past 30 years is any guide, South Koreans are able to adapt remarkably fast to a challenge. "I'm a great believer in the power of necessity," says Kim Kyung Won, a former South Korean ambassador to the U.S. "When it becomes absolutely necessary to change, we'll change. The present crisis has helped to focus our minds and in this regard, it's a blessing in disguise."

*Article 25*

*FAR EASTERN ECONOMIC REVIEW,* May 9, 1996

# Between God And Mammon

In Malaysia, Muslims are learning to live in the modern world—and many like it.

By Simon Elegant

Kuala Lumpur's bustling Central Market is a magnet for young Malaysians. The huge barn-like space envelops a warren of stalls proffering trendy fripperies from batik scarves to instant antiques. Among the crowds of shoppers one afternoon, a knot of young girls stands out: dressed in almost complete *purdah*—dark blue or black head-to-toe robes and wimple—eyes downcast, they whisper to each other behind raised hands.

Then, as though in deliberate contrast, a looser group sways past, teenagers of both sexes, long hair swinging free, laughing and talking a little too loudly, uniformly dressed in tight jeans and T-shirts proclaiming their preference for heavy-metal bands like Iron Maiden and Black Sabbath.

Both groups of teenagers are ethnically Malay, and, by definition, Muslims. And to some Malaysians, a scene like the one in the market vividly illustrates the dire threat facing Islam in their country, a sign of the divisions in the Muslim community as it struggles to adapt to the enormous change that three decades of booming economic growth have wrought. For others, though, the existence of such side-by-side contradictions is powerful evidence that their religion is not only coping with the onslaught of the modern world, but that it is flourishing.

"Malaysia is on the cutting edge of the changes in the Islamic world," says Karim Raslan, a 30-something lawyer in Kaula Lumpur. "We are the most urbanized, the most industrialized Islamic country in the world. In Malaysia," Raslan concludes proudly, gesturing out his office window at Kaula Lumpur's bristling skyline, "Islam works."

In a quiet residential suburb just 16 kilometres from the city centre, a cracked and weather-beaten wooden sign bears the green and white colours of the Parti Islam Malaysia, or Pas. It carries much the same message, though with an entirely different meaning. *"Islam boleh,"* the relic of last year's general election proclaims, "Islam can."

To Nik Aziz Nik Mat, the party's senior leader and chief minister of the northeastern state of Kelantan, the slo-

# *All the Right Reasons*

In Bukit Tunku, one of Kuala Lumpur's most exclusive neighbourhoods, one group of buildings seems out of place amid the mix of colonial-era bungalows and more modern homes. A campus-like complex of vaguely Moorish design is the home of the Institute for Islamic Understanding. Ikim, as the institute is known, is a government-financed think-tank that seeks to meld Islam and the modern world.

Ikim also hopes to dispel the sneaking suspicion felt by some Muslims in Malaysia that aspects of the country's rapid growth have been at odds with their religion. "The trouble is that someone comes along and tells you that your ordinary life isn't enough to be a good Muslim," says social activist Chandra Muzaffar. "People

get a little uneasy when a preacher comes along and says, 'Here's chapter and verse.' They don't have the arguments at their fingertips to refute it and they become a little doubtful."

It is the institute's task to give those middle-of-the-road Muslims the arguments they need. One salient example is the acceptability or otherwise of Kuala Lumpur's roller-coaster stockmarket, where the line between investment and gambling is "as thin as an onion skin," according to Subky Latiff of the Islamic party, Pas.

Not surprisingly, Ismail Ibrahim, who heads the think-tank, doesn't see it that way. He points out that officials have already made numerous modifications to

Malaysia's financial system, to comply with the dictates of the Koran. They have, for example, introduced non-interest-bearing bank accounts and special Islamic banks, pawn shops and insurance companies. "Being a good Muslim doesn't mean you reject the entire financial system, just that you have to change or modify the existing system.

"Greed is not acceptable of course, but Islam doesn't oppose materialist ambition." Be it fundamentalism or greed, the soft-spoken Ismail concludes, "moderation is the most important criterion for a Muslim. We concentrate on educating people to be moderate."

■ **Simon Elegant**

gan's meaning is simple: Islam can thrive in the modern world without making any compromises. He does not hesitate to contrast his party's version of Islam with that of Prime Minister Mahathir Mohamad's ruling United Malays National Organization.

"Umno declares a policy based on secularism. We declare that our struggle is based on Islam," he says. "They will do anything and call it religion. This is just to get people to vote for them. If Pas didn't exist, I don't know what would happen to Islam in Malaysia."

Nik Aziz's party managed to win only seven seats in the federal parliament in last year's general elections. Pas did hang onto its power base in Kelantan, now the only opposition-controlled state assembly in the country. The victory there was mostly fuelled by regional loyalties, though, and most analysts would agree that the election was a signal that Muslims in Malaysia broadly prefer the secular, tolerant Islam of Mahathir and Umno to the stricter vision espoused by Pas and conservative *mullahs*.

For many Malaysians, it is axiomatic that the country's multi-ethnic society makes a Middle-Eastern style upsurge in fundamentalism unthinkable. "We've always been a crossroads. It forces people to deal with non-Muslims," says one Malay professional in Kuala Lumpur. "We can't huddle in exclusively Muslim groups."

"There's no way Pas' views will become ascendant in this country," agrees social activist and academic Chandra Muzaffar. "Unless there's massive corruption, and Umno becomes corrupt, but that's not happening now and probably never will."

And yet, for all the proudly touted benefits economic growth has brought, the sometimes wrenching changes that have accompanied the boom have sparked deep unease among many Muslims in the country. The erosion of traditional Malay *kampung* or village values through rapid urbanization, television and the consumerist mentality it brings have helped to spark a quiet but intense revival of interest in Islam among Malays.

"Twenty years ago, I was going to keep this as a museum piece to show my children," says Subky Abdul Latiff. Subky, a Pas council member and the party's spokesman in Kuala Lumpur, doffs his *kopiah*, a knitted white skull cap, and waves it to emphasize his point. "Now 80% of Muslims have a cap and wear it. Nobody asked them to do it, but they did it anyway. Moral people wear caps."

To many Malays, though, the issue is exactly who—and what—is moral. For Pas there is no question. In the past, the state government has attempted to change the state's penal code so that it would include such Islamic punishments as stoning for adultery and amputation

of hands for theft. The move—which would have required a change to Malaysia's constitution—was blocked by the federal government. On a smaller scale, the Pas government recently decided to enforce the segregation of sexes in supermarket checkout lines.

Seeking strict application of Islamic laws isn't confined to Pas-controlled Kelantan, either. Religious matters are under the control of Peninsular Malaysia's states, which enforce Islamic dictates with varying degrees of enthusiasm. In the southern state of Johor, which neighbours Singapore and chalks up the country's fastest growth rates, state religious authorities are attempting to institute public caning as a punishment for adultery.

All this profoundly alarms liberal Muslims such as Noraini Osman, a co-founder of a group of professional Malay women called Sisters in Islam. She laments what she sees as the instinctive attempt to apply brute force to address problems triggered up by the collision of Islam with the modern world.

"There's a fair amount of moral panic on their part from what they see in the streets," she says, speaking of traditionalist groups such as Pas and those among the country's Islamic teachers and scholars who press for the imposition of the harsher penalties the Koran prescribes. Noraini cities as an example the decision by the Pas government in Kelantan to bar women from working at night because of fears they might be assaulted. "You can't solve the problem by trying to control women, confining them and forcing them to conform. It's as though you were a doctor and you couldn't find the solution to a problem with a patient's leg so you decide to cut off the leg."

One group that seeks middle ground is the Malaysian Youth Movement, known by its Malay acronym, Abim. Current Deputy Prime Minister Anwar Ibrahim helped to found the group during the first flush of the Islamic resurgence in the 1970s. Its agenda includes educational programmes designed to help what Abim—and many Malaysians—see as the group most likely to come adrift from their Islamic moorings in the face of modern life: young Malays, many of them fresh from the kampungs, who come to the cities to work in factories.

"Factory workers lose their identity because of the pressure of industrialization," says Mohamad Nur Manuty, Abim's president. "It is not easy to bring them back." Abim relies on a combination of counselling, motivational talks and programmes, seeking to persuade rather than lecture, he says. "We have to offer them friendship rather than speakers who come to give a sermon and condemn them."

On the opposite side of the spectrum from these alienated young Muslims are their compatriots who revolt against modern life's emptiness and seek solace in something stronger than the pieties of conventional organized Islam. The fundamentalist sect Al-Arqam—which ran communes for its members and boasted a leader who claimed regular dialogues with the Prophet Mohamad—was one such refuge. The government disbanded the group in 1995 and detained its leader for spreading what the authorities labelled "deviationist" teachings.

Only a tiny portion of Muslims join such sects, though. The vast majority of Malays are exploring the centre ground between fundamentalism and apostasy, says Chandra Muzaffar. He argues that continued rapid economic development will not turn Malaysia's Muslims away from their faith. Rather, he says, it will ultimately prompt them to take a much more active role in determining for themselves what is Islamic, what is moral.

"Very, very few Muslims renounce their faith," Chandra says. "But more and more will interpret the Koran for themselves and say, 'these are my rights.' They will be an increasingly important factor."

Simon Elegant is the REVIEW's Arts & Society editor.

---

*Article 26*

FAR EASTERN ECONOMIC REVIEW, August 15, 1996

## INVESTMENT

# Enter at Own Risk

After the political snakepit, the quicksand. Investors who wade into Burma despite human-rights criticism find that rickety infrastructure and a heavy state hand can pose trouble, too.

**By Gordon Fairclough in Kanbauk, Burma**

French oil company Total's rain-soaked base-camp in southern Burma is ringed with guard posts and double barbed-wire fences. In the centre are two underground bunkers. "In case of rocket attack," explains Jean-Claude Ragot, Total's stocky, cigar-smoking operations manager. "We lost five people last year. We have to be careful."

The workers were killed by guerrillas fighting Rangoon's military government. Now, crews travel with army escorts as they lay the groundwork for a 670-kilometre pipeline that will carry natural gas from wells in the Andaman Sea to a power plant in Thailand. The troops won't protect Total against attacks from another direction, though: Europe and its human-rights groups, who say pipeline revenues will prop up Burma's repressive regime.

The French oil company faces more than political risks as it builds Burma's biggest foreign-investment project. Its odyssey also reveals the myriad daily challenges that crop up as companies do business in one of Asia's least-developed countries: Total has had to build its own roads, airfield and wharf. It has also had to bridge two large rivers in order to bring in its heavy equipment and supplies.

Total and other companies investing in Burma are pioneers braving one of the region's last commercial frontiers. Infrastructure is antiquated and inadequate, and there's little hope that multilateral lenders will finance improvements if Burma's politics don't change. The country's 45 million people are among the world's poorest and least educated—only one in four children completes primary school. National income is less than $300 per person. And the government continues to dominate much of the economy—despite assurances that it has abandoned socialism for the free market.

Investors plunge in anyway, although many find there's more pain than gain. Among the intrepid are Western oil companies and mining firms, staking their claims to the country's natural riches. Southeast Asian businessmen have put their money into hotels, real estate and light manufacturing. Japan's big trading companies have also set up shop, gambling that Burma will become the next low-cost production base for their country's labour-intensive industries.

What spurs them on? "The country has potential," says Satoru Takahashi, chief rep-

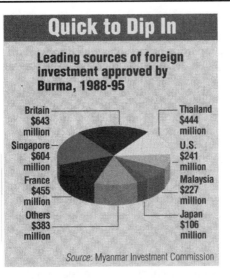

## Quick to Dip In

**Leading sources of foreign investment approved by Burma, 1988-95**

Britain $643 million
Singapore $604 million
France $455 million
Others $383 million

Thailand $444 million
U.S. $241 million
Malaysia $227 million
Japan $106 million

*Source*: Myanmar Investment Commission

resentative in Rangoon of Bank of Tokyo-Mitsubishi. "They have many natural resources and cheap labour." Indeed, Burma used to be one of Asia's wealthiest countries. The fertile Irawaddy Delta was the region's rice bowl. The country also has gas, teak and minerals. But the

generals who rule Burma drove the economy into the ground during 26 years of socialist isolation.

Now, they've reversed themselves and opened the doors to foreign investors. "We can't industrialize without the help of the developed countries," says Set Maung, an economic adviser to the government. "We need their technology. We need their capital. That is why we are trying to attract as much foreign investment as possible."

To that end, the State Law and Order Restoration Council (Slorc), as the junta calls itself, promulgated a liberal foreign-investment law in 1989. It has approved more than $4 billion in investment projects, much of it in oil and gas. It has also allowed private commercial banks to set up shop, and says the banks may form joint ventures with foreign partners. The generals have also given more economic freedom to Burma's farmers and small-time entrepreneurs.

The resulting uptick in economic activity has created thousands of new jobs.

# *Second Rate*

No one is wearing red suspenders or power ties. There aren't even any computers in Rangoon's foreign-exchange trading centre. But, says trader Aung Myint Lwin, there's still plenty of action.

As dozens of people mill about, many clutching mobile phones and plastic bags crammed with cash, the trader explains that Burmese demand for U.S. dollar foreign-exchange certificates has been soaring. Indeed, in mid-July, there just weren't enough certificates to go around. The kyat, which had been trading at about 140 to the dollar, hit 172 before dropping back to about 150 at the end of the month.

Aung Myint Lwin chalks the jumpiness up to consumer demand for new telephone lines (which have to be paid for in dollars) and heavy buying by a few firms that owe dollars for imports they've acquired.

More uncertainty lies ahead as the government continues to liberalize Burma's foreign-exchange system. There's a grossly overvalued official rate of about 6 kyat to the dollar. But the government has been steadily expanding that range of transactions for which the market rate is accepted. Both Burmese and foreigners can now trade foreign-exchange certificates, which the government has issued

since 1993. They can also use certificates to open foreign-currency bank accounts. Their transactions are made easier by the trading centre, which opened late last year. All these developments have served to minimize the effect of the official exchange rate and, practically speaking, allowed a devaluation of the kyat.

"The official exchange rate is still there, but it is irrelevant," says Set Maung, a government economic adviser. Businessmen and World Bank officials wouldn't use the word irrelevant—many complain the system can make bookkeeping a nightmare. One hotelier who earns dollars from foreign tourists says he pays most of his payroll and other expenses in kyat. But he's obliged to keep books at the official conversion rate—a practice that makes it look as though he's losing a lot of money even though he's not. "You send a chief financial officer over here, and he'd have to go back in a straitjacket," he says.

Many firms keep separate kyat and dollar accounts. Myanmar Knitwear Manufacturing, for example, uses left-over fabric to make inexpensive clothes which it sells locally. That's how the company

earns the kyat it needs to pay employees and meet local expenses.

Most damaging to the economy, according to the World Bank, is that the official exchange rate distorts Burma's international trade. The overvalued kyat encourages state agencies and enterprises to buy imports, which seem cheap. It also discourages exports, which seem unprofitable. The distortion has a broad effect because the state controls more than half of Burma's exports and a third of imports. The World Bank, in a recent report, concluded that scrapping the official exchange rate would help Burma export more and import less.

The Burmese government fears an official devaluation could lead to panic, speculation and a collapse of the currency that would send prices spiralling upward. Government economist Set Maung says "we do not yet have a sufficient amount of foreign-exchange reserves to defend our currency."

The World Bank, plays this concern down. "For much of the population, a significant portion of the price adjustment has already taken place," its report says.

■ **Gordon Fairclough**

High-rise buildings are springing up in downtown Rangoon, where the streets are clogged with private cars and taxis. New shops, restaurants and hotels abound.

But there are nevertheless serious doubts about whether Burma, officially Myanmar, is on its way to becoming an Asian tiger. The World Bank and Asian Development Bank say recent reforms do not go far enough. And an American Embassy report released in August says Burma's economic growth "may prove unsustainable in the medium and long terms" unless investment in infrastructure and education rises.

The country's policies certainly don't seem to be putting it on a trajectory of improvement. The fiscal conservatism, high investment and small state sectors that characterize Asia's success stories are nowhere to be found. Private investment as a share of GDP has been declining since 1990, and only a tiny number of state enterprises have been privatized. Burma's government keeps spending far more than it earns. The deficit in the year ending March 31, 1995, was more than 6% of GDP.

The generals spent more than 45% of the 1995 budget on defence. And that doesn't include purchases of foreign hardware, such as Chinese tanks and artillery, which aren't accounted for in government statistics. Meanwhile, the proportion of spending which goes to education, health and other social services, at 22.8%, has been falling since 1991.

The government pays for its spending spree by printing money, running up the arrears on its foreign debt, and borrowing from domestic banks. In fact, Burmese banks lend more than 80% of their money to the government and state enterprises. Private borrowers are crowded out.

"There's still a socialist mentality," notes one Sino-Burmese businessman who has returned to the country. He and his family fled in the 1960s after the military government nationalized all they owned.

The state firms get better access to utilities and government permits. In addition, state firms and government agencies dominate Burma's international trade.

The state sector accounts for more than half of Burma's exports and more than a third of its imports. The government already monopolizes trade in rice, teak and many minerals. And these days,

foreign exchange-hungry state agencies are buying up Burma's beans and pulses—among the main agricultural exports—to sell overseas. Private traders, whose work was made legal in 1989, complain they're being forced out of business. "Government ministries and departments have an easier time getting the export licences," says one elderly trader. "They are the traders now."

With little in the way of capital and few opportunities to take advantage of, prospective Burmese businessmen don't have much of a chance to rise. That's bad news for foreign investors who might have sought independent partners. "The private sector is very small. So most negotiating is done with the government," says Kosuke Ito, Rangoon general manager of Japanese trading company Nissho Iwai. "The government says it will privatize, but is still seeking its own business, so there is a conflict."

At the end of March 1995, only 30% of foreign investors in Burma had found private-sector partners. The rest had joined hands with the military and government. The military's holding company, Union of Myanmar Economic Holdings, is a popular joint-venture partner. Forty percent-owned by the Defence Ministry's procure-ment division, the company owns a large industrial estate near the Rangoon airport. Its foreign partners include Daewoo, Korean textile maker Segye and other large firms. Other investors have hooked up with government ministries and state enterprises.

Investors find that having a government partner can shield them from pervasive corruption. A bureaucrat's salary doesn't buy what it used to, and many petty officials have perfected the art of exacting special payments for every service they perform. While this kind of corruption helps investors cut through red tape, it also raises the cost of doing business.

The country's other major disability is infrastructure. "It's terrible," says Halpin Ho, president of the Ho Group.

Ho was nine years old when his family left Burma in 1964. They ended up in Thailand, where they built a profitable jewellery business. In the early 1990s, Ho's family was looking to escape Thailand's rising labour costs. So Ho was sent to Burma to take a look. He wasn't impressed: The port and road networks were a mess, electricity blacked out regularly, and it was almost impossible to make a

phone call from one end of Rangoon to the other.

"We couldn't do what we wanted to do, which was set up a factory. So we decided to build infrastructure," says Ho, dressed in a traditional Burmese longyi and a light-blue Perry Ellis shirt. His company is completing its second hotel project—a lakefront property patterned on an ancient Burmese palace.

Ho now has an even grander scheme in the works. He wants to build a city-within-a-city, a protective enclave to shelter business from the harsh external environment. The Thuwanna New Business District "will be world-standard, state-of-the-art," says Ho, pointing at an architectural model of sprawling towers and plazas. Among the features: fibre-optic cables, video-conferencing facilities and a Western-style supermarket.

That's fine for executives, but few manufacturers are going to find it economical to wade into Burma lugging their own infrastructure. What's more, wider shortcomings will continue to inhibit industrialization: a clogged port, bad roads and insufficient electrical power.

The biggest bottleneck is the Rangoon port. There are only two cranes for unloading container ships, and one of them is often out of service. With trade having grown over the past few years, it's now common to have scores of vessels waiting to unload on any given day. Some ships wait in the estuary for weeks—an expensive proposition for anyone moving goods in and out of Rangoon.

The mess at the port prompted the general manager of a multinational consumer-goods company to try a different route. His soaps and shampoos are trucked from Bangkok to Ranong on the Andaman Sea and ferried across to Burma's Victoria Point. A wooden schooner then sails them up the monsoon-battered coast to Rangoon.

The well-tanned American says his worst fear is that one of the ships will capsize in a storm: "Losing a boatload of uninsured product wouldn't be too good."

Takahashi of Bank of Tokyo-Mitsubishi shares the concern. "You cannot make production plans with such a poor port situation," he says. The shipping costs make manufacturers wary of starting operations in Burma. New factories will rely on a lot of imported inputs, and reliable supplies will be essential.

The good news is that foreign investors from Singapore and Hong Kong are building a new container port across the river from Rangoon, which may be in operation by the end of the year. But even then, traders will face obstacles.

Poor roads, train tracks and water networks also hold the economy back. They leave large parts of the fertile countryside beyond reach of the market. That's despite buyers' enthusiasm: Nissho Iwai's Ito says he and his colleagues comb the country looking for agricultural goods to satisfy Japan's demand for imported foods.

"There are a lot of things we want to buy," says Ito. "The price at the site is very cheap." But "it can take weeks" to get to Rangoon—and that means spoiled goods and missed opportunities for Burmese farmers.

Some of these problems may have private-sector solutions. Besides working on the port, foreign investors are also building industrial estates. They would no doubt snap up electricity and telecommunications contracts too, if the government were to let them.

Other projects, like irrigation works, roads and bridges will probably have to be built by the public sector. The government has been funding such public works using its own money and relying heavily on the forced labour of its citizens. In 1994, for example, the government used forced- and prison-labour to restore the moat around the palace at Mandalay. Earlier this year, human-rights groups blasted the Slorc for using forced labour to build a railway line in the South. Now state media show images of soldiers doing the same work.

But without foreign aid and lending from multilateral institutions, it's unlikely Burma will be able to lay the groundwork for future economic growth. By 1990 all donor countries but China had stopped giving Burma assistance. The army had cracked down violently on anti-government demonstrations in 1988 and refused in 1990 to acknowledge the results of elections in which its opponents won more than 80% of the vote. The United States and other Western countries have also acted to prevent a resumption of lending from the World Bank and International Monetary Fund.

The barriers to cheap money aren't just political. The Asian Development Bank said in August that Burma's economic reforms were lagging behind those elsewhere in Southeast Asia and that this could hinder access to ADB loans. Economic policy in Burma is "at present not necessarily up to our standards," said senior bank official Noritada Morita.

Japan has reinstituted some limited aid programmes since the release of opposition leader Aung San Suu Kyi from house arrest in July 1995. But major outside assistance isn't likely to resume until there is some progress towards a political settlement between the military government and Suu Kyi's opposition National League for Democracy. The recent deaths in prison of two Suu Kyi supporters has further darkened the junta's image. In an effort to force the government to compromise with the NLD, the U.S. and European countries have been threatening economic sanctions. Suu Kyi has appealed for sanctions in an effort to force the government to negotiate with her.

"We do not think now is the time for any foreign company to invest in Burma," Suu Kyi said in recent television interview with Asia Business News, owned by Dow Jones, publisher of the REVIEW. "These investments only benefit a privileged few," she said. Suu Kyi called on foreign tourists to stay away from the country during "Visit Myanmar Year," which is set to begin in November.

Even if sanctions are not imposed, Western companies still run a heavy political risk by doing business in Burma. Pro-democracy activists in the U.S. and Europe have been pressing shareholders to protest company involvement in Burma, and have mounted consumer boycotts. Some American state legislatures and city governments have even voted not to do business with companies that have invested in Burma. PepsiCo sold off its 40% stake in a Burmese Pepsi bottler in April. Europe's Carlsberg and Heineken both announced in July that they were scrapping plans to set up breweries. In retaliation, Burma has banned imports of the two brands.

Even non-Western companies can feel the activists' sting. Just ask Joe Pang. The head of Hong Kong's Victoria Garment Manufacturing has four factories in Rangoon. He has had to scramble to keep his order book full after some

of his high-profile U.S. customers—including Eddie Bauer, Liz Claiborne and Macy's—stopped buying from him. Pang said of his customers who were worried about protesters: "They told me: 'They'll picket our stores. We don't need that kind of problem.'"

But despite this pressure, many European and American firms continue to source garments in Burma. One of Pang's factories, which makes knitwear, still sells more than 70% of its output to the U.S. It still makes Mickey Mouse jerseys for U.S.-based American Character Classics, for instance. The rest of the orders are from Europe.

It looks as though some companies are still willing to take a chance on Burma, despite the difficulties. Oil, gas and mining concerns are there because they have to get in first to stake their claim to these resources. Other companies, largely from Southeast Asia, have focused on businesses in which they can earn dollars—such as hotels and tourism. Or they choose businesses where their assets, such as real estate, stand to appreciate.

Japanese firms, too, have flocked to Burma. Most are not investing much money, however. Instead, they are moving slowly to lay the groundwork for a major presence in the future. Japan's business leaders think Burma should be the next site for their labour-intensive manufacturing operations. And they have been pressing their government to restart concessionary loans for infrastructure.

"Today's operations are not commercially viable," admits Mike Nagai, general manager of Mitsui's Burma office. "But we believe this country has big potential." Over the past two years, Mitsui has worked to draft a master plan for the country's industrialization. Its cornerstone is a project that will use supplies of natural gas from the Gulf of Martaban to produce fertilizer and electrical power. Mitsui, Total and American oil company Unocal are now doing a feasibility study. Mitsui is also building an industrial estate near the Rangoon airport. But, Nagai says, without major infrastructure improvements, Burma's economy will never take off. "The private sector can't do it all," he says. "International organizations have got to give their support."

That is likely only if Burma's military leaders and its democratic opposition can solve their differences. "The only thing that is blocking the kind of growth we want here is politics," sighs one Burmese businessman.

*Article 27*

*CURRENT HISTORY*, December 1996

# Narcopolitics in Burma

While undoubtedly enjoying widespread popular support," Aung San Suu Kyi and her National League for Democracy "lack a coherent strategy to counter SLORC. It also appears that actions taken by the West have had little impact. Political change in Burma seems to depend on when, if ever, ASEAN begins to pay less attention to geopolitical security concerns and economic gains than to human rights and the rapid spread of narcotics in the region."

## BERTIL LINTNER

A little over a year after Burmese opposition leader and Nobel Peace Prize winner Aung San Suu Kyi's release from house arrest in Rangoon last July, politics in Burma has come nearly full circle.

Suu Kyi had been detained in July 1989 after a year of confrontation between her party, the National League for Democracy (NLD), and the ruling military junta, the State Law and Order Restoration Council (SLORC). Her detention had caused an international outcry, which raised hopes that her release would end the conflict and lead to a dialogue between the NLD and SLORC. Those hopes were dashed only three months after Suu Kyi's release when the government newspaper, *The New Light of Myanmar,* resumed its attacks on Suu Kyi and the movement she was trying to revive after years of repression.

In November 1995, one month after the newspaper attack, the handful of NLD representatives to the National Convention—a body of 700 delegates SLORC had charged with drafting a new constitution—walked out. The convention, they said, did not represent the wishes of the Burmese people.

The NLD had won a landslide victory in a general election in May 1990, while Suu Kyi was still under house arrest, cap-

turing 392 out of 485 seats in the National Assembly. But the assembly was never convened. Instead, SLORC, contrary to earlier promises not to interfere with the constitutional process, called the National Convention. The convention included only 97 delegates from those who had been elected in May 1990, most from the NLD. The more than 600 remaining delegates were hand-picked by the military. The NLD felt that it had entered the National Convention under duress while Suu Kyi was in detention. With its leader free again, the NLD evidently thought it had the strength to claim its 1990 election victory.

The walkout backfired badly. Repression increased, and when the NLD attempted to convene a congress in Rangoon this May, SLORC reacted harshly, arresting 258 people, 238 of whom had been elected to parliament in 1990. Most were released after questioning, but several were sentenced to long prison terms. In September, a second attempt by the NLD to gather its scattered forces provoked an even stronger response, more than 800 people were taken into custody, and between 40 and 50 remain in detention. At least 11 were sentenced to long prison terms; the stiffest sentence was meted out to Aung San Suu Kyi's aide, Win Htein, who received 14 years.

Perhaps even more significantly, on September 27, 1996, SLORC sealed off the capital's University Avenue, where Suu Kyi lives. Until then Suu Kyi's home had been the venue for weekly gatherings since her release from house arrest. Every Saturday she had spoken from her compound to crowds of

BERTIL LINTNER, *a Bangkok-based correspondent for the* Far Eastern Economic Review, *is the author of four books on Burma, the most recent of which is* Burma in Revolt: Opium and Insurgency since 1948 *(Boulder, Colo.: Westview, 1994).*

thousands of people. Although the barricades on University Avenue were removed a few days later, they went up again the following Saturday, and continue to go up whenever SLORC suspects people are about to gather outside her house, indicating that the public rallies will no longer be tolerated.

Suu Kyi's telephone lines also have been cut whenever there is a gathering outside her home, leaving her unable to communicate with her followers or with the outside world. Although no official detention order has been issued and the junta insists that Suu Kyi is "free to go wherever she likes," she is in fact under virtual house arrest—and the revival of her democracy movement has been quashed.

## THE NEWEST PARIAH STATE

Although successful at home, the most recent crackdown caused a backlash in the international arena. In early October 1996, President Bill Clinton slapped a visa ban on members of SLORC, their family members, and others who "benefited from policies that are impeding the transition to democracy in Burma." The month before, the United States Congress had passed legislation obliging the president to prohibit new investments by American businesses in Burma "if SLORC physically harms, re-arrests, or exiles Aung San Suu Kyi, or continues its repression of the democracy movement." While American companies had successfully lobbied Congress to water down another bill that would have triggered outright sanctions against Burma, sanctions now seem unavoidable.

A privately initiated boycott movement has also gathered speed in the United States as local governments enacted laws banning the purchase of goods and services from companies doing business in Burma. In October, Apple Computer announced that it was pulling out of Burma to avoid being penalized by the Commonwealth of Massachusetts. The city of San Francisco has begun scrutinizing the United States-based Motorola, Swedish telephone giant Ericsson, Japan's Mitsubishi Heavy Industries, and other companies that have placed bids for two large city projects. Under San Francisco's tough new legislation, the bid of any company doing business in Burma would be rejected.

The October sweep against the NLD also prompted the European Union to condemn SLORC. The union's foreign ministers called for the immediate release of the hundreds of NLD members who had been detained by the military authorities. The ministers stopped short of mentioning sanctions, but said they wished to "emphasize the need for a genuine dialogue to commence without delay between SLORC and the NLD."

In Canberra, Foreign Minister Alexander Downer ordered the Australian ambassador in Rangoon to protest the crackdown to the junta "in the strongest terms." In Tokyo, Foreign Ministry spokesman Seiroku Kajiyama told a news conference that "Japan cannot overlook moves that run counter to the democratization of Burma."

But SLORC seemed unmoved by this international outcry and continued its campaign against what was left of the NLD inside the country—as well as striking back at critics abroad. On October 11, *The New Light of Myanmar* ran a lengthy commentary by "U Byatti," believed to be the pseudonym of a high-ranking SLORC spokesman. It was written in the junta's quaintly jumbled, archaic English, but the message was clear.

The author of the article ridiculed "[t]raitorous axe-handles" inside and outside the country, condemned the United States government, and perhaps inadvertently, expressed SLORC's views on Burma's political future and its position in regional power politics. Suu Kyi would "never come to get a legal stand in the political sphere of Myanmar [the SLORC renamed Burma "Myanmar" in 1989] . . . and . . . Myanmar will never be an American-style democracy."

The article then raised the issue of the West's threats to impose sanctions against Burma: "Myanmar people will not shrink away or waver simply at mere mention of America . . . There still exist many centers of power in the world. One center of power is China with common borders and good traditions of friendly relations with Myanmar." U Byatti then referred to American moves in 1993 to impose sanctions against another Asian pariah state, North Korea, which he claimed had been thwarted by China: "[I]t should be noted that the US cannot have its way in Asia without China's consent."

When SLORC assumed power in September 1988, it massacred thousands of pro-democracy demonstrators in Rangoon and in other cities and towns across the country. This crackdown elicited an even stronger international outcry than is seen at present. All foreign aid was eliminated, and trade was curtailed substantially. China quickly filled this vacuum by opening its border with Burma to trade, extending loans to Rangoon, and selling massive quantities of arms and ammunition to Burma's armed forces.

The military had stepped in, not to overthrow the ruling Burma Socialist Program Party (BSPP), but to shore up a regime overwhelmed by popular protest. In short, the military simply dropped its civilian fig leaf to assume direct power through SLORC. A massive military buildup, with Chinese assistance, helped the junta survive its first difficult years in power. The armed forces grew from an estimated 180,000 soldiers before the bloody events of 1988 to more than 300,000 today. The final goal is said to be a 500,000-strong military machine.

The once poorly equipped Burmese army suddenly found itself in possession of hundreds of new light infantry weapons as well as battle tanks, jet fighters, and patrol boats. The military increased its visibility in all fields and tightened its grip on the country. It appeared the massive demonstrations of 1988 had shaken the military regime out of its complacency.

## THE SLORC WAY TO CAPITALISM

"The Burmese Way to Socialism"—the stated ideology of the BSPP—had led to economic ruin, with Burma, once one of Asia's most prosperous countries, being forced to apply for least developed country status with the UN. Industrial production had fallen even in real terms, the country's external debt was mounting, and foreign exchange reserves in September 1988 were estimated to be a mere $10 million to $20 million.

The junta discarded the socialist state ideology after assuming power and in November 1988 introduced a new, fairly liberal foreign investment law. Given the unsettled political situation, it was not surprising that the initial response was lukewarm, even from investors in the region. But foreign investment gradually picked up, especially in the potentially lucrative energy sector. Burma is believed to have considerable untapped reserves of oil and gas. The American firms Unocal and Texaco, France's Total, and other oil companies began in late 1989 to invest millions in Burma.

Although the abolition of the disastrous Burmese Way to Socialism had been initially motivated by a desire to survive economically, the military soon discovered that a number of other benefits came with foreign investment and liberal domestic economic policies. Many officers became rich through kickbacks and private business deals, dampening any dissent that had existed among the rank and file during the turbulent years of 1988 and 1989.

The military as an institution has also benefited from the new economic policies. The preferred local partner for most foreign companies—and not always by choice—has been the Union of Myanmar Economic Holdings. Set up in February 1990, UMEH has become one of the country's largest companies, with registered capital of 10 billion kyats—$1.6 billion at the official exchange rate, or $67 million at the prevailing black market rate. Significantly, 40 percent of this powerful company is owned by the armed forces' Directorate of Procurement.

SLORC realized that to avoid another uprising, the public would have to benefit from its policies. It needed to woo popular opinion from the NLD, which had propagated free trade and economic liberalization before SLORC adopted similar ideals. Today, Suu Kyi and the NLD claim that SLORC's economic policies have benefited only a privileged few. But the fact remains that after years of socialist austerity, privately owned enterprises, including family-run hotels, shops, and small factories, have mushroomed in Burma.

While Western companies have been restrained by human rights concerns, Asian countries have been quick to take advantage of Burma's new economic policies—an eagerness due only in part to Burma's image as the emerging "tiger" in a region that is economically the fastest growing in the world. U Byatti may have bragged about Burma's close friendship with China as a warning to the United States. But that friendship—especially massive Chinese arms shipments to Burma—has also been a cause for regional concern, and a major reason why the Association of Southeast Asian Nations (ASEAN) has not heeded Western calls to isolate SLORC.

In theory, both the West and ASEAN want to see the healthy development of democracy in Burma. The West wants to encourage it through diplomatic, political, and economic pressure, while ASEAN officially believes that a policy of "constructive engagement" would be more effective in achieving the same goal. In reality, the aim of ASEAN's constructive engagement is not to entice SLORC

to become more democratic, but to pull it away from its most important ally since 1988: the People's Republic of China.

Singapore has been especially active in Burma, investing more than $900 million and promoting official visits. A study by Australian defense analyst Andrew Selth in 1996 by the Strategic and Defense Studies Center of the Australian National University, noted that Singapore is emerging as an alternative source of weapons procurement for the Burmese, offering better and more sophisticated equipment than the Chinese.

---

"[E]xport of opiates alone appears to be worth as much as all legal exports," or $922 million at the official exchange rate.

---

According to Selth, Burma's Singapore-supplied munitions include surface-to-air missile systems, mortars, automatic rifles, and small arms ammunition. Selth notes that "Singapore may also be training Burmese military personnel in the use of modern information technology systems and other electronic equipment being provided to the Burmese *tatmadaw* [the armed forces] by Singaporean companies." Political support from Singapore also came after the crackdown against the NLD this May, when Senior Minister Lee Kuan Yew declared: "At the end of the day, the opposition in Burma has to face the realities of life. The one instrument of effective government there is the army."

When the Danish Carlsberg and Dutch Heineken beer companies gave in to pressure from prodemocracy groups and pulled out of Burma shortly after the crackdown, Singaporean companies quickly replaced them. Fraser and Neave stepped in to fill Heineken's slot, and Tiger Beer may become the replacement for Carlsberg. Other Singaporean firms have invested in everything from trading and hotels to manufacturing. Approved Singaporean investment in Burma totaled $896 million by 1996, and is steadily increasing.

Singapore has emerged as the leading source of foreign investment in Burma since the economy was opened in 1988. Britain comes in second on the list with $809 million worth of commitments, but that figure includes companies registered in the British Virgin Islands and similar tax havens. France is number three with $465 million, almost exclusively made up of Total's investment in the energy sector. Other major investment includes $422 million from Thailand, $420 million from Malaysia, $241 million from the United States, and $106 million from Japan.

China's somewhat lower profile in Burma in the last two years lends credence to the suggestion that ASEAN's policy of constructive engagement has been successful in wooing SLORC from China. In September, shortly before the most recent crackdown, Malaysia, another close trading partner, endorsed Burma's application for membership in ASEAN when it celebrates its twentieth anniversary next year. The Philippines and to some extent Thailand have expressed reservations about admitting Burma before it has accepted at least some political pluralism. But ASEAN's traditional policy has been not to interfere in the "internal affairs" of member countries, which means Burma may well become a member of the group in 1997.* Any sanctions imposed by Western countries against Burma would then be largely ineffective, since Singaporean companies would replace the departing Western companies (as was seen in the case of Carlsberg and Heineken).

It is also clear that the divergent opinions on how to approach the Burmese problem do not represent an East-West divide, as ASEAN governments often insist when rejecting calls for tougher action against SLORC. A number of nongovernmental organizations and other lobby groups in ASEAN countries strongly disagree with their governments' policies toward Burma. The Thailand-based Asian Forum for Human Rights and Development, which includes some of Thailand's brightest talents and most influential nonpartisan political activists, stated in a report released after the crackdown in October that "ASEAN policy is fraught with dangers. An impoverished and strife-torn Burma would contribute to increased smuggling of arms and drugs, trafficking in women, and the outflow of refugees and illegal immigrants . . . ASEAN should strive to promote peace and democracy in Burma."

## OPIATES FOR THE MASSES

The Asian Forum's concerns are not unfounded. An estimated 400,000 Burmese are working illegally in Thailand alone, and each year thousands of girls from Burma are being sold into prostitution there and elsewhere in Southeast Asia. Perhaps even more worrisome is Burma's booming export of drugs. Western and Asian narcotics officials estimate that the production of illicit narcotics in the Burmese sector of the Golden Triangle—the area where the borders of Burma, Laos and Thailand intersect—has nearly tripled since SLORC's formation.

According to the United States government, the 1987 harvest for Burma alone yielded 836 tons of raw opium; by 1995, production had increased to 2,340 tons. The area under poppy cultivation increased from 92,300 hectares in 1987 to 142,700 in 1989 and 154,000 in 1995. The potential heroin output soared from 54 tons in 1987 to 166 tons in 1995, making drugs the country's growth industry—one that continues to expand, despite government claims to the contrary.[1]

Under SLORC, Burma has become the world's leading producer of heroin and opium. In June 1996, the United States embassy in Rangoon released a report charging that "export of opiates alone appears to be worth as much as all legal exports," or $922 million at the official exchange rate. The report also said that the Burmese government "makes no perceptible effort to bar investments funded by the production or export of narcotics."

According to the report, the barriers between the legal and extralegal economies have weakened partly because of the government's policy of "openly welcoming investment without any consideration of the likely original source of the funds." The report noted significant investment in hotels and construction by companies closely associated with known drug traffickers.

Meanwhile, the embassy report said, gross legal investment declined from about 21 percent to about 18 percent of GDP, foreign direct investment fell from 9.3 percent to 5 percent of GDP, the government's external arrears nearly doubled to $1.5 billion, and its stock of external debt (excluding debt for military imports) grew to $5.5 billion, thus painting a much gloomier picture of the Burmese economy than is usually presented by Asian sources.

## PLAYING THE ETHNIC CARD

The heroin boom in Burma is the direct outcome of another element of SLORC policies. In the wake of the 1988 massacres, more than 8,000 pro-democracy activists fled Burma's urban centers for the border areas near Thailand, where a multitude of ethnic insurgents, not involved in the narcotics trade, were active. The military feared an alliance between the ethnic rebels along its frontiers and the pro-democracy activists.

However, these rebel groups along the Thai border (Karen, Mon, Karenni, and Pa-O) were unable to provide the urban dissidents with more than a handful of weapons. None of the ethnic groups could match the strength of the Communist Party of Burma (CPB), whose 10,000 to 15,000 troops then controlled a 20,000-square-kilometer territory along the Sino-Burmese frontier in the northeast.

Unlike the ethnic insurgents, the CPB had vast quantities of arms and ammunition that had been supplied by China between 1968 and 1978, when it was Beijing's policy to support communist insurrections in Southeast Asia (a fact carefully avoided in the SLORC's official rhetoric; "eternal friendship" is said always to have dominated Sino-Burmese relations). Although the aid had virtually ceased by 1980, the CPB still had vast stockpiles of munitions, probably enough to last for at least ten years of guerrilla war.

Despite government claims of a "communist conspiracy" during the 1988 uprising, there was at that time no linkage between the anti-totalitarian, pro-democracy movement in central Burma and the orthodox, Marxist-Leninist CPB. However, given their strong desire to avenge the massacres, it is plausible to assume that the urban dissidents would have accepted arms from any source. Thus it became imperative for the SLORC to neutralize as many of the border insurgencies as possible, especially that of the CPB.

A situation potentially even more dangerous for SLORC arose in March and April 1989 when the hill-tribe rank and file of the CPB—led by its military commanders, who also came from the various minorities of its northeastern base area—mutinied against the party's aging, mostly Burman, political leadership.

On April 17, 1989, ethnic Wa mutineers from the CPB's army stormed the party headquarters at Panghsang on the Yunnan bor-

---

[1] It takes 10 kilograms of raw opium, plus chemicals, to make 1 kilogram of heroin. "Potential heroin output" is therefore equivalent to opium output divided by 10. However, not all raw opium is refined into heroin, because a substantial amount of opium is consumed locally in its raw form.

der. The old leaders and their families escaped to China, and the former CPB army soon split along ethnic lines and formed four regional resistance armies. Ethnic minority rebels along the Thai border sent a delegation to Panghsang to negotiate with the main Wa component of the CPB mutineers soon after the breakup of the old party. The possibility of a linkup between the four groups and the ethnic minority groups along the Thai border, as well as with the urban dissident refugees, worried SLORC.

But the authorities in Rangoon reacted faster, with more determination, and with much more to offer than the ethnic rebels. Within weeks of the CPB mutiny, the chief of Burma's military intelligence, Major-General (now Lieutenant-General) Khin Nyunt, traveled to the border to meet the former communist commanders, and alliances of convenience were forged between Burma's military authorities and various groups of mutineers. In exchange for promises not to attack government forces and to sever ties with other rebel groups, the CPB mutineers were granted unofficial permission to engage in any kind of business to sustain themselves. Rangoon also promised to launch a "border development program" in the former CPB areas.

Ironically, at a time when almost the entire population of Burma had turned against the regime, thousands of former insurgents rallied behind the ruling military. The threat from the border areas was thwarted and the regime was safe, but the consequences for the country and the outside world have been disastrous. "Business" in the northeast inevitably means opium and heroin.

Within a year of the CPB mutiny, American and Chinese intelligence sources claimed that there were more than 20 new heroin refineries in the former CPB areas west of the Salween River. Former communist commanders have become some of the richest men in Burma. Many have invested their drug profits in real estate, hotels, construction, and even supermarkets in Rangoon, Mandalay, and other cities.

With the collapse of the communist insurgency, several smaller ethnic rebel armies also gave in. SLORC claims it has made peace with 16 former rebel groups. In January 1996, the world was stunned by a spectacle in the eastern Shan hills, bordering Thailand. Army helicopters landed in Homong, the headquarters of the Mong Tai Army (MTA) of Golden Triangle drug lord Khun Sa, where they were greeted by thousands of guerrillas standing at attention, their weapons at their feet. Nearly 15,000 MTA soldiers surrendered to the authorities and handed over assault rifles, machine guns, rocket launchers, and even SA-7 surface-to-air missiles. Until then the MTA had been the strongest and best-armed rebel group fighting the government.

Khun Sa himself left in one of the helicopters for Rangoon, where the government claimed it would keep him "for interrogation" and assured the world that he would be dealt with "according to the laws" of Burma. The United States, which had indicted the warlord on drug trafficking charges in 1989, demanded his extradition, but American government sources say Rangoon ignored even requests to know more about Khun Sa's whereabouts.

A month after the spectacular ceremony at Homong, ten new business companies were registered in Rangoon, all with strong links to Khun Sa. He was seen being driven around Rangoon in a four-wheel drive vehicle, escorted by army officers; it became increasingly clear that he had simply moved his business activities to Rangoon. His drug trafficking continued unabated, but not through Thailand as before.

Instead, Khun Sa appears to have forged an alliance of convenience with Lin Mingxian, a former CPB warlord along the Yunnan frontier who has also entered into a peace agreement with the government. The combined groups and their allies have sent vast amounts of drugs across the border to China. In March 1996, Chinese government authorities in Guangdong province confiscated in a single sweep more than 300 kilograms of pure heroin that had entered the country from northeastern Burma.

In response, the United States and others have accused the Burmese government of complicity in the drug trade. "The drug trade in the Shan State continues virtually unchecked," the United States State Department wrote in a March 1996 report on narcotics in Burma. "Burmese authorities lack the resources, the ability or the will to take action against ethnic drug trafficking groups with whom they have negotiated cease-fires. Groups known to be involved in the heroin trade, such as the United Wa State Army and the Kokang militia [both components of the former CPB], remain heavily armed and enjoy complete autonomy in their base areas. Although the Burmese government claims that these groups have committed themselves to drug control as part of their cease-fire agreements, the Burmese government has been either unwilling or unable to get these groups to reduce heroin trafficking or opium production." The report concluded that as a result of this situation, money laundering has become a growing problem in Burma, where drug-related proceeds are reinvested in legitimate commerce, having "a widespread impact on the Burmese economy."

## SLORC'S PAYOFF

When the Burmese generals set up SLORC in September 1988, the entire population opposed them, they were condemned internationally, and Burma verged on bankruptcy. Eight years later, through a combination of extremely harsh repression, Machiavellian policies, and other governments' geopolitical concerns, the Burmese armed forces have emerged more powerful—militarily, politically, and even economically—than at any time in the country's history.

While undoubtedly enjoying widespread popular support, the NLD seems to lack a coherent strategy to counter SLORC. It also appears that actions taken by the West have had little impact. Political change in Burma seems to depend on when, if ever, ASEAN begins to pay less attention to geopolitical security concerns and economic gains than to human rights and the rapid spread of narcotics in the region.

**Editor's note:** Burma (Myanmar) and Laos were admitted into ASEAN on July 23, 1997, in Subang Jaya, just one day before the start of the thirtieth ASEAN Ministerial Meeting.

*Article 28*                    THE CHRISTIAN SCIENCE MONITOR, September 30, 1997

# Little House on the Paddy
## Life in a northern Vietnam village

**By Cameron W. Barr**
Staff writer of The Christian Science Monitor

**MINH SON, VIETNAM**

AT day's end there is a pretty view of rolling green hills from a porch in this village in northern Vietnam. The evening breeze shuffles the leaves on the eucalyptus trees and the sun's angled rays grace the rice paddies with a luminous sheen.

Life is good for farmer Hoang Van Quang, his wife, Nguyen Thi Hanh, their three children, and two in-laws—Mr. Quang's mother and his younger sister. The family's animals are just one sign of prosperity: A water buffalo glares from its paddock, four pigs grunt and roll over in their sty, and underfoot, eight ducklings and 35 chickens peck their way toward table-readiness.

It is no thanks to socialism, but this family is in the middle of an economic great leap forward. Everyone is anticipating the day, a year or two from now, when they can trade in their wood house for the sturdy prestige of brick. The parents are proud that their two daughters do well in school and hope they will eventually attend a teachers' college in Hanoi, Vietnam's capital, about 45 miles to the south.

Not too long ago, everyone in this village farmed collectively. Whistles went off at 7 a.m. and then at 11 a.m. to mark the morning shift, and afternoon work hours ran from 1 p.m. to 5 p.m. About five years ago—Quang doesn't remember exactly—the government gave him "land-usage certificates" that effectively granted the family ownership of several acres of paddy, as well as land to raise vegetables and fruit trees.

Technically, "the people" hold title to all the land in Vietnam. But Quang and his wife consider that they have "full

**THE FAMILY:** *Squatting, from right: Nguyen Thi Hanh, daughters Huong and Phuong. At back from right: Grandmother Do Thi Bat, son Quyen, and Hoang Van Quang.*

autonomy" over their property. "If we work hard, we get more; if we work less, we get less," Quang says. And they set their own schedule.

The end of collective farming was part of a massive shift in Vietnam's economy that began in the late 1980s. The Communist planners in Hanoi decided that state-controlled socialism—absent aid from the Soviet Union—would lead to disaster and embraced a policy of free-market reforms. The country is still poor, but many people are a lot less poor than they once were.

With the rice already transplanted and the children on vacation, the days of late summer aren't the most hectic in the year. Today, Ms. Hanh has washed

**LEARNING ENGLISH:** *Sisters Phuong and Huong struggle with pronunciations in their English-language textbook.*

**ALL IN A DAY'S WORK:** *Nguyen Thi Hanh carried just-washed sweet potato leaves from the stream running near the house to feed the family's four pigs. During the days of late summer, when the rice from their paddies has already been transplanted, the pace of life is slower for Ms. Hanh. 'Life goes on,' she says with a smile. 'If I don't finish something today, I can always do it tomorrow.'*

(DAVE HERRING—STAFF)

**SIMPLE POSSESSIONS:** *Their one-room house has a clay-tile roof, a dirt floor, and three large wooden beds where the seven family members sleep on thin, straw mats. They also own an electric fan, a television set, and a battery-powered clock.*

Photos by
Melanie Stetson Freeman—staff

some sweet potato leaves that will be fed to the pigs, done the laundry, and set some corncobs to dry in the sun. "Life goes on," she smiles. "If I don't finish something today, I can always do it tomorrow."

The one-room house has a clay-tile roof, a dirt floor, and three large wooden beds where the seven family members sleep on thin straw mats. An electric fan hangs from the roof, along with bundles of mosquito netting over the beds. A battery-powered clock tells the time.

The kitchen is a separate, smaller building where Hanh cooks over an open fire. A cupboard holds a few metal pots,

bowls, and plates. The meals mostly center on rice and animals the family raises. "If we want some meat, we kill a chicken," Quang says. Every two or three weeks they visit a nearby town to shop for fish sauce, salt, soap, and other necessities of life.

The money to buy these things comes from selling produce or slaughtering a pig. The family doesn't have a savings plan. "If I get some money, I usually spend it right away," Quang explains.

A tall bamboo pole at the edge of the wide, brick porch supports the television antenna. Like parents everywhere, Quang and Hanh worry about how much time

the children spend in front of the tube. "During the school year," the father says, fingering a remote control swathed in protective plastic wrap, "we try to keep it off so the kids keep studying."

Huong, the elder of the two daughters, doesn't seem to need much prodding. She brings out a worn English textbook to show two American visitors and begins trying out phrases.

A brand new straw hat with a bow hangs over one of the beds. The parents explain, beaming, that Huong received it for doing such a good job in school.

---

*Article 29*

THE CHRISTIAN SCIENCE MONITOR, April 3, 1998

# Vietnam's Communists Eye New Vices as Market Worries Rise

*Warning against lavish weddings hints at party's concern over market effects on society*

**By Minh T. Vo**

Special to The Christian Science Monitor

HANOI AND HO CHI MINH CITY, VIETNAM

To the young and hip in Ho Chi Minh City, the Dash Rush restaurant is more than a fast-food outlet serving novelties such as hamburgers: It is also a popular place to hold a wedding banquet.

In Hanoi, those looking for something more stylish can rent the ballroom of the five-star Hanoi Daewoo Hotel, where some 700 people attended a recent event.

Vietnam's young brides and grooms have more choices of large venues than ever. But not everyone is happy about this.

The government has launched a campaign against big wedding parties, using its press and brandishing unspecified punishments.

"Many families, including those of senior officials, have held big wedding parties or funerals to gain prestige or money," said the official Vietnam News. "These phenomena have become social ailments and degrade traditional morals

MELANIE STETSON FREEMAN—STAFF
**SIGNS OF THE TIMES:** *Huge ads for foreign products tower over the streets of Ho Chi Minh City. The influx of Western goods came after Communist-run Vietnam adopted market reforms.*

and the people's thrifty, modest, and fine way of living."

## Socialism vs. markets

For a good part of the past decade, Vietnam's state-run media have periodically, and unsuccessfully, rallied to stamp out prostitution and illicit drugs. This latest addition to the government's list of social vices underscores the ruling Communist Party's predicament as it tries to reconcile socialist ideals with a burgeoning market economy.

Hanoi's leaders, watching how other Asian nations handle similar problems, see nearby Thailand as a mixed model. While Thailand allows private business to be dynamic, it also allows "too much of a widening gap between the rich and the poor, the cities and the rural areas," says government economic adviser Do Duc Dinh.

## Opening in 1986

Ever since Vietnam embarked on its economic reforms known as *doi moi* in 1986, the gap between the rich and the poor has steadily grown. Moreover, some areas of the country have benefited more than others from the market economy. Ho Chi Minh City, the nearby Dong Nai province, and Hanoi alone attracted some 60 percent of the pledged foreign capital last year, yet they account for just 12 percent of the 75 million people in Vietnam. All this is not lost upon the Communist Party, which draws much of its power base from rural areas where some 80 percent of the population live.

Though some people complain that the pronouncement against big wedding parties is a case of excessive Big Brother intervention, the Vietnamese government sees it as a necessary step to defuse political unrest. Last year, a string of protests erupted in several provinces as villagers complained about low wages, tax increases, and corruption among local officials.

## Vice worries conservatives

Some Western analysts believe that the uprisings fueled conservative elements within the party's ruling Politburo and slowed the pace of economic reforms. As a result, direct foreign investment in new projects fell by almost half last year compared with 1996. This was the first time that investment growth in Vietnam declined since *doi moi* was initiated.

"As the government courts international interest, it simultaneously constrains investors with tight restrictions on advertising spending and a long licensing process," says a Western businessman who declined to be identified.

The market has not grown as much as many international companies had expected, and some firms have moved out or scaled down operations. Dutch airline KLM Royal suspended its flights to Ho Chi Minh City in March.

This is in stark contrast to just four years ago, when the United States lifted its embargo against Vietnam and foreign investors rushed in, attracted to the country's relatively educated population, low-cost labor, and opening economy. "The reforms in the early '90s were quite radical by any standards," says International Monetary Fund representative Erik Offerdal.

These days, investors are less enthusiastic, and they are increasingly concerned about the government's often-conflicting policies of freeing the market and tightening controls.

According to Daewoo's public relations manager in Hanoi, Phan Hong Nga, the South Korean conglomerate's apartment building adjacent to its hotel had a low occupancy rate in 1996 and early 1997 because companies were uncertain about the market. "Investors in Vietnam are quite cautious and unwilling to sign a long-term lease—which is understandable," she says. Ms. Nga adds that the building now allows three-month leases.

Government officials "haven't seen the need for further reforms in recent years," says Mr. Offerdal. "It has been several years since significant market reforms have been implemented."

There are signs, however, that Vietnam will kick-start its economy again. Last September, the Communist Party Central Committee changed its leadership by naming two market reformers to the posts of president and prime minister: Tran Duc Luong and Phan Van Khai.

## New leader's direction

Yet Hanoi-based foreign businessmen caution that it is too early to tell what the new leadership will mean to the economy. In late December, conservative Army official Le Kha Phieu was elected Communist Party secretary general, traditionally the most powerful member of the triumvirate. Mr. Phieu has a record of opposing a free-market system, and he is seen as a

counterbalance to the new president and prime minister.

However, since assuming his new post, Phieu has said that he favors economic reforms. "We will continue to carry out renovation," the Nhan Dan daily reported him as saying.

Some businessmen warn that Phieu's recent statements in the official press cannot be taken at face value. "I doubt that he could have changed his ideology just because he has a new title," says one Ho Chi Minh City-based businessman who spoke on condition of anonymity. "A leopard can't change his spots."

Other analysts are more optimistic. "The reforms will definitely continue at a fast pace," says Mr. Dinh, the government economic adviser.

Offerdal agrees, pointing out that Vietnam's decisionmaking process is based on consensus: "I don't think that any one person can change Vietnam's commitment to market reform."

Vietnam's leadership overhaul came at a particularly difficult time. Vietnamese products' competitiveness fell as other Asian currencies plummeted. South Korea, Vietnam's largest investor last year, is tending to its problems at home. And investment from other East Asian nations, which together with South Korea accounted for some 70 percent of Vietnam's trade last year, may continue to decline as the region deals with its financial crisis.

Though the government forecasts GDP growth of 9 percent this year, many Western economists believe this figure is optimistic. "I don't think that it can be achieved given the regional situation," says Offerdal.

## Control above reform

Ironically, the regional troubles and last year's disappointment may prove to be an "impetus for reforms," Offerdal says. "Over the past year, it's become apparent that new initiatives are needed."

However, party leader Phieu indicated that Communist control must still be incorporated in the government's economic plans.

"Maintaining political stability is the fundamental condition to carry out the renewal process," he told the official Nhan Dan daily newspaper recently.

# Credits

# Sources for Statistical Reports

U.S. State Department, *Background Notes* (1998).

C.I.A. *World Factbook* (1997).

World Bank, *World Development Report* (1998).

UN *Population and Vital Statistics Report* (January 1998).

*World Statistics in Brief* (1998).

*The Statesman's Yearbook* (1998–1999).

Population Reference Bureau, *World Population Data Sheet* (1998).

*World Almanac* (1998).

# Glossary of Terms and Abbreviations

**Animism**  The belief that all objects, including plants, animals, rocks, and other matter, contain spirits. This belief figures prominently in early Japanese religious thought and in the various indigenous religions of the South Pacific.

**Anti-Fascist People's Freedom League (AFPFL)**  An anti-Japanese resistance movement organized by Burmese students and intellectuals.

**ANZUS**  The name of a joint military-security agreement originally among Australia, New Zealand, and the United States. New Zealand is no longer a member.

**Asia Pacific Economic Cooperation Council (APEC)**  Organized in 1989, this body is becoming increasingly visible as a major forum for plans about regional economic cooperation and growth in the Pacific Rim.

**Asian Development Bank (ADB)**  With contributions from industrialized nations, the ADB provides loans to Pacific Rim countries in order to foster economic development.

**Association of Southeast Asian Nations (ASEAN)**  Established in 1967 to promote economic cooperation among the countries of Indonesia, Malaysia, the Philippines, Singapore, Thailand, and Brunei.

**British Commonwealth of Nations**  A voluntary association of nations formerly included in the British Empire. Officials meet regularly in member countries to discuss issues of common economic, military, and political concern.

**Buddhism**  A religious and ethical philosophy of life that originated in India in the fifth and sixth centuries B.C, partly in reaction to the caste system. Buddhism holds that people's souls are endlessly reborn and that one's standing with each rebirth depends on one's behavior in the previous life.

**Capitalism**  An economic system in which productive property is owned by individuals or corporations, rather than by the government, and the proceeds of which belong to the owner rather than to the workers or the state.

**Chaebol**  A Korean term for a large business conglomerate. Similar to the Japanese *keiretsu*.

**Chinese Communist Party (CCP)**  Founded in 1921 by Mao Zedong and others, the CCP became the ruling party of the People's Republic of China in 1949 upon the defeat of the Nationalist Party and the army of Chiang Kai-shek.

**Cold War**  The intense rivalry, short of direct "hot-war" military conflict, between the Soviet Union and the United States, which began at the end of World War II and continued until approximately 1990.

**Communism**  An economic system in which land and businesses are owned collectively by everyone in the society rather than by individuals. Modern communism is founded on the teachings of the German intellectuals Marx and Engels.

**Confucianism**  A system of ethical guidelines for managing one's personal relationships with others and with the state. Confucianism stresses filial piety and obligation to one's superiors. It is based on the teachings of the Chinese intellectuals Confucius and Mencius.

**Cultural Revolution**  A period between 1966 and 1976 in China when, urged on by Mao, students attempted to revive a revolutionary spirit in China. Intellectuals and even Chinese Communist Party leaders who were not zealously communist were violently attacked or purged from office.

**Demilitarized Zone (DMZ)**  A heavily guarded border zone separating North and South Korea.

**European Union (EU)**  An umbrella organization of numerous Western European nations working toward the establishment of a single economic and political European entity. Formerly known as the European Community (EC) and European Economic Community (EEC).

**Extraterritoriality**  The practice whereby the home country exercises jurisdiction over its diplomats and other citizens living in a foreign country, effectively freeing them from the authority of the host government.

**Feudalism**  A social and economic system of premodern Europe, Japan, China, and other countries, characterized by a strict division of the populace into social classes, an agricultural economy, and governance by lords controlling vast parcels of land and the people thereon.

**Greater East Asia Co-Prosperity Sphere**  The Japanese description of the empire they created in the 1940s by military conquest.

**Gross Domestic Product (GDP)**  A statistic describing the entire output of goods and services produced by a country in a year, less income earned on foreign investments.

**Hinduism**  A 5,000-year-old religion, especially of India, that advocates a social caste system but anticipates the eventual merging of all individuals into one universal world soul.

**Indochina**  The name of the colony in Southeast Asia controlled by France and consisting of the countries of Laos, Cambodia, and Vietnam. The colony ceased to exist after 1954, but the term still is often applied to the region.

**International Monetary Fund (IMF)**  An agency of the United Nations whose goal it is to promote freer world trade by assisting nations in economic development.

**Islam**  The religion founded by Mohammed and codified in the Koran. Believers, called Muslims, submit to Allah (Arabic for God) and venerate his name in daily prayer.

**Keiretsu**  A Japanese word for a large business conglomerate.

**Khmer Rouge**  The communist guerrilla army, led by Pol Pot, that controlled Cambodia in the 1970s and subsequently attempted to overthrow the UN–sanctioned government.

**Kuomintang**  The National People's Party (Nationalists), which, under Chiang Kai-shek, governed China until Mao Zedong's revolution in 1949; it continues to dominate politics in Taiwan.

**Laogai**  A Mandarin Chinese word for a prison or concentration camp where political prisoners are kept. It is similar in concept to the Russian word *gulag*.

**Liberal Democratic Party (LDP)** The conservative party that ruled Japan almost continuously between 1955 and 1993 and oversaw Japan's rapid economic development.

**Martial Law** The law applied to a territory by military authorities in a time of emergency when regular civilian authorities are unable to maintain order. Under martial law, residents are usually restricted in their movement and in their exercise of such rights as freedom of speech and of the press.

**Meiji Restoration** The restoration of the Japanese emperor to his throne in 1868. The period is important as the beginning of the modern era in Japan and the opening of Japan to the West after centuries of isolation.

**Monsoons** Winds that bring exceptionally heavy rainfall to parts of Southeast Asia and elsewhere. Monsoon rains are essential to the production of rice.

**National League for Democracy** An opposition party in Myanmar that was elected to head the government in 1990 but that has since been forbidden by the current military leaders to take office.

**New Economic Policy (NEP)** An economic plan advanced in the 1970s to restructure the Malaysian economy and foster industrialization and ethnic equality.

**Newly Industrializing Country (NIC)** A designation for those countries of the developing world, particularly Taiwan, South Korea, and other Asian nations, whose economies have undergone rapid growth; sometimes also referred to as newly industrialized countries.

**Non-Aligned Movement** A loose association of mostly non-Western developing nations, many of which had been colonies of Western powers but during the cold war chose to remain detached from either the U.S. or Soviet bloc. Initially Indonesia and India, among others, were enthusiastic promoters of the movement.

**Opium Wars** Conflicts between Britain and China in 1839–1842 and 1856–1866 in which England used China's destruction of opium shipments and other issues as a pretext to attack China and force the government to sign trade agreements.

**Pacific War** The name frequently used by the Japanese to refer to that portion of World War II in which they were involved and which took place in Asia and the Pacific.

**Shintoism** An ancient indigenous religion of Japan that stresses the role of *kami,* or supernatural gods, in the lives of people. For a time during the 1930s, Shinto was the state religion of Japan and the emperor was honored as its high priest.

**Smokestack Industries** Heavy industries such as steel mills that are basic to an economy but produce objectionable levels of air, water, or land pollution.

**Socialism** An economic system in which productive property is owned by the government as are the proceeds from the productive labor. Most socialist systems today are actually mixed economies in which individuals as well as the government own property.

**South Pacific Forum** An organization established by Australia and other South Pacific nations to provide a forum for discussion of common problems and opportunities in the region.

**Southeast Asia Treaty Organization (SEATO)** This is a collective-defense treaty signed by the United States and several European and Southeast Asian nations. It was dissolved in 1977.

**Subsistence Farming** Farming that meets the immediate needs of the farming family but that does not yield a surplus sufficient for export.

**Taoism** An ancient religion of China inspired by Lao-tze that stresses the need for mystical contemplation to free one from the desires and sensations of the materialistic and physical world.

**Tiananmen Square Massacre** The violent suppression by the Chinese Army of a prodemocracy movement that had been organized in Beijing by thousands of Chinese students in 1989 and that had become an international embarrassment to the Chinese regime.

**United Nations (UN)** An international organization established immediately after World War II to replace the League of Nations. The organization includes most of the countries of the world and works for international understanding and world peace.

**World Health Organization (WHO)** Established in 1948 as an advisory and technical-assistance organization to improve the health of peoples around the world.

# Bibliography

## GENERAL WORKS

Mark Borthwick, *East Asian Civilizations: A Dialogue in Five Stages* (Cambridge: Harvard University Press, 1988). The development of philosophical and religious thought in China, Korea, Japan, and other regions of East Asia.

Richard Bowring and Peter Kornicki, *Encyclopedia of Japan* (New York: Cambridge University Press, 1993).

Barbara K. Bundy, Stephen D. Burns, and Kimberly V. Weichel, *The Future of the Pacific Rim: Scenarios for Regional Cooperation* (Westport, CT: Praeger, 1994).

Commission on U.S.–Japan Relations for the Twenty-First Century, *Preparing for a Pacific Century: Exploring the Potential for Pacific Basin Cooperation* (Washington, DC: November 1991). Transcription of an international conference on the Pacific with commentary by representatives from the United States, Malaysia, Japan, Thailand, Indonesia, and others.

Susanna Cuyler, *A Companion to Japanese Literature, Culture, and Language* (Highland Park, NJ: B. Rugged, 1992).

William Theodore de Bary, *East Asian Civilizations: A Dialogue in Five Stages* (Cambridge: Harvard University Press, 1988). An examination of religions and philosophical thought in several regions of East Asia.

Syed N. Hossain, *Japan: Not in the West* (Boston: Vikas II, 1995).

James W. McGuire, ed., *Rethinking Development in East Asia and Latin America* (Los Angeles: Pacific Council on International Policy, 1997).

Charles E. Morrison, ed., *Asia Pacific Security Outlook 1997* (Honolulu: East-West Center, 1997).

Seijiu Naya and Stephen Browne, eds., *Development Challenges in Asia and the Pacific in the 1990s* (Honolulu: East-West Center, 1991). A collection of speeches made at the 1990 Symposium on Cooperation in Asia and the Pacific. The articles cover development issues in East, Southeast, and South Asia and the Pacific.

Edwin O. Reischauer and Marius B. Jansen, *The Japanese Today: Change and Continuity* (Cambridge: Belknap Press, 1995). A description of the basic geography and historical background of Japan.

## NATIONAL HISTORIES AND ANALYSES

### Australia

Boris Frankel, *From the Prophets Deserts Come: The Struggle to Reshape Australian Political Culture* (New York: Deakin University [St. Mut.], 1994). Australia's government and political aspects are described in this essay.

Herman J. Hiery, *The Neglected War: The German South Pacific and the Influence of WW I* (Honolulu: University of Hawaii Press, 1995).

David Alistair Kemp, *Society and Electoral Behaviors in Australia: A Study of Three Decades* (St. Lucia: University of Queensland Press, 1978). Elections, political parties, and social problems in Australia since 1945.

David Meredith and Barrie Dyster, *Australia in the International Economy in the Twentieth Century* (New York: Cambridge University Press, 1990). Examines the international aspects of Australia's economy.

### Brunei

Wendy Hutton, *East Malaysia and Brunei* (Berkeley: Periplus, 1993).

Graham Saunders, *A History of Brunei* (New York: Oxford University Press, 1995).

Nicholas Tarling, *Britain, the Brookes, and Brunei* (Kuala Lumpur: Oxford University Press, 1971). A history of the sultanate of Brunei and its neighbors.

### Cambodia

David P. Chandler, *The Tragedy of Cambodian History, War, and Revolution since 1945* (New Haven: Yale University Press, 1993). A short history of Cambodia.

Michael W. Doyle, *UN Peacekeeping in Cambodia: UNTAC's Civil Mandate* (Boulder: Lynne Rienner, 1995). A review of the current status of Cambodia's government and political parties.

Craig Etcheson, *The Rise and Demise of Democratic Kampuchea* (Boulder: Westview Press, 1984). A history of the rise of the Communist government in Cambodia.

William Shawcross, *The Quality of Mercy: Cambodia, Holocaust, and Modern Conscience; with a report from Ethiopia* (New York: Simon & Schuster, 1985). A report on political atrocities, relief programs, and refugees in Cambodia and Ethiopia.

Usha Welaratna, ed., *Beyond the Killing Fields: Voices of Nine Cambodian Survivors* (Stanford, CA: Stanford University Press, 1993). A collection of nine narratives by Cambodian refugees in the United States and their adjustments into American society.

### China

Julia F. Andrews, *Painters and Politics in the People's Republic of China, 1949–1979* (Berkeley: University of California Press, 1994). A fascinating presentation of the relationship between politics and art from the beginning of the Communist period until the eve of major liberalization in 1979.

Ma Bo, *Blood Red Sunset* (New York: Viking, 1995).
A compelling autobiographical account by a Red Guard during the Cultural Revolution.

Jung Chang, *Wild Swans: Three Daughters of China* (New York: Simon and Shuster, 1992).
An autobiographical/biographical account that illuminates what China was like for one family for three generations.

Kwang-chih Chang, *The Archaeology of China,* 4th ed. (New Haven: Yale University Press, 1986).

___, *Shang Civilization* (New Haven: Yale University Press, 1980).
Two works by an eminent archaeologist on the origins of Chinese civilization.

Nien Cheng, *Life and Death in Shanghai* (New York: Penguin Books, 1988). A view of the Cultural Revolution by one of its victims.

Qing Dai, *Yangtze! Yangtze!* (Toronto: Probe International, 1994).
Collection of documents concerning the debate over building the Three Gorges Dam on the upper Yangtze River in order to harness energy for China.

John King Fairbank, *China: A New History* (Cambridge: Harvard University Press, 1992).
An examination of the motivating forces in China's history that define it as a coherent culture from its earliest recorded history to 1991.

David S. G. Goodman and Beverly Hooper, eds., *China's Quiet Revolution: New Interactions between State and Society* (New York: St. Martin's Press, 1994).
Articles examine the impact of economic reforms since the early 1980s on the social structure and society generally, with focus on changes in wealth, status, power, and newly emerging social forces.

Richard Madsen, *China and the American Dream: A Moral Inquiry* (Berkeley: University of California Press, 1995).
A history on the emotional and unpredictable relationship the United States has had with China from the nineteenth century to the present.

Jim Mann, *Beijing Jeep: A Case Study of Western Business in China* (Boulder, Westview Press, 1997).
A crisp view of what it takes for a Westerner to do business in China.

Suzanne Ogden, *China's Unresolved Issues: Politics, Development, and Culture* (Englewood Cliffs: Prentice Hall, 1992).
A complete review of economic and cultural issues in modern China.

Li Zhisui, *The Private Life of Chairman Mao* (New York: Random House, 1994). Memoirs of Mao's personal physician.

**Hong Kong**

"Basic Law of Hong Kong Special Administrative Region of the People's Republic of China," *Beijing Review*, Vol. 33, No. 18 (April 30–May 6, 1990), supplement.

Ming K. Chan and Gerard A. Postiglione, *The Hong Kong Reader: Passage to Chinese Sovereignty* (Armonk, NY: M. E. Sharpe, 1996).
A collection of articles about the issues facing Hong Kong during the transition to Chinese rule after July 1, 1997.

Berry Hsu, ed., *The Common Law in Chinese Context* in the series entitled *Hong Kong Becoming China: The Transition to 1997* (Armonk, NY: M. E. Sharpe, Inc., 1992).
An examination of the common law aspects of the "Basic Law," the mini-constitution that will govern Hong Kong after 1997.

Walter Hatch and Kozo Yamamura, *Asia in Japan's Embrace: Building a Regional Production Alliance* (Cambridge: Cambridge University Press, 1996). Discusses the future likelihood of Japan building an exclusive trading zone in Asia.

Benjamin K. P. Leung, ed., *Social Issues in Hong Kong* (New York: Oxford University Press, 1990).
A collection of essays on select issues in Hong Kong, such as aging, poverty, women, pornography, and mental illness.

Jan Morris, *Hong Kong: Epilogue to an Empire* (New York: Vintage, 1997).
A detailed portrait of Hong Kong that gives the reader the sense of actually being on the scene in a vibrant Hong Kong.

Mark Roberti, *The Fall of Hong Kong: China's Triumph and Britain's Betrayal* (New York: John Wiley & Sons, Inc., 1994).
An account on the decisions Britain and China made about Hong Kong's fate since the early 1980s.

Frank Welsh, *A Borrowed Place: The History of Hong Kong* (New York: Kodansha International, 1996).
A presentation on Hong Kong's history from the time of the British East India Company in the eighteenth century through the Opium Wars of the nineteenth century to the present.

**Indonesia**

Amarendra Bhattacharya and Mari Pangestu, *Indonesia: Development, Transformation, and Public Policy* (Washington, DC: World Bank, 1993).
An examination of Indonesia's economic policy.

Frederica M. Bunge, *Indonesia: A Country Study* (Washington, DC: U.S. Government, 1983).
An excellent review of the outlines of Indonesian history and culture, including politics and national security.

Philip J. Eldridge, *Non-government Organizations and Political Participation in Indonesia* (New York: Oxford University Press, 1995).
Examination of Indonesia's nongovernment agencies (NGOs).

Audrey R. Kahin, ed., *Regional Dynamics of the Indonesian Revolution: Unity from Diversity* (Honolulu: University of Hawaii Press, 1985).

A history of Indonesia since the end of World War II, with separate chapters on selected islands.

Hamish McConald, *Suharto's Indonesia* (Australia: The Dominion Press, 1980).

The story of the rise of Suharto and the manner in which he controlled the political and military life of the country, beginning in 1965.

Susan Rodgers, ed., *Telling Lives, Telling Histories: Autobiography and Historical Immigration in Modern Indonesia* (Berkeley, CA: University of California Press, 1995).

Reviews the history of Indonesia's immigration.

David Wigg, *In a Class of Their Own: A Look at the Campaign against Female Illiteracy* (Washington, DC: World Bank, 1994).

Looks at the work that is being done by various groups to advance women's literacy in Indonesia.

## Japan

David Arase, *Buying Power: The Political Economy of Japan's Foreign Aid* (Boulder: Lynne Rienner Publishers, Inc., 1995).

An attempt to explain the complexities of Japan foreign-aid programs.

Michael Barnhart, *Japan and the World since 1868* (New York: Routledge, Chapman, and Hall, 1994).

An essay that addresses commerce in Japan from 1868 to the present.

Marjorie Wall Bingham and Susan Hill Gross, *Women in Japan* (Minnesota: Glenhurst Publications, Inc., 1987).

An historical review of Japanese women's roles in Japan.

John Clammer, *Difference and Modernity: Social Theory and Contemporary Japanese Society* (New York: Routledge, Chapman, and Hall, 1995).

Dennis J. Encarnation, *Rivals beyond Trade: America Versus Japan in Global Competition* (Ithaca: Cornell University Press, 1993).

Explains how the economic rivalry that was once bilateral has turned into an intense global competition.

Mark Gauthier, *Making It in Japan* (Upland, PA: Diane Publishers, 1994).

An examination of how success can be attained in Japan's marketplace.

Walter Hatch and Kozo Yamamura, *Asia in Japan's Embrace: Building a Regional Production Alliance,* (Cambridge: Cambridge University Press, 1996).

Discusses the future likelihood of Japan building an exclusive trading zone in Asia.

Paul Herbig, *Innovation Japanese Style: A Cultural and Historical Perspective* (Glenview, IL: Greenwood, 1995).

A review of the implications for international competition.

Harold R. Kerbo and John McKinstry, *Who Rules Japan? The Inner-Circle of Economic and Political Power* (Glenview, IL: Greenwood, 1995).

The effect of Japan's politics on its economy is evaluated in this essay.

Hiroshi Komai, *Migrant Workers in Japan* (New York: Routledge, Chapman, and Hall, 1994).

Focus on the abundance of the migrant labor supply in Japan.

Makoto Kumazawa, *Portraits of the Japanese Workplace: Labor Movements, Workers, and Managers* (Boulder: Westview Press, 1996).

Translated into English from Japanese, the book includes reviews of the workplace lifestyle of bankers, women, steel workers, and others.

Solomon B. Levine and Koji Taira, eds., *Japan's External Economic Relations: Japanese Perspectives,* special issue of *The Annals of the American Academy of Political and Social Science,* January 1991.

An excellent overview of the origin and future of Japan's economic relations with the rest of the world, especially Asia.

E. Wayne Nafziger, *Learning from the Japanese: Japan's Pre-War Development and the Third World* (Armonk, NY: M. E. Sharpe, 1995).

Presents Japan as a model of "guided capitalism," and what it did by way of policies designed to promote and accelerate development.

Nippon Steel Corporation, *Nippon: The Land and Its People* (Japan: Gakuseisha Publishing Co., 1984).

An overview of modern Japan in both English and Japanese.

Asahi Simbun, *Japan Almanac 1998* (Tokyo: Asahi Shimbun Publishing Company, 1997).

Charts, maps, statistical data about Japan in both English and Japanese.

Patrick Smith, *Japan: A Reinterpretation* (New York: Pantheon Books, 1997).

A discussion of the rapidly changing Japanese national character.

## Korea: North and South Korea

Chai-Sik Chung, *A Korean Confucian Encounter with the Modern World* (Berkeley, CA: IEAS, 1995).

Korea's history and the effectiveness of Confucianism are addressed.

Donald Clark et al., *U.S.–Korean Relations* (Farmingdale, NY: Regina Books, 1995).

A review on the history of Korea's relationship with the United States.

James Cotton, *Politics and Policy in the New Korean State: From Rah Tae-Woo to Kim Young-Sam* (New York: St. Martin's, 1995).

The power and influence of politics in Korea are examined.

James Hoare, *North Korea* (New York: Oxford University Press, 1995).

An essay that addresses commerce in Japan between 1868 and the present.

Dae-Jung Kim, *Mass Participatory Economy: Korea's Road to World Economic Power* (Landham, MD: University Press of America, 1995).

Korean Overseas Information Service, *A Handbook of Korea* (Seoul: Seoul International Publishing House, 1987).
A description of modern South Korea, including social welfare, foreign relations, and culture. The early history of the entire Korean Peninsula is also discussed.

___, *Korean Arts and Culture* (Seoul: Seoul International Publishing House, 1986).
A beautifully illustrated introduction to the rich cultural life of modern South Korea.

Callus A. MacDonald, *Korea: The War before Vietnam* (New York: The Free Press, 1986).
A detailed account of the military events in Korea between 1950 and 1953, including a careful analysis of the U.S. decision to send troops to the peninsula.

Christopher J. Sigur, ed., *Continuity and Change in Contemporary Korea* (New York: Carnegie Ethics and International Affairs, 1994).
A review of the numerous stages of change that Korea has experienced.

### Laos

Sucheng Chan, ed., *Hmong: Means Free Life in Laos and America* (Philadelphia: Temple University Press, 1994).

Arthur J. Dommen, *Laos: Keystone of Indochina* (Boulder: Westview Press, 1985).
A short history and review of current events in Laos.

Joel M. Halpern, *The Natural Economy of Laos* (Christiansburg, VA: Dalley Book Service, 1990).

___, *Government, Politics, and South Structures of Laos: Study of Traditions and Innovations* (Christiansburg, VA: Dalley Book Service, 1990).

### Macau

Charles Ralph Boxer, *The Portuguese Seaborne Empire, 1415–1825* (New York: A. A. Knopf, 1969).
A history of Portugal's colonies, including Macau.

W. G. Clarence-Smith, *The Third Portuguese Empire, 1825–1975* (Manchester: Manchester University Press, 1985).
A history of Portugal's colonies, including Macau.

### Malaysia

Mohammed Ariff, *The Malaysian Economy: Pacific Connections* (New York: Oxford University Press, 1991).
The report on Malaysia examines Malaysia's development and its vulnerability in world trade.

Richard Clutterbuck, *Conflict and Violence in Singapore and Malaysia, 1945–1983* (Boulder: Westview Press, 1985).
The Communist challenge to the stability of Singapore and Malaysia in the early years of their independence from Great Britain is presented.

K. S. Jomo, ed., *Japan and Malaysian Development: In the Shadow of the Rising Sun* (New York: Routledge, 1995).
A review of the relationship between Japan and Malaysia's economy.

Gordon Means, *Malaysian Politics: The Second Generation* (New York: Oxford University Press, 1991).

R. S. Milne, *Malaysia: Tradition, Modernity, and Islam* (Boulder: Westview Press, 1986).
A general overview of the nature of modern Malaysian society.

### Myanmar (Burma)

Michael Aung-Thwin, *Pagan: The Origins of Modern Burma* (Honolulu: University of Hawaii Press, 1985).
A treatment of the religious and political ideology of the Burmese people and the effect of ideology on the economy and politics of the modern state.

Aye Kyaw, *The Voice of Young Burma* (Ithaca, NY: Cornell SE Asia, 1993).
The political history of Burma is presented in this report.

Chi-Shad Liang, *Burma's Foreign Relations: Neutralism in Theory and Practice* (Glenview, IL: Greenwood, 1990).

Mya Maung, *The Burma Road to Poverty* (Glenview, IL: Greenwood, 1991).

### New Zealand

Bev James and Kay Saville-Smith, *Gender, Culture, and Power: Challenging New Zealand's Gendered Culture* (New York: Oxford University Press, 1995).

Patrick Massey, *New Zealand: Market Liberalization in a Developed Economy* (New York: St. Martin, 1995).
Analyzes New Zealand's market-oriented reform programs since the Labour government came into power in 1984.

Stephen Rainbow, *Green Politics* (New York: Oxford University Press, 1994).
A review of current New Zealand politics.

Geoffrey W. Rice, *The Oxford History of New Zealand* (New York: Oxford University Press, 1993).

### Papua New Guinea

Robert J. Gordon and Mervyn J. Meggitt, *Law and Order in the New Guinea Highlands: Encounters with Enga* (Hanover: University Press of New England, 1985).
Tribal law and warfare in Papua New Guinea.

David Hyndman, *Ancestral Rainforests and the Mountain of Gold: Indigenous Peoples and Mining in New Guinea* (Boulder: Westview Press, 1994).

Bruce W. Knauft, *South Coast New Guinea Cultures: History, Comparison, Dialectic* (New York: Cambridge University Press, 1993).

### The Philippines

Frederica M. Bunge, ed., *Philippines: A Country Study* (Washington, DC: U.S. Government, 1984).

Description and analysis of the economic, security, political, and social systems of the Philippines, including maps, statistical charts, and reproduction of important documents. An extensive bibliography is included.

Manual B. Dy, *Values in Philippine Culture and Education* (Washington, DC: Council for Research in Values and Philosophy, 1994).

James F. Eder and Robert L. Youngblood, eds., *Patterns of Power and Politics in the Philippines: Implications for Development* (Tempe: AZ: ASU Program, SE Asian, 1994).
A review of the impact of politics and its power over development in the Philippines.

**Singapore**

Lai A. Eng, *Meanings of Multiethnicity: A Case Study of Ethnicity and Ethnic Relations in Singapore* (New York: Oxford University Press, 1995).

Paul Leppert, *Doing Business with Singapore* (Fremont, CA: Jain Publishing Co., 1995).
Singapore's economic status is examined in this report.

Hafiz Mirza, *Multinationals and the Growth of the Singapore Economy* (New York: St. Martin's Press, 1986).
An essay on foreign companies and their impact on modern Singapore.

Nilavu Mohdx et al., *New Place, Old Ways: Essays on Indian Society and Culture in Modern Singapore* (Columbia, MO: South Asia, 1994).

**South Pacific**

C. Beeby and N. Fyfe, "The South Pacific Nuclear Free Zone Treaty," Victoria University of Wellington *Law Review,* Vol. 17, No. 1, pp. 33–51 (February 1987).
A good review of nuclear issues in the Pacific.

William S. Livingston and William Roger Louis, eds., *Australia, New Zealand, and the Pacific Islands since the First World War* (Austin: University of Texas Press, 1979).
An assessment of significant historical and political developments in Australia, New Zealand, and the Pacific Islands since 1917.

**Taiwan**

Joel Aberbach et al., eds., *The Role of the State in Taiwan's Development* (Armonk, NY: M. E. Sharpe, 1994).
Articles address technology, international trade, state policy toward the development of local industries, and the effect of economic development on society, including women and farmers.

Bih-er Chou, Clark Cal, and Janet Clark, *Women in Taiwan Politics: Overcoming Barriers to Women's Participation in a Modernizing Society* (Boulder: Lynne Rienner Publishers, 1990).
Examines the political underrepresentation of women in Taiwan and how Chinese culture on the one hand and

modernization and development on the other are affecting women's status.

Stevan Harrell and Chun-chieh Huang, eds., *Cultural Change in Postwar Taiwan* (Boulder: Westview Press, 1994).
A collection of essays that analyzes the tensions in Taiwan's society as modernization erodes many of its old values and traditions.

Dennis Hickey, *United States–Taiwan Security Ties: From Cold War to beyond Containment* (Westport: Praeger, 1994).
Examines U.S.–Taiwan security ties from the Cold War to the present and what Taiwan is doing to ensure its own military preparedness.

Chin-chuan Lee, "Sparking a Fire: The Press and the Ferment of Democratic Change in Taiwan," in Chin-chuan Lee (ed.), *China's Media, Media China* (Boulder: Westview Press, 1994), pp. 179–193.

Robert M. Marsh, *The Great Transformation: Social Change in Taipei, Taiwan, since the 1960s* (Armonk, NY: M. E. Sharpe, 1996).
An investigation of how Taiwan's society has changed since the 1960s when its economic transformation began.

Robert G. Sutter and William R. Johnson, *Taiwan in World Affairs* (Boulder: Westview Press, 1994).
Articles give comprehensive coverage of Taiwan's involvement in foreign affairs.

**Thailand**

Medhi Krongkaew, *Thailand's Industrialization and Its Consequences* (New York: St. Martin, 1995).
A discussion of events surround the development of Thailand since the mid-1980s with a focus on the nature and characteristics of Thai industrialization.

Ross Prizzia, *Thailand in Transition: The Role of Oppositional Forces* (Honolulu: University of Hawaii Press, 1985).
Government management of political opposition in Thailand.

Susan Wells and Steve Van Beek, *A Day in the Life of Thailand* (San Francisco: Collins SF, 1995).

**Vietnam**

Chris Brazier, *The Price of Peace* (New York: Okfam Pubs. U.K. [St. Mut.], 1992).

Ronald J. Cima, ed., *Vietnam: A Country Study* (Washington, D.C.: U.S. Government, 1989).
An overview of modern Vietnam, with emphasis on the origins, values, and lifestyles of the Vietnamese people.

Chris Ellsbury et al., *Vietnam: Perspectives and Performance* (Cedar Falls, IA: Assn. Text Study, 1994).
A review of Vietnam's history.

D. R. SarDeSai, *Vietnam: The Struggle for National Identity* (Boulder: Westview Press, 1992).
A good treatment of ethnicity in Vietnam and a national history up to the current involvement in Cambodia.

## PERIODICALS AND CURRENT EVENTS

*The Annals of the American Academy of Political and Social Science*
c/o Sage Publications, Inc.
2455 Teller Rd.
Newbury Park, CA 91320
Selected issues focus on the Pacific Rim; there is an extensive book-review section. Special issues are as follows:
"The Pacific Region: Challenges to Policy and Theory" (September 1989).
"China's Foreign Relations" (January 1992).
"Japan's External Economic Relations: Japanese Perspectives" (January 1991).

*Asian Affairs: An American Review*
Helen Dwight Reid Educational Foundation
1319 Eighteenth St., NW
Washington, DC 20036-1802
Publishes articles on political, economic, and security policy.

*The Asian Wall Street Journal,* Dow Jones & Company, Inc.
A daily business newspaper focusing on Asian markets.

*Asia-Pacific Issues*
East-West Center
1601 East-West Rd.
Burns Hall, Rm. 1079
Honolulu, HI 96848-1601
Each contains one article on an issue of the day in Asia and the Pacific.

*The Asia-Pacific Magazine*
Research School of Pacific and Asian Studies
The Australian National University
Canberra ACT 0200, Australia
General coverage of all of Asia and the Pacific, including book reviews and excellent color photographs.

*Asia-Pacific Population Journal*
Economic and Social Commission for Asia and the Pacific
United Nations Building
Rajdamnern Nok Ave.
Bangkok 10200, Thailand
A quarterly publication of the United Nations.

*Canada and Hong Kong Update*
Joint Centre for Asia Pacific Studies
Suite 270, York Lanes
York University
4700 Keele St.
North York, Ontario M3J 1P3, Canada
A source of information about Hong Kong emigration.

*Current History: A World Affairs Journal*
Focuses on one country or region in each issue; the emphasis is on international and domestic politics.

*The Economist*
25 St. James's St.
London, England
A newsmagazine with insightful commentary on international issues affecting the Pacific Rim.

*Education about Asia*
1 Lane Hall
The University of Michigan
Ann Arbor, MI 48109
Published 3 times a year, it contains useful tips for teachers of Asian Studies. The Spring 1998 issue (Vol. 3, No. 1) focuses on teaching the geography of Asia.

*Indochina Interchange*
Suite 1801
220 West 42nd St.
New York, NY 10036
A publication of the U.S.–Indochina Reconciliation Project. An excellent source of information about assistance programs for Laos, Cambodia, and Vietnam.

*The Japan Foundation Newsletter*
The Japan Foundation
Park Building
3-6 Kioi-cho
Chiyoda-ku
Tokyo 102, Japan
A quarterly with research reports, book reviews, and announcements of interest to Japan specialists.

*Japan Quarterly*
Asahi Shimbun
5-3-2 Tsukiji
Chuo-ku
Tokyo 104, Japan
A quarterly journal, in English, covering political, cultural, and sociological aspects of modern Japanese life.

*The Japan Times*
The Japan Times Ltd.
C.P.O. Box 144
Tokyo 100-91, Japan
Excellent coverage, in English, of news reported in the Japanese press.

*The Journal of Asian Studies*
Association for Asian Studies
1 Lane Hall
University of Michigan

Ann Arbor, MI 48109
Formerly *The Far Eastern Quarterly;* scholarly articles on Asia, South Asia, and Southeast Asia.

*Journal of Southeast Asian Studies*
Singapore University Press
Singapore
Formerly the *Journal of Southeast Asian History;* scholarly articles on all aspects of modern Southeast Asia.

*Korea Economic Report*
Yoido
P.O. Box 963
Seoul 150-609
South Korea
An economic magazine for people doing business in Korea.

*The Korea Herald*
2-12, 3-ga Hoehyon-dong
Chung-gu
Seoul, South Korea
World news coverage, in English, with focus on events affecting the Korean Peninsula.

*The Korea Times*
The Korea Times Hankook Ilbo
Seoul, South Korea
Coverage of world news, with emphasis on events affecting Asia and the Korean Peninsula.

*Malaysia Industrial Digest*
Malaysian Industrial Development Authority (MIDA)
6th Floor
Industrial Promotion Division
Wisma Damansara, Jalan Semantan
50490 Kuala Kumpur, Malaysia
A source of statistics on manufacturing in Malaysia; of interest to those wishing to become more knowledgeable in the business and industry of the Pacific Rim.

*The New York Times*
229 West 43rd St.
New York, NY 10036
A daily newspaper with excellent coverage of world events.

*News from Japan*
Embassy of Japan
Japan–U.S. News and Communication
Suite 520
900 17th St., NW
Washington, DC 20006
A twice-monthly newsletter with news briefs from the Embassy of Japan on issues affecting Japan–U.S. relations.

*Newsweek*
444 Madison Ave.
New York, NY 10022
A weekly magazine with news and commentary on national and world events.

*Pacific Affairs*
The University of British Columbia
Vancouver, BC V6T 1W5
Canada
An international journal on Asia and the Pacific, including reviews of recent books about the region.

*Pacific Basin Quarterly*
c/o Thomas Y. Miracle
1421 Lakeview Dr.
Virginia Beach, VA 23455-4147
Newsletter of the Pacific Basin Center Foundation. Sometimes provides instructor's guides for included articles.

*South China Morning Post*
Tong Chong Street
Hong Kong
Daily coverage of world news, with emphasis on Hong Kong, China, Taiwan, and other Asian countries.

*Time*
Time-Life Building
Rockefeller Center
New York, NY 10020
A weekly newsmagazine with news and commentary on national and world events.

*U.S. News & World Report*
2400 N St., NW
Washington, DC 20037
A weekly newsmagazine with news and commentary on national and world events.

*The US-Korea Review*
950 Third Ave.
New York, NY 10022
Bimonthly magazine reviewing cultural, economic, political, and other activities of The Korea Society.

*The World & I: A Chronicle of Our Changing Era*
2800 New York Ave., NE
Washington, DC 20002
A monthly review of current events plus excellent articles on various regions of the world.

# Index

5133